The Juvenile Skeleton

The Juvenile Skeleton

Louise Scheuer
*Honorary Senior Lecturer, Department of Anatomy and Developmental Biology,
Royal Free and University College Medical School, University College, London,
UK*

Sue Black OBE
*Professor of Anatomy and Forensic Anthropology, Faculty of Life Sciences,
University of Dundee, UK*

Contributions to Chapter 5 by
Helen Liversidge
*Clinical Lecturer, Department of Oral Growth and Development, Queen Mary
School of Medicine and Dentistry, London University, UK*

Illustrations by
Angela Christie

ELSEVIER
ACADEMIC
PRESS

AMSTERDAM BOSTON HEIDELBERG LONDON NEW YORK OXFORD
PARIS SAN DIEGO SAN FRANCISCO SINGAPORE SYDNEY TOKYO

Elsevier Academic Press
84 Theobald's Road, London WC1X 8RR, UK
http://www.elsevier.com

Elsevier Academic Press
525 B Street, Suite 1900, San Diego, California 92101-4495, USA
http://www.elsevier.com

British Library Cataloguing in Publication Data
A catalogue record for this book is available from the British Library

Library of Congress Cataloguing in Publication Data
A catalogue record for this title is available from the Library of Congress

ISBN 0-12-102821-6

Typeset by Keyword Typesetting Services Ltd,
Wallington, Surrey SM6 9AA
Printed and bound in Great Britain by
MPG Books, Bodmin, Cornwall
04 05 06 07 9 8 7 6 5 4 3 2 1
MP

Contents

Preface

Developmental Juvenile Osteology (Academic Press, 2000) arose from the dissatisfaction and frustration of teaching and studying without the assistance of a text dedicated to the juvenile human skeleton. It was written as a reference volume, aiming to provide detailed information on the development of the skeleton from its earliest embryological stage through to its final adult form. It brought together, for the first time, detailed and fully illustrated descriptions of every bone at each critical developmental stage with an extensive bibliography that consolidated and centralised the widely disparate relevant literature. The book was received well by reviewers, colleagues and students but confirmed suspicions that it was rather unwieldy and expensive for a student teaching text.

The present book, *The Juvenile Skeleton*, has been written in response to those comments and requests for an additional text that is more specifically tailored to the needs of students of skeletal biology, anthropology, archaeology and forensic science. It is designed to be a core teaching text that is both more manageable and affordable than *Developmental Juvenile Osteology* but retains and develops the elements that proved to be most informative and useful in the original volume.

This text assumes that readers will have considerable previous knowledge and familiarity with the adult skeleton as the format has been markedly reduced by the removal of much of the general and detailed information pertaining to the adult. Consequently, this has resulted in a reduced bibliography with reference made to key papers only. Readers are therefore advised to refer to the original text for more detailed information. The content of the text has been updated and restructured to provide a more accessible learning resource but still retains all the original illustrations and descriptions of the juvenile skeleton, which have now been supplemented by several new drawings. Metrical information has been omitted and this has been transferred to an accompanying laboratory manual that is specifically designed to aid in the practical identification, sideing and ageing of juvenile material in the laboratory, mortuary or the field.

Chapter 1 discusses the provenance, identification and interpretation of the juvenile component of a skeletal collection and chapter 2 considers bone as a tissue, highlighting the different modes of formation, growth and maturation. Chapter 3 offers a very brief outline of early human embryonic development as an introduction to the more detailed bone specific descriptions found in subsequent chapters. Chapters 4 to 11 consider the development of each element of the human skeleton from the early embryological stages to final adult form and the chapters are arranged in a logical topographical order. Chapter 4, the

Head and Neck, commences with a description of the early development of the skull as a whole before it details each of the individual components. In *Developmental Juvenile Osteology* the principles of ageing from the teeth were included in the Head and Neck Chapter but in this text the dentition is awarded a Chapter of its own. We thank Dr Helen Liversidge, an acknowledged authority on tooth development and ageing, who has contributed to Chapter 5 by updating the review and adding descriptions of tooth morphology. Chapters 6 through 11 consider the remainder of the axial skeleton and the appendicular skeleton as in the original text.

Working again with the exceptional talents of our illustrator, Angela Christie, has proved to be a true pleasure and inspiration. She has created some new drawings that we believe make a welcome and necessary addition to the original text. Our acknowledgement and thanks remain with those previously listed in *Developmental Juvenile Osteology*. We also acknowledge the assistance of our editor, Elaine Leek and extend our thanks to Andrew Richford, Chris Jarvis and Deena Burgess of Elsevier who have looked after the production of this new text.

Louise Scheuer
Sue Black

CHAPTER ONE

Juvenile Skeletal Remains: Provenance, Identification and Interpretation

The correct identification of the skeletal components of juvenile remains is fundamental to their subsequent analysis and interpretation. This is true regardless of whether they are of archaeological or forensic origin. A lack of familiarity with immature remains may lead to incorrect classification as either 'non-human' or indeed 'of uncertain origin'. This would have a major impact on the validity and results of any investigation and so a successful outcome will rely heavily on this most basic step of accurate recognition. Without such a confirmation it is virtually impossible to progress with the analysis and establish the number of individuals represented, let alone their identity.

In the investigation of human remains, basic biological identity is assessed through the determination of the four principal parameters of sex, age at death, stature and ethnicity. However, it is only the estimation of age at death that can be determined with any degree of reliability from the juvenile skeleton. Sex determination using morphological characters is tentative at best and the age of the individual is so closely linked to stature that it is generally used to predict height. Ethnic identity is difficult to establish in the adult and in the child it is virtually impossible as there are very little data available upon which to base a determination.

This basic biological identity is used for different purposes depending on the aims of the investigator. Skeletal biologists, physical anthropologists and palaeo-demographers use the information to construct demographic profiles of popula-tions from both historic and prehistoric times and then draw conclusions about lifestyle, death rates and life expectancies. In a skeletal assemblage that includes subadult specimens, the identification and age at death of the juvenile compo-nent will be particularly relevant as it is deemed a reflection of the overall health and wellbeing of that population.

It is equally important that forensic scientists can also recognize juvenile components of the skeleton and establish age at death to assist in determining, or to confirm, the identity of an individual. Forensic anthropology uses the biological identity to attempt to determine 'personal' identity and this demands absolute accuracy, as it is only when the deceased has been given a name that an investigation can proceed.

The determination of age has significant clinical applications where it is sometimes more important to assign a child to a particular stage of develop-ment regardless of their actual age. In clinical specialties such as orthopaedic surgery, growth hormone treatment or orthodontics, a critical window of time may then be identified for corrective treatment to ensure that intervention will not impede development and sufficient time remains for catch-up growth.

Occasionally the legal system requires an assignment of age so that appropriate procedures may be observed, for example, where there is a statutory age for criminal responsibility. In certain countries, refugees lacking personal documents may be obliged to prove adult status in order to obtain a residence permit.

This chapter considers the basic concepts of growth and age and then attempts to distinguish the many different categories of database from which information on the developing skeleton is drawn. It then summarizes the estimation of age from skeletal and dental material. Finally, aspects of documentation, sampling, representativeness and sexing that are particularly associated with the juvenile component of a skeletal assemblage are discussed.

Growth

Growth is a term that is used to describe progressive changes in size and morphology during the development of an individual. In general, it is positively correlated with age and so estimation of age at death utilizes the many incremental changes that occur during development. Growth consists of two factors, an increase in size and increase in maturity, and while these two elements are usually closely integrated, their relationship is not linear. For example, a girl of 7 years may be several centimetres taller than her friend of the same age. Similarly, two boys, both aged 13 years, can be at very different stages of skeletal and sexual maturity.

Growth rates vary between the sexes, between individuals of the same population and between populations themselves. The underlying basis of this variation is genetically determined but the influence of environmental factors is critical in controlling the expression of the growth process. This interplay between genetic and environmental influences is the basis of the 'nature versus nurture' argument. In spite of much research, the causal picture remains far from clear as it is almost impossible to study the effect of a single factor acting alone. Also the effects of that factor on an individual may vary depending at which stage of development it acts.

Genetic inheritance is the background for differences of size and maturity between the sexes, which, although small, can be discerned, even before birth (Choi and Trotter, 1970; Pedersen, 1982). These show in the timing of ossification and mineralization of teeth (Garn *et al.*, 1966; Mayhall, 1992). Postnatally, skeletal maturation is more advanced in girls than boys (Pyle and Hoerr, 1955; Brodeur *et al.*, 1981) but bone mineral density is less in girls than boys, the latter having larger and longer bones (Maresh, 1970; Specker *et al.*, 1987; Miller *et al.*, 1991). As puberty approaches, sexual dimorphism increases by differential hormone secretion and this is reflected in the adolescent growth spurt. Although the timing varies between individuals of the same sex (early and late maturers), girls are, in general, about two years in advance of boys in maturity at the same age. The later growth spurt in boys allows more growth beforehand and therefore has its greatest influence at a different critical phase of growth. It results in a greater adult size, predominantly because muscle mass increases rapidly during this period, which affects overall skeletal robusticity (Tanner, 1978). Some studies show that, as in childhood, bone mineral density and accumulation of peak bone mass varies between the sexes at puberty. Recently, however, Baxter-Jones *et al.* (2003) have questioned the significance of this.

By far the most important negative environmental factors are those of under-nutrition and exposure to disease, which usually lead to a slowing of the growth rate and an inability to realize maximum growth potential. These influences can in turn be dependent on circumstances such as socio-economic status or environmental and psychological adversity (Haeffner *et al.*, 2002; Komlos and Kriwy, 2002). Many of these factors dominate most strongly in infancy and childhood but can also, in extremes, be known to affect growth and development before birth. Starvation conditions in Russia and the Netherlands during World War II caused a significant decline in birth weight and vitality of infants (Antonov, 1947; Smith, 1947). The effects of poor growth in the early years, often following a failure to achieve optimum size and weight at birth, have been shown to affect both susceptibility to disease and final adult size (Frisancho *et al.*, 1970: Clark *et al.*, 1986; Barker *et al.*, 1993; Marins and Almeida, 2002). Maternal under-nutrition appears to be one of the links in the causal chain between socio-economic factors and fetal growth (Lechtig *et al.*, 1975). Nutrition and disease have long been accepted as factors in raised childhood morbidity and mortality rates in countries with low socio-economic levels. Even in countries with a general high standard of living, minority groups with a low income raise children who show delayed postnatal ossification rates and tooth emergence times (Garn, Nagy *et al.*, 1973; Garn, Sandusky *et al.*, 1973a). The variability of growth and some of the factors responsible are discussed in detail in Tanner (1962, 1978), Sinclair (1978) and a comprehensive survey of variation in the growth of children worldwide, which can be found in Eveleth and Tanner (1990).

Age

Chronological age is the actual age of the individual. However, the relationship between growth and chronological age is not linear and therefore the concept of 'biological' age is used to indicate how far along the developmental continuum an individual has progressed. Biological age may be expressed as either skeletal age or dental age and it is generally recognized that the relationship between chronological age and dental age is stronger than that for chronological and skeletal age. Skeletal age can be estimated from the times of appearance and fusion of ossification centres and the size and morphology of the bones (see below). Dental age may be expressed in terms of the time of emergence of teeth or the state of maturation of their mineralization (see below and Chapter 5). Both skeletal and dental age require the individual to be compared to a known standard and this in turn will introduce areas of incompatibility. For these reasons, the establishment of age at death from juvenile remains, whilst more reliable than that for adults, is always an estimation.

Many different terms are used to designate the phases of the lifespan of an individual and while a few are established clinical definitions, others are not universally accepted. Their usage varies in different contexts and in different countries. Some of the different systems and terminology are reviewed here.

Prenatal age

In the prenatal period chronological age *per se* does not technically exist, as it is rarely possible to establish a definite starting point (i.e. fertilization) with any certainty. The actual known date of insemination is rarely known and tends to be restricted to cases of rape or assisted fertilization. Clinicians and embryologists record age slightly differently (O'Rahilly, 1997). In the clinical context, the only known date is usually that of the first day of the last menstrual period (LMP) of the mother but even the accuracy of this date may be affected by factors such as post-fertilization bleeding, inconsistencies of maternal recollection or intentional falsification. In addition, the period between insemination and fertilization is itself slightly variable. Clinically, normal term is calculated as 280 days (40 weeks/10 lunar months). The ranges of weights and lengths of a baby at term are population-dependent but for forensic purposes in the UK are taken as 2550–3360 g, 28–32 cm crown–rump length (CRL) and 48–52 cm crown–heel length (CHL) (Knight, 1996). Gestational age is also frequently estimated in the live newborn infant by evaluation of its neurological maturity (Dubowitz and Dubowitz, 1977; Dubowitz *et al.*, 1999). Some of the common terms used by clinicians and embryologists are given in Table 1.1.

Embryologists calculate age from the time of fertilization (postovulation), which takes place approximately two weeks after the first day of the last menstrual period and anatomical prenatal age averages 266 days (9.5 lunar months). This can vary with the interval between ovulation and fertilization and it is extremely rare to know the actual age of an embryo (Tucker and O'Rahilly, 1972). Historically, age was expressed in terms of the crown–rump rump length, crown–heel length or foot length of the embryo (Streeter, 1920; Noback, 1922; Scammon and Calkins, 1923).

Because of the variation that inevitably occurs when a single criterion such as age is used, it is difficult to make valid comparisons between embryos of the same size but of obviously different developmental stages. This problem was overcome in the human embryo and also in a number of commonly used laboratory animals, by a practice called 'staging'. This entails the division of the first eight postovulatory weeks (the embryonic period proper) into 23 stages, originally called 'Streeter developmental horizons' but now known as 'Carnegie stages'. Each stage is characterized by a number of external and internal morphological criteria, which are independent of size but indicative of maturity. Staging was initiated by Streeter (1942, 1945, 1948, 1951) and continued by O'Rahilly and co-workers (O'Rahilly and Gardner, 1972, 1975; O'Rahilly and Müller, 1986; Müller and O'Rahilly, 1994, 1997). Details of the morphological criteria can be found in O'Rahilly and Müller (2001)

In the fetal period (from 8 weeks to term), a satisfactory staging system is not yet available and the stage of development is still usually expressed in terms of CRL or related data. CRL itself is a rather inexact measurement and actual sizes do vary considerably, although the morphological differences between fetuses become less obvious as term approaches. O'Rahilly and Müller (2000, 2001) advise the use of greatest length (GL), the length of the fetus minus leg length. This is because the crown and rump are not always evident

Table 1.1 Terms accepted by clinicians and embryologists

Embryo	First 8 weeks of intra-uterine life
Fetus	From 8 weeks intra-uterine life to birth
Trimester	A third of the time of normal pregnancy, thus 1st, 2nd and 3rd trimesters
Preterm	From <37 weeks (258 days) LMP
Full-term	From 37–42 weeks (259–293 days) LMP
Post-term	>42 weeks (294 days) LMP
Stillbirth	Infant born dead after gestational period of 28 weeks (UK definition)

and do not exist in very young embryos and GL is the length measurement of ultrasound so that comparison may easily be made with living individuals. However, GL is very similar to CRL which was the measurement used in older studies. Texts that provide equivalent ages vary slightly, but there is, nevertheless, an accepted correlation of ranges of CRL or GL with age. The time scale for the whole prenatal period and for the embryonic (first 8 weeks) period are shown in Tables 1.2 and 1.3.

The relationship between various measurements and gestational age was discussed by Birkbeck (1976). More recently, Croft *et al.* (1999) used obstetrical ultrasound to determine the most suitable parameters for ageing formalin-fixed human fetuses. They found that both foot length and head circumference were superior to CRL, which, after the first trimester, was inaccurate due to distortion of the spine caused by compression in storage. This would also apply to GL. Sherwood *et al.* (2000) examined a series of spontaneous abortuses to provide a means of obtaining accurate ages for fetuses between 15 and 42 weeks. They found that skeletal measurements taken from radiographs provide better estimates than either anthropometric or ultrasound measurements.

Postnatal age

The terminology used to designate stages of the postnatal life varies both in different countries and as used by clinicians, auxologists and evolutionary and skeletal biologists. Some of these are accepted definitions but usage varies as to other commonly used terms (Table 1.4).

The time period between the end of childhood and the beginning of adult life is termed **juvenile** by Acsádi and Nemeskéri (1970) and **adolescence** by the WEA – Workshop for European Anthropologists (Ferembach *et al.*, 1980). In skeletal terms, both define the beginning of adult life as coinciding with the closure of the spheno-occipital synchondrosis, and this event is stated in most standard anatomical texts to occur between 17 and 25 years, which is almost certainly inaccurate. Recourse to the original literature from observations on dry skulls, cadavers and histological sections and radiographs report this as occurring between the ages of 11 and 15 years, around the time of eruption of

Table 1.2 Time scale of whole prenatal period

Days	Weeks PF	Months	GL (mm)
1–28	1–4	1	0.1–3
29–56	5–8	2	8–30
57–84	9–12	3	40–80
85–112	13–16	4	100–140
113–140	17–20	5	150–190
141–168	21–24	6	200–230
169–196	25–28	7	240–265
197–224	29–32	8	270–300
225–252	33–36	9	305–325
253–266	37–38	9.5	330–335

PF, Post fertilization.

Adapted from O'Rahilly and Müller (2001)

Table 1.3 Time scale of embryonic period proper

Pairs of somites	Carnegie stage	Size GL (mm)	Age days*	Approx. weeks
	1	0.1–0.15	1	
	2	0.1–0.2	2–3	
	3	0.1–0.2	4–5	1
	4	0.1–0.2	6	
	5	0.1–0.2	7–12	2
	6	0.2	17	
	7	0.4	19	
	8	0.5–1.5	23	3
1–3	9	1.5–2.5	25	
4–12	10	2.0–3.5	28	4
13–20	11	2.5–4.5	29	
21–29	12	3–5	30	
30+	13	4–6	32	
	14	5–7	33	5
	15	7–9	36	
	16	8–11	38	
	17	11–14	41	6
	18	13–17	44	
	19	16-18	46	
	20	18–22	49	7
	21	22–24	51	
	22	23–28	53	
	23	27–31	56	8

* Post fertilization.

Adapted from O'Rahilly and Müller (2001)

Table 1.4 Some terms used by clinicians, skeletal and behavioural biologists

Perinate	Around the time of birth
Neonate*	First 4 weeks after birth
Infant*	Birth to the end of the first year
Early childhood	To the end of the fifth year, often pre-school period
Late childhood	About 6 years to puberty
Puberty	A physiological term describing the beginning of secondary sexual change at about 10–14 years in girls and 12–16 years in boys
Adolescence	Used by some authors interchangeably with puberty and by others as referring to the period of behavioural and psychological change accompanying puberty

*Accepted definitions.

Table 1.5 Time of closure of the spheno-occipital synchondrosis

	Age (yr)		Numbers		
	Female	Male	Female	Male	Method
Powell and Brodie (1963)	11–14	13–16	193	205	Radiographic
Konie (1964)	10.5–13.5	12.5–16	162	152	Radiographic
Melsen (1972)	12–16	13–18	44	56	Histological
Ingervall and Thilander (1972)	>13.75*	>16	21	32	Histological
Sahni et al. (1998)	13–17	15–19	34	50	Direct inspection
			27	46	CT scans

*Never open.

the second permanent molars (Table 1.5). Thus most of the time period defined by these two schemes would be eliminated.

In some European countries yet another system of terms is used by skeletal biologists (Table 1.6), but again has the disadvantage of being defined by the time of closure of the spheno-occipital synchondrosis.

Cox (2000) has stressed that the present 'obsession' with age has driven us to try to determine accurate age at death for past populations regardless of what meaning this may have had at that time. For much of the past historical period, the majority of people would have been illiterate and innumerate and consequently age was probably not exactly known, nor indeed relevant. The important phases of life would have been biological and physical, such as weaning, dependence on parents, puberty and the attainment of adulthood with the important additions of female fertility and menopause. Behavioural biologists have used these more meaningful phases of the lifespan that refer to physical attributes or physiological states independent of actual chronological age. An example of this is that given by Bogin (1997), shown in Table 1.7. This again gives different meanings to the terms **juvenility** and **adolescence**. Cameron and Demerath (2002) considered the impact of factors related to growth and development in relation to disease outcomes later in life. They also used four general growth periods – intra-uterine, infancy, mid-childhood and adolescence.

In the UK and North America, the terms **immature**, **subadult** and **non-adult** are also used for any stage of life that is not truly adult, i.e. when all growth plates are closed. Gradually, however, in more recent publications the term **juvenile** is replacing these terms and it is used as such in the present text.

Table 1.6 Terms used in some European countries by skeletal biologists

Infans I	Birth to 7 years (until emergence of 1st permanent molars)
	Sometimes divided into:
Infans Ia	Birth to 2 years
Infans Ib	2–7 years
Infans II	7–14 years (between emergence of 1st and 2nd permanent molars)
Juvenil	Period until closure of spheno-occipital synchondrosis
Adult	Onset of suture closure

Knussmann (1988) after Martin and Saller (1959)

Table 1.7 Terms used by some behavioural biologists

Infancy	Period of time when the young is dependent on the mother for nourishment via lactation – duration may vary from a few months to about 3 years depending on the society
Childhood	Period after weaning when the child is still dependent on adults for feeding and protection. This coincides with the period of rapid brain growth, a relatively small gut and immature dentition
Juvenility	Period at the completion of brain growth and the beginning of eruption of the permanent dentition
Adolescence	Beginning at puberty and including the adolescent growth spurt
Adulthood	From the end of the growth spurt, the completion of the permanent dentition, the attainment of adult stature and reproductive maturity

Chronological age is normally of course calculated from the day of birth but, while this may appear to be rather obvious, as with all biological criteria, it is subject to errors. Even when age appears to be known, it is sometimes, on careful perusal, found to be inaccurate (see below – Documentation).

Source material

The methodologies that have been developed for the evaluation of age at death have been derived from a variety of skeletal sources. The data recorded before birth are from an entirely different source from those obtained post-natally and observations commonly use different techniques. In general, early development has been studied on aborted embryos and fetuses and there is a limited amount of information from ultrasound. In contrast, much postnatal information comes from radiographs of living children, although there are a few radiological and histological studies on postmortem and amputated limbs. There is also a wealth of archaeological data from skeletons of individuals whose age at death has been estimated from morphological criteria. Because of this variety of skeletal sources and methods of observation, it is vital in any study of individuals of unknown age, that, if at all possible, the provenance of the material used in comparison be known and, where appropriate, comparable.

Prenatal material

Studies of early human development were carried out on embryos obtained from spontaneous or elective abortions and, while the latter may technically be considered to constitute a normal sample, the former may have exhibited abnormalities that would negate the usefulness of the data. A number of factors, including single or multiple occupation of the uterus, nutrition of the mother and the introduction of teratogenic components such as alcohol, nicotine and other drugs, could affect development and in most cases such information would have been unknown (Roberts, 1976).

Both skeletal and dental structures have been studied by a variety of methods. Until the end of the nineteenth century remarkably detailed observations were made from gross dissections. A review can be found in Noback (1943, 1944). Drawings of the fetal skeleton by Kerckring (1717), Albinus (1737) and Rambaud and Renault (1864) are still some of the best recordings taken from gross specimens and are a salutary lesson in observation.

Subsequently, three principal methods were used:

1 Histological examination of microscopical serial sections.
2 Examination of alizarin-stained whole embryos.
3 Radiological observations.

Each of these methods has a different sensitivity for the detection of mineralized tissue and consequently age estimates will vary depending on the method used.

Histology

Bone is a tissue that is defined in histological terms and therefore its critical detection must, by definition, be by histological techniques (O'Rahilly and Gardner, 1972). It is the most sensitive method and observations using histology nearly always result in earlier reported times of appearance of bone than for any other method. The examination of serial sections is time-consuming and laborious work but most of the classical papers describing the human embryonic skeleton have been made by this method (Fawcett, 1910a; Macklin, 1914, 1921; Lewis, 1920; Grube and Reinbach, 1976; Müller and O'Rahilly, 1980, 1986, 1994; O'Rahilly and Müller, 1984).

Alizarin stain

Examination of alizarin-stained embryos involves 'clearing' of whole specimens with potassium hydroxide followed by staining with alizarin red S. This was only used in the very early stages of development when the embryo was small enough to be transparent but it provided a good overall picture of the embryo, especially the establishment of periosteal bone collars and mineralization of tooth germs (Zawisch, 1956; Meyer and O'Rahilly, 1958; Kraus and Jordan, 1965). However, the method is not specific for actual formation of bone and some accounts have used the first sign of osteoid as the beginning of ossification. Use of this method has therefore brought forward the range of reported times of appearance of ossification centres. Its disadvantages are that it destroyed the soft tissues and so ruined the use of the specimen for further examination and it could only be used in the very early period when the embryo was small enough to be transparent (O'Rahilly and Gardner, 1972).

Radiological

Radiological examination can be used at any period of life and leaves the specimen intact but it is the least sensitive method for detection of calcified tissue. Even after enhancement by soaking in silver solutions, calcification is not detected until a sufficient quantity of material has accumulated to render the tissue radiopaque. Also, as both bone and cartilage are radiopaque, the presence of trabeculae must be seen for the presence of bone to be confirmed (Roche, 1986). Observations using radiology provide dates that are at least one week later than those made from alizarin or histology (Noback, 1944).

During the later fetal period, data were derived from aborted fetuses and stillbirths and size measurements were made on either dry bone or from standard radiographs. More recently, clinical ultrasound observations have provided data on living individuals *in utero*.

The study of fetal osteology by Fazekas and Kósa (1978) contains much valuable information, including measurements of most bones of the skeleton from three lunar months to term. However, the age/bone-size correlations involve an inherent circular argument as their material, being of forensic origin, was essentially of unknown age. For their study, fetuses were grouped according to crown–heel length, each group being assigned an age at half-lunar month intervals in accordance with the widely accepted correlation between body length and age using Haase's rule (Fazekas and Kósa, 1978). Their 'regression diagrams' (graphs) are of body length as the independent variable against bone length as the dependent variable. While there is undoubtedly a close correlation between fetal age and size, as grouping was based on crown–heel length, all the bones, especially those of the lower limb that actually contribute to body length, inevitably show a high correlation and lie virtually on a straight line. 'Modified regression diagrams' show age in lunar months superimposed onto these graphs.

Other length data can be found in Balthazard and Dervieux (1921), Hesdorffer and Scammon (1928), Moss et al. (1955), Olivier and Pineau (1960), Olivier (1974), Keleman et al. (1984), Bareggi et al. (1994a, 1996) and Huxley and Jimenez, (1996). Length measurements from radiographs can be found in Scheuer et al. (1980) and Bagnall et al. (1982). Measurements from this source are, of necessity, cross-sectional (see below) and in addition may have introduced some abnormal data.

Starting from the early 1980s, there have been increasingly detailed data provided on long bone lengths, and skull and thorax size from ultrasound studies (Jeanty et al., 1981; O'Brien et al., 1981; Filly and Golbus, 1982; Jeanty et al., 1982; Seeds and Cefalo, 1982; Bertino et al., 1996). These 'ages' commence from conception and have to be adjusted if dates are established from LMP (McIntosh, 1998). Ultrasound norms are derived either from cross-sectional surveys or from longitudinal surveys that involve a limited number of observations per pregnancy (Bertino et al., 1996).

Postnatal material

Nearly all information on postnatal known age data has come from systematic, longitudinal radiological growth studies of living children. These were carried out between about 1930 and 1960 before the full risk of repeated exposure to X-rays was appreciated and are therefore non-repeatable. They involved large groups of children, mostly of middle-class, white Europeans or North Americans of European origin, who were radiographed, often three times during the first year of life and then at 6-monthly, and then yearly intervals until cessation of growth in height. This continued exposure to radiography may in itself have had a damaging effect on development. The 'normal' growth data were originally compiled for clinical purposes. First, screening programmes could identify individuals at risk, who might then benefit from treatment and response could be evaluated by paediatricians. Second, larger groups were used to reflect the general health of the population in particular communities or between social classes (Tanner, 1978). Other studies, some limited to fewer bones and shorter time periods, are by Ghantus (1951), Anderson et al. (1964) and Gindhart (1973). The data are now of course three generations old and therefore changes in the so-called secular trend, or tendency for increase in height, weight and decrease in age of maturity, need to be taken into account in their use as comparison populations. Some of the published studies in the USA and UK are included in Table 1.8.

In addition to these large longitudinal surveys, there have been other studies, either of a cross-sectional nature or, as often happens, a mixture of the two. Both offer a different type of information and have their merits and disadvantages (Tanner, 1962, 1978). The statistical methods and sampling problems encountered in large studies of this kind are discussed by Goldstein (1986), Healy (1986) and Marubini and Milani (1986). Briefly, a longitudinal

Table 1.8 Large scale studies of growth and development

Institution	Main researchers
The University of Colorado — The Brush Foundation	Maresh, Hansman
Case Western Reserve, Ohio	Todd, Greulich, Hoerr, Pyle
The Fels Institute, Yellow Springs, Ohio	Garn and colleagues
The Harpenden Growth Study	Tanner and colleagues[†]
The Oxford Child Health Survey	Hewitt, Acheson and colleagues

[*]See bibliography.
[†]for updated references, see P. Wraith (2003).

study consists of following the same group of individuals over a period of time, whereas a cross-sectional study measures a number of people once only at a particular time in their development. Longitudinal studies, especially those that extend over a number of years, are expensive and time-consuming, and require great commitment on the part of both the investigators and subjects. They are the only way to reveal true individual differences in growth velocity such as those that occur in the adolescent growth spurt. As there is always a drop-out rate in recording, so-called longitudinal studies are rarely exclusively longitudinal, and often include, by necessity, some cross-sectional data. Because cross-sectional data collection only requires a single measurement (or set of measurements) for each individual, it is potentially easier to include greater numbers. Essentially, it will give information about whether an individual has reached a certain stage of development compared with the mean for that age group.

Many of the large growth studies were used to compile reference atlases specific to a particular joint or topographical region. They consist of a series of standards, separate for males and females, usually at 6-monthly intervals, each of which was compiled from approximately 100 films judged to be the most representative of the anatomical mode. The atlas of the hand and wrist (Greulich and Pyle, 1959) illustrates development of the primary centres of the carpus, secondary centres for the metacarpals, phalanges and distal ends of the radius and ulna. The atlas of the foot and ankle (Hoerr *et al.*, 1962) shows development of the primary centres of the tarsus and secondary centres of the calcaneus, metatarsals, phalanges and distal ends of the tibia and fibula. Similarly the atlas of the elbow (Brodeur *et al.*, 1981) illustrates the development of secondary centres in the distal humerus and proximal radius and ulna; and that of the knee (Pyle and Hoerr, 1955) shows the appearance of the patella and secondary centres of the distal femur and proximal tibia and fibula.

The skeletal age of an individual can be estimated by comparing the pattern of appearance of the ossification centres on a radiograph with the maturity stages in the atlas. However, this inspectional technique suffers from a number of disadvantages. First, systematic and variable errors occur in evaluation (Mainland, 1953, 1954, 1957; Cockshott and Park, 1983; Cundy *et al.*, 1988). Second, there are methodological objections to this way of assessing maturation (Acheson, 1954, 1957). It presupposes a fixed pattern and order of development in the appearance of centres, which is by no means the case in all individuals. There is also necessarily a certain time interval between standard films so that a distinction can be made between successive standards. However, this is often too long for good matching to take place. Finally, Garn and Rohmann (1963) and Garn, Blumenthal *et al.* (1965) warn that, as a general rule, ossification centres appearing in early postnatal life tend not to be normally distributed but are particularly skewed. As the mean and median no longer coincide, data presented with percentiles are more accurate than those with means, and the atlas method cannot take this into account.

Improvements on the inspectional atlas technique were developed by Acheson (1954, 1957) and Tanner *et al.* (1983). The appearance of metaphyseal ends of the long bones and the epiphyses of each region was awarded a score in units as change in shape occurred during development. In this way, each individual bone element was allowed to make its own contribution to a total maturity score, regardless of the order of development of individual units. It thus avoided the assessor being compelled to match an individual's X-ray to a standard picture in an atlas and so circumvented the problem of a fixed order of development. As the ossification sequence is also sexually dimorphic, the 'score' method had the added advantage that it allowed direct comparison between the sexes, because the units were those of maturity and not time (Garn *et al.*, 1966). It proved to be a more accurate procedure than the direct inspectional method but was obviously more laborious and time-consuming. The principle is similar to that used for assessing mineralization stages of tooth development in the estimation of dental age (see Chapter 5).

In general, size appears to be more affected by adverse circumstances than is maturity but the majority of studies have recorded diaphyseal measurements of the major long bones. Until recently, apart from the changes in shape used in the scoring methods and isolated case reports in the clinical literature, the use of detailed developmental morphology of ossification centres has been a neglected area of osteology (Scheuer and Black, 2000). Fazekas and Kósa (1978) comment briefly on fusion of major elements of the skull and Redfield (1970) and Scheuer and MacLaughlin-Black (1994) have related the size and morphology of elements of the occipital bone to age. Paucity of information on the anatomy of all these bony elements is undoubtedly due to the difficulty in obtaining juvenile skeletal material for study. Post-mortem specimens are fortunately rare, and rightly difficult to obtain, because of the sensitivity and obvious emotional consequences of a child's death.

There is, however, a large body of data from dry bone measurements from archaeological material from Africa, Europe and North America. Most of the data consists of measurements of the long bones of undocumented archaeological populations where age has been estimated, often from dental development, thus entailing a double set of estimations (Scheuer and Black, 2000: appendix 3). The documented length data commonly used for comparison with archaeological collections is that from the University of Colorado (Maresh, 1943, 1955, 1970).

Searches of archaeological skeletal collections lacking age at death data have shown that epiphyses, especially those of the later developing group, are particularly rare, which is partly due to the age profile of most of the samples. Children succumb to adverse environmental circumstances in the early years of life, but if they survive the first 5 years, few die in later childhood. Material from the ages of 6–12 years is particularly rare. It is fairly common to find early forming epiphyses, such as those of the proximal humerus, distal radius, proximal and distal femur and tibia, but those that make a later appearance and then fuse early, for example elbow epiphyses, are extremely rare. Improved knowledge of timing of skeletal development and the ability to recognize these small elements would undoubtedly result in a better retrieval rate during skeletal excavations. Obviously, age estimation will be determined with greater accuracy using those bone elements that undergo distinct changes within a relatively short time range. Together with diaphyseal length, this aspect of evaluating maturity, could then improve accuracy of age estimation.

The reported times of fusion are very variable and, as with the times of appearance, this is due to different methods of observation and also to the fact that variability increases with increasing age. Stevenson (1924), Todd (1930) and Stewart (1934) carried out early studies of fusion using dry bone and radiographs. In their investigation of the Korean War dead, McKern and Stewart (1957) used Stevenson's (1924) categories of fusion and although their data were more extensive in number, their sample was necessarily restricted to active males of military age. As a result, their 'late union' group of epiphyses probably displayed the full range, but their 'early union' group was inevitably truncated at its lower end. Their conclusions pointed to a constant order irrespective of age and to the innominate bone as being the best indicator throughout the particular age range studied (17–23 years). Webb and Suchey (1985), in a forensic series, reported on large numbers of both sexes in a study of ageing from the anterior iliac crest and medial clavicle. These epiphyses are different from those of the long bones in that they fuse relatively soon after formation and so different staging categories were employed. Results showed that both bones were useful, at least in the forensic situation, where a complete cadaver was present, which meant that their first stage of 'no epiphysis present' was capable of confirmation. Again it was emphasized that the best indicators of age are those whose ranges of fusion are the most restricted in time.

There are several methodological problems involved with reporting epiphyseal union. The degree of union is generally divided into at least four morphological phases – no fusion, commencement of fusion, advanced fusion and complete fusion (Stevenson, 1924; McKern and Stewart, 1957). However, some authors have condensed this to only three stages (Hasselwander, 1910), whilst others have expanded it to five (MacLaughlin, 1990) or even nine stages (Todd, 1930). The distinction between different stages can be difficult to identify and as expected, intra- and inter-observer errors increase as the process of union is divided into an ever-increasing number of stages. Radiographic studies are either confined to atlases of limited regions of the body, as discussed above, or appear as scattered reports in the clinical literature. Again, as with appearance times, there is the similar problem of matching an individual to a particular atlas pattern.

It is also difficult to correlate observations from dry bone with those from radiographs. It is obvious in bone specimens whether or not fusion has begun and indeed whether or not external fusion is completed as bridges of bone are seen at the periphery of the epiphyseal/metaphyseal junction. However, much of the research in this area has used radiographic images, which have the distinct disadvantage of providing only two-dimensional information (Haines *et al.*, 1967). Epiphyseal union (epiphyseodesis) commences with the formation of a mineralized bridge and ends with the complete replacement of the cartilaginous growth plate (Haines, 1975). Although this entire process can extend over quite a considerable period of time, it can also occur quite rapidly within the space of a matter of months and so in this situation it is often difficult to capture a critical moment in dry bone specimens, let alone in radiographic images. Much of the detailed histological information is therefore extrapolated from animal models and so must be viewed with caution when applying it to human conditions (Dawson, 1929; Smith and Allcock, 1960; Haines and Mohuiddin, 1962; Haines, 1975).

Timing of fusion is much affected by variation in the onset of the adolescent growth spurt and not all accounts give total age ranges or gender differences.

The inability to determine sex in juvenile skeletal remains until adolescent sexual dimorphism is well under way complicates the use of fusion times to estimate age in this group until secondary sexual characters are reflected in the skeleton.

More recently, following the tragic events in the Balkans, Rwanda and Sierra Leone, information on war crimes is providing further skeletal data. Forensic anthropologists now have the opportunity to examine more recent remains of previously undocumented populations, assess techniques and modify methods accordingly if necessary.

Estimation of skeletal age

To establish the skeletal age of an individual from a bone, or bone element, it is necessary to identify it in one of its three phases of development. First, the time at which the ossification centre appears; second, the size and morphological appearance of the centre; and finally, where appropriate, the time of fusion of the centre with another centre of ossification. Because the various bones of the skeleton are very different in function, growth pattern and timescale of development, these three phases will not necessarily apply either to all bone elements, or to all situations that require estimation of age. There are considerable methodological problems associated with all these phases.

Appearance of ossification centres

Ossification centres form throughout the entire period of skeletal development. Because in their earliest stages they are indistinguishable from each other, they are identified by their anatomical position rather than their distinctive morphology. They therefore require the presence of soft tissue to hold them in place to allow identity to be established.

Ossification in the prenatal period is almost exclusively represented by development of primary centres of ossification, although the secondary centres around the knee may appear in the last few weeks before term. The times of appearance of primary centres of ossification are quite variable on account of two main factors. First, as discussed above, age itself in the prenatal period is not easy to establish and second, the ability to detect bone formation depends on what method of observation is used (Youssef, 1964; Wood *et al.*, 1969; O'Rahilly and Gardner, 1972). Appearance of secondary centres typifies postnatal skeletal development, although some smaller primary centres, for example carpals, do develop in this period. It occupies a wide timespan from just before birth through to early adult life.

In summary, the formation times of ossification centres:

- Are useful in a clinical context to rapidly establish the developmental status of an individual by reference to a standard maturity stage. Treatment of, for example, hormonal pathology may then be carried out at an optimum time.
- May be employed to assign an estimated age to an individual of disputed age using maturity status as in the clinical context. A variety of circumstances could include a legal situation.
- Are of little use in the estimation of the age at death of individuals forming part of a skeletal assemblage as it is unlikely that very early ossification centres would be recovered or indeed identified. The only exception is perhaps the study of mummified material by a variety of imaging techniques as the soft tissues keep the centres in their natural anatomical position.

- May be of use in forensic situations. If the body is decomposed but intact, radiological and histological techniques may be employed, although the latter are likely to be of poor quality. The presence of ossification in the calcaneus, talus (and possibly cuboid) and the appearance of secondary centres in the distal femur and proximal tibia usually denote a full term fetus and are therefore of direct legal significance (Knight, 1996).

Morphology and size of ossification centres

During development, each ossification centre assumes its own unique morphology. This permits identification in isolation and does not therefore rely on the presence of soft tissue to maintain its anatomical position. Once a bone element reaches a critical morphological stage it can be recognized and age may then be assessed, either from its size or from its morphological appearance. This approach to ageing is of value over a wide timespan, extending from midfetal life onwards to the adult stage.

Most of the available data from the prenatal period relate to lengths of the diaphyses of major long bones. Diaphyses have been measured directly on alizarin-stained fetuses, on dry bone, or by means of standard radiography and by ultrasound. In the postnatal period, data on lengths of diaphyses are drawn from the many cross-sectional and longitudinal surveys described above.

Radiological data, necessarily limited to standard two-dimensional views, of a limited number of bones may be found in developmental atlases of joints of the elbow, wrist, knee and ankle. With few exceptions, other bones are only represented by case reports in the clinical literature. A detailed account of the bony anatomy of the primary centres and epiphyses of all the bones of the skeleton may be found in Scheuer and Black (2000) and in this volume.

In summary, the size and/or morphology of ossification centres:

- Are useful in a clinical context to assess maturity. The most common application at the present time is the use of preterm ultrasound to monitor fetal development. Morphological changes in the bones can be used to provide maturity scores.
- May be of value in a forensic clinical situation for example the ageing of detained individuals awaiting judicial investigation or presenting for immigration purposes.
- May be used in age estimation of juveniles in both archaeological and forensic assemblages.

Fusion of ossification centres

Cessation of activity in the growth plate results in fusion between centres of ossification. Timing of fusion, which may take place at any time from mid- to late fetal life until the end of the third decade, varies greatly in different parts of the skeleton, partly in response to the function of the soft tissues with which that element is associated. For example, the parts of the skeleton that enclose the brain and spinal cord reach union either before birth or during early childhood, reflecting the precocious development of the central nervous system. Many of the bones of the skull form from single centres and fuse at sutures. More complex bones, such as the temporal, occipital and sphenoid, are formed from several centres that fuse together either prenatally or by early childhood. The vertebral centra and arches also fuse by early childhood. Long bones, on the other hand, are among the last areas of the skeleton to reach maturity and this is in part due to the delayed spurt in muscle growth, especially in the adolescent male. Interestingly, the clavicle, which is regarded as the first long bone to show signs of ossification, has an epiphysis at its medial end that is probably the last of the secondary centres to fuse. Therefore fusion times can span nearly 30 years.

As with times of appearance of ossification centres, the reported times of fusion are very variable. This is due to several factors. First, variability of all skeletal parameters increases with increasing age as external influences continue to act on the skeleton. Second, as with appearance of centres, different methods of observation, whether on dry bone or radiographs, affect the reported times. Third, reporting is affected by the use of different fusion categories and intra- and interobserver errors. Finally however the greatest effect is caused by the present inability to correctly sex juvenile skeletal remains through much of the age range. The onset of the adolescent growth spurt varies greatly between the sexes and among individuals and it is only when this is well under way that secondary sexual characters begin to be reflected in the skeleton. In addition, not all accounts in the literature state their age ranges or sex categories.

In summary, timing of fusion of ossification centres:

- Is useful in a clinical context to signify the normal cessation of growth or to identify premature fusion as a sign of pathological disturbance.
- Is useful in age at death estimations from archaeological remains although it is complicated by the inability to assign sex. The determined age ranges must, by necessity, be wider in material where the sex is unknown.
- May be used to estimate age of forensic remains if the sex is known from soft tissues or other factors. If only skeletal remains are present, then the problem discussed above is still relevant.

Estimation of dental age

Estimating age from the teeth has several advantages over skeletal ageing. First, teeth survive inhumation well, which is especially relevant for skeletal biologists and palaeontologists. Second, the development of both the deciduous and permanent teeth can be studied over the entire range of the juvenile life-span, beginning in the embryonic period and lasting until early adult life. Finally, it is commonly observed both in living populations that, for a given chronological age, dental age shows less variability than does skeletal age (Lewis and Garn, 1960; Demirjian, 1986; Smith, 1991), and this has also been confirmed in an archaeological population of documented age (Bowman et al., 1992). Dental development is less affected than bone by adverse environmental circumstances such as nutrition and disturbances of endocrine function (Garn et al., 1959; Lewis and Garn, 1960; Garn, Lewis and Blizzard, 1965; Garn, Nagy et al., 1973; Garn, Sandusky et al.,1973a; Demirjian, 1986). While the causes are not fully understood, a possible reason is that the development of all the deciduous dentition and part of the permanent dentition takes place before birth in a protected environment whereas skeletal growth and development, albeit having a strong genetic basis, is exposed for an increasing length of time to external factors such as variations in nutrition, socio-economic status and possibly climate.

Eruption of the teeth and their stage of mineralization have been used in dental ageing. It is accepted that the process of mineralization is genetically determined (Lewis and Garn, 1960; Tanner, 1962; Garn, Lewis and Kerewsky, 1965; Garn, Sandusky et al., 1973b), whereas eruption appears to be affected by systemic influences such as nutrition or local conditions, for example, early loss of deciduous precursors or inadequate space in the jaws (Fanning, 1961; Haavikko, 1973; Brown, 1978). Eruption is the whole process by which a tooth moves from the dental crypt to full occlusion in the mouth but nearly all studies of eruption are actually confined to emergence of the teeth and are incorrectly referred to as eruption (Demirjian, 1986). Clinically, emergence is defined as the time when the first part of the tooth pierces the gingiva or, radiographically, shows the resorption of supporting alveolar bone on the surface. On dry bone, tooth emergence is usually defined as being synonymous with a tooth cusp appearing at, or above the level of the surface of the alveolar bone. It is therefore a single event in time whose occurrence is not accurately known whereas mineralization is a continuous process that may be observed at defined points in the whole lifespan of the tooth. However, in many clinical and forensic situations, observance of tooth emergence is the only practical means on which to base an age estimate and this is supported by a large database for comparison (see Chapter 5).

The estimation of age using stages in the mineralization of teeth visualized on radiographic images, while more accurate than the use of emergence times, has several disadvantages. First, it requires training and experience in the reading of the several complex methods. Second, problems arise with the study of stages that occur during infancy and early childhood, mainly concerned with the difficulties of radiographing very young children and, as with skeletal development, there are ethical concerns about exposure to X-rays. Finally, there are many methodological problems causing discrepancies in results that are due to sampling and different statistical methods (Smith, 1991). Both emergence and mineralization stages of teeth are considered in more detail in Chapter 5.

Documentation

It is rare that the age and sex of the individuals comprising an archaeological collection are known but there are a few skeletal collections where the remains are of documented origin (Scheuer and Black, 2000). The term 'documented' is sometimes applied to a collection, meaning that its overall historical dates and origins are known, for example, Ubelaker and Pap (1998). However, it is more usually interpreted as consisting of a collection of individuals of known sex and age at death (Molleson and Cox, 1993; Cunha, 1995; Scheuer and Black, 1995). In this case, the remains of the deceased must be associated with some means of plausible identification, the principal one being a coffin plate that gives at least the name, and therefore sex, and also the age at death. Often, in the case of infants and children, the date of birth is also on the coffin plate. Occasionally, there may be additional documentary information from birth and death certificates and parish records of baptisms, marriages and burials.

All documentary evidence should be viewed with caution, especially if different sources do not concur with each other. Dates of birth may be incorrectly recalled. Todd (1920) reported that, in the Terry Collection, the listed ages at death for adults displayed peaks at around 5-year intervals, indicating that perhaps in later life people giving information tend to round to the nearest quinquennium. Lovejoy *et al.* (1985), investigating records in the Hamann–Todd Collection in Cleveland, Ohio, discovered gross discrepancies between 'stated' and 'observed' ages. Dates of birth or death may also be deliberately falsified for personal reasons. For example, in some developing countries, parents are known to falsify the age, particularly of their sons, to obtain preferential educational opportunities or of their daughters for matrimonial motives.

Sampling and representativeness

By its very nature, an archaeological skeletal sample is bound to be biased. It is necessarily cross-sectional in nature and therefore differs significantly from a living sample. In addition, burial in a particular place is affected by a variety of factors, including social and economic conditions and religious beliefs. After burial, subsequent skeletonization and preservation of the bones are in turn affected by the physical conditions of the burial place and these may include temperature, type of soil, coffin design or disturbance by humans and predators. Even in a carefully planned excavation, it is not always possible to recover all the material from the ground in a good enough condition to contribute useful information towards scientific evaluation of individual skeletons. As a result, the true age profile of the original population will always remain uncertain and therefore conclusions drawn from a demographic profile constructed from such data may be far from realistic (Waldron, 1994).

The juvenile component of the sample can be especially biased in particular ways that do not affect the adults. For instance, the juveniles in many archaeological populations consist of individuals that were subject to illness, or deficiency of some sort and therefore cannot represent the normal healthy children that may have gone on to constitute the adult population. However, this criticism may only apply if the individuals suffered from chronic disease or malnutrition, whereas many illnesses, for example plague and childhood infectious diseases, probably killed people before they had time to manifest effects on the skeleton. Saunders and Hoppa (1993) reviewed the literature for evidence of reduced or retarded growth in skeletal samples and the issue of biological mortality bias. They concluded that while the potential for bias exists, errors introduced by the larger methodological difficulties outweigh the small amount of error in interpretation of past population health. King and Ulijaszek (1999) surveyed the current literature on environmental factors that can influence growth. They concluded that the biological evidence suggests that growth faltering can be the result of insults that are archaeologically invisible. Saunders and Barrans (1999), however, are more optimistic about identifying determining factors that cause infant mortality by studying cause of death and dietary reconstruction from skeletal material.

Some palaeoepidemiologists mistakenly refer to their long bone measurements as growth curves. They are not true growth curves, or measures of growth velocity as used by auxologists, because these can only be observed on longitudinal follow-up studies. Saunders *et al.* (1993a) discussed methodology in relation to the production of so-called 'skeletal growth profiles' and have argued that confidence intervals rather than standard deviations should be used to report variation as they control sample size as well as variance.

Another factor that is often thought to bias a demographic profile is the under-representation of the immature component of a skeletal sample. Overall numbers of juveniles are often found to be lower than might be expected for the time and conditions of the period and this can seriously bias any conclusions drawn from death rates. Occasionally, this supposition can be corroborated by documentary evidence (Scheuer, 1998). It has been argued that the low numbers, especially of infants, are due to the relative fragility and poor preservation of the remains (Kerley, 1976; Johnston and Zimmer, 1989; Goode *et al.*, 1993) and that the physicochemical properties of infant bones were responsible for the scarcity in cemeteries (Guy *et al.*, 1997). However, this could also be attributed to the low retrieval rate of juvenile bones at the time of excavation, rather than to the nature of the material (Sundick, 1978). Deficiencies of skill and failure to recognize small unfused parts of the immature skeleton are thought by some researchers to play a large part in the incompleteness of many juvenile remains. Although some of the bones, particularly those of the calvaria and face, often do not survive inhumation intact, many bones useful for estimating age such as the base of the skull, parts of the vertebrae and most long bones can, and do survive as well as those of the adult under similar conditions.

One known reason for the smaller than expected number of young juveniles in some assemblages was the widespread habit of excluding infants and young children from burial in the same location as adults, so that they are under-represented in certain ossuaries and cemeteries. This selective process was sometimes dependent on a belief system of the community or due to economic circumstances. The pre-historic Iroquoians of southern Ontario buried infants along pathways, believing that it could affect the fertility of passing women (Saunders, 1992). In the Romano-British period, infant skeletons were found under the doorsteps of houses in St. Albans on the supposition that this would bring good luck to the household. Documentary evidence from both the St Bride's and Spitalfields Collections indicate a discrepancy between records of infant deaths and the numbers in crypt and cemetery samples (Cox, 1995; Scheuer and Bowman, 1995; Scheuer, 1998). Given the high infant death rate in Victorian England, it is likely that economic factors, such as the cost of funeral expenses, must have played a significant part in the decision concerning juvenile disposal.

Various methods have been employed to make use of juvenile material previously thought to be too damaged to include in a skeletal analysis. Measurements of fragmentary long bones, other than total length, have been used successfully by Hoppa (1992) with Anglo-Saxon remains and by Hoppa and Gruspier (1996) with protohistoric Canadian remains. However, comparison between the samples revealed significant differences and it was suggested that population-specific models would be necessary to make use of this method. Goode *et al.* (1993) have used a standardized method that would include any individual on a single plot, even if only represented by a single long bone.

Sexing

Undoubtedly the largest single problem in the analysis of immature skeletal remains is the difficulty of sexing juveniles with any degree of reliability. Males and females mature at different times and different rates, especially in the adolescent period. The growth spurt occurs at different times, both in individuals of the same sex, and also between girls and boys. As a result, any estimated age category is necessarily wider than it would be, had the sex been known. As quantitative differences of size and rate of growth between males and females are of little use in sexing skeletal remains, a large literature has accumulated on morphological differences, mostly centred on those regions that are most sexually dimorphic in adults, such as the pelvis, cranium, mandible and teeth.

It has been reported that the general shape of the pelvis, particularly the greater sciatic notch and the subpubic angle, shows that sexual dimorphism exists from an early age (Chapter 10). Fazekas and Kósa (1978) related the length of the greater sciatic notch to its depth and to the length of the ilium and the femur and reported 70–80% success rates in sexing. However, Schutkowski (1987), using discriminant function analysis on the same data, achieved an accuracy of just 70%. Schutkowski (1993) has also described differences in the greater sciatic notch and mandible in a documented collection but this has yet to be tested on a comparable series. Weaver (1980) proposed that the morphology of the sacro-iliac joint might be useful in sex determination but tests of the method by Hunt (1990) and Mittler and Sheridan (1992) have shown that it may have very limited use. Loth and Henneberg (2001) recently published a method that proposed that in early childhood, consistent shape differences between male and female mandibles could be used to predict sex with an accuracy of 81%. A blind test of the method by Scheuer (2002) showed that there was an overall accuracy of only 64%, that the method sexed males more reliably than females and that observer consistency was low. All these examples point to important principles if methods are to be universally applicable. They need always to be tested on a separate population, different from that on which the method was derived and by a person other than those who originally devised the method.

Molleson *et al.* (1998) scored discrete traits of the orbit and mandible in a sample of known sex adults and juveniles. Sex was correctly inferred in almost 90% of adults and 78% of juveniles and when the same traits were scored in a large skeletal assemblage of unknown sex, there was a concordance between facial characters, pelvic sizing and size of mandibular canines. This suggests that these traits could be useful in attempting to sex juveniles under carefully controlled conditions in a specific population, but more work is necessary should a larger assemblage become available. Although there are undoubtedly skeletal morphological differences between the sexes from an early age, it appears that they do not reach a high enough level for reliable determination of sex until after the pubertal modifications have taken place.

Both the permanent and deciduous dentition has been shown to be sexually dimorphic but levels are very small, especially in the latter, when both intra- and inter-observer error can outstrip differences in size and so become a significant factor in the analysis. There are reports of successful sex determination from the teeth on archaeological populations of unknown sex using discriminant function techniques but they are in reality 'concordances' between dental and skeletal indicators and not tests of accuracy (Ditch and Rose, 1972; Rösing, 1983).

An interesting approach to the problem of sexual dimorphism in archaeological populations has recently been developed and discussed by Humphrey (1998). Based on the concept that different parts of the skeleton vary in the proportion of adult size attained both at birth and postnatally, a method was introduced for analyzing the sexual differences in the growth of the postcranial skeleton. It was demonstrated by analysis of separate male and female cross-sectional growth patterns that sexual dimorphism occurs in many parts of the skeleton that complete their growth prior to adolescence. This sort of approach may possibly provide an insight into a morphological method of distinguishing males and females during the childhood period but again would need preliminary work on both adults and juveniles for the specific population in question.

Following from forensic principles, the isolation and amplification of DNA from archaeological bone should prove to offer potential advances through the sex-typing of genetic material. Breakdown products of the amelogenins, the organic components of the enamel of teeth, are sometimes preserved in archaeological material. These proteins are produced by a gene with copies on the X and the Y chromosomes, and have been used in sex determination (Lau *et al.*, 1988; Slavkin, 1988; Stone *et al.*, 1996; Blondiaux *et al.*, 1998). At the present time, genetic methods are limited by problems of contamination and degradation and are both time-consuming and expensive but the recent development of DNA LCN (Low Copy Number) might help to overcome this problem. The field of genetic investigation changes very rapidly and the perceived barrier between forensic and archaeological investigation is narrowing. Such research will revolutionize the analysis of skeletal remains although expense is bound to be a major factor in large archaeological collections.

Conclusions

In conclusion, it would appear that better recognition of all elements of the immature skeleton could lead to improved retrieval of the juvenile component of skeletal remains, which in turn can only have a beneficial effect on the final skeletal analysis. Also, various methods that make use of previously discarded remains could enlarge the size of many subadult samples.

The major problem in the skeletal analysis of juvenile remains still to be resolved is the ineffectiveness of most methods of morphological sexing. New methods will undoubtedly be devised, but the material on which they are tested must be documented. Any new method for sex determination and age estimation needs a rigorous standard against which to test its validity and reliability and this can only be achieved on a sample of known biological identity. While the majority of scholars do detail their sexing and ageing methods, there is a tendency to refer to confirmation of age and sex when both the original and the derived data were observed from anatomical parameters, thus resulting in a circular argument.

The other main difficulty lies in the choice of an appropriate sample with which to compare any markers that might reflect defects of growth and development. Skeletal assemblages are by necessity cross-sectional in nature and come from different temporal periods, geographical locations and gene pools. Ideally, an appropriate sample for comparison should come from a similar background to the material studied but this is often not possible. Caution must be used when applying standards derived from relatively recent material to ancient human remains because an archaeological sample may not show the same relationship between chronological and skeletal age as that displayed by the reference sample. Bocquet-Apel and Masset (1982, 1985, 1996) represent an extreme idea that a demographic profile of unknown remains will be bound to reflect the range of the sample with which it is compared, but many scholars feel that this is too critical a view. Various methods have been developed in an attempt to alleviate these problems. Instead of comparing the diaphyseal lengths directly with a comparative sample, the percentage of adult length attained at different ages may make a more realistic comparison. In addition to these theoretical problems, there are many living populations for which there are no metric or morphological data, thus reducing the database for comparisons.

Truly documented samples are one of the most valuable resources to which a skeletal biologist has access. Such collections are obviously very limited and should be treasured and maintained in good order so that improved methods of establishing biological parameters of identity may be tested. Only then can the identity of a forensic specimen be attempted with any reliability and relevant and reasonable conclusions be drawn from the skeletal remains of past peoples.

CHAPTER TWO

Bone Development

Mammalian bone arises from the differentiation of pluripotential embryonic tissues. At some sites this involves the replacement of a cartilaginous model and at others, the conversion of a membranous template. Historically, great emphasis has been placed on the distinction between a bone whose precursor is formed from virtually avascular hyaline cartilage (**endochondral**) and one that, in contrast, arises from the direct transformation of a highly vascular membrane (**intramembranous**). Indeed, it is generally not appreciated that there are two quite distinct types of intramembranous or mesenchymal ossification. First, that which is considered to be more phylogenetically ancient and gives rise to **dermal** bones (generally held to be indicators of an evolutionary distant exoskeleton or armour – Smith and Hall, 1990; Carter and Beaupré, 2001) and second, **perichondral** bone that is formed in the immediate vicinity of the highly vascular perichondrium by direct apposition from perichondral osteoblasts.

It is not clear why certain bones preform in cartilage and others develop directly in mesenchyme, and indeed some authors have erroneously claimed that it is of no consequence, as the final outcome is virtually identical. Yet there are very distinct differences in the resultant bone morphology, which reflect the interaction between function and cellular origin and organization. Intramembranous ossification results in either dense compact or diploic bone (e.g. bones of calvarium, shaft of femur, or compact covering of carpals) whereas endochondral ossification results in trabecular or cancellous bone formation (Fig. 2.1). Put very simply, intramembranous ossification forms the compact, regularly organized bone that is exposed on the external surface whereas endochondral ossification produces the somewhat haphazard cancellous structure found in the internal aspect of some bones. All bones exhibit intramembranous ossification to a varied degree but only some exhibit endochondral ossification. In addition, dermal ossification progresses in virtual topographical isolation in the cranium with little or no delicate cancellous development, whereas perichondral and endochondral ossification generally operate in unison to produce bones of a mixed cortical and cancellous nature and are widely distributed throughout the postcranial skeleton with limited representation in the skull.

It has been suggested that dermal bones originate from a condensation of cells derived from the neural crest whereas all other bones (perichondral and endochondral) arise from mesenchymal cell condensations. Recent research illustrates that the cellular components of the two modes of intramembranous bone formation do behave in different ways, perhaps reflecting their distinct embryological origins. It should, however, be noted that much of the cellular

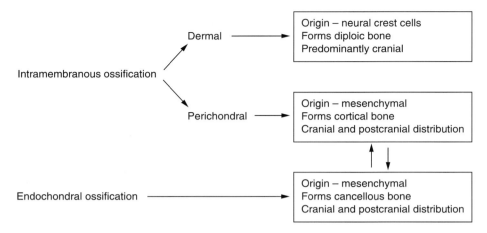

Figure 2.1 A summary of the basic modes of bone formation.

research has concentrated on quail/chick chimeras or transplantation research in the mouse, and extrapolation to the human skeleton must be regarded with some caution (Caplan *et al.*, 1983; Carter and Beaupré, 2001). However, in support of the theory, differences in cellular behaviour have been reported in plastic and reconstructive human facial surgery, where the successful grafting of bone to a new location relies heavily on the cells behaving and growing in a manner that is appropriate to their new translocation site. Therefore, correct selection of the appropriate bone type is critical, as unpredictable or inappropriate cellular behaviour might seriously compromise a successful surgical and aesthetic outcome (Smith and Abramson, 1974; Zins and Whitaker, 1979, 1983; Kusiak *et al.*, 1985; Moskalewski *et al.*, 1988; Scott and Hightower, 1991; Sullivan and Szwajkun, 1991; Chole, 1993).

In evolutionary terms, intramembranous bone formation is the more primitive mode of ossification and cladograms of the proposed phylogeny of bone development (Carter *et al.*, 1998) indicate that although phosphatic skeletons occurred in early Cambrian deposits (500+ million years BP) the first clear evidence of true dermal intramembranous ossification was found in the cranial skeleton of Ordovician agnathans (500 million years BP). The earliest incidence of perichondral intramembranous ossification is not well documented, but it may be present in heterostracans of the later Ordovician period. Endochondral ossification first appears around 100 million years later in Osteichthyes (bony fish) of the Devonian period (around 350 million years BP). It is generally regarded that such a marked alteration and adaptation in the manner of bone formation must be linked to the functional requirements of an altered postcranial skeleton, which is integral to the successful migration of fish onto land and thus the development of the first Devonian tetrapods (Smith and Hall, 1990). Therefore, in phylogenetic terms, it would appear that dermal intramembranous ossification predated perichondral intramembranous ossification, which in turn predated endochondral ossification and it is likely that each developed in response to changing functional requirements. It is interesting to note that this pattern is also generally adhered to in the ontogenetic development of the human skeleton with dermal bones being the first to commence ossification followed by perichondral ossification with endochondral formation often being the last type to appear.

The simple endochondral postcranial ossification seen in the Devonian period did not appear to alter substantially for 200 million years, until in the Jurassic period animals like *Sapheosaurus* displayed discrete accessory islands of endochondral ossification at the extremities of long bones. These additional, or secondary endochondral centres appeared to evolve independently in many vertebrate lineages and tended to occur more frequently in larger animals. These are generally recognized as early forms of 'epiphyses' and illustrate very clearly the cumbersome and often inappropriate osteological terminology that persists from early texts.

The precursor of the future bone generally commences osteogenesis at a constant locus. This initial site of ossification is traditionally known as the **primary centre** and can form either as a result of intramembranous (dermal or perichondral) or endochondral ossification. Strictly speaking, a 'primary centre' is purely a temporal indication of the initial locus of ossification in a particular bone. For example, the primary centre of ossification for the frontal bone occurs via dermal intramembranous ossification in the region of the superciliary arch in prenatal week 6, whereas that for the femur occurs via perichondral intramembranous ossification in the region of the midshaft around prenatal week 7 and that for the calcaneus occurs via endochondral development in the centre of the cartilage mass around prenatal month 5. Therefore following this definition, there can only be one primary centre of ossification for each bone as it must be the label applied to the centre that forms first. However, the accepted classification system allows there to be, for example, three primary centres for the innominate (pubis, ilium and ischium) and often in excess of sixteen for the sphenoid. Perhaps the traditional definition of a 'primary centre' needs some redefinition.

Classification based on age alone is not sufficient as, whilst the majority of 'primary centres' appear in the embryonic and fetal period, a few develop as late as the pre-adolescent years of childhood (e.g. the pisiform of the hand at around 8–10 years). Therefore a more complex multi-layered definition of a primary centre is required to cover the confusing classification of these structures.

A primary centre of ossification may be defined as:

1   The initial locus of ossification in the template of a skeletal element. This centre may go on to form the *entirety* of the adult bone (e.g. sesamoids, carpals and all tarsals except the calcaneus – endochondral ossification) or will form the majority of the future adult bone, which can in turn fuse with smaller additional centres of ossification (e.g. shaft of long bone, coracoid of scapula – perichondral ossification).
2   All centres formed by dermal intramembranous ossification. The skull is therefore formed entirely from primary centres of ossification.

Table 2.1 summarizes the mode of ossification of the individual skeletal elements that comprise the skull. It should be noted that it is generally only those bones that form the base of the skull that display endochondral ossification as the majority of the skull is formed by intramembranous ossification. Table 2.2 summarizes the mode of ossification for the postcranial primary centres.

Whilst the impetus for dermal bone development is probably protective with regards to the development of the central nervous system, perichondral intramembranous centres of ossification may develop in response to the *in utero* stretching of surrounding soft tissue structures. It has been found that involuntary embryonic muscular contractions encourage bone formation at the site of the muscle attachment (Carter and Beaupré, 2001). For example, in the neural arches of the vertebral column, plaques of perichondral bone develop

Table 2.1 Type of initial bone formation in the development of the different skeletal elements of the skull

	Intramembranous	Endochondral
Occipital	Squamous — interparietal Squamous — supra occipital	Partes laterales Pars basilaris
Temporal	Otic capsule (small part) Squamous Tympanic Styloid process	Otic capsule (major part)
Ossicles	Malleus, incus and stapes	
Sphenoid	Greater wing (major part) Medial pterygoid Lateral pterygoid Hamulus Conchae	Greater wing (small part) Body — pre and post Lesser wing
Parietal	Whole bone	
Frontal	Whole bone	
Nasal	Whole bone	
Ethmoid	Whole bone	
Inferior concha	Whole bone	
Lacrimal	Whole bone	
Vomer	Whole bone	
Zygomatic	Whole bone	
Maxilla	Whole bone	
Palatine	Whole bone	
Mandible	Majority of bone	Condyle and symphysis

Table 2.2 Type of initial bone formation in the postcranial primary centres of ossification

	Perichondral	Endochondral
Hyoid	Greater and lesser horns	Body
Larynx	Thyroid and cricoid	
Vertebral column and sacrum	Neural arches Anterior arch C1	All centra, dens, Lateral masses of sacrum
Sternum		Manubrium, sternebrae, xiphoid
Ribs	Whole bone	
Pectoral girdle	Scapula, clavicle	
Major long bones	Diaphyses	
Hand	Phalanges, metacarpals	Carpals, sesamoids
Innominate	Ilium, ischium and pubis	
Patella		Whole bone
Foot	Phalanges, metatarsals	Tarsals, sesamoids

in the region of the lamina as the stresses are relayed from the contraction of the muscles of the neck and back to the perichondrium via Sharpey's fibres.

Similarly, in long bones such as the femur, it is believed that the bending stresses set up by proximal and distal muscle contractions result in intermittent bending moments in the cartilaginous shaft template, that focus in the midshaft region and thereby initiate perichondral ossification (Carter and Beaupré, 2001). These authors suggested that mild axial tension and hydrostatic tensile stresses in pluripotential tissue enhance bone formation and that axial and hydrostatic compression tend to promote chondrogenesis. It has been shown that babies born with neuromuscular dysfunction often display reduced diaphyseal diameters and a decreased volume of bone (Rodriguez et al., 1988; Dietz, 1989).

It has also been suggested that bone may preferentially form in a location that is protective to an immediate neurological structure (suggesting a neurological based biochemical stimulator). This osteogenic localization occurs in all three primary centres of the innominate, where bone forms initially in the vicinity of the three main nerve trunks to the lower limb, in the clavicle in response to the brachial plexus and in the ribs in relation to the neurovascular intercostal bundles (Laurenson, 1963).

Primary centres that form directly via endochondral ossification are to be found only in the carpals, tarsals, centra of the vertebral column, sternebrae and sesamoids. These are bones that are difficult to identify in the early stages of their development as they are represented by little more than amorphous nodules. They only attain their characteristic morphology when the advancing ossification front approaches the perichondrium and then a thin layer of cortical bone is laid down via intramembranous ossification to produce a recognizable surface, e.g. talus or calcaneus.

The primary centre of ossification does not always expand to fill the entire cartilaginous area of the precursor template and in some regions (generally associated with joint surfaces or sites of muscle/ligament attachment) separate **secondary centres** of ossification develop, usually in the postnatal period. These are often also collectively referred to as **epiphyses** and abut onto a growth plate or metaphyseal surface.

There are fundamentally three types of secondary centres of ossification and these are summarized in Table 2.3.

1   Many secondary centres form substantial areas of bone that tend to be located at the extremities of long bones (i.e. appendicular), often encompass the entire synovial articular surface and form via endochondral ossification, thereby being ostensibly cancellous in nature with only a thin outer compact shell. By experimentation, using finite element analysis, Carter and Beaupré (2001) illustrated that areas of cartilage exposed to intermittent octahedral shear stresses experience an acceleration in ossification thereby encouraging the development of an isolated additional centre of ossification within a cartilage mass. In contrast however, these same distortional forces appear to inhibit ossification in the region of the articular cartilage and in the growth plate that separates the primary from the secondary centre. The only substantial secondary centre in this group that does not follow this rule is the greater trochanter of the femur. This may be because it originally develops as part of a continuous cap with the head before it becomes separated by the development of the neck in the second year (see Chapter 11). The secondary centres found at the extremities of long bones form the usual textbook description of epi-

Table 2.3 Type of initial bone formation in the postcranial secondary centres (epiphyses) of ossification

	Articular cancellous	Articular flake/smear	Non-articular lig./musc.
Vertebral column and sacrum		Costal processes Auricular surface sacrum Lateral margin sacrum	Transverse processes Spinous processes Apex of axis
Sternum		Sternoclavicular joint Chondrosternal junction	
Ribs		Articular tubercle Head	Non-articular tubercle
Clavicle		Medial and lateral	
Scapula		Subcoracoid Glenoid	Angle and apex of coracoid Acromion, medial border Inferior angle
Humerus	Proximal and distal		Medial and lateral epicondyles
Radius	Proximal and distal		
Ulna	Proximal (beak) and distal		Proximal and apex
Hand	Metacarpals and phalanges		
Innominate		Acetabulum Superior ossific nodule (pubis)	Anterior inferior iliac spine Ischial spine, Iliac crest Ischial tuberosity and ramus
Femur	Head, greater trochanter* and distal		Lesser trochanter
Tibia	Proximal and distal		Tibial tuberosity
Fibula	Proximal and distal		
Foot	Metatarsals and phalanges		Calcaneus

*See associated text for explanation.

physes and of endochondral ossification, but there are at least two other forms of secondary centres to be considered.

2   Certain articular surfaces do not form from large cancellous masses but rather develop via small, flat islands of cortical-type bone that spread over the surface of the joint rather like smearing thin putty, e.g. glenoid of scapula, sacro-iliac articulation, medial clavicle, sternum, manubrium and acetabulum of innominate, and it is interesting to note that they do not occur in the appendicular skeleton, being restricted to the axial and girdle regions.

3   In addition, not all secondary centres occur in association with joints but some are formed at sites of ligamentous or muscular attachment. These secondary centres tend to form slivers of varying sized 'caps' and may form in a manner that is more reminiscent of perichondral ossification as they may develop in response to the stresses set up by muscle/ligament attachments. This type of secondary centre can be found in areas of the skeleton such as the crest of the ilium, transverse processes of the vertebrae, inferior angle of the scapula and calcaneus.

Primary and secondary centres are separated by an organized cartilaginous region of rapid growth (**growth plate**, **epiphyseal plate**, **physis**) (see below). When the rate of cartilage proliferation is exceeded by the rate of osseous deposition, then the growth plate will start to narrow and eventually will be replaced by bone so that **fusion** will occur between the primary and secondary centres. This event marks the end of longitudinal bone growth and whilst the time of fusion is relatively well documented, it can show a considerable degree of variation (see Chapter 1). Last (1973) likened the times of appearance and fusion of centres of ossification to telephone numbers, being sufficiently haphazard that recourse to a book should always be recommended as it is impossible to keep them all in one's memory.

The actively developing surface of the primary and secondary centre on either side of the growth plate is always represented by the characteristic ridge and furrow or billowed appearance of a **metaphyseal** surface. This morphology indicates the grooves left by the extensive vascularity of the region as bone formation is intimately related to a rich blood supply.

Each bone has at least one nutrient artery that enters via a **nutrient foramen**. The number and direction of such foramina have excited a considerable amount of research, with the latter being considered an indicator of the **growing end** of the bone. This is obviously a misnomer as (in long bones in particular, where this description is generally levied) both ends of a bone grow, but one is generally dominant and therefore contributes to a greater percentage of the final adult length (see below).

Pre-osseous development

Mesenchymal condensation

Mesenchyme is the meshwork of embryonic connective tissue from which all other connective tissues of the body are formed, including cartilage and bone. Mesenchymal cells migrate to sites of future osteogenesis and there differentiate into osteogenic cells as a result of cellular interactions and locally generated growth factors (Hall, 1988). This local instruction ensures that bone does not develop in inappropriate sites.

The first sign of future potential bone formation occurs in the early embryonic period as a localized condensation of the mesenchyme (skeletal blastema). Cellular condensations may arise as a result of either increased mitotic activity or an aggregation of cells drawn towards a specific site (Hall and Miyake, 1992). Signaling agents such as retinoids seem to be responsible for controlling *Hox* gene expression so that cells are given positional addresses (Tickle, 1994). For example, this results in a humerus developing in the arm and not in the foot.

As the mesenchyme begins to condense, the cells become more rounded, concomitant with a reduction in the amount of intercellular substance (Streeter, 1949). This stage is referred to as the precartilage blastema (Hamilton and Mossman, 1972; Glenister, 1976; Atchley and Hall, 1991). The formation of mesenchymal condensations has been associated with the formation of gap junctions that permit intercellular communication (Hall and Miyake, 1992). Each cell begins to secrete a basophilic matrix, rich in collagen filaments along with other substances, including chondroitin sulphate, indicating a differentiation into chondroblasts. As development continues, the levels of hyaluron decrease following an increase in hyaluronidase. Hyaluron blocks chondrogenesis, so its removal permits cellular differentiation (Knudson and Toole, 1987). As the levels of hyaluron decrease, so the levels of chondroitin sulphate increase (Toole and Trelstad, 1971). It appears that hyaluron may be necessary for cellular aggregation and therefore essential for the accumulation of a sufficient number of precartilage cells to initiate the transition from mesenchyme to cartilage (Grüneberg, 1963; Ogden, 1979). A number of factors, such as a mutation or the introduction of a teratogen may be responsible for the reduction in size of a mesenchymal condensation. If this condensation does not reach a critical size/mass, then the onset of chondrification may be retarded or even aborted. There is a substantial volume of evidence from *in vitro* cultures to suggest the requirement of a minimum cell number before prechondrogenic cells can differentiate (Steinberg, 1963; Flickinger, 1974; Solursh, 1983). A similar requirement has also been documented for pre-osteogenic cells (Thompson *et al.*, 1989; Nakahara *et al.*, 1991). Interestingly, this may go some way towards an explanation for the phylogenetic loss of certain skeletal structures (Hall, 1984). The embryonic potential to produce certain skeletal structures that will ultimately be suppressed can be retained. For example, snakes retain the mesenchymal condensations that would indicate impending limb formation. However, they remain small and so may fail to meet the prerequisite cellular quantity threshold so that they ultimately regress. Occasionally some of these suppressed structures do develop beyond the condensation stage and are then classified as atavistic traits (Hall, 1984). Conversely, should a condensation become excessively large, it can subsequently lead to abnormally large skeletal elements (Hall and Miyake, 1992).

As the tissue continues to mature, there is a continued separation of the cells by matrix deposition and so the tissue soon takes on the appearance of early hyaline cartilage. Gardner (1963) reported that such cellular condensations, which will ultimately lead to cartilage formation, could be distinguished at a very early age from the predominantly fibrous condensations that lead to the formation of intramembranous bone. This ease of identification is partly due to the early presence of a well-defined perichondrium.

Chondrification

Chondrogenesis is initiated by a response to an extracellular matrix-mediated interaction either via a basal lamina or via an ectodermal–mesenchymal interaction (Syftestad and Caplan, 1984; Hall, 1988). For example, interaction with the basal lamina of the notochord and neural tube increases the rate of differentiation of the paraxial mesoderm. The production of type II collagen in mesenchymal cells is a clear indication of chondrogenic potential.

The cells at the periphery of the blastema condense to form a bilaminar perichondrium whose inner layer is host to chondroblasts that will be responsible for appositional growth of the developing cartilage anlage. Interstitial growth of the cartilage model continues via cellular division. Such growth can only be maintained whilst the matrix is sufficiently pliable to permit expansion (Serafini-Fracassini and Smith, 1974; Glenister, 1976).

The question of maintained nutrition to the deepest areas of a cartilage anlage is a well-documented scientific debate. Whilst many texts incorrectly state that cartilage is an avascular structure, it is equally well known that cartilages will maintain viability either by diffusion from a blood source (usually perichondral) or via vascular bundles travelling in cartilage canals (Fig. 2.2). The presence of vascular canals within a cartilaginous mass is not a new discovery, as they were first described by Hunter in 1743. Despite the production of an anti-angiogenic factor (Kuettner and Pauli, 1983), it is known that vascular canals are present from a very early age (Haines, 1933; Brookes,

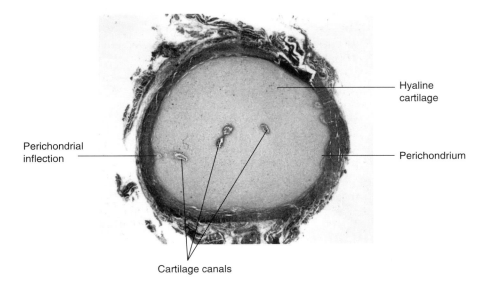

Figure 2.2 Transverse section of fetal costal cartilage canals (Masson's stain × 1 objective).

1971; Moss-Salentijn, 1975). Interestingly, their presence is not restricted to large cartilage masses as one might expect if their function was simply to supplement nutrition, but they have also been found in, for example, the epiphyses of fetal phalanges (Gray *et al.*, 1957). The canal is formed by an inflection of the deep layer of the perichondrium and carries a small central artery or arteriole surrounded by numerous venules and perivascular capillaries (Hurrell, 1934; Wilsman and Van Sickle, 1972). The arteriole of a canal enters the cartilage matrix at a groove or sulcus and terminates by division into a capillary glomerulus. The capillaries are lined by fenestrated endothelium and the pericytes are thin, facilitating the transfer of nutrients and metabolites. The capillaries recombine to form a venule that rejoins the perichondral network via the same channel as the parent arteriole. The loose connective tissue that surrounds the blood vessels is continuous with the perichondrium and is rich in fibroblasts, connective tissue fibres, undifferentiated mesenchymal cells and macrophages. Also present are unmyelinated nerve fibres and lymphatic vessels and the entire cartilage canal is bathed in interstitial fluid, facilitating metabolic exchange throughout its entire length (Lufti, 1970; Wilsman and Van Sickle, 1972).

Given the production of anti-angiogenic factors, it is unlikely that embryonic chondrogenic condensations are in fact actively invaded by blood vessels, but it is well established that osteogenic condensations are (Hall, 1983, 1988). Thompson *et al.* (1989) suggested that the pre-osteogenic condensation must release an angiogenic factor that encourages vascularization.

Engfeldt and Reinholt (1992) summarized the chondrification stage of development as beginning with a morphogenetic phase of development and ending with a cytodifferentiation phase. The former is characterized by migration of the mesenchymal cell populations, cellular division and proliferation and cellular interactions. The latter is characterized by synthesis and secretion of cartilaginous proteoglycans and type II collagen.

There is the additional matter of small regions of so-called 'secondary cartilage' to be considered. This seems to be temporary cartilage that is found in bones that will typically develop via dermal intramembranous ossification, e.g. the mandible and the clavicle (de Beer, 1937; Koch, 1960; Andersen, 1963). Small regions of cartilage also form in dermal intramembranous bones wherever rapid development is taking place, e.g. cranial sutures and alveolar ridges, and they may arise in response to a requirement for a localized alteration in growth rate (Jones, personal communication).

Ossification

De novo mineralization

The *de novo* mineralization of connective tissue is surrounded by a long tradition of controversial theories that have subsequently been upheld or refuted by the development of relatively new histo- and biochemical techniques. Two discoveries were of particular importance in this regard – the identification of matrix vesicles by Bonucci in 1967 (although not named as such until Anderson in 1969) and the process of epitactic nucleation that was first described by Neuman and Neuman (1953). Matrix vesicles are double-membrane bound, round or ovoid structures (0.1–0.2 μm in diameter) that are often found between collagen fibrils in small clusters about halfway between adjacent chondrocytes (Bonucci, 1967, 1971; Boyan *et al.*, 1990). These small extracellular structures are the recognized induction sites of mineralization (Fig. 2.3). They develop as small buds from the plasma membrane of chondrocytes and are released following retraction of the supporting microfilament network (F-actin) of the cell surface microvilli (Hale and Wuthier, 1987; Wuthier, 1989; Sela *et al.*, 1992). Matrix vesicles are a universal phenomenon of mesenchymal tissues and this was implied, although not fully appreciated, as early as 1931 by Charles Huggins (cited in Anderson, 1990). Huggins found that if the transitional epithelium from a dog's bladder was transplanted into the rectus sheath of that same animal then bone would form wherever the mesenchymal cells of the sheath came into contact with the epithelium. It is thought that the matrix vesicles may provide both the necessary enzymes and environment to concentrate both calcium and phosphates sufficiently to overcome the threshold for crystallization (Hunter, 1987).

In cartilage, calcium is bound to anionic groups of proteoglycans and therefore is not directly available for precipitation. A localized increase in phos-

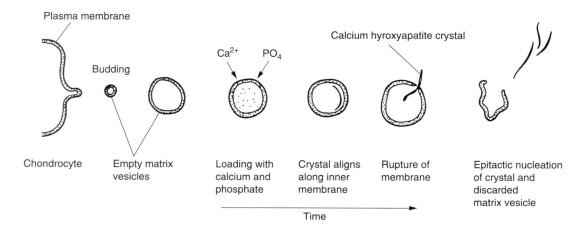

Figure 2.3 *De novo* mineralization via matrix vesicles (after Sela *et al.*, 1992).

phate levels serves to displace some of the calcium from the proteoglycans by ion-exchange mechanisms, thereby raising the calcium and phosphate product above the threshold for precipitation of calcium hydroxyapatite ($Ca_{10}[PO_4]_6[OH]_2$). It is known that the inner membrane of the matrix vesicle is rich in phosphatidyl-serine, a calcium-binding phospholipid (Wuthier, 1989). It has also been shown that to initiate the mineralization process *in vitro*, modest amounts of adenosine triphosphate (ATP) are required (Ali and Evans, 1973).

Initial mineralization occurs along the inner membrane of the matrix vesicle (Fig. 2.3). Calcium is attracted to this membrane by phosphatidylserine and various other calcium-binding proteins. A localized increase in phosphate levels occurs via the presence of phosphatases, including alkaline phosphatase. Thus the initial phase of mineralization is brought about by a complex interaction between calcium-binding molecules and phosphate-metabolizing enzymes (Anderson and Morris, 1993). The initial nuclei of hydroxyapatite are thought to be somewhat unstable and so a protective micro-environment is required where the levels of calcium and phosphate can be both concentrated and controlled (Sauer and Wuthier, 1988). The crystallites of hydroxyapatite initially form as small needle or plate-like structures aligned along the inner membrane of the vesicle (Moradian-Oldak *et al.*, 1991; Akisaka *et al.*, 1998).

As the crystals increase in size they rupture the membrane and so break free from the protective environment of the matrix vesicle (Eanes and Hailer, 1985). These 'seed' crystals are now exposed to the extracellular fluid and serve as templates for new crystal proliferation – epitactic nucleation (Neuman and Neuman, 1953). In this extravesicular phase, collagen provides a favourable environment for nucleation and propagation of the hydroxyapatite seeds (Arsenault, 1989). Although some authors believe that the crystallites are deposited at specific sites along the collagen fibrils, mainly in the spaces between the tropocollagen molecules, others consider that most lie outwith the confines of the fibrils in the extrafibrillar volume (Lees and Prostak, 1988; Weiner and Traub, 1989; Bonucci, 1992; Traub *et al.*, 1992; Mundy and Martin, 1993). As the matrix becomes heavily mineralized the matrix vesicles are fragmented and destroyed, as they serve no further purpose (Fig. 2.3). The histological appearance of *de novo* mineralization is illustrated in Fig. 2.4.

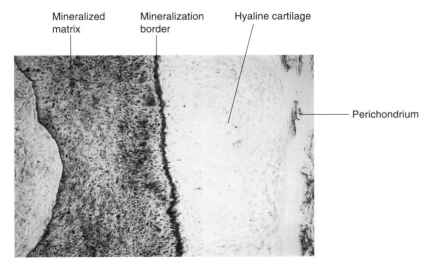

Figure 2.4 *De novo* mineralization of costal cartilage (ground section × 2.5 objective).

Intramembranous ossification

In terms of both phylogeny and ontogeny, intramembranous ossification is the first to develop and continues throughout life in the form of subperiosteal apposition. Indeed, this form of ossification is expressed in every bone in the human skeleton, although most texts tend to dwell only on the embryonic range of its spectrum. Its earliest stages of development are perhaps less complicated than its later stages, which are represented by bone modelling and remodelling which continues throughout life (see below).

Intramembranous ossification is defined as the direct mineralization of a highly vascular connective tissue membrane. It occurs in two forms – dermal and perichondral. The clavicle is probably the first bone in the human skeleton to show evidence of bone formation and osteoprogenitor cells can be detected in the differentiating mesenchyme from approximately day 39 in the 6th week of intra-uterine life. It is widely accepted that ossification commences via the process outlined above for *de novo* mineralization. The crystals expand spherically within the osteoid (the organic matrix of bone) thereby forming bone nodules, which subsequently fuse to form seams of woven bone (Bernard and Pease, 1969; Marvaso and Bernard, 1977). Perhaps as a result of a breaching of a threshold potential, once a sufficient number of these nodules have been deposited in the mesenchymal matrix, there is evidence of vascular invasion. Proliferation of the centre of ossification does tend to be located around a capillary network (Hamilton and Mossman, 1972; Hansen, 1993) and it has been suggested by Thompson *et al.* (1989) that the osteogenic cells may in fact secrete an angiogenic factor that actively encourages vascular invasion. The intimate relationship between osteogenic cells and vascularity is further evidenced by the fact that the osteoblasts are always polarized so that they secrete with their 'backs' aligned next to a blood vessel.

Fine trabeculae of early bone can be detected between adjacent differentiating mesenchymal cells and these will extend and expand into a diffuse network of bony spicules. Intervascular sprouts of bone extend to enclose the blood vessels as more mesenchymal cells differentiate into osteoblasts. This primary spongiosa begins to thicken with the laying down of more osteoid on the surfaces of the trabeculae. The primary trabeculae radiate centrifugally from the centre of ossification and increase in length by accretion to their free ends (Weinmann and Sicher, 1947; Ogden, 1979). Small secondary trabeculae develop at right angles to the primary struts helping to enclose the vascular spaces, and as the rate of bone growth slows, primary osteonal systems form.

The mesenchyme on the surface of the developing bone begins to condense and form the fibrovascular periosteum that will remain actively osteogenic throughout life. As each successive layer of bone is laid down on the surface, osteoblasts become trapped in the matrix and are transformed into osteocytes occupying the lacunae in the interstitial bony substance. Some fetal and neonatal bones present with an incomplete cortex in which the underlying trabeculae are visible. This is not a pathological condition but is probably little more than an intermittent stage, indicating as yet incomplete development of the periosteal layer of compact bone.

Haversian systems (first identified by Clopton Havers in 1691) develop almost exclusively in compact bone (Cohen and Harris, 1958; Cooper *et al.*, 1966). Although they epitomize the microscopic appearance of adult bone they are also found in **woven bone**, which is the most immature type of developing bone and is typical of young fetal bones. Woven bone tends to form very quickly, is poorly organized and relatively weak. When viewed under polarized light it appears similar to the weave of fabric, hence its name. It appears as a randomly interconnecting labyrinth that houses large vascular spaces. Osteoblast-mediated apposition of **concentric lamellae** on the walls of the vascular spaces reduces them to such an extent that eventually only a small canal persists around the central blood vessel. Thus a **primary osteon** (Haversian system) develops with its Haversian canal and associated neuro-vascular contents. At the periosteal surface, blood vessels become incorporated into the circumferential lamellar structure laid down by the periosteum and become surrounded by several layers of concentric lamellae, thereby forming a primary osteon in this location.

Lamellar bone is more mature, forms slowly, is well organized, consists of parallel layers and constitutes almost all of adult compact bone. It appears in two distinct patterns that have been likened to plywood architecture (Giraud-Guille, 1988). In the first of these, the collagen fibres are parallel in each lamella but change by 90° at the interface with the next lamella. In other regions, this can be replaced by a helicoidal arrangement where the collagen fibres constantly change their direction so that the individual identification of a lamella is almost impossible. Both of these patterns of collagen orientation lead to birefringence when a section is viewed under polarized light (Ascenzi and Bonucci, 1967). This alteration in fibre orientation imparts great resilience and strength to the tissue.

The **primary bone** that is formed by early primary Haversian systems is short-lived and is soon remodelled into a more complex tissue comprised of longitudinally orientated cylindrical secondary Haversian systems (secondary osteons). The existing primary bone is removed and replaced with new lamellar bone by osteoblasts and osteoclasts that operate together in a basic multicel-lular unit or BMU. This generally consists of approximately 9–10 osteoclasts and several hundred osteoblasts operating in unison (Jaworski et al., 1981). A BMU operates in a predictable pattern – activation, resorption and formation (ARF) (Jaworski et al., 1983), although there are in fact six identifiable phases in the sequential development of a secondary osteon. These are as follows:

1 Activation – this involves the recruitment of precursor cells to form the BMU. It has been reported that this phase can take up to 3 days to complete (Martin et al., 1998).

2 Resorption – in this stage the newly differentiated osteoclasts begin to resorb the primary bone at a rate of approximately 40–50μm per day. This collection of 9–10 osteoclasts forms the so-called 'cutting cone'. The secretion of acids demineralizes adjacent bone and then enzymes dissolve the collagen. The tunnel that is cut by the osteoclasts is more or less longitudinal to the axis of the bone but there is some evidence to suggest that it spirals slightly at an angle of curvature of approximately 12° (Petrtyl et al., 1996).

3 Reversal – this marks the stage of transition between the leading osteo-clastic cutting cone and the following osteoblastic region of bone forma-tion.

4 Formation – osteoblasts align along the periphery of the tunnel cut by the osteoclasts and begin to lay down concentric lamellae at a closing rate of approximately 1–2 μm per day and is commonly called the 'closing cone' (Polig and Jee, 1990). The tunnel is not completely infilled, as it is neces-sary to house a nutrient artery in the central Haversian canal. The aver-age formation phase takes approximately 3 months to complete in the adult (Martin et al., 1998).

5 Mineralization – following deposition of the osteoid the process of mineralization commences by the growth of mineral crystals between the layers of collagen fibrils (Landis, 1995). Mineralization can continue for up to 6 months, so that newly formed osteons can exhibit very different mechanical properties from more mature osteons, which will exhibit a greater proportion of mineralization.

6 Quiescence – the osteoclasts are no longer required in this stage and the remaining osteoblasts either convert into osteocytes or are removed. The secondary osteon is fully mature at this stage and able to fully participate in its primary roles of tissue metabolism and mechanics.

Endochondral ossification

The process of endochondral ossification is most frequently described in relation to the development of the long bones. However, the first step in long bone development is in fact intramembranous in nature, as there is no direct replacement of cartilage *per se*. The perichondrium in the region of the centre of the long bone diaphysis begins to thicken and the osteoprogenitor cells give rise to osteoblasts. Bruder and Caplan (1989) termed these 'stacked cells', and described them as a layer of 4–6 cells that completely surrounds the cartilage. Interestingly, they stated that the osteogenic differentiation in this region progressed independent of any chondrogenic activity in the cartilage anlage of developing bone. The osteoblasts surround capillaries from the perichondral arterial network and secrete osteoid, which is quickly mineralized (matrix vesicles have been identified in this location). In this way a discrete bone collar or constricting cuff forms around the midshaft region (Fig. 2.5). Above and below this region the perichondrium is continuous with the now appropriately named periosteum. Bruder and Caplan (1989) also suggested that such a restrictive bone collar would initiate a nutrient diffusion barrier that might be directly responsible for the hypertrophy of the chondrocytes in the centre of the cartilage model. The bone in this area will be remodelled as growth progresses, but in essence, it can be said that the compact bone of the mature diaphysis of each long bone is almost entirely periosteal and therefore intramembranous in origin.

The periosteum retains its osteogenic potential throughout life but it has been noted that in the earlier years bone formation can become somewhat exuberant such that excess new woven bone is formed at such a rate that its

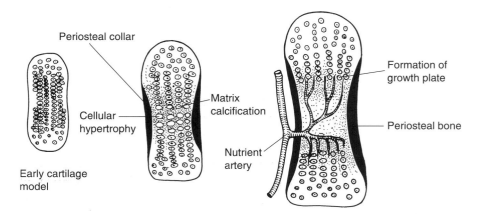

Figure 2.5 The early stages of long bone diaphyseal ossification.

remodelling into more mature bone may be somewhat delayed (Shopfner, 1966). Such so-called 'periosteal reactions' are quite commonly found in immature bones (Malmberg, 1944; Caffey and Silverman, 1945; Tufts *et al.*, 1982; Aoki *et al.*, 1987; Anderson and Carter, 1994; Lewis and Roberts, 1997) and are not necessarily, as has been suggested, an indication of inflammatory reaction/infection, stress or even child abuse. They can be identified radiologically as a 'double contour' effect which is most commonly seen between 2 and 6 months of age in otherwise healthy children. These contours later disappear with no treatment or change in clinical management and are therefore probably normal (Glaser, 1949; Hancox *et al.*, 1951). Shopfner (1966) suggested that increased activity of the periosteum may arise when it is not tightly bound to the underlying cortex, perhaps as a result of sparse or shortened Sharpey's fibres. In 35% of his sample there was no evidence of any other clinical condition. It is also possible that this situation may arise following asynchrony in the rate of growth of the physis cartilage and the periosteum, resulting in periosteal tension and reactive apposition (Jones, personal communication).

True endochondral ossification occurs within the cartilage core of the anlage (template). The chondrocytes in the centre of the cartilage begin to enlarge and the cytoplasm becomes vacuolated (Fig. 2.5). The cells degenerate and the intercellular matrix becomes compressed into septae (primary areolae) that ultimately mineralize due to the presence and involvement of matrix vesicles. A vascular bud then penetrates the periosteal collar forming an **irruption canal**, thereby permitting osteogenic invasion of the cartilage core and the development of marrow spaces. Whilst several periosteal vessels may initially penetrate the bony ring, usually only one will become dominant and develop into the nutrient artery. The traditional view of subsequent events is that osteoid is laid down in the residual walls of the calcified cartilage and the newly introduced osteoprogenitor cells convert this into woven bone, thereby forming an internal trabecular network. It is not clear whether the function of such internal struts in the midshaft region is to provide support for the haemopoietic tissue of the developing marrow cavity or to provide an internal framework to underpin the developing cylindrical shaft. However, it is clear that following cortical drift in the midshaft region of the more mature thick compact bone of the diaphysis, short thick endosteal struts are all that are likely to remain of the endochondral element of diaphyseal ossification (Jones *et al.*, 1999). However, in the proximal and distal extremities of the more mature diaphysis, an abundance of cancellous struts are retained, presumably indicating that their presence is necessary/desirable for force dissipation. Bruder and Caplan (1989) forcefully stated that the embryonic cartilage model *does not* provide scaffolding for new bone formation but rather serves as a target for future bone marrow elements. It is at this stage, when a periosteal collar has been formed and endochondral ossification has commenced in the core, that the primary centre of ossification of a long bone is said to have developed.

Not only does endochondral ossification play a critical role with regards to the longitudinal growth of a long bone (growth plate – see below), but it is also the mode of ossification encountered in the epiphyses of the long bones, the centra of the vertebral column, sternebrae, carpals, tarsals and in fact any region of the skeleton that displays significant volumes of cancellous or trabecular bone. In these areas, the first sign of impending ossification occurs when isogenous cell groups in the centre of the cartilaginous mass begin to hypertrophy. Matrix vesicles have been identified in these locations and it is highly probable that they form the initial site of *de novo* crystallite formation. The region is subsequently invaded by osteogenic vascular mesenchyme, probably via the cartilage canals that have been identified even in the youngest human fetal epiphyses (Weinmann and Sicher, 1947; Brookes, 1958, 1971; Wilsman and Van Sickle, 1972). Arterial invasion normally occurs at a number of sites via a vascular arcade, which explains the multitude of nutrient foramina generally found in the non-articular regions of epiphyses (Brookes, 1971). Following the pattern of endochondral ossification seen in the long bone diaphyses, bone is laid down in these centres along the mineralized cartilage septae and subsequently remodelled into the characteristic thicker trabeculae of recognizable cancellous bone. Bone can only grow via accretion and so, as the ossification centre enlarges, its cartilaginous periphery becomes a proliferative zone permitting an increase in size in a radial direction. The cartilaginous cell columns are generally directed towards the growth plate.

The growth plate and bone growth

Due to the rigid nature of the matrix component of bone, osseous tissue cannot increase in size by interstitial development and so grows by a well-balanced process of apposition and resorption that constitutes bone modelling. Shortly after formation of the primary centre of ossification, an organized region of rapid growth (growth plate) will develop between the epiphysis and the diaphysis, which is primarily responsible for the increase in length of the developing diaphysis (Rang, 1969). This region is often referred to as the epiphyseal plate or the physis and whilst the latter is appropriate as it is the Greek term for 'growth', the former is inappropriate as this plate does not play a part in the increase in size of the epiphysis (Siegling, 1941).

The traditional description of a growth plate is that found at the extremities of a long bone diaphysis (Fig. 2.6). These are generally described as being discoid in shape and are responsible not only for the longitudinal growth of the shaft but also for its diametric expansion. The division of the growth plate into distinct zones is artificial but helpful for the appreciation of the histological appearance, although unfortunately the terminology used is not universal. However, it is the function of each zone that is important and not its name.

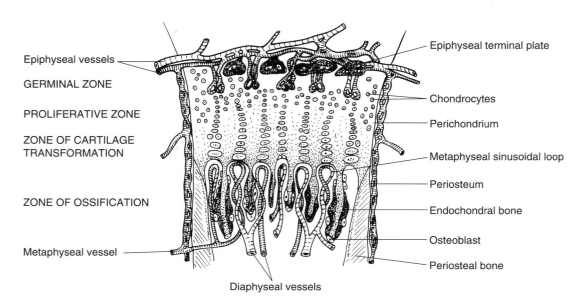

Figure 2.6 A summary of the major features of a diaphyseal growth plate.

The zone furthest away from the diaphysis and closest to the epiphysis is called the resting or **germinal zone**. In this area the chondrocytes are small, quiescent and randomly distributed. These cells receive a vascular supply from the epiphyseal vessels that penetrate the terminal plate (see below). In the adjacent **proliferative zone**, the chondrocytes increase in size as they accumulate glycogen. The cells exhibit mitotic division and become arranged in longitudinal pillars or palisades of initially wedge-shaped cells. These palisades make up almost half the height of a growth plate and are the sites of new cartilage formation that will ensure the continued longitudinal expansion of the diaphysis. Although the majority of mitotic divisions occur in a transverse plane, Lacroix (1951) and Serafini-Fracassini and Smith (1974) have explained the paradox of their contribution to the lengthening of the shaft. Following mitosis, the daughter cells do indeed lie side by side but the cells are wedge-shaped and orientated so that their narrow edges overlap considerably. As the cells migrate towards the metaphysis, the narrow edges expand so that the cell is ultimately rectangular and as a result the originally oblique intercellular septum becomes transverse and the cells align in a longitudinal direction.

The chondrocytes start to hypertrophy in the **zone of cartilage transformation**, in preparation for their replacement by bone. In this region there is a progressive degeneration of the cellular component, with an increase in hydroxyapatite deposition via matrix vesicles. Any intercellular connections are removed as the vascular invasion by metaphyseal sinusoidal loops advances. Rather than degenerating, some of the cells in this region may be released into the next zone where transformation into osteoblasts may occur. In the **zone of ossification**, osteoblasts form a layer of bone on the remnants of the mineralized cartilage of the preceding zone. This bone undergoes re-organization through osteoclastic activity and the subsequent addition of new bone.

As the primary ossification centre expands towards the epiphyses, the periosteal collar remains slightly in advance of the endochondral replacement, although it will eventually adopt a position level with the hypertrophic zone. This region, comprising the extremity of the periosteal collar, peripheral physis and fibrovascular tissue, is referred to as the zone of Ranvier and is important for diametric expansion (Ogden, 1979). Diametric or transverse expansion occurs by cell division and matrix expansion within the growth plate and by cellular addition from the periphery at the zone of Ranvier (Speer, 1982; Rodriguez *et al.*, 1992). This small, wedge-shaped zone of cells governs the control of relative diametric proportions between the expanding diaphysis and epiphysis. To maintain proportions within a bone, the diaphysis must remodel in the transverse plane as it expands longitudinally (see below). New layers of bone are laid down at the periosteal margin (apposition) whilst bone is removed from the endosteal surface (resorption). This complementary relationship ensures a relatively constant ratio between bone addition and bone loss. Obviously, when one or other of these processes no longer maintains that balance, then disorders of excess or insufficient cortical mass will ensue.

Appositional bone growth via the periosteum was discovered almost by accident around 1736 by Mr Belchier, a surgeon at Guy's Hospital (Holden, 1882). He was dining with a friend who happened to be a calico printer and they were eating a leg of pork when he noted that the bones were red and not white. On making further enquiries he found that the pig had been fed on the refuse from the dyeing vats, which contained a substantial quantity of madder (Eurasian vegetable dye from *Rubia tinctorum*). As a direct result of this fortuitous discovery, many of the earlier studies on bone growth and development were performed on animals that were fed on madder. More recently, of course, this form of bone growth has been observed by tetracycline labelling and radio-isotopes such as [85]Sr (Milch *et al.*, 1958; Shock *et al.*, 1972).

Much is made in the literature about the 'growing end' of a long bone. Obviously, this is an inappropriate description as both ends of a long bone exhibit growth. It actually refers to the fact that one extremity of the shaft may contribute to a larger proportion of the overall diaphyseal development than the other. It has been suggested that growth is equal at both ends until birth but that after that event one extremity becomes dominant (Brookes, 1963). In all long bones, except the fibula, the general rule is that the growing end is represented by the epiphysis that is the first to appear and the last to fuse. It is also recognized that the angles of obliquity of the nutrient foramina conform to this pattern so that in the upper limb they are directed towards the elbow and in the lower limb, away from the knee (Hughes, 1952; Mysorekar, 1967; Patake and Mysorekar, 1977). In this way, the nutrient foramen is directed away from the growing end of the bone and therefore the faster-growing ends are located at the shoulder and wrist in the upper limb and around the knee in the lower limb. If only one extremity of a long bone bears an epiphysis (e.g. metacarpals), then the nutrient foramen is generally directed away from the epiphyseal end.

Hales (1727) and later Hunter (1837) were probably the first to note and study the phenomenon of unequal growth in the extremities of long bones. Hales (1727) pierced two small holes in the tibia of a chick and sacrificed the animal 2 months later. He found that the distance between the marks had remained constant but that the shaft had grown in length and had increased more at one end than at the other. Many other researches have since repeated the experiment but probably the two most quoted are Bisgard and Bisgard (1935) on goats and the findings of Digby (1915) on human material.

The typical physis described at the extremity of a long bone diaphysis is only one type of growth plate. The epiphysis (or indeed primary centre, e.g. in a carpal or tarsal bone) has its own growth plate, which is more appropriately described as a growth zone as it approximates to the shape of the developing structure (Fig. 2.7). It is represented by a proliferative zone of cartilage cells that are modelled into cancellous bone by the progressive centrifugal expansion of endochondral ossification. In this situation the bony nucleus of the developing epiphysis is homologous with the metaphyseal region of a long bone and forms the initial osseous growth site. As the ossification centre expands in the epiphysis of a long bone, it is inevitable that it will eventually approximate to the growth plate of the diaphysis (Fig. 2.7). Juxtaposition of the epiphyseal spherical growth plate with the developing cartilaginous model of the diaphysis results in the formation of a temporary bipolar physis (Ogden, 1979). The epiphyseal contribution is eventually replaced by a subchondral growth plate, which is also known as the **terminal plate**. This plate is formed when the trabeculae of the epiphysis unite to form a sealing plate that ensures the separate containment of the respective marrow spaces (Weinmann and Sicher, 1947).

As bone maturity approaches, cartilage proliferation slows and the growth plate becomes quiescent and gradually thins. The juxtaposed subchondral bone of the epiphysis thickens, while a similar thickening occurs at the corresponding metaphyseal surface. In this way, dense parallel bone plates (sclerotic lines) begin to form on either side of the remaining physis (Ogden, 1979). This double layer of bone tends to persist throughout life (often beyond 70 years of age) in many of the long bones and can be detected radiographically, when it is known as the 'epiphyseal line, scar or ghost' (Cope, 1920; MacLaughlin, 1987; Martin

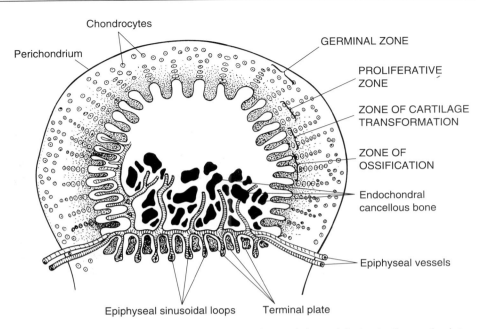

Figure 2.7 A summary of the major features of an epiphyseal (spherical) growth plate.

et al., 1998). There is rapid replacement of the cellular palisades by metaphyseal bone and vascular shoots will ultimately pierce the thin cartilaginous plate and unite with the epiphyseal vessels. Ossification occurs concomitant with this invasion, forming initial bony bridges that will ultimately lead to fusion of the diaphysis to the epiphysis. Depending upon the size of the bone, perforation may only occur at one site or in the cases of larger bones there may be many sites of vascular breakthrough. There seem to be few rules as to whether epiphyseal union commences peripherally or centrally and in fact it seems to be bone, and possibly individual, dependent (Haines, 1975).

Obviously, the spherical growth plate is also the means whereby small cancellous bones such as the carpals and tarsals increase in size. Expansional growth will cease when the interstitial expansion of the cartilage template no longer keeps pace with the advancing front of endochondral ossification and it comes into contact with the enveloping perichondrium. Via intramembranous ossification, the periosteum will then form a thin covering shell of compact bone. Further bone growth will, by necessity, involve the processes of apposition and resorption for continued remodelling (see below).

An insult to the growth plate, whether developmental, hereditary, disease- or trauma-related, may result in an abnormal growth rate, which can either stimulate or inhibit growth at the plate. For this reason, precise surgical management of growth plate abnormalities is extremely important to ensure not only the continued bilateral symmetrical growth of the bones but also to safeguard against foreshortening of the limb (De Campo and Boldt, 1986; Young *et al.*, 1986; Nilsson *et al.*, 1987). There are many factors that can cause a disturbance of the normal functioning of the growth plate and the aetiology of such disorders is most conveniently considered under the somewhat traditional headings of congenital (genetically programmed disorders, chromosomal abnormalities and developmental disorders), infection, nutrition, trauma, physical injury, vascular factors, hormonal imbalance and neoplasm (Rang, 1969).

The growth plate represents a site of potential weakness in the bone, which subsequently decreases its resilience to withstand trauma. Approximately 15% of all fractures in children involve the growth plate (Salter and Harris, 1963; Ogden, 1981). Males tend to sustain physeal injuries more frequently than females and this may be due either to social factors (i.e. greater degree of physical activity) or to the extended duration of the physis in the male. Interestingly, distal growth plates tend to be affected more frequently than proximal ones in all long bones. The prognosis following physeal fracture is obviously highly dependent upon the nature and site of the fracture and the integrity of the blood supply (Adams and Hamblen, 1992).

The normal growth and development of a bone is inextricably linked to its vascular, and in particular its arterial, supply. In fact, the onset and maintenance of ossification is dependent upon an uninterrupted nutritive flow. There are three principal arterial networks associated with the developing bone and each fulfils a different functional role (Fig. 2.8). The **diaphyseal** arteries are synonymous with nutrient arteries and are generally derived from an adjacent major systemic artery. They enter a bone via its nutrient foramen (Havers, 1691), which leads into a nutrient canal. There is no branching within the canal but once the vessel enters the medullary cavity it normally divides into ascending and descending medullary branches (Crock, 1996; Brookes and Revell, 1998). The direction and source of arterial blood flow in the cortex has been a long-standing topic of much debate. The historical views tended to support the theory that the cortex derives its superficial peripheral supply from periosteal vessels, while its deeper layers are supplied by medullary vessels (Lewis, 1956; Trueta and Morgan, 1960; Trueta and Cavadias, 1964; Skawina and Gorczyca, 1984). However, Brookes and Harrison (1957) suggested that in youth, the arterial input to the cortex is in fact predominantly

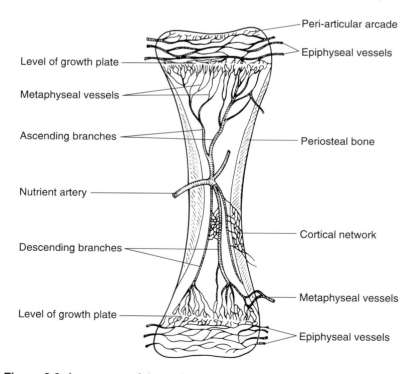

Figure 2.8 A summary of the main arterial supply to a developing long bone.

medullary in origin. Modern research has confirmed that in the young (<35 years) there is no periosteal supply to the cortical bone, but it is entirely medullary in origin and therefore operates in a centrifugal manner (Dillaman, 1984; Skawina *et al.*, 1994; Bridgeman and Brookes, 1996; Brookes and Revell, 1998). However, it has been suggested that the cortical supply becomes increasingly periosteal in nature with advancing age due to medullary ischaemia brought on by atherosclerosis of the medullary vessels (Bridgeman and Brookes, 1996). In advancing years (70+), the cortical supply is reported to be almost entirely periosteal in nature.

The ascending and descending branches of the medullary vessel branch profusely throughout the cavity and terminate in helical loops in the vicinity of the metaphyseal zone. Here they anastomose with the **metaphyseal** vessels, which are also direct branches from adjacent systemic vessels. They are aligned vertical to the growth plate and are uniformly dispersed throughout the cancellous bone. The active metaphysis obtains its blood supply not only from the metaphyseal vessels but also from branches of the sinusoidal medullary loops in the zone of ossification. In fetal bone, the metaphyseal vessels support the entire width of the growth plate but in the postnatal years they tend to be responsible for maintenance of the cells in the zones of cartilage transformation and ossification (Brookes and Revell, 1998).

The **epiphyseal** arteries are derived from peri-articular vascular arcades that form on the non-articular bone surfaces. Branches of these vessels can be identified in the cartilage canals of the epiphyseal mass as early as the 9th prenatal week (Haraldsson, 1962; Brookes and Revell, 1998). The epiphyseal mass is a discrete vascular zone with limited or no anastomoses occurring with the adjacent metaphyseal vessels. In postnatal long bones it has been shown that the epiphyseal vessels penetrate through the juxtaposed subchondral (terminal) plate to supply the germinal and proliferative zones of the growth plate (Brookes and Revell, 1998). Thus the overall viability of the growth plate to maintain normal bone growth and development is dependent upon the integrity of these vessels. Should damage occur to these arteries then growth arrest will occur. Whilst it has been shown that some degree of arterial anastomosis exists, it is generally insufficient to fully compensate when a major vessel is damaged (Brookes, 1957) and so an interruption to normal growth is unavoidable.

Probably one of the best known indicators of growth arrest (delay) is the presence of radiodense lines or bands in the diaphyses of the growing long bones, although they are not solely restricted to this location (Sontag, 1938; Stammel, 1941). However, they are most frequently encountered in the proximal end of the tibia and the distal end of the femur (Kapadia, 1991; Kapadia *et al.*, 1992; Aufderheide and Rodriguez-Martin, 1998). First described by Wegner in 1874, they have been variously called Harris lines (Harris, 1926, 1933), growth arrest lines (Ogden, 1984a) or even recovery lines (Park and Richter, 1953; Park, 1964) depending upon the considered mode of formation (Fig. 2.9). These radiopaque lines form as a result of stress, whether biological, mechanical or even psychological. The normal maladies of childhood such as measles, mumps and chickenpox can be sufficient to induce the formation of such a stress marker (Gindhart, 1969). As a result of the insult, it has been noted that the cartilaginous growth plate diminishes in size following decreased chondrogenesis, although the advancing front of mineralization continues (Eliot *et al.*, 1927). Whilst proliferation of the cartilage slows, the osteoblasts continue bone formation so that the undersurface of the cartilage plate becomes an almost impenetrable barrier. When normal growth is resumed or the restrictive factor is removed, the Harris line continues to thicken, as there

Proximal

Harris lines

Harris lines

Distal

Figure 2.9 Harris lines at both the proximal and distal extremities of a juvenile tibial shaft.

is a delay whilst osteoclastic activity penetrates the bony plate before a normal rate of activity can be resumed (Park and Richter, 1953). In cross-section, the radiopaque line appears as a latticework of trabeculae and is composed of discontinuous projections of compact bone that end in the marrow cavity (Garn *et al.*, 1968; McHenry, 1968).

Several studies have attempted to determine the age of formation of these lines using information on the percentage of growth that occurs at each end of the growing bone at a given age (Hunt and Hatch, 1981; Maat, 1984; Hummert and Van Gerven, 1985; Byers, 1991). It should be borne in mind of course that when the bone recommences its growth after cessation of the upset then such trabecular struts are susceptible to remodelling and therefore resorption (Kapadia, 1991; Kapadia *et al.*, 1992).

There is a delicate balance between bone formation and bone resorption during bone modelling and remodelling, with an abnormality in one or the other leading to extensive pathological change. Intramembranous subperiosteal apposition and resorption is a critical component of the ongoing remodelling of the skeleton throughout life (Enlow, 1963; Garn, 1970; Martin *et al.*, 1998). Not only is remodelling necessary to allow bone growth and development, but, of course, it is essential for repair following traumas, including fracture. It should therefore be borne in mind that continued subperiosteal apposition is a form of intramembranous ossification.

As a bone develops it must not only increase in length and width but also alter its shape and composition to accommodate the changing stresses and strains that are placed upon it in this dynamic stage. Bone **modelling** therefore involves the sculpting of a developing bone by the removal of bone in some locations with a concomitant addition in other places. Bone development is a continuous activity involving mutually dependent actions of bone-forming cells (osteoblasts) and bone removal cells (osteoclasts). Such geometric alterations are witnessed in almost all bones, irrespective of whether they form by intramembranous or endochondral ossification. Obviously, bone modelling is markedly reduced once the individual attains maturity.

Remodelling involves the removal of bone that was formed at an early time and its replacement with new bone. It has been estimated that approximately 5% of adult compact bone is renewed every year, and an astonishing 25% of cancellous bone (Martin *et al.*, 1998). Remodelling tends to occur more as a coordinated operation between bone formation and resorption, tends not to affect the overall size and shape of the bone, is episodic and continues throughout life (Enlow, 1963; Garn, 1970). The function of remodelling is thought to be essentially reparative in nature by the elimination of microscopic damage that could eventually lead to fatigue failure.

Remodelling of bone can be used as a means of determining the age of the bone. As the osteons are remodelled, so the proportion of bone 'debris' such as woven bone, primary osteons, osteon fragments, etc. to new osteons will alter. This has been utilized by anthropologists to establish an age at death using microscopic sections of compact bone. The usefulness of this technique lies in its ability to establish age in the adult when often there are few other methods available. However it is a complex laboratory process and cannot realistically be undertaken by the amateur. Whilst Amprino (1948) and Hattner and Frost (1963) recognized the relationship between bone turnover and age, Kerley (1965) is attributed with being the first to apply it to anthropological problems. Although revisions were made to his original technique (Kerley and Ubelaker, 1978), this work remains the ground-breaking research in the field and it has since been used by many investigators (Ahlqvist and Damsten, 1969; Singh and Gunberg, 1970; Bouvier and Ubelaker, 1977; Thompson, 1979; Ericksen, 1991; Stout *et al.*, 1994; Walker *et al.*, 1994; Cool *et al.*, 1995; Watanabe *et al.*, 1998).

Whilst most anthropologists recognize the value of this approach, there are certain limitations to be taken into consideration (Lazenby, 1984; Aiello and Molleson, 1993). For example, the accuracy of this approach will vary between different populations depending upon factors such as health, nutrition, etc. Factors such as the choice of bone, the sample site and the amount required must be carefully selected. However, these problems are not specific to this technique alone but apply to many methods of age determination. The true benefit of histological age determination probably lies in the ability to assign an age at death from relatively small fragments of bone, although the effect of diagenesis must be borne in mind (Bell, 1990; Bell *et al.*, 1996).

CHAPTER THREE

Early Embryonic Development

This chapter is a brief synopsis of very early embryogenesis, in order to prevent unnecessary repetition in the following chapters. For a fuller account the reader should refer to specific embryology texts (e.g. O'Rahilly and Müller, 2001). Details on early skeletal development of individual bones can be found in subsequent relevant chapters.

At the end of the second week following fertilization (stages 5 and 6), the cells that will form the embryo are arranged as a circular bilaminar embryonic disc of about 0.2 mm in diameter. The upper layer, or **epiblast**, consists of columnar cells that lie adjacent to the amniotic cavity. The lower layer of the disc, or **hypoblast**, is composed of cuboidal cells that form the roof of the secondary umbilical vesicle. Both these layers are continuous peripherally outside the embryonic area with extra-embryonic tissues (Fig. 3.1).

Starting at stage 6 (about day 17), cells of the epiblast are involved in a complex re-arrangement of cell populations that establishes bilaterality of the embryo and the formation of the three germ layers. It begins with the formation of the **primitive streak**, a proliferative zone of cells in the caudal part of the part of the epiblast that starts to migrate ventrally in the median plane (Fig. 3.2). The rostral end of the primitive streak may be distinct and is known as the **primitive node**, which is hollowed by the **primitive pit**. The first cells to replace the hypoblast form the definitive **endoderm**. (Fig. 3.3) The remaining cells form intra-embryonic **mesoderm** between the epiblast

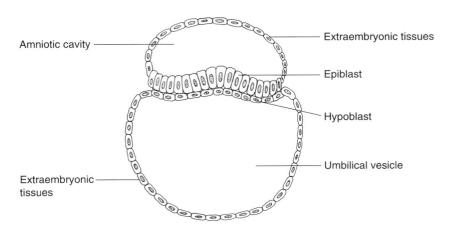

Figure 3.1 The bilaminar disc at the end of week 2.

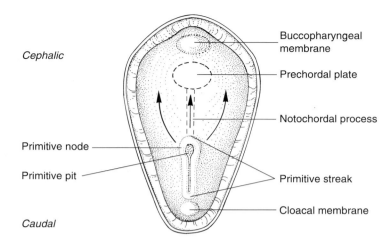

Figure 3.2 The primitive streak.

and the endoderm and produce two midline structures, the **prechordal plate** and the **notochordal process**. The prechordal plate, anchored into the endoderm, is a localized, thickening cephalic to the notochordal process and is thought to be an important source of cephalic mesenchyme and possibly endoderm. The notochordal process is a rod-like bar of cells extending rostrally from the primitive node to the prechordal plate. Its primary function is the induction of the neural plate and it goes through several changes before becoming the definitive notochord (stages 8–11). It takes part in the maintenance of the neural floor plate and is involved in signalling to the sclerotomal part of the paraxial mesoderm. Once the three germ layers are fully established, the remaining surface epiblast is known as the **ectoderm**. At the cephalic and caudal ends of the embryo the ectoderm and endoderm are closely related and form the **buccopharyngeal** and **cloacal** membranes, respectively. These two membranes, which later break down, form the oral and cloacal ends of the gut tube (Figs 3.2 and 3.8).

The establishment of the three germ layers of the embryo is fundamental to the subsequent development of the major systems of the body, although the notion of their separate development is an oversimplification. The study of morphogenetic mechanisms has revealed that there are complex interactions between cells from different layers and many structures have contributions from more than one layer.

By stage 8 (about 23 days), the embryonic disc is about 1 mm in length and is pyriform-shaped, being wider rostrally. The beginnings of the nervous system are seen as the thickened **neural plate**, which lies in the midline over the

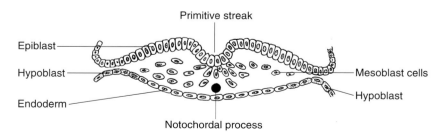

Figure 3.3 The trilaminar disc – stage 8 (3rd week).

notochord from the primitive node to the prechordal plate, and laterally over the paraxial strip of mesoderm. The neural plate enlarges rapidly and develops a median sulcus, **neural groove** and the margins become raised as **neural folds** (Fig. 3.4). The folds gradually meet over the top of the groove, beginning at the junction between the future brain and spinal cord, and fusion proceeds both rostrally and caudally to form a hollow **neural tube**, which subsequently detaches itself from the surface ectoderm (Fig. 3.5a–c). This process is known as neurulation. Anteriorly, the tube enlarges and it is possible to distinguish the three major subdivisions of the brain: **prosencephanon** (forebrain), **mesencephanlon** (midbrain) and **rhombencephalon** (hindbrain). The tube temporarily remains open at **rostral** and **caudal neuropores**, which eventually close by the stages 11 and 12 (about 30 and 31 days) respectively (Fig. 3.6). A special population of cells, the **neural crest** (ectomesenchyme), forms at the lateral margins of the neural folds between the neural and somatic ectoderm between stages 9 and 13 ($3\frac{1}{2}$–$4\frac{1}{2}$ weeks). The cells of the neural crest differentiate first at the junction of the midbrain and hindbrain and then detach from the epithelium and become mesenchymal and migratory in nature. They invade the intra-embryonic mesoderm and by a process of epithelio-mesenchymal interaction, contribute to a wide range of skeletal and dental tissues.

As the neural folds are forming, the bilateral **paraxial mesoderm** alongside the notochord thickens, while laterally, it connects to a narrower band of **intermediate mesoderm**. This in turn is continuous with a flatter band called the **lateral plate** (Fig. 3.7). The paraxial mesoderm in the region of the hindbrain becomes subdivided lengthways into a series of rounded whorls of cells, which, in the chick, mouse and rat, have been called **somitomeres** and this formation proceeds cephalocaudally as the embryo grows. These structures have not yet been identified in the human embryo but their behaviour is assumed to follow the general mammalian pattern. The seven pairs rostral to the mid-myelencephalon are said to remain as somitomeres but caudal to this

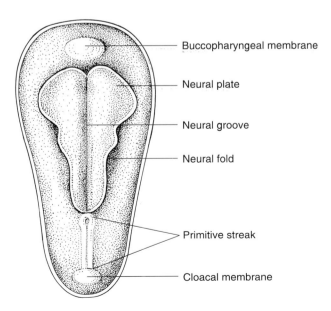

- Buccopharyngeal membrane
- Neural plate
- Neural groove
- Neural fold
- Primitive streak
- Cloacal membrane

Figure 3.4 The position of the neural plate.

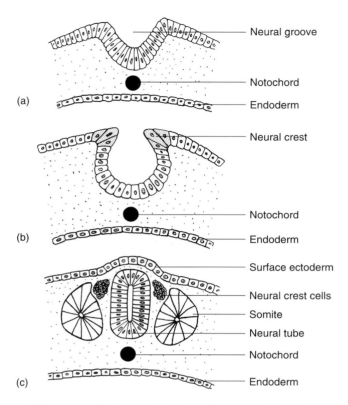

(a)

Neural groove

Notochord

Endoderm

(b)

Neural crest

Notochord

Endoderm

(c)

Surface ectoderm

Neural crest cells

Somite

Neural tube

Notochord

Endoderm

Figure 3.5 Neurulation – stages 9–11 (4th week).

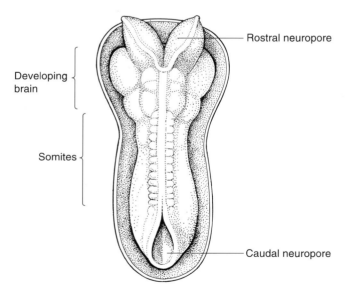

Rostral neuropore

Developing brain

Somites

Caudal neuropore

Figure 3.6 Embryo showing neuropores and somites – stage 10–11 (4th week).

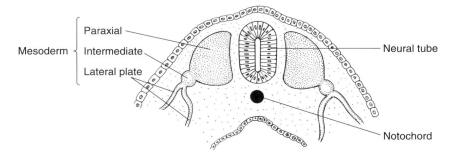

Figure 3.7 Divisions of the mesoderm.

point they develop into discrete blocks or segments called **somites**. They develop during the same period as the formation of the neural crest, i.e. during stages 9–13 ($3\frac{1}{2}$–$4\frac{1}{2}$ weeks). There are probably 38–39 pairs but they are never all visible at one time and several of the terminal pairs later regress. Each somite consists of three parts: a ventromedial **sclerotome**, which forms the basis of the future postcranial skeleton, a dorsolateral **dermatome** and a dorsomedial **myotome**, which will develop into the skin and muscles respectively of the body wall and limbs. The first four or five pairs of somites are incorporated into the occipital region, while the successive eight pairs form the cervical region with the most cranial of these also taking part in the formation of the occiput. The next 12 somite pairs form the thoracic vertebrae and the bones, striated muscles and dermis of the thorax. Some cells from the lower cervical and upper thoracic somites migrate laterally to form the structures of the upper limb buds. Of the next 10 somite pairs, the upper five form the lumbar column and the dermis and striated muscles of the abdominal wall, while the lower five form the sacrum and its associated structures. As with the upper limb, cells from the lumbar and upper sacral somites contribute to the development of the structures of the lower limb. The remainder of the somite pairs will form the coccygeal region of the embryo (for further details see Chapter 6).

During the 3rd and 4th weeks, other fundamental changes are taking place in the embryo that are only outlined here. Differential growth causes a folding of the embryo both cephalocaudally and laterally to assume its definitive shape (Fig. 3.8). In the very early stages, the prechordal plate and cardiogenic area lie in front of the anterior tip of the notochord. The rapid overgrowth of the nervous system produces a head fold during which the buccopharyngeal membrane and pericardium tilt a full 180° ventrally in a process known as reversal. Thus, the future mouth (stomodeum) and pharyngeal region is bounded dorsally by the developing forebrain and notochord and below by the heart tube in its pericardial cavity. In a similar manner, during the formation of the tail fold, the cloacal membrane and connecting stalk, originally posterior, also come to lie ventrally (Fig. 3.8).

During the 3rd and 4th weeks the first external signs of the formation of the ear, eye and nose show as ectodermal thickenings. The **otic placodes** (discs), which give rise to the inner ear, are situated lateral to the hindbrain region, the **lens discs** are associated with the lateral aspects of the forebrain and the **nasal placodes** are found on the frontonasal process of the future face.

During the 4th and 5th weeks of development, a series of **pharyngeal** (branchial) **arches** are formed in the lateral walls of the pharyngeal region of the foregut (Fig. 3.9). They develop in a rostrocaudal sequence during stages

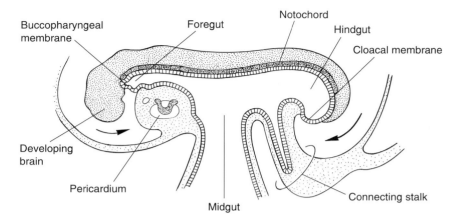

Figure 3.8 Folding of the embryo – stages 9–11 (4th week).

10–13 (between the 28th and 32nd days) and form a series of bars, each with a mesenchymal core covered by ectoderm and lined by endoderm. Between the bars lie the external **pharyngeal grooves** (clefts) and the internal **pharyngeal pouches**, where the ectoderm and endoderm are in contact. The arches are transient structures with the first four being fairly prominent and it appears from experimental evidence on animal models, that they contain contributions from the neural crest. The fifth arch is rudimentary and short-lived and this and the sixth arch cannot be recognized externally. Some of the skeletal structures derived from the arches develop in cartilage, which subsequently ossifies, while others develop directly from mesenchyme. Skeletal elements of the first (mandibular) arch form within the maxillary and mandibular processes and so contribute to the upper and lower jaws, Meckel's cartilage in the mandible and the major part of the malleus and incus of the middle ear. The second (hyoid) arch gives rise to the styloid process of the temporal bone, part of the hyoid bone and the stapes of the middle ear. The rest of the hyoid bone forms from the third arch, while the fourth and sixth arches contribute to the cartilages of the larynx. The external auditory meatus,

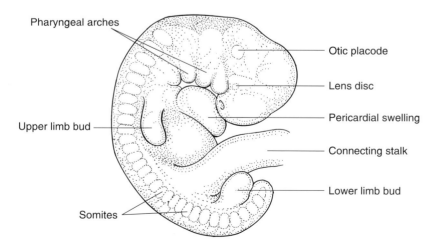

Figure 3.9 Embryo at stage 13–14 (about 5 weeks).

the tympanic cavity and the auditory (pharyngotympanic/Eustachian) tube are remnants of the first cleft and pouch (see Chapter 4).

At stages 12 and 13 (during the 5th week) the **limb buds** appear as small projections from a lateral ridge on the ventrolateral aspect of the trunk (Fig. 3.9). The early development of both limbs is similar, but the timing of the upper limb precedes that of the lower limb by about 2 days (see Chapter 9).

CHAPTER FOUR

The Head and Neck

This chapter includes not only the skull and mandible but also the hyoid and larynx. The cervical vertebrae are considered together with the rest of the vertebral column in Chapter 6.

The skull is the most complex region of the axial skeleton. It both supports and protects the brain and special sense organs and accommodates the first part of the gut and respiratory tract. The skull may be divided functionally into two parts. The **neurocranium**, or braincase, consists of a base and vault whose side walls and roof (calvaria) provide a bony protective covering. Attached anteriorly is the face, the upper part forming the skeleton of the orbits and nose, and the lower part, together with the mandible, constituting the mouth and jaws, or **viscerocranium.**

The terminology used in human cranial embryology is principally derived from the literature of comparative morphology, and a very brief synopsis of development of the vertebrate skull is introduced here so that the subsequent description of the early embryology of the human skull may be more easily appreciated. In the earliest forms of vertebrates there was both an inner (endo-) and an outer (exo-) skeleton. The **endoskeleton** consisted of a cartilaginous braincase, or **chondrocranium**, to which were attached capsules that surrounded organs of special sense, and a **jaw** skeleton composed of visceral (branchial/pharyngeal) arch cartilages which, in later forms, became secondarily attached to the skull. The **exoskeleton**, which covered the anterior end of the body as a protective bony shield, developed in relation to the skin, hence the term dermal bone (see also Chapter 2). During the course of vertebrate evolution, the basic pattern of the chondrocranium has been conserved, albeit with additional new elements in later vertebrates. On the other hand, the exoskeleton has been greatly reduced but some derivatives still exist in mammals.

The vertebrate chondrocranium consists of a **basal plate** of fused cartilages to which are attached three pairs of capsules (otic, optic and nasal) that support and protect the organs of hearing, sight and smell. Posteriorly, the paired **parachordal cartilages** surround the anterior end of the notochord and have the **otic capsules** attached laterally. In front of the notochord the plate is composed of paired **trabeculae cranii** which, for descriptive purposes, can be divided into a **hypophyseal** area around the pituitary posteriorly and an **interorbitonasal** element anteriorly, to which are attached the **nasal** and **optic** capsules. The side wall of the braincase was incomplete in early vertebrates but, in subsequent mammalian evolution, which involved enlargement of the brain, a new element, the **ala temporalis**, formed. The roof of the chondrocranium was also incomplete but represented by three bands of cartilage called the synotic tecta connecting, from anterior to posterior, the orbital cartilages, the otic capsules and the posterior cartilages (Jarvik, 1980).

The second component of the endoskeleton is derived from a variable number of cartilaginous **pharyngeal** (visceral) **arches**, which develop in the floor and walls of the pharynx. In aquatic forms, they support the gills but their function and subsequent development varies in different groups of land animals. In early jawed vertebrates, the first two arches were involved in the formation and support of the jaws but in higher vertebrates they became incorporated into the skull, ear and skeleton of the neck. For instance, Meckel's cartilage is a prominent but transient structure from the lower element of the first (mandibular) arch seen in the embryos of all mammals. Reichert's cartilage, from the second (hyoid) arch, contributes to the temporal and hyoid bones, and parts of the post-hyoid arches take part in the formation of the larynx.

Remains of the original dermal armour that comprised the exoskeleton have become highly modified and homologies between different groups are far from clear. One theory holds that, in higher vertebrates, these original dermal bones contribute to the cranial vault, the orbital and nasal cavities, the jaws and pectoral girdle. An alternative idea of head morphology is that the anterior part of the skull is not directly related to previous forms but is an entirely new construction (Gans and Northcutt, 1983; Northcutt and Gans, 1983).

In the human skull, some bones develop endochondrally from a cartilaginous template and others form intramembranously directly in mesenchyme (see Chapter 2). Three large and complex bones, the occipital, temporal and sphenoid, contain constituent parts with both intramembranous and endochondral origins. The major part of the **nose** and the **cranial base** are preformed in cartilage. The latter comprises the basal, lateral parts and lower squama of the occipital bone, the petromastoid portions of the temporals, the body, the lesser

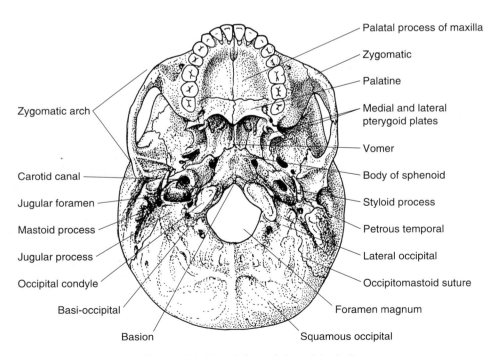

Figure 4.1 Basal view of the adult skull.

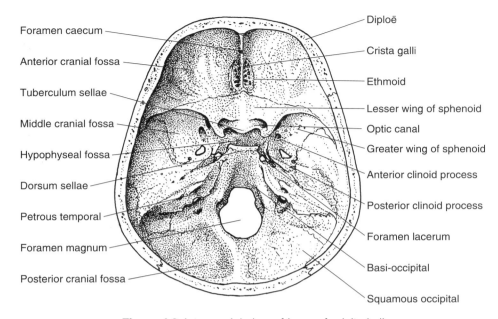

Figure 4.2 Intracranial view of base of adult skull.

wings and medial parts of the greater wings of the sphenoid, and the ethmoid and inferior conchae (Figs 4.1 and 4.2). The bones of the **vault** arise directly in membranous tissue to cover the rapidly expanding brain. They include the frontal, parietals, greater wings of the sphenoid, squamous parts of the temporals and the upper squama of the occipital bone (Figs 4.3 and 4.4). Most of the remainder of the bones of the skull, which constitute the **face** and form around the nasal capsule, also develop directly in membrane. They are repre-

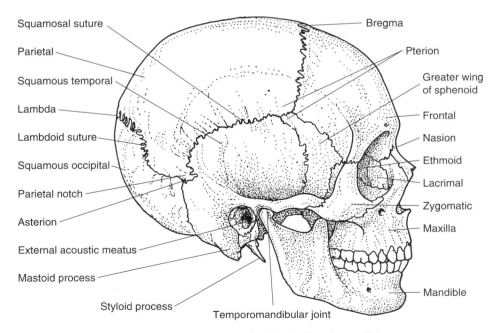

Figure 4.3 Lateral view of adult skull and mandible.

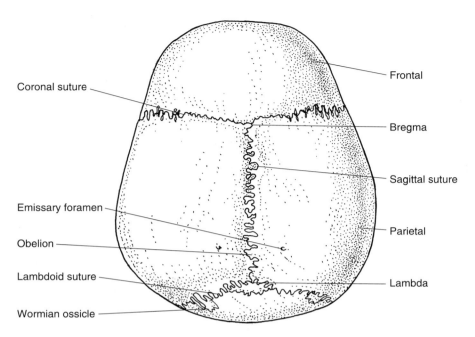

Figure 4.4 Superior view of adult skull.

sented by the maxillae, palatines, nasals, lacrimals, zygomatics and the vomer (Figs 4.1, 4.3 and 4.5).

Derivatives of pharyngeal arches contribute to the maxilla, mandible, ear ossicles, styloid process of the temporal, hyoid bone and the larynx. Much of the cranial base undergoes ossification during prenatal development but some cartilaginous synchondroses remain until early adult life when growth ceases.

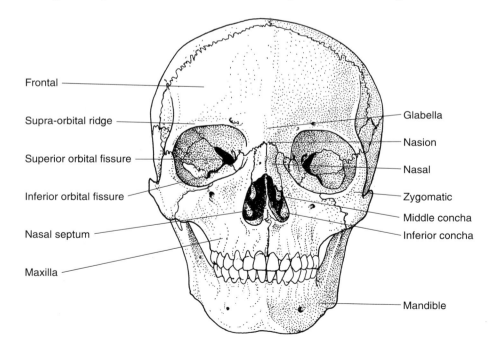

Figure 4.5 Anterior view of adult skull and mandible.

Some cartilage is retained throughout life in the nasal alae, the external ear and part of the auditory (Eustachian) tube. Fusion between parts of compound bones occurs over a wide time range extending from fetal life, through infancy to early childhood. Articulations between most of the bones of the vault and face are composed of fibrous sutures, most of which are well developed during infancy.

Early development of the human skull

To prevent needless repetition, this section contains an outline of the early development of the human skull as a whole up to the end of the embryonic period. Details may be found in Macklin (1914, 1921), Lewis (1920), Youssef (1964), Müller and O'Rahilly (1980, 1986, 1994) and O'Rahilly and Müller (1984). Development from the beginning of the fetal period is included under each individual bone.

The **blastemal** skull develops in the embryonic mesenchyme that surrounds the developing brain and primitive pharynx. The first signs of the **cranial base** are mesenchymal masses that appear in the occipital area during the 4th week of intra-uterine life. These gradually spread anteriorly and, by the beginning of the 2nd month, encompass the pituitary region and then penetrate the territory of the nasal septum beneath the forebrain. The posterior part of the cranial base is penetrated obliquely by the notochord (Fig. 4.6), which leaves the dens of the axis and enters the basal area, where, at first, it lies dorsally between the hindbrain and the occipital mesenchyme. It then passes ventrally to lie in the dorsal wall of the pharynx and finally ends just in front of the region that is to become the dorsum sellae of the sphenoid (Müller and O'Rahilly, 1980; David *et al.*, 1998). At about the 5th week, the otic placodes, composed of specialized neurepithelial cells, sink below the surface ectoderm and become encased in mesenchyme to form the **otic capsules** which gain attachment to the occipital part of the basal plate. Meanwhile, the basic organization of the face is being laid down (see below).

At the beginning of the 2nd month, the cranial base begins to chondrify as separate foci gradually fuse to form a continuous but incomplete cartilaginous

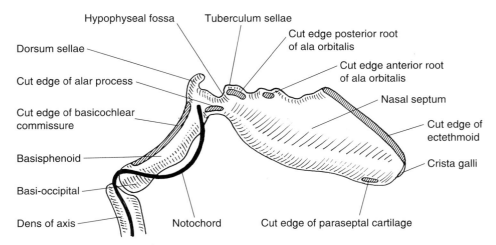

Figure 4.6 The central stem of the chondrocranium (redrawn after Müller and O'Rahilly, 1980).

mass, the **basal plate** (Fig. 4.7). Names given to the cartilages of the human cranial base vary, depending on the supposed derivation from an ancestral condition, but commonly accepted accounts may be found in Sullivan and Lumsden (1981) and Sperber (1989). The central stem (Fig. 4.6) is angled in the region of the hypophyseal fossa into chordal and prechordal parts. Cranial base angulation changes greatly during early fetal development as reflected by the rapidly growing brain and extension of the neck region. This is measured at the pre-chordal/ chordal junction, by lines from nasion to sella (mid-hypophyseal fossa), and sella to basion (Figs 4.2 and 4.5). It angulates to about $130°$ in the 7 week embryo (cartilaginous stage), between $115°-120°$ at 10 weeks (pre-ossification stage) and then widens again to between $125°$ and $130°$ by 20 weeks as the cranial base ossifies The prechordal cranial base increases in length and width sevenfold whilst the posterior part grows only fivefold as these changes keep pace with the rate of development of the different parts of the brain (Sperber, 1989). Growth of the different segments of the fetal skull is detailed by Ford (1956).

For descriptive purposes, the chondrocranium during the embryonic period can be conveniently divided from posterior to anterior as occipital, otic, sphenoidal (orbitotemporal) and ethmoidal areas (Figs 4.6–4.8). In the **occipital** region, the paired parachordal cartilages join to form the basi-occipital part of the basal plate, which lies anterior to the foramen magnum. This is at first deeply notched anteriorly but later becomes more rounded in shape. On either side lie the ex-occipitals, which give rise to the lateral parts of the occipital bone. They develop jugular tubercles that separate the hypoglossal canals from the jugular fossae. The ex-occipitals are continued superiorly into the occipital plates (squamae), which at first are not united in the mid-dorsal line, so that

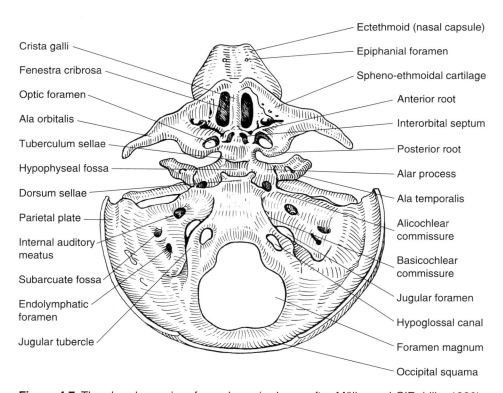

Figure 4.7 The chondrocranium from above (redrawn after Müller and O'Rahilly, 1980).

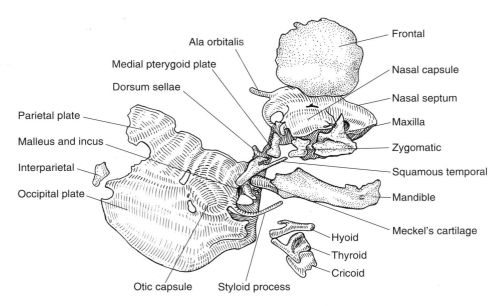

Figure 4.8 The chondrocranium with membrane bones from the right side (redrawn after Müller and O'Rahilly, 1980).

the foramen magnum is incomplete posteriorly. Initially, a thin band of cartilage, the tectum posterius (synoticum), joins the occipital plates but later the whole inferoposterior occipital region is formed by the cartilaginous occipital plate.

The **otic capsules** lie lateral to the basal plate and are joined to it by basicochlear commissures. Each may be divided into a cochlear and a canalicular part. The internal auditory meatus, the endolymphatic foramen and the subarcuate fossa are obvious and the internal carotid artery and the VIIth (facial) cranial nerve are exposed on the rostral surface. Joined to the canalicular parts of the otic capsules by capsuloparietal commissures are two areas of cartilage called parietal (mastoid/nuchal) plates. They are incomplete superiorly but joined posteriorly to the occipital plate and so partially cover the posterolateral part of the occipital area.

In the **sphenoidal region** the basisphenoid (postsphenoid) cartilage is continuous posteriorly with the basi-occipital and has the dorsum sellae protruding superiorly. On either side of the hypophyseal fossa is an alar process over which the internal carotid artery runs in an anterior direction. The alar processes join the bases of the greater wings (alae temporales) to the body and are themselves connected posteriorly, via the alicochlear commissures, to the otic capsules. In the midline, anterior to the postsphenoid, is the interorbital septum, which forms the presphenoid part of the body between the tuberculum sellae and the limbus sphenoidalis. It is connected to a lesser wing (ala orbitalis) on each side by two roots, a pre-optic (anterior/ventral) and a postoptic (posterior/dorsal/metopic) root, between which lies the optic foramen. The maxillary nerve runs forward to a cleft between the greater and lesser sphenoidal wings. At first this is wide open but later becomes filled in medially as the foramen rotundum forms, and laterally, as the rest of the wing develops in membrane.

The **ethmoidal region** consists of a mesethmoid cartilage in the midline that contributes to the nasal septum. The prominent crista galli protrudes superiorly. On either side are the nasal capsules composed of small paraseptal cartilages and ectethmoid cartilages from which the ethmoidal labyrinths develop. At first, they are incomplete, having side walls with a developing middle conchae but almost no floor except the inturned edges where the inferior conchae form. Superiorly, the anterior half has a roof, but posteriorly are the open fenestrae cribrosae. Epiphanial foramina in the roof allow passage of the anterior ethmoidal nerves. The posterior ends of the nasal capsules are joined to the orbital wings of the sphenoid by spheno-ethmoidal cartilages, which support the developing frontal lobes of the brain.

Ossification of the chondrocranium begins posteriorly before chondrification is complete in the whole mass anteriorly. At the beginning of the 2nd month the first ossification centres appear in the tectum posterius region of the occipital squama as the supra-occipital bone begins to ossify.

The **vault** of the skull appears at the end of the first prenatal month, as lateral curved plates of mesenchyme that gradually spread both downwards to meet the forming cartilaginous base and upwards to meet each other over the top of the developing brain. Most of the bones ossify directly in this mesenchyme and the sides of the vault are temporarily connected superiorly by three incomplete bands of cartilage called tecta but these ill-defined cartilaginous remnants soon disappear (Fawcett, 1910a, 1923). By the end of the embryonic period, (Fig. 4.8) ossification can be seen posteriorly in the interparietal part of the occipital, laterally in the squamous temporal, medial pterygoid plate and the frontal bones. The goniale, which develops into the anterior process of the malleus, is represented by a small spicule of bone close to the end of Meckel's cartilage. Early ossification centres for the maxillae and zygomatic bones can be seen in the side wall of the nasal capsule and those for the palatines and bilateral plates of the vomer lie in the posterior part of the nasal cavity. The parietals, tympanic parts of the temporal bones, nasal and lacrimal bones start to ossify slightly later in the fetal period (O'Rahilly and Gardner, 1972).

The basic organization of the **face** begins at the end of the 4th week when five swellings appear around the stomodeum. The mandibular (first pharyngeal) arch gives rise to bilateral maxillary and mandibular processes above and below the stomodeum and a median frontonasal process develops in the forehead area over the anterior end of the forebrain (Fig. 4.9a). During the 5th week, nasal placodes appear on the frontonasal process and the mesenchyme on either side of these ectodermal thickenings forms the medial and lateral nasal folds (processes). The placode invaginates beneath the surface to become the nasal pit. By a process of differential growth, the medial folds meet together to become the intermaxillary segment (Fig. 4.9b), which forms the bridge and centre of the nose, the philtrum of the upper lip and the premaxillary area (primary palate) (Fig. 4.10a,b). The lateral nasal folds join with the maxillary processes to form the sides of the nose and the cheek area (Fig. 4.9c).

Deep to the surface, the maxillary processes form palatal shelves (Fig. 4.10), which at first hang down beside the tongue. They subsequently rotate to a horizontal position and join with each other to complete the posterior growth of the palate (secondary palate). The nasal septum grows down from the base of the skull and fuses to the midline of the palate. In this way the primitive pharyngeal cavity is separated into bilateral nasal cavities above and an oral cavity below (Fig. 4.10c). The transition of the palatal shelves from a vertical to a horizontal position takes place over a relatively short period of time between 7 and 8 weeks. However, the shelves remain vertical slightly longer in females, which could account for the greater incidence of cleft palate in girls (Burdi and Silvey, 1969a, 1969b). The basic morphology of the face and palate is laid down

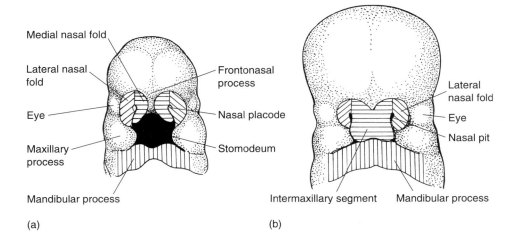

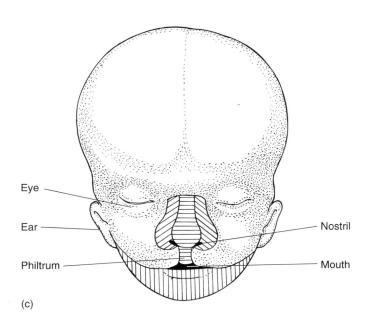

Figure 4.9 The formation of the face: (a) 5 weeks; (b) 7–8 weeks; (c) 10 weeks.

between 4 and 10 weeks. Diewert (1985) has studied details of major growth changes that take place during this period.

The neurocranium has a very rapid rate of growth concurrent with the precocious development of the brain and reaches 25% of its growth by birth, 50% by 6 months of age, 75% by 2 years and almost completes its growth by 10 years (Sperber, 1989). The circumference of the head almost doubles from midfetal life to birth and the biparietal diameter (BPD), as measured by ultrasound, is one of the common parameters by which normal development is monitored during pregnancy.

The growth of the vault and eyes in their contained orbits follow the rapid pattern of neural growth whilst the lower part of the facial complex is primarily related to the development of the dentition and muscles of mastication. This results in a skull in the fetus, infant and young child that has very different

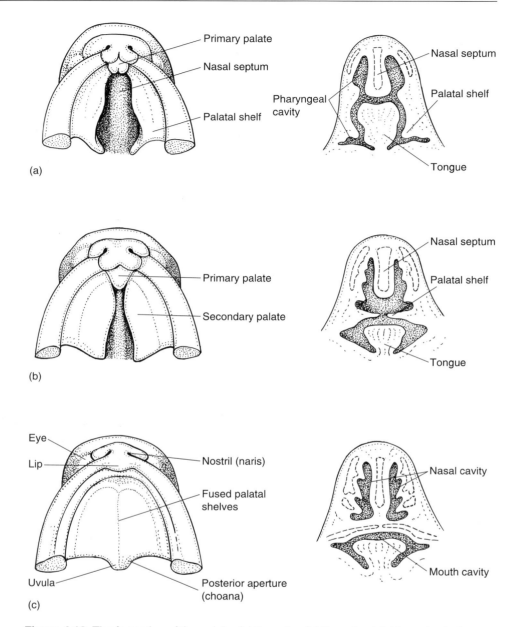

Figure 4.10 The formation of the palate: (a) 7 weeks; (b) 8 weeks; (c) 10 weeks. Left row – looking into roof of the mouth; right row – coronal sections through nose and mouth.

proportions from that seen in later childhood, adolescence and adult life, hence the large head and eyes and relatively small face of infants and young children (Figs 4.11–4.14). At birth, the face is 55–60% of the breadth, 40–45% of the height and 30–35% of the depth of the adult value (Krogman, 1951). Calvarial to facial proportions are about 8:1 at birth, 4:1 at 5 years and about 2.5:1 in adult life (Sperber, 1989).

The **pharyngeal arches** are transitory structures that form in the lateral walls and floor of the pharynx of all mammalian embryos. In the human embryo they develop in a craniocaudal sequence between 22 and 29 days. The first three are fairly prominent but the rest of the series are rudimentary

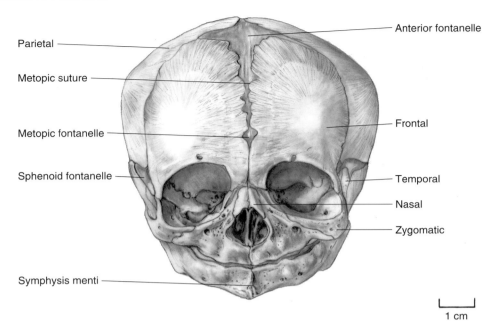

Parietal

Metopic suture

Metopic fontanelle

Sphenoid fontanelle

Symphysis menti

Anterior fontanelle

Frontal

Temporal

Nasal

Zygomatic

1 cm

Figure 4.11 Anterior view of fetal skull and mandible.

and short-lived. Some of the structures that arise from the branchial arches develop in cartilage, which subsequently ossifies, and others are formed directly in mesenchyme.

During the embryonic period, Meckel's cartilages are represented by elongated cartilaginous rods, which extend inferiorly from the otic capsules to converge at an angle in the floor of the mouth. The upper end of each rod

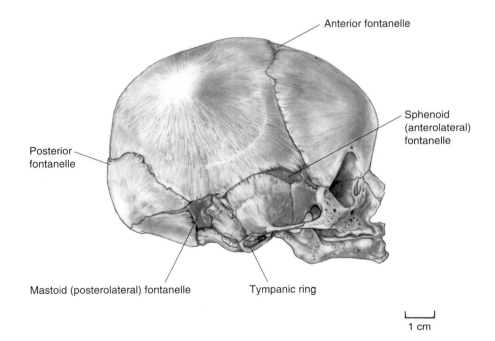

Anterior fontanelle

Sphenoid (anterolateral) fontanelle

Posterior fontanelle

Mastoid (posterolateral) fontanelle

Tympanic ring

1 cm

Figure 4.12 Lateral view of fetal skull and mandible.

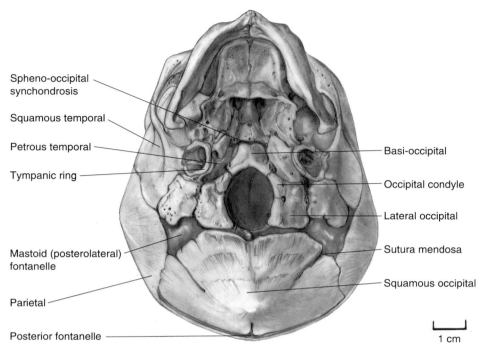

Spheno-occipital synchondrosis

Squamous temporal

Petrous temporal

Tympanic ring

Mastoid (posterolateral) fontanelle

Parietal

Posterior fontanelle

Basi-occipital

Occipital condyle

Lateral occipital

Sutura mendosa

Squamous occipital

1 cm

Figure 4.13 Basal view of fetal skull and mandible.

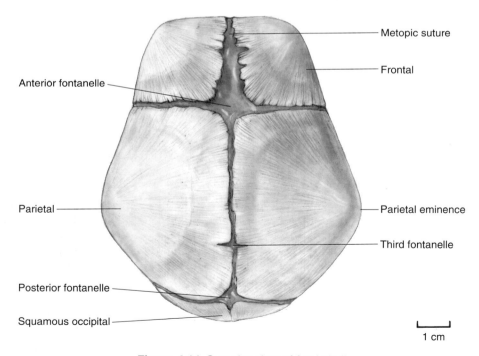

Metopic suture

Frontal

Anterior fontanelle

Parietal

Parietal eminence

Third fontanelle

Posterior fontanelle

Squamous occipital

1 cm

Figure 4.14 Superior view of fetal skull.

forms the malleus and incus, which at this stage are still attached to the cartilage, but later become separated by mesenchyme. On the lateral side of Meckel's cartilage the mandible is well ossified in membrane. The second arch cartilage is represented by the stapes, the styloid process of the temporal bone and part of the hyoid bone. At this stage, the stapes is disc-shaped with a small central foramen. The cartilaginous styloid process is attached to the otic capsule above and projects downward from the base of the skull. Derivatives of subsequent pharyngeal arches are represented by contributions to the hyoid and laryngeal cartilages that lie below Meckel's cartilage (Fig. 4.8). It is not clear which pharyngeal arches give rise to the larynx, as the number of arches beyond the fourth, and particularly the actual existence of the fifth arch in the human embryo, is in some doubt. With the present state of knowledge it does not seem possible to assign various laryngeal components to specific arches (O'Rahilly and Tucker, 1973).

There is a vast literature on the growth and development of the skull as a whole that lies beyond the scope of this text. Much of it is in dental and orthodontic papers, and further information, including details of the main planes and osteometric landmarks used in radiological cephalometric analysis, can be found in other texts (Knussmann, 1988; Sperber, 1989; Enlow and Hans, 1996).

I. THE OCCIPITAL

The occipital bone forms part of the base of the skull and the posterior wall of the cranial cavity. It articulates with the parietals superolaterally, the petromastoid parts of the temporals inferiorly and laterally and the sphenoid anteriorly (Figs 4.1–4.4). The bone consists of four parts – the squamous, two lateral and a basal part, all of which form the boundaries of the foramen magnum.

Ossification

Ossification of the occipital arises from a variable number of centres, which join during fetal life to form the four principal components of the bone (Fig. 4.15). The **squama occipitalis** (pars squama) is subdivided into a **pars interparietalis** and a **pars supra-occipitalis,** which fuse in the central part of the **sutura mendosa** during prenatal life. The interparietal part, which is the only section that is truly a squamous bone, forms part of the posterior wall of the cranial cavity extending up to the lambda. It occupies a triangular area bounded by the highest nuchal line and the posterior borders of the two parietal bones. The supra-occipital part forms the most posterior part of the skull base, defines the centre of the posterior border of the foramen magnum and articulates anteriorly with the lateral occipitals at the **sutura intra-occipitalis posterior**. The two **partes laterales/condylares** (lateral/ex-occipitals) form the lateral boundaries of the foramen magnum and articulate anteriorly with the **pars basilaris** (basi-occipital) at the **sutura intra-occipitalis anterior**. The basilar part forms the anterior margin of the foramen magnum and articulates anteriorly with the sphenoid at the **spheno-occipital synchondrosis**. All four main parts of the bone articulate with the temporal bone.

Ossification in the **squamous** part of the occipital bone is visible between 8 and 10 weeks of intra-uterine life (Noback, 1944; Noback and Robertson, 1951). Ossification centres can be seen by alizarin staining or by examination

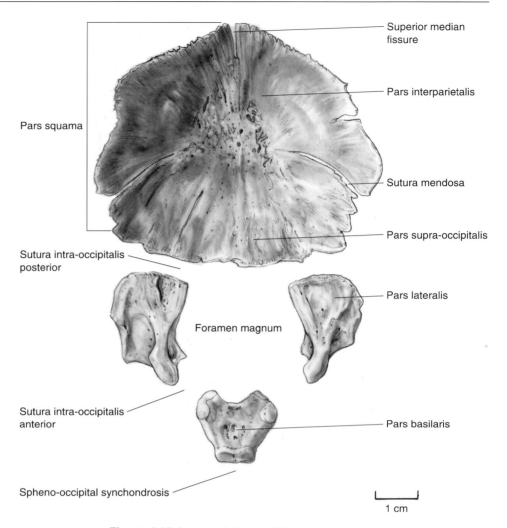

Superior median fissure

Pars interparietalis

Pars squama

Sutura mendosa

Pars supra-occipitalis

Sutura intra-occipitalis posterior

Pars lateralis

Foramen magnum

Sutura intra-occipitalis anterior

Pars basilaris

Spheno-occipital synchondrosis

1 cm

Figure 4.15 Intracranial view of the perinatal occipital.

of histological sections before they are visualized radiographically (O'Rahilly and Gardner, 1972). During the 8th week (stage 23), two small areas of bone representing the supra-occipital and interparietal portions can be seen: a small area of perichondral bone in the tectum posterior on the outer aspect of the chondrocranium and above it on each side of the median plane, an intramembranous centre (O'Rahilly and Gardner, 1972; Müller and O'Rahilly, 1980). In studies of the developing fetal cranium by Kjær and colleagues, the sequence of appearance of the ossification centres was shown to be very consistent (Bach-Petersen and Kjær, 1993; Kjær et al., 1993).

The major part of the supra-occipital part is preformed in cartilage and ossification starts at the end of the embryonic period proper from either a single centre (Macklin, 1921; Noback, 1944) or a pair of centres (Mall, 1906; Müller and O'Rahilly, 1980) which rapidly fuse together forming a solid plate of bone at the posterior border of the skull (Frazer, 1948; Fazekas and Kósa, 1978; Matsumura et al., 1993, 1994). The interparietal part ossifies from several intramembranous centres. The detailed observations of Srivastava (1992) and Matsumura et al. (1993) agree fundamentally but, unfortunately, different terms have been used for the same parts of the developing bone. Early in the 9th week, a small pair of centres appear in the membrane above the ossifying supra-occipital. These fuse with each other and then join with the supra-occipitals to form the **torus occipitalis transversus,** the part of the adult bone which lies between the superior and highest nuchal lines. This small membranously formed area is called the 'intermediate segment' by Srivastava (1992) and the 'primary interparietal' by Matsumura *et al.* (1993). Srivastava considers that this part, and the endochondrally ossified part to which it fuses, constitute the supra-occipital. However, further studies by Matsumura *et al.* (1994) indicate that this division of bone forming either endochondrally or intramembranously is an over-simplification. They observed that the supra-occipital part is indeed preformed in cartilage and the part that forms immediately superior to it appears in membrane. However, the first formed supra-occipital bone becomes covered on both the internal and external surfaces with fine periosteal cancellous bone, which appears to spread from the membrane formed bone above. Interestingly, a similar process occurs in the maxilla. From the 5th fetal month the supra-occipital bone is a three-layered structure consisting of a solid core of rough, spongy bone between two layers of trabecular meshwork. These appearances were originally described by Zawisch (1957) and have been confirmed by Niida *et al.* (1992).

The true **interparietal** part of the bone, above the highest nuchal line, is formed from a variable number of ossification centres that develop in the membrane above the supra-occipital during the 3rd and 4th intra-uterine months. Srivastava (1992) describes a lateral plate on each side, both formed from medial and lateral centres and, above this, two medial plates composed of superior and inferior centres. Matsumura *et al.* (1993) call the medial and lateral plates 'secondary interparietals' and observed that the medial centres always appeared before the lateral ones. The use of the terms primary and secondary interparietal centres is misleading as both are, in truth, primary ossification centres. There is much variation in the pattern of fusion of these centres causing this part of the skull to be subject to numerous anomalies. However, as most of the descriptions are of adult specimens, it is not possible to deduce their true embryological origins. They have been regarded either as normal variants or as non-metric traits (Berry and Berry, 1967; Ossenberg, 1976; Saunders, 1989) and there appears to be no agreement as to their aetiology.

Rambaud and Renault (1864), Augier (1931) and O'Rahilly and Meyer (1956) describe an inconstant 'pre-interparietal' centre and Matsumura *et al.* (1993) describe fetal skulls with occasional further ossification centres, which they also call pre-interparietals. They appear anterior to the main part of the interparietal bone. The authors view them as a group of separated bones that form in the triangular territory of the central lambdoid region, whose bases are situated higher than the highest nuchal line and distinct anatomically from the small sutural bones that sometimes form in this location. Srivastava (1992) considers that the term pre-interparietal is a misnomer to be avoided and maintains that all the bones developing in the region of the lambdoid suture are sutural or Wormian bones with their own separate ossification centres. Bennett (1965) found that there was a positive correlation between the occurrence of Wormian bones and the length of the basi-occiput in three different populations and concluded that their formation was not under direct genetic control, but represented secondary sutural characteristics, which are brought about by stress. Ossenberg (1970) noted an increased frequency of posterior Wormian bones in skulls that had been deformed by the pressure of cradleboards and bandages. However, El-Najjar and Dawson (1977) concluded that there is a genetic predisposition for these to form and that they were not the result of deformation. Gottlieb (1978) reported that in deformed skulls there was an increase in sutural complexity in the upper part of the lambdoid suture and, if Wormian bones were present, then there was an increase in their numbers compared to normal skulls.

Between 3.5 and 5 prenatal months, the supra-occipital and interparietal parts of the bone start to fuse together in the middle of the bone but there is sometimes a small aperture in the centre between the two parts, the inio-endinial canal, to accommodate a vascular channel between the occipital veins and the confluence of sinuses (O'Rahilly, 1952; O'Rahilly and Meyer, 1956). Fusion is incomplete laterally and this is called the lateral 'fissure' by Srivastava (1992) and the lateral 'incisure' by Niida *et al.* (1992) but is much more commonly known as the **sutura mendosa**. Niida *et al.* considered that lateral fusion is prevented by the existence of the **tectum synoticum poster-ior**, one of the three roof elements of the chondrocranium existing in the territory of the interparietal from about 10–16 prenatal weeks (Fawcett, 1923; Jarvik, 1980), which interferes with the extension of the bone trabeculae in this area. It also represents the future site of the posterolateral fontanelle (Fig. 4.12).

Noback (1944) and Moss *et al.* (1956) reported that the cartilaginous part of the squama has a different growth rate from the interparietal part. The latter, together with the other bones of the vault, has a rapid growth rate up to 12–13 prenatal weeks, which is related to the early precocious growth of the cerebral hemispheres. The supra-occipital part is related to the slower growth rate of the cerebellar hemispheres, which start to enlarge at about the end of the 3rd prenatal month. Confirming this, Fazekas and Kósa (1978) reported that from the 'fifth to the tenth lunar months' the maximum width of the squama is in the interparietal part above the sutura mendosa but by the perinatal period the longitudinal and transverse measurements are very similar. These proportions have also been confirmed in Japanese fetuses by Ohtsuki (1977) who measured the thickness of the occipital squama from 4 fetal months until birth.

By the perinatal period the pars squama has adopted a shallow, bowl-shaped appearance, which is composed of an inferior, thicker supra-occipital portion set at an angle to the thinner, fan-shaped interparietal part (Fig. 4.15). At the junction, is the prominent external occipital protuberance on the convex (external) surface in the median plane. There is usually a median fissure of variable length at the superior angle of the interparietal part, which is continuous with the posterior fontanelle (Figs 4.13 and 4.14). From here, the bone slopes down to the sutura mendosa that may extend up to half way from the midline and is continuous laterally with the mastoid (posterolateral) fontanelle (Fig. 4.12). Up to the perinatal stage, the interparietal part is extremely thin with fragile, feathery borders but later, these thicken and become finely serrated. The lateral borders of the supra-occipital are also serrated and are continuous with the inferior border that is thickened on either side of the midline where it will eventually fuse with the lateral occipitals.

There is an occasional midline ossicle, or process, in the posterior margin of the foramen magnum (Fig. 4.16). This structure was recognized by early anatomists and was originally described by Kerckring (1717) and illustrated by Albinus (1737). Kerckring observed that it appeared in the 4th or 5th fetal month and fused with the supra-occipital before birth. Sometimes, instead of a separate ossicle, this area is represented by a projecting tongue of bone, called the manubrium squamae occipitalis by Virchow or the opisthial process

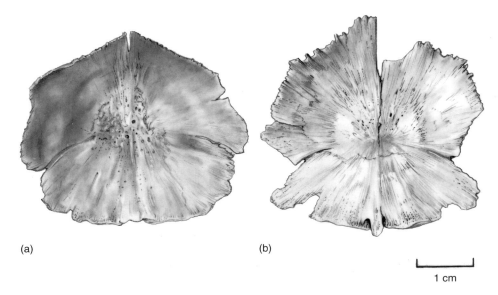

(a)

(b)

|_____|
1 cm

Figure 4.16 Perinatal pars squama. (a) Straight lower border, slightly thickened in the centre; (b) a damaged archaeological specimen with a process of Kerckring.

(O'Rahilly and Meyer, 1956) but is more commonly known as the process of Kerckring. It is described and illustrated by Schultz (1917), Toldt (1919), Limson (1932), Redfield (1970) and Shapiro and Robinson (1976b, 1980) amongst others. Caffey (1953) believed that it could still be visualized as late as the first few months of life if a Towne projection radiograph of the skull was taken. Matsumura *et al.* (1994) indicated that the ossicle sometimes appears when the inner surface of the newly formed supra-occipital is covered with periosteal bone from above, but its aetiology remains uncertain.

Schultz (1917) and Caffey (1953) describe other ossicles that develop laterally in the cartilaginous plate between the supra-occipital and the pars lateralis. They vary in number and size and fuse by the end of the first year with the lower edge of the supra-occipital only, but never with the pars lateralis.

Vascular and neural markings begin to show on the intracranial surface of the bone in the perinatal period and details have been described by Vignaud-Pasquier *et al.* (1964). Radiographs of children's skulls normally show patchy areas of diminished density called digital impressions or convolutional rarefactions, which are most prominent in the posterior and lower lateral calvarial bones. Davidoff (1936) and Macauly (1951), scoring their appearance in different age groups, found that they rarely appeared before 18 months of age but then increased rapidly up to 4 years, reaching a plateau between 7 and 9 years. Although the aetiology is still unknown, they occur maximally during a period of very active growth of the brain and calvaria and are thought in some way to reflect the adaptation of the two tissues to one another. Contrary to previous suggestions, it is now considered unlikely that they are due to increased intracranial pressure (Du Boulay, 1956).

The centres for the **partes laterales** start to ossify endochondrally on either side of the foramen magnum 8 and 9 prenatal weeks. Noback (1944), Bach-Petersen and Kjær (1993) and Kjær *et al.* (1993) reported the onset of ossification as arising above the hypoglossal canal but Zawisch (1957) described two perichondral centres for each bone, the posterior being the larger. Ossification spreads to form quadrilateral plates whose long axes run anteroposteriorly. During the early fetal period, two limbs, which will eventually enclose the hypoglossal nerve, begin to develop from the anteromedial corner of the bone. The posterior condylar canal is present from an early fetal stage, immediately posterior to the occipital condyle.

The neonatal pars lateralis (Fig. 4.17) has a thickened medial border that forms the lateral boundary of the foramen magnum. It meets the wedge-shaped posterior border, which fuses postnatally with the supra-occipital, at a right angle. This ends laterally at a rounded angle that at this stage is open to the mastoid (posterolateral) fontanelle. The lateral border articulates with the mastoid part of the temporal bone (Fig. 4.13). The anterolateral corner has a rounded profile and forms the occipital border of the jugular foramen. It may have one or more spicules of bone along its length, meeting reciprocal processes from the petrous temporal bone, which divide the foramen into one or more compartments (Dodo, 1986). During the first year, the bone posterior to the foramen extends laterally to form the quadrangular jugular process.

At the anteromedial angle the jugular (upper) and condylar (lower) limbs project from the bone. The upper limb bears the jugular tubercle on its intracranial surface whilst the inferior surface of the lower limb forms the posterior two-thirds of the occipital condyle. At first the rounded ends of the two limbs articulate with reciprocal surfaces of the dual facet on the posterolateral border of the pars basilaris (see below) thus forming the hypoglossal canal. Between the ages of one and 3 years, the condylar limb develops a hooked extension, which grows towards, and eventually fuses with the jugular limb, thus excluding the pars basilaris from forming part of the border of the canal. The hypoglossal canal then lies entirely within the territory of the pars lateralis (Fig. 4.18). The canal is often partially or fully divided and this condition may be present from an early fetal age (Dodo, 1980).

The ossification centre for the **pars basilaris** appears in the basal plate anterior to the foramen magnum between the 11th and 12th weeks of prenatal life (Macklin, 1921; Noback, 1944; Noback and Robertson, 1951, Fazekas and Kósa, 1978). Kjær (1990a, 1990b), Kjær *et al.* (1993) and Kyrkanides *et al.*

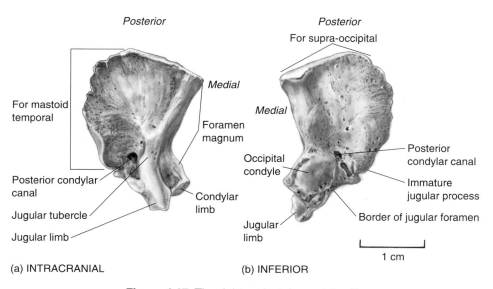

(a) INTRACRANIAL   (b) INFERIOR

Figure 4.17 The right perinatal pars lateralis.

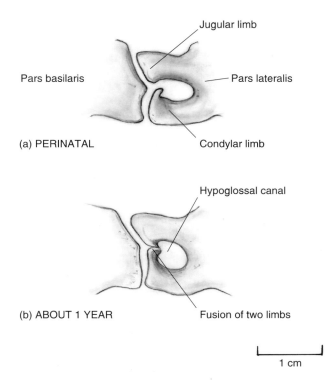

Figure 4.18 Formation of the hypoglossal canal.

(1993) observed the centre in their radiographic series between 11 and 13 weeks. They divided the early development from 12 to 21 weeks into five maturity stages, which correlated closely with age, crown–rump and humeral length.

This part of the occipital bone becomes recognizable from about the 3rd prenatal month and with advancing age, its characteristic features are intensified. At first, the bone is spindle-shaped but about the beginning of the 4th month it becomes more triangular. The base, facing the foramen magnum, is V-shaped but during the next two weeks it assumes a U-shaped curve and the basilar contributions to the occipital condyles become more obvious at the tips of the inferior surface. At the same time, the sides become parallel and the bone adopts a more quadrilateral shape. By the 7th prenatal month, the lateral margins are angulated outwards at about the midpoint and the bone assumes a trapezoid shape.

The perinatal pars basilaris is a robust bone (Fig. 4.19). The inferior surface is flattened and the intracranial surface is slightly concave from side to side and pitted with nutrient foramina. The anterior surface, which forms one side of the spheno-occipital synchondrosis, is D-shaped with the straight edge on the intracranial surface. The posterior border, contributing to the foramen magnum, is thickened and forms a semi-lunar curve, each horn of which bears a third of an occipital condyle inferiorly. The border reaches adult size at about the age of 2 years. The lateral border is divided into two parts. Anterior to the angle, it articulates with the petrous temporal bone whilst posteriorly there are two distinct facets, which articulate with the jugular and condylar limbs of the pars lateralis (see above). The pharyngeal tubercle,

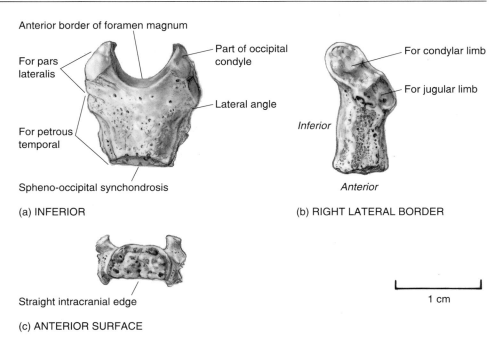

Anterior border of foramen magnum

For pars lateralis

Part of occipital condyle

For condylar limb

For jugular limb

Lateral angle

Inferior

For petrous temporal

Spheno-occipital synchondrosis

Anterior

(a) INFERIOR

(b) RIGHT LATERAL BORDER

Straight intracranial edge

1 cm

(c) ANTERIOR SURFACE

Figure 4.19 The perinatal pars basilaris.

the attachment for the posterior pharyngeal raphé, on the inferior surface cannot usually be identified until the second or third year of life.

Immediately anterior to the tubercle there may be a depression or foramen, the incidence of which varies in different populations (Collins, 1928). This has been variously named the fossa pharyngea, fovea bursa, mediobasal bursa or canalis basilaris chordae and is thought, by most authorities, to be the remnant of the path taken by the fetal notochord (chorda dorsalis) as it emerges from the developing vertebral column to enter the cranial base (see Early Development of the Human Skull). The fossa normally closes during the 3rd month of prenatal life. Discussion of its incidence and aetiology are given in Huber (1912) and Schultz (1918a). More recently, the concept that this remnant could result in the formation of a Tornwaldt's cyst has gained credence (Bonneville *et al.*, 1980; Currarino, 1988; Beltramello *et al.*, 1998; Jacquemin *et al.*, 2000). Because of the confusion in terminology and the different interpretation given to MRI scans, it is not entirely clear if clinical observers have distinguished between this foramen in the occipital bone and the sphenoidal canal, which is an unfused part of the pre- and postsphenoid parts of the body of the sphenoid bone (see Sphenoid).

The changing proportions throughout the development of the pars basilaris, together with the fact that it tends to survive inhumation intact, have been used as a means of ageing immature skeletons. However, the osteological landmarks used for taking measurements have not always been clearly defined. Redfield (1970), in a useful and carefully observed study, included both the pars basilaris and the partes laterales to identify seven developmental stages as an aid to ageing and described, but did not illustrate, the measurements. Fazekas and Kósa (1978) reported dimensions of all parts of the bone and illustrated measurements with photographs. However, the landmarks on both the pars basilaris and lateralis are not the same as those of Redfield (Fig. 4.20). The differences in the measurements are described and evaluated

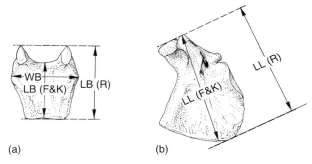

(a)   (b)

Figure 4.20 Measurements of the (a) pars basilaris and (b) pars lateralis.
LB (R)   Redfield's maximum length of pars basilaris
LB (F&K)   Fazekas and Kósa's mid-sagittal length of pars basilaris
WB   Width of pars basilaris
LL (R)   Redfield's length of pars lateralis
LL (F&K)   Fazekas and Kósa's length of pars lateralis

by Scheuer and MacLaughlin-Black (1994). In essence, if only the pars basilaris is available, the sagittal length is greater than the width in individuals less than 28 prenatal weeks. If the maximum length is less than the width, then the individual is more than 5 months *post partum*. If however both the pars basilaris and the pars lateralis are available, and they are of approximately the same length, then the fetus is less than 7 months *in utero*. In the perinatal period, the pars lateralis has a faster growth rate and is longer than the pars basilaris. After this time, the pars lateralis is always longer than the basilaris but the latter has always a greater width than length.

A variety of anomalies occur around the foramen magnum as the occipito-vertebral border is an embryological unstable junction (see also Chapter 6). Causes are not certain but most probably happen at a very early stage of embryological development when there is incomplete segmentation of the occipital and cervical sclerotomes. The neural arches are primarily affected, indicating involvement of the denser part of the sclerotome. Barnes (1994) has reviewed this subject in some detail and divides abnormalities into two groups depending on whether there is a cranial or caudal shift in the normal position of the occipitovertebral border. Caudal shifting is more common and can result in occipitalization of the atlas vertebra (Shapiro and Robinson, 1976a; Black and Scheuer, 1996a), basilar impression (Peyton and Peterson, 1942; Hadley, 1948) or the presence of a paracondylar process (Anderson, 1996). Cranial shifting may result in a variety of conditions including transverse basilar clefting (Kruyff, 1967; Johnson and Israel, 1979). Anatomical abnormalities vary from minor and symptomless to extensive, resulting in major neurological and vascular problems.

Fusion of the individual parts of the occipital bone starts in the perinatal period and continues until the age of 5 or 6 years. The lateral sections of the sutura mendosa, which extend about half way to the median plane, start to close from about 4 months *post partum* (Redfield, 1970) and are normally virtually closed, but not necessarily obliterated, by the end of the first year of life (Molleson and Cox, 1993). Fazekas and Kósa (1978) state that they can persist until the age of 3 or 4 years. Reinhard and Rösing (1985) reported that the suture may remain in 25%, 10% and 1% of skulls at the age of 4 years, 5–6 years and 11–15 years respectively and Keats (1992) shows a 17-year-old male skull with persistent mendosal sutures. Abnormalities in the normal pattern of fusion of the ossification centres of the interparietal part of the bone can produce many varieties of Inca (Wormian) bones.

The lateral occipitals fuse with the supra-occipital part of the squama between the first and third years at the **sutura** (synchondrosis) **intra-occipitalis posterior**. This is often referred to as the 'innominate synchondrosis' in the clinical literature (Caffey, 1953; Shapiro and Robinson, 1976b). Molleson and Cox (1993) reported that in a small skeletal sample of infants and children of documented age, the suture fused between 2 and 4 years. Redfield (1970), examining individuals of estimated age at death, found that the suture was fused and obliterated in about half of the bones by the fifth year, which is later than all other accounts. Exceptionally, traces of the suture may remain into adult life (Smith, 1912). Fusion starts where the partes laterales meet the mastoid parts of the temporal bones and proceeds medially. The last part to fuse is at the posterior border of the foramen magnum where the open sutures on each side may leave a tongue of bone between them (Fig. 4.21). This must be distinguished from the process of Kerckring (see above), which is a much earlier structure (Fig. 4.16).

Complete fusion of the lateral occipitals with the basi-occipital at the **sutura** (synchondrosis) **intra-occipitalis anterior** takes place between the ages of 5 and 7 years but can start as early as 3–4 years of age (Tillmann and Lorenz, 1978). Moss (1958) remarked that the hyaline cartilage between the bones of both the anterior and posterior intra-occipitalis synchondroses are reduced to sutural dimensions well before final fusion takes place and this difference in the definition of fusion may account for the wide range of times reported. Fusion starts internally and proceeds outwards, often leaving a small gap across the occipital condyles. Redfield (1970) distinguished this from the 'dimple or fossa', which lies over the hypoglossal canal and noted that few condyles younger than 12 years of age are smooth. Tillmann and Lorenz (1978) also

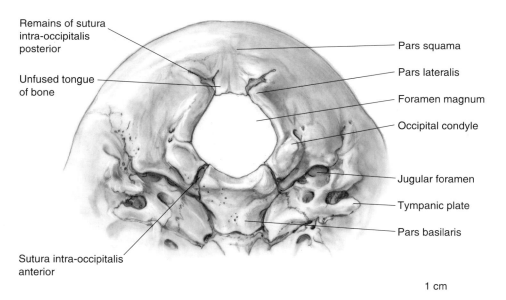

Remains of sutura intra-occipitalis posterior

Unfused tongue of bone

Sutura intra-occipitalis anterior

Pars squama

Pars lateralis

Foramen magnum

Occipital condyle

Jugular foramen

Tympanic plate

Pars basilaris

1 cm

Figure 4.21 The sutura intra-occipitalis posterior. Drawn from a skull of dental age 18 months. Fusion is almost complete except for a small tongue of bone at the posterior border of the foramen magnum. The sutura intra-occipitalis anterior is still open.

commented on a strip of unossified cartilage that sometimes divides condyles even into adult life but rejected a developmental cause in favour of a still unknown mechanical explanation. This final fusion of the parts of the occipital bone halts any further growth in size of the foramen magnum, other than an increase in robusticity of its margins by subperiosteal deposition and this is necessarily mirrored by a concurrent completion of the atlas (see Chapter 6). It reflects the well-documented precocious maturation of the human central nervous system.

The age range of the closure of the spheno-occipital synchondrosis (Fig. 4.13), at between 18 and 25 years, is overestimated as reported in most standard anatomical texts (Frazer, 1948; Grant, 1948; Williams et al., 1995). Ford (1958) and Scott (1958), in reviewing growth of the cranial base, also state that closure occurs between 17 and 25 years of age. Irwin (1960), in a tomographic study, found that the synchondrosis was complete by 18 years but did not distinguish between the sexes. Large series were reviewed by Powell and Brodie (1963), Konie (1964), Melsen (1969, 1972), Ingervall and Thilander (1972) and Sahni et al. (1998) (see Chapter 1 and Table 1.5). They all report closure times during adolescence with females being on average two years in advance of males. Melsen (1969), in observations on dry skulls of unknown age, notes that fusion occurs after the eruption of the permanent canines, premolars and second molar teeth and Konie (1964) found that the closure age coincided with skeletal age as estimated from hand–wrist X-rays (Greulich and Pyle, 1959). It seems likely that the slight discrepancies observed may be due to differences in methodology but the closure of the synchondrosis almost certainly occurs during the adolescent rather than the young adult period. Closure occurs first on the intracranial surface and proceeds towards the base of the skull.

It appears that the fusion times of both the intra-occipital and the spheno-occipital synchondroses are related to significant maturational events. The posterior intra-occipital fusion occurs at between 2 and 4 years of age when the deciduous dentition has erupted into the mouth and is nearing completion. The anterior fusion is usually complete by the age of 6 years when the period of rapid brain growth has reached its peak and the permanent molars are starting to erupt. Spheno-occipital fusion occurs at the end of the adolescent growth spurt and when the permanent dentition (except the third molars) is nearing completion (see Bogin, 1997 and Chapter 1, Table 1.7).

A small area between the occipital and temporal bones does not fuse until early adult life. This is the cartilaginous jugular growth plate (jugular synchondrosis/petro-exoccipital articulation), a small triangular or quadrangular area, situated just posterolateral to the jugular foramen in the occipitotemporal suture (Figs 4.1 and 4.2). Maat and Mastwijk (1995) found that, in a Dutch series, fusion did not begin until after the age of 22 years and that bilateral fusion was complete at 34 years. Hershkovitz et al. (1997) reported on a larger series (Hamann-Todd collection of black and white American populations) and found that small proportions underwent complete union before 20 years of age (7–10%) or remained open after 50 years (5–9%). It was concluded that the chance of finding individuals above the age of 40 years with a completely open suture was less than 13% and this area might be useful in assigning age in the young adult. The authors' 'anatomical perspective' in dividing the petro-occipital articulation into three regions is somewhat misleading. Only part of the petro-exoccipital articulation is the jugular growth plate. The rest of the suture between the exoccipital and the whole of the suture with the supra-occipital as far as the lateral angle is not 'petro-' at all but in fact the occipitomastoid suture.

Practical notes

Sideing/orientation of the juvenile occipital (Figs 4.15, 4.17, 4.19)
Pars lateralis – identification is possible by midfetal life. Sideing depends on identifying the condylar and jugular limbs of the hypoglossal canal, which extend anteromedially. The greater part of the occipital condyle lies on the inferior surface of the condylar limb.

Pars basilaris – the bone is identifiable by midfetal life although it differs from its neonatal appearance in being longer and not so angled laterally. By 7 fetal months it is readily identifiable. The inferior surface is fairly flat and parts of the occipital condyles can usually be seen at the tips of the posterior curve. The intracranial surface is slightly concave.

Bones of a similar morphology
Pars squama – fragments of the squama are probably indistinguishable from fragments of other vault bones or scapula unless a characteristic part, such as the process of Kerckring, is present. The inferior part of the supra-occipital part of the bone that borders the foramen magnum is more robust than other vault bones in the perinatal period.

Pars lateralis – at the perinatal stage, a single pars lateralis viewed from the intracranial surface is very similar in shape to the dorsal surface of the scapula of the opposite side as the jugular limb extends from the bone in a manner very like the scapular spine (Fig. 4.22). However in any one individual, the scapula is larger overall and the blade is more extensive than the body of the pars lateralis, which has the occipital condyle on its inferior surface (see Chapter 8, Scapula).

Pars basilaris – an isolated pars basilaris is similar in shape to the manubrium sterni but at the perinatal stage of development the basilaris is a substantial, solid bone whilst the manubrium is barely more than a thin disc (see Chapter 7, Sternum). From the perinatal stage until the pars basilaris fuses

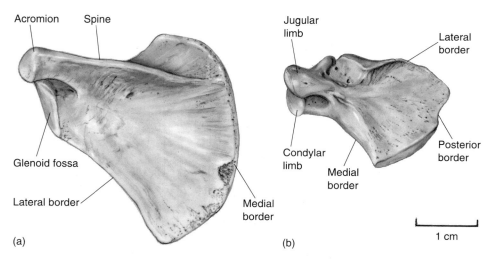

(a)

Acromion   Spine

Glenoid fossa

Lateral border

Medial border

(b)

Jugular limb

Lateral border

Condylar limb

Medial border

Posterior border

1 cm

Figure 4.22 (a) Dorsal view of the perinatal left scapula; (b) intracranial view of the right pars lateralis from the same skeleton. Note the superficial similarity.

with the rest of the occipital, the manubrium is always smaller and thinner and has less well-defined borders.

Morphological summary

Prenatal

Wks 8–10	Ossification centres for supra-occipital, interparietal, pars lateralis appear in that order
By mth 5	Supra-occipital and interparietal parts of squama fuse centrally at the sutura mendosa
By mth 7	Pars basilaris develops lateral angle
By mth 8	Pars lateralis longer than pars basilaris
Birth	Represented by: pars basilaris
	2 partes laterales
	pars squama
By mth 6	Pars basilaris width always greater than length
During yr 1	Median sagittal suture and remains of sutura mendosa normally close
	Jugular process develops on pars lateralis
	Vascular and neural markings become apparent
Yrs 1–3	Fusion of partes laterales to squama
Yrs 2–4	Hypoglossal canal complete excluding pars basilaris
Yrs 5–7	Fusion of pars basilaris and partes laterales
Yrs 11–16 (females)	Fusion of spheno-occipital synchondrosis
Yrs 13–18 (males)	Fusion of spheno-occipital synchondrosis
Yrs 22–34	Closure of jugular growth plate

II. THE TEMPORAL

The temporal bones form part of the base of the skull and the lateral walls of the cranial cavity. Each bone is a compound structure composed of four main parts: the petromastoid, squamous, tympanic and styloid process.

The petromastoid part may be further subdivided into a petrous portion occupying the space between the greater wing and body of the sphenoid and the occipital bone in the base of the skull (Fig. 4.2) and a mastoid portion, situated behind the external auditory meatus and articulating with the squamous occipital bone and the postero-inferior border of the parietal (Figs 4.1 and 4.3).

The squamous part forms part of the lateral wall of the cranial cavity and the lateral wall of the middle ear. It articulates with the greater wing of the sphenoid and parietal bones and incorporates the articular surface of the temporomandibular joint and the zygomatic process, which, with the temporal process of the zygomatic bone, forms the zygomatic arch (Figs 4.1 and 4.3).

The tympanic part of the bone is a quadrilateral plate lying below the squamous part and anterior to the mastoid process. Its posterior part forms most of the bony external acoustic meatus whose inner end accommodates the tympanic membrane (Fig. 4.3).

The styloid process projects antero-inferiorly from the tympanic plate. Its tip is connected to the superior horn of the hyoid bone by the stylohyoid ligament (Figs 4.1 and 4.3).

The ear forms an integral part of the temporal bone and both the internal carotid artery and the VIIth (facial) and VIIIth (vestibulocochlear) cranial nerves pass through the bone. The inner ear includes the membranous labyr-

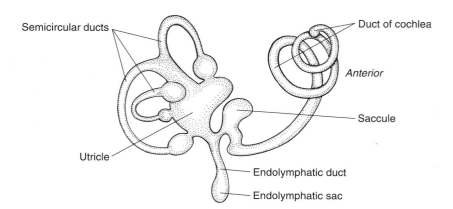

Figure 4.23 The right membranous labyrinth from the lateral side.

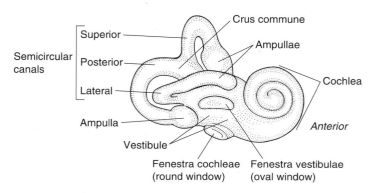

Figure 4.24 The right osseous labyrinth from the lateral side.

inth (Fig. 4.23) containing the peripheral receptors for hearing and balance, enclosed within the osseous labyrinth (Fig. 4.24), a system of interconnecting cavities in the petrous part of the bone. The space between the bone and the membranous labyrinth is filled with perilymph, a fluid akin to cerebrospinal fluid. The petrous bone also forms the medial wall, floor and roof of the middle ear cavity (tympanum) (Fig. 4.25), which is responsible for the transmission of sound waves from the exterior to the inner ear via a chain of three auditory ossicles (Fig. 4.26).

Early development of the ear

The development of the ear and the surrounding temporal bone is a complex process involving the interaction of several different embryonic tissues. A neurectodermal placode, with additions from neural crest, gives rise to the membranous labyrinth at an early embryonic stage. The surrounding osseous labyrinth develops endochondrally from paraxial mesoderm with additional mesenchyme derived from the neural crest. Both the styloid process and the auditory ossicles develop perichondrally from branchial arch tissue and the external and middle ear spaces arise from associated grooves and pouches. The squamous and tympanic parts of the bone develop from mesenchyme by intramembranous ossification.

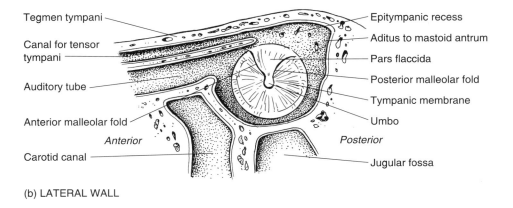

Tegmen tympani

Canal for tensor tympani

Auditory tube

Anterior malleolar fold

Anterior

Carotid canal

Epitympanic recess

Aditus to mastoid antrum

Pars flaccida

Posterior malleolar fold

Tympanic membrane

Umbo

Posterior

Jugular fossa

(b) LATERAL WALL

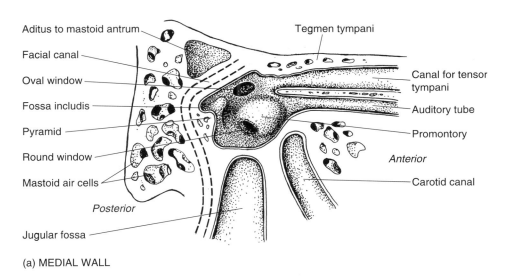

Aditus to mastoid antrum

Facial canal

Oval window

Fossa includis

Pyramid

Round window

Mastoid air cells

Posterior

Jugular fossa

Tegmen tympani

Canal for tensor tympani

Auditory tube

Promontory

Anterior

Carotid canal

(a) MEDIAL WALL

Figure 4.25 The right middle ear.

Because of this complex development from different embryological components, congenital atresia may affect one part of the ear and leave another part unaffected or modifications may occur in associated structures, including the sigmoid sinus and the facial nerve. Clinical accounts (Altmann, 1955; Gill, 1969; De La Cruz *et al.*, 1985) suggest that the most frequent malformations involve the outer and middle ear only. Males are affected more than females and there is a bias towards unilateral involvement of the right ear. Anatomical and archaeological cases have been described by Greig (1927a) and Hodges *et al.* (1990).

The first signs of **ear** development are evident during the 3rd week of embryonic life as dorsolateral thickenings on either side of the head at the level of the myelencephalon region of the hindbrain. These epidermal placodes develop into the **membranous labyrinth** of the internal ear. Each placode sinks below the surface forming an **otic**/auditory **vesicle** the mouth of which closes off to form an **otic sac,** which, for a time, is attached to the surface ectoderm by a stalk (Fig. 4.27a). Between the 5th and 7th weeks a fold sepa-

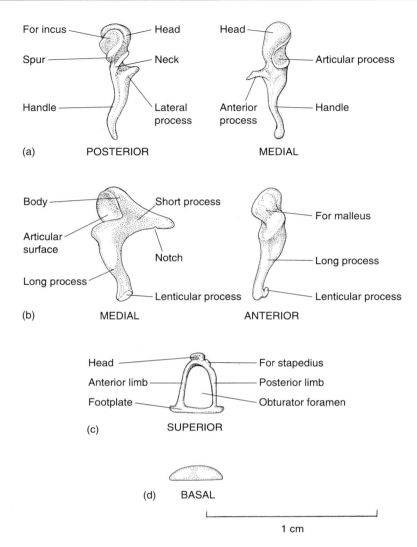

Figure 4.26 The right ear ossicles: (a) malleus; (b) incus; (c) stapes; (d) stapes footplate.

rates off part of the vesicle, which will develop into the **endolymphatic appendage**. This later develops into a duct that lies in the bony vestibular aqueduct ending in a sac that protrudes to lie in a hollow on the posterior surface of the petrous bone between the two layers of dura mater. Further folds separate the remainder into two parts: a dorsal part (pars superior/vestibularis) forming the utricle and semicircular ducts, and a ventral part (pars inferior/cochlearis), differentiating slightly later, forming the saccule and cochlear duct (Fig. 4.27b). The membranous labyrinth is fully differentiated by week 25 of fetal life. Further details may be found in Bast *et al.* (1947) and Streeter (1942, 1945, 1948, 1951) and the precise sequence of events in staged human embryos may be followed in O'Rahilly (1983).

Between 4 and 5 weeks, the primordia of the **tympanic cavity** and **auditory tube** develop from the **tubotympanic recess**. This is a diverticulum from the primitive pharynx derived from the first, and possibly second pharyngeal pouches. The exact derivation of the tissues is in some doubt and is

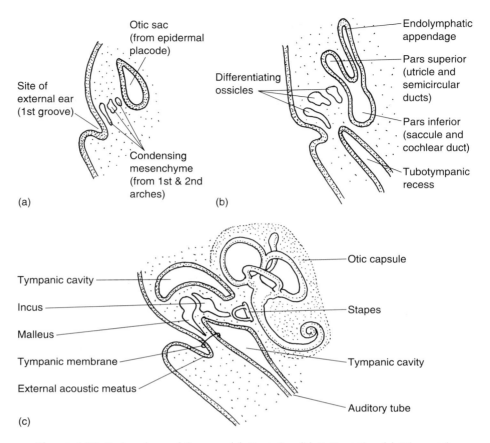

Figure 4.27 Embryology of the ear: (a) 3 weeks; (b) 5–7 weeks; (c) 8th month.

discussed in detail by Frazer (1910a, 1914, 1922) and Kanagasuntheram (1967). The first branchial groove, which will form the **external auditory meatus**, extends medially from the external surface towards the recess leaving an area of mesenchyme between the two spaces in which the auditory ossicles develop from branchial arch tissue.

By 8 to 9 weeks, the mesenchyme surrounding the developing otic vesicles condenses to form the cartilaginous **otic capsules**, part of which will eventually develop into the osseous labyrinths. At this stage, they form prominent lateral bulges in the base of the chondrocranium (see Early Development of the Human Skull). The anterior **cochlear** part and posterior **canalicular** part of each capsule is separated by a sulcus. In the canalicular part, the subarcuate fossa, endolymphatic foramen and eminences of the semicircular canals soon become obvious. The cochlear part displays a wide internal auditory meatus, through which pass the VIIth (facial) and VIIIth (vestibulocochlear) cranial nerves. The internal carotid artery lies in a groove beneath the cochlear part and the facial nerve passes straight through the internal meatus and exits at the facial foramen in the anterior sulcus. A little later, a small projection, the mastoid process, develops posteriorly and the shelf of the tegmen tympani, which will form part of the roof of the middle ear, begins to project from the capsule (Macklin, 1914, 1921).

Whilst the cartilaginous otic capsule is developing it is, at the same time, being resorbed to make way for the perilymphatic fluid-filled spaces around the membranous labyrinth. These start in the region of the vestibule and spread to the cochlear duct. The last part of the capsule to be transformed is around the semicircular ducts and their ampullae. By about 11 weeks, the spaces eventually form a continuous gap, the **periotic cistern**, between the membranous and bony labyrinths, which is filled with perilymph. Further details may be found in Streeter (1918).

The **auditory ossicles** are at first embedded in mesenchyme (see above) but, as the tympanic cavity enlarges, its mucous membrane covers the ossicles and acts as mesenteries, partially separating tympanic spaces (Proctor, 1964). The epithelium of the cleft, the intervening mesenchyme and the epithelium of the pouch, each contribute a layer to the trilaminar tympanic membrane. Between 5 and 6 weeks, the blastemal mass attached to the ends of the **first and second arches** is grooved and partially separated by the facial nerve. One side will develop into the **malleus** and **incus** and the other will become the **stapes** (Anson et al., 1960). By 8 weeks, the three blastemal ossicles are separated by joint cavities and becoming cartilaginous. The head, body and manubrium of the malleus are recognizable, although it is still associated with the end of Meckel's cartilage. The body and crura of the incus are likewise obvious and the short crus is in contact with the otic capsule. At this stage the stapes has an annular shape and is fused to the otic capsule, which will provide part of its footplate. The goniale, the primordium of the anterior process of the malleus, is visible (Macklin, 1921; Müller and O'Rahilly, 1980) and is the only ossicular structure to form in membrane. The long-held classical view of the single mesenchymal origin for each of the ossicles has been modified by the detailed studies of Hanson et al. (1962). The head of the malleus and the body and short crus of the incus are derived from first arch tissue. The manubrium and long crus of the incus, as well as the head and crura of the stapes arise from the second arch. Additional to branchial arch tissue are the independent membranous anterior process of the malleus and part of the footplate of the stapes that develop from the otic capsule. Between 9 and 15 prenatal weeks, the cartilaginous ossicles acquire their recognizable adult morphology and size (Richany et al., 1954). By the second half of prenatal life, the main morphology of the ear is in place (Fig. 4.27c).

The **styloid** part of the temporal bone develops from the cartilage of the second pharyngeal arch. At 8 or 9 weeks, the cranial end of the arch becomes attached to the otic capsule and the anlage of the styloid extends inferiorly and medially from the base of the chondrocranium (Macklin, 1921; Müller and O'Rahilly, 1980) (Fig. 4.8).

At about 10 weeks, the **tympanic ring** is represented only by a small nodule of cells surrounded with a little osseous matrix in the angle between the handle of the malleus and Meckel's cartilage (Macklin, 1921).

Ossification

The ossification of the temporal bone is unique in two ways. First, the osseous labyrinth, the auditory ossicles and the tympanic ring reach full adult proportions by the middle of prenatal life and there is no subsequent postnatal increase in size. Second, unlike any other bones, the capsular portion of the petrous bone does not undergo remodelling, and so the first formed endochondral bone is retained throughout life. Interestingly, the otic capsule portion of the petrous temporal is one of the few bones that is spared from pathological change in Paget's disease, whose chief characteristic is a distortion of the normal remodelling process (Ortner and Putschar, 1985). In contrast to the otic capsule, the mastoid, squamous and parts of the tympanic change greatly in shape and proportion during postnatal life.

Ossification of the petrous part of the temporal (**pars petrosa)** proceeds firstly by the formation of the bony labyrinth immediately surrounding the otic capsule and then by extensions from this which contribute to the extracapsular part of the bone. Ossification of the **otic capsule** is almost all endochondral except for small parts, which form in membrane. Ossification begins only when the cartilaginous capsule, with its contained membranous labyrinth, has reached adult proportions. At this point, apart from the endolymphatic duct and sac, further growth of all the internal structures ceases. The first formed endochondral bone is not replaced by Haversian bone but keeps its primitive, relatively avascular structure. There are conflicting accounts of the number of ossification centres that contribute to the formation of the otic capsule. The definitive work is by Bast (1930), who makes it clear that, in the human embryo, there may be up to fourteen separate centres, the first of which appears at 16 weeks in the outer part of the capsule overlying the first turn of the cochlea. Once begun, the process is very rapid and the greater part of the capsule is ossified by the 23rd prenatal week. There is considerable variation in the order of appearance and some of the centres may be of the inconstant, accessory variety. They appear to arise in groups, in relation to nerve terminations, the internal acoustic meatus and the semicircular canals. Each centre is trilaminar consisting of an inner layer surrounding the labyrinthine spaces, a middle layer made up of scattered islands of calcifying cartilage (globuli ossei), which lie in marrow spaces and an outer periosteal layer. Vascular osteogenic buds lay down endochondral bone and then further bone (called endochondrial bone by Bast) is formed on the surface of the remaining cartilage. Fusion between the centres takes place without intermediate zones of epiphyseal growth so that no suture lines can be seen. Ossification takes place rapidly around the immediate area of the cochlear part of the membranous labyrinth but it is slower in the canalicular area. Spoor (1993) reported that there were no changes in size of the bony labyrinth as seen on CT scans after the ossification of the otic capsule at approximately the 24th prenatal week. Bonaldi *et al.* (1997) measured the region of the round window and its fossula from 4 months of fetal life to the adult stage and found that, although there were very minor differences in shape of the window itself, adult dimensions are reached during fetal development. There is a burst of activity in the perinatal period when the capsule finally attains its petrous character.

Several channels of communication still exist between the interior of the bony labyrinth and external structures. The internal acoustic meatus carries the facial and vestibulocochlear nerves and labyrinthine vessels to the internal ear and the subarcuate fossa transmits the subarcuate artery to the periotic bone. The vestibular aqueduct and the cochlear canaliculus transmit the endolymphatic duct and the periotic duct respectively, the latter communicating with the subarachnoid space in the posterior cranial fossa.

The petrous bone first becomes recognizable in midfetal life (Fig. 4.28). It is irregularly shaped with a rounded **anterior cochlear** end and a more expanded **canalicular posterior** end. Medially, the **internal acoustic meatus** lies anterior to the larger and wider **subarcuate fossa**. Above this, the uncovered curves of the anterior and posterior semicircular canals lie at right angles to each other. The superior surface is smooth and bears opposite to the internal meatus, the **facial foramen** for the passage of the facial nerve into

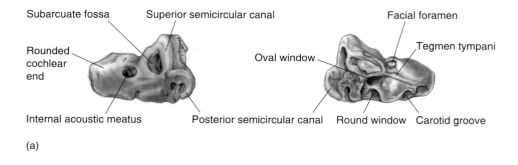

(a)

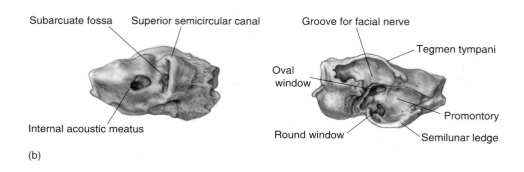

(b)

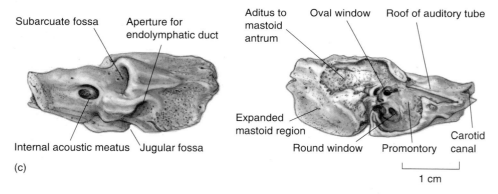

(c)

1 cm

Figure 4.28 Ossification of the right pars petrosa: (a) midfetal life; (b) about 7 months *in utero*; (c) late fetal life. Left row – medial side, anterior is to the left; right row – lateral side, anterior is to the right.

the tympanic cavity. Beneath this, the lateral surface forms the irregular medial wall of the future middle ear. In its centre is the oval window, above which is a minute aperture leading to a groove, the partially formed **facial canal**, which bends postero-inferiorly over the oval window. Just inferior and posterior to the oval window is the fossula of the **fenestra cochleae** in which the round window can be seen facing backwards. The inferior surface is slightly grooved anteriorly where the internal carotid artery passes under it but there is, as yet, no carotid canal. Posteriorly, is the smooth jugular part of the bone. The last regions of the canalicular part to ossify are the posterior and lateral canals and the lateral aspect of the superior canal as they continue to grow for some time after the rest of the internal ear has reached maximum size (Bast, 1930). This whole area spreads posteriorly towards the future mastoid part of the bone.

In the second half of intra-uterine life the ossification of most of the **extra-capsular** areas of the petrous bone takes place by extension from the outer periosteal layer of the capsule. The facial foramen becomes covered by a plate of bone which is continued laterally as the **tegmen tympani.** It starts to ossify by prenatal week 23 (Kenna, 1996) and eventually forms the roof of the middle ear, the antrum and part of the wall of the auditory tube. The **canal for the facial nerve** is formed partly by extension from the otic capsule with contributions from the second branchial arch. At first, the nerve lies in a groove on the lateral wall of the canalicular part of the capsule but by 26 weeks, together with the stapedius muscle and blood vessels, it is partially enclosed in a bony sulcus. Between the oval and round windows, the **promontory**, related to the basal turn of the cochlea, forms a bulge in the wall. The inferior edge of the lateral surface of the bone forms a **semilunar ledge**, which will eventually support the lower part of the tympanic ring. Between 24 and 29 prenatal weeks, a further petrosal ledge, the **jugular plate,** extends laterally and begins to form part of the floor of the middle ear (Spector and Ge, 1981).

During late fetal life, the arcuate fossa and the internal auditory meatus are about equal in size (Fig. 4.28) and the aperture of the **endolymphatic duct** can be seen inferior to them. The extracapsular parts of the bone expand further and a tongue of bone curves inferiorly from the anterior part of the semilunar ledge to form the entrance of the **carotid canal**. Behind this are the forming **jugular fossa** and the expanding mastoid part of the bone. The bony section of the **auditory tube** can be seen as a definite groove leading anteriorly from the middle ear.

The main **tympanic cavity** is complete by prenatal week 30. The **epitympanum**, the superior space leading posteriorly to the mastoid antrum and anteriorly to the double canal for the auditory tube and the tensor tympani muscle, is complete by week 34. The facial canal is gradually enclosed by the end of the first year of life (Anson et al., 1963), although up to 25% of canals may have dehiscences (Sataloff, 1990). Although pneumatization of the extracapsular parts of the bone starts at about 35 weeks, it does not accelerate until after birth when air replaces amniotic fluid in the middle ear. It proceeds throughout infancy and early childhood (Bast and Forester, 1939) and may even continue at the petrous apex into early adult life (Shambaugh, 1967). Three principal groups of air cells are formed in the fetus and undergo postnatal growth until puberty. They open into the mastoid antrum, the main cavity and the auditory tube (Ars, 1989).

The **squamous** part of the temporal bone (**pars squama**) starts to ossify in membrane in the 7th or 8th week of intra-uterine life (Noback and Robertson, 1951; Anson et al., 1955; O'Rahilly and Gardner, 1972; Müller and O'Rahilly, 1980). Bach-Petersen and Kjær (1993) identified it radiographically at about 9 to 10 weeks. Most accounts describe a single centre at the base of the zygomatic process from which ossification spreads. However, Augier (1931) described and illustrated a zygomatico-squamosal centre and a second squamomastoid centre posterior to it. Fazekas and Kósa (1972) described three independent centres which unite by the 3rd lunar month, the first being near the base of the zygomatic process, the second for the main part of the squama and a third posterior part, the last two centres being separated by a deep fissure until the 8th month. The bone in the 9th week is described by Macklin (1914, 1921) as a thin, narrow plate just lateral to the upper parts of the malleus and incus terminating in a pointed zygomatic process above the root of which there is a small foramen. The squama itself is short supero-inferiorly and the edges are serrated both behind and in front.

By mid-fetal life the squamous temporal is recognizable as it has assumed more adult proportions (Fig. 4.29). The **squama** is a delicate, almost flat semicircular plate with finely serrated edges. About a third of the way along the lower border, the **zygomatic process** projects anteriorly from a thickened root below which is a small curved plate which will become the **mandibular fossa**. Postero-inferior to the root of the zygomatic process is the **scutum**, a triangular extension with a sharp inferior angle that later becomes pneumatized. On the medial surface, the scutum is delimited superiorly by a ledge of bone, which fuses with the tegmen tympani postnatally (see below).

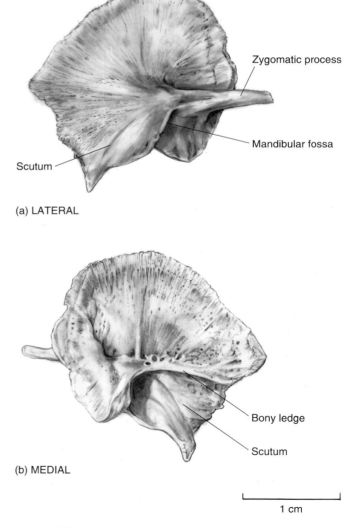

(a) LATERAL

(b) MEDIAL

1 cm

Figure 4.29 The right perinatal pars squama.

A detailed histological account of the development of the **tympanic** part of the temporal bone (**pars tympani**) can be found in Anson *et al.*, (1955) and Ars (1989). At about 9 weeks, the primary ossification centre is seen between the first and second branchial arches, anterior to the cartilaginous anlage of the incus. It is posterior to the mandible and inferior to the squamous plate, both of which have already commenced ossification. About a week later, the centre that will become the anterior horn becomes joined by intermediate mesenchymal tissue to four or more other centres arranged in a C-shape. Two weeks later the ossification centres fuse to form an incomplete ring that has expanded to twice its original size, with its anterior part now adjacent to the ossified anterior process of the malleus (goniale). The ring appears radiologically at about 12–13 weeks (Bach-Petersen and Kjær, 1993). By 19 weeks the diameter of the ring has increased by 3.5 times and the **tympanic sulcus** has begun to form on the inner surface although the tympanic membrane is still not lodged within it.

The tympanic ring (Fig. 4.30) is usually recognizable in isolation from about halfway through fetal life. It is deficient at the upper **tympanic incisure** (notch of Rivinus), which is framed by **anterior** and **posterior horns**. Medially, just below the larger anterior horn, is a transverse groove, the **mallear gutter**, which accommodates the anterior process of the malleus. The groove is delimited above by a ridge, the **crista spinarum**, whose ends form **anterior** and **posterior tympanic spines**. The lower, inner end of the mallear gutter protrudes as the **anterior tympanic tubercle**. The **posterior tympanic tubercle** lies about half way down the posterior limb of the ring. The inner surface of the ring is grooved by the **sulcus tympanicus** for the attachment of the tympanic membrane. By 35 weeks it has attained almost full adult dimensions and there is a localized fusion of the posterior segment to the squamous part of the bone (Anson *et al.*, 1955). At term, the ring is slightly more robust and is usually fused to the squamous part of the temporal at its open ends, the anterior being attached postero-inferior to the root of the zygomatic process and the posterior fusing to the pointed end of the scutum. Here there is a sharp projection at the petrotympanic fissure where the chorda tympani branch of the facial nerve leaves the middle ear cavity (iter chordae anterius). At this stage it is possible to look through the ring into the tympanic

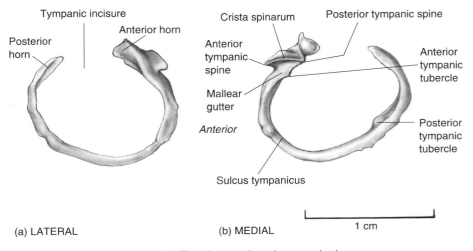

(a) LATERAL   (b) MEDIAL   1 cm

Figure 4.30 The right perinatal tympanic ring.

cavity of a dry skull and see the auditory ossicles and the oval and round windows.

The **styloid process** ossifies from the second branchial arch. The centre for the base of the process appears in the perinatal period (Augier, 1931) followed by several more centres for the main part of the process during the third and fourth years of life (Rambaud and Renault, 1864).

In summary, at birth, the petrous part of the bone is well ossified. The pointed anterior end has, as yet, an incomplete carotid canal. On the medial side the internal acoustic meatus and the subarcuate fossa are about equal in size and the aqueduct of the vestibule is usually somewhat smaller. From the superior surface the tegmen tympani projects laterally over the open wall of the middle ear cavity, which is delimited below by the semilunar ledge. The structures of the medial wall of the middle ear, including the oval and round windows, are obvious. Posteriorly, a small mastoid part of the bone is visible. The squamotympanic section of the bone consists of a delicate squama separated by a ridge of bone on the medial side from a partially pneumatized scutum. The tympanic ring is attached below the root of the zygomatic process by its anterior and posterior ends.

Postnatal growth and fusion

In the perinatal period, the combined squamotympanic part of the bone fuses to the petromastoid part along various segments. First, the ledge on the medial surface of the squamous bone fuses to the reciprocal lateral edge of the tegmen tympani at the internal petrosquamous suture. The scutum, which becomes increasingly pneumatized during this period, thus becomes the lateral wall of the epitympanic recess of the middle ear. Second, the external petrosquamous (squamomastoid) suture is formed where the posterior border of the squamous part fuses with the mastoid section of the bone. This suture often remains evident into adult life. Gradually the squamous part extends inferiorly, covering the anterior part of the petromastoid and contributing to the tip of the rapidly growing mastoid process. Even after pneumatization, the air cells from the two parts may be divided by a septum of bone (Korner's septum). Finally, the lower part of the tympanic ring fuses with the semilunar ledge at the lower border of the tympanic cavity.

During the first year of life, the anterior and posterior tympanic tubercles enlarge, grow towards each other across the ring and eventually fuse leaving a second opening, the foramen of Huschke, below the main auditory meatus (Fig. 4.31). During the same period the tympanic plate grows laterally, gradually converting the ring into the bony external auditory meatus. Anderson (1960) reported that the anterior tubercle made the major contribution to the formation of the foramen and the posterior tubercle showed an inferior direction of growth. Later still, fingers of bone grow in from the edges of the foramen of Huschke, which gradually closes by about the age of 5 years (Reinhard and Rösing, 1985; Ars, 1989), although the foramen may persist as a permanent feature in a significant proportion of adult skulls, depending on the population. Weaver (1979) and Curran and Weaver (1982) described a method for ageing the infant and child temporal bone using stages based on the growth of the tympanic plate. The first stage is described as 'tympanic ring not developed' and the second 'tympanic ring incomplete'. The stages are misleading as the ring is, in fact, fully developed by midfetal life but unfortunately the method

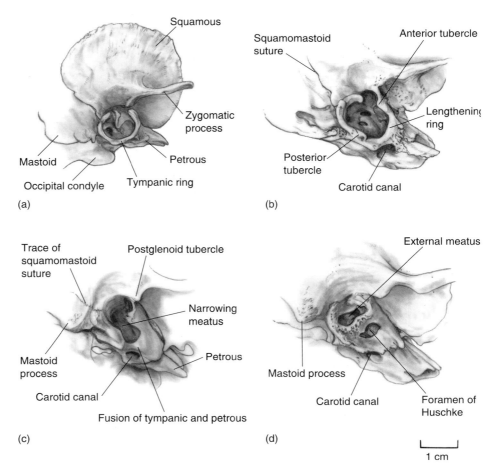

Figure 4.31 The formation of the foramen of Huschke. Drawn from skulls with dental ages of: (a) birth; (b) 6 months; (c) 1 year; (d) 2.5 years.

has been quoted and illustrated in many other texts, including Krogman and Işcan (1986).

The bony meatus continues to grow laterally displacing the ring from the external osseous opening and this causes a considerable change in orientation of the plane of the tympanic membrane. At term, it is almost horizontal but by 4–5 years of age it has acquired its more vertical adult position (Eby and Nadol, 1986; Ars, 1989). The growth of the plate also extends posteriorly and inferiorly to enclose the base of the styloid process in its vaginal sheath and a tongue of bone encloses the anterior border of the carotid canal. This eventually fuses with the petrous base but can be seen as a separate entity in some skulls until puberty. On the inferior surface of the petrous bone, an edge of the tegmen tympani protrudes between the growing tympanic plate and the glenoid fossa, thus splitting the squamotympanic fissure into a petrotympanic part posteriorly and a petrosquamous part anteriorly.

Recent advances in technology and surgery have made cochlear implantation in profoundly deaf young children possible. In order to attach wires onto the skull surface, it has been necessary to record accurate measurements of those parts of the bone that show significant postnatal growth. In a radiological and histological study, Eby and Nadol (1986) found that a very slight increase in width of the tympanic cavity occurred in the first 6 months of life. Mastoid width and depth increased rapidly up to the age of 7 years with no apparent sexual dimorphism. Mastoid length, on the other hand, showed two periods of growth, the first occurring before 7 years and the second phase between 9 and 15 years in females and 11 and 19 years in males. Dahm *et al.* (1993) recorded a doubling in depth of the external auditory canal from birth to adulthood, with most of this occurring in the first 6 months of life. They confirmed the growth in all directions of the mastoid process and noted that the digastric ridge was only visible in bones older than 6 months of age. Simms and Neely (1989) measured the growth of the lateral part of the temporal bone, including the squama, from birth to adult life and found that there was very rapid growth increase in dimensions from birth to four years after which growth slowed dramatically but continued until age 20.

Both the time and pattern of fusion of parts of the styloid process are very variable. Normally the base and other separate ossified sections fuse to form a styloid process in late puberty or early adult life. Common variations include non-fusion throughout life or fusion together with the ossified ligament and superior horns of the hyoid bone. Lengelé and Dehm (1988) recorded short and long types of hyoid bones and concluded that the short ones were the result of ossification of the base alone whereas those of the long group were the result of fusion to other ossified segments.

The fusion of the petrous temporal to the lateral occipital at the jugular growth plate (petro-exoccipital synchondrosis/jugular synchondrosis) is described under Occipital bone.

Ossification of the auditory ossicles

Ossification of the **auditory ossicles** begins at 16 weeks *in utero* and each bone has a different pattern of ossification and remodelling. Cartilage is retained on the articular surfaces and on the manubrium of the malleus, the short crus of the incus and the stapedial base.

Between 16 and 17 weeks the ossification centre for the **malleus** appears as a plaque of periosteal bone at the head near its junction with Meckel's cartilage. It spreads rapidly forming a shell around the ossicle except for the manubrium, which retains a cartilaginous covering around an endochondral bony centre until the perinatal period (Richany *et al.*, 1954). The anterior process (goniale), which was formed in membrane, finally fuses with the main part of the ossicle at about 19 weeks (Anson *et al.*, 1960). At the same time, the malleus loses its proximity to Meckel's cartilage, which is starting to undergo de-organization although the anterior ligament of the malleus is thought to be a remaining part.

The ossification centre of the **incus** appears slightly before that of the malleus, at about 16 weeks, as a thin layer of perichondral bone on the anterior part of the long crus, which spreads rapidly to completely invest the surface of the ossicle. The main bulk of the ossicle then becomes converted into dense bone by late fetal life (Richany *et al.*, 1954). The incus, unlike the other two ossicles, is subject to remodelling, particularly in the long crus, at any time during life, although Lannigan *et al.* (1995) report that it often results in resorption without regrowth.

Ossification of the **stapes** starts about two weeks later than in the incus and malleus and takes a very different course. The other two ossicles keep the relative shape, size and bulk of their original cartilage anlage. The stapes undergoes such extensive resorption and remodelling that the final bone is actually less bulky than the fetal model. Richany *et al.* (1954) described a single perichondral centre that appears on the obturator surface of the base of the stapes at about 18 weeks of prenatal life but Dass and Makhni (1966) described, and illustrated three centres appearing at about the same age. These fuse to form a U-shaped ossified area which gradually spreads up both crura towards the head until the whole ossicle is converted to bone at about 24 weeks. As soon as a shell of bone has covered the whole surface, resorption begins and it loses most of its bulk, so that at 6 prenatal months the stapes has acquired its relatively gracile adult structure. Both crura are converted to three-sided pillars of bone that open towards the obturator foramen (Richany *et al.*, 1954). The base and the head are also hollow on their obturator surfaces, but are bilaminar, consisting of a layer of cartilage and bone (Anson *et al.*, 1948). Dass *et al.* (1969) describe resorption continuing into postnatal life.

Practical notes

Sideing/orientation of the juvenile temporal
Pars petrosa – (Fig. 4.28) the perinatal bone can be recognized at about midfetal life and the descriptions can be found in the main text. Sideing of the perinatal bone depends on identifying the middle ear cavity, which lies laterally, and the intracranial surface, which is medial. On the lateral surface, the smooth mastoid part of the bone lies posterior to the semicircular ledge to which the tympanic ring may be fused. On the intracranial surface the anteriorly pointing subarcuate fossa lies above the oval internal auditory meatus.
Pars squama – (Fig. 4.29) this part of the bone assumes adult morphology by midfetal life. Sideing depends on identifying either the zygomatic process, which points anteriorly from the lateral surface, or the triangular pneumatized scutum with a straight anterior border lying below the ledge. Fragments of the rest of the squama are probably indistinguishable from other calvarial fragments.
Pars tympani – (Fig. 4.30) the tympanic ring assumes its characteristic shape by midfetal life. It is difficult to side until late fetal life when it is more robust and the sulcus for the tympanic membrane has developed on the medial side. At the superior tympanic incisure the anterior horn is more robust than the posterior horn, which tapers off to a point. By birth, the ring is usually partly fused to the pars squama.

Sideing the auditory ossicles
A magnifying glass facilitates examination of these small bones.
Malleus – (Fig. 4.26a) place with the head pointing superiorly and the manubrium inferiorly. Turn so that the slender anterior process is pointing downwards and the articular surface for the incus is visible on the head. The short lateral process points to the side from which the bone comes.
Incus – (Fig. 4.26b) place with the short crus pointing horizontal and the long crus pointing inferiorly. Turn so that the lenticular process is pointing upwards and the superior half of the articular surface for the malleus is visible. The short crus points to the side from which the bone comes.
Stapes – (Figs 4.26c,d) place with the head pointing superiorly and the long crus pointing inferiorly. Turn so that the footplate has its flat surface below and its rounded surface uppermost. The more curved and slightly more robust

posterior crus is on the side from which the bone comes. It is sometimes difficult to side a stapes as many of the features are not at all well defined.

Morphological summary

Prenatal

Wks 3–25	Development of membranous labyrinth
Wks 6–16	Cartilaginous anlagen of ossicles developing
Wks 7–8	Ossification centres for pars squama and goniale appear
Wk 9	First ossification centre for pars tympani appears
Wks 9–15	Development of cartilaginous otic capsule
Wk 12	Centres for tympanic ring joined together
Wk 16	First ossification centre for otic capsule appears; ossification centre for incus appears
Wks 16–17	Ossification centre for malleus appears
Wk 18	Ossification centre(s) for stapes appear(s)
Wk 19	Goniale fuses to malleus
Wk 30	Tympanic cavity complete except for lateral wall
Wk 35	Epitympanum complete
	Pneumatization of petromastoid starts
	Posterior segment of ring fuses to squamous part
Birth	Bone usually represented by 2 parts: petromastoid and squamotympanic
During yr 1	Petromastoid and squamotympanic parts fuse
	Anterior and posterior tympanic tubercles commence growth
Yrs 1–5	Growth of tympanic plate and formation of foramen of Huschke
	Mastoid process forming

III. THE SPHENOID

The sphenoid lies in the centre of the skull and this is the key to an appreciation of its anatomy. It articulates with the ethmoid, frontal, zygomatics, parietals, squamous and petrous temporals, vomer and occipital (Figs 4.1–4.3). It consists of: a central body, lying in the skull base; two lesser wings contributing to the anterior cranial fossa and the orbits (Fig. 4.32); two greater wings which lie in the middle cranial fossa and form part of the lateral walls of the cranial cavity and the orbits; and paired medial and lateral pterygoid plates extending vertically beneath the skull base.

Ossification

The sphenoid bone ossifies from a large number of centres, and accounts in the literature vary as to their exact number. Most of the centres fuse during prenatal life and, again, the pattern is variable. However, it is convenient to divide them into five main groups: those for the body, the lesser wings, the greater wings, the pterygoid plates and the sphenoidal conchae.

The **body** is formed endochondrally from anterior (basi-/presphenoid) centres and posterior (basi-/postsphenoid) centres. Fusion between the two groups of centres at the synchondrosis intrasphenoidalis takes place at the tuberculum sellae, which is at the junction of the prechordal and chordal regions of the skull base (see Early Development of the Human Skull).

Centres for the **presphenoid** part of the body appear at 12–14 prenatal weeks and usually consist of bilateral single, or double, centre(s) medial to

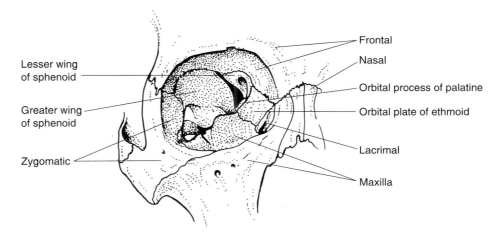

Figure 4.32 Anterior view of the right orbit showing bones that contribute to its walls.

the optic foramen (Augier, 1931; Kier, 1966). Kodama (1976a) distinguished a constant pair of main centres, a pair of anterior accessory centres, a 'corporal deep centre' composed of two parts and an occasional pair of posterior accessory centres and an occasional middle centre. By about 24 weeks, the main centres have fused together to form the medial wall of the optic foramen. Formation of the interoptic region, which will become the jugum, is variable and may be formed, either by extension of the presphenoid centres or by the formation of a median, unpaired rostral centre, at about 19–20 weeks. This lower part of the body, which will eventually form the crest, rostrum and ethmoid spine derives from the corporal deep centre (Kodama, 1976a). The anterior wall of the sella turcica at this stage is still cartilaginous and gradually ossifies in the last trimester by the posterior and medial growth of the presphenoid centres. These extend from the superior to the inferior surface of the body but may still not be fully ossified until the end of the first year of life (Kier, 1968).

The **postsphenoid** centres for the body form in the base of the sella turcica and are normally paired (Kodama, 1976b), but again, there may be an additional median centre. They appear at about 13 prenatal weeks and are usually united by 16 weeks (Noback, 1944; Arey, 1950). Sasaki and Kodama (1976) distinguished pairs of medial basisphenoid and lateral basisphenoid centres which showed distinct individual differences in size and pattern of fusion. Kjær (1990b, 1990c), in a series of 145 fetuses, also identified different patterns of ossification. There were single and double ossification centres for the postsphenoid, with the single pattern being the more common. The most lateral part of the body, which will form the carotid sulcus and lingula, develops from a separate endochondral centre in the cartilaginous alar processes (see Early Development of the Human Skull). They join with the main postsphenoid centres some time after the 4th month.

The presphenoid part of body (Fig. 4.33a) is an inverted Y-shaped bone with the single stem facing anteriorly and two limbs pointing posteriorly. The superior surface is relatively smooth and the inferior surface bears a blunt finger-like projection pointing antero-inferiorly. Each posterior limb has three surfaces: the supero-anterior and superoposterior are set at right angles and are articular for the lesser wings. The inferoposterior surfaces of both sides are approximately at right angles and form the upper boundaries of the cruciform space between the pre- and postsphenoid parts of the body.

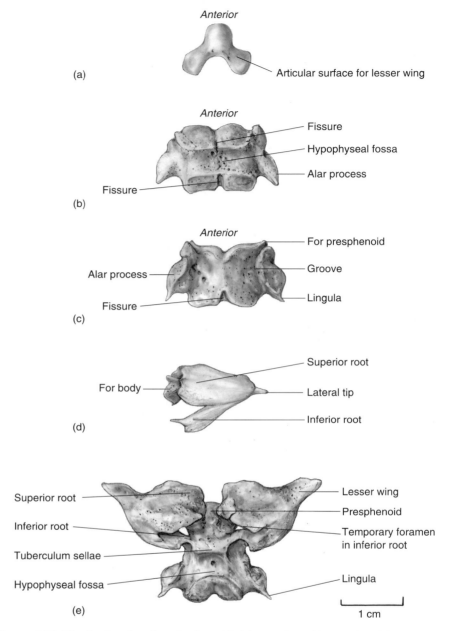

(a)

Anterior

Articular surface for lesser wing

(b)

Anterior

Fissure

Hypophyseal fossa

Alar process

Fissure

(c)

Anterior

For presphenoid

Groove

Alar process

Lingula

Fissure

(d)

For body

Superior root

Lateral tip

Inferior root

(e)

Superior root

Inferior root

Tuberculum sellae

Hypophyseal fossa

Lesser wing

Presphenoid

Temporary foramen
in inferior root

Lingula

1 cm

Figure 4.33 The fetal and perinatal sphenoid: (a) presphenoid, superior; (b) postsphenoid superior; (c) postsphenoid, inferior; (d) right lesser wing; (e) lesser wings fused to body.

The postsphenoid part of body (Figs 4.33b,c) becomes recognizable by about the 5th month of prenatal life. It is a roughly quadrilateral bone about twice as wide as it is long with two lateral alar projections extending postero-inferiorly. The centre of the superior surface is concave anteroposteriorly forming the shallow hypophyseal fossa from which the blunt alar processes slope away laterally. The anterior and posterior surfaces of the body may be divided by deep central fissures indicating the dual origin from two ossification centres. Later the alar processes become separated inferiorly from the

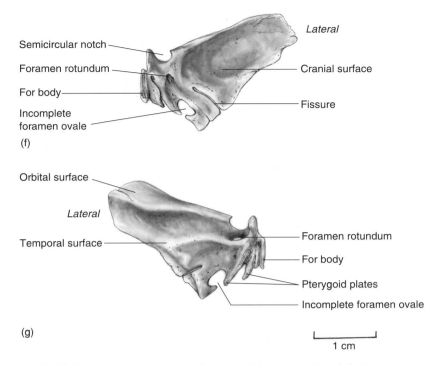

Semicircular notch

Foramen rotundum

For body

Incomplete
foramen ovale

Lateral

Cranial surface

Fissure

(f)

Orbital surface

Lateral

Temporal surface

Foramen rotundum

For body

Pterygoid plates

Incomplete foramen ovale

(g)

1 cm

Figure 4.33 (f) right greater wing, superior; (g) right greater wing, inferior.

main part of the body by the carotid sulcus. They develop sharp projections pointing anteriorly, which articulate with the presphenoid part of the body and the posterior processes become the lingulae. Covell (1927) recorded the size of the sella turcica during fetal life and reported that the mean dimensions at birth were 0.89 cm, 0.54 cm and 0.29 cm for the transverse, AP and vertical diameters respectively.

The ossification centres for the **lesser wings** (alipresphenoid) are formed in the orbitosphenoid (ala orbitalis) cartilages at about 12 prenatal weeks. This region has been described in detail by Fileti (1927), Kier (1966) and Kier and Rothman (1976) in studies on the development of the optic canal. Between 12 and 16 weeks two centres form on the superior and lateral sides of the cartilaginous optic foramen that rapidly fuse together. They may appear before, or at the same time, as the presphenoid centres for the body. By 16 weeks, the optic foramen is almost surrounded by bone. A small linear process, the anteroinferior segment of the optic strut (posterior root/crus posterior), extends from the lesser wing and fuses with the postsphenoid centre of the body to form the inferolateral border of the optic foramen. At this stage the foramen resembles a keyhole with the ophthalmic artery occupying the inferior, narrower part and the optic nerve above it in the wider part. The optic canal, as opposed to the foramen, starts to form during the 5th month of prenatal life with the formation of a second, or posterosuperior strut, which joins the lesser wing to the presphenoid centre of the body. Normally at this time, the ophthalmic artery takes up a more superior position above the second strut and becomes incorporated into the dural sheath of the optic nerve. So for a relatively short time the optic strut is composed of the two segments enclosing a transitory foramen between them, which on its closure, forms the cranial opening of the optic canal.

There are three developmental malformations that can be associated with this stage of development. The 'figure of 8' anomaly occurs when the second strut develops above, instead of below, the ophthalmic artery and so it, and the optic nerve, occupy separate foramina at the cranial entrance to the canal. It would appear to be this arrangement that is described in the literature as a duplicated optic canal. The 'keyhole' anomaly occurs when the second strut does not develop at all, or is very rudimentary, so causing absence of the posterior wall of the canal. The orbital opening then retains its primitive fetal arrangement with the artery lying in the narrow part below the nerve. There is also a very rare condition, reported by LeDouble (1903), which occurs when neither of the struts is formed and the optic canal and superior orbital fissure remain confluent. The 'metopic foramen', described by Augier (1931), as transmitting an aberrant ophthalmic vein, was interpreted by Kier as the transitory foramen in the unfused optic strut.

The lesser wing (Fig. 4.33d) becomes recognizable about half way through fetal life as a small flat piece of bone shaped like an arrow-head with the tip of the wing pointing laterally. The superior root, called the anterior crus by Kodama (1976c), is slightly flatter and wider than the inferior root (posterior crus). Later the difference between the two roots becomes more obvious and the upper root develops a posteromedial projection, which will articulate with the presphenoid part of the body.

Both endochondral and intramembranous ossification centres contribute to the formation of the **greater wings**. The intramembranous centre for each wing appears lateral to the cartilaginous foramen rotundum at about 9–10 prenatal weeks and gradually expands to form the major part of the wing. At about 13 weeks cartilage starts to ossify in the region where the maxillary nerve branches from the trigeminal ganglion 'like a bent forefinger'. This is the endochondral centre for the medial part of the wing (Fawcett, 1910b) and when this joins the lateral intramembranous centre, the foramen rotundum is complete. The inconstant foramen of Vesalius marks the junction of the endochondral and membranous portions of the wing so that the foramen ovale, being lateral to this, is entirely within the membranous part. Its margins are represented by a medial process and a lateral tongue of bone, which normally fuse behind the mandibular nerve to complete the foramen. This usually takes place either late in fetal life or during the first year (Augier, 1931) but occasionally fusion may never take place and the foramen ovale remains open to the petrosphenoid suture. The foramen spinosum is normally complete by the second year (Frazer, 1948). The posterior limitations of both the foramen ovale and the foramen spinosum are variable (Kier and Rothman, 1976; Sasaki and Kodama, 1976). James et al. (1980) interpret the inconstant pattern of grooves and foramina as being caused by the variable nature of the emissary middle meningeal veins passing to the pterygoid plexus.

The intramembranous centre for the **medial pterygoid plate** can be seen medial to the developing tensor veli palati muscle at about 9–10 fetal weeks but the **hamulus** develops separately from cartilage at about the 3rd month and rapidly ossifies. The **lateral plate** also ossifies in membrane during the early part of the 3rd month (Fawcett, 1905a). Both the medial and lateral plates become fused to the under surface of the greater wing between the 6th and 8th prenatal months.

The morphology of the greater wing and pterygoid plates (Figs 4.33f,g) becomes recognizable about half way through fetal life. The wing can be divided into a posteromedial third and an anterolateral two-thirds by a line running through the foramen rotundum anteriorly and a fissure running for a variable distance into the bone towards it from the posterior surface. Medially there is a complex surface for articulation with the alar process on the lateral surface of the body. The incomplete foramen ovale can be seen on the posterior surface of the bone but the foramen spinosum is still incomplete. The lateral two-thirds of the wing has three surfaces. The anterior surface is relatively thicker than the other two and turns up at right angles to form part of the lateral wall of the orbit. Its upper border, just above the opening of the foramen rotundum, forms a semicircular notch at the medial end of the superior orbital fissure. The gently concave upper (cranial) surface tapers down to the thin, serrated lateral and posterolateral border and the inferior surface is reciprocally convex. At its medial end, the lateral and medial pterygoid plates project downwards. They are closer together anteriorly than posteriorly and the lateral plate extends further posteriorly.

The **sphenoidal conchae** develop from ossification centres which appear on the medial part of the cartilaginous cupola of the nasal capsule, the future ethmoidal bone, between 4 and 6 months (Schaeffer, 1910a; van Gilse, 1927). Further lower centres are added during the perinatal period and growth continues after birth.

The order in which the different parts of the bone **fuse** together is variable but the lesser wings always fuse with the presphenoid part of the body in about midfetal life as the optic foramina are forming (Fig. 4.34). Reports of the time of fusion of the pre- and postsphenoid parts of the body are very variable. Augier (1931), for instance, stated that it can occur as early as 17 weeks *in utero*, or be delayed until after birth. Certainly fusion as late as the postnatal period is difficult to reconcile with Kier's description of the formation of the optic canal, which has the posterior root joining the postsphenoid part of the body at the time of the formation of the optic foramen.

Clinical descriptions of unfused centres add to an inconsistent account of timing. Ortiz and Brodie (1949) described the appearance on radiographs of unfused pre- and postsphenoidal centres in almost a third of 139 newborn infants. Shopfner *et al.* (1968) recorded the incidence of a so-called sphenoidal cleft from 750 radiographs and found that it was present in 64% of infants of less than a month in age and then progressively decreased to 3% at 3 years. They described the histological structure of the cleft as similar to that of the spheno-occipital synchondrosis. It is difficult to distinguish between these descriptions and those of the craniopharyngeal canal. This is an occasional foramen in the floor of the sella turcica, which may end in the vomer (Cave, 1931) or pass straight through the bone to emerge on the base of the skull (Arey, 1950). Bowdler (1971) reported that these so-called craniopharyngeal canals were seen as vertical transradiant regions on X-rays of some neonatal and infant skulls, but are rare in the adult. Earlier workers attributed these to the remains of the hypophyseal recess (of Rathké), which forms part of the developing pituitary gland. Arey (1950) and Lowman *et al.* (1966) made detailed studies of dry skulls and sections of early embryos and confirmed that the remains of Rathké's pouch disappear at 8–9 weeks of fetal life and suggested that the canals provide a channel for vessels concerned with the ossification of the body of the bone. They would therefore be comparable to the large foramina seen on the posterior surface of juvenile centra that are associated with the basivertebral veins (see Chapter 6). Currarino *et al.* (1985) described a second type of canal, the large craniopharyngeal canal. It occupies most of the floor of the sella, tapers inferiorly and appears to be pathological as it is prone to be associated with cranial abnormalities such as meningo-encephalocoeles.

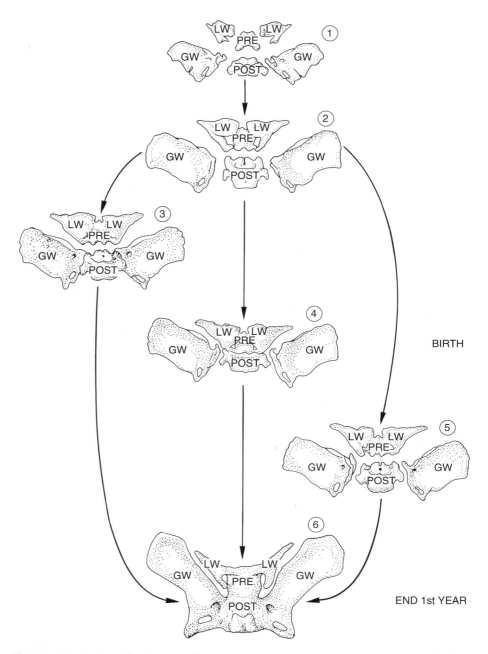

Figure 4.34 Fusion of sphenoid. Centre column usual order of fusion; right and left columns are possible variations.
PRE   Presphenoid part of body   LW   Lesser wing
POST Postsphenoid part of body   GW   Greater wing

A further divergence from the normal fusion is an illustrated description by Sprinz and Kaufman (1987) in a study of perinatal Egyptian crania. The lateral side of the pre- and postsphenoid parts of the body were fused leaving a space that was commonly triangular or funnel-shaped in the centre, which they called the sphenoidal canal and interpreted as the remaining central, unfused area. They distinguished this canal from the craniopharyngeal canal which, when present, occurs more posteriorly. Certainly their photographs and descriptions are a commonly observed appearance in the perinatal period. A similarly shaped foramen is often seen at the junction of the body and dens of the incompletely fused axis vertebra (see Chapter 6).

In summary, at **birth** (Fig. 4.34: **1–6**), the bone is usually represented by three parts (**4**): the body with attached lesser wings and two separate greater wings each with attached pterygoid plates (centre column). The fusion of the two parts of the body may be delayed until after birth (**5**) (right column) or, the other less common order of fusion is that the greater wings fuse to the post-sphenoid part of the body before birth (**3**) (left column). However, by the end of the first year of life, all parts of the bone have usually consolidated into a single structure (**6**). In the Spitalfields juvenile crania, Molleson and Cox (1993) found fusion had already occurred between the body and the greater wings by the 5th postnatal month.

The jugum is undeveloped in the perinatal period as the lesser wings are separated by a cleft, which is filled in by bone during the first year. The ante-roposterior growth of the jugum is variable and is reflected in the reciprocity of the widths of the jugum and sulcus (Fig. 4.35). The posterior margin of the jugum, the limbus sphenoidale, may remain separate from the underlying pre-sphenoid for several years leaving a cleft between them. By adulthood, the two structures fuse (Kier, 1968).

Van Alyea (1941), Fujioka and Young (1978) and Wolf *et al.* (1993) recorded the appearance of the **sphenoidal sinus** from radiographs. Pneumatization is first seen at about 6 months of age and is an extension from the nasal cavity into the conchal area, which gradually spreads into the presphenoid part of the body. It can extend into the basisphenoid by age 4 years and is present in 50% of individuals by 8 years and 95% by 12 years. According to Vidić (1968), the dorsum sellae and the posterior clinoid processes are pneumatized in about 20% of individuals between the ages of 12 and 20 years. The sphenoidal con-chae gradually become attached to the ethmoid bone by resorption of interven-ing cartilage. The time of fusion is very variable as it may begin as early as 4 years of age, or be delayed until puberty (Lang, 1995).

Acheson and Archer (1959), Latham (1972), Underwood *et al.* (1976) and Chilton *et al.* (1983) recorded the postnatal growth of the sella. As the distance between the sella and the foramen caecum of the ethmoid (Fig. 4.2) remains constant after about the seventh year, there is probably little growth at the

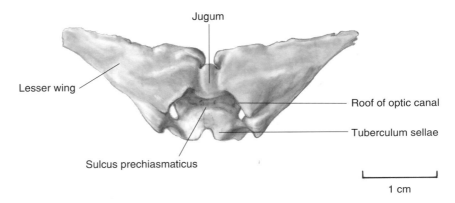

Figure 4.35 Immature jugum sphenoidale.

spheno-ethmoidal suture after the end of the first decade (Scott, 1958). Latham (1972) reported histological evidence of bone resorption in the posterior wall of the fossa for at least the first 10 years of life. This resulted in the upward and backward movement of the sella point, which would not have been obvious by measurements taken on radiographs alone.

Knott (1974) used the increase in distance between the centres of the right and left foramen rotundum, as recorded from radiographs, as one of the parameters in a longitudinal study of cranial growth. Increase in size in individuals between the ages of 6 and 26 years ranged from 3.2 mm to 8.3 mm. The spheno-occipital synchondrosis at birth is wide and extends superiorly to include the region of the dorsum sellae and posterior clinoid processes (Moss-Salentijn, 1975). This remains largely cartilaginous for at least 5 years after birth (Latham, 1966, 1972) and there are still small areas of cartilage up to the age of puberty (Ingervall and Thilander, 1972). The synchondrosis ossifies by extension from the posterior part of the body (Augier, 1931). Its age of closure is discussed under the Occipital bone.

Practical notes

Sideing/orientation of the juvenile sphenoid (Fig. 4.33)

Body – recognition of this part of the bone will depend on the state of fusion (see text) but by late fetal life the pre- and postsphenoid parts are normally fused together and the hypophyseal fossa has assumed its characteristic shape (Figs 4.33a–c).

Lesser wing – this part of the bone becomes recognizable by midfetal life. It resembles an arrowhead with the superior root anterior and flatter than the narrower posterior root. Both lesser wings are usually fused to the body before birth and form a characteristic-shaped bone (Fig. 4.33d,e).

Greater wing – this is usually recognizable by midfetal life. Sideing depends on recognizing the concave intracranial surface with the obvious foramen rotundum pointing anteriorly and a posterior fissure in the bone. The pterygoid plates are attached inferiorly. Both wings normally fuse to the body soon after birth (Figs 4.33f,g).

Morphological summary	
Prenatal	
Wks 9–10	Medial pterygoid plate and lateral part of greater wing commences ossification
Wks 12–14	Centres for postsphenoid part of body appear; centres for lesser wings appear
Early mth 3	Lateral pterygoid plate commences ossification; centre for hamulus appears
Wk 13	Centre for medial part of greater wing appears
Mths 4–6	First ossification centres for sphenoidal conchae appear
Mth 5	Ossification centre for lingula appears Lesser wings usually fused to body
By mth 8	Pterygoid plates fused to greater wings Pre- and postsphenoid parts of body usually fused together
Birth	Usually represented by two parts: body with lesser wings attached; two separate greater wings with attached pterygoid plates

During yr 1	Greater wings fuse to body
	Foramen ovale is completed
	Sinus commences pneumatization
By yr 2	Foramen spinosum is completed
By yr 5	Dorsum sellae ossified
Yr 4 – puberty	Sphenoidal conchae fused to ethmoid

IV. THE PARIETAL

The right and left parietal bones form a large part of the side walls of the cranial cavity. They articulate at the sagittal suture with each other, with the squamous occipital, the mastoid and squamous parts of the temporals, the greater wings of the sphenoid and the frontal (Figs 4.3 and 4.4). In common with other bones of the cranial vault they are composed of an inner and outer table of compact bone sandwiching the cancellous, erythropoietic **diploë** between them.

Ossification

There is no agreement on either the time of appearance or the number of ossification centres for the parietal bone. The major reason for this lies in the variety of methods used to study the intramembranous development of the bones of the cranial vault (see Chapter 1). Mall (1906), Noback (1944) and Noback and Robertson (1951) reported that, in alizarin-stained fetuses, the bone can be seen between 7 and 8 weeks of intra-uterine life. A single centre, corresponding to the site of the future parietal eminence, is described by Rambaud and Renault (1864) and Pendergrass and Pepper (1939). However Mall (1906), Augier (1931) and Frazer (1948) describe two centres, one above the other, which rapidly unite. Noback (1944) reported that 8 out of 9 fetuses showed evidence of ossification from two centres. Limson (1932) described a perinatal skull with a completely divided left parietal in which each part possessed a distinct protuberance, suggesting development from separate centres. The early fusion of two centres could be the explanation of the hourglass-shaped bone described and illustrated by Mall (1906) or a bipartite bone (Shapiro, 1972; Anderson, 1995). Noback also stressed that the ossification centre is not necessarily coincident with the parietal eminence, which occurs at the region of greatest curvature and is thought to be a response to the mechanical stimulus of the growth of the underlying brain and dural tracts.

Moss *et al.* (1956) studied the rate of growth of the calvarial bones of the skull between 8 and 20 prenatal weeks and recorded an interphase at about 12.5 weeks. This coincides with the time when the major portions of the fetal brain have attained their definitive topographical relations and the tentorium cerebelli has ceased its backward migration in relation to the overlying neuro-cranial capsule. The bones then assume a size and shape roughly proportional to their position in the adult skull. Silau *et al.* (1995) described the detailed radiographic appearance at the tuber, the sagittal suture and the anterior fontanelle, and the general shape of the bone between 14 and 21 prenatal weeks. Ohtsuki (1977, 1980) measured various parameters of the fetal parietal bone from the 5th month until birth and found a fairly constant rate of increase in area whereas the increase in thickness shows some deceleration as term is approached.

The later development of the bone is described by Noback (1943, 1944), O'Rahilly and Twohig (1952) and Fazekas and Kósa (1978). At about 5 months the bone appears as a delicate, ellipsoidal membranous disc with a thickened central eminence from which a fine network of trabeculae radiate outwards. At first, the individual borders and angles are not identifiable but after the 6th month, the margins of the bone begin to straighten out and the angles take on their characteristic shapes (Fig. 4.36). The frontal border is gently concave and finely serrated ending laterally at the sphenoidal angle which points acutely forwards. The sagittal border usually runs directly posteriorly from the rounded frontal angle for about two-thirds of its length. This is the position of the **obelion**, and there may be a parietal notch in the bone (Fig. 4.37) after which the serrations on the border become more fringe-like as it slopes away towards the rounded occipital angle at the posterior fontanelle. The occipital border is also finely serrated and may contain one or two slits. The squamosal border is usually divided into two sections, a posterior blunt portion and an anterior curved part, to accommodate the mastoid and squamous parts of the temporal bone respectively. In the early postnatal period, the bone thickens and the mature structure of inner and outer tables with diploë between them quickly develop.

The region of the obelion (Fig. 4.4) is the site of many bony variants and developmental anomalies, which may be limited to the bone, but can also involve the scalp or central nervous system (Currarino, 1976). At the site of the parietal notch there may be a fissure (incisura), a small parietal fontanelle or parietal foramina of varying sizes. The remnants of the parietal notch may remain as a thin cleft in one or both bones, where it is often seen in routine X-rays that can simulate a fracture. Notches on each side of the sagittal border can be so wide as to form a **sagittal fontanelle** (third fontanelle/fontanelle obélique/Gerdy's fontanelle). It is often present at birth, where it has been

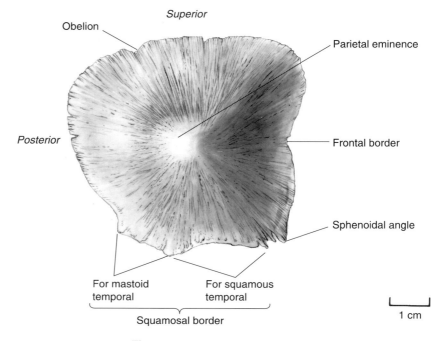

Figure 4.36 The right perinatal parietal.

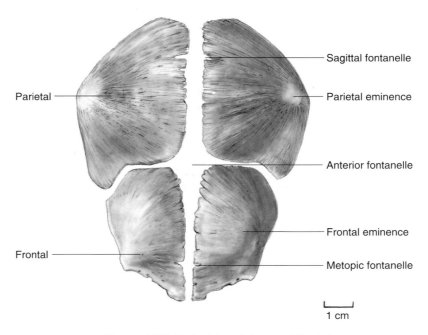

Figure 4.37 Perinatal parietals and frontals.

recorded in 50–80% of perinatal skulls (Paterson and Lovegrove, 1900; Augier, 1931). Adair and Scammon (1927) recorded a 30% incidence during the first postnatal month and followed its progress in a series of healthy newborns. There is evidence however, of an increased incidence of the third fontanelle in babies born with Down's syndrome and other abnormalities (Chemke and Robinson, 1969; Tan, 1971). Normally both fissures and the fontanelle disappear before, or soon after, birth but rarely exist after the third postnatal trimester, although occasionally one may remain as a median parietal foramen. More usually there are small parietal foramina not exceeding 1 mm in diameter, which transmit a vessel connecting the superior sagittal sinus, the diploic veins and the surface veins of the scalp. However, accounts of grossly enlarged foramina, up to the size of 3 or 4 cm, are commonplace in the anatomical literature (Turner, 1866; Greig, 1892, 1917, 1927b; Symmers, 1895; Paterson and Lovegrove, 1900; Cave, 1928; Stibbe, 1929; Boyd, 1930; Stallworthy, 1932). They can be unilateral or bilateral and are sometimes connected by a suture that crosses the sagittal suture at right angles. Pendergrass and Pepper (1939), Hollender (1967), Murphy and Gooding (1970) and Fein and Brinker (1972) have followed their development in consecutive radiographs in individual patients. At birth there is a large unossified midline defect, which is gradually filled in by tongue-like growths of bone from the centre. The aetiology of the condition is not clear but from clinical accounts it is obvious that there is some inherited factor, as the anomaly has been traced through at least five generations in some families (Greig, 1917; Alley, 1936; Irvine and Taylor, 1936; Pepper and Pendergrass, 1936; Travers and Wormley, 1938; O'Rahilly and Twohig, 1952; Fein and Brinker, 1972). An unknown factor, regarded as an erratic hereditary defect of ossification, causes the bone formation to cease, leaving bilateral foramina of varying sizes. Warkany and Weaver (1940) reviewed the anomaly in relation to other heredofamilial disorders. In some cases, the bone never attains its normal thickness and a condition known as biparietal thinness (biparietal osteodystrophy) is seen in the adult (Greig, 1926; Cave, 1927; Camp and Nash, 1944; Bruyn and Bots, 1977).

Craniolacunia (lacunar skull/Lückenschädel) is an abnormality of the calvarial bones of the skull, which develops during fetal life and is present at birth. It differs from the normal digital impressions that only appear after the first year (see Occipital). Kerr (1933) and Doub and Danzer (1934) described the condition in the newborn and Maier (1934) claimed the first prenatal, radiological diagnosis. The bones of the cranial vault have large, rounded areas of decreased density outlined by a web-like pattern of thicker bone bars and ridges whilst the cranial base remains normal. It nearly always occurs in conjunction with other malformations, commonly spina bifida, hydrocephalus and meningocoele (Vogt and Wyatt, 1941). Hartley and Burnett (1943a, 1943b) illustrated the skeletal and radiological appearance of affected vault bones, some of which show actual perforations that they termed craniofenestria. Early reports suggested that increased intracranial pressure could be the most likely aetiological factor but this has not been substantiated as it occurred in skulls of normal size. Hartley and Burnett (1944) suggested that dietary deficiency might be the cause as the condition appeared more often in babies from mothers of a financially poorer class. It also occurred more frequently in those children who were conceived during the starvation winters of World War II in Holland (van Waalwijk and Boet, 1949). The aetiology is still far from clear and Caffey (1993) classifies it as a probable dysplasia of the calvaria and its internal periosteum that is practically always associated with meningocoele and with the Arnold–Chiari (Chiari II/Treacher–Collins/mandibulofacial dysostosis) malformation (Stovin et al., 1960).

Ortiz and Brodie (1949) studied the postnatal growth of the bone from birth to 3 months of age and reported that, after recovery from moulding of the skull during labour, dolicocephalic and brachycephalic skull types could be distinguished at a very early period. In both types the parietals rise markedly on a lateral view of the head radiograph. Young (1957) measured growth increase on radiographs in a longitudinal series of 20 boys from one month to 16 years. The parietal, as measured by the arc from bregma to lambda, increased its maximum curvature rapidly until about the 9th postnatal month after which growth slowed and the bone became progressively more flattened.

Practical notes

Sideing/orientation of the juvenile parietal (Fig. 4.36)
It is unusual in perinatal skulls to recover a complete separate parietal as many bones of the vault are damaged. Sideing will depend on the ability to distinguish the four borders and angles from each other. The sharp, protruding sphenoidal angle lies at the antero-inferior corner. There may be a parietal notch or foramen near the posterior end of the sagittal border and the squamosal (inferior) border becomes characteristically bevelled soon after birth.

Bones of a similar morphology
Small fragments of the parietal bone are probably indistinguishable from other vault fragments unless a characteristic marking is present. Structures to be aware of include: venous sinus grooves with granular foveolae, grooves for

meningeal vessels, a distinct parietal foramen near a serrated border, temporal lines and characteristic bevelling on the squamosal border.

Morphological summary

Prenatal

Wks 7–8	Two centres of ossification form which rapidly fuse
By mth 6	Borders and angles become definitive
	There may be a sagittal fontanelle
Birth	Single bone with prominent eminence
	Sagittal fontanelle usually obliterated
Childhood	Gradually takes on the appearance of the adult bone as the diploë
	develop and the eminence becomes less obvious

V. THE FRONTAL

The frontal is an irregular, bowl-shaped bone that articulates with the parietals, greater wings of the sphenoid, zygomatics, frontal processes of the maxillae, lacrimals, nasals and the cribriform plate of the ethmoid (Figs 4.2–4.5). It is both calvarial and facial, forming part of the roof and side walls of the cranial cavity, the floor of the anterior cranial fossa, and the roofs of the orbits (Fig. 4.32). These functionally different parts are reflected in its morphological form (Moss and Young, 1960).

Ossification

There has been much disagreement about both the number of centres and the manner in which the frontal bone ossifies. This was in part due to misinterpretation of the development of the somewhat complex structure at both ends of the supra-orbital ridges and also to the attempts of early zoologists and anatomists to homologize parts of the human frontal bone with pre-and postfrontal elements of pre-mammalian skulls. Inman and Saunders (1937) reviewed the previous extensive literature and carried out a careful and definitive study on fetal and infant frontal bones from the 6th week of intra-uterine life to the 10th postnatal month.

Each half of the bone ossifies from a single centre, which appears in membrane between 6 and 7 weeks. At first each centre has an oval-shaped form whose long axis lies in the region of the supraciliary arch which forms the lower part of the squama and the anterior portion of the orbital plate. Ossification spreads as a network of radiating trabeculae, at first more rapidly in the pars frontalis than in the pars orbitalis. The rapid expansion upwards has led to many accounts of the centre of ossification being in the region of the frontal eminence but this does not appear to be the case (Inman and Saunders, 1937; Noback, 1943, 1944). This first burst of ossification gives rise only to that part of the supraciliary arch medial to the future supra-orbital notch. The lateral two-thirds of the arch and the zygomatic process develop later between 10 and 12 weeks, thus separating the orbital cavity from the temporal fossa. This process, which includes the formation of the linea temporalis and a fissure for the attachment of the membrane of the anterolateral fontanelle, tends to accentuate the appearance of a separate ossification centre. A similar process occurs at the medial end of the supraciliary ridge where the orbital plate is slow to ossify and this is complete by about 13 weeks.

The bone becomes recognizable at the end of the first trimester of prenatal life. It is a fragile, oval-shaped dome whose long axis runs from anteromedial to posterolateral (Fig. 4.38). The anterior edge is thickened at the orbital margin, which may show a supra-orbital notch or foramen. The orbital plate is extremely slight and thin. As the bone develops the frontal plate grows more rapidly and by about the 5th month, the anteroposterior length is greater than its lateral width.

Moss *et al.* (1956) measured four parameters of the prenatal frontal bone and found, that like the parietal, there is a definite interphase in rate of growth at between 12 and 13 weeks. Ohtsuki (1977) recorded developmental changes in thickness between 4 months and term.

In the last 2 months of prenatal life, the bone is more substantial (Fig. 4.39a). The inferomedial angle of the bone, which will form the glabella, shows transverse striations and from here the medial border is fairly smooth for a short distance. About halfway between the frontal eminence and the medial border there may be a foramen, which is continuous with a groove or slit joining it to the medial border. This is the site of the metopic fontanelle (see below). More posteriorly, the medial edge of the bone is very finely serrated and then slopes away laterally to form the margin of the anterior fontanelle. There is a rounded posterior angle at the lateral edge of the fontanelle and from here the coronal margin is also serrated as far as the lateral end of the supra-orbital ridge. Here the bone is thickened for the zygomatic articulation, which at this stage is an elongated triangle containing a groove whose apex points posteriorly (Fig. 4.39b). The lateral edge of the supra-orbital margin is sharp and the medial third smooth as in the adult bone.

Both the thickened articulations for the maxilla and nasal bones and the undulations in the orbital plate become obvious in the perinatal period. There are differering accounts of the development of the nasal spine. Both Rambaud and Renault (1864) and Augier (1931) state that this part of the bone develops from a double cartilaginous centre between 2 and 8 years of age but Inman and Saunders (1937) were unable to see a separate centre. They noted that the nasal spine became obvious in radiographs at about 10 years of age.

At birth, the frontal bone is composed of two symmetrical halves, which are separated from each other by the metopic suture (Figs 4.11, 4.14 and 4.37). The anterosuperior angles meet the parietal bones at the diamond-shaped **anterior fontanelle**, which is the largest of the fetal fontanelles. Dimensions are

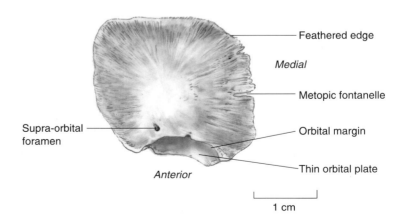

Supra-orbital foramen

Feathered edge

Medial

Metopic fontanelle

Orbital margin

Thin orbital plate

Anterior

1 cm

Figure 4.38 The right fetal frontal.

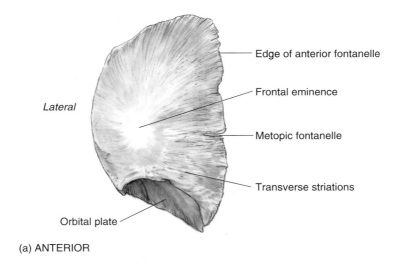

(a) ANTERIOR

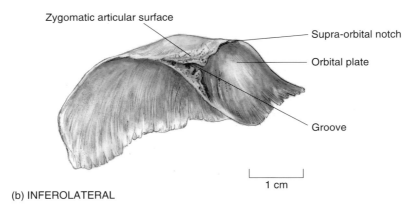

1 cm

(b) INFEROLATERAL

Figure 4.39 The right perinatal frontal.

very variable (Popich and Smith, 1972; Duc and Largo, 1986) but tend to increase in the first month of life as the shape of the vault settles after moulding in the birth canal. The size of the fontanelle does not appear to be significantly related to sex, head circumference or bone age, or be predictive of time of closure; 38% of fontanelles are closed by the end of the first year, 96% by 2 years. It is not uncommon for the fontanelle and its contiguous sutures to contain separate ossicles (Barclay-Smith, 1909; Willock, 1925; Girdany and Blank, 1965), which may be present at birth or develop later. They do not seem to interfere with normal growth and usually fuse with the surrounding bones before the 5th year of life. The frontal arm of the sagittal suture regularly reaches below the level of the frontal tuberosities, and in about 15% of infants it persists to birth or into postnatal life. In some cases the entire frontal arm of the suture is open, but more usually the upper part closes and the lower open part is then known as the metopic fontanelle (Schultz, 1929). It usually contains lateral emissary veins and, with age, adopts a more posterior location as the bone grows in height. Traces may remain, as in the parietal bone, as a median, or two lateral paramedian, frontal foramina which may be connected by an orthometopic suture which is sometimes reduced to a bony, star-shaped scar (Schultz, 1918b, 1929; Augier, 1931). A persistent metopic fontanelle (cranium bifidum occultam frontalis) is one of the signs of cranio-cleido dysostosis (Epstein and Epstein, 1967; Jarvis and Keats, 1974) (see also Chapter 8).

Fusion of the metopic suture normally takes place during the first year (Molleson and Cox, 1993) but completion can last until the 4th year. It starts to close just above the nasal end but many older skulls show a short, irregular suture just above the junction with the nasal bones. In a number of individuals, varying with the population, the suture is retained in its entirety into adult life (Bryce and Young, 1917; Limson, 1924; Jit and Shah, 1948; Woo, 1949a; Berry and Berry, 1967; Ossenberg, 1970; Das et al., 1973; Berry, 1975; Agarwal et al., 1979; Ajmani et al., 1983). The terminology of this condition, usually referred to as **metopism**, is confusing and its use in the literature has not been consistent. The remnant of any part of the suture remaining after about 2 years of age is usually called a **sutura metopica persistens** (Reinhard and Rösing, 1985). Wood Jones (1953) described a complete suture as appearing typically dentate from the nasion to about 2 cm anterior to the bregma, the pars bregmatica, when it becomes more simple in structure. The partial metopic suture is typically complex in form in its supranasal section (Das et al., 1973; Agarwal et al., 1979; Ajmani et al, 1983).

All theories concerning metopism focus on reasons for the non-fusion of the two parts of the frontal bone and none is very convincing (Bolk, 1917; Bryce and Young, 1917; Ashley-Montagu, 1937; Hess, 1945). Its presence is not related either to skull shape or to cranial capacity but is positively correlated with an increase in frontal curvature (Bolk, 1917; Schultz, 1929; Woo, 1949a). Torgersen (1950, 1951) followed its incidence in 16 Norwegian families and argued for a genetic basis.

A more interesting question is why in the vast majority of individuals the interfrontal suture closes much earlier than the rest of the sagittal suture, rather than why the suture remains open in a minority of cases. Because of its morphology and position, the frontal bone plays a major part in connecting the facial and neurocranial skeleton. Ethmoid centres cease growth at about 2 years of age, so that the early fusion of the halves of the frontal could be a way of maintaining maximum stability in the region of the fronto-ethmoidal-nasal suture system. However, if there is premature fusion of the metopic suture (metopic synostosis), severe defects in the orbital region and compensatory expansion in other cranial areas occur (Kolar and Salter, 1997). It is obviously essential for increase in width to take place at the interfrontal suture until ethmoid centres have completed their growth. Both ethmoid and normal metopic fusion occur at about the time of completion of eruption of the deciduous dentition, when there are maximum masticatory forces on the facial skeleton. Experimental approaches, such as those of Hylander et al. (1991) and Ross and Hylander (1996), on the mechanical forces on the facial and anterior calvarial skeleton, may throw further light on the reasons for the early closure of the interfrontal suture. The mechanics at the cellular level (Hall, 1967; Manzanares et al., 1988) also seem to suggest that the formation of chondroid tissue, which is involved in the closure of the interfrontal suture, is linked to the action of forces exerted in different directions on the sutural space.

Young (1957) recorded postnatal growth of the bone in boys aged from one month to 16 years and Meredith (1959) in girls from 5 to 15 years. After a rapid increase in chord, arc and thickness measurements the bone becomes increasingly more arched until the 3rd year, reflecting early brain enlargement. After this time, there is a deceleration of growth leading to a flattening of the bone.

Obviously adjustments also have to be made both to the growth of the frontal sinus and to the facial skeleton.

The sinus starts development in fetal life, either as a mucosal evagination at the anterior end of the middle meatus of the nose or from anterior ethmoidal cells but does not pneumatize the frontal bone until the postnatal period. Expansion begins at the age of 3.5 years (Lang, 1989; Wolf *et al.*, 1993), is level with the orbital roof between 6 and 8 years (Caffey, 1993) and then increases slowly until puberty. Dimensions in childhood are given by Wolf *et al.* (1993). Brown *et al.* (1984) made detailed measurements from radiographs in 49 males and 47 females from the age of 2 years until over 20 years. Over half of the subjects had a sinus visible on first examination but the mean age of appearance was 3.25 years in boys and 4.58 years in girls. This agrees with Maresh (1940), who gave an age range of 2 to 6 years. As expected, the main period of enlargement coincided with the pubertal growth spurt, the end of which was about 13 years in girls and 15 years in boys. Thus the period of growth was shorter and the mean final size was smaller in girls than in boys. Lang (1989) reported that the sinus may go on increasing in size well into the fourth decade of life. Once adult size and shape has been established, the frontal sinuses are unique to each individual and this may be used to advantage by forensic scientists for purposes of identification (Schuller, 1943; Ubelaker, 1984; Krogman and Işcan, 1986; Harris *et al.*, 1987; Yoshino *et al.*, 1987; Kullman *et al.*, 1990). Absent or hypoplastic sinuses are characteristic of Down's syndrome (trisomy 21) or Apert's syndrome (acrocephalosyndactyly) but occasionally the condition appears to be unrelated to pathological conditions.

Practical notes

Sideing/orientation of the juvenile frontal (Fig. 4.39)
In the perinatal period, it is unusual to recover a complete separate frontal as most bones of the vault are damaged. Sideing and orientation rely on recognizing the orbital margin, which is thickened and often survives inhumation. The sharp, projecting margin is on the lateral side and ends in the thickened, triangular articular surface for the zygomatic bone.

Bones of a similar morphology
Small fragments of the frontal bone are probably indistinguishable from other vault fragments unless a characteristic part of the bone is present. Only the frontal bone has orbital rims and orbital plates set at an angle to the rest of the bone. There may be traces of frontal air sinuses or the highly characteristic crista frontalis.

Morphological summary

Prenatal	
Wks 6–7	Primary centre of ossification appears
Wks 10–13	Zygomatic process and medial angular processes start ossifying
By mth 5	Anteroposterior longer than mediolateral length
Birth	Represented by right and left halves
Yrs 1–2	Anterior fontanelle closed
Yrs 2–4	Metopic suture normally closed

VI. THE NASAL BONE

The right and left nasal bones form the bridge of the nose and articulate with each other, the frontal bone, perpendicular plate of the ethmoid, nasal septal cartilages and the frontal processes of the maxillae (Figs 4.3, 4.5 and see 4.43).

Ossification

The nasal bones develop in membrane in the dense mesenchyme overlying the cartilaginous nasal capsule. They are first visible histologically at 9–10 weeks (Macklin, 1914; Sandikcioglu *et al.*, 1994) and become recognizable in radiographs a little later (O'Rahilly and Meyer, 1956; Sandikcioglu *et al.*, 1994). Most accounts describe a single ossification centre for each bone although there are reports, not well substantiated, of a second, medial endochondral centre (Augier, 1931; Frazer, 1948).

Limson (1932) commented on the variety in size and shape of fetal nasal bones and distinguished four distinct classes according to overall shape, the percentage frequencies being different in black and white fetuses. Niida *et al.* (1991), using scanning electron microscopy, distinguished three separate patterns of trabecular bone growth in Japanese fetuses. The most common was a concentric arrangement in the lower part and a vertical arrangement in the upper part of the bone. The patterns, already apparent in the fetus, were thought to be responsible for the variations that are common in the adult bone. Fazekas and Kósa (1978) measured the length and breadth of the dry bone throughout fetal life and Sandikcioglu *et al.* (1994) recorded the length from radiographs from about 3–7 'lunar months'. Although the measurements were not strictly comparable, both showed a relatively linear rate of growth in length.

Because of its extreme fragility, the nasal bone is probably not identifiable in isolation before the third trimester of prenatal life. It can be recognized from its adult morphological shape although it differs in size and overall proportions (Fig. 4.40). An obvious articular surface on the medial border for the corresponding bone does not develop until late in fetal life.

At birth, the bone is surprisingly robust. The borders are smooth and the vascular foramen can usually be seen in the lower half of the bone (Fig. 4.41). Its length is about twice the breadth across the lower part of the bone (Fazekas and Kósa, 1978; Lang, 1989) but its overall shape, even at this stage, is quite variable. After one year of age, the bone starts to increase in length in its lower part so that by puberty it is about three times as long as it is wide. Both the serrated superior border and the nasal spine develop after the age of 3 years about the time that ossification is proceeding inferiorly in the perpendicular plate of the ethmoid. Enlow and Bang (1965), in a study of the maxilla and its

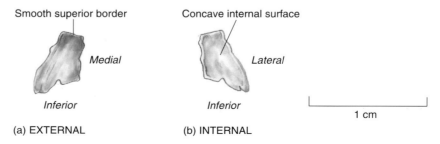

Figure 4.40 The right fetal nasal.

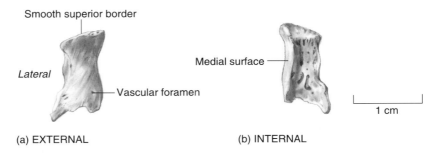

Figure 4.41 The right perinatal nasal.

neighbouring bones, observed that the outer and inner surfaces of the nasal bones show typical appositional and resorptive surfaces respectively as the bone grows in size and noted that there was much individual variation in size and shape.

Anomalies of the nasal bones may vary from unilateral or bilateral agenesis, through hyperplasia to hyperdevelopment (Duckworth, 1902; Wahby, 1903; Augier, 1931; Barnes, 1994). Dedick and Caffey (1953) reported that, in rare cases where the nasal bones failed to mineralize, the condition may be associated with Down's syndrome. In the absence of separate nasal bones, the neighbouring frontal or maxillary bones may compensate by sending a process into the normal territory of the nasal.

In young children the nasofrontal and frontomaxillary sutures are both level with the roof of the nasal cavity whereas in older children and adults the nasofrontal suture is somewhat higher (Fig. 4.42). This is caused by the overlapping nature of the suture so that, as it develops, the nasion ascends on the frontal bone with age and becomes closer to the upper orbital margin in adults than in children. Because of this changing relationship, Scott (1956) warned that the nasion cannot be used as evidence of the growth and separation of the frontal and maxilla. It must be used with care as a fixed point when measurements are taken on radiographs.

Practical notes

Sideing/orientation of the juvenile nasal (Fig. 4.41)
The bone does not become recognizable in isolation until late fetal life as it is small and fairly fragile but by birth it is more robust. It is narrower superiorly than inferiorly. The medial border is shorter than the lateral border and bears the thickened articular surface for the bone of the opposite side.

Morphological summary	
Prenatal	
Wks 9–10	Ossification centre appears for each bone
Mths 9–10	Medial articular border develops
Birth	Morphology similar to adult except:
	length to width proportion different
	borders are smooth
	vascular foramen is in lower half of the bone.
About yr 3	Nasal spine develops and superior border becomes serrated
Puberty	Adopts adult morphology and size

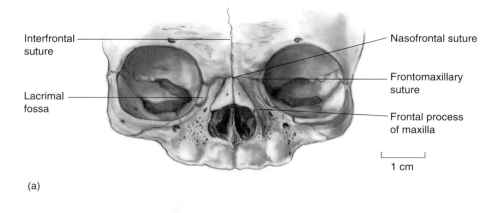

Interfrontal suture

Lacrimal fossa

Nasofrontal suture

Frontomaxillary suture

Frontal process of maxilla

1 cm

(a)

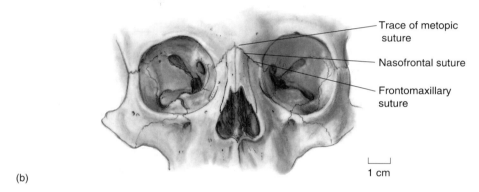

Trace of metopic suture

Nasofrontal suture

Frontomaxillary suture

1 cm

(b)

Figure 4.42 Frontonasal sutures. (a) Perinatal – nasofrontal and frontomaxillary sutures at same level. Note triangular nasal bone. (b) Child of 8 years – nasofrontal sutures superior to frontomaxillary sutures.

VII. THE ETHMOID

The ethmoid is a component of the nasal cavity and orbits and also lies in the anterior cranial fossa (Fig. 4.32). It occupies the ethmoidal notch of the frontal bone and also articulates with the sphenoid, vomer, maxillae, lacrimal and nasal bones and the septal cartilage (Figs 4.2, 4.3 and 4.43). It consists of a horizontal cribriform plate, a midline perpendicular plate and two lateral labyrinths.

Ossification

The first centres of ossification appear in the middle conchal region of the labyrinths of the ethmoid bone during the 5th prenatal month (Vidić, 1971). In general, ossification spreads from inferior to superior and medial to lateral and there may be several centres for the main concha, the bulla and the uncinate process (Augier, 1931). The ethmoidal and frontal sinus systems begin to develop as air cells which bud out from the superior and middle meatuses to invaginate the ectethmoidal part of the nasal capsule (see

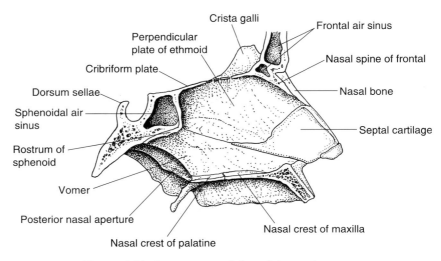

Figure 4.43 Components of the adult nasal septum.

Early Development of the Human Skull). Ossification extends into the superior concha and then slowly spreads into intercellular septa as far as the orbital laminae, which form as the external surfaces of ethmoidal cells so that by about 6 months, each labyrinth is almost completely ossified. At birth, the bone consists of the two bony labyrinths held together by the cartilaginous cribriform and perpendicular plates. In the perinatal period, an individual labyrinth may be identified by its characteristic adult morphology, although it is rarely recovered owing to its extremely fragile nature (Fig. 4.44). It is a slim rectangle, the medial side of which is 'wrinkled' bone forming the upper and middle conchae. The lateral side is the smooth orbital plate that forms a more or less continuous covering except at the anterior end where open air cells are usually visible.

The cribriform plate and the upper part of the perpendicular plate start to ossify quite rapidly during the first year of life, the external parts by ossification spreading from the labyrinth and the internal parts from paramedian centres. From 4 to 8 months *post partum* the internal and external sections unite, commencing in the posterior third. The crista galli ossifies either by extension from the internal part of the cribriform plate or from a separate centre of ossification and there may be an occasional centre for the tip

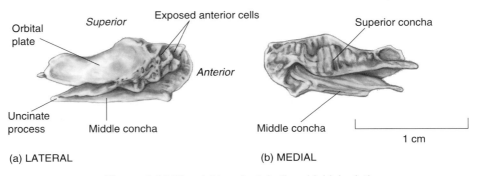

Figure 4.44 The right perinatal ethmoidal labyrinth.

(Augier, 1931). It may deviate laterally or be pneumatized. Growth in length and width of the cribriform plate ceases by the age of 2–3 years, when it fuses with the labyrinths (Ford, 1958; Scott, 1959). After this, the width of the labyrinths can only increase by surface deposition during further pneumatization on the orbital side (Scott, 1959). The orbital plate may be divided by sutures or show dehiscences. Measurements of the ethmoidal sinuses at birth and during childhood are given by Wolf *et al.* (1993). The most anterior group of air cells sometimes give rise to the frontal air sinuses (Schaeffer, 1916), which start to pneumatize the frontal bone in early childhood (see Frontal bone). Pneumatization may spread into the uncinate process (Schaeffer, 1910a) and ethmoidal air cells may also invade the sphenoid, maxilla and lacrimal bones.

The lower part of the perpendicular plate ossifies later and more slowly. An ossification centre appears in the mesethmoid cartilage during the first year and bone gradually spreads in the cartilaginous septum towards the vomer (see ossification of Vomer). At first, only the edge of the ossifying area is thickened and the rest of the plate is very thin and may be perforated (Cleland, 1862). Verwoerd *et al.* (1989) reported on the radiological appearances of the nasal septum from birth to 30 years of age. No ossification was visible in the upper part of the septum during the first year but the alae of the vomer showed clearly. Ossification began in the upper, posterior part of the septum and gradually enlarged antero-inferiorly towards the vomer, the lower rim of the bony area becoming obvious. The age at which the ossification reached the vomer varied between 3 and 10 years of age. There was usually an unossified posterior part of the septum, the 'sphenoidal tail', between the thickened rim of the perpendicular plate and the line of fusion of the vomerine alae. From 10 years of age until the late teens there was a progressive expansion of ossification in the perpendicular plate at the expense of the cartilaginous septum and overlap was visible radiologically. Bony integration between the two structures took place between 20 and 30 years of age. It is common for the nasal septum to show deviation (see Vomer).

Practical notes

Sideing/orientation of the juvenile ethmoid (Fig. 4.44)

The ethmoidal labyrinth is usually ossified by the 7th month of fetal life and resembles the adult in its morphology. The smooth orbital plate lies laterally and the wrinkled conchal surface is medial. The free edge of the middle concha is inferior and pointed posteriorly. Air sinuses can usually be seen anteriorly on the superior surface. A whole ethmoid is not usually recognizable until some time after birth as the perpendicular plate does not start to ossify until the first year of life.

Bones of a similar morphology

Small fragments of any of the pneumatized bones could be mistaken for the ethmoidal labyrinth. Probably the only recognizable parts are the crista galli or a large part of the nasal septum in late juvenile life.

Morphological summary

Prenatal

Mth 5	Ossification centres appear in the cartilage of the conchal regions of the labyrinth.

Birth	Represented by two labyrinths joined by cartilage
Yrs 1−2	Cribriform plate and crista galli ossify and fuse with labyrinths
Yrs 3−10	Ossified perpendicular plate reaches vomer and 'sphenoidal tail' usually visible posteriorly
Yr 10− puberty	Progressive expansion of ossification into nasal septum
Yrs 20−30	Ethmoid and vomer fuse

VIII. INFERIOR NASAL CONCHA

Functionally the inferior nasal concha should be viewed as a detached part of the ethmoid bone. It lies below the ethmoidal labyrinth in the lateral wall of the nose (Fig. 4.5) and is covered with mucous membrane on both sides. It is a delicate plate of bone, boat-shaped in outline, with two surfaces, two ends and two borders.

Ossification

The inferior concha develops in the lateral wall of the nasal capsule. As with the other conchae, it is part of the ectethmoid cartilage (see Early Development of the Human Skull), which forms the incomplete floor (solum nasi) of the nasal region before the palatal shelves develop. It is the first part of the region to ossify and appears before any of the ethmoid centres. According to Augier (1931), a single ossification centre appears at about 16 weeks in the middle of the cartilaginous anlage and rapidly grows inferiorly towards the free edge. It loses continuity with the capsule during ossification and so develops into an independent bone. Limson (1932) describes a second bony plate, which appears at the inferior border of the first centre during the 7th month. During the later part of fetal life it spreads upwards as a corrugated mass of bone and covers the medial surface of the upper plate. The maxillary process appears first and is recognizable in the 7th month whilst the ethmoidal and lacrimal processes do not develop until the 8th month. At birth, the bone has all the characters of the adult bone except that it is more wrinkled and the processes of the superior border are less obvious (Fig. 4.45). It frequently fuses with the maxilla before middle life (Augier, 1931; Frazer, 1948) and may also fuse with the uncinate process of the ethmoid bone (Augier, 1931).

Practical notes

Sideing/orientation of the juvenile inferior concha (Fig. 4.45)

Recovery of an isolated juvenile inferior concha would be a rare event as it is a very fragile bone and correct sideing would depend on the completeness of the specimen. The medial surface is wrinkled and convex and the lateral surface is smoother and concave. The posterior end is more pointed than the anterior and the inferior border is thickened and incurved.

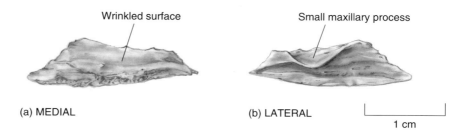

(a) MEDIAL (b) LATERAL 1 cm

Figure 4.45 The right perinatal inferior concha.

Bones of a similar morphology

Parts of an inferior concha would be very difficult to distinguish from fragments of the labyrinths of the ethmoid bone.

Morphological summary	
Prenatal	
Wk 16	Single ossification centre appears
Mth 7	Maxillary process develops
Mth 8	Ethmoidal and lacrimal processes develop
Birth	Adult morphology except more wrinkled and lacrimal, maxillary and ethmoid processes less well developed
Postnatal	Frequently fuses with maxilla but timing very variable

IX. LACRIMAL

The lacrimal is probably the most delicate of all the bones of the body and, despite its small size, quite variable in morphology. It lies at the anterior edge of the medial wall of the orbit and articulates with the frontal and ethmoidal bones and with the maxilla and the inferior nasal concha (Figs 4.3, 4.32). It has two surfaces and four borders.

Ossification

The lacrimal bone develops in membrane on the surface of the nasal capsule. It arises from a single ossification centre at about 10 pretal weeks (Macklin, 1921; Noback and Robertson, 1951) in a cleft in the chondrocranium between the posterior maxillary process and the posterior prominence with the nasolacrimal duct lying immediately lateral to it (Macklin, 1921). The main part of the bone forms first, followed by the crista and then the hamulus, with the orbital part last. Rambaud and Renault (1864) describe two calcified tracks, which would explain the occasional bipartite bone. There is occasionally a separate inferior ossicle for the hamulus (Augier, 1931). In fetuses between 5 and 8 months the orbital part of the bone is very small compared to the facial part but by birth the two parts have become nearly equal in size (Limson, 1932). The perinatal bone is long and slim supero-inferiorly with the facial and orbital parts separated by the lacrimal crest (Fig. 4.46). It may not articulate directly with the orbital plate of the ethmoid until after birth. There are two periods of more rapid growth in length of the nasolacrimal duct: first from 7 months to 3

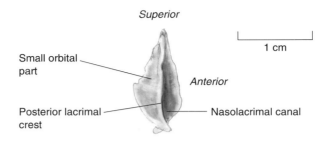

Figure 4.46 The right perinatal lacrimal.

years and second between 12 and 14 years. They are thus temporally related to the eruption of the deciduous dentition and the second permanent molars.

There are reports of failure of ossification that may lead to the lacrimal being rudimentary or absent. Its territory is then occupied by the ethmoid bone or the maxilla.

Practical notes

Sideing/orientation of the juvenile lacrimal (Fig. 4.46)

It is unlikely that the lacrimal bone would be recovered in isolation owing to its extremely fragile nature. The lacrimal crest lies on the lateral side and ends inferiorly in the lacrimal hamulus.

Bones of a similar morphology

Fragments of the orbital plate of the ethmoid have a similar structure to the lacrimal, which could only be identified if a characteristic part such as the crest or hamulus were preserved.

Morphological summary	
Prenatal	
Wk 10	Single ossification centre appears
Birth	Long slim bone with narrow section posterior to crest
Yrs 2–3	Assumes adult morphology

X. THE VOMER

The vomer is a thin, trapezoid-shaped plate of bone that lies in the midline and forms part of the nasal septum. It articulates with the sphenoid, ethmoid and palatine bones, and with the maxilla and septal cartilage (Figs 4.1 and 4.43). It has two surfaces and four borders.

Ossification

The vomer develops from two intramembranous centres that appear in the mucoperichondrium at the lower border of the nasal septum during the 9th week of uterine life (Fawcett, 1911; Macklin, 1914, 1921; Müller and O'Rahilly, 1980). Histologically they appear as two slender strips of bone, widest in the middle and tapering off towards their ends. After about two weeks, they fuse at their lower borders beneath the septal cartilage to form a V- or U-shaped bone. Later still, this becomes Y-shaped in coronal section. The vomerine groove, which extends from the sphenoid posteriorly to the premaxillary area in front, supports the lower edge of the septal cartilage, the posterior part of which will ossify later as the perpendicular plate of the ethmoid. The vomer is visible radiographically at about 11 weeks (O'Rahilly and Meyer, 1956). In a histological and radiological study, Sandikioglu *et al.* (1994) reported fusion at a mean age of 17 prenatal weeks, which began posteriorly. The bone assumed its Y-shaped form between 19 and 23 weeks and, from the lateral aspect, looked fan-shaped with bony trabeculae spreading from the base.

The vomer in the third trimester of prenatal life is boat-shaped consisting of two leaves of bone joined inferiorly into a single lamina with a flattened base (Fig. 4.47). Each leaf has a feathery free edge and is pointed and almost vertical anteriorly. Posteriorly, the two leaves open out to form a scoop-shaped end that develops into the vomerine alae.

The involvement of the paraseptal (Jacobsonian) cartilages in the development of the vomer is complex and has remained a matter of some controversy. Fawcett (1911) described the vomer invading and ossifying the posterior end of the anterior paraseptal cartilages that he believed originated in the roof of the nasal capsule. Augier (1931) described the paraseptal cartilages ossifying independently into paraseptal ossicles, which then fused with the vomer later in the perinatal period or even after birth. Eloff (1952) agreed with Augier on the existence of independent paraseptal ossicles but could not confirm Fawcett's finding of fusion with the vomer. More recently, Wang *et al.* (1988) attempted to elucidate the fate of the paraseptal cartilages, which they believed originated directly from the antero-inferior part of the septal cartilage as it grows down to meet the palatal shelves. They were unable to identify any separate paraseptal ossicles and agreed with Fawcett that the vomer invades the posterior end of the paraseptal cartilages whilst the anterior end seems to be resorbing. The time of ossification varied greatly from 14 to 32 weeks *in utero*. They were also unable to identify any posterior paraseptal cartilages. The paraseptal cartilages

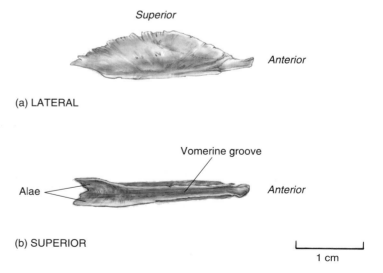

Superior

Anterior

(a) LATERAL

Vomerine groove

Alae

Anterior

(b) SUPERIOR

1 cm

Figure 4.47 Perinatal vomer.

obviously contribute to the development of the bone, although their exact relationship is far from clear. The vomer therefore appears to have contributions from both membranous and cartilaginous elements. The role of the paraseptal cartilages and the surgical approaches to cartilaginous remnants were reviewed by Beck (1963).

The postnatal growth of the vomer is intimately connected with the growth of the nasal septum as a whole and the consequent increase in size of the facial skeleton (Scott, 1953, 1967). Takahashi (1987), in a study of septal deformity, gave a detailed account of the changes in the vomer and distinguished nine phases of development. The downward spread of ossification in the perpendicular plate of the ethmoid reaches the vomer during early childhood and contact between the two structures induces further ossification at the open edges of the vomerine groove. By the age of 10 years, the height of the posterior edge of the nasal septum is about 80% of its adult size (Scott, 1967). The superior left and right edges of the vomer fuse, converting the groove into a vomerine canal by the age of puberty. In early adult life, there is usually a fusion with the perpendicular plate of the ethmoid (see above) and later the bone undergoes compaction and thinning and also increases in height.

Incomplete ossification may lead to perforations in the bone or to a narrow cavity between the two sides. Most of the variations in the shape of the vomer play a part in the clinical condition of deviated septum (Takahashi, 1987). Deviation is rarely seen in the newborn or before the age of 7 years and so may be related to the growth of the maxillae after the appearance of the deciduous dentition (Augier, 1931; Frazer, 1948). It appears to be more common in whites and males. Rarely, the sphenoidal sinus may project inferiorly and pneumatize the vomer (Lang, 1989).

Practical notes

Orientation of the juvenile vomer (Fig. 4.47)
The boat-shaped bone is composed of two laminae, which are fused inferiorly. They are more pointed and closer together anteriorly.

Bones of a similar morphology
The complete vomer is unlikely to be mistaken for any other bone as it has a characteristic shape. However, fragments would be indistinguishable from other delicate nasal and facial fragments.

Morphological summary	
Prenatal	
Wks 9–10	Two ossification centres appear
Wks 11–12	Fusion at the lower edges of the two leaves of bone
Mths 3–5	Change from U-shaped to Y-shaped base
Birth	Boat-shaped bone composed of two laminae
Yrs 3–10	Fusion of perpendicular plate of ethmoid to vomerine groove
Yr 10 –	
puberty	Assumes adult size and proportions
Yrs 20–30	Fuses with perpendicular plate of ethmoid

XI. THE ZYGOMATIC

The zygomatic (malar /jugal) forms the prominence of the cheek and separates the orbit from the temporal fossa. It articulates with the maxilla, the greater wing of the sphenoid, and the zygomatic processes of the frontal and temporal bones (Figs 4.1, 4.3 and 4.5). It is an irregular shape and has three surfaces, two processes and five borders.

Ossification

The single ossification centre for the bone develops in the mesenchyme below and lateral to the orbit during the 8th week of intra-uterine life (Noback and Robertson, 1951; O'Rahilly and Gardner, 1972) and evidence for two or three separate centres appears doubtful, at least in Europeans. The bone appears as a triangular squama with the temporal process most advanced and the frontal process the last to form (Augier, 1931). By the 9th week it already bears a resemblance to the adult bone, being an incurved quadrilateral with four angles. The border between the cranial and ventral angles forms the part that will articulate with the maxilla. (Macklin, 1914, 1921). At first, the temporal process is the most obvious but it does not complete the zygomatic arch until late in fetal life, or occasionally after birth. The ossification centre becomes apparent radiologically by about 11 to 12 weeks (O'Rahilly and Meyer, 1956; Bach-Petersen and Kjær, 1993).

   By the end of the first half of prenatal life, the zygomatic is sufficiently similar to the adult bone to be recognizable although the proportions are somewhat different. It is also comparatively large and robust and is therefore one of the most frequently recovered complete juvenile cranial bones. Perinatally, it is a gracile triradiate bone with slender frontal, temporal and maxillary processes, which project from a relatively small, curved body (Fig. 4.48). The three surfaces have the same relationship to each other as in the adult bone but the borders of the bone are different because the height of the facial skeleton is relatively small at this stage. The inferior border bears a prominent notch about a third of the way from the medial end and this marks the future angle between the antero-inferior and postero-inferior borders. The postero-medial border just touches the frontal bone and then articulates with the

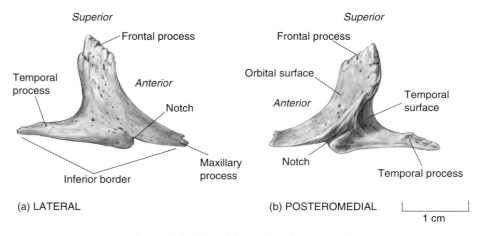

(a) LATERAL (b) POSTEROMEDIAL 1 cm

Figure 4.48 The right perinatal zygomatic.

greater sphenoidal wing. There is a big non-articular area below this as the inferior orbital fissure is relatively large at this stage and the inferior part of the border articulates with the maxilla obliquely along the middle of the orbital floor.

During infancy and early childhood, the zygomatic develops to keep pace with the rapid growth of the maxilla, which increases in height and width to accommodate the deciduous dentition. This causes a change in position of the articulation with the maxilla and angulation at the notch on the inferior border. The infra-orbital zygomaticomaxillary suture shifts from the middle to the lateral side of the orbital floor and the antero-inferior and the postero-inferior borders become defined. By the time of completion of the eruption of the deciduous dentition, the bone has assumed adult proportions. Both the tuberculum marginale and the eminentia orbitalis become palpable during the second or third year of life. At about the same time, the ends of the frontal and temporal processes become serrated. As the development of a malar tubercle is a secondary sexual characteristic, it is not usually obvious much before puberty.

Practical notes

Sideing/orientation of the juvenile zygomatic (Fig. 4.48)
The bone is recognizable in isolation from midfetal life and by the perinatal period is surprisingly large and robust compared to other facial bones. Sideing depends on orientating the convex triradiate external surface correctly. The curved orbital surface faces medially and the notched border is inferior. The concave temporal surface and the slender temporal process point posteriorly.

Bones of a similar morphology
A complete zygomatic bone is readily recognizable but fragments of one of its processes could be confused with pointed parts of other cranial bones such as the zygomatic process of the temporal or lesser wing of sphenoid.

Morphological summary	
Prenatal	
Wk 8	Single ossification centre appears
Mth 6	Adopts recognizable morphology
Birth	Slender triradiate bone with notched inferior border
Yrs 2–3	Adopts adult proportions with serrated frontal and temporal processes
	Tuberculum marginale and eminentia orbitalis palpable
Puberty	Malar tubercle may be obvious in males

XII. THE MAXILLA

The maxillae form a large part of the visible surface of the lower face and nasal aperture. They also extend inwards to take part in the floor and lateral walls of the nasal cavity, the floors of the orbits (Fig. 4.32) and the anterior part of the roof of the oral cavity and they bear all the upper teeth. The right and left bones join with each other in the midline of the hard palate (Fig. 4.49) and articulate with the zygomatics, frontal, nasals, lacrimals, inferior conchae,

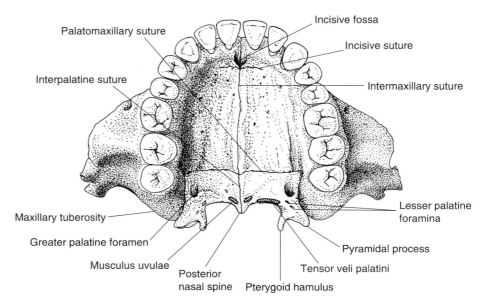

Figure 4.49 The adult hard palate.

ethmoid and palatine bones (Figs 4.1, 4.3 and 4.5). Each maxilla consists of a body from which four processes extend.

The most common anomalies of the maxilla are caused by abnormalities at the blastemal stage of development. Failure of the normal morphogenesis of the frontonasal and median nasal processes (see Early Development of the Human Skull) result in different types of defects. These include cleft lip and palate, absence of the premaxillary region (Walker, 1917; Derry, 1938), various forms of facial clefting and Binder's syndrome (hypoplasia of the median nasal prominence (Horswell *et al.*, 1987). Frontonasal process field defects seen in archaeological material have been reviewed by Barnes (1994). Information on clinical conditions can be found in Stricker *et al.* (1990).

Ossification

Accounts of the ossification of the human maxilla have been bedevilled with disagreements about the supposed presence of a separate premaxilla (os incisivum) based on the partial separation of the adult bone by the incisive (premaxillary) suture (fissure) that is sometimes present on the palatal aspect in the adult. As stressed by Noback and Moss (1953) and Jacobson (1955), the argument has been further complicated by similar terms being used for both the mesenchymal processes and the ossification centres. Ossification centres are independent of, and secondary to, the fusion of the early mesenchymal facial processes and their boundaries do not coincide. Further confusion has been created by attempts to homologize the parts of the human maxilla with the separate premaxilla and maxilla that exist in other mammals, particularly primates. A full review of the literature from the time of Vesalius may be found in Ashley-Montagu (1935).

No agreement exists on whether there are separate centres of ossification for the premaxillary and maxillary parts of the bone. Separate centres have been reported by Chase (1942), Woo (1949b), Noback and Moss (1953), Shepherd and McCarthy (1955), Kraus and Decker (1960) and Latham (1970). However, Fawcett (1911), Jacobson (1955) and Wood *et al.* (1967, 1969) stated categorically that there is no separate premaxillary ossification centre. Wood *et al.* (1969) described the whole bone developing from a lamina of osteoid tissue that may contain separate foci of calcification which rapidly fuse together. They attribute the observations of supposed separate centres to misinterpretation of material; alizarin staining showing only calcification but not the preliminary formation of osteoid tissue, and serial sections possibly being viewed at too high a level to see the continuous osteoid lamina at the base of the bone.

There is also controversy regarding the subsequent development of the maxilla and there are two main interpretations based on its developing appearance. The overgrowth theory (Ashley-Montagu, 1935; Wood Jones, 1947; Woo, 1949b) described the maxillary part gradually covering the premaxillary centre on the facial aspect thus obliterating the incisive suture, which remains only on the palatal aspect. The other view (Chase, 1942; Noback and Moss, 1953; Kvinnsland, 1969a) is that the two parts of the bone fuse together at the incisive suture, which then becomes obliterated on the facial aspect but remains open in the palate. Other studies adopted an intermediate position. Shepherd and McCarthy (1955) described a mixture of fusion and overgrowth with erosion of the premaxillary territory by the maxilla. Kraus and Decker (1960) described a secondary overgrowth of bone, the external trabecular network, which obliterated the incisive suture. This type of development is similar to that described by Matsumura *et al.* (1994) in the supra-occipital (see Occipital bone) where the endochondrally formed bone is overgrown by cancellous bone formed in the membranous interparietal above it. Wood *et al.* (1969, 1970) followed the course of ossification on the frontal aspect of the body and frontal process of the maxilla. They regarded the so-called 'incisive suture' as not a true suture in that it never truly separates parts of the bone at any stage in its development and preferred the term 'incisive fissure' for the feature that undoubtedly exists at an early stage. However, as emphasized by O'Rahilly and Gardner (1972), the existence of a separate bony element does not depend on a separate centre of ossification and these differing accounts do not preclude the convenient use of the term 'premaxilla' for that part of the bone that lies in front of the incisive suture and bears the incisor teeth (Dixon, 1953).

The early development of the maxilla is described in detail by Fawcett (1911), Dixon (1953) and Jacobson (1955). The first ossification centre is seen during the 7th week of prenatal life (Stage 19) in the membranous tissue covering the anterior part of the nasal capsule. At this stage, the tongue is high in the undivided pharyngeal cavity and the palatal shelves are still vertical (see Early Development of the Human Skull – Fig. 4.10a). The centre is just above that part of the dental lamina that gives rise to the canine tooth and where the anterior superior alveolar nerve branches from the infra-orbital nerve. The definitive parts of the maxilla spread rapidly from this centre. Dixon (1953) envisaged the bone as functionally subdivided into neural and alveolar areas. Outer and inner neural plates, which develop into the zygomatic (malar) process and the inner orbital margin respectively, form on either side of the anterior superior nerve, which runs forward to reach the incisor teeth. Under the nerve, the ossific tissue rejoins to form a subneural plate that develops into the infra-orbital groove in which the nerve lies in the floor of the orbit. About two weeks later, two further limbs extend superiorly and inferiorly from the centre to form the frontal and alveolar processes. The latter eventually develops into a gutter that houses the dental lamina. From the junction of the two processes ossification spreads medially into the palatal shelves, which by then have reached a horizontal position (Figs 4.10b,c). Small centres of secondary cartilage are present at both the upper end of the frontal process on the outer side of the lacrimal duct and at the alveolar border of the zygomatic process, but these quickly become converted to bone.

Descriptions of the radiographic appearance of the developing maxilla emphasize a maxillary centre at 7–8 weeks followed by a premaxillary centre at 9–10 weeks (Kjær, 1990d). O'Rahilly and Meyer (1956) described and illustrated its structure at about 11–12 weeks. A gap can be seen between the palatine processes of the premaxillary and maxillary parts and there is a prominent anterior nasal spine. Njio and Kjær (1993) described the gross, radiological and histological appearance of both the incisive fissure and the maxillopalatine sutures. They concluded that the latter is likely to have a function in the anteroposterior growth of the bony palate whilst the former is associated with accommodation of the increased volume of tissue during development of the dentition.

The prenatal maxilla towards the end of the embryonic period is described and illustrated in detail by Macklin (1914, 1921), Augier (1931) and Müller and O'Rahilly (1980). The main body of the bone is small, the nasal notch, the infra-orbital margin and all four processes are recognizable. The frontal process, triangular in shape, lies on the side wall of the ectethmoid part of the nasal capsule in front of the epiphanial foramen with the lacrimal bone above, and the paraseptal cartilage below it. Its derivation from the premaxillary and maxillary parts sometimes shows as a cleft. The zygomatic process points dorsolaterally but at this early stage, there is a wide interval between it and the zygomatic bone. The alveolar process is an irregular, crescentic groove with rough edges filled with developing tooth germs. At this stage, the palatine process is still not completely developed and is represented by a shelf of bone extending from the inner alveolar area towards the midline. It is divided into maxillary and premaxillary parts but does not meet either the bone from the opposite side or the palatine bone posteriorly. The infra-orbital nerve lies in a groove in the bone of the orbital floor. Later it usually becomes closed over in the anterior part of the orbital floor and emerges on the facial aspect through the infra-orbital foramen. Variations in the formation of the infra-orbital suture are described by Schwartz (1982) and Bollobás (1984a). Occasionally the foramen remains open at the infra-orbital margin into adult life (Turner, 1885).

The maxillary sinus starts development between 10 and 12 prenatal weeks as a small epithelial sac outpouching from the infundibulum of the middle meatus into the ectethmoid cartilage (Schaeffer, 1910b; Van Alyea, 1936). At first, it lies above the floor of the nose and medial and superior to the infra-orbital foramen but these relationships change as pneumatization proceeds into the ossifying maxilla (see below).

The whole of the palatal process consists of a thin plate of bone until the late fetal period. After this, the medial surface anterior to the incisive canal increases in height as it becomes the interdental septum between the central incisor teeth germs. The growth of the whole alveolar process is complex and develops in close relationship to the developing deciduous and permanent tooth germs (Scott, 1959). A series of radiographs, with corresponding dissections, of fetal specimens from 3 to 10 prenatal months shows the developing tooth germs *in situ* (Boller, 1964). Other details have been reported by Kraus (1960), Schwartz (1982) and Bollobás (1984b). In general, the alveolar crypts develop in an anteroposterior direction with the lingual lamina in advance of the buccal lamina. The interalveolar septa are the last parts to complete each crypt. At 11 weeks of intra-uterine life, the crypts of the deciduous incisors start formation and septa form between the tooth germs about 2 weeks later. The crypts of all the teeth from the central incisors to the first molars are complete by about 17–18 prenatal weeks.

The perinatal maxilla (Fig. 4.50) has a very small body so that the tooth germs are close to the orbital floor. Although the air sinus is very small, its bony outline can be seen as a spindle-shaped depression in the lateral wall of the nose immediately lateral to the inferior concha. It is about 10 mm long, 3 mm wide and 4 mm high, is radiographically identifiable and is usually circular or pyramidal in shape in the living (Cullen and Vidić, 1972; Wolf *et al.*, 1993). All the air sinuses contain amniotic fluid at birth and do not become fully aerated until about 10 days *post partum* (Wasson, 1933). A prominent infra-orbital foramen is visible on the anterior surface and may still be open superiorly and continuous with the groove in the floor of the orbit. The frontal process is lanceolate in shape with the anterior lacrimal crest prominent on the outer surface although the oblique ethmoidal crest on the nasal aspect is only faintly marked. The slender zygomatic process extends posterolaterally from above the infra-orbital foramen and consists almost entirely of a triangular articular surface for the zygomatic bone. The palatal process is thin except for the medial border. Anteriorly, the pre-maxillary part of the bone displays racial differences. There is a less prominent anterior nasal spine and more alveolar prognathism in black individuals compared to white (Limson, 1932). Between the central incisors there is a smooth interdental septum behind which the incisive canal runs almost vertically. Posteriorly, the bone then becomes thinner as it forms the main part of the intermaxillary suture. The incisive fissure on the palatal surface extends from the incisive fossa medially to a variable position at its lateral end. It may be continuous with a fissure on the nasal aspect of the frontal process or end in alveolar bone. According to Schwartz (1982), this may be between the crypts of the lateral incisor and canine, at the middle, or even posterior to the canine crypt. Detailed discussion of these variable positions appears to be based on assumptions about direct derivation of the premaxilla and maxilla from embryological mesenchymal processes. The calcified crowns of the deciduous teeth cause prominent bulges on the external border of the alveolar process and the inferior view of the maxilla is dominated by the curve formed by the alveolar crypts, which envelop the palate. The first three dental crypts are triangular and arranged in a cuneiform pattern. The apices of the central incisor (i^1) and canine (c) face lingually whilst the lateral incisor (i^2) fits between them with its apex facing in a labial direction. The crypt of the first molar (m^1) is rectangular and that of the second deciduous molar (m^2) is still incomplete and continuous posteriorly with the infratemporal fossa (Fig. 4.50c). The infratemporal surface of the body only becomes identifiable late in fetal life as it lies postero-inferior to the orbital floor and superior to the alveolar process and both these structures are late to ossify fully posteriorly.

The alveolar bone in infants consists mainly of fine cancellous bone, which is constantly undergoing remodelling as the dentition forms. Van der Linden and Duterloo (1976) distinguish four stages that take place in bone of the alveolar socket immediately surrounding each developing tooth, each of which is related to a specific morphological stage of crown or root development. They illustrate the appearance of the crypts both before and after the removal of the deciduous and permanent tooth germs.

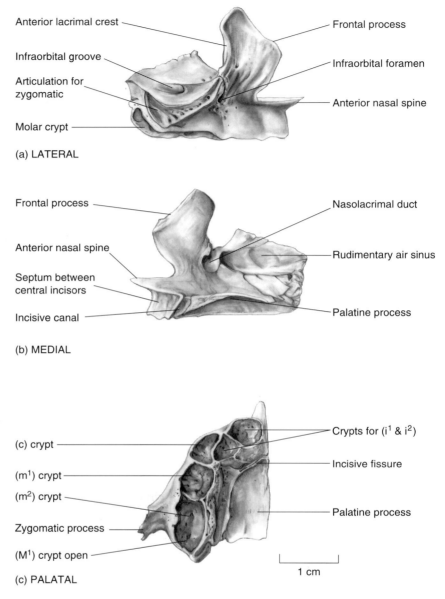

Anterior lacrimal crest

Frontal process

Infraorbital groove

Infraorbital foramen

Articulation for zygomatic

Anterior nasal spine

Molar crypt

(a) LATERAL

Frontal process

Nasolacrimal duct

Anterior nasal spine

Septum between central incisors

Rudimentary air sinus

Incisive canal

Palatine process

(b) MEDIAL

Crypts for (i^1 & i^2)

(c) crypt

Incisive fissure

(m^1) crypt

(m^2) crypt

Zygomatic process

Palatine process

(M^1) crypt open

1 cm

(c) PALATAL

Figure 4.50 The right perinatal maxilla.

The maxillary tuberosity as such does not exist during childhood as its place is taken by the posterior extensions of the alveolar processes. After eruption of the second and third molars the tuberosity then becomes closely related to the pyramidal process of the palatine bone (Scott, 1967).

Postnatal growth of the maxilla is rapid and related to different functional areas of the anterior part of the skull. The increase in size of the eyeballs and the nose both influence the development of main part of the body. The growth of the nasal septum carries the maxilla downwards and forwards, more anteriorly in the first decade and more vertically in the second. Enlow and Bang (1965) described growth by sutural activity and cartilaginous expansion up to the age of about 7 years, after which overall apposition becomes the dominant mechanism of growth. This occurs mainly at the alveolar region, the facial surface and the posterior border (Scott, 1967). Björk and Skieller (1977) followed the growth of the maxilla from 4 years to adult life radiographically by using metallic implants in living patients.

The contained air sinus enlarges by resorption and deposition of bone surfaces. By 4 years of age, pneumatization has reached laterally to the infra-orbital foramen and inferiorly to the attachment of the inferior concha (Wolf *et al*. 1993). By 8 or 9 years, it has reached beyond the infra-orbital foramen and by 12 years has reached the same level as the floor of the nose inferiorly and as far as the molar teeth laterally (Van Alyea, 1936; Wolf *et al*. 1993). By puberty, its lower limit is usually below that of the nose but the size and shape can be very variable (Schaeffer, 1910b). Dimensions of the sinus from birth to adulthood may be found in Maresh (1940) and Lang (1989).

The other major influence on the growth of the maxilla is the need for space for the increasing number and size of teeth. As the eruption of the deciduous dentition nears completion, the calcified crowns of the permanent central and lateral incisor teeth can be seen through foramina in the palatal process behind the corresponding deciduous incisor teeth. These are the openings of the gubernacular canals occupied by fibrous cords that connect the tooth follicles of the permanent teeth to the overlying mucous membrane. With the formation of each subsequent molar tooth, the posterior wall of the crypt of the tooth anterior to it is completed, leaving the newly formed crypt behind it open to the infratemporal fossa. Thus, at about one year of age, the crypt of the second deciduous molar (m^2) completes formation and that of the first permanent molar (M^1) is open posteriorly. After about 3 years of age, the second permanent molar (M^2) socket is open (Fig. 4.51). In dry skulls the maxillary tuberosity appears to remain partially unossified until the third molar (M^3) becomes properly surrounded by alveolar bone. However, Norberg (1960) distinguished a sutural line between the bone formed by the follicular sac of the second permanent molar and that of the maxilla proper. This would seem to concur with later observations on experimental animals that the alveolar bone is derived from the tooth germ and is therefore of a different origin from that of the main body of the maxilla with which it fuses (Ten Cate and Mills, 1972; Freeman *et al*., 1975).

The time of closure of the incisive suture is very variable. Although the facial aspect of the suture closes in infancy, the internal aspect in the region of the incisive canal between the two maxillae is slow to fuse and about one-third remain unfused into the adolescent period (Behrents and Harris, 1991). The palatal aspect of the suture may close laterally as early as the perinatal period, where the palatal processes fuse with the alveolar bone (Schwartz, 1982), but the medial part often remains open into adult life. Mann *et al*. (1987) found that the earliest age at which total obliteration of the suture occurred was 25 years. Sejrsen *et al*. (1993) studied the suture and its enclosed premaxillary area in a series of medieval Danish skulls. They showed that the degree of closure of the suture was related to tooth maturation and took place soon after the crowns of the permanent incisors has reached their final width. The size of the premaxillary area appeared to be related to tooth spacing and was reduced in some cases of tooth agenesis. Both these observations, and those of Njio and Kjær (1993) on the prenatal structure of the suture, suggest that the function of the suture is likely to be directly related to the maturation of the anterior tooth germs rather than general increase in size of the palate. (Palatal growth as a whole is considered under the Palatine bone).

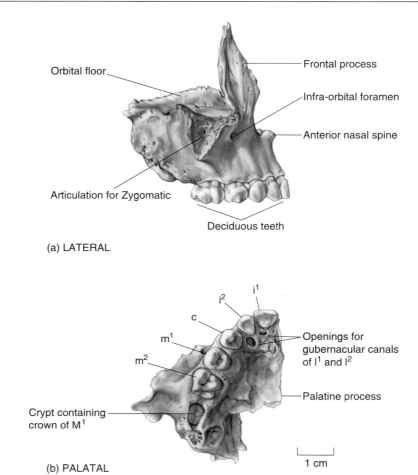

Orbital floor

Frontal process

Infra-orbital foramen

Anterior nasal spine

Articulation for Zygomatic

Deciduous teeth

(a) LATERAL

Openings for gubernacular canals of I^1 and I^2

Palatine process

Crypt containing crown of M^1

1 cm

(b) PALATAL

Figure 4.51 The right maxilla of a child of dental age 4–5 years.

Scott (1967) described three main periods of skull growth. During the first, which extends from late fetal life until about the third year, all the sutural systems are very active as the brain, eyeballs and tongue increase in size. By the end of the first year, the greater wings of the sphenoid unite with the body and the two parts of the frontal bone commence fusion. Within the next two years, the mesethmoid unites with the labyrinths and this limits growth of the craniofacial suture system. The second phase is from the third to the tenth year. Surface deposition generally replaces sutural growth as the main method of development although there is still some enlargement at the lambdoid, coronal and circum-maxillary sutures and growth is still active at the spheno-occipital synchondrosis. The distance from the pituitary fossa to the spheno-ethmoidal suture reaches adult dimensions (Brodie, 1941), as does the distance from the fossa to the foramen caecum (Ford, 1958). By about 10 years, when the third period begins, adult dimensions have been reached by the cranial and orbital cavities, the upper nose and the petrous parts of the temporal bones. During this time, the spheno-occipital synchondrosis ceases to be a growth centre and growth slows in the nasal septum. Growth by bone deposition is still marked at the alveolar processes, the orbital margins and muscular processes including the zygoma and the pterygoid plates. During all three phases, growth of the mandible continues to keep pace with that of the skull (see below).

There is a large amount of information in the dental and anatomical literature on the postnatal growth of the face in relation to the development and eruption of the dentition. Details of the growth of the face and its sutures are outwith the scope of this text and further details can be found in dental and orthodontic texts (Scott, 1954, 1956, 1957, 1967; Enlow and Hans, 1996).

Practical notes

Sideing/orientation of the perinatal maxilla (Fig. 4.50)
The maxilla does not ossify completely until late fetal life and is a relatively fragile bone, especially in the alveolar region. Sideing relies on orientating the bone so that the dental crypts lie inferiorly, the frontal process extends anterosuperiorly and the palatal process points medially.

Bones of a similar morphology
Fragments of damaged alveolar processes of the maxilla and mandible may appear similar but the supporting bone in the mandible is narrow with compact and dense cortices. In the maxilla, the bone related to the alveolar process is the thin, flat nasal or orbital floor.

Morphological summary	
Prenatal	
Wk 6	Ossification centre(s) appear(s)
By wk 8	Body and four processes identifiable
Wks 10–12	Maxillary sinus starts to develop
Wk 11	Formation of crypts for deciduous dentition
Wks 14–16	Deciduous tooth germs start to form
Wks 17–18	All deciduous crypts completed
Birth	Main parts of bone present
	Sinus rudimentary
	Crowns of deciduous teeth in crypts
	Calcification of first permanent molar commenced
Infancy and childhood	Gradual increase in size of body of bone
	Increase in size of sinus
	Eruption and replacement of deciduous teeth
By yrs 12–14	All permanent teeth except third molars emerged (further details of teeth in Chapter 5)

XIII. THE PALATINE

The palatine bones contribute to the posterior part of the roof of the mouth and floor and lateral walls of the nose, the medial wall of the maxillary sinuses and the orbital floors (Fig. 4.32). Each bone consists of horizontal and perpendicular plates (laminae) set at right angles to each other. Orbital and sphenoidal processes are attached to the superior border of the perpendicular plate and a pyramidal process extends posterolaterally from the junction of the two plates. The right and left bones join with each other in the midline of the palate and also articulate with the maxillae, inferior conchae, ethmoid and sphenoid bones

(Figs 4.1 and 4.49). Together with the vomer, the palatine bones form the skeleton of the posterior choanae, which lead from the nasal cavity into the nasopharynx.

Ossification

The ossification centre for the perpendicular plate of the palatine appears at about 7–8 weeks on the medial aspect of the nasal capsule between the primitive oropharyngeal cavity medially and a palatal nerve bundle laterally (Fawcett, 1906). At this stage of development, the mesenchymal palatal processes are hanging vertically beside the tongue, which is still high in the pharyngeal cavity (Fig. 4.10). About a week later, as the palatal shelves take up a horizontal position, the ossification centres assume a boomerang-like shape as bone begins to spread into them. By about 10 weeks, the orbital and sphenoidal processes are visible as outgrowths from the perpendicular plate and are separated by a shallow notch. At first, the orbital process is directed upwards and forwards and faces the maxilla but later turns upwards and backwards and forms a small part of the orbital floor (Fig. 4.32). During fetal life there is a prominent groove for the medial pterygoid plate (Fawcett, 1906).

The palatine is recognizable in isolation from about midfetal life when it assumes the main morphological features of the adult bone, although the relative proportions of its component parts are different. In the perinatal period (Fig. 4.52), the thin horizontal plate is almost square. The medial border is slightly thickened for the sagittal suture and the palatine crest may be seen running transversely across the oral surface. The perpendicular plate is about the same height as the width of the horizontal plate and is also very thin. On its nasal surface the conchal crest for articulation with the posterior end of the inferior concha is just above the junction of the two plates, reflecting the small height of the nasal cavity compared to the adult. The groove leading down to the greater palatine foramen is obvious on the maxillary surface. A notch separates the orbital and sphenoidal processes that extend from the upper border, the former being the larger and turning laterally and the latter inclining medially. The pyramidal process, extending posterolaterally, is relatively larger than in the adult but bears the same recognizable morphology. Up to about the age of 3 years, the horizontal and perpendicular plates are about equal in size. After this time, the growth rate of the perpendicular plate increases to keep pace with the rapid increase in size of the face and nasal

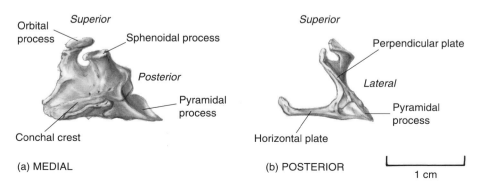

(a) MEDIAL   (b) POSTERIOR   1 cm

Figure 4.52 The right perinatal palatine.

cavity during childhood. By puberty, its height is about twice the width of the horizontal plate.

Growth of the palate

The palate is a septum dividing the first part of the alimentary and respiratory tracts (Fig. 4.49). It is bounded laterally by the alveolar processes of the maxillae and extends from behind the mouth and nostrils anteriorly to the junction of the naso- and oropharynx posteriorly. The anterior four-fifths consists of the bony (hard) palate and is composed of the palatal processes of the maxilla and the horizontal laminae of the palatine bones, which meet in the midline at the continuous intermaxillary and interpalatine sutures. Partial or complete sutures in the palate delineating extra ossicles or complete supernumerary bones have been described and illustrated by Ashley-Montagu (1940) and Woo (1948). The latter named them 'anterior' or 'posterior medio-palatine bones' respectively, depending upon their position in the maxillary or palatine part of the hard palate. In the dry skull the posterior border of the palate, together with the medial pterygoid plates and the inferior surface of the sphenoidal body form the posterior choanae. The right and left sides are divided by the vomer. In the living, the muscular (soft) palate is attached to the posterior border of the hard palate and is composed of the aponeuroses and fibres of the tensor veli palatini, levator palati and uvulae muscles.

Prenatal growth of the palate as a whole has been studied by Freiband (1937), Kraus (1960), Lebret (1962), Burdi (1965), Ewers (1968), Kvinnsland (1969a), Latham (1971) and Silau et al. (1994). Kraus (1960) distinguished eight morphological stages of development between 7 and 18 weeks. Only two of 151 specimens were reported to show separate premaxillary and maxillary ossification centres. Networks of bony trabeculae spread out into the palatine processes from the region of the canine tooth germ. At first, the maxillary and palatine components are separated from each other and from the opposite side so that the developing plates of the vomer can be seen between them. By about 13 weeks, both maxillary processes reach the midline but the bony palatine processes do not fuse until after 18 weeks. Up to this time, increase in length is more rapid than that in width. After this, length increases in a linear fashion, with the maxillary component contributing approximately two-thirds and the palatine component one-third (Silau et al., 1994). Palatal width increases more rapidly as growth at the midpalatal suture and the buccal surfaces of the alveolar processes is very active, and this leads to the typical broad infantile palate (Ewers, 1968). At term, the length and width are approximately equal.

Postnatally, growth at the midpalatal suture slows and ceases between 2 and 4 years of age. Appositional growth at the alveolar margins continues to widen the palate particularly posteriorly until about the age of 7 (Sperber, 1989). Increase in height appears to cease after 9 years of age (Knott and Johnson, 1970) but increase in length takes place up to adult life. Melsen (1975) found that until the age of 13–15 years growth occurred at the transverse (maxillo-palatine) suture and also by apposition at the tuberosity of the maxilla. After this, sutural growth appeared to cease but appositional growth continued for some years. The morphology of the suture changed during the growth period from a broad, sinuous type in infants to a typical squamous suture in childhood when the palatine overlapped the maxilla on the cranial side. Growth in width at the midpalatal (sagittal) suture continued up to about the age of 16 in girls and 18 in boys. Again, the nature of the suture changed from a simple infantile Y-shaped structure enclosing the vomer, through an increasingly sinuous type in childhood to a densely interdigitated type by puberty. The nasal cavity increases in height throughout childhood, with bone apposition on the oral side and resorption on the nasal side. This is accompanied by an increase in depth of the palatal arch from an almost flat palate at birth to an arched palate at puberty, mainly caused by the alveolar bone around erupting teeth. Further details of palatal growth may be found in orthodontic texts (e.g. Lavelle and Moore, 1970; Foster *et al.*, 1977; Enlow and Hans, 1996).

Slavkin *et al.* (1966) measured the position of the greater palatine foramen posterior to the last molar tooth from birth to 18 years of age. As each tooth erupted, the position of the foramen moved posteriorly due to sutural growth at the transverse palatine suture and appositional growth at the posterior palatine processes. Sejrsen *et al.* (1996) used a similar method to measure palatal growth in a series of medieval child and adult crania. They concluded that the growth increment between the incisive foramen and the transverse palatine suture was greater than that between the transverse suture and the greater palatine foramen. The distance between the greater palatine foramen and the posterior margin of the palate did not increase significantly with age, which argues against significant appositional growth at the posterior border. Growth in width appeared to continue into adult life. There is little data on the age at which palatal sutures start to close. Persson and Thilander (1977) investigated the intermaxillary and transverse palatine sutures on histological sections of autopsy material in the adolescent and young adult age ranges. They concluded that there was great variation between individuals and, although sutures may show obliteration during the juvenile period, any marked degree was rare until the third decade. Any closure that was observed seemed to be more rapid on the oral rather than the nasal side and in the posterior more often than the anterior part of the intermaxillary suture.

Practical notes

Sideing/orientation of the juvenile palatine (Fig. 4.52)
In spite of its seemingly fragile nature, an isolated palatine bone often survives intact due to its central position and protection from surrounding bones. It is sometimes recovered still attached to the maxilla. The horizontal plate is rectangular and the perpendicular plate has two processes extending superiorly from it. The relatively robust pyramidal process extends posterolaterally from the side to which the bone belongs.

Bones of a similar morphology
There is no complete bone that looks similar. Fragments of the palatine are unlikely to be identified, except perhaps the pyramidal process which bears some similarity to the pointed lateral end of the lesser wing of the sphenoid. However, the fine structure of each is characteristic.

Morphological summary

Prenatal

Wks 7–8	Ossification centre for perpendicular plate appears
Wk 10	Orbital and sphenoidal processes start to develop
Wk 18	Palatal processes fuse
Midfetal life	Has adopted adult morphology but not proportions

Birth	Horizontal and perpendicular plates are about equal in width and height
	Orbital process does not contain air cells
From yr 3	Perpendicular plate starts to increase in height
	Pneumatization may commence in orbital process
Puberty	Assumes adult morphology and proportions

XIV. THE MANDIBLE

The lower jaw is the only skeletal element of the head, apart from the ossicles of the middle ear, to enjoy independent movement. It articulates with the mandibular fossae of the squamous temporal bones at the synovial temporo-mandibular joints (Fig. 4.3). The mandible gives attachment to the muscles that form the floor of the mouth and the tongue, to the muscles of mastication and also bears all the lower teeth. Each half of the mandible consists of a horizontal body and a vertical ramus.

Ossification

The mandible is the second bone in the body (after the clavicle) to commence ossification. A centre for each half of the bone appears during the 7th week of intra-uterine life (Stage 18) lateral to Meckel's cartilage in the ventral part of the first pharyngeal arch (Mall, 1906; Noback and Robertson, 1951; Dixon, 1958; O'Rahilly and Gardner, 1972). Before ossification can begin, the ectome-senchyme within the lower jaw must react with the epithelium of the mandib-ular arch and there is evidence that the presence of the trigeminal nerve is also essential for the induction of ossification (Sperber, 1989). Also, Jacobsen et al. (1991) described an archaeological adult mandible in which there was unilat-eral absence of the mandibular canal and foramen, and teeth from the second premolar to the second molar. They suggest that the nerve was also absent and that this observation supports the evidence that interaction between nerve tissue and tooth formation at an early stage is essential for normal develop-ment.

Detailed descriptions of the initial stages of mandibular ossification are given by Fawcett (1905b, 1905c, 1930) and Low (1905, 1909). The centre is first seen as a delicate lamella on the lateral aspect of Meckel's cartilage between the lateral incisor and canine tooth germs. The inferior alveolar nerve lies between the bone and Meckel's cartilage and gives off its mental branch, which at first lies in a notch on the superior border of the bone. Ossification spreads rapidly until there is a sheet of bone from the midline to the auriculotemporal nerve posteriorly. From this lateral plate, the bone spreads beneath the nerve and a medial plate forms between the nerve and the cartilage so that vertical sections appear V-shaped around the nerve, and then Y-shaped as the base of the bone (splenium) thickens. The terms medial and lateral alveolar plates (walls) were considered inappropriate by Symons (1951) as the tooth germs are well above the bone at this stage. True alveolar bone on either side of the developing teeth is formed above the level that bridges over the nerve.

The coronoid process differentiates topographically within the temporal muscle mass in the 7th week and by 8 weeks unites with the main part of the ramus (Spyropoulos, 1977). Kvinnsland (1969b) noted a difference in degree of ossification between the medial and lateral walls, which were distinct as far back as the angle. At 10 weeks, the medial wall, in close relation to

Meckel's cartilage, was more active whereas the lateral wall, continuous with the coronoid and condylar regions, was less well ossified. The angle at this stage was very obtuse so that the condylar process was nearly in direct line with the body. By 12 weeks, the angle and the coronoid and condylar processes were well ossified and the mental foramen was visible on the lateral wall.

The lower jaw at the end of the embryonic period is described and illustrated by Macklin (1914, 1921), Augier (1931) and Müller and O'Rahilly (1980). Meckel's cartilage appears as a long rod of mature cartilage that is continuous posteriorly with the malleus and is enlarged and flattened anteriorly where it meets its fellow of the opposite side at a wide angle in the midline. The cartilage is covered laterally for three-quarters of its length by a plate of bone whose lower border runs parallel with it. In the centre is the large mental foramen. Posteriorly, the upper end is notched and separated from the zygomatic process of the temporal bone in the region of the future condyle and, anterior to this, a thin projecting spur shows the position of the future coronoid process. The lateral surface of the body is a rounded, vertical ridge and the medial wall is serrated with the gutter between them occupied by developing tooth germs. In front of the mental foramen, spicules of bone pass from one alveolar wall to the other to cover in the mental and incisive nerve canals.

At about week 10, the anterior end of the perichondrium of Meckel's cartilage, from the mental foramen to the symphysis, shows signs of incipient ossification and this section of the cartilage becomes incorporated into the bone. Kjær (1975, 1997) reported that, before this ossification began, the two halves of Meckel's cartilage were fused at a 'rostral connection' across the midline for a short time and then separated. Although this has been described and named the 'rostral process' in the rat (Bhaskar, 1953; Bhaskar *et al.*, 1953) and the mouse (Frommer and Margolies, 1971), this is the only report of midline fusion in the human embryo. More posteriorly, from the mental foramen to the lingula, the cartilage disappears completely by 24 weeks (Friant, 1960; Sperber, 1989). The extreme posterior end becomes converted into the malleus, incus, anterior ligament of the malleus and the sphenomandibular ligament (Bossy and Gaillard, 1963).

Between 12 and 14 weeks, secondary cartilages develop in the region of the condylar and coronoid processes, and a small number of cartilaginous nodules can be seen at the symphysis. Goret-Nicaise and Dhem (1982) studied the histological and microradiographic structure of the symphyseal region and maintain that the tissue in both the extremities of the hemi-mandibles and in the ossicles (ossicula mentalia) differs from both bone and calcified cartilage and suggest it be designated chondroid tissue. The condylar cartilage develops in the cellular blastema covering the dorsal extension of the bony mandible and soon becomes a 'carrot-shaped wedge' that passes down the ramus to end at the base of the coronoid process (Fawcett, 1905c; Charles, 1925). About two weeks later, the temporomandibular joint is clearly defined and the posterior end becomes covered by articular hyaline cartilage (Symons, 1952; Blackwood, 1965). At first, the cone-shaped mass of the condylar cartilage reaches well forwards but by the 4th month, it starts to be replaced by bone. By 5 months, all that remains is a narrow strip of cartilage immediately beneath the condyle (Symons, 1951). The coronoid cartilage becomes rapidly converted to bone and all traces of the cartilage have usually disappeared by the 6th month. The ossicles at the symphysis ossify about the 7th prenatal month and fuse with the anterior part of the body during the first year of life. The condylar cartilage, however, continues to act as the main growth centre until the beginning of the third decade of life

(Rushton, 1944; Blackwood, 1965). At about 5 months, the replacement of early woven bone by lamellar bone is initiated. It is suggested that this replacement of woven bone by mature Haversian systems at such an early stage of ontogeny is related to the fact that the mandible is subjected to intense activity from sucking and swallowing (Goret-Nicaise and Dhem, 1984).

The shape of the dental arch and the proportionate growth of the prenatal maxilla and mandible have been much studied (Burdi, 1965, 1968; Scott, 1967; Lavelle and Moore, 1970). At 6 weeks, the mandible is further advanced than the maxilla but 2 weeks later, the maxilla has overtaken it in size. By 11 weeks, they are equal in size then again the maxilla becomes larger between 13 and 20 weeks. At birth, they are about equal with the mandible retrognathic to the maxilla. The rapid postnatal growth of the mandible should lead to a normal occlusion but inadequate size or overgrowth can result in abnormal occlusal positions (Sperber, 1989). A series of radiographs with corresponding dissections of fetal specimens from 3 to 10 months shows the developing tooth germs *in situ* (Boller, 1964).

The perinatal mandible (Fig. 4.53) consists of a body and a ramus of about half its length that extends posteriorly in an almost straight line so that the head of the condyle is at the same level as the superior surface of the body. The outer surface of the body is flattened anteriorly but becomes rounded just above the base, at the level of the canine and first molar crypts by the bulging tooth germs contained within it. The mental foramen lies about two-thirds of the way from the base of the bone with its entrance pointing anteriorly. The mylohyoid line and mental spines can be seen on the inner surface. The angle between the body and ramus is obtuse, measuring about 135–145°. The articular surface of the condyle points posteriorly and between it and the thin pointed coronoid process there is a wide, shallow notch. The prominent mandibular foramen, with a well-formed lingula, lies in the centre of the inner surface of the ramus. The crypts for the two incisor tooth germs (i_1 and i_2) are rounded or oval and the mesial wall of the central incisor crypt forms the U-shaped symphyseal surface (Fig. 4.53b). The inferior edge of the surface curves away so that there is a gap between the two sides when the two halves of the mandible are articulated together. The canine crypt (c) is triangular in shape with its base on the labial side and its apex pointing lingually. The crypt for the first deciduous molar (m_1) is square and behind it is a long, rectangular crypt that extends into the ramus. This is imperfectly divided by an incomplete interdental septum at its base and contains the tooth germ of the second deciduous molar (m_2) and the forming crown of the first permanent molar (M_1). The detailed appearance of the alveolar bone and crypts during the development of the deciduous dentition is described and illustrated by van der Linden and Duterloo (1976).

Postnatally, the mandible undergoes more variation in shape and greater increase in size than any other facial bone. It has to grow in harmony both with development of the deciduous and permanent dentition, with changes of size and shape of the maxilla and with increase in width of the cranial base. Growth at the symphysis is limited, as the right and left halves of the body join at the midline during the first year of life. Fusion starts on the outer and inferior surfaces and proceeds towards the inner and superior surfaces. Using archaeological populations, Becker (1986) suggested a fusion date between 7 and 8 months and Molleson and Cox (1993) found that in the Spitalfields collection the two halves of the mandible were always separate before 3 months of age but that most had fused by 6 months.

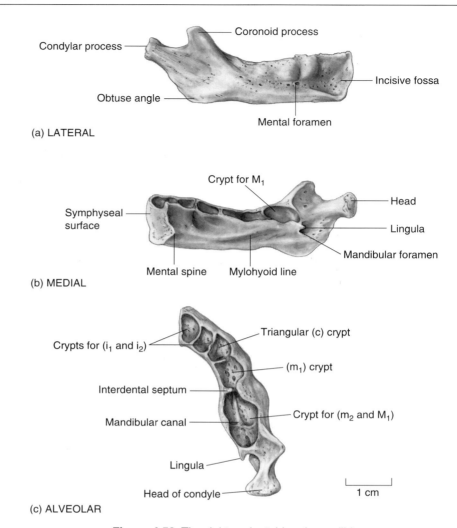

(a) LATERAL

(b) MEDIAL

(c) ALVEOLAR

Figure 4.53 The right perinatal hemi-mandible.

As early as 1878 Humphry, carrying out experimental work on the pig, forecast most of the results of subsequent studies of mandibular growth. Growth has since been studied in archaeological specimens (Murphy, 1957), in living patients via the implant method (Björk, 1963), by histological examination of ground sections of dry bone (Enlow and Harris, 1964) and by Fourier analysis (Ferrario *et al.*, 1996).

The condyle plays a major role in the development of the lower jaw and its role is reviewed by Scott (1967) and Meikle (2002). It causes a downward and forward movement of the mandible from the cranial base. At first, there is an increase in length of the body because of the almost straight line formed by the body and ramus. The angle at birth is between 135 and 150° but soon afterwards it decreases and this becomes most obvious at about the time of the completion of the deciduous dentition when it is between 130 and 140° (Jensen and Palling, 1954) (Fig. 4.54).

Alveolar bone is deposited at the superior surface of the body as the deciduous dentition develops but, once the occlusal plane is established, it maintains a stable relationship with the lower border of the body (Brodie, 1941). The

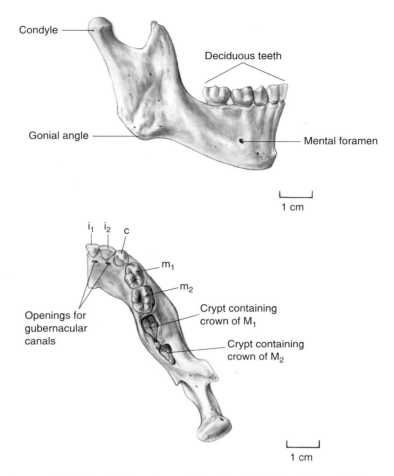

Condyle

Deciduous teeth

Gonial angle

Mental foramen

1 cm

i_1 i_2 c

m_1

m_2

Openings for
gubernacular
canals

Crypt containing
crown of M_1

Crypt containing
crown of M_2

1 cm

Figure 4.54 The right hemi-mandible of a child of dental age 4–5 years.

concomitant decrease in the mandibular angle, together with a rapid growth in height of the ramus, results in the condyle reaching a higher level than the occlusal plane of the teeth. The angle measures between 120 and 130° after the eruption of the second permanent molars (Jensen and Palling, 1954). To maintain constant relationships during progressive increases in size, bone deposition occurs on the posterior border of the ramus and resorption on the anterior border. In this way, the ramus is backwardly displaced and the posterior part of the body is lengthened making further space for developing teeth. As in the maxilla, each succeeding crypt occupies the same position relative to the surrounding structures, in this case, the mandibular canal and the anterior border of the ramus (Symons, 1951).

To keep pace with increase in width of the cranial base there is an overall widening of the mandibular body by resorption and deposition with consequent increase in bigonial width. A similar mechanism occurs at the mandibular notch and in the neck to further define their shape. The mental foramen lies below a line between the canine and first deciduous molar until the completion of eruption of the deciduous dentition. It subsequently moves posteriorly relative to the dentition, first lying under the first molar and then between the first and second molars. The foramen also changes its position vertically as the alveolar process increases in depth. At birth, it points anteriorly and upwards but there is a change during childhood, so that in the adult the neurovascular bundle occupies a posteriorly placed groove (Warwick, 1950). This is possibly brought about by differential rates of growth in the bone and periosteum as the body grows in length.

The chin alters considerably during childhood. Its depth increases rapidly after the eruption of the incisor teeth (Fig. 4.55) to make space for the developing roots but the triangular mental area is variable in shape in different individuals. Brodie (1941) reported a rapid growth until the age of about 4 years, after which growth slowed. Meredith (1957) found that the concavity of the chin changed from very shallow at 4 years of age to a distinctly concave shape at 14 years. The crowns of the permanent incisors (I_1 and I_2) can usually be seen through the openings of the gubernacular canals on the lingual surface of the symphyseal region behind the deciduous teeth between 3 and 4 years of age (Fig. 4.54b).

Most sexual dimorphism starts to appear in the skeleton at puberty but, as nearly all the increase in craniofacial growth takes place before this time, it would seem reasonable to expect differences in growth between boys and girls in the craniofacial bones in childhood. There have been many studies in this area which suggest that sexual dimorphism in both the face and mandible does exist from quite an early age (Newman and Meredith, 1956; Hunter and Garn, 1972; Walker and Kowalski, 1972; Baughan and Demirjian, 1978; Buschang *et al.*, 1983, 1986; Schutkowski, 1993; Humphrey, 1998). However, its manifestation is complex, and dimorphism does not usually reach a sufficiently high level to allow useful positive determination of sex until after the skeletal changes that take place at puberty. Molleson *et al.* (1998) found that the mandibular angle and the shape of the chin proved useful in determination of sex in juvenile skulls but indicated that this needs to be tested on larger samples of known sex. Loth and Henneberg (2001) identified a shape difference in the anterior body and symphyseal region that could distinguish between males and females from 7 months to 4 years of age. When tested on a different population, the accuracy was not as high as the original and distinguished male individuals better than females (Scheuer, 2002).

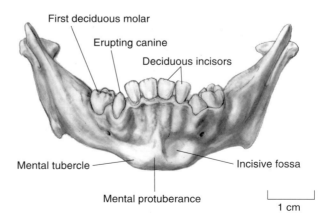

Figure 4.55 The formation of the chin. Mandible of a child of dental age about 1 year.

Practical notes

Sideing/orientation of the juvenile mandible (Fig. 4.53)

The mandible is identifiable in isolation by midfetal life. The two halves remain separate until the first or second year of life. To side a complete half mandible, the coronoid and condylar processes extend posterosuperiorly and the anterior end of the body curves medially.

Bones of a similar morphology

Fragments of the alveolar area may appear similar to those of the maxilla but the bone of the body beneath the crypts of the mandible is relatively thick and rounded, whereas that related to the crypts of the maxilla is part of the thin nasal or orbital floor. The condyle bears similarities to the acromial end of a scapular spine, the acetabular end of a perinatal pubis and to the pedicle end of some of the vertebral half arches (Figs 6.27, 8.7a, 10.5).

Morphological summary

Prenatal	
Wk 6	Ossification centre develops lateral to Meckel's cartilage
Wk 7	Coronoid process differentiating
Wk 8	Coronoid fuses with main mass
About wk 10	Condylar and coronoid processes recognizable
	Anterior part of Meckel's cartilage starting to ossify
Wks 12–14	Secondary cartilages for condyle, coronoid and symphysis appear
Wks 14–16	Deciduous tooth germs start to form
Birth	Mandible consists of separate right and left halves
During yr 1	Fusion at symphysis
Infancy and	Increase in size and shape of bone
childhood	Eruption and replacement of deciduous teeth
By yrs 12–14	All permanent teeth emerged except third molars

XV. THE HYOID

The hyoid bone forms part of the rather insubstantial skeleton of the anterior part of the neck. It does not normally articulate directly with other skeletal structures but is suspended by muscles and ligaments from the base of the skull and the mandible above, and connected to the larynx and sternum below. It consists of a central body, two greater and two lesser horns that give attachment to muscles of the tongue, pharyngeal wall and anterior neck from the mandible to the thoracic inlet.

Early development

The hyoid develops from the second and probably the third pharyngeal arches. The medial parts of the second and third arch bars meet at their ventral ends to form the body of the hyoid whilst the dorsal portions project posteriorly to form the lesser and greater horns. A cartilaginous centre appears in the body at about 5 weeks of intra-uterine life and by the 7th week the hyoid body and both horns have chondrified and at this stage the greater horns may be attached directly to the superior horns of the thyroid cartilage of the larynx (Frazer, 1910b; Müller *et al.*, 1981) (Fig. 4.8).

Macklin (1921) and Müller and O'Rahilly (1980) described the appearance of the hyoid cartilage at the end of the embryonic period. It resembles the adult form but the body is slightly V-shaped with a notch or groove in the lower surface which, at this stage is continuous with the upper edge of the thyroid cartilage of the larynx. Koebke (1978) described the later prenatal development of the relationships between the horns and the body. Tompsett and Donaldson (1951) reported that the body of the hyoid appeared as a radio-opacity in 75% of 500 newborn infants but that care must be taken to distinguish it from the anterior arch of the atlas, which was ossified in 20%.

Ossification

Ossification has been reported in the body and greater horns as early as 30 prenatal weeks (Reed, 1993) but may not be present until the first few months of life (Parsons, 1909). Reed found that, radiographically, ossification was always visible in the body at the age of 4 months and by the end of the first year had invaded the rest of the body. In lateral view on a radiograph, the body initially appeared crescentic, changing to triangular in early childhood and then square in early adolescence.

In early childhood, the body of the bone consists of a curved bar with rounded margins which is deeply concave posteriorly (Fig. 4.56a). In later childhood, the anterior surface of the body is composed of two unequal parts set at an angle to each other. The upper section is wider than the lower and divided by a central projecting ridge or knob of bone, which separates small hollows providing attachment for the geniohyoid and genioglossus muscles. The lower section is narrower and relatively unmarked (Fig. 4.56b). Reed (1993) reported that from childhood onwards, the width of the body was significantly greater in boys than in girls. Ossification was first seen in the medial end of the greater cornua after the age of 6 months and this gradually extended posteriorly throughout childhood and adolescence. By late adolescence, the bone reaches adult size and proportions. The body has a square outline with the anterior surface being composed of upper and lower sections of about equal width. The lower section is then also divided by a central ridge for attachment of bilateral muscles connecting the hyoid to the sternum and scapula (Fig. 4.56c). The lesser horns and the distal end of the greater horns do not usually complete ossification until puberty and may well remain unossified throughout life.

Normally, both the greater and lesser horns eventually fuse with the body but timing is very variable. Evans and Knight (1981) found fusion of the greater horns and the body at 18 years and also non-fusion in the eighth and ninth decade. O'Halloran and Lundy (1987), in a review of 300 autopsy cases, reported that although fusion generally increased with age, it did not normally occur until the third decade. These findings are of interest to the forensic pathologist as fracture of the hyoid bone is a well recognized indicator of strangulation although only a third of such victims actually have a fractured hyoid. Fracture is rare in infants and children but becomes increasingly likely in adults with advancing age (Ubelaker, 1992). It is probably more likely to be related to the degree of ossification or fusion of the greater horns to the body (Pollanen and Chiasson (1996).

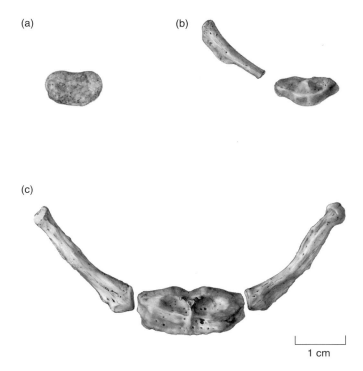

(a)

(b)

(c)

1 cm

Figure 4.56 The development of the hyoid bone: (a) body of hyoid – male aged 2 years 6 months; (b) body and damaged greater horn – female aged 8 years 7 months; (c) adult body with separate greater horns.

Practical notes

Orientating/sideing of the juvenile hyoid (Fig. 4.56c)

In a complete hyoid the body faces anteriorly and the greater horns extend superoposteriorly. An isolated body is convex anteriorly and the smaller, biconcave section of the anterior surface faces superiorly. Isolated greater horns are difficult to side if not well marked. The wider anterior end can usually be distinguished from the tubercle at the posterior end and the lower surface tends to be smoother than the upper surface, which has muscle markings.

Bones of a similar morphology

The body of the hyoid bone is similar to an unfused anterior arch of atlas, both having a concave posterior surface (see Chapter 6: Fig. 6.13d). An isolated anterior arch of the atlas has a tubercle in the middle of its anterior surface whilst a hyoid body is usually divided into two horizontal sections set at an angle to each other. If the two bones from the same individual are compared, the atlas is more robust and about twice the size of the hyoid. Isolated fragments of the greater horn may look like ossified horns of the laryngeal thyroid cartilage.

Morphological summary

Prenatal

Wk 5	Cartilaginous centre for body appears
Wk 7	Body, greater and lesser horns chondrified
Birth	Ossification centres may be present in the upper part of the body and ventral ends of greater horns
By yr 2	Body usually completely ossified
Puberty	Body and most of greater horns ossified.

XVI. THE LARYNX

The larynx is composed of cartilages, ligamentous membranes and muscles and lies opposite the third to the sixth cervical vertebrae in the anterior part of the neck. It is connected to the hyoid bone above and the trachea below. The principal cartilages are the single thyroid, cricoid and epiglottic cartilages and the paired arytenoids, corniculates and cuneiforms. The epiglottis, together with small paired corniculate and cuneiform cartilages are composed of fibro-elastic cartilage which has little tendency to ossify. However, the thyroid, cricoid and arytenoids are composed of hyaline cartilage and may calcify or ossify within the young adult time period.

Early development

Chondrification of the thyroid, cricoid and arytenoid cartilages starts at the beginning of the 8th week (Stage 20). Bilateral centres appear in the laminae of the thyroid cartilage and, about a week later, they become joined cranially and caudally leaving the mesenchymal thyroid copula in the centre. This chondrifies separately and by 12 weeks has joined the laminae. Bilateral centres for the cricoid arch and the arytenoids appear at the same time as those for the thyroid cartilage (Doménech-Mateu and Sañudo, 1990). The shape of the cartilages at the end of the embryonic period have been described in some detail by Macklin (1921), Hast (1970), Müller and O'Rahilly (1980) and Müller *et al.* (1981). The thyroid cartilage is composed of two laminae, which may still be unfused in the midline so there is no laryngeal prominence or thyroid notch. It is directly joined to the hyoid bone as the upper edges are continuous with the body of the hyoid cartilage. The superior horns are a direct prolongation of the greater horns of the hyoid (Fig. 4.8). Both superior and inferior thyroid tubercles and an oblique line are present on each lamina and there is normally a foramen, the foramen thyroideum, where chondrification is incomplete near the posterior border. The cricoid cartilage has already adopted its signet-ring form but the right and left halves of the posterior lamina are set at an angle causing the lumen to be triangular rather than circular. Tucker *et al.* (1977) comment on this shape in relation to intubation injuries in the infant larynx and Too-Chung and Green (1974) reported that the different rate of growth of sagittal and coronal diameters in the juvenile cricoid compensates for this early inequality. The arytenoid cartilages are composed of young cartilage and have distinct muscular and vocal processes. They are still joined to the cricoid by mesenchymal condensations as the crico-arytenoid joints are as yet undeveloped and there are no corniculate or cuneiform cartilages at this stage. The epiglottis is composed of mesenchyme and fibro-elastic cartilage does not appear until the 5th month (Tucker and Tucker, 1975). León *et al.* (1997) have investigated the incidence of the foramen thyroideum in embryos, fetuses and adults. This is a foramen situated in the posterior superior part of the thyroid lamina. It occurred in 57% of prenatal larynges but only 31% of adults and in the latter the foramen is always traversed by a nerve or vessel. They proposed that it represents a failure of the complete fusion of the fourth and sixth arches which, when present, may be invaded by neurovascular elements. If this does not occur, then the foramen chondrifies completely and disappears.

By the end of the second trimester, the laryngeal cartilages have adopted their neonatal form, which is morphologically similar to that of the adult (Fig. 4.57). The hyoid and thyroid horns become separated by the thyrohyoid membrane and the former connection between them is sometimes represented by small triticeal cartilaginous nodules. The fetal larynx is higher in the neck with respect to the vertebral column compared to its postnatal position, the tip of the epiglottis to the lower border of the cricoid cartilage reaching from C1 to C3/4 (Roche and Barkla, 1965; Müller and O'Rahilly, 1980; Magriples and Laitman, 1987). At birth, the larynx lies between C2 and superior C4 and there is then a marked descent between birth and 3 years as the lower rim of the cricoid cartilage reaches the C4/5 level. This has important clinically consequences during intubation of infants and small children because, as the larynx descends, so a greater number of vertebrae can be flexed and the upper respiratory tract becomes easier to access (Westhorpe, 1987). There is little change after this period until puberty when, with the growth of the thyroid cartilage, the larynx approaches the adult position.

The larynx begins to display sexual dimorphism towards the end of the pubertal growth spurt. In the male, the size of the thyroid laminae is larger and the angle between them is more acute, allowing a greater length for the vocal cords and thus a deeper voice. Kahane (1978) found that, although there

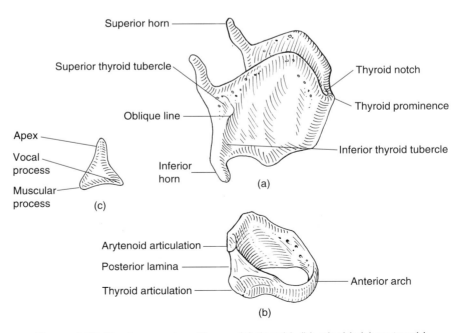

Figure 4.57 The laryngeal cartilages: (a) thyroid; (b) cricoid; (c) arytenoid.

appeared to be no sexual dimorphism in the prepubertal larynx, females were closer to their adult counterparts than males and therefore had less growth per unit time to reach maturity. Harjeet and Jit (1992) reported that sexual dimorphism occurred in Indian subjects between the ages of 13–15 years in both sexes but that increase in size in males could continue until the age of 40 years.

Ossification

Calcification of the laryngeal and tracheal cartilages has been reported in infancy (Nabarro, 1952; Russo and Coin, 1958; Goldbloom and Scott Dunbar, 1960). This is very rare and must be regarded as pathological.

Later calcification and ossification of the laryngeal cartilages have been much studied (Roncallo, 1948; Keen and Wainwright, 1958; Yoshikawa, 1958; Hately et al., 1965; Harrison and Denny, 1983; Curtis et al., 1985; Turk and Hogg, 1993). Keen and Wainwright (1958) reported that 79% of males and 21% of females show some ossification before the age of 30, the earliest being 18 years in males and 25 years in females. Hately et al. (1965) reported earliest ossification as 16.5 years in females and 18 years in males and other authors show similar figures. It thus appears that it is quite common to find ossification beginning towards the end of the second decade and into the young adult age range.

Details of different studies vary, but two principles appear to be established. First, ossification, especially in the thyroid cartilage, and to a lesser extent in the cricoid cartilage, follows a progressive pattern. Second, although the pattern is very similar in different individuals, its timing is highly variable and appears not to be sex related. In the thyroid cartilage (Fig. 4.58a) ossification begins near the postero-inferior border of the lamina and then extends into the inferior horn and along the whole inferior border. It then extends upwards in the posterior border of the lamina towards the superior horn before spreading into the main part. Often an anterior midline tongue forms, and it is common for there to be one or two 'windows' of unossified, or less ossified, material in the centre of each lamina. Eventually the whole cartilage may ossify to produce an 'os thyroideum'. Normally it is only the first two stages that would be seen in the young adult age range. In the cricoid cartilage (Fig. 4.58b) ossification starts at the superior edge of the posterior lamina and then spreads down the sloping lateral sides towards the anterior arch. This stage may be seen in the young adult but eventually, the whole cricoid may ossify. There appear to be no accounts of arytenoid ossification in young adults.

Evidence that there may be a genetic basis for the timing and pattern of ossification comes from studies of identical twins (Vastine and Vastine, 1952). The same pattern was seen in the hyoid and laryngeal cartilages in five pairs of twins ranging in age from 13 to 64 years.

Fatty and cellular marrow may be seen in both the thyroid and cricoid (Keen and Wainwright, 1958). Partially calcified or ossified laryngeal cartilages may be mistaken for a foreign body in a cervical radiograph (O'Bannon and Grunow, 1954; Zoller and Bowie, 1957; Hately et al., 1965; Morreels et al., 1967).

In summary, although most studies have demonstrated a gradual increase in ossification in both sexes with advancing age, there is no correlation between actual age and the degree of ossification. Nor is there a substantial difference in

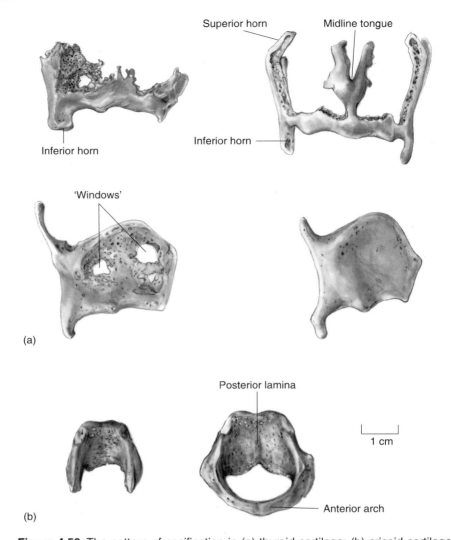

Figure 4.58 The pattern of ossification in (a) thyroid cartilage; (b) cricoid cartilage.

pattern between the sexes and it is therefore an unsuitable parameter with which to attempt ageing and sexing of skeletal remains. It is unfortunate that Krogman and Işcan (1986) quote an age-related pattern (Cerný, 1983) that appears to have been based on only five individuals.

There is some reported sexual dimorphism in the radiological appearance of the bony texture of the thyroid cartilage, in that the ossification is more homogeneous and hazy in the male, and more irregular and dense in the female. It is interesting that this corresponds to the trabecular and sclerotic type of calcification that is typically seen in male and female costal cartilages (see Chapter 7 and Scheuer and Black, 2000). It appears that cartilage always retains its potential to calcify and ossify in the normal manner. Recently, matrix vesicles and asbestoid (giant collagen) fibres have been demonstrated for the first time in the thyroid cartilage of young adults (Kirsch and Claassen, 2000).

Practical notes

Orientation/sideing of the juvenile larynx (Figs. 4.57 and 4.58)

The laminae of the thyroid cartilage (or 'os thyroideum') are joined **anteriorly** and open **posteriorly** and the thyroid notch is **superior**. The **superior** horns are thinner and longer than the **inferior** horns.

The **posterior** lamina of the cricoid cartilage (or 'os cricoideum') is quadrilateral in shape and the **lateral** borders slope down to a narrow **anterior** arch.

Bones of a similar morphology

At the excavation stage, awareness that there may be an ossified or partially ossified larynx greatly increases recovery if careful searches are made in the cervical region. Small fragments of ossified laryngeal cartilages would be difficult to recognize in isolation and horns of the thyroid cartilage have a similar morphology to hyoid greater horns.

Morphological summary

Prenatal	
Wk 8	Cartilaginous centres for the thyroid, cricoid and arytenoids appear.
By mth 6	Cartilages adopt adult morphology.
Birth	Adult morphology but larynx position high in the neck.
By yr 3	Larynx descends to childhood position
Puberty	Larynx adopts adult position; sexual dimorphism begins
By end of second decade	Calcification and ossification may begin in thyroid and cricoid cartilages

CHAPTER FIVE

The Dentition

Teeth are the only skeletal structures of the living body that are in part visible to the naked eye. Their composition, anatomy and development are also quite different from the rest of the skeleton and, in addition, they tend to be more resistant than bone to the effects of inhumation. As a result, the study of teeth forms a large and important part of the investigations of palaeontologists, anthropologists, skeletal biologists and forensic scientists. In common with many mammals, humans are diphyodont; that is, they have two generations of teeth: the deciduous, or 'milk', teeth and the permanent teeth. Deciduous teeth begin to form at about 6 weeks *in utero* and the last permanent tooth does not reach completion until early adult life, so that the development and maturation of both sets cover almost the whole of the juvenile lifespan. In fact, they have proved to be one of the most accurate indicators of age at death, especially in immature individuals.

Terminology

Teeth are arranged in both the upper and lower jaws in the form of a dental arch (arcade), or so-called catenary curve (like a chain suspended from two points). Both halves of each jaw contain the same number of teeth and for descriptive purposes are called the right and left, upper and lower quadrants. The deciduous and the permanent dentition both contain two incisors and a canine tooth in each quadrant and these are commonly referred to as anterior teeth. Behind them are the cheek, or posterior teeth, which consist of two molars in the deciduous series. These are replaced by premolars in the permanent dentition, and the arcade is normally completed posteriorly by a further three permanent molars. There are therefore 20 deciduous and 32 permanent teeth. In summary, the dental formulae for the deciduous dentition is:

$$\text{i } \frac{2}{2} \text{ c } \frac{1}{1} \text{ m } \frac{2}{2}, \text{ often individually named di1, di2, dc, dm1, dm2}$$

and that for the permanent dentition is:

$$\text{I } \frac{2}{2} \text{ C } \frac{1}{1} \text{ PM } \frac{2}{2} \text{ M } \frac{3}{3}$$

often individually named I1, I2, C, PM1, PM2, M1, M2, M3

Figures given a super- or subscript position in relation to the letter designate a maxillary or mandibular tooth, respectively. For example, a right mandibular first deciduous molar will be Rdm$_1$ and a left maxillary second premolar will be

LPM^2. Terminology can appear somewhat confusing, as clinical dentistry has several systems of shorthand to identify tooth position and these differ from that used by both zoologists and palaeontologists. For example, the latter often refer to the premolars as PM3 and PM4 as they are the remaining pair of a series of four premolars found in many mammals.

The two most common systems in clinical use are the Zsigmondy and the FDI (Fédération Dentaire International, 1971). The Zsigmondy system, in common use by clinicians, assigns letters a–e to the deciduous teeth and numbers 1–8 to the permanent teeth in each quadrant and the mouth is displayed diagrammatically, as if the observer is facing the patient (Fig. 5.1a). Thus d‾| is a right mandibular first deciduous molar and |5‾ is a left maxillary second premolar. The FDI system assigns two digits to each tooth, the first of which designates the appropriate quadrant and the second, the number of the tooth. The quadrants are numbered:

1 permanent right upper	5 deciduous right upper
2 permanent left upper	6 deciduous left upper
3 permanent left lower	7 deciduous left lower
4 permanent right lower	8 deciduous right lower

Thus, the same two teeth in the FDI system would be numbered as 84 (lower right first deciduous molar) and 25 (upper left second premolar; Fig. 5.1b). The FDI system appears to be less straightforward than the Zsigmondy system, but was developed for the purpose of entering individual teeth into a computer database.

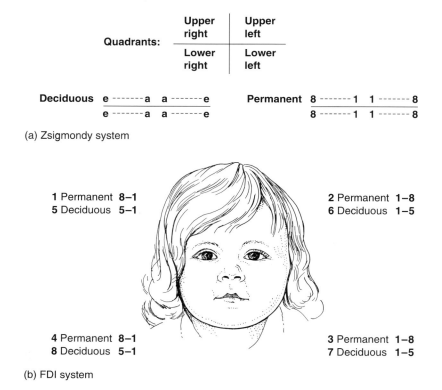

Figure 5.1 Terminology of tooth position. (a) Zsigmondy system; (b) FDI system.

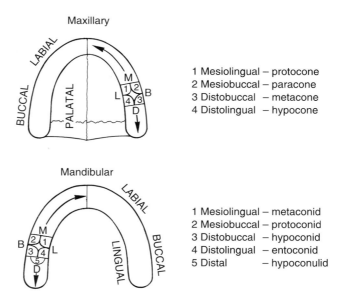

Figure 5.2 Dental arcades and molar cusp terminology.
B   buccal   D   distal
L   lingual   M   mesial

Each tooth has surfaces named according to the position in the dental arcade and its relationship to the morphology of the mouth. The surfaces of all teeth that face towards and away from the median sagittal plane are called respectively mesial and distal. The mesial and distal surfaces of neighbouring teeth that face each other are termed approximal. The anterior teeth, incisors and canines, have outer labial surfaces and inner palatal or lingual surfaces relative to the lips, palate or tongue and the cutting edges are termed incisal. Posterior (cheek) teeth, premolars and molars, have outer buccal surfaces and inner palatal or lingual surfaces relative to the cheeks, palate or tongue. Their surfaces that meet teeth of the opposite jaw are termed occlusal. In a clinical situation, the positions of cusps of the premolar and molar teeth are similarly designated but, again, zoologists and palaeontologists use a different terminology. This again derives from comparative mammalian dental anatomy, the corresponding terms being shown in Fig. 5.2. Equivalent teeth in the maxilla and mandible are termed isomeres, whereas those in the opposite right and left quadrants are called antimeres.

The mature tooth

The human tooth is composed of three types of hard tissue – dentine, enamel and cementum – each of which is different in composition from bone. The major part of both the crown and root of each tooth consists of dentine, which is covered by enamel on the crown and by a thin layer of cementum around the root. The junction between enamel and cementum occurs at the neck, or cervix. Surrounding the cervical one-third of the crown in some teeth there is often a prominent bulge known as the cingulum. The innermost section of each tooth is occupied by the pulp chamber and root canal, composed of loose connective tissue containing nerves and blood vessels, which gain access to the pulp through the apex of the root. Each tooth is anchored by fibres of the periodontal ligament, which run from the cementum of the root to the alveolar bone of the jaw (Fig. 5.3). Covering the alveolar bone and attached around the tooth is the gum, or gingiva. Details of the gross anatomy and light and electron microscopy of the tissues of the tooth may be found in Berkovitz *et al.* (2002), Bhaskar (1980), Aiello and Dean (1990), Hillson (1996) and Ten Cate (1998).

It is important to recognize the normal appearance of developing teeth on an X-ray as one of the most commonly used methods of ageing relies on developmental stages as seen on radiographs (Fig. 5.4). X-rays also provide information on unerupted teeth that is not available when the jaw is viewed with the naked eye. Enamel is the most radiopaque tissue of the tooth and so the crown, or developing crown of a tooth can be distinguished as the whitest part. Dentine and cementum contain less radiopaque material than enamel and therefore appear greyer, but they are not easily distinguished from one another as their density is similar and in addition, cementum is extremely thin. The soft tissues of the pulp cavity and the periodontal ligament are radiolucent and appear dark in radiographs. Two parts of the supporting alveolar bone stand out on radiographs: the lamina dura, the layer of compact bone that lines the tooth socket and the alveolar crest, which is the gingival margin of the alveolus. The appearance of the crest depends on the space between the teeth, often producing points between the anterior teeth and flat crests between the cheek teeth. In a healthy erupted tooth, the alveolar crest is just below the level of the cervical margin of the tooth.

Each tooth develops within the alveolar bone of the jaw from a soft tissue tooth germ that is subsequently mineralized. The crown and part of the root is formed before eruption commences. Eruption is the movement by which a tooth advances from the alveolar crypt to its functional occlusal position in the mouth and can be regarded as a potentially lifelong process. Depending on the tooth, between one-third and three-quarters of the root is formed by the time of emergence into the mouth (Gleiser and Hunt, 1955; Grøn, 1962) and the remainder of root growth, including the maturation of its apex, continues after emergence has occurred. A tooth may be stimulated to overerupt at any time in response to local conditions, such as the loss of an antagonist (Fanning,

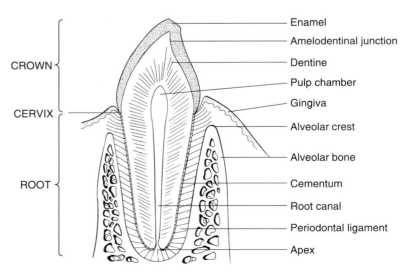

Figure 5.3 Section through a mandibular tooth to show tissues.

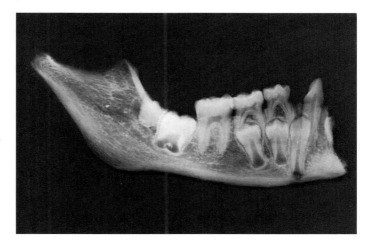

Figure 5.4 Radiograph of part of a hemi-mandible from a Romano-British archaeological specimen from Peterborough. The deciduous canine, first and second molars and the first permanent molar are in occlusion. Unerupted teeth visible are the permanent canine, both premolars, the partially complete second permanent molar and part of the crown of the third molar.

1962), or to compensate for attrition, so that different fractions of the crown and root are visible in the mouth during the life history of a single tooth. Any part of the tooth visible in the mouth is termed the clinical crown and this obviously comprises less than the anatomical crown during emergence. In fully emerged teeth, the cementum/enamel junction (CEJ) is just subgingival. Only with gingival recession and/or continuous emergence to compensate for attrition, does the CEJ become visible intra-orally in life. However, in certain pathological conditions, such as periodontal disease (and therefore often in old age), where there is continued loss of attachment of the periodontal ligament from the alveolar crest, the visible part of the tooth above the gingival margin sometimes consists of the anatomical crown plus part of the upper section of the root covered with cementum, hence the term 'long in the tooth'. In this case, the clinical crown comprises more than the anatomical crown (Fig. 5.5). In skeletal material where gingival tissues are absent, the anatomical crown is always at, or above, the level of the crestal alveolar bone, even in juvenile specimens where a tooth is fully erupted.

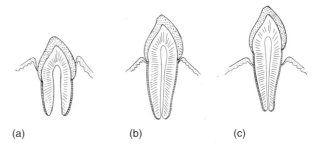

(a) (b) (c)

Figure 5.5 Anatomical and clinical crowns. (a) Emerging tooth, clinical < anatomical crown; (b) healthy tooth in occlusion, anatomical = clinical crown; (c) over-erupted tooth clinical > anatomical crown. Tissues as in Fig. 5.3.

Tooth morphology

Brief descriptions of the morphology of the deciduous and permanent dentition follow but the reader is directed to the many excellent dental texts for further detail (Van Beek, 1983; Brown, 1985; Hillson, 1996, White, 1991; Berkovitz *et al.*, 2002; Ash and Nelson, 2003). Metrical variation is described by Kieser (1990) and non-metrical variation by Hillson (1996) and Scott and Turner (2000). Photographs of the *in situ* state of the dentition from late fetal life to adulthood may be found in van der Linden and Duterloo (1976).

Incisors have an incisal edge extending from the mesial angle to the distal angle, while the canine has a single pointed cusp that slopes towards the widest part of the crown at the contact points. The palatal/lingual surface of anterior teeth may show marginal ridges and/or a cingulum that vary in expression, particularly in maxillary teeth. The occlusal surface of posterior teeth is composed of cusps and ridges as well as grooves or fissures and pits. The mesial and distal marginal ridges of the occlusal surface connect the cusps to form the functional occlusal table. Each tooth type is described in order to distinguishing between the dentitions (deciduous or permanent, with the exception of premolars), the jaws (maxillary or mandibular), the number (first, second or third) and side of the jaw (left or right). Buccal and lingual views of individual deciduous teeth are illustrated in Fig. 5.6; buccal and lingual views of permanent teeth are illustrated in Figs 5.7 and 5.8. The palate and mandible showing occlusal surfaces of the deciduous and permanent dentition *in situ* are illustrated in Figs 5.9 and 5.10.

Incisors
Place in dentition
Deciduous incisors (di1 and di2/a and b) are the first and second teeth from the midline in the deciduous dentition. The permanent incisors (I1 and I2/1 and 2) are the first and second teeth from the midline in the permanent dentition.

Deciduous or permanent
Features that distinguish deciduous and permanent incisors are:

- size
- crown margin.

Deciduous incisors have smaller crowns and roots compared to permanent incisors but are similar in shape. Deciduous incisors are characterized by a prominent cervical enamel margin. The short crown height makes deciduous incisors appear rounder and more bulbous than permanent incisors.

Maxillary or mandibular
Features that help identify maxillary from mandibular incisors include:

- crown size
- crown shape
- expression of the cingulum
- root shape and apex curvature
- crown root alignment.

The maxillary incisor crowns are wider in the mesiodistal dimension than mandibular incisors. They also have a more pronounced cingulum than mandibular incisors and occasionally the marginal ridges may be rounded making

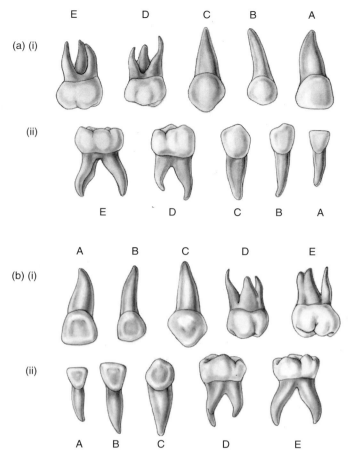

Figure 5.6 Deciduous teeth: (a) (i) maxillary − labial/buccal view; (ii) mandibular − labial/buccal view; (b) (i) maxillary − palatal view; (ii) mandibular − lingual view.

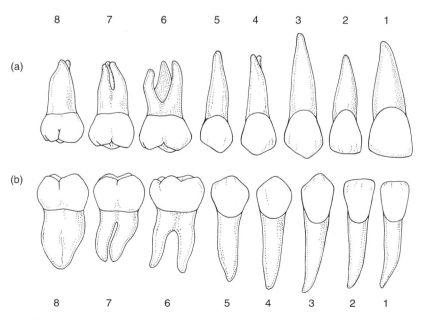

Figure 5.7 Permanent teeth: (a) maxillary − labial/buccal view; (b) mandibular − labial/buccal view.

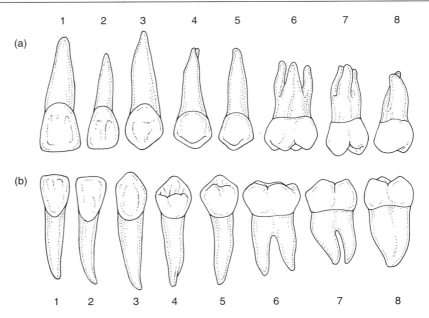

Figure 5.8 Permanent teeth: (a) maxillary – palatal view; (b) mandibular – lingual view.

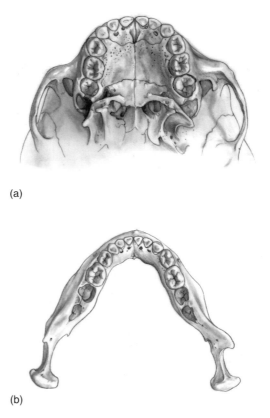

Figure 5.9 (a) Palate of child of dental age approximately 4 years showing occlusal view of deciduous maxillary teeth and unerupted developing permanent molars. (b) Mandible of same child showing occlusal view of mandibular deciduous teeth and unerupted permanent molars.

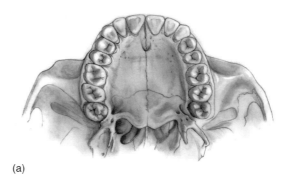

(a)

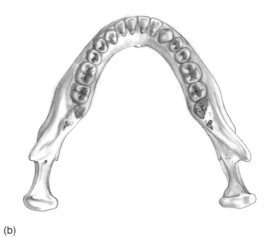

(b)

Figure 5.10 (a) Palate of an adolescent showing occlusal view of permanent maxillary teeth with third molars still not fully erupted. (b) Mandible of an adolescent showing occlusal view of permanent mandibular teeth with third molars still not fully erupted.

the incisor shovel shaped. The roots of the maxillary central incisors are straight and robust while the root apices of most other permanent incisors tend to incline distally. The roots of permanent mandibular incisors may be narrowed mesiodistally so that they are oval in cross section with a groove on the distal surface. Roots of maxillary incisors are more round in cross section.

Central or lateral
Features that help identify central from lateral incisors include:

- crown size
- incisal angle of crown
- crown root alignment
- root length and shape.

Maxillary central incisors are larger than maxillary lateral incisors, the mesiodistal width being greater in both dentitions. In the mandible, central incisors are narrower mesiodistally than lateral incisors and may be considerably smaller in size. Viewed from the buccal aspect, the incisal edge of maxillary central incisors are straight while the incisal edge of maxillary lateral incisors slope towards the distal side giving them a shorter distal crown height. This pattern is also found in the mandibular incisors but the difference is slight. The distal incisal angle of mandibular lateral incisors is rounded compared to the mandibular central incisor. The mandibular lateral incisor crown is slightly twisted on the root viewed from the occlusal surface, the incisal edge deviating distally in a lingual direction. The crown and root are aligned in all other incisors.

The root of the maxillary central incisor is considerably stouter than the lateral incisor. In the mandible, the deciduous central incisor root is considerably shorter than the lateral incisor root. In the permanent dentition, the mandibular incisors have similar roots that are flattened mesiodistally. Root length is slightly longer and longitudinal grooves may be more marked on the mandibular lateral than on the central incisor.

Left or right side

Features that help identify left from right sides are:

- mesial and distal incisal angles
- enamel curvature of the crown margin approximally
- root curvature.

The mesial incisal angle of all incisors forms a right angle compared to the rounded distal angle. The enamel margin of incisors is more sinuous on the mesial than on the distal surface, making the mesial crown height shorter than the distal crown height. Curvature of root apices is usually distal.

Canines

Place in dentition

Both deciduous canines (dc/c) and permanent canines (C/3) are the third tooth from the midline, forming the corner of the mouth.

Deciduous or permanent

Distinguishing features relate to:

- tooth size
- crown margin.

The deciduous canines are smaller than the permanent canines, with proportionally longer roots. The enamel at the crown margin is considerably thicker in the deciduous canine crown compared to the permanent, making the deciduous crown appear short and stout and the neck constricted.

Maxillary or mandibular

Maxillary and mandibular canines in both the deciduous and permanent dentitions resemble each other so that if isolated canines are heavily worn, these teeth are difficult to distinguish. Features that identify maxillary from mandibular canines include:

- crown and cingulum size
- mesial crown surface
- position of contact areas
- mesial crown and root alignment.

Maxillary canines are larger in both mesiodistal and buccolingual dimensions compared to mandibular canines making the mandibular canines appear slimmer in both dentitions. The palatal cingulum is more substantial in maxillary canines than mandibular canines and this is particularly noticeable in the permanent canines. The lingual surface in mandibular canines is flatter, similar to the adjacent incisors. Both deciduous and permanent maxillary canines have a convex mesial crown surface from the crown margin to the contact point after which it becomes flatter. In mandibular canines, the mesial crown surface forms a larger contact area with the incisor and the surface forms a straight line with the root.

Left or right side

Features that help identify left from right sides include:

- approximal crown convexity
- mesial slope of crown and length of mesial and distal slopes
- position of the contact points
- enamel curvature of the crown margin approximally
- root shape and inclination.

The distal crown surface of all canines is markedly convex compared to the flatter mesial surface and the distal marginal ridge is thicker than the mesial marginal ridge. From the buccal view, the mesial slope from the cusp tip to the contact point is flat while the distal slope is concave. The deciduous maxillary canine differs in two aspects from other canines. The mesial slope of the crown is longer than the distal slope, whereas in all other canines the mesial slope is shorter than the distal slope. The contact points of the deciduous maxillary canine are at similar levels, while in other canines the distal contact point is in the middle third and the mesial contact point is towards the incisal margin. The crown margin is more sinuous on the mesial than the distal root surface. The large root often inclines distally and may display a distal groove.

Premolars

Place in the dentition

These form the fourth and fifth permanent teeth (PM1 and PM2/ 4 and 5) from the midline and replace the deciduous molars. Isolated premolars are often difficult to distinguish especially if the cusps are worn.

Maxillary or mandibular

Features that distinguish maxillary and mandibular premolars include:

- crown outline
- cusp proportion
- root number.

Viewed from the occlusal, the maxillary crowns are oval in shape, made up of two distinct cusps, whilst the outline of the mandibular crowns is circular. Viewed from the occlusal surface, maxillary premolars have two cusps of similar size divided by a central fissure, while mandibular premolars are dominated by a larger buccal cusp and smaller lingual cusp(s). The first maxillary premolar is distinguished from other premolars as it has two roots while all other premolars have a single root.

First or second

Characteristics that identify these teeth include:

- relative cusp size
- fissure extension over the mesial marginal ridge
- root shape.

The first premolar takes on features of the canine with a dominant buccal cusp while the second premolar is more molariform with cusps that are similar in size.

Maxillary premolars – the **first** has two roots while other premolars have a single root. The crowns have a buccal and palatal cusp separated by a straight fissure. In the first premolar, this fissure extends across the mesial marginal ridge onto the mesial crown surface. From the approximal surface, it has sharper cusps than the second premolar with the palatal cusp being shorter than the buccal. The larger buccal cusp forms the wider mesiodistal part of the crown and the mesial crown surface and root trunk surface have a concavity known as the canine fossa. The **second premolar** has more rounded cusps that are similar in size and height. The cusps are shorter and the root longer than the first premolar and there is a convex mesial crown surface. Viewed from the buccal aspect, the mesial slope of the buccal cusp in the first premolar is longer than the distal slope. Both the second premolar (and canine) have a buccal cusp with a shorter mesial than distal slope.

Mandibular premolars – the **first** is dominated by a larger, pointed buccal cusp and a much smaller, short, rounded lingual cusp. Viewed occlusally, the buccal cusp is placed centrally over the root. Two occlusal pits lie on either side of the central enamel ridge; a smaller mesial occlusal pit that may extend into a mesiolingual groove, and a larger distal pit. Viewed from the approximal surface, the crown has a marked lingual inclination with a convex buccal crown surface and flatter lingual surface. The root may be grooved on the mesial surface. The **second premolar** is larger than the first, with rounded cusps that are more equal in size and height. The lingual cusp may be subdivided into two cusps, but is shorter than the buccal cusp. The occlusal surface also has two pits; a larger distal and a smaller mesial pit connected by a fissure that curves around the larger buccal cusp. Viewed from the buccal or lingual surface, the mesial marginal ridge is higher than the distal marginal ridge.

Left or right side
Features that differentiate left and right teeth include:

- cusp position
- cusp height
- mesial crown surface
- root curvature.

Maxillary – in the **first** premolar, the occlusal fissure extends across the mesial marginal ridge onto the mesial crown surface. In addition, the mesial crown and root surface of this tooth is slightly concave forming the canine fossa. The buccal cusp of the first premolar is higher than the palatal cusp. The **second** premolar has cusps that are more similar in size and height.

Mandibular – the **first** premolar has a central enamel ridge. The smaller mesial occlusal pit may extend into a mesiolingual groove and there is a larger distal pit. The root may be grooved on the mesial surface. The occlusal surface of the **second** premolar has two pits; a larger distal and a smaller mesial pit connected by a fissure that curves around the large buccal cusp. Viewed from the buccal or lingual surface, the mesial marginal ridge is higher than the distal marginal ridge. Premolar roots may show some distal curving of the root apices.

Molars

Place in the dentition

Deciduous molars (dm1 and dm2/ d and e) are the fourth and fifth teeth from the midline. Permanent molars (M1, M2 and M3/ 6, 7 and 8) are the sixth, seventh and eighth teeth from the midline.

Deciduous or permanent

The crowns of deciduous first molars are unlike any other teeth, but the root pattern is similar to other molars. Second deciduous molar crowns are similar in shape to permanent molar crowns but smaller so general comments about molars include the second deciduous molar. Third molars (wisdom teeth) show much variation in shape.

Features that distinguish deciduous from permanent molars are:

- crown size and shape
- thickness of the enamel at the crown margin
- root size and shape.

Both the crowns and roots of deciduous molars are smaller than those of permanent molars. Deciduous molars have a prominent cervical enamel margin making the cervix appear narrow and the crown bulbous. The distinguishing feature of deciduous first molars is the pronounced enamel tubercle (named after Zuckerkandl) on the mesiobuccal crown margin that often extends onto the root surface. Root shape differs between the dentitions with roots of deciduous molars being slimmer and more curved than those of permanent molars. Deciduous molar roots arise from a very short root trunk and show marked divergence, allowing space for the developing premolar crowns. Deciduous molar roots converge apically, although this feature is not apparent if the root is partly resorbed during exfoliation or if it is damaged postmortem. Roots of permanent molars are longer and more robust than deciduous molar roots.

Maxillary or mandibular

Features that help to identify maxillary from mandibular molars include:

- cusp arrangement
- crown outline
- root number and position.

The crowns of **permanent maxillary molars** are wider buccolingually than mesiodistally and consist of three or more cusps. The largest is the mesiopalatal followed by the two smaller buccal cusps and the smallest distopalatal cusp. The crown of maxillary molars is rhombic in shape and characterized by an oblique enamel ridge that runs from the mesiopalatal to the distobuccal cusp. The fissure on the distal side of this ridge extends onto the palatal surface and is helpful in distinguishing maxillary from mandibular molars. There are usually three roots: a large palatal root that diverges from the two smaller mesiobuccal and distobuccal roots. This divergence can be explained by the presence of the maxillary sinus (antrum), which is in close proximity to maxillary molar and occasionally premolar roots. The buccal arch length of the maxillary dentition is considerably greater than the palatal arch length, accommodating two buccal roots in maxillary molars. The crowns of **permanent mandibular molars** are wider mesiodistally than buccolingually and are made up of four or more cusps. Crowns are inclined lingually with a flat lingual surface and a convex buccal surface. These teeth have two roots that are flattened mesiodistally and curve distally.

First or second deciduous molar
Features that distinguish these teeth are:

- crown size and shape
- cusp number
- arrangement and fissure pattern.

The **deciduous maxillary first molar** crown is quadrilateral in outline and consists of two buccal and two palatal cusps that appear as ridges and are not clearly separated. Viewed from the occlusal surface, the buccal cusps are considerably wider mesiodistally than the palatal cusps. The mesiobuccal crown margin of this tooth may show a pronounced bulge. The **deciduous maxillary second molar** crown is larger than the first molar and is square in outline. It is made up of four cusps, the largest being the mesiopalatal followed by the mesiobuccal cusp. An oblique ridge runs from this cusp to the distobuccal cusp. Occasionally an extra cusp (named after Carabelli) occurs on the mesiopalatal surface of this cusp. This can take the form of a pit, groove or cusp and may also be present on the maxillary permanent first molar.

The **deciduous mandibular first molar** is rectangular in outline, with a considerably larger mesiodistal width than buccolingual dimension. The crown is lingually inclined so that the buccal cusps lie over the centre of the occlusal surface giving the tooth a small occlusal table. The **deciduous mandibular second molar** crown is rectangular in outline made up of three buccal and two lingual cusps. This tooth is larger than the deciduous mandibular first molar but smaller and similar in shape to the permanent mandibular first molar.

First, second or third permanent molar
Features that distinguish these teeth include:

- crown shape
- size
- number of cusps
- root size and divergence.

Maxillary molars – the **first** molar is the largest maxillary tooth crown, consisting of four cusps in decreasing size: mesiopalatal, mesiobuccal, distobuccal and distopalatal. Viewed from occlusally, the outline is rhombic and the buccolingual dimension is slightly larger than the mesiodistal width. The mesial palatal surface may have an additional cusp. The **second** molar is smaller than the first, with a narrower mesiodistal width, but closely resembles it in shape. Distinguishing features include reduced distal cusps or an absent distopalatal cusp. No cusp of Carabelli is present and the roots may curve more than the maxillary first molar. The palatal root is less divergent and the buccal roots are closer together than in the maxillary first molar, or may even be fused. The **third** molar varies considerably and is usually smaller than other molars. It is triangular in outline and made up of three or more cusps, the largest being the palatal and the shortest, the distobuccal. The distopalatal cusp is small or absent. The three roots are shorter than those of other permanent maxillary molars and are often fused and inclined distally.

Mandibular molars – the **first** molar is the largest mandibular tooth and is rectangular in shape with three buccal and two lingual cusps. The occlusal surface has a central groove with mesial and distal fossae. This tooth has a root trunk and two substantial roots that are broad buccolingually and curve distally. The **second** molar crown is rectangular in outline and smaller than the first molar crown. It has four equal sized cusps having lost the distal cusp. The central fissures form a cross on the occlusal surface and the fissures between the buccal and the lingual grooves may extend onto the buccal and lingual surfaces of the tooth. The lingual cusps are higher and sharper than the buccal cusps. Like all permanent mandibular molars, the crown is inclined lingually and the lingual surface is flat compared to the buccal surface. The roots of this tooth differ from the permanent mandibular first molar by being less divergent and less curved. The **third** molar is rectangular in outline and made up of four or more cusps. The mesial crown margin may have a contact point showing interproximal wear. The two roots tend to be shorter and less divergent or fused compared to other mandibular molars.

Left or right side
Features that help in identifying side rely on:

- number and position of cusps
- direction of the oblique ridge (maxillary)
- crown outline
- buccal and lingual surface (mandibular)
- root number and curvature.

Deciduous first molars – the outline is characteristic. Viewed from the occlusal surface, the buccal cusps are considerably wider mesiodistally than the palatal cusps and the mesial outline is angular where this tooth contacts the canine. The distal margin of the tooth is rounded, making a wider contact area with the bulbous crown of the second deciduous molar. The mesial cusps of the **mandibular** tooth are larger and higher than the distal cusps with the mesiobuccal cusp being the largest. An enamel ridge separates the occlusal surface into a small mesial and larger distal fossa. The buccal cusps are not well defined but the lingual cusps are separate and sharper.

Other maxillary molars – the oblique ridge of other crowns runs from mesiopalatal to distobuccal with a distinct fissure between the larger mesiopalatal cusp from the distopalatal cusp. The largest cusp of the permanent first molar crown is the mesiopalatal, but the mesiobuccal is the highest. The buccal cusps are sharper than the rounded palatal cusps. Viewed from the occlusal surface, the crown outline has rounded mesiopalatal and distobuccal edges while the mesiobuccal and distopalatal edges have more acute angles. The mesial cusps are wider buccolingually than the distal cusps. These features may be less noticeable on permanent maxillary second and third molars. The permanent maxillary third molar has three or more cusps, the largest being the palatal with a small or absent distopalatal cusp. These teeth also have three roots, a larger palatal root and two buccal roots that curve distally.

Other mandibular molars – these have four or five cusps. Viewed from the occlusal surface, the mesial outline of the crown is flat and the distal outline is rounded. They also have larger mesial cusps making the tooth wider buccolingually than at the distal cusps. The buccal surface is rounded compared to the flatter lingual surface. In the permanent first molar, the mesial marginal ridge is higher than the distal marginal ridge viewed from the buccal aspect. The larger mesial root is flatter than the distal root, with a longitudinal groove on the mesial surface. The distal root is shorter and rounder and may not be as curved. These features are less obvious in the permanent second and third molars but they all share pointed lingual cusps compared to buccal cusps and a flat lingual surface compared to the convex buccal surface. Most roots of molars show some degree of distal curvature.

General chronology of tooth development

Although the development of the dentition is a continuous process that extends from embryonic to early adult life, it may be divided into a number of stages that are visibly active in the mouth as bouts of tooth emergence separated by apparently more quiescent periods. Within the jaws, however, there is continuous growth throughout most of embryonic and fetal life and postnatally until 18–20 years. By birth, all the teeth of the deciduous dentition and the first permanent molars have started to mineralize. By the age of about 3 years the deciduous dentition has emerged into the mouth and completed root formation. During the first year, the permanent first molar and anterior teeth begin formation and between the ages of 2 and 4 years, mineralization in the premolars and second molars is initiated. The third molars commence formation between 6 and 12 years of age.

The emergence of all the permanent teeth, except the third molars, takes place in two stages, between the ages of about 6 and 8 years and again between 10 and 12 years, separated by two relatively inactive periods. In the first active stage, the first permanent molar appears behind the second deciduous molar. At the same time, the deciduous incisors are shed and replaced by their permanent successors. The usual emergence order is the mandibular central incisor, followed by the maxillary central and the mandibular lateral incisors about a year later. The maxillary laterals are normally the last incisors to appear. There is then a quiescent period of 1.5–2 years before the second visibly active stage commences. This involves shedding deciduous canines and molars and their replacement by permanent canines and premolars, together with the emergence of the second permanent molars. Thus, the first active period begins with the emergence of the first molars at about 6 years and the second period ends at about 12 years with the emergence of the second molars.

Third molars in humans appear late in development and are said to be more variable in their development, size, shape and presence. They usually commence formation between 6 and 12 years, complete their crowns in 4 years and emerge and complete development during adolescence or early adulthood. Garn *et al.* (1962) compared the variability in timing to other posterior teeth and found it no different from the general biological trend that variability increases directly with mean age of attainment. Stewart (1934) compared their emergence to other skeletal markers and found it was variable in relation to the closure of both long bone epiphyses and the spheno-occipital synchondrosis. In a large French Canadian sample, crown mineralization began at 9.8 years and was complete about 5 years later, with females being in advance of males, as with the development of other molar teeth. However, further developmental emergence and root completion was faster in males, apex maturation occurring about 1.5 years earlier in males (Levesque *et al.*, 1981).

The total time taken for an individual tooth to develop is considerable, lasting from 2–3 years for the deciduous teeth and up to 8–12 years for the permanent teeth. In general, anterior tooth crowns take 4–5 years and molar tooth crowns 3–4 years. This means that roots take approximately 6–7 years to grow. Normal emergence is correlated between antimeres and isomeres rather than neighbouring teeth (Garn and Smith, 1980), but if there is early loss of deciduous predecessors, or malocclusion, there may be delayed emergence (Fanning, 1961, 1962; Maj *et al.*, 1964; Anderson and Popovich, 1981).

Sex differences exist in developmental timing of the deciduous dentition. Boys are in advance of girls in the prenatal stages (Burdi *et al.*, 1970a; Garn and Burdi, 1971). There is also a sequence precedence, established very early in development, for tooth formation and emergence, with the anterior teeth more commonly having a mandibular precedence and the posterior teeth tending to a maxillary precedence (Burdi *et al.*, 1970b, 1975).

There is a large volume of literature on emergence times of both the deciduous and permanent teeth from all parts of the world and reports vary greatly in the size of the samples and in the methodology of recording. The timing of emergence or sequencing of the deciduous teeth appears to differ only slightly between the sexes or regions of the world (reviewed by Liversidge, 2003). However Tanguay *et al.* (1986) pointed out that although a sex difference in deciduous tooth emergence in young children was observed relative to chronological age, there was no significant difference between the length/height of an individual child and the time of tooth emergence. They suggested that clinical standards might be more accurate and efficient if scaled relative to height, as reflecting general physical development, rather than age. McGregor *et al.* (1968) also found that young children who are tall or heavy for their chronological age tended to have more teeth in the mouth than those who were smaller and lighter. Evidence on difference in timing between populations is equivocal, but reported differences appear to be small and it is difficult to isolate the effects of socio-economic status with its consequent nutritional effects. Shedding, or exfoliation, of the deciduous teeth begins at about the same time in boys as in girls, but sex differences increase with age, girls being in advance of boys (Fanning, 1961; Haavikko, 1973; Nyström *et al.*, 1986).

There is more general agreement about the development of the permanent dentition as differences are more apparent. The timing of emergence of the first two permanent teeth in two African groups (Ghana and one Kenyan study) are considerably earlier than other worldwide groups, although the pattern for other teeth, groups and regions is not clear (Liversidge, 2003). Evidence from sibling studies points to a genetic component influencing the sequence of development (Garn *et al.*, 1956; Garn and Lewis, 1957; Barrett *et al.*, 1964; Garn and Burdi, 1971; Kent *et al.*, 1978; Garn and Smith, 1980; Smith and Garn, 1987). Sex differences in both mineralization and emergence are usually in reverse of those for the deciduous dentition, girls being in advance of boys by about 6 months, with the exception of the third molar. The difference is most marked in the emergence times for the canine teeth. Studies on tooth crown size in individuals with sex chromosome anomalies and their normal male and female relatives have demonstrated that genes on the X and Y chromosomes have differential effects on growth. This would explain the expression of sexual dimorphism of size, shape and number of teeth and differences in the proportions of enamel and dentine (Alvesalo, 1997).

Indications for differences in timing between populations are stronger in the permanent than in the deciduous dentition (Liversidge, 2003) and some studies have taken into account socio-economic levels (Garn *et al.*, 1973b; De Melo e Freitas and Salzano, 1975). There is also evidence for difference in sequencing between populations (Dahlberg and Menegaz-Bock, 1958) and it is possible that sequencing could be affected by seasonality (Nonaka *et al.*, 1990). As with the deciduous dentition, some studies suggest that emergence of the permanent teeth is also related to general somatic development (Maj *et al.*, 1964; Helm, 1969). Filipsson (1975) and Moorrees and Kent (1978) developed methods based on the number of emerged teeth in living children. Estimating age from the number of deciduous teeth in the mouth is reviewed by Townsend and Hammel (1990). Estimated age from the number of erupted permanent teeth was found to be more accurate than using individual tooth eruption (Gillett, 1997).

Age may be estimated using tooth emergence, but is not as accurate as some other methods (see below). In the living child, a tooth is normally recorded as having emerged if any part of the crown has broken through the gum. In a skull, emergence is usually defined as the appearance of the tip of the tooth, or its cusps, at the same level as the alveolar crest. In either case, it is not usually possible to know the exact time of the event, as it may have happened at an unknown time before the examination of the child or skull. However, there are some occasions when the use of tooth emergence times is the only possible option, for example, in some fieldwork or forensic situations, where radiography is not practicable and speed and expense are paramount. Tables 5.1 and 5.2 give ages of the alveolar and clinical emergence of the deciduous and permanent dentition. Because of the wide age range of each stage of third molar development, it is not a very useful estimator of age at death in a forensic situation, where accuracy is all important. Regression formulae and probabilities that an individual has reached the medicolegally important age of 18 years are given by Mincer *et al.* (1993).

Early development of the teeth

The first indications of dental development are visible in the early embryonic period before even the nose and mouth cavities are completely separated by formation of the secondary palate (Chapter 4). At about 28 days, an island of ectodermal epithelial thickening appears on each side of the maxillary processes and on the dorsolateral aspects of the mandibular arch. Additional thickenings appear about a week later on the lateral borders of the frontonasal process (see Fig. 4.9). The maxillary and frontonasal islands coalesce and the mandibular thickenings join in the midline. They form continuous arch-shaped plates, the **primary epithelial bands** in both the upper and lower jaws from which the vestibular and dental laminae develop (Nery *et al.*, 1970). On the

Table 5.1 Times of emergence (years) of the deciduous dentition

		Alveolar		Clinical	
		Mean	SD	Mean	SD
Maxilla	i^1	0.34	0.11	0.85	0.02
	i^2	0.62	0.11	0.95	0.02
	c	1.05	0.26	1.60	0.03
	m^1	0.81	0.12	1.33	0.02
	m^2	1.29	0.32	2.43	0.03
Mandible	i_1	0.27	0.14	0.67	0.02
	i_2	0.66	0.36	1.10	0.02
	c	1.05	0.30	1.64	0.03
	m_1	0.89	0.23	1.35	0.02
	m_2	1.38	0.11	2.26	0.03

Adapted from Liversidge and Molleson (2004) and Lysell *et al.* (1962).

Table 5.2 Times of emergence (years) of the permanent dentition

		Boys				Girls			
		Maxillary		Mandibular		Maxillary		Mandibular	
Tooth	Stage	Median	Disp	Median	Disp	Median	Disp	Median	Disp
I1	alv	6.2	2.2	5.9	1.9	6.1	0.9	5.8	1.1
	clin	6.9	2.2	6.3	1.8	6.7	1.7	6.2	1.4
I2	alv	7.3	3.3	6.9	2.0	7.0	2.3	6.5	1.4
	clin	8.3	3.2	7.3	1.9	7.8	2.2	6.8	1.8
C	alv	11.2	3.1	9.8	2.8	9.3	3.2	8.8	1.6
	clin	12.1	3.6	10.4	3.0	10.6	3.7	9.2	2.7
PM1	alv	9.8	3.6	9.6	3.3	9.0	2.8	9.1	2.3
	clin	10.2	3.6	10.3	4.6	9.6	3.5	9.6	3.8
PM2	alv	11.1	4.1	10.3	4.4	9.5	3.5	9.2	4.2
	clin	11.4	3.8	11.1	4.4	10.2	4.1	10.1	4.5
M1	alv	5.3	1.9	5.3	0.9	5.3	1.2	5.0	1.0
	clin	6.4	1.6	6.3	1.4	6.4	1.4	6.3	1.4
M2	alv	11.4	2.8	10.8	2.6	10.3	2.3	9.9	2.7
	clin	12.8	3.2	12.2	3.6	12.4	3.0	11.4	3.6
M3	alv	17.7	3.9	18.1	5.5	17.2	6.3	17.7	6.0

alv: alveolar emergence; clin: clinical emergence; Disp: difference between 90th and 10th percentile.

Table from Haavikko (1970)

labial side, apoptosis of the central cells of the **vestibular lamina** results in the formation of a sulcus, the **oral vestibule**, which will separate the lips and cheeks from the tooth-bearing alveolar bone.

From each **dental lamina** ten swellings, the **enamel organs**, are budded off, which subsequently produce the enamel crowns of the teeth. Beneath each epithelial component is an aggregation of mesenchymal tissue, the **dental papilla**, derived from neural crest cells, which have migrated from the caudal mesencephalic and rostral metencephalic regions of the neural tube. The dentine, cementum and pulp of each tooth are derived from the dental papilla. The study of tooth development has provided much insight into induction mechanisms and tissue interactions (Lumsden and Buchanan, 1986; Mina and Kollar, 1987; Lumsden, 1988; Linde, 1998). By the tenth week the elements derived from these two tissues become surrounded by a capsular **dental follicle** and each unit, or **tooth germ**, develops into a deciduous tooth. For descriptive purposes bud, cap and bell stages are distinguished before the late bell stage, when mineralization begins (Fig. 5.11). As with bone, the production of both enamel and dentine involve the deposition of an organic matrix, which is subsequently mineralized. Dentine is formed first, followed closely by enamel, with the two tissues being laid down between the original two components of the tooth germ. **Ameloblast** cells from the inner layer of the original epithelial enamel organ produce enamel and also induce the outer layer of the mesenchymal papilla to differentiate into **odontoblasts**, which form dentine. A layer of epithelial cells, known as Hertwig's **epithelial root sheath**, covers the future root and in the cheek teeth some of these cells invaginate to produce multi-rooted teeth. Cells of the dental follicle are involved in the production of **cementum**, the **periodontal ligament** and part of the surrounding alveolar bone. Permanent teeth that have deciduous predecessors develop as down-

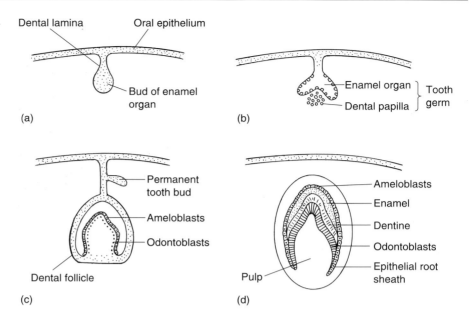

Figure 5.11 Tooth development: (a) bud stage; (b) cap stage; (c) bell stage; (d) late bell stage.

growths from the dental lamina on the palatal or lingual side of their respective deciduous tooth germs. The permanent molars arise from an extension of the dental lamina posterior to the deciduous molars. Details of dental histodifferentiation may be found in Ten Cate (1998).

Mineralization

Mineralization of the tooth germ can be viewed as the equivalent of the ossification stage of bone formation. As with studies of ossification, prenatal observations are from entirely different source material than those obtained postnatally. Similarly, detection of mineralization depends on the technique used and reported timing is also affected by the inaccuracies incurred in the estimation of fetal age (see Chapter 1). Postnatal observations of mineralization are nearly all from cross-sectional and longitudinal radiological studies of living populations, some of the latter employing the same children that took part in the long-term skeletal growth studies discussed in Chapter 1.

Prenatal dental development has been studied histologically by serial sectioning, dissection and alizarin staining of fetal tooth germs and by radiology. Some authors reported that there are discrepancies in recorded timing of developmental stages, albeit smaller than in the ossification process, depending on whether the tooth germs are dissected or examined radiologically (Logan and Kronfeld, 1933; Kronfeld, 1935; Garn *et al.*, 1959; Nolla, 1960). Mineralization can be detected histologically up to 6 months before it can be seen on radiographs, as initially both enamel and dentine are not very radiopaque (Hess *et al.*, 1932). As a result, mineralization times from radiographs are usually shorter than the actual times taken for full crown and root formation.

Kraus (1959a) and Kraus and Jordan (1965), using dissection and staining techniques, demonstrated that initial mineralization began earlier than had previously been reported using other methods. Calcification proceeded faster mesiodistally than vertically and between 13 and 18 weeks *in utero* showed a sigmoid type of growth curve (Kraus, 1959b). Formation times of crown soft tissue, initiation of mineralization and maturation of enamel observed by all three techniques were reported by Nomata (1964). Lunt and Law (1974) reviewed previous studies on times of initial mineralization and produced a modified chronology table, which agrees with later histological work by Sunderland *et al.* (1987). Lunt and Law's (1974) timing appears to be about 2 weeks in advance of the times given by Sunderland *et al.* (1987), but is an example of the difference incurred in recording fetal age from fertilization or from LMP (see Chapter 1).

The sequence of prenatal mineralization in the deciduous teeth starts with the central incisor followed by the first molar, lateral incisor, canine and second molar. The maxillary central incisors and first molars are usually seen before those in the mandible. The lateral incisor appears first in the maxilla, but subsequent development is ahead in the mandible. Sunderland *et al.* (1987) reported mineralization in the mandibular canine before that in the maxilla, but it occurred simultaneously in the maxillary and mandibular second molars. Both Turner (1963) and Kraus and Jordan (1965) are in agreement that the sequence of calcification in the molar cusps of both the maxillary and mandibular teeth is mesiobuccal, mesiolingual, distobuccal, distolingual, with the distal cusp of the mandibular molar being the last to form.

Metrical studies of fetal molar tooth germs from 12 weeks to term have been reported by Butler (1967a, 1967b; 1968), who concluded that the initial growth of the tooth germ and its subsequent calcification are independent processes. Kjær (1980) studied the development of the mandible and its anterior deciduous teeth and found that, up to about 19 prenatal weeks, the development of the lateral incisor was in advance of that of the central incisor. It was suggested that the envelopment of Meckel's cartilage by bone at the site of the canine tooth germ influenced the lateral incisor germ first. However, Deutsch *et al.* (1984) found that from 20 prenatal weeks, the crown height of both the mandibular and maxillary anterior teeth proceeded in order of central incisor, lateral incisor and canine. Using gravimetric methods, Stack (1964, 1967, 1971) demonstrated that during the last trimester, fetal age is linearly related to the square root of the weight of mineralized tissue in the deciduous anterior teeth and Deutsch *et al.* (1981, 1984) confirmed that both the weight and crown height of the anterior teeth were correlated with fetal age. Initiation of mineralization, as visualized by alizarin staining, takes place in the first permanent molars between 28 and 32 prenatal weeks, the mandibular germs being slightly in advance of those of the maxilla (Christensen and Kraus, 1965).

The mineralization status of the deciduous teeth and first permanent molars has been tested against other methods for the estimation of gestational age. Luke *et al.* (1978) tested the Kraus and Jordan (1965) stages of molar calcification and Stack's (1964) gravimetric method on fetuses whose LMP ages and crown–rump lengths were reliably known. Although the mean error produced by each method was similar, the correlation coefficients between actual and estimated ages were higher with the gravimetric method. They concluded that between 24 and 42 weeks of gestation, dental methods were more reliable in the estimation of gestational age than crown–rump length.

Kuhns *et al.* (1972) correlated radiographic tooth mineralization with chest radiographs and knee ossification in premature infants and again found dental age correlated better with gestational age than did skeletal age. Lemons *et al.* (1972) attempted the estimation of age in small-for-dates babies from 2 weeks before the expected date of delivery, by correlating mineralization of the teeth with the appearance of the distal femoral epiphysis. They also confirmed that fetal age could be determined with greater accuracy from dental rather than skeletal development, but the method had a limited use as tooth germs could only be visualized sufficiently clearly if the fetus was in breech position with the head well clear of the pelvis.

At birth, the deciduous incisors have about 60–80% of their crowns complete and the incisal edges are usually elaborated into three small cuspules, or mamelons, which wear flat soon after emergence. In spite of this initial shape, there is no evidence that mineralization proceeds from more than a single centre, as had been previously suggested, the lobed appearance being merely a function of depressions in the amelodentinal junction (Kraus, 1959a). Canine crowns are a simple conical shape and are approximately 30% formed by birth. The first deciduous molars have a complete occlusal cap of mineralized tissue, the maxillary tooth being more fully calcified than the other molars. The mandibular molars lack the characteristic pattern of grooves and pits, which only develop with later postnatal deposition of enamel (Kraus and Jordan, 1965). The crown of the second molar tooth normally has calcified cusps continuous with a large central area of uncalcified occlusal surface (Kraus and Jordan, 1965). Calcification may be present on as many as four cusp tips of first permanent molars at birth (Christensen and Kraus, 1965). Radiographic assessment of tooth formation in early postnatal life is documented in Nyström and Ranta (2003).

In archaeological specimens, the fragile ring of mineralized tissue in the second deciduous molars rarely remains intact and it is often difficult to recover the tiny calcified cusps of the first permanent molars. Most maxillary and mandibular incisors reach maximum crown size between birth and 3 postnatal months but the canines can take up to 14 months to reach maximum size. The first permanent molars grow more slowly, but finally attain a total weight that is 2–2.5 times that of the deciduous molars (Stack, 1968). Postnatal changes in the size, morphology and weight of the deciduous dentition have been detailed by Deutsch et al. (1985). The accuracy of these standards tested on a crypt sample of known age between birth and 1 year was found to be high and accuracy during the first postnatal year was highest for deciduous molar tooth length (Liversidge et al., 1993; Liversidge, 1994). Mays et al. (1995) also found that there was a highly significant relationship between permanent molar crown height and dental age amongst juveniles from an archaeological population of unknown age. Details of the appearance of the enamel matrix in decalcified sections from birth to 2.5 years, useful for age estimation in a forensic context, have been reported by Calonius et al. (1970).

The literature on the prenatal development of the teeth is complex and historical reviews may be found in Garn et al. (1959), Lunt and Law (1974) and Smith (1991). Many of the early studies give no clear indication of methods, ageing or sample size. However, it seems unlikely that there will be many new studies on the very early developmental stages because of the rarity of fetal tissue. Also, in the UK at least, radiographic studies *per se* are unlikely to be ethically approved as radiographs of young children are only taken if treatment is needed (Liversidge and Molleson, 1999). Information on the initiation of mineralization and the completion of crown and root formation of the deciduous teeth taken from Sunderland et al. (1987), Kronfeld and Schour (1939), Smith (1991) and Liversidge and Molleson (2004) is shown in Table 5.3.

The majority of postnatal studies of mineralization have been radiological surveys of varying sizes. Starting with the classic study of the life history of the permanent mandibular first molar by Gleiser and Hunt (1955), defined stages

Table 5.3a Chronology of the deciduous dentition: *Beginning of mineralization (weeks post fertilization)*

Tooth	50th percentile	Range
di1	15	13–17
di2	17	14–19
dc	19	17–20
dm1	16	14–17
dm2	19	18–20

From Sunderland *et al.* (1987)

Table 5.3b Chronology of the deciduous dentition: *Age of crown completion of mandibular teeth (years)*

	MFH			LM	
	Mean	±2SD	K&S	Mean	SD
di 1	—	—	0.1–0.2	0.10	0.20
di 2	—	—	0.2	0.32	0.07
dc	—	—	0.7	0.81	0.12
Females	0.7	0.4–1.0	—	—	
Males	0.7	0.4–1.0	—	—	
dm 1	—	—	0.5	0.48	0.18
Females	0.3	0.1–0.5	—	—	
Males	0.4	0.2–0.7	—	—	
dm 2	—	—	0.8–0.9	0.92	0.26
Females	0.7	0.4–1.0	—	—	
Males	0.7	0.4–1.0	—	—	

MFH, data of Moorrees, Fanning and Hunt (1963a) from Smith (1991).
K&S, data of Kronfeld and Schour (1939) from Smith (1991).
LM, data of Liversidge and Molleson (2004).

of crown and root development were assessed from panoramic or lateral radiographs to construct chronological time scales of normal tooth growth. Most employed 11–14 stages, but the number varied in different studies as stages were either interpolated or omitted. Crown stages start with first evidence of mineralization and then coalescence of the cusps, followed by complete cusp outline, then half, three-quarters and completion of the crown. This is followed by root initiation, and usually by fractions of root completion with an added cleft formation stage in multi-rooted teeth. Some surveys used additional stages for maturation of the root apex. Accepted standard stages are shown in Fig. 5.12 and their abbreviations in Table 5.4.

Chronologies using stages of mineralization are reviewed by Demirjian (1986) and Smith (1991). Data are available for a variety of teeth, or combinations of mostly mandibular teeth, and nearly all are of children from European or European-derived populations of North America. Many studies use cumulative distribution methods to produce age-of-attainment schedules; that is, the

Table 5.3c Chronology of the deciduous dentition: *Age of root completion of mandibular teeth (years)*

	MFH			LM	
	Mean	±2SD	K&S	Mean	SD
di 1	—	—	1.5	1.98	0.11
di 2	—	—	1.5–2.0	2.39	0.40
dc	—	—	3.25	3.51	0.35
Females	3.0	2.3–3.8	—	—	
Males	3.1	2.4–3.8	—	—	
dm 1	—	—	2.25	2.91	0.35
Females	1.8	1.3–2.3	—	—	
Males	2.0	1.5–2.5	—	—	
dm 2	—	—	3.0	3.54	0.74
Females	2.8	2.2–3.6	—	—	
Males	3.1	2.4–3.9	—	—	

Abbreviations as Table 5.3b.

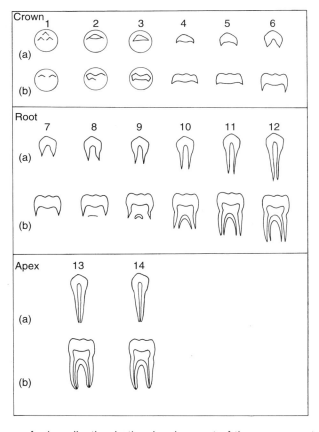

Figure 5.12 Stages of mineralization in the development of the crown, root and apex of permanent teeth as defined by Moorrees *et al.* (1963b). (a) Single-rooted teeth; (b) mandibular molars. Abbreviations are given in Table 5.4.

Table 5.4 Standard abbreviations of tooth formation stages

1	C_i	Initial cusp formation
2	C_{co}	Coalescence of cusps
3	C_{oc}	Cusp outline complete
4	$Cr_{1/2}$	Crown half complete
5	$Cr_{3/4}$	Crown three-quarters complete
6	Cr_c	Crown complete
7	R_i	Initial root formation
8	Cl_i	Initial cleft formation
9	$R_{1/4}$	Root length quarter
10	$R_{1/2}$	Root length half
11	$R_{3/4}$	Root length three-quarters
12	R_c	Root length complete
13	$A_{1/2}$	Apex half closed
14	A_c	Apical closure complete

From Moorrees *et al.* (1963b)

proportion of children who had reached a particular developmental stage was plotted against the midpoint of each age group.

The most commonly used method in estimation of age in archaeological material is that of Moorrees *et al.* (1963a, 1963b) and it is one of the few studies based on radiographs from birth and is therefore the most suitable radiographic method to assess dental age during early childhood and infancy. However, the timing of some stages of the permanent canine, first molar and incisors are considerably earlier than other radiographic and histological data and accounts of its accuracy vary (Saunders *et al.*, 1993b; Liversidge, 1994).

In growth-related studies of older archaeological populations, accuracy cannot be tested, as the individuals are of unknown age. However, tooth formation standards have been applied in an attempt to compare differences between populations. This has identified methodological problems such as systematic and patterned differences in tooth formation timing, which have complicated their use (Owsley and Jantz, 1983).

Another type of mineralization study was developed by Demirjian *et al.* (1973) to estimate dental maturity in children of known age, using subjects of French Canadian origin. The number of stages was reduced to eight with a detailed description, radiograph and line drawing of each stage. Each tooth was assigned a score depending on its state of development. Weighted scores were then added to produce a total maturity score, which was plotted against age. This was the same principle as that used to estimate skeletal maturity from wrist bone age (Tanner *et al.*, 1983). It was modified by Demirjian and Goldstein (1976), the sample size increased (Demirjian, 1986), and data for individual teeth documented (Demirjian and Levesque, 1980), including third molars (Levesque *et al.*, 1981). Numerous studies around the world report an advancement in dental maturity compared to the original French Canadian sample (Liversidge, 2003). Recent adaptation of the scoring system was presented from data of Belgian children with reported high accuracy (Willems *et al.*, 2001).

Studies testing accuracy of dental age estimation on recent skeletal remains are complicated by a small or uneven age range, inappropriately used methods and results that are difficult to compare with other investigations (Saunders *et al.*, 1993b; Liversidge, 1994). What is clear, is that estimating age is more accurate in younger than older age groups. This is a common finding, as variability increases with age when environmental influences have a cumulative effect (Garn et al., 1959; Haavikko, 1970; Anderson et al., 1976).

All radiographic studies vary somewhat, depending on the number of formation stages used, the time interval between examinations and the intra- and interobserver error (Pöyry et al., 1986). Training and experience in the reading of dental radiographs is essential in order to recognize 'crown complete' stage, as well as fractions of crown and root development. It is obviously easier to assess these in longitudinal studies, where successive radiographs of the same individual are available. In cross-sectional studies, evaluation has to be made by comparing each tooth with more mature neighbouring teeth and this is inevitably less accurate.

Smith's (1991) review chapter on tooth formation stages in the assessment of age is essential reading. She stresses that data collected for various tooth chronologies have been subjected to different statistical procedures and many studies are not comparable with each other as the underlying variables are fundamentally different. As a result, it is likely that some of the conclusions that claim population and other differences are more likely to be due to the use of statistical treatments, or to sampling effects, rather than real differences between samples. There are also a number of gaps in the present knowledge of tooth development stages. The majority of samples are truncated in the early age ranges, owing to scarcity of very young children and the problems incurred in radiographing them. Ages are usually available for mandibular teeth only, as there is little information on maxillary teeth, owing to the practical difficulties of visualizing them. There is also sparse information on both deciduous and permanent incisors mainly due to the difficulty of visualizing anterior teeth. Some samples have an uneven distribution of ages, or do not give variances, and there is also very little information other than from white, European-derived populations. Most clinical studies are expressed as either age-of-attainment of a growth stage, or produced for maturity assessments. The timing of stages of permanent tooth formation of Moorrees et al. (1963b) have been presented with standard deviation by Harris and Buck (2002). Few chronologies are suitable for age prediction. Smith (1991) re-worked the data of Moorrees et al. (1963b) so that each tooth may be assessed independently, making it more suitable for use with archaeological or fragmented remains (Table 5.5). The mean of the ages attributed to any available teeth can then be designated as the dental age. As most of this type of material is likely to be of unknown sex, the average of the male and female estimates would be appropriate. Timing of deciduous tooth formation and eruption has been adapted in a similar way (Liversidge and Molleson, 2004). Two studies testing the accuracy of age estimation on individuals of known age using the revised data of permanent teeth (Smith, 1991) are contradictory. Liversidge (1994) found the age-of-prediction tables to be significantly more accurate, whereas Saunders et al. (1993b) found no substantial difference between age-of-attainment and the age-of-prediction tables although it is unclear how this was calculated.

Other methods of age estimation

Tooth length
There have been a few studies on living children, which have produced reference charts based on tooth length alone in relation to age (Israel and Lewis,

Table 5.5 Estimation of age (years) from the permanent mandibular dentition

Stage	I1	I2	C	PM1	PM2	M1	M2	M3
Female								
C_i	—	—	0.6	2.0	3.3	0.2	3.6	9.9
C_{co}	—	—	1.0	2.5	3.9	0.5	4.0	10.4
C_{oc}	—	—	1.6	3.2	4.5	0.9	4.5	11.0
$Cr_{1/2}$	—	—	3.5	4.0	5.1	1.3	5.1	11.5
$Cr_{3/4}$	—	—	4.3	4.7	5.8	1.8	5.8	12.0
Cr_c	—	—	4.4	5.4	6.5	2.4	6.6	12.6
R_i	—	—	5.0	6.1	7.2	3.1	7.3	13.2
Cl_i	—	—	—	—	—	4.0	8.4	14.1
$R_{1/4}$	4.8	5.0	6.2	7.4	8.2	4.8	9.5	15.2
$R_{1/2}$	5.4	5.6	7.7	8.7	9.4	5.4	10.3	16.2
$R_{2/3}$	5.9	6.2	—	—	—	—	—	—
$R_{3/4}$	6.4	7.0	8.6	9.6	10.3	5.8	11.0	16.9
R_c	7.0	7.9	9.4	10.5	11.3	6.5	11.8	17.7
$A_{1/2}$	7.5	8.3	10.6	11.6	12.8	7.9	13.5	19.5
A_c	—	—	—	—	—	—	—	—
Male								
C_i	—	—	0.6	2.1	3.2	0.1	3.8	9.5
C_{co}	—	—	1.0	2.6	3.9	0.4	4.3	10.0
C_{oc}	—	—	1.7	3.3	4.5	0.8	4.9	10.6
$Cr_{1/2}$	—	—	2.5	4.1	5.0	1.3	5.4	11.3
$Cr_{3/4}$	—	—	3.4	4.9	5.8	1.9	6.1	11.8
Cr_c	—	—	4.4	5.6	6.6	2.5	6.8	12.4
R_i	—	—	5.2	6.4	7.3	3.2	7.6	13.2
Cl_i	—	—	—	—	—	4.1	8.7	14.1
$R_{1/4}$	—	5.8	6.9	7.8	8.6	4.9	9.8	14.8
$R_{1/2}$	5.6	6.6	8.8	9.3	10.1	5.5	10.6	15.6
$R_{2/3}$	6.2	7.2	—	—	—	—	—	—
$R_{3/4}$	6.7	7.7	9.9	10.2	11.2	6.1	11.4	16.4
R_c	7.3	8.3	11.0	11.2	12.2	7.0	12.3	17.5
$A_{1/2}$	7.9	8.9	12.4	12.7	13.5	8.5	13.9	19.1
A_c	—	—	—	—	—	—	—	—

From Moorrees *et al.* (1963b), modified by Smith (1991)

1971; Ledley *et al.*, 1971; Carels *et al.*, 1991) or in combination with other radiographic measures of tooth growth (Mörnstad *et al.*, 1994). They appear to give good information for maturity assessment. Results from direct observation of developing teeth in the Spitalfields archaeological collection of known age at death individuals indicate that the age of crown completion is later than that reported in radiographic studies (Liversidge, 1995). This is partly due to the condition known as 'burnout', where the last formed enamel in the cervical region is not seen at all on dental X-rays. There is also difficulty in visualization of the whole of the curving cementum/enamel junction in a two-dimensional radiograph. The enamel contour extends on the buccal and lingual surfaces 2–4 mm more towards the root than on the mesial and distal surfaces. Also, enamel on the buccal and lingual surfaces can occur up to 2 years after initial root formation begins on the approximal surfaces. Recent histological studies (see below) agree with this. Regression equations to estimate age from the lengths of deciduous and some permanent teeth are from Liversidge *et al.*

Table 5.6 Estimation of age (years) from tooth length of the deciduous dentition

di1	$-0.653 + 0.144 \times$ length ± 0.19
di2	$-0.581 + 0.153 \times$ length ± 0.17
dc	$-0.648 + 0.209 \times$ length ± 0.22
dm1	$-0.814 + 0.222 \times$ length ± 0.25
dm2	$-0.904 + 0.292 \times$ length ± 0.26

Tooth length (mm) = distance from cusp-tip or mid-incisal edge to developing edge of crown or root in the midline; only appropriate if root is incomplete, i.e. tooth still growing.

From Liversidge *et al.* (1998).

(1998) (Tables 5.6 and 5.7). Liversidge and Molleson (1999) corrected and extended these data for permanent teeth. They include the earliest and latest age for when they are appropriate as well as dispersion. The accuracy of some of these methods (Mörnstad *et al.*, 1994; Liversidge and Molleson, 1999; Carels *et al.*, 1991) was higher for children aged 8–9 years compared to children aged 12–13 years (Liversidge *et al.*, 2003). In this study, the Carels *et al.* (1991) method was least accurate and the tooth with the highest accuracy was the canine (Liversidge and Molleson, 1999). None of these quantitative methods have been tested on younger children.

Tables and charts

Many skeletal studies use estimated ages derived from the mean stage of development of the dentition as a whole, compared to a chart or atlas. The most commonly used are by Schour and Massler (1941), van der Linden and Duterloo (1976) and Ubelaker (1978). The last, although originally adapted for Native Americans, has been widely used with many different samples and is recommended by the WEA (Ferembach, *et al.* 1980, Fig. 5.13). Comparing an individual with a set stage in an atlas is easy and rapid but, as with skeletal atlases, difficulties occur with matching. Dentally, this happens when numbers of teeth, or sequencing between the two, do not match.

Table 5.7 Estimation of age (years) from tooth length of some permanent teeth

		Max t/l
I1	$0.237 - 0.018 \times$ length $+ 0.042 \times$ (length)$^2 \pm 0.21$	<11.3
I^2	$-0.173 + 0.538 \times$ length $+ 0.003 \times$ (length)$^2 \pm 0.14$	<9.9
I$_2$	$0.921 - 0.281 \times$ length $+ 0.075 \times$ (length)$^2 \pm 0.12$	<9.8
C	$-0.163 + 0.294 \times$ length $+ 0.028 \times$ (length)$^2 \pm 0.25$	<9.8
M1	$-0.942 + 0.441 \times$ length $+ 0.010 \times$ (length)$^2 \pm 0.25$	<11.5

Length: maximum tooth length in mm; max t/l: maximum tooth length on which data based.

From Liversidge *et al.* (1998)

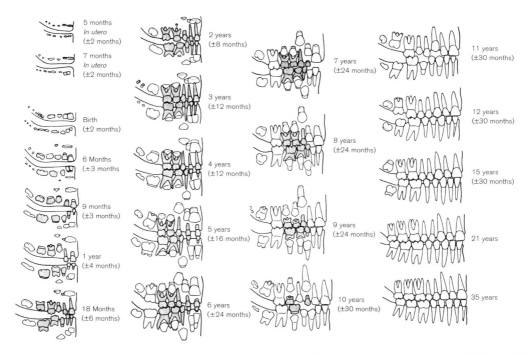

Figure 5.13 Chart of development of the teeth from 5 months *in utero* to 35 years. From WEA (1980) after Ubelaker (1978).

However, accuracy of age estimation on a large sample of known age juveniles below the age of 5.4 years from the Spitalfields crypt was found to be higher using the Schour and Massler atlas than by other methods (Liversidge, 1994).

Another method in common use is the chart developed by Gustafson and Koch (1974), which includes both deciduous and permanent teeth. It was compiled from the accumulated data of about 20 different studies, regardless of histological or radiological observations, or of the application of different statistical methods. It is based on four recognizable stages of development: initiation of mineralization, crown completion, tooth emergence and root completion. These are drawn as triangles on the chart, the base representing the range and the apex the mean. Age is estimated by placing a ruler across the available teeth and adjusting to 'best fit'. The authors tested it on a sample of 41 children of known age and found that an individual could be aged with an accuracy of ±2 months and that the 95% confidence interval for a single estimation was ±4.79 months. It has been tested independently on children of known age by Crossner and Mansfield (1983), who found it to be reliable irrespective of sex or race. Hägg and Matsson (1985) found that it was more accurate for males than for females, but that its precision (intra- and inter-observer variability) was low, presumably because of the difficulty of its application. Reported overall accuracy for a known age crypt sample between birth and 5 years was 0.1 ± 0.37 years (Liversidge, 1994).

Dental microstructure

All the dental hard tissues show incremental lines that occur during the laying-down of their organic matrix and subsequent mineralization and there is a considerable volume of literature concerned with age estimation that makes use of this process. A long-established method for ageing in adults using cementum apposition, secondary dentine formation and other associated criteria was established by Gustafson (1950) and modified by Johanson (1971) and Maples and Rice (1979). It was compared with other methods against a known modern population by Lucy *et al.* (1994) and Lucy and Pollard (1995) have offered an alternative statistical analysis of Gustafson's data. Further techniques have been tested by Charles *et al.* (1986) and Condon *et al.* (1986). Their use in archaeological skeletal remains is hampered by the damage and possible diagenesis that occurs to cementum and dentine and the majority of the methods are only applicable in the young adult and adult age ranges.

Incremental lines in enamel provide a much more accurate method of age determination and their use in the estimation of age at death of a child from an archaeological site was first reported by Boyde (1963). The method is based on the recognition of two types of lines visible in enamel. Cross-striations occur along the length of the enamel prisms and it is generally accepted that they result from a circadian rhythm inherent in the rate of enamel matrix secretion by ameloblasts (reviewed by FitzGerald, 1998; Dean, 2000). Fairly regular numbers of cross-striations appear between darker and coarser lines, the striae of Retzius, which form with a repeat interval of 8–11 with a modal value of 9 (FitzGerald *et al.*, 1996; Hillson, 1996), although there are variations (Huda and Bowman, 1994). Enamel is first laid down appositionally over the cusps and then secreted over the sides of the teeth, where the striae pass from the amelodentine junction to the surface. Here the overlapping layers, or imbricational enamel, are recognized as perikymata. The method has since been extended to estimate age in juvenile fossil hominids (Bromage and Dean, 1985; Dean *et al.*, 1986, 1993) and Dean and Beynon (1991) have used cross-striation counts, perikymata counts and root formation times to calculate the age of an unknown child from the Spitalfields archaeological collection. They found that incremental markings in the enamel were internally consistent between three different teeth of the same individual. Also, the estimates of average rate of root growth of the three teeth were consistent with each other and with the calculated chronological age of the child. Huda and Bowman (1995) have since used this technique to identify individual juvenile skulls in a sample of commingled remains between 1 and 4 years of age, by correlating them with information on their respective coffin plates. The advantage of this procedure is that it provides a much more accurate age at death estimate than can be obtained with previous mineralization standards. It is also an absolute method of age determination without reference to the growth standards of a particular population. Its disadvantages are that it is destructive of valuable or rare material, requires the facilities of a hard tissue laboratory, experience in technique and in addition, is both expensive and very time consuming. For these reasons, it is unlikely to become routinely used for the ageing of juveniles in samples of skeletal remains, although it could well be applied to an occasional forensic case. Recently, data from sections of permanent anterior crowns have been presented to estimate the timing of linear hypoplasia (Reid and Dean, 2000).

The neonatal line, described independently by Rushton (1933) and Schour (1936), is a pronounced incremental line formed at birth or very soon afterwards. It can be seen on all teeth that start mineralization before birth, that is, all the deciduous teeth and usually at least the mesiobuccal cusp of the first permanent molar. Enamel prisms change direction as they cross the neonatal line and on the postnatal side they appear to be less tightly packed (Whittaker and Richards, 1978). The visualization of the line could be of significance for medicolegal reasons, where it is important to determine if an infant was live-born or stillborn. In practice, the neonatal line can be visualized by light micro-scopy if the child has survived for about 3 weeks after birth, or by electron microscopy, within a day or two after birth (Whittaker and MacDonald, 1989). Change in the normal location of the line in relation to the cervix of the tooth or a double neonatal line may indicate that the child has suffered premature birth or prolonged neonatal disruption of health (Skinner and Dupras, 1993; Huda and Bowman, 1995).

Chemical methods

There have been several attempts to estimate age at death from the teeth by measurement of biochemical norms. For instance, the calcium/phosphorus ratio in peritubular dentine increases significantly with age (Kósa *et al.*, 1990) and the rate of racemization of D and L enantiomers of aspartic acid residues in the collagen of dentine is accurately time-dependent (Whittaker, 1992). Problems such as diagenesis caused by soil organisms have complicated the use of chemical methods thus far, but they provide a potentially interesting field for further investigation.

Conclusions

Detailed reviews of the principles and methods involved in the estimation of juvenile age from dentition can be found in Smith (1991) and Liversidge *et al.* (1998). Recommendations include:

- As many teeth as possible should be aged separately and a mean taken to give an age interval for a stated specific confidence interval.
- If age of attainment data are used, allowance must be made for the fact that any growth stage only becomes evident some time after the event. This means that the child is *older than* the last observed growth event. The type of data adapted for prediction (Smith 1991, Liversidge and Molleson 2004) is likely to estimate age more accurately.
- Teeth at stages of formation that are clearly defined and more easily seen (such as initial cusp formation [C_i], crown complete [Cr_c], initial root cleft formation [Cl_i]) are likely to give more accurate age estimates than subjective fractions of crown or root growth.
- Some knowledge of crown height and root length of the group is prudent if these stages are used in ageing. This can be done by examining fully formed crowns and roots in young adults of the group under study.
- In infancy and early childhood, the atlas of Schour and Massler (1941), Ubelaker (1978) or the chart of Gustafson and Koch (1974) are recom-mended. Standards drawn from radiographic studies are suitable for this age group only if they include very young children from birth.
- For older age groups, selection of the least variable mandibular teeth (Haavikko, 1974) may lead to greater accuracy. These are:

<10 years: M_1, M_2, PM_1, I_1
>10 years: M_2, PM_1, C.

CHAPTER SIX

The Vertebral Column

The vertebral column extends in the midline from the base of the skull above to the pelvis below and then beyond as the rudimentary coccyx (Fig. 6.1). It is a curved, flexible, vertical pillar of bone, formed from a number of individual components (vertebrae) that articulate above and below with each other, thus forming a segmented structure.

Although somewhat variable, there are normally 33 vertebrae in the adult column, of which 24 are true (presacral) and 9 are false. The true vertebrae are

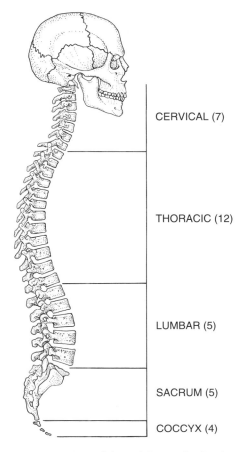

CERVICAL (7)

THORACIC (12)

LUMBAR (5)

SACRUM (5)

COCCYX (4)

Figure 6.1 Lateral view of the adult vertebral column.

to be found in the region of the neck (7 cervical), the chest (12 thoracic) and the small of the back (5 lumbar). The nine false vertebrae occur in two parts in the adult, with the upper five fusing to form the sacrum, which is the central axis of the pelvic girdle, and the remaining four fusing to form the diminutive coccyx.

The **cervical** column extends from the base of the skull and its articulation with the occipital bone above to the articulations with the first thoracic vertebra below at the root of the neck. The **thoracic** column articulates with the last cervical vertebra above and the first lumbar vertebra below and laterally with the paired thoracic ribs. The **lumbar** column extends from the last thoracic vertebra above to the first sacral vertebra below at the lumbosacral angle. The **sacrum** articulates with the last lumbar vertebra above, with the uppermost coccygeal segment below and laterally with the innominates at the sacroiliac articulations to form the pelvic girdle. The **coccygeal** segment of the column is a vestigial structure showing considerable variation in both morphology and number of components and its base articulates with the last sacral vertebra above.

Early development

The earliest stages of the development of the column are considered in Chapter 3. The development of a segmented structure requires a code of patterning to be laid down in the very early stages of development and comparative studies have shown the evolutionary preservation of a so-called 'segmentation clock'. It is widely held that this genetic segmentation mechanism is expressed within the presomitic mesoderm, generating a temporal periodicity that ultimately converts into a spatial periodicity (Pourquie, 2001).

In the 4th week of intra-uterine life, the **sclerotome** develops a central cavity that becomes populated by diffuse core cells. It ruptures on the medial side and cells from its ventromedial wall, along with core cells, migrate towards the notochord anteriorly and the developing neural tube posteriorly (Fig. 6.2).

The ventral portion of the migrating sclerotome surrounds the notochord so that by the end of the 4th week it becomes encased in a continuous investment of mesenchyme. In very general terms this region will go on to develop into the vertebral centrum. The dorsal region of the sclerotome migrates to surround the neural tube and essentially forms the precursor of the neural arch.

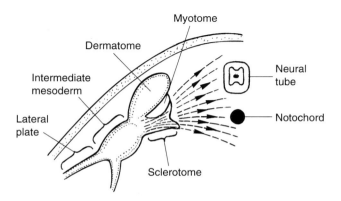

Figure 6.2 Diagrammatic representation of the embryonic migration of the cells of the sclerotome.

Grafting experiments have shown that the normal development of the centrum depends upon the proximity of the notochord (or perhaps more precisely, the perinotochordal cellular sheath – Müller and O'Rahilly, 1994) and, following ablation, the centrum fails to develop (Fleming *et al.*, 2001).

Similarly, for normal development of the neural arches to occur, an inductive signal is required from the neural tube (Campbell *et al.*, 1986; Jacobson and Sater, 1988; Gurdon *et al.*, 1989). If a defect occurs in the early development of the neural tube then failure to close (spinal dysraphism) may result. This neurological failure most commonly occurs at the cranial and caudal neuropores, explaining why the majority of developmental defects in the dorsal part of the column occur at the extremities of the structure. Failure of closure of the cranial neuropore can lead to anencephaly, which is incompatible with prenatal survival and failure of closure of the caudal neuropore can lead to partial or complete sacral agenesis. The ensuing disability is minimized providing the S1 and preferably S2 components develop normally, as the individual may only experience neurological disruption in the lower limbs, although incontinence and impotence are also possible consequences. If sacral agenesis is complete, then the individual will experience more profound lower limb dysfunction in association with the inability to walk or stand due to the loss of the bony stress trajectories to the innominates and thereby the means to physically withstand the transfer of body weight to the ground.

Following a neural tube defect, it appears that the inductive signal is either absent or insufficient to initiate normal development of the neural arches and spina bifida can result. This is a developmental abnormality involving failure of the laminae of one or more neural arches to fuse in the midline. It is important to make the distinction between spina bifida and cleft vertebrae as only the former involves a neural tube defect. Cleft vertebrae are a result of non-union of the bony elements and are not necessarily indicative of a serious congenital neurological defect (Barnes, 1994). True spina bifida will result in the edges of the affected bone being displaced outwards due to the bulging pressure of the underlying neurological tissues. The most innocuous form of this defect is spina bifida occulta where a restricted number of vertebrae are affected and there is an absence of either spinal or meningeal herniation. This most commonly occurs in the lumbosacral region, is often asymptomatic and has a reported incidence of 3–18% in the general population (Shore, 1931; Saluja, 1988). A tuft of hair, a dimple or a small pigmented area on the adjacent skin frequently indicates the underlying location of this defect. Spina bifida cystica occurs where gross deficiencies of the vertebral arch exist or when several vertebrae are affected so that the meninges may protrude through the defect, resulting in a meningocoele. In some cases, the spinal cord itself may protrude beyond the limits of the spinal canal, resulting in the formation of a myelomeningocoele and consequent neurological disturbances are almost inevitable.

Recent clinical research has indicated that there are strong genetic and nutritional influences on the incidence of spina bifida abnormalities. It has been shown that maternal diets low in either folic acid or selenium severely impair zinc metabolism, which is a vital element for normal neural tube development (Zimmerman and Lozzio, 1989; Shelby, 1992). Dietary supplements of folic acid are now regularly recommended to all women attempting to conceive in an effort to reduce the relatively high incidence of spina bifida, particularly in older mothers. In the USA, folic acid is routinely added to grain products such as cereals and breads.

The pattern for the future development of the vertebral column is set during the 3rd and 4th weeks of intra-uterine life, which makes the earliest stage of pregnancy a critical window for teratogenic influences. The complexity of the embryology of the axial skeleton leaves it vulnerable to many potential developmental abnormalities and it is important to realize that these can occur at any stage from the formation of the presomitic mesoderm right through to the eventual ossification of the cartilage anlage.

Chapter 3 considers the earliest stages of development of the central axis and the formation and organization of the somites and the sclerotomes and this should be considered before the later development of this column is considered. There is a traditional resegmentation theory, which states that during migration each segmental sclerotome splits into a smaller and more loosely arranged cranial part and a larger and more densely organized caudal part. This structure then resegments (Tanaka and Uhthoff, 1981; Bagnall *et al.*, 1988) with the caudal part of one sclerotome fusing with the cranial part of the sclerotome segment below, to form an intersegmental structure, which then goes on to develop directly into the segmented precursor of the vertebral column (Fig. 6.3). It is noteworthy that although the future vertebral bodies reputedly develop from a recombined segment of the sclerotome, it is likely that the neural arches, pedicles and costal elements develop almost entirely from the more dense caudal part of each segmental sclerotome (Verbout, 1985; Selleck and Stern, 1991). This may explain why, in the typical adult vertebra, the pedicles that originally arise from the caudal portion of the sclerotome are generally attached towards the upper pole of the vertebra. The surrounding structures, e.g. the muscles, nerves and blood vessels, maintain their original segmental pattern. The seven cervical vertebrae are actually formed from eight cervical sclerotome segments. The cranial portion of the first vertebral segment fuses with the caudal portion of the fourth occipital segment, which is then incorporated into the formation of the base of the skull (Fig. 6.4). This explains why there are eight pairs of cervical spinal nerves and only seven cervical vertebrae. Similarly, it explains why in the cervical region, the spinal nerves exit from the column above the vertebra of the corresponding number, whereas in the remaining regions of the column they exit below the vertebra of the corresponding number. The segmental spinal nerves are then free to exit from the vertebral canal in the space between two adjacent vertebrae to supply

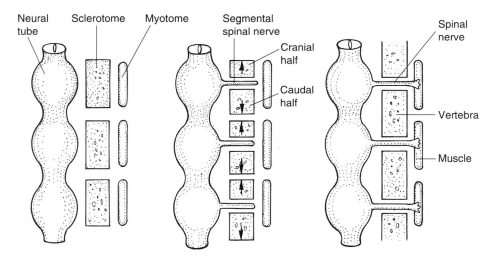

Figure 6.3 Diagrammatic representation of the embryonic recombination of the sclerotome.

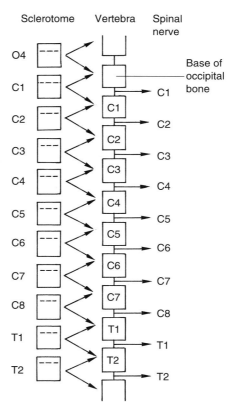

Sclerotome   Vertebra   Spinal
                          nerve

Figure 6.4 Embryonic differentiation of the upper regions of the vertebral column (redrawn after Larsen, 1993).

their appropriate segmental dermatome and myotome as they essentially maintain their original segmental position.

This resegmentation theory has been widely accepted as the mechanism for formation of the vertebral column, but several authors have suggested an alternative approach that is very convincing given the detailed embryological specimens that are illustrated in the Uhthoff text in particular (Baur, 1969; Verbout, 1976; Richenbacher *et al.*, 1982; Dalgleish, 1985; O'Rahilly and Benson, 1985; Müller and O'Rahilly, 1986; Uhthoff 1990a; O'Rahilly and Müller, 1996). It is suggested that the resegmentation theory was based on a fundamental misconception as it represented an incomplete and therefore inexact extrapolation of information that was only seen in the earlier embryological stages. The differentiation between the more densely packed caudal section of a sclerotome and its less densely packed cranial section can be identified in early embryological sections when the sclerotome occupies a more lateral position prior to the onset of medial migration. However, once the cells have reached the midline, these authors consider the differentiation to be non-existent and argued that the proponents of the resegmentation theory had accepted that the observed changes were temporal rather than spatial, and this is where Uhthoff (1990a) believed that the error had been made. He strongly advocated that the changes were both temporal and spatial and that extrapolation of the situation that could be observed when the migrating cells were in the lateral position were incorrectly superimposed on the final definitive vertebral anlage in the midline. Thus, no account had been taken of any drift alterations in the relative positions of the migrating cells and while the vertebral column is indeed formed via a segmental process, there is unlikely to be any true resegmentation of the structure. In agreement with Dalgleish (1985), Müller and O'Rahilly (1994) stated that the centra develop from the perinotochordal territory and not from the sclerotome halves. Rather, they may develop from chondrific centres that originate in the somite-derived tissue surrounding the notochord – the perinotochordal tube.

In summary therefore, their alternative theory proposes that cells spread out from the ventral sclerotome segments to form an essentially unsegmented cellular perinotochordal sheath that surrounds the notochord. Dense and loose zones, separated by a relatively cell-free interzone, eventually form in this sheath with the loose cephalic zone being the precursor of the vertebral centrum and the denser caudal zone being the precursor of the disc. The centra are therefore formed directly from the perichordal sheath. Cells from the dorsal region of the sclerotome and probably from the dense caudal zone will pass medially and develop into the neural arch and associated ribs with the serial segmentation of the arches believed to be dependent on the presence and influence of the spinal ganglia. But the principle difference between the two theories is that the secondary formation, of the ventral aspect of the segmented structure in particular, is not rigidly dependent upon the original sclerotome segmentation.

Whichever theory is correct, the notochord and developing neural tube are enclosed within a mesenchymal template by the 28th intra-uterine day and this represents the blastemal stage of vertebral development. Small lateral mesenchymal condensations (costal processes) arise in association with the lateral surface of the neural arch of all developing vertebrae at this stage. However, it is only in the thoracic region that these will separate from the developing vertebral mass and elongate into ribs, although all costal processes retain the potential to develop independently in any region of the column. This is often seen in the cases of cervical ribs, which generally occur in association with C7 but can also be found less frequently associated with C6 and C5. Lumbar ribs are less common but when they do arise it is usually in association with the first lumbar vertebra.

During the 6th week of intra-uterine life, up to six chondrification centres may appear in the mesenchymal template (Fig. 6.5a). Typically, there is one centre for each lateral half of the centrum, but these will fuse together shortly after formation to form a single centre. In this region, the notochord becomes increasingly restricted and regresses until it eventually disappears. However, in the space between developing vertebrae, the notochord expands, forming the nucleus pulposus of the future intervertebral disc (Peacock, 1951) (Fig. 6.6). If one of these chondrification centres fails to develop, then the pathological conditions of either hemi- or butterfly vertebrae may arise, which manifest as a congenital scoliosis.

After the 6th month of prenatal life, the notochordal cells within the nucleus pulposus undergo mucoid degeneration and are replaced by cells from the inner aspect of the annulus fibrosus. This degeneration continues until the second decade of life, by which time all the true notochordal cells have disappeared. Persistence of notochordal tissue results in 'notochordal remnants' that may subsequently develop into a chordoma, a slow-growing neoplasm most frequently located in either the basi-occiput or in the lumbosacral region. In addition, failure of proper regression of the notochord may facilitate the formation of Schmorl's nodes by creating a defect in the cartilaginous end-plate through which intervertebral disc material may prolapse into the vertebral

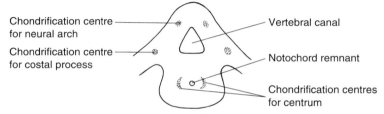

Chondrification centre for neural arch

Chondrification centre for costal process

Vertebral canal

Notochord remnant

Chondrification centres for centrum

(a) Blastemal stage with chondrification centres – approx. 6 prenatal weeks

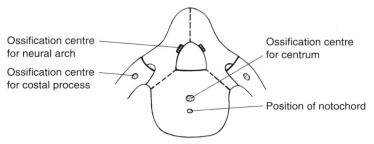

Ossification centre for neural arch

Ossification centre for costal process

Ossification centre for centrum

Position of notochord

(b) Cartilaginous stage with primary centres of ossification – approx. 11-12 prenatal weeks

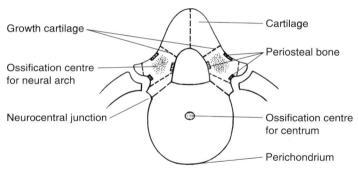

Growth cartilage

Ossification centre for neural arch

Neurocentral junction

Cartilage

Periosteal bone

Ossification centre for centrum

Perichondrium

(c) Ossification centres at approx. 13-14 prenatal weeks
(redrawn after Chandraraj and Briggs, 1991)

Figure 6.5 The development of the vertebral anlage: (a) blastemal stage – approximately 6 prenatal weeks; (b) cartilaginous stage – approximately 11–12 prenatal weeks; (c) ossification – approximately 13–14 prenatal weeks (redrawn after Chandraraj and Briggs, 1991).

body. It is believed that these nodes may give rise to congenitally weak spots in the cartilaginous end-plates, which may lead to other vertebral orthopaedic conditions and may in fact be the first indicators of degenerative disc disease. Some authors believe that Schmorl's nodes may develop as a post-traumatic condition (Kornberg, 1988), or indeed as a result of vascular channel regression, resulting in weak spots or scars into which the disc can herniate (Harris and MacNab, 1954; Chandraraj *et al.*, 1998).

Each half of the cartilaginous neural arch develops from a single centre, which commences chondrification at around 6 prenatal weeks (Fig 6.5a). These will eventually spread into the regions of the transverse and articular processes and anteriorly into the pedicles. A further two chondrification centres appear at the junctions between the centrum and the neural arch and by

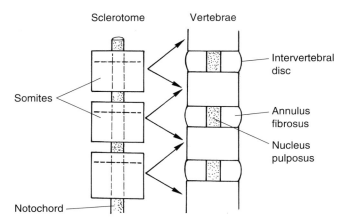

Figure 6.6 The embryological fate of the notochord (redrawn after Larsen, 1993).

lateral extension form the costal elements in the thoracic region and contribute to the transverse processes in the other regions of the column (Maat *et al.*, 1996). By expansion of all the chondrification centres, a solid cartilaginous vertebral unit is formed when chondrific fusion finally occurs at the spinous process in the 4th prenatal month. Defects in this normal sequence of events can result in posterior arch anomalies, which can occur on either an isolated basis or may be related to defects in adjacent bone formation. For example, the 'absent pedicle complex' results from a failure of development and formation of the more ventral part of the chondrification centre of the neural arch at 6 prenatal weeks (Schwartz *et al.*, 1982). This can be explained by the necessity to achieve a critical size or mass, which can override basic phylogenetic and ontogenetic templates (see Chapter 2).

When ossification does commence at around 10 weeks, thoracic ribs will separate from the neural arches through the development of costovertebral joints (Fig. 6.5b) while in the cervical, lumbar and sacral regions the costal processes will maintain continuity with the transverse processes in particular (Tsou *et al.*, 1980). The type of vertebra (cervical, thoracic, etc.) is established very early on in development and so it is perhaps not surprising to find that if a portion of thoracic somites is transplanted into the cervical region, ribs will still develop in this location (Kieny *et al.*, 1972; Goldstein and Kalcheim, 1992).

More detailed information on the embryonic and fetal development of the vertebral column can be found in Wyburn (1944), Sensenig (1949), Verbout (1985), Töndury and Theiler (1990), Christ and Wilting (1992) and O'Rahilly and Müller (2001).

A discussion on the development of the vertebral column would not be complete without a brief mention of *Hox* genes, which have revolutionized the understanding of developmental processes (Burke *et al.*, 1995). A *Hox* axial code has been identified that appears to specify developmental position or regional identity along the craniocaudal axis. It is believed that each *Hox* gene represents an overlapping domain and as such provides specific positional information. Kessel and Gruss (1991) suggested that each individual vertebra might be based upon a unique *Hox* code and so its ultimate form will be dependent upon the successful expression of that code (Johnson and O'Higgins, 1996). It is clear that this rapidly expanding field of research will continue to dominate the field of vertebrate development and direct the course of experimental research in the future. A simple and clear discussion of homeo-box genes can be found in Weiss et al. (1998).

Ossification

Primary centres
The ossification of the cartilaginous anlage begins at the end of the 2nd pre-natal month. While it is agreed that a single ossification centre develops for each half of the neural arch, the situation is more contentious for the centrum. Some authors have stated that there is a single ossification centre (Birkner, 1978; Ogden, 1979) while others maintain that there are paired centres, one anterior and one posterior, that fuse shortly after formation (Cohen et al., 1956; Hollinshead, 1965; Fazekas and Kósa, 1978). However, Tanaka and Uhthoff (1983) have shown that when two ossification centres do arise, they are always connected by a bony bridge, which carries a blood vessel. Therefore, it can be said that each typical vertebra is formed from at least three and in some instances possibly four separate primary centres of ossification (Fig. 6.5c). While there are regional and individual bone variations in the patterns and timings of ossification, there are some basic principles that apply to the centra and the neural arches in general.

Centra
The ossification of the centrum is initiated dorsal to the relative position of the notochord within the cartilaginous anlage and so represents true endochondral ossification (Fig. 6.5c). This primary centre first appears in the lower thoracic and upper lumbar regions (T10–L1) between the 9th and 10th prenatal weeks (Fig. 6.7). Ossification in the centra progresses in a bi-directional pattern, appearing at successively higher and lower levels, reaching the fifth lumbar vertebra by the end of the 3rd prenatal month, and the second cervical vertebra certainly by the end of the 4th month.

The morphology and development of the juvenile centrum is heavily influ-enced by its profuse vascular supply (Fig. 6.8) (Ratcliffe, 1981, 1982). According to Skawina et al. (1997) ossification commences in the region of the notochord remnants and they suggested that the notochordal cells contain an angiogenic-inhibiting factor that delays vascular penetration into this region. As a result, a vertebral centrum from the first trimester of pregnancy shows an axial avas-cular area around the notochord region, resulting in a ring-shaped area of ossification. They proposed that if the vascular penetration into this area was abnormally delayed then it could give rise to congenital malformations, such as a persistent notochordal canal or even cleft vertebral bodies (Hensinger and MacEwan, 1975). The notochord essentially disappears by the end of the first trimester, when the blood vessels then advance centrifugally to increase the size of the centre and centripetally to invade the previously avascular region. Each centre is normally supplied by paired (i.e. segmental) posterior (nutrient) arteries accompanied by a venous network (Willis, 1949; Ferguson, 1950; Crock et al., 1973). Ratcliffe (1982) noted that the arterial supply to the centrum undergoes fundamental changes throughout growth. He noted that the extensive intra-osseous arterial anastomotic networks found in the centra of the infant and young child started to reduce in number around 7 years of age and continued to do so until approximately 15 years. By adolescence, he found that the blood supply to the vertebral body was zoned into isolated regional

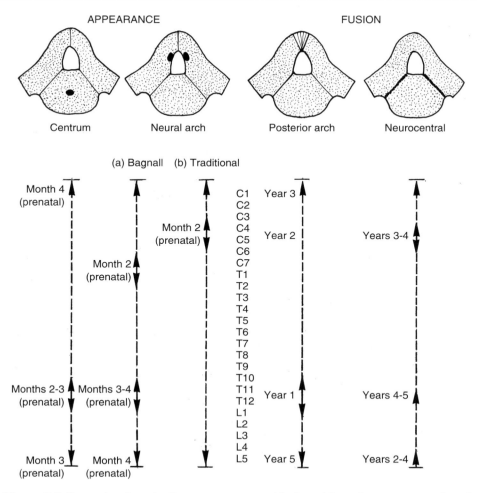

Figure 6.7 General pattern for the appearance and fusion of the primary centres of ossification in the presacral vertebrae.

compartments and felt that this might serve to explain the distribution of angiogenic-related osseous pathological conditions.

In general terms the vertebral bodies receive their arterial supply from a rich arborescent plexus that courses the length of the column and is fed by segmental arteries (Harris and Jones, 1956; Guida *et al.*, 1969; Brookes and Revell, 1998). Each segmental artery gives off a number of anterior central branches that penetrate the anterior and lateral surfaces of the centrum (Rothman and Simeone, 1975). The anterior central branches are largest on the anterior aspect of the centrum, where they penetrate into the core of the bone in the embryological segmental position. These prominent vascular channels are obvious in the middle of the anterior surface of the juvenile centrum (Fig. 6.9a), although they will eventually reduce in size as a layer of compact bone is laid down on this surface and by puberty there is little evidence of the anterior vascular foramina. These vascular channels are most prominent on the anterior surfaces of the thoracic vertebrae, possibly due to the size of the posterior intercostal arteries. At the level of the transverse process, the segmental artery bifurcates into a ventral and a dorsal branch. The dorsal branch gives off the spinal artery, which passes medially across the pedicle before

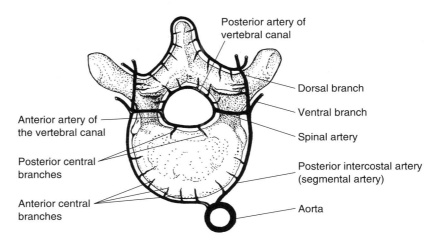

Figure 6.8 The arterial supply of a typical adult vertebra.

bifurcating into the anterior and posterior arteries of the vertebral canal. The anterior artery courses along the posterior surface of the centrum and sends perforating posterior central arteries into the dorsal surface of the centrum. Unlike the anterior channels, these posterior vascular foramina tend to persist even into adulthood as the basivertebral foramina, which transmit the basivertebral veins to the anterior internal vertebral veins. As the anterior and posterior central perforating arteries pass across the superior and inferior surfaces of the centrum they form vascular radiating channels, which produce the characteristic billowed appearance of both the juvenile centrum and later the vertebral body (Donisch and Trapp, 1971) (Fig. 6.9c). It is only when the annular epiphyses of the body have fused that these furrows are no longer visible. It is important to remember at this stage that the adult vertebral

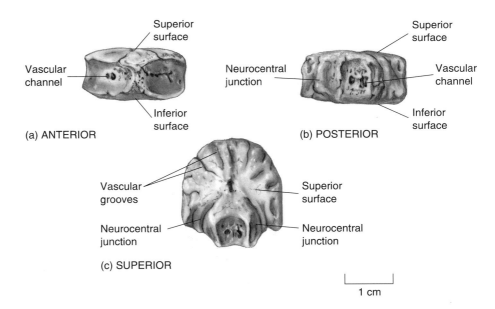

Figure 6.9 A typical juvenile vertebral centrum (T8 from a child of approximately 4 years).

body is derived from the juvenile centrum plus a small portion of the neural arch on each side. Thus, the adult vertebral body equates to more than the juvenile centrum and so in developmental terms it is incorrect to use the term 'vertebral body' as the term 'centrum' is more appropriate (MacLaughlin and Oldale, 1992).

Agenesis of the centrum is rare and can result either from a disruption to the ventral part of the migrating sclerotome, the failure of chondrification or ossification centres to appear or develop, or indeed through a deficiency in the vascular supply (Tsou et al., 1980). In this situation, the neural arch elements may continue to develop normally and the pedicles may fuse anterior to the spinal cord resulting in a congenital kyphosis (Tsou et al., 1980). If untreated, aplasia of the centrum leads to rapidly progressive spinal deformity and neurological defects (Lorenzo et al., 1983).

Neural arches

Ossification of the neural arches commences on the inner surface of each hemiarch (Fig. 6.5b) as a perichondral lamella from which osteogenesis extends into the cartilage anlage (Richenbacher et al., 1982). Technically therefore, the neural arches initially form via intramembranous perichondral ossification. Periosteal lamellar bone is first observed on the internal (canal) surface of an arch around week 12. By week 13, periosteal bone appears on the external (laminar and pedicular) surface, as the zone of hypertrophying cartilage has extended across the arch. Periosteal vessels then invade the calcifying mass and introduce osteogenic cells, which begin to lay down spicules of bone. The ossification centre eventually resembles a curved growth zone with three separate growth cartilages – one for the region of the pedicle, one for the lamina/spinous process and one for the transverse process (Fig. 6.5c). Ossification and subsequent growth of the neural arch therefore occurs centripetally (Chandraraj and Briggs, 1991).

This peripheral initiation of ossification supports the theory by Bagnall et al. (1977b) that the stimulus for the commencement of ossification in the neural arches is the attachment of muscles involved in early prenatal reflexes. They proposed that these neurological reflexes initiated muscle contraction, thereby stimulating bone development on the perichondral surface of the cartilage template at the site of the muscle attachment. They found that primary centres of ossification for the neural arches first appeared in the lower cervical and upper thoracic regions in the 2nd prenatal month and then spread upwards and downwards in a fairly orderly fashion towards the mid-thoracic region (Fig. 6.7). Bagnall et al. (1977b) proposed that this initiation of ossification was concomitant with the head jerk reflex (gasp reflex) seen in the fetus around week 10. By the 12th week, a second group of centres appeared in the lower thoracic and upper lumbar regions, spreading up towards the mid-thoracic and down to the lower lumbar and sacral regions in a fairly ordered sequence, with the neural arches of L5 being the last to develop towards the end of the 4th month. Bagnall et al. (1977b) proposed that the initiation for this second group of ossification centres arose again from muscle contraction associated with reflex movements in the fetal lower limbs. Thus, they suggested that both the initiation and the mode of ossification differed between the centra and the neural arches and that they therefore developed independently of each other, explaining why there is no apparent integrated pattern of timing of ossification (Fig. 6.7). Hill (1992) also reported that early embryonic and fetal movements are vital to align the trabeculae within bones.

The more widely held and traditional view of ossification in the neural arches (Fig. 6.7) is that it commences in the cervical region in the 2nd prenatal month and is essentially monodirectional in a craniocaudal sequence (Mall, 1906; Fawcett, 1907; Noback and Robertson, 1951; Fazekas and Kósa, 1978; Ogden, 1979; Budorick et al., 1991; Bareggi et al., 1993). A third theory is that neural arch ossification appears at three distinct locations and then each progresses independently in a cranial and caudal direction. Ford et al. (1982) stated that the first group to appear was in the lower cervical and upper thoracic regions, followed by a second group in the upper cervical region and finally by a third group in the lower thoracic and upper lumbar region.

In an attempt to get away from this controversy of different developmental sequences, Bareggi et al. (1994b) simply correlated the total number of centres present in a column and related this to fetal crown–rump measurements. They found that this offered a simple and reliable method for establishing the maturity of a fetus.

Regardless of which of the developmental sequence theories is accepted, it is clear that all three primary vertebral centres are present in all presacral vertebrae, certainly by the end of the 4th prenatal month, if not earlier (Budorick et al., 1991). It is also true that in the cervical region, the ossification centres for the neural arches are present before the centra, whereas in the lower thoracic and upper lumbar regions, the centra may appear before the neural arches. In the upper to mid-thoracic regions the primary ossification centres for the centra and neural arches probably appear simultaneously (Fig. 6.7). Thus, in regional terms the maturation of the centra parallels the maturation of the notochord, while the pattern of maturation in the vertebral arches parallels that of the somites and therefore the peripheral nervous system (Sperber, 1989; Kjær et al., 1993). This serves to reinforce Bagnall's theory of independent development through the possibility of differing embryological origins and influences.

Fusion of neural arches

During the first year of postnatal life, the neural arches commence fusion posteriorly at the spinous process (Fig. 6.7). This occurs initially in the lower thoracic and upper lumbar regions in the latter part of the first year and progresses in a systematic cranial and caudal direction so that the cervical arches may not fuse until the beginning of the second year and the lowest lumbar may not fuse until the end of the 5th year. Therefore, in any individual below the age of 6 years some degree of non-fusion of the primary elements of the presacral vertebral spinous processes should be expected. The histological make-up of this junction is not, however, simply a plug of mesenchyme or cartilage, but is in fact a true growth plate which plays an integral part in the overall co-ordinated increase in size of the developing vertebra to accommodate early neurological maturation (Maat et al., 1996).

Spondylolysis is defined as a separation in the neural arch, excluding that which can occur in the midline as a result of failure of the laminae to unite at the spinous process (Merbs, 1996). Such separation usually occurs through the isthmus separating the superior from the inferior articular facets (pars interarticularis). This is a uniquely human condition as its incidence is closely related to the development of the lumbar curvature (Letts et al., 1986).

Neurocentral fusion

Fusion between the primary centres of the neural arches and the centra occurs ventral to the pedicles at the neurocentral junction between 2 and 5 years of age. The adult vertebral body is formed from the centrum and the paired anterior extensions (boutons) of the pedicles. It is important to remember that the head of the costal process only ever articulates with the lateral surfaces of these boutons and never directly with the centrum (Fig. 6.10).

Histologically, the growth plate at the neurocentral junction (epiphysis arcus vertebrae) clearly displays growth columns on both its anterior and posterior aspects and therefore is responsible for contributing not only to growth in the neural arch but also in the centrum (Maat *et al.*, 1996). Even when the neurocentral junctions have begun to fuse, their position remains clearly marked externally by a crescentic impression whose concavity is directed dorsolaterally on both the cranial and caudal aspects of the body. Thus, the pedicular bouton of the neural arch element forms a wedge that extends across the full height of the future vertebral body, with its upper and lower boundaries being limited by the cranial and caudal annular rings respectively. The morphology of this wedge has been likened, appropriately, to a carpenter's dovetail joint (Maat *et al.*, 1996). Evidence of the neurocentral junction is maintained throughout adult life and persists as a permanent bilateral plate of bone inside the dorsolateral region of every adult vertebral body that is not completely obliterated by advanced age-related remodelling. The persistence of this dense plate of bone makes this region of a vertebra extremely suitable for the strategic positioning of pedicular screws in spinal surgery (Maat *et al.*, 1996). It is also interesting to note that vertebral fracture lines seem to avoid the region of the neurocentral junction in the adult partly explaining the typical pattern seen in traumatic burst fractures of a vertebra (Panjabi *et al.*, 1994).

Neurocentral fusion tends to occur first in the lumbar region, followed closely by the cervical segment, with the thoracic vertebrae generally being the last to close. It is perhaps for this reason that the crescentic impressions of this junction are most frequently seen in the thoracic region of the juvenile column as they tend to persist longer in this area. It is likely that all neurocentral junctions will be closed by the fifth and certainly the sixth year, although the impressions will still be visible for some considerable time thereafter.

Premature osseous fusion, either anteriorly at the neurocentral junctions or posteriorly at the spinous process, would preclude further canal widening and thus impair proper diametric increase of the canal. Improperly timed fusion may be the mechanism of spinal stenosis in conditions such as achondroplasia (Ogden, 1979).

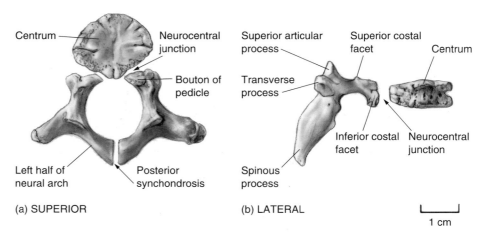

(a) SUPERIOR   (b) LATERAL   1 cm

Figure 6.10 A typical thoracic vertebra from a child of approximately 1.5 years.

Cervical vertebrae

The embryological development of the first two cervical vertebrae is complicated and sufficiently different from that of the more typical vertebrae to require some further detailed discussion (Fig. 6.11).

The caudal part of the fourth occipital sclerotome fuses with the cranial part of the first cervical sclerotome segment to form the proatlas (zoological term). In some lower vertebrates this remains a separate bone located between the occipital bone above and the first cervical vertebra below, but in man it is probably assimilated into the occipital condyles and the apex (ossiculum terminale) of the odontoid process of the axis (Shapiro and Robinson, 1976a; Müller and O'Rahilly, 1994). The caudal part of the first cervical sclerotome segment forms the lateral masses and anterior and posterior arches of the atlas (O'Rahilly *et al.*, 1983). The remainder of the dens develops from the fusion of the caudal part of the first cervical segment with the cranial part of the second cervical sclerotome. The true centrum of the axis and its neural arch is then formed from the fusion of the caudal part of the second cervical sclerotome segment with the cranial part of the third cervical sclerotome. Müller and O'Rahilly (1994) identified three complete centra that develop in the region of the atlanto-axial region, although they are related to only 2.5 sclerotomes and two neural arches. They concluded that these three centra, which they termed the 'xyz' complex, belong ontogenetically to the axis so that the atlas does not appear to possess a central element.

David *et al.* (1998) reported that chondrification commenced in the lateral masses of the atlas around day 45, by which time the embryonic centrum of C1 had already become detached. The anterior tubercle of C1 develops from a separate chondrification centre around 50–53 days, which coincides with chondrification of the anterior arch. The intervertebral foramina of C1 and C2 are simply grooves by day 45 but have converted into foramina by day 58. At day 45, the odontoid process is simply represented by the embryonic centra of C1 and C2, but by day 58 it is well developed and extends above the level of C1 and actually reaches into the foramen magnum, thereby forming the so-called 'third occipital condyle' (Müller and O'Rahilly, 1980; O'Rahilly *et al.*, 1983).

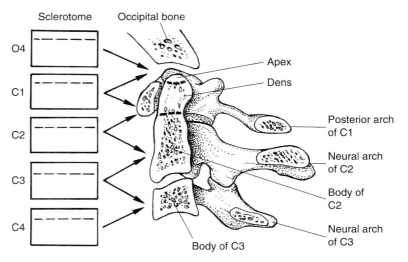

Figure 6.11 Embryological differentiation of the upper cervical vertebrae.

There is some evidence that, in phylogenetic terms, the craniovertebral junction moves caudally as vertebrae are assimilated into the posterior segment of the skull. This is therefore a phylogenetically inconstant region of the column and, given the complexity of its embryological derivation, it is not surprising that a relatively high incidence of congenital and acquired abnormalities is seen in this region.

It is generally recognized that the **atlas** ossifies from three primary centres of ossification (Fig. 6.12) and is recognizable in isolation from the 4th prenatal month. A centre appears for each of the lateral masses, posterior to the articular pillar, in the 7th week of intra-uterine life. These centres increase in size and form the majority of the upper and all of the lower synovial articular facets (Castellana and Kósa, 1999). Ossification spreads backwards from these primary centres to form the two halves of the posterior arch and laterally to form the thick posterior bar of the transverse process (Fig. 6.13a). It has been reported that in approximately 2% of cases in the second year of life, a separate ossification centre may arise which forms the posterior tubercle (Connor *et al.*, 2001).

At birth, the atlas is represented by two bony masses, which display larger concave articular facets on their upper surface (Fig. 6.13a) and smaller flatter articular facets on their lower surface (Fig. 6.13b). A relatively large nutrient foramen can usually be found on the inferior surface at the junction between the limits of the inferior articular facet and the transverse process. The groove for the vertebral artery is present behind the superior articular facet and the posterior arches are curved towards the midline. The anterior bar is not present at this stage and the superior articular facet may look somewhat foreshortened (at the neurocentral junction), as the remainder of the surface will form from the anterior centre of ossification. At this stage, the transverse process is only represented by a thick posterior bar, but this will eventually fuse with a thinner anterior bar, which develops from the ventrolateral aspect of the articular pillar between the third and fourth years (Fig. 6.13c). It is clear that the posterior tubercle is formed from the thick posterior bar, as fusion with the anterior bar, to complete the foramen transversarium, occurs anterior to the posterior tubercle. Thus, in the atlas, the posterior tubercle represents the end of the true transverse process. The foramina transversaria are therefore formed by the fusion of the anterior and posterior bars as they pass around the ascending position of the vertebral artery. The foramina are usually near to

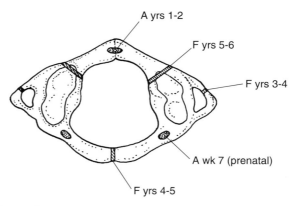

Figure 6.12 Times of appearance (A) and fusion (F) of the primary centres of ossification of the atlas.

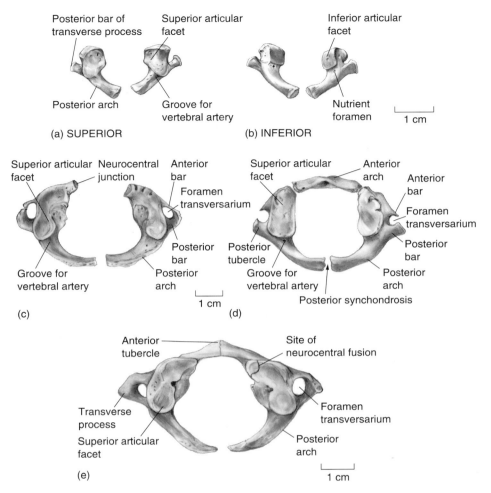

Posterior bar of transverse process

Superior articular facet

Inferior articular facet

Posterior arch

Groove for vertebral artery

Nutrient foramen

1 cm

(a) SUPERIOR

(b) INFERIOR

Superior articular facet

Neurocentral junction

Anterior bar

Foramen transversarium

Groove for vertebral artery

Posterior arch

Posterior bar

1 cm

(c)

Superior articular facet

Anterior arch

Anterior bar

Foramen transversarium

Posterior tubercle

Groove for vertebral artery

Posterior bar

Posterior arch

Posterior synchondrosis

(d)

Anterior tubercle

Site of neurocentral fusion

Transverse process

Superior articular facet

Foramen transversarium

Posterior arch

1 cm

(e)

Figure 6.13 The development of the atlas: (a) perinatal superior surface; (b) perinatal inferior surface; (c) male aged 3 years 4 months; (d) child aged between 2 and 3 years; (e) spina bifida atlantis – female aged 8 years 7 months.

completion by years 3–4. Occasionally, the foramen transversarium of the atlas may be absent or sufficiently rudimentary to obviously exclude the passage of the vertebral artery (Vasudeva and Kumar, 1995). Since the presence of the vertebral vessels are an important factor in the genesis of the foramen, a variation in its course will influence the presence/absence and indeed the form, of the foramen transversarium. Therefore, if the foramen is not going to develop, this will be apparent by 3 years of age, if not earlier.

The morphology of the atlas remains virtually unchanged for the first year following birth, with the major growth emphasis being placed on an increase in overall size. In the first or second year, ossification commences in the cartilaginous mass of the anterior arch either as a single centre, paired centres, multifocal nodules or from ossification bars that spread directly from the lateral masses (Fig. 6.14), although the most common form arises from a single separate centre. As a result, the pattern of fusion in the anterior arch will depend upon the manner in which it originally ossified. A separate anterior arch of the atlas is probably identifiable at 3–4 years of age. It appears as a short bar of bone that has a downward-projecting tubercle on its anterior sur-

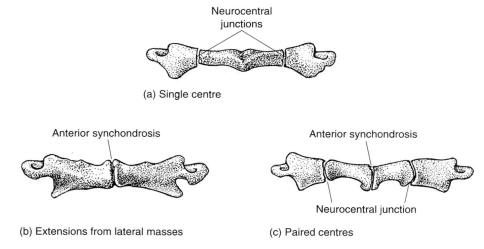

Figure 6.14 Variation in the mode of development of the anterior arch of the atlas.

face (for the attachment of the anterior longitudinal ligament) and a smooth articular facet on its posterior surface for articulation with ventral aspect of the dens (Fig. 6.13d). It is likely that this centre arises via intramembranous perichondral ossification in response to the pull of the anterior longitudinal ligament and additional evidence for this mode of ossification arises from the variant where the anterior bar is formed directly from a continuation of the lateral masses.

The posterior arch usually fuses in the fourth or even fifth year, although it is not unusual for it to remain open even in the adult (Fig. 6.13e). Non-union of the posterior arch (spina bifida atlantis) is not an uncommon asymptomatic anomaly and has a reported incidence of around 1% (Motateanu *et al.*, 1991).

The anterior (effectively neurocentral) junctions may not close until the fifth or sixth year at the earliest (Fig. 6.12). The line of union between the anterior arch and a lateral mass passes across the anterior aspect of the superior articular facet, thereby mimicking the pattern of fusion seen in the occipital condyles (see Chapter 4) but very different from the pattern seen throughout the remainder of the column where the superior articular facet forms entirely within the neural arch component. However, it should be noted that the pattern is similar to that seen for the formation of a vertebral body where the centrum articulates with bouton thereby forming the future adult articular surface of the vertebral body. It has been suggested that the large kidney shape of the superior articular facets of the atlas, which not infrequently present as two separate articular areas, are represented by a fusion between a more dorsally located facet (equivalent to the superior articular facet of other vertebrae) and a more ventrally located facet (equivalent to the anterior extensions of the pedicular bouton in other vertebrae). This fusion of articular areas suggests that there is no true pedicular boundary to the foramen transversarium as is seen in C3 through to C7. An almost identical situation is seen for the axis and it is not until the articulation between the inferior facet of C2 and the superior one of C3 is reached that the characteristic vertical pillar of synovial articulations commences. It is clear therefore that whilst a basic pattern of vertebral morphology is retained in these two uppermost vertebrae there has been extensive modification to allow adaptation to the specific functional requirements of the region.

Endochondral growth occurs prior to fusion at all junctions, ensuring an overall integrated expansion of the vertebral canal as the three ossified units grow away from each other (Maat et al., 1996). C1 reaches close to its final adult size by 4–6 years of age, after which there is little increase in the width of the vertebral canal, only a growth in the overall robusticity of its bony limits to facilitate increased muscle mass attachment (Tulsi, 1971; Ogden, 1984b). This early limitation on the size of the vertebral canal is a clear indication of the well-documented precocious maturation of the human central nervous system.

Hypoplasia of the atlas with a complete posterior arch is rare and seems to occur predominantly in male Asians and most display myelopathic symptoms usually as a result of atlal stenosis. It is thought that it may arise through premature fusion of either the neurocentral or the posterior cartilaginous synchondroses (May et al., 2001; Urasaki et al. 2001).

The occipito-atlanto-axial region is both a phylogenetically and ontogenetically inconstant region of the axial skeleton. Its embryological development is complex and gives rise to a high incidence of congenital and acquired abnormalities. Occipitalization or assimilation of the atlas occurs as a result of the maldevelopment of the craniovertebral junction from an incomplete segmentation of the first cervical sclerotome segment during the early embryonic period. The fusion between the occipital bone and the atlas may be localized or extensive and it can be uni- or bilateral (Green, 1930; Nayak, 1931; Pate, 1936; Stratemeier and Jensen, 1980; Kalla et al., 1989). In the majority of cases, the fusion is localized to the region of the atlanto-occipital joint (McRae and Barnum, 1953; Black and Scheuer, 1996a). Around 10% of cases of assimilation of the atlas are asymptomatic, but it can present with weakness or ataxia of the lower limbs, numbness or pain in the extremities and a dull ache in the upper neck and occipital region (Malhotra and Leeds, 1984). These symptoms are thought to arise following the abnormally high position of the dens in relation to the medulla oblongata. Incomplete incorporation or failure of segmentation of the last occipital and C1 sclerotomes leads to a spectrum of fusional anomalies and accessory structures, many of which are asymptomatic.

A caudal shift in the position of the atlanto-occipital demarcation, causing an assimilation of the atlas into the occipital bone, is more common than a cranial shift, which results in an occipital vertebra (see Chapter 4). However, this phenomenon of cranial–caudal border shifting is not clearly understood, but it is thought that the cause may lie more with the neural arch components of these transitional vertebrae, rather than with the centra. As the neural arches develop from the more dense caudal part of the sclerotome, it may be that the formation of the sclerotomic fissure is responsible for the delay in proper segmentation between two adjacent regions.

The **axis** ossifies from five primary centres of ossification (Fig. 6.15) – one for each half of the neural arch, one for the true centrum of the axis, and one for each half of the body of the dens. In keeping with the prevailing pattern of ossification in the cervical region, the centres of ossification for the neural arches appear before the centra (between 7 and 8 weeks of intra-uterine life). In each half, the ossification centre appears dorsal to the articular pillar and a nutrient foramen generally persists in this region on the inferior surface, posterior to the inferior articular facet. Ossification spreads backwards into the laminae and anteriorly to the neurocentral junction initially via perichondral ossification. As with the atlas, the first part of the foramen transversarium to form is the posterior boundary and this is represented in the perinatal axis by a small, laterally projecting spicule of bone, which is considerably more gracile than that seen in the atlas (Fig. 6.16a). As with the atlas, the posterior tubercle

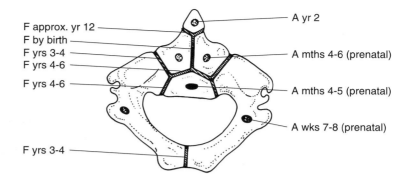

F approx. yr 12
F by birth
F yrs 3-4
F yrs 4-6
F yrs 4-6

A yr 2
A mths 4-6 (prenatal)
A mths 4-5 (prenatal)
A wks 7-8 (prenatal)

F yrs 3-4

Figure 6.15 Times of appearance (A) and fusion (F) of the primary ossification centres of the axis.

is present at an early stage of development and is therefore unlikely to be costal in origin. Even from an early age, the neural arches are robust compared with the other cervical arches and end in a slightly bulbous terminal area that is deflected laterally to form the precursor of the bifid spinous process seen in the adult. Only the lateral two-thirds of the superior articular facet is formed from

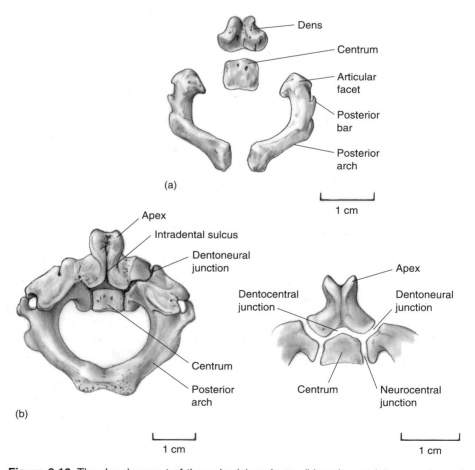

Dens
Centrum
Articular facet
Posterior bar
Posterior arch

(a)

1 cm

Apex
Intradental sulcus
Dentoneural junction

Apex
Dentocentral junction
Dentoneural junction

Centrum
Posterior arch

Centrum
Neurocentral junction

(b)

1 cm

1 cm

Figure 6.16 The development of the axis: (a) perinate; (b) male aged 3 years 4 months.

the neural arch component, as the remainder will be formed when the odontoid process fuses at the dentoneural synchondrosis (note the similarities between the pattern of formation of the superior articular process of C1 above and that of the occipital bone in Chapter 4).

The true centrum of the axis commences ossification from a single endochondral centre between the 4th and 5th months of intra-uterine life (Wollin, 1963; Sherk and Nicholson, 1969). Around the same time, two laterally placed ossification centres appear in the odontoid process, which rapidly coalesce so that the intradental synchondrosis fuses, certainly by the time of birth and possibly as early as 7 or 8 months *in utero*, to form the characteristic forked appearance of the upper aspect of the juvenile dens (Freiberger *et al.*, 1965; Kline, 1966; Michaels *et al.*, 1969; Rezaian, 1974; Juhl and Seerup, 1983; Ogden, 1984c).

Although the neural components of the axis can be identified in isolation from approximately 4–5 prenatal months, the centres for the centrum and the dens are only clearly recognizable towards the end of prenatal life and realistically around the time of birth. The perinatal dens is slightly pyramidal in shape with a broader base that passes up towards a forked apex (Fig. 6.16a). The axial centrum is very similar in morphology to all other cervical centra except that it has a horizontal superior surface that is the same size as the horizontal inferior surface and is therefore not the characteristic wedge-shape of the lower cervical vertebrae (see below). In addition, it is the largest of the cervical centra in all dimensions. Therefore, the perinatal axis presents as four separate bones, each of which is theoretically identifiable in isolation from an early age.

A longitudinal midline (intradental) sulcus is found on the posterior surface of the dens and this persists certainly until 3 or 4 years of age (Fig. 6.16b), when it begins to fill in, initially from below, concomitant with the period of development for the ossiculum terminale (see below). A posteriorly tilted dens can be detected, particularly on radiographs, and it is thought that this arises due to uncoordinated growth on the anterior and posterior aspects of the dens (Swischuk *et al.*, 1979).

The posterior synchondrosis between the neural arches, fuses between 3 and 4 years of age (Fig. 6.16b) and at approximately the same time, the dens is fusing laterally to the neural arches at the dentoneural synchondrosis. This fusion line passes across the superior articular facet, so that the medial one-third of the facet is formed by the dens and the lateral two-thirds by the neural arch (keeping in continuity with the location seen in both C1 and the occipital bone). The inferior articular facet is formed entirely within the neural arch component. This fusion of the anterior and posterior elements effectively halts any further substantial growth in the dimensions of the vertebral canal, apart from minor areas of continued subperiosteal remodelling. As with the atlas, this precocious fusion again clearly displays the early maturation of the central nervous system. Therefore, between 3 and 4 years of age, the axis may be represented by only two bony components (Fig. 6.16b). The larger element is formed from the fusion of the neural arches with the dens and the smaller element represents the true centrum of the axis.

At this stage, the transverse processes, and therefore the foramina transversaria, are near to completion. The posterior bar of the transverse process extends anterolaterally from the laminar section of the neural arch element, while the more slender anterior bar is formed from a posterolateral outgrowth from the superior articular region. Between the ages of 3 and 5 years, the foramina transversaria will be completed by fusion of the anterior and posterior bars. In this way, the medial boundary of the foramen transversarium of the axis is formed directly by the lateral border of the superior articular facet (see C1 above).

The dentocentral junction and the paired neurocentral junctions fuse between 4 and 6 years of age (Rezaian, 1974; Dyck, 1978). All lines of fusion usually disappear by 9–10 years, although a small horizontal crevice may remain for quite some time in the region of the posterior dentocentral junction, as this is generally the last region to complete fusion (Fullenlove, 1954). It is thought that this might prove to be a site of potential weakness if there is trauma to this region.

At approximately 2 years of age, a small ossific nodule (ossiculum terminale) appears in the cartilage plug (chondrum terminale) that fills the apical cleft (Freiberger *et al.*, 1965; Dyck, 1978). This nodule increases in size and eventually fuses with the 'v'-shaped apex of the dens at around 12 years of age (Fig. 6.15). Therefore, a forked apex to the axis is usually indicative of an age younger than 12 years. However, the ossiculum may persist as a separate ossicle in one of every 200 cases (Todd and D'Errico, 1926), when it is clinically known as 'ossiculum terminale persistens Bergmen' and is generally asymptomatic. A separate bone in this situation can however arise following trauma involving stress to the apical ligament of the dens. A detailed understanding of the timing of appearance and fusion of axial elements is critical in clinical evaluations, as it is not uncommon for normal variations to be misdiagnosed as fracture sites.

Odontoid abnormalities can result in biomechanical atlanto-axial instability, which can of course be fatal, so perhaps it is not surprising that there is a considerable amount of clinical research into developmental abnormalities and the effects of trauma in this region (Burke and Harris, 1989).

The traditional view of the odontoid process is that it represents the displaced centrum for the first cervical vertebra, but this is certainly too simplistic a viewpoint. Jenkins (1969) found that a dens of some form or another is present in all mammals except the Cetacea. He proposed that the dens evolved as an addition to the atlas body as a means of replacing the midline atlanto-axial articular surfaces, which were lost when the mammalian atlanto-axial joint became specialized for rotational movement.

Fractures of the odontoid generally arise from impact trauma, such as severe falls or automobile accidents. The odontoid peg rarely fractures in children less than 7 years and trauma in this age group is more likely to result in damage to the dentocentral growth plate. It is thought that if damage is not treated, then it can result in resorption of the dens, leading to either a hypoplastic dens or indeed total agenesis, which is rare (Gwinn and Smith, 1962; Fielding, 1965; Freiberger *et al.*, 1965; Anderson, 1988). An odontoid fracture in a child older than 7 years frequently manifests below the level of the superior articular facet, in the position of the most recently fused dentocentral synchondrosis. This is a site of potential weakness for a considerable number of years even after fusion as the dentocentral cartilaginous disc first ossifies peripherally, leaving a cartilaginous centre that may persist even into adulthood. This is considered to support the view that the dens is truly the displaced body of C1, as this peripheral form of fusion at the dentocentral junction is consistent with the type of fusion that occurs between the annular epiphyses of, for example, two adjacent sacral bodies. However, as will be discussed later, there is some debate as to whether the annular rings are indeed epiphyseal in nature.

Stillwell and Fielding (1978) and Fielding *et al.* (1980) believed that following a fracture in the dentocentral region, there may be some compromise to the blood supply at the base of the dens and a clinical condition known as 'os odontoideum' could result (Wollin, 1963). This manifests as persistent neck discomfort with pain that can be transferred to the upper limbs and between the shoulder blades, a resistance to cervical extension and in extreme cases, transient paraplegia or tetraplegia. Radiologically, this presents as a separate ossicle in the normal position of the dens that is not attached to the vertebral body of C2. This can result in extreme atlanto-axial instability with significant risk for spinal cord injury unless a halo-cast is employed. Traction of the skull in this situation is to be avoided as it can increase the instability and does not permit close juxtaposition of the odontoid fragment to the main body of the bone (Ryan and Taylor, 1984). It is thought that the dystopic position of the fragment occurs following an upward pull on the tip by the alar ligaments (Spierings and Braakman, 1984). Schuller *et al.* (1991) considered that os odontoideum could be either congenital or traumatic in origin, with the rather meagre evidence for congenital aetiology arising from the identification of this condition in one individual suffering from Klippel–Feil syndrome.

A traumatic aetiology with subsequent non-union is the more widely accepted theory (Fielding and Griffin, 1974; Hawkins *et al.*, 1976; Hukuda *et al.*, 1980). The dentocentral synchondrosis prevents vascularization of the dens by direct extension of vessels from the centrum of C2. Thus, the arterial supply to the dens is achieved via arteries that enter either in the region of the apex or from small arteries that lie just medial to the facet joints (Schiff and Parke, 1973) although there is also evidence of a large contribution from the ascending pharyngeal artery (Haffajee, 1997). Thus, following a fracture at the base of the dens, the dentocentral growth plate may be damaged but the dens itself will survive as it has its own independent blood supply, although the inferior portion may be resorbed. The presence of an os odontoideum in identical twins in the absence of trauma, suggests that there may even be a genetic component to this condition (Kirlew *et al.*, 1993).

A rare congenital condition arises when the odontoid process fails to separate from the anterior arch of the atlas and becomes fused in what would be considered to be the location of the atlantal vertebral body (Cave, 1930; Olbrantz and Bohrer, 1984). Less than ten cases of this type have been reported in the clinical literature and the patient obviously experiences restricted rotational movement of the head, especially when the lower cervical vertebrae are fixed in position. This condition probably arises when normal resegmentation occurs with subsequent failure of sclerocoele formation in the caudal half of the first and cranial half of the second cervical sclerotome segments, resulting in an abnormality of the synovial joint formation.

The **third** to **seventh cervical vertebrae** develop in accordance with the general ossification pattern for any typical vertebra, as given above. Each is formed from three primary centres of ossification, which are all recognizable from midfetal life (Fig. 6.17). The neural arches are the first to show evidence of ossification, appearing at the end of the 2nd prenatal month and they are characterized by the presence of the developing foramen transversarium, which will not be complete until 3–4 years of age. The centra commence ossification a little later, appearing in C7 at the beginning of the 3rd prenatal month and finally reaching C3 certainly by the beginning of the 4th (Noback and Robertson, 1951). They have a flat inferior surface, which may even tend towards being slightly convex, while the superior surface is flat posteriorly but slopes downwards anteriorly (Fig. 6.17a). Thus, the superior surface has a

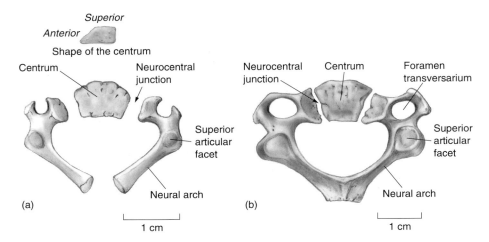

Figure 6.17 Development of a typical cervical vertebra: (a) perinate; (b) male aged 3 years 4 months.

smaller horizontal area than the inferior surface and the whole structure is wedge-shaped anteriorly (note the different appearance of the C2 centrum). At birth each cervical vertebra is represented by three separate bony elements (Fig 6.17a).

All cervical laminae unite posteriorly within the second year and neurocentral fusion is complete in the cervical segment between the ages of 3 and 4 years (Fig. 6.17b). It is only once neurocentral fusion takes place that the synovial uncovertebral joints of Luschka can form on the sloping and elevated articular sides of the neural element of the vertebral body. These joints are therefore technically absent at birth but will be well developed by around 6 years. Their function is to allow the intervertebral disc to maintain rotational function in harmony with the intervertebral joints (Boreadis and Gershon-Cohen, 1956; Penning, 1988).

Therefore, in the second year each cervical vertebra may be represented by two bony elements (Fig. 6.17b) but by the end of the fourth year, fusion will have occurred and each vertebra will be represented by a single bony element and so close to adult morphology is achieved.

The costal processes of C7 (and sometimes C5 and C6) develop independent of the transverse processes and ossify from centres that appear around the 6th prenatal month (Meyer, 1978). These centres remain independent from the vertebral column until around 4–10 years, when they generally fuse with the transverse process of the last cervical vertebra. However, there is a differential rate of growth between the costal process and the transverse process of C7 such that at an early age, the costal element may extend lateral to the transverse process (Keating and Amberg, 1954) but as the time for fusion approaches, the transverse process catches up and they become of equal length. This differential growth rate and the late fusion of the two processes have frequently resulted in clinical misdiagnoses of a cervical rib in children (Southam and Bythell, 1924; Weston, 1956).

A true **cervical rib** cannot therefore be correctly diagnosed until the child is in excess of 10 years of age (Black and Scheuer, 1997). This rather late fusion may explain the phenomenon of cervical ribs being apparently more frequent in radiographs of the new born than is reflected in the incidence in the adult population as a whole (Keating and Amberg, 1954). A cervical rib may possess a definite head, neck and tubercle and the shaft can vary quite considerably in size (Fig. 6.18). Only one-third of cases will present with clinical symptoms and the degree of development of the shaft generally dictates whether the rib will remain asymptomatic. Cervical ribs are generally bilateral, although symptoms are more frequently expressed on the right- than on the left-hand side (probably because of the position of the brachiocephalic trunk) and they are reported to be more common in females (Adson and Coffey, 1927). Symptoms do not generally appear until late adolescence or early adulthood, as the growth of the rib is not completed until 25 years of age. The lower trunk of the brachial plexus and the subclavian vessels are likely to be affected by the presence of a cervical rib, although it may not be discovered until the patient starts to complain of nervous or vascular disruptions. These symptoms generally include pain in the forearm and hand, muscle wastage along the C8 distribution, cyanosis, paraesthesia of the forearm and fingers and weakened radial and ulnar pulses. Although the aetiology of cervical ribs is unknown, there is some evidence for a familial predisposition towards the condition (Southam and Bythell, 1924; Gladstone and Wakeley, 1932; Purves and Wedin, 1950).

It is generally recognized in the surgical literature that when cervical ribs are well developed, the symptoms are more commonly vascular than neurological (Ross, 1959). This is believed to result from the superior displacement of the brachial plexus by one segment (prefixed plexus) so that there is limited neurological compression on the lower cervical spinal nerves. However, arterial compression with a concomitant poststenotic dilatation is much more common in this situation, due to the position of the cervical rib in relation to the subclavian artery.

Smaller cervical ribs tend to be attached to the first thoracic rib by a fibrous band that fuses with the scalene tubercle on the superior surface of the latter rib. The presence of this restrictive band generally causes compression on the lower trunk of the brachial plexus, but rarely causes any vascular complications (Ross, 1959). Larger cervical ribs can either articulate with the cartilage of the first thoracic rib or in rare cases extend as far anteriorly as the manubrium. In this location, the subclavian artery is forced to pass over the site of the articulation, where it may be further compressed by the attachments of the scalenus anterior muscle. Symptoms are most effectively alleviated by resection of the cervical rib and the first reported operation for this procedure was in St Bartholemew's Hospital, London in 1861. Tenotomy of the scalenus anterior

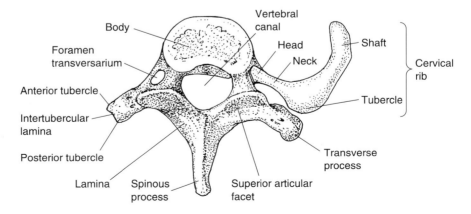

Figure 6.18 The superior surface of the adult seventh cervical vertebra showing a cervical rib on the right side.

muscle has also been undertaken with limited success in the case of larger cervical ribs (Davis and King, 1938).

Interestingly, some texts state that the presence of cervical ribs is atavistic, as there is an evolutionary trend towards a reduction in the total number of ribs (Jones, 1913). The evidence for this seems to rest with the fact that animals that develop limb buds require greater mobility in the region of the girdles and that the presence of cervical ribs in this location would be functionally intrusive. In more recently evolved mammal groups, the limb buds tend to cover several vertebral segments and nerves from these segments grow outward at approximately right angles to the vertebral column and into the developing buds. As the column grows in length and the position of the root of the limb buds remains static, the nerves are forced to adopt an oblique course to reach the developing limbs. It is here that a conflict arises between the nerves and the developing ribs. Large nerve trunks that press on comparatively small ribs will impede their growth and stunt them so that they ultimately merge with the transverse processes of the vertebrae. Therefore, the degree of development of the cervical rib depends on the nature of the obstruction in its path and if the brachial plexus is prefixed (i.e. comes off one segment higher), then it is free to develop and grow as it would in more primitive animal groups (Davis and King, 1938). In this way there are few neurological complications, but due to the involvement of the subclavian artery more anteriorly, vascular symptoms may arise. If this is true, then it is difficult to interpret the finding that cervical ribs are more common in man than in any of the apes.

Elongated anterior tubercles at the C5–6 levels have been found concomitant with a narrowing of the disc space and deformity of the vertebral bodies and it has been suggested that elongation of the anterior tubercles may be indicative of incomplete segmentation of this specific region of the column. This hypertrophy of the costal element of the cervical vertebra has been likened to the development of cervical ribs and although the incidence of this condition is not common, it is sufficiently important to note in clinical situations as it can be misdiagnosed as a pathological finding such as osteochondroma, avulsion fracture or paravertebral calcification (Lapayowker, 1960; Applbaum et al., 1983).

The presence of cervical ribs and anomalies associated with the transverse processes has led to considerable speculation regarding the developmental origins of the structure and the influence of the structures enclosed within the foramen transversarium. The pillar of bone associated with the superior articular facet forms the posterior boundary of the foramen transversarium, whilst the true transverse process (posterior bar) forms the posterolateral boundary and terminates in the posterior tubercle. The costal process of a typical cervical vertebra is represented by the anterior bar, which terminates in the anterior tubercle and is connected to the posterior tubercle by an intertubercular lamina of bone forming a shallow neural groove for the passage of the anterior (ventral) roots of the spinal nerves. Therefore, the costal element, which is the homologue of the thoracic rib, forms the entire transverse element apart from the posterior bar, which in fact represents the true transverse process (Fig. 6.19). The anterior bar and tubercle are said to be homologous with the head of the rib, while the intertubercular lamina is equivalent to the neck of the rib. The posterior tubercle is homologous with the tubercle of the rib and in the cervical region there is no equivalent to the rib shaft unless a cervical rib develops (Cave, 1975). Accessory articulations arising from the anterior tubercles have been reported and this intercostal articulation is thought to be homologous with pattern of fusion of the lateral masses of the sacrum (Cave, 1934).

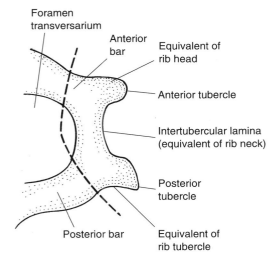

Foramen
transversarium

Anterior
bar

Equivalent of
rib head

Anterior tubercle

Intertubercular lamina
(equivalent of rib neck)

Posterior
tubercle

Posterior bar

Equivalent of
rib tubercle

Figure 6.19 The developmental origins of the transverse process of a typical adult cervical vertebra.

All **thoracic vertebrae** develop in accordance with the general ossification pattern for any typical vertebra, as given above. The primary centres of ossification are present in each of the three primary elements by the end of the 3rd month of intra-uterine life and are identifiable in isolation by the end of the 4th prenatal month. The centres for the neural arches of the first two thoracic vertebrae are first to appear in week 8 and by the end of week 10 an ossification centre is present in each half arch of the thoracic segment (O'Rahilly *et al.*, 1990b). The ossification centres for the centra appear during week 9 in the mid- to lower thoracic region and by the end of week 10 each centrum of the thoracic segment will show ossification. Thus, in the upper regions of the thoracic column, the ossification centres for the neural arches are the first to appear, while in the mid- to lower thoracic levels ossification commences in the centra prior to that in the arches (Noback and Robertson, 1951; Birkner, 1978). The costal elements elongate and extend around the thoracic region as ribs and these will be considered in detail in Chapter 7. It is sufficient to say at this stage that the costal elements of the thoracic segment commence ossification in the 8th to 9th prenatal weeks and their development progresses independent of that in the vertebrae. At birth, each thoracic vertebra is represented by three bony masses (Fig. 6.10) – a centrum anteriorly and paired neural arches posteriorly.

The laminae unite posteriorly within the first and often into the second year of life, with the lower thoracic usually the first to show union. Neurocentral fusion commences in the lower thoracic region in the third and fourth years and will be completed in most of the thoracic segment by the fifth and certainly the entire segment by the sixth year. Neurocentral fusion occurs anterior to the site of articulation with the ribs, as the ribs always remain associated with the neural arch component of the vertebrae and never articulate directly with the centrum. Therefore, in years 1–2, each thoracic vertebra will be represented by two bony masses and it is only from around the age of 6 years that each is represented by only a single bony structure. A rare condition of persistent neurocentral synchondrosis has been reported (March, 1944).

The **lumbar vertebrae** develop in accordance with the general ossification pattern for any typical vertebra as given above, although there are reports of some rare developmental anomalies (Roche and Rowe, 1951; Stelling, 1981).

Ossification commences in the centra of the upper lumbar vertebrae in weeks 9–10 and reaches L5 by the end of the 3rd prenatal month. Ossification commences in the neural arches of the upper lumbar vertebrae in the 11th week and reaches L5 in the 4th prenatal month. Thus, it is a general rule that, in the lumbar segment of the column, the centra develop in advance of the neural arches. As with all the other presacral vertebra, the lumbar vertebrae are readily identifiable from the end of the 4th prenatal month. At birth, each lumbar vertebra is represented by three bony masses – a centrum anteriorly and paired neural arches posteriorly.

It is reported that the synovial articular facets do not adopt their characteristic vertical position until the child starts to walk at approximately 1 year (Lanz and Wachsmut, 1982) and may indicate an adaptation to bipedal locomotion. The laminae unite towards the end of the first year in L1–L4, but fusion may not occur in L5 until the fifth year of life, if at all, as spina bifida in the last lumbar segment is not uncommon. Neurocentral fusion commences between the second and third years for L5 and fusion is generally completed in the lumbar segment by the fourth year.

There is considerable disagreement as to the ultimate fate of the true transverse process and the costal elements of the lumbar vertebrae and the degree of involvement of the accessory and mamillary processes. Both Fazekas and Kósa (1978) and Ogden (1979) considered that the lumbar 'transverse process' is formed from the fusion of the true transverse process with the costal element. The former authors stated that the accessory and mamillary processes only develop around 6–8 years of age as muscle mass starts to increase. Frazer (1948) also concluded that the processes were sites of muscle attachment, with the accessory process representing the true transverse process, being the site of attachment of the longissimus thoracis muscle. He concluded that the mamillary process was a site of attachment for the multifidus muscle and that the 'transverse process' was predominantly costal in origin. Last (1973) agreed that the 'transverse process' was costal in origin, but stated that the true transverse process was represented by a small mass of bone that is grooved by the posterior ramus of the lumbar spinal nerve and that the mamillary and accessory processes belonged to this true process. Whatever the actual origin of the lumbar transverse process, it does not start to develop and become visibly detectable until the end of the first and the beginning of the second year of life.

Lumbar ribs are most commonly associated with the first lumbar vertebra, are less frequent than cervical ribs, generally bilateral, more common in females and can result in considerable discomfort in the region of the lower back (Steiner, 1943).

The ossification pattern in the **sacrum** is complex as it develops from approximately 21 separate primary centres of ossification (Fig. 6.20). Each of the five sacral segments is represented by the usual three primary centres seen in all other vertebrae, but in addition, the first to third, and sometimes fourth, sacral segments also incorporate paired lateral (costal) elements. These form the ventral aspect of the alae or wings of the sacrum and are the site of articulation with the auricular surface of the innominate bone at the sacro-iliac joint.

Sacra from individuals younger that 4 prenatal months are said to be straight, with the natural concavity of the bone not developing until after this age. The

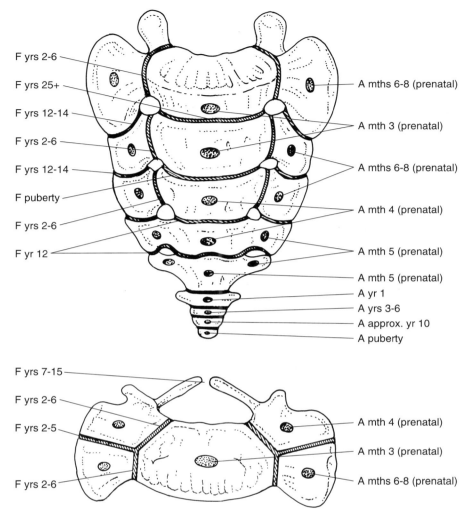

F yrs 2-6

F yrs 25+

F yrs 12-14

F yrs 2-6

F yrs 12-14

F puberty

F yrs 2-6

F yr 12

A mths 6-8 (prenatal)

A mth 3 (prenatal)

A mths 6-8 (prenatal)

A mth 4 (prenatal)

A mth 5 (prenatal)

A mth 5 (prenatal)

A yr 1

A yrs 3-6

A approx. yr 10

A puberty

F yrs 7-15

F yrs 2-6

F yrs 2-5

F yrs 2-6

A mth 4 (prenatal)

A mth 3 (prenatal)

A mths 6-8 (prenatal)

Figure 6.20 The times of appearance (A) and fusion (F) of the primary ossification centres of the sacrum and coccyx.

sacrum alters shape again when the individual starts to adopt upright posture and commence walking as the promontory is forced downwards and forwards, thereby also altering the shape of the pelvic inlet (Morton, 1942).

In the 3rd month of prenatal life, ossification centres appear in the first and second sacral centra. By the 4th month, ossification is evident in the centra of the third and fourth sacral segments and in the neural arches of S1–3. By the 5th month, ossification occurs in the centrum of S5 and in the neural arches of S4–5. The paired costal elements of S1–3 appear between prenatal months 6 and 8. Thus, all primary centres are generally present by birth, although some may be represented by no more than a small ossific nodule. Therefore, each element of the sacrum only becomes recognizable in isolation within the first year of life (Fig. 6.21). At this stage, the laminae of S1 are gracile and short in comparison to the bulk of the remainder of the neural arch. The superior articular facets are much larger than the inferior facets, which lie at the lateral extent of the inferior border of the lamina. The remainder of the neural

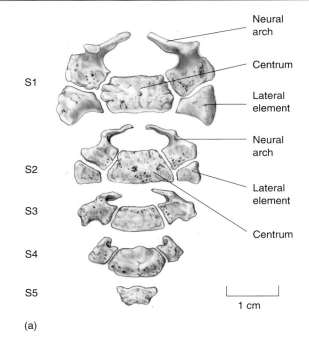

(a)

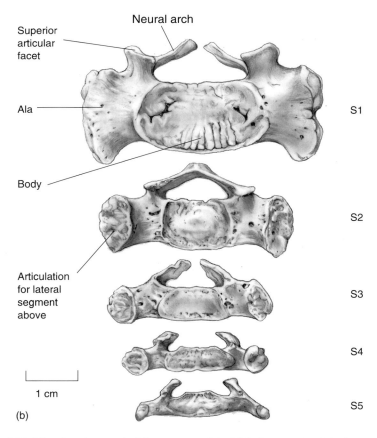

(b)

Figure 6.21 The development of the sacrum: (a) child of approximately 1 year; (b) child of between 7 and 8 years.

element is square in shape and has a billowed articular surface on its medial aspect for articulation with the centrum. On its anterior aspect is another billowed surface for articulation with the lateral element, which forms the ala or wing of the sacrum. The inferolateral border bears a small oval facet that abuts onto an identical facet on the superolateral aspect of the neural arch of the second element. The morphology of the second sacral neural arch is very similar to that of the first, although considerably reduced in size. By the time the third and fourth sacral neural arches are reached there is frequently no articulation with a lateral element and the laminae are considerably reduced in size.

The sacral centra are identifiable by their increased height and also by the concave shape of the anterior surface. The centra are wider anteriorly than posteriorly and the upper two centra show paired billowed articular surfaces on their lateral borders (Fig 6.21a). Of these two surfaces, the anterior one is for articulation with the lateral/costal element and the posterior one is for articulation with the neural element. Although the centra decrease in size from above to below, the superior surface is noticeably larger than the inferior surface.

The lateral (costal) elements can only be identified with any certainty in the first two segments (Fig 6.21a). If they arise at other sacral levels they often appear as little more than small, indistinct, spherical nodules of bone. The lateral elements are pyramidal in shape, with their apices facing medially for articulation with the centrum and their bases facing laterally to form the auricular surface of the sacro-iliac joints. The anterior surface is concave, forming the identifiable curvature of the sacral alae and the inferior surface is also concave, forming the upper margin of the sacral foramen (Fig. 6.21a). The posterior surface is billowed for articulation with the anterior aspect of the neural element.

The sacro-iliac joint forms in the 2nd month of prenatal life (see Chapter 10) and is not completed until the 7th prenatal month (Schunke, 1938). At birth, the sacro-iliac joint resembles that of quadrupeds, being straight and parallel to the vertebral column. Due to the mechanical forces induced by growth, posture and locomotion, the joint curves in a caudodorsal direction to adopt the classical adult morphology (Bellamy *et al.*, 1983). At birth the surface area of the joint has been calculated to be 1.5 cm^2, 7 cm^2 at puberty and 17.5 cm^2 in adulthood (Brooke, 1924).

Each half neural arch unites with its costal element in years 2–5, before uniting with the centrum slightly later in years 2–6. Therefore, by 6 years of age, all primary centres have fused in each sacral segment except posteriorly at the spinous processes (Fig. 6.21b). The laminae fuse posteriorly between 7 and 15 years of age and each sacral segment remains separate until puberty, when the lateral elements commence fusion and secondary centres appear.

O'Rahilly *et al.* (1990a) proposed that the lateral elements of the sacrum were not costal in origin, as the costal and transverse processes fused more posteriorly. They suggested that in fact the alar regions of the sacrum were new developments of bone and were restricted only to the sacrum. This is borne out to some extent by the fact that the alae of the sacrum articulate with the centra, which is a situation that does not arise in any other region of the column.

There is very little information available regarding the ossification of the **coccyx**. The consensus of opinion proposes that each coccygeal segment arises from a single centre of ossification although separate centres may be present for the cornua of the first segment (Fig. 6.20). The ossification centre for the first coccygeal body appears either towards the end of prenatal life or certainly within the first year of life concomitant with the centres for the cornua. The centre for the second body appears between years 3 and 6, that for the third body around 10 years of age and that for the fourth body around puberty. It has been suggested that the appearance of the ossification centres is earlier in males (Frazer, 1948). The centres for the coccyx appear as indistinct ossific nodules but it is only as puberty is approached that they will begin to adopt the final recognizable adult form.

Secondary centres

It is generally held that the typical vertebra possesses five epiphyses or secondary centres of ossification. These occur at the tips of the transverse and spinous processes and as annular rings that cover the periphery of the superior and inferior surfaces of the vertebral bodies. Most texts concur that the secondary centres appear at the beginning of puberty (12–16 years) and finally fuse at the end of puberty (18+ years), and certainly by 24 years of age.

Hindman and Poole (1970) reported that the ossified **annular epiphyses** (which, being deficient posteriorly, are more horseshoe- than ring-shaped) can be detected on radiographs as early as 2–6.5 years as distinct calcified rings that commence ossification by 13 years. In fact, there is some debate as to whether these rings ought to be called 'epiphyses' as they may simply represent initial calcification and ultimate ossification in the vertebral end plate. They do not cover the entire surface of the vertebral body but are located only around the periphery, as their main function may be to serve as anchor points for the annulus fibrosus of the intervertebral disc. In most quadrupeds, however, these rings cover the entire area of the endplate and display characteristic histological growth columns that clearly take an active part in the increase in height of the vertebral body (Töndury and Theiler, 1990). In a very convincing histological study of growth in the vertebral body, Bick and Copel (1950, 1951) showed that the annular rings do not take part in the active metaphyseal surface of a developing human vertebral body and so only fuse with the vertebral surface when it has completed growth in the later pubertal period. Schmorl (cited in Bick and Copel, 1950) used the term 'randleiste', meaning 'rim moulding', to describe the annular rings, and if indeed they are not epiphyseal in nature, then perhaps it is perfectly normal for them to be present in younger individuals. Interestingly, Bick and Copel found a higher frequency of early calcification of these rings in females and suggested that it may be hormonally induced. What is clear is that the appearance of ossification in the annular rings may not be a reliable indicator of the age of skeletal material, but perhaps the age at which they fuse to the vertebral body may be considered to be more meaningful.

There is an alarming paucity of detailed information concerning vertebral secondary centres of ossification and most publications offer little more than a basic outline of the times and patterns of development and fusion. Needless to say, each region displays its own pattern of epiphyseal development and within that, certain individual vertebrae are of specific interest. From our experience, the appearance and fusion of these centres cannot be used to identify a specific age at death, but their presence does indicate a time around puberty which is in itself an extremely variable event in terms of onset, duration and cessation and of course highly sex-specific.

It is generally stated that the **typical cervical vertebra** has six epiphyses, one for the tip of each transverse process, a ring for both the superior and inferior surfaces of the body (if indeed these are epiphyses, see above) and one for each terminal ending of the bifid spinous process. Avulsion fractures of the superior rings often occur after extreme flexion of the cervical column, while avulsion of the inferior rings often follows extremes of extension. It is debatable whether epiphyses exist for the transverse processes of C3–7 as, developmentally, they do not represent the true transverse processes but are in fact costal in origin. If epiphyses do exist they are likely to be restricted to the posterior tubercles and to be highly transitory in nature. The epiphyses for the spinous processes are small, flake-like structures that probably do not exist as separate entities but fuse directly with the process as it forms. The spinous process for C7 is different in this respect, first because it is not bifid in nature and second because the epiphysis is considerably larger and more readily identifiable than in any of the other cervical vertebrae.

The annular rings first start to fuse to the bodies in the upper cervical region and then fuse in a progressively caudal direction. The rings lie around the periphery of the body and pass upward to cover the uncinate processes. Buikstra et al. (1984) examined the pattern of annular epiphyseal union in 32 black females from the Terry collection. They noted that, at any given age, the more cranially placed vertebrae tend to be at a more advanced stage of maturation than their more caudal counterparts. They found that union had commenced in their 17–19 years age group and that it was complete by 25 years.

Figure 6.22 shows a summary of the appearance and fusion times of the constant cervical ossification centres.

The **atlas** is reported to show epiphyses at the tips of the transverse processes, but if these do exist, they are likely to be small, fugacious, flake-like structures associated with the posterior aspect of the process. Figure 6.12 shows a summary of the appearance and fusion times of the atlantal ossification centres.

The **axis** usually possesses five secondary ossification centres, although this rises to six if the ossiculum terminale is considered to be epiphyseal in nature. There are two flake-like epiphyses for the transverse processes that probably do not exist as separate structures but fuse to the process as they form. In addition, there are two distinct plate-like epiphyses for the bifid spinous process. The inferior annular ring is the first to commence fusion in the cervical column. It can display an interesting phenomenon whereby a tongue of bone passes upwards from the posterior border of the annular ring on the posterior surface of the dens to terminate in the region of the dento-central junction (Fig. 6.23). This does not occur on all axes but does seem to arise concomitant with a notched posterior border of the inferior surface of the axial body. It would appear that this was first reported by Scheuer and Black (2000) and its phylogenetic and ontogenetic origins are uncertain. Figure 6.15 shows a summary of the appearance and fusion times of the axial ossification centres.

Most reports state that each **typical thoracic vertebra** possesses at least five epiphyses – two annular rings, two for the tips of the transverse processes and one for the spinous process. However, in the upper regions of the column, separate epiphyseal flakes can exist for the costal articular surfaces of the transverse processes (Fig. 6.24a). These are thin plates of bone and are likely to fuse as they form and never manifest as separate centres. They cover the medial costal articular surface, while the epiphysis of the lateral area that extends out onto the tip of the transverse process, arises from a separate, more clearly defined epiphysis.

In the first seven thoracic vertebrae, the annular epiphyses commence fusion in the region of the costal demi-facet and sends thin, scale-like prolongations to

(a)

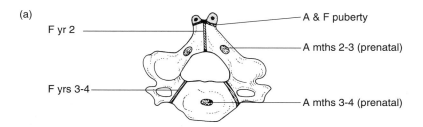

F yr 2 ——————— A & F puberty

——————— A mths 2-3 (prenatal)

F yrs 3-4 ———————

——————— A mths 3-4 (prenatal)

(b)

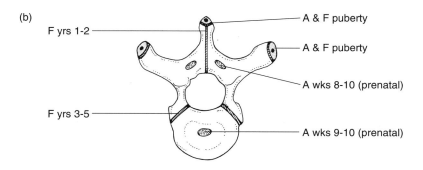

——————— A & F puberty

F yrs 1-2 ———————

——————— A & F puberty

——————— A wks 8-10 (prenatal)

F yrs 3-5 ———————

——————— A wks 9-10 (prenatal)

(c)

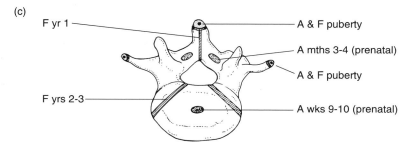

F yr 1 ——————— A & F puberty

——————— A mths 3-4 (prenatal)

——————— A & F puberty

F yrs 2-3 ———————

——————— A wks 9-10 (prenatal)

Figure 6.22 Appearance (A) and fusion (F) times of the (a) cervical; (b) thoracic; (c) lumbar vertebrae.

cover these articular surfaces (Fig 6.24a). In the lower thoracic vertebrae separate flakes arise for the costal articular surfaces, independent of the annular ring, as they are topographically removed from it (Fig. 6.24b). The annular rings first begin to fuse at the extremities of the thoracic segment and then progressively towards the middle, so that the annular rings of T5–6 are often the last to fuse. It is only once annular fusion is complete that the crescentic depressions indicating the position of the neurocentral junctions are finally covered.

Albert and Maples (1995) examined the pattern and charted stages of union of ring epiphyses in thoracic and upper lumbar vertebrae from 55 cadavers. They identified three stages of union and separated each into an early and a late phase, thereby effectively using a six-stage process. They found that there was no evidence of epiphyseal union prior to 14 years in females and 16 years 4 months in males. The youngest female to show complete union in any vertebra was 18 years and the youngest male was 18 years 9 months. The youngest

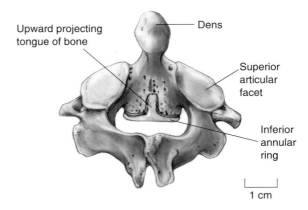

Figure 6.23 Prolongation of the inferior annular ring onto the posterior surface of the body of the axis in a female aged between 16 and 18 years.

female to show complete union in all the vertebrae was 25 years and the youngest male was 24 years 2 months. Although they could not confirm any clear pattern to the sequence of union from T1 to L2, they did suggest that union might commence in the T8–12 region in advance of the T2–7 region. However, they could not uphold the finding of McKern and Stewart (1957), who suggested that T4 and T5 were always the last to complete union. Further, Albert and Maples could not identify any differences regarding the sequence of union between the superior and inferior ring epiphyses.

Only Last (1973) reported the presence of two secondary epiphyses for the mamillary processes of the last thoracic vertebra, which are stated to appear in the early twenties.

Figure 6.22 shows a summary of the appearance and fusion times of the constant thoracic ossification centres.

Each **lumbar vertebra** is reported to have seven secondary centres of ossification – one for each mamillary process and transverse process, two annular rings and one for the spinous process. The centres for the mamillary processes are said to be the first to appear and those for the transverse and spinous

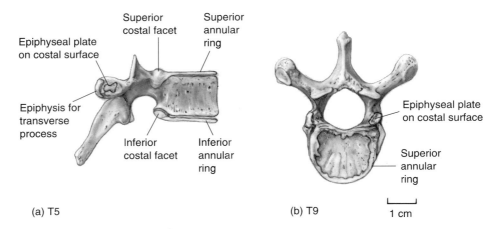

Figure 6.24 The annular epiphyses of the upper and lower thoracic region in a female aged between 16 and 18 years.

processes are the last, with those for L5 appearing before those for L1. The ring epiphyses for L5 also appear and fuse before those for L1. The posterior aspects of the ring epiphyses in this region are susceptible to stress-related factors.

Figure 6.22 shows a summary of the appearance and fusion times of the constant lumbar ossification centres.

The number of secondary centres of ossification in the **sacrum** is not constant and it is likely that it varies between any two individuals. There are 14 constant centres (Fig. 6.25), representing ten annular rings for the five sacral bodies, two auricular epiphyses for the sacro-iliac joints and two epiphyses for the lateral margins of the sacrum below the level of the sacro-iliac joint. In addition there are a number of variable elements, including small, flake-like epiphyses in the position of the fused spinous processes on the median sacral crest and on the transverse processes, which are represented by the lateral sacral crest. In addition, small epiphyseal nodules can occur anywhere at the junctions between any two individual sacral vertebrae.

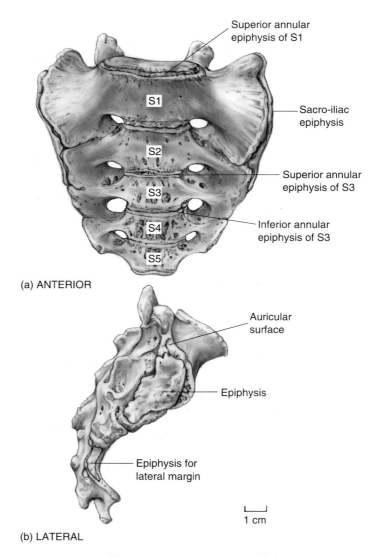

(a) ANTERIOR

(b) LATERAL

Figure 6.25 The constant epiphyses of the sacrum.

The lateral (costal) elements of the primary sacral centres start to fuse with each other around 12 years of age. This first occurs in the lower regions of the sacrum, with the lateral masses of S1 and S2 being the last to fuse towards the end of puberty. At this stage, the annular epiphyses have formed and they too commence fusion in a caudocranial direction. As a general rule, if spaces can be detected between the sacral vertebral bodies, then the individual is younger than 20 years of age. If the space only occurs between S1 and S2, then the individual is likely to be younger than 27 years of age, and complete union is often not seen until 25+ years. Spondylolysis in the sacrum is rare, as it tends to occur as a result of a stress-related fracture produced by the movement of the affected vertebra relative to the vertebra below. As the sacrum is a fixed bone, spondylolysis in this region must occur before fusion of the vertebral bodies, when there is still movement possible between adjacent, bones, i.e. in the case of S1 around the time of puberty or before (Merbs, 1996).

The epiphysis of the sacro-iliac joint generally develops from a number of discrete ossific islands that eventually coalesce to form a thin sheet of bone that covers the articular surface and dips into the demarcation lines between the lateral costal elements certainly between S1 and S2 but also between S2 and S3 (Fig. 6.25). This epiphysis appears around 15–16 years of age and fuses by 18+ years when the costal elements will also have completed union. It is probable that the epiphyses for the lateral margin follow a similar time schedule for appearance and fusion.

Figure 6.20 shows a summary of the appearance and fusion times of the sacral ossification centres.

There do not appear to be any constant epiphyseal structures associated with the **coccyx**. However, when the coccyx becomes incorporated into the sacrum, vestiges of annular rings may occur. Fusion of the coccygeal segments is variable but some degree of union generally occurs in the third decade although union between the first and second segments can be delayed until the fourth decade.

Curvatures and growth of the column

The vertebral column is not a straight pillar of bone but consists of several curved segments that act like independent springs and so bestow considerable flexibility and resilience to the structure as a whole. The curvatures are described as either primary or secondary, with the former being concave anteriorly and the latter convex anteriorly. In the fetus, the vertebral column is flexed in a 'C' shape with the concavity facing anteriorly, and this shape is fundamentally maintained until birth (Fig. 6.26). Crelin (1973) noted that the vertebral column of the neonate is so flexible that when dissected free it can easily be bent (flexed or extended) into a perfect semicircle. It is generally held that once the child starts to hold its head up independently, around 2–3 months *post partum*, a compensatory secondary curve, which is convex anteriorly, develops in the cervical region. However, Bagnall *et al.* (1977a) found the cervical curve to be present in the 10-week fetus and proposed that it might arise in direct response to the well-documented reflex movements of the fetal head *in utero*. Once the child begins to sit up unaided, around 6–8 months *post partum*, a further secondary compensatory curve, which is also convex anteriorly, develops in the lumbar region. It is generally recognized that the primary curves are maintained through the shape of the bony vertebrae whilst the secondary curves arise from a modification in shape of the intervertebral discs.

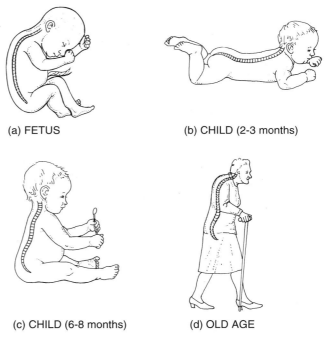

(a) FETUS

(b) CHILD (2-3 months)

(c) CHILD (6-8 months)

(d) OLD AGE

Figure 6.26 Changes in the curvature of the vertebral column with advancing age.

With age, discs may degenerate and the integrity of the secondary curves becomes impaired. The column may then revert to its original primary curves, thereby partly explaining the curved shape of the vertebral column in the elderly.

The vertebral column grows at a faster rate than the spinal cord, such that the adult vertebral column is 22 times longer than that of the fetus, whilst the adult spinal cord is only 12 times longer than that of the fetus (Reimann and Anson, 1944). This explains why the adult cord terminates at such a relatively high vertebral level. At 20 weeks of intra-uterine life, the cord extends as far as L4 and by term it lies between L2 and L3 and, interestingly, maldevelopments of the vertebral column tend to be associated with a lower terminal level of the spinal cord (Barson, 1970; O'Rahilly *et al.*, 1980). The cord reaches its adult location, between L1 and L2, by 2 months *post partum*.

It has also been shown that between 9 and 13 years, growth in the length of the female column exceeds that found in the male (Taylor and Twomey, 1984). This differential growth pattern ultimately leads to the female possessing a more slender vertebral column, which is more likely to buckle in the coronal plane than the relatively shorter, wider vertebral column of the male. It has been suggested that this might be a contributory factor in the greater prevalence of scoliosis among adolescent females.

Practical notes

Identification of juvenile vertebrae
Cervical vertebrae – The juvenile atlas and axis are both readily identifiable at birth and may in fact be recognizable from as early as the 4th prenatal month. Similarly, the remainder of the cervical vertebrae are well developed

at birth. Their neural arches bear the characteristic precursor of the foramina transversaria and the laminae are long and slender (Fig. 6.27). The centra are identifiable as they have a flat horizontal inferior surface and a superior surface that is flat posteriorly but slopes anteriorly so that they are wedge-shaped. Identification of individual centra is not possible, other than by following the premise that they increase in size as the segment is descended. However, the neural arches can be identified and this relies on the fact that as the segment is descended, the true transverse element (posterior bar) adopts a more lateral position relative to the superior articular facet (Fig. 6.27). In addition, the posterior bar increases in robusticity and becomes squarer in shape in the lower cervical region. Once neurocentral fusion has occurred, identification of individual vertebrae follows the morphology seen in the adult (Scheuer and Black, 2000).

Thoracic vertebrae – Thoracic centra can be separated from cervical centra as they are rounder in shape and of an even height, although the T1 centrum is essentially cervical in shape (Fig. 6.28). By T10, the transverse width of the

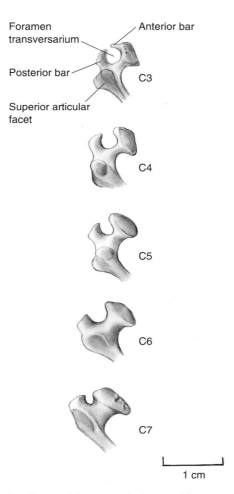

Figure 6.27 Changes in the shape of the posterior bar and foramen transversarium in the perinatal cervical neural arches.

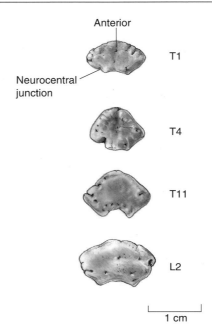

Figure 6.28 Variation in the shape of the perinatal thoracic and lumbar centra.

centrum exceeds the anteroposterior dimensions and by T12, the centrum is clearly lumbar in shape, being more robust and wider in its transverse dimensions. Other than the extremes of the segment, individual identification of centra is extremely difficult and relies on all centra of the segment being present so that they can be ranked according to size and small shape alterations. Further, we have been unable to detect any differences that would allow the superior and inferior surfaces of a young juvenile centrum to be identified.

Identification of individual half thoracic arches is extremely difficult and in our opinion, only upper, middle and lower regions can be separated with any degree of certainty (Fig. 6.29). The morphology of T1, and to a lesser extent T2, are sufficiently different from the middle, more typical, thoracic vertebrae that they can be identified with relative ease. T1 has the longest and most slender laminae of the thoracic segment and possess a well-developed butting facet associated with the superior articular facet (Scheuer and Black, 2000). Further, the inferior articular facets of T1 and T2 are to be found in the angle that is formed between the transverse process and the pedicle.

The middle thoracic segment comprises T3–10. These are the typical thoracic neural arches, which if viewed from above, are roughly T-shaped, with the cross bar being represented by the transverse process and the pedicle and the leg of the T being represented by the lamina. As the thoracic segment is descended, a number of changes gradually occur that allow an individual half arch to be roughly placed – the transverse processes become more robust, reduce in size and come to be more horizontally placed; the laminae become more square in shape; the superior borders of the laminae change from being sloped in the upper vertebrae to being more horizontal in the lower vertebrae; and the inferior articular facets come to adopt a more posterior position, closer to the site of the future spinous process.

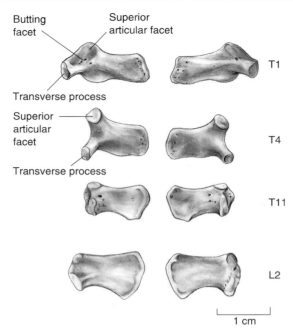

Butting facet

Superior articular facet

Transverse process

Superior articular facet

Transverse process

T1

T4

T11

L2

1 cm

Figure 6.29 Variation in the shape of the perinatal thoracic and lumbar half neural arches.

The neural arches of T11 and T12 adopt a transitional morphology between that of the more typical thoracic arches above and the lumbar arches below. The transverse processes are reduced in size and may not be obvious in T12 and the laminae are squarer in shape, with a more vertical posterior edge in the position of the synchondrosis. In T12, the direction and morphology of the superior articular facets is essentially thoracic in nature, while the inferior articular facets are fundamentally lumbar, indicating the transitional nature of this vertebra.

Once neurocentral fusion has occurred, then the identification of individual vertebrae essentially follows the adult morphology (Scheuer and Black, 2000).

Lumbar vertebrae – The lumbar centra can be separated from any others not only by their size and robusticity, but also because the height of the centrum is increased and the transverse diameter exceeds the anteroposterior diameter (Fig. 6.28). Only the L5 centrum can be identified with any certainty as it adopts adult morphology early in fetal life, being markedly wedge-shaped, with the anterior height exceeding the posterior height. As with the thoracic centra, we have been unable to establish any means of identifying the superior from the inferior surface.

The lumbar half neural arches can be separated from any others by the lack of transverse processes, the robusticity and virtually horizontal position of the pedicles, a reduction in size of the superior articular facets, which adopt a more posterior position, the location of the inferior articular facets on the posterior surface of the laminae close to the position of the future posterior synostosis, and the square, blade-like shape of the laminae that possess a slight concavity along their inferior borders (Fig. 6.29).

Sacral vertebrae – The upper sacral centra are readily identifiable by the presence of the paired billowed surfaces on their lateral borders for articulation with the neural arch posteriorly and the costal element anteriorly. The centra decrease in size from S1 to S5 and the superior surface has a greater area than the inferior surface (Fig. 6.21).

The neural arches of the upper sacral vertebrae are readily identifiable, due to the presence of two billowed articular surfaces, which gives the structure a club-like appearance. The anterior area is for articulation with the costal element, while the more medially located surface is for articulation with the centrum (Fig. 6.21). Once fusion of the various elements commences, identification essentially follows the guidelines given by Scheuer and Black (2000).

It is unlikely that the **coccygeal** components of the developing column can be identified in isolation until much later in the skeletal development and so their identification is probably somewhat inconsequential.

Sideing/orientation of juvenile vertebra

Centra – Orientation of the anterior arch of the atlas is difficult, as it is essentially a square piece of bone. The anterior surface is somewhat convex, while the posterior surface is slightly concave and bears the midline atlanto-axial articulation. Identifying the superior from the inferior border is very difficult and relies heavily on being able to place the bone in its correct anatomical position to judge a 'best fit' scenario.

Orientation of the dens relies on being able to identify the slightly convex base that articulates with the centrum of C2 inferiorly and the forked appearance of the superior aspect. In addition, the intradental sulcus is most obvious on the posterior aspect. Correct orientation of the centrum of C2 is very difficult, as it is essentially a rectangular block. The superior and inferior articular surfaces are obvious, but distinguishing anterior from posterior is very difficult.

Orientation of the cervical centra relies on being able to identify the superior metaphyseal surface, which has a smaller horizontal area compared to the relatively larger inferior metaphyseal surface. In addition, the anterior aspect of the body slopes downwards, producing a wedge-shaped appearance.

We have been unable to identify any reliable means for distinguishing between the upper and lower metaphyseal surfaces of the thoracic and lumbar juvenile centra. However, the anterior and posterior aspects can always be separated, due to the convexity of the anterior margin, the concavity of the posterior margin and the more dorsally located neurocentral junctions (Fig. 6.30).

Unlike the cervical centra, the sacral centra display a relatively larger superior metaphyseal surface compared to the smaller inferior surface. In addition, the centra are always wider anteriorly and narrower posteriorly.

Neural arches – Sideing of the arches of the atlas rely on being able to identify the relatively larger superior articular facet, which is rounded from the smaller, more oval-shaped inferior facet. The posterior arch passes backwards from the articular facet.

In the axis, the laminae slope inferolaterally on their outer aspect, leaving a distinct concavity on the inner aspect at the junction between the neurocentral region and the laminae proper.

In the cervical half-neural arches, the laminae also slope inferolaterally and the superior facet faces posterolaterally, while the inferior facet slopes ante-

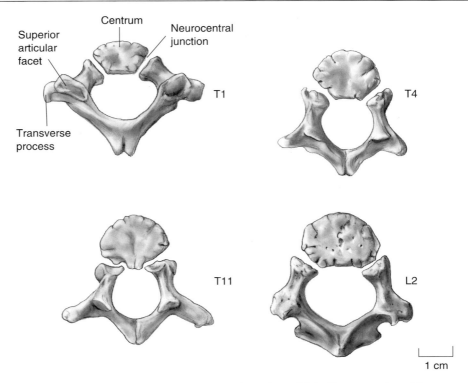

Figure 6.30 The thoracic and lumbar vertebrae in a child of between 2 and 3 years.

romedially. In the thoracic segment, the transverse process is always on the same aspect of the bone as the superior articular facet and it generally slopes downwards from the inferior border. The superior articular facet tends to be perched on the superior border, while the inferior facet is entirely located on the dorsal surface of the laminae. The sideing of half-lumbar arches is more difficult and relies on the fact that the superior border is more horizontal and the inferior border is somewhat hook-shaped.

For the sacral half arches, the superior articular facets are considerably larger than the inferior facets, which lie at the lateral extent of the inferior border of the lamina.

The costal elements of the sacral vertebrae are pyramidal in shape, with a concave anterior surface and a billowed posterior articular surface. The upper surface of the first is non-articular, while its lower surface is metaphyseal. Both surfaces of at least the second segment are metaphyseal in nature and so more difficult to orientate.

Bones of a similar morphology

The centra may be confused with developing sternebrae, but the latter are much thinner and at an early stage the morphology is not distinct, whereas the centra are always clearly defined. Half-neural arches can be confused with ribs because of their angulation but their size and the lack of a well-defined long shaft should remove the chances of confusion. The anterior arch of the atlas could be confused with the body of the hyoid bone (see Chapter 4), although the latter displays a more deeply scooped posterior surface.

Morphological summary

Prenatal

Mth 2	Ossification centres appear for lateral masses of C1 and neural arches of C2–T2
Mth 3	Ossification centres appear for centra of C4–S2; neural arches of T3–L2; costal elements (ribs) in thoracic region
Mth 4	Ossification centres appear for centra of C2–3 and S3–4; neural arches of L3–S3; paired centres for odontoid process. All primary ossification centres for the presacral vertebrae are present by this age (except anterior arch of C1)
Mth 5	Ossification centres appear for centrum of S5 and neural arches of S4–5
Mth 6	Ossification centres appear for costal process of C7 and for lateral elements of S1–3
Mth 7	Intradental fusion
Mth 8	Ossification centres for Co1 and cornua may appear

Birth	All primary centres of ossification are present with the exception of the more distal coccygeal segments and the anterior arch of C1. Intradental fusion has occurred
Yr 1	Posterior fusion of the laminae commences in the thoracic and lumbar regions. Co1 present
Yr 2	Ossification of the anterior arch of the atlas. Ossification commences in ossiculum terminale. Fusion of posterior synchondrosis in C3–7 and complete in most thoracic and upper lumbar vertebrae. Transverse processes starting to develop in lumbar region. Annular rings may be present
Yrs 3–4	Foramen transversarium complete in all cervical vertebrae. Midline sulcus on posterior surface of dens filling in. Fusion of posterior synchondrosis of axis and dentoneural synchondrosis. Neurocentral fusion in C3–7, all thoracic and lumbar vertebrae. Neurocostal fusion in S1 and S2. Co2 appears
Yrs 4–5	Posterior fusion of the atlas. Dentocentral fusion commencing in the axis. Commencement of fusion of neurocostal elements of S1 and S2 to centra. Laminae unite in L5
Yrs 5–6	Neurocentral fusion in the axis. Axis complete, apart from fusion of ossiculum terminale. Costal fusion can commence in C7. Primary centres fused in all thoracic vertebrae. Primary centres fused in all lumbar vertebrae, apart from mamillary processes. Primary centres fused in all sacral segments, apart from region of posterior synchondrosis. Anterior arch of atlas fuses. Posterior fusion complete in lumbar segment. Development of unco-vertebral joints of Luschka in cervical region
Yrs 6–8	Mamillary processes develop in lumbar segment. Commencing fusion of posterior synchondrosis in sacrum
Yr 10	Co3 appears. Continued fusion of posterior synchondrosis in sacral region. Costal fusion complete in C7
Yr 12	Dens complete following fusion of ossiculum terminale. Costal elements and central regions of the bodies start to fuse in the lower sacrum
Puberty	Co4 appears. All epiphyses appear. Posterior sacrum is completed
Early 20s	Most epiphyses fused and column is virtually complete, except for fusion between bodies of S1 and S2
25+ yrs	Column complete and fusion of coccygeal segments may commence

Morphological summary (Fig. 6.12)

C1	At birth	2 parts	2 lateral masses
	By yr 2	3 parts	2 lateral masses, anterior arch
	4–6 yrs	2 parts	Posterior and anterior arches
	6 yrs+	1 part	Fusion of arches

Morphological summary (Fig. 6.15)

C2	Late prenatal	5 parts	2 half neural arches, centrum, 2 dental centres
	Birth	4 parts	2 half neural arches, centrum, dens
	By 3 yrs	4 parts	neural arch, centrum, dens, ossiculum terminale
	3–4 yrs	3 parts	dentoneural, centrum, ossiculum terminale
	By 6 yrs	2 parts	dentoneurocentral fusion, ossiculum terminale
	By 12 yrs	1 part	fusion of ossiculum terminale
	Puberty	1 part	epiphyses appear and fusion completed

Morphological Summary (Fig. 6.22)

C3–C7	Birth	3 parts	2 half neural arches, centrum
	By 2 yrs	2 parts	neural arch, centrum
	By 4 yrs	1 part	neurocentral fusion
	Puberty	1 part	epiphyses appear and fusion completed

Morphological summary (Fig. 6.22)

T1–T12	Birth	3 parts	2 half neural arches, centrum
	By 2 yrs	2 parts	neural arch, centrum
	By 6 yrs	1 part	neurocentral fusion
	Puberty	1 part	epiphyses appear and fusion completed

Morphological summary (Fig. 6.22)

L1–L4	Birth	3 parts	2 half neural arches, centrum
	In yr 1	2 parts	neural arch, centrum
	By yr 4	1 part	neurocentral fusion
L5	Birth	3 parts	2 half neural arches, centrum
	By yr 5	1 part	neural and then neurocentral fusion
	Puberty	1 part	epiphyses appear and fusion completed

Morphological summary (Fig. 6.20)

Sacrum

Birth	21 parts	all primary centra: S1–S3 in 5 parts – 2 half neural arches, centrum, 2 lateral elements. S4–S5 in 3 parts – 2 half neural arches, centrum
2–6 yrs	5 parts	all elements fused apart from posterior synchondroses
12–14 yrs	Variable	fusion between lateral elements and union of lower sacral segments
Puberty	1 part	epiphyses appear and commence union, lateral and central fusion in caudocranial direction
25+	1 part	fusion of bodies of S1 and S2 ventrally

Morphological summary (Fig. 6.20)

Coccyx

Yr 1	1 part	Co 1 develops
By 6 yrs	2 parts	Co1 and 2 present
By 10 yrs	3 parts	Co1—3 present
Puberty	4 parts	all coccygeal centres present
Post puberty	Variable	variable fusion of primary centres

CHAPTER SEVEN

The Thorax

The thoracic cage comprises an anterior midline sternum, 12 thoracic vertebrae posteriorly and a lateral series of 12 pairs of ribs (Fig. 7.1). The sternum is comprised of three parts – an upper manubrium, a middle mesosternum and a lower xiphoid process. Ribs 1–10 articulate with the thoracic vertebral column behind and with the sternum in front via their costal cartilages, but the eleventh and twelfth ribs do not articulate anteriorly and are therefore termed floating ribs. Ribs 1–6 (and sometimes 7) articulate directly with the sternum via their costal cartilages and are termed vertebrosternal ribs. Ribs 7–10 articulate with the sternum via a common cartilaginous bar called the costal margin and are termed vertebrochondral ribs.

The thorax is an osteo-cartilaginous framework that surrounds and protects the principal viscera of respiration and circulation although its primary function probably resides in its intimate involvement with the mechanism of respiration.

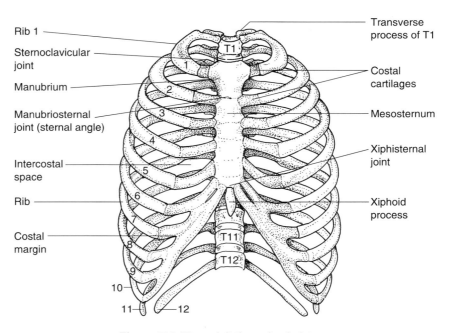

Figure 7.1 The adult thoracic skeleton.

Early development of the thorax

The sternum was originally considered to be an embryological derivative of the mesenchymal somite arrangement that gives rise to the vertebral column, ribs, intercostal and anterior abdominal musculature. However, it was clearly shown by Chen (1952) in mice and Seno (1961) in chicks, that the sternum is in fact developed from the same lateral somatopleuric mesenchyme that gives rise to the pectoral muscles and so is fundamentally of appendicular and not axial derivation. The bilateral mesenchymal precursors of the sternum develop immediately ventral to the primordia for the clavicle and ribs but are in fact independent from them in their development. The line of division between the somite-derived structures and the lateral plate mesodermal structures is the future chondro-sternal junction (Ogden *et al.*, 1979a).

At approximately 6 weeks of fetal life a pair of **lateral sternal plates** can be identified embedded in the anterior chest wall, which are independent both of each other and the developing ribs (Fig. 7.2a). These mesenchymal bars first become associated with the upper six (or seven) ribs on each side and eventually fuse to their anterior extremities. Similar condensations then appear and connect the anterior ends of ribs 7–10, which eventually fuse with that of the ribs above. As the ribs increase in length, so the sternal plates migrate medially towards each other and it is then that chondrification commences. Around the 9th prenatal week, the sternal plates begin to fuse with each other (Fig. 7.2b) in the midline and do so in a craniocaudal direction (Ogden, 1979). These plates should only fuse once the heart has descended into the thorax and a failure of fusion results in the clinical condition of ectopia cordis, where the heart is exposed to the exterior. A rare condition of cleft sternum is strongly associated with ectopia cordis (Chang and Davis, 1961) and, not surprisingly, there is a strong correlation between developmental abnormalities in this region and congenital heart defects in general (Fischer *et al.*, 1973).

Three mesenchymal masses appear at the superior extremity of the lateral plates around 6 weeks of prenatal life (Fig. 7.2a). The **presternal mass**

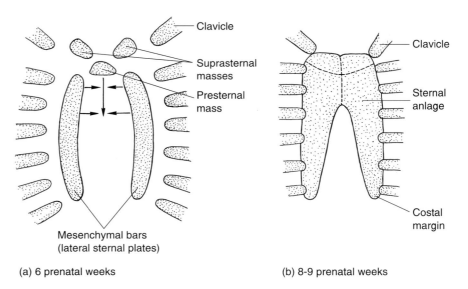

(a) 6 prenatal weeks   (b) 8-9 prenatal weeks

Figure 7.2 A diagrammatic representation of the embryological development of the sternum (redrawn after Larsen, 1993).

(median sternal anlage) lies inferior to the paired **suprasternal masses** and will eventually fuse with all but the most lateral part of the suprasternal section to form the upper part of the manubrium, while the remainder of the two lateral masses take part in the formation of the sternoclavicular joint (Whitehead and Waddell, 1911; Klima, 1968). The presternal mass appears later than the lateral sternal plates and it is thought to be embryologically derived from the pectoral girdle (Currarino and Silverman, 1958).

To fully understand the early development of the ribs, it is advised that the relevant section in Chapter 6 is consulted, as only a brief summary will be considered here.

The rib primordia arise from the costal outgrowths of the neural arch portion of the vertebral anlage (see Fig. 6.5) and are almost entirely derived from the caudal half of the sclerotome (Sensenig, 1949; Ogden, 1979; Verbout, 1985). This embryological origin explains why each typical rib has a major articulation with only one vertebra, namely that which also develops from the same caudal sclerotome portion and why there is only a minor articulation with the vertebra above. By the time the tenth rib is reached, there is no articulation with the vertebra above as the rib remains fully within the realms of its embryological cohort.

The rib primordia penetrate into the body wall between two adjacent segmental myotomic plates and eventually become associated with the sternal mesenchymal plates, as described earlier (Fig. 7.2). Ribs 1–6 (vertebrosternal) curve around the body wall to reach the developing sternal plates whilst ribs 7–10 (vertebrochondral) are progressively more oblique and shorter, only reaching the costal cartilage of the rib above and thereby contributing to the costal margin. The junction between the sclerotome derivatives (ribs) and the lateral plate mesoderm derivatives (sternum) persists as the chondrosternal articulations.

Chondrification commences in the posterior section of the rib primordium around day 36 of intra-uterine life. It progresses ventrally, and as growth also occurs in this direction, the sternal plates become approximated and eventually meet and fuse in the midline. Therefore, the normal growth of the ribs is critical to the proper location of the sternal plates. By the time these plates have finally met, ossification has commenced in the ribs. Once ossification begins, the synovial costovertebral joints commence development and so the rib separates from the vertebral anlage (Tsou et al., 1980). Failure of this joint formation will result in congenital costovertebral fusion and whilst this is generally asymptomatic when restricted to one segment, if several segments are involved then respiratory limitations will ensue.

The shape of the developing ribs is greatly influenced by the structures that they grow around. Therefore, the upper ribs are modified by the shape of the underlying lung buds and developing heart, while the lower ribs grow to accommodate the bulk of the abdominal viscera, such as the liver (Geddes, 1912).

Rib abnormalities, such as bifidity, flaring, fusion or bridging, generally arise from irregular segmentation either in association with the vertebral anlage or with abnormal segmentation in the sternum (Sycamore, 1944; Barnes, 1994). These abnormalities are relatively common and generally asymptomatic. Congenital fusion of ribs should not, of course, be confused with post-traumatic fusion of fractures. The latter is a more common event and identification of an intercostal callus formation should prevent confusion.

I. THE STERNUM

Ossification

In the cartilaginous state, the sternum is a continuous non-segmented structure (Fig. 7.2b). However, once ossification commences, this ceases to be the case and the future development is a reflection of true metamerism. The ribs are segmental structures and their influence has been shown to be directly responsible for the relatively late ontogenetic segmentation of the sternum. Removal of the rib anlage in the experimental condition, results in the development of a non-segmented sternum (Chen, 1952). It has been suggested that the tips of the ribs inhibit the spread of chondroblastic proliferation to the adjacent cartilage of the sternum and therefore the cartilage remains relatively immature in these locations and so is resistant to ossification (Currarino and Silverman, 1958).

Premature synostosis is rare at these junctions but it can be detected as early as 6 months *post partum* and results in a pigeon chest deformity or *pectus carinatum* where the sternum projects forwards while the lateral regions of the chest are flattened, resulting in a keel-like condition. This condition can also arise due to rickets. The segmentation of the sternum may arise as a result of the high magnitude of compressive hydrostatic stress in the regions of the developing sternum adjacent to the costal facets. These stresses have been shown to slow the process of endochondral ossification so that the initial zones of bone formation occur away from these areas in the intercostal regions of the developing sternum (Wong and Carter, 1988; Carter and Beaupré, 2001).

It is generally agreed that ossification commences in the sternum once sternal bar fusion has begun. As union takes place in a craniocaudal direction, so the appearance of the centres of ossification also occurs in this direction. Should ossification commence before plate fusion has fully taken place, then two centres of ossification may result, one in each bar remnant.

Primary centres
Appearance
The primary centre of ossification for the manubrium is generally the first to develop and this occurs within the 5th prenatal month (Paterson, 1904; Noback and Robertson, 1951; Fazekas and Kósa, 1978; Ogden, 1979). It is not uncommon for the manubrium to develop from more than one centre of ossification, although there is generally one major centre and a variable number of smaller centres (Ashley, 1956a). These centres will, however, quickly coalesce to form one major centre (Fig. 7.3). Currarino and Swanson (1964) found that the manubrium developed from two centres, one above the other, in 90% of children suffering from Down's syndrome.

In the early stages of development, the manubrium is difficult to identify as it is represented by little more than small, undifferentiated bony nodules (Fig. 7.4a). However, by approximately 6 months *post partum* it starts to adopt a more recognizable appearance, with relatively flat anterior and posterior surfaces, straight sides in the upper two-thirds for the first costal cartilage articulation and a small oval facet inferiorly for the manubriosternal joint (Fig. 7.4b).

The mesosternum ossifies from a variable number of ossification centres. As a rule, either a single or multiple centres will arise in the area of the cartilaginous mesosternum, at regular intervals between the sites of costal cartilage attachment. Ashley (1956b) suggested that the variability in the pattern of

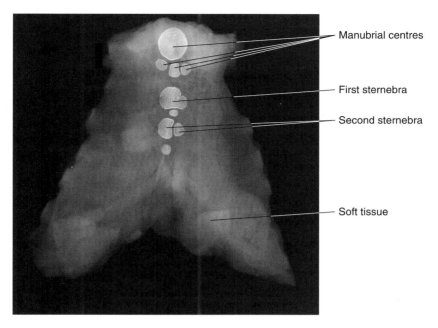

Figure 7.3 Radiograph of the sternal plate from a male aged 9 months (*post partum*). Note the multiple centres for the developing manubrium and the irregular morphology of the centres in the mesosternum.

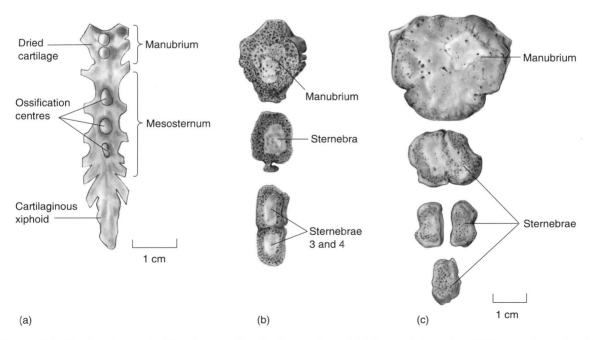

(a)   (b)   (c)

Figure 7.4 The development of the sternum. Ossification centres at (a) 8 prenatal months; (b) 3 years 4 months; (c) 8 years 7 months.

fusion indicated that the mesosternum was 'held in a plastic stage of phyloge-netic development', as similar variations are found in other primates. These sites of ossification develop into sternebrae, and so the first sternebra develops in the midline between the sites of articulation of the second and third costal cartilages. Similarly, the second sternebra develops between the sites of articulation of the third and fourth costal cartilages and so on. A total of four individual sternebrae will develop and these will eventually fuse to form the adult mesosternum (Fig 7.5). The first and often the second sternebra will develop from single centres of ossification, while the third and fourth may develop from paired centres. A higher frequency of bilateral centres is to be expected in the lower sternebrae, due to the relatively late fusion of the sternal plates in this region (Figs 7.3 and 7.4c).

It has been proposed that much of the morphological variation seen in the sternum may result from the pattern and number of ossification centres. Ashley's (1956a) type I sterna are narrow with parallel sides and they may result from each sternebra forming from a single centre. Type II sterna also have parallel sides but are much wider than type I and it has been proposed that they may arise from sternebrae that form from bilateral ossification centres. Type III sterna are intermediate in form, being narrow in the upper part and wider in the lower part (piriform) and it is proposed that they may develop from upper sternebrae formed from single centres and lower sternebrae that form from bilateral centres (Wong and Carter, 1988).

A midline sternal foramen is a relatively common defect found in the region of sternebrae 3 and 4 and it is not uncommon for it to be mistaken for a gunshot wound in the forensic situation. It is thought to result from a defective or delayed fusion of the sternal plates, resulting in bilateral ossification at that

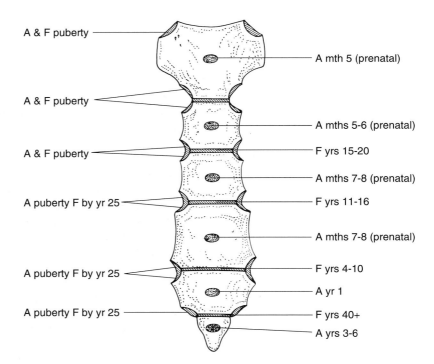

Figure 7.5 Times of appearance (A) and fusion (F) of the primary ossification centres of the sternum.

level, with concomitant non-fusion of the ossification centres (Cooper *et al.*, 1988). A sternal foramen has been identified in approximately 4% of European and some 13% of East African remains (Ashley, 1956a) and it is more common in males than females. That a sternal foramen is a developmental defect is verified by the fact that it is not traversed by any anatomical structure.

The ossification centre for the first sternebra generally appears in the 5th or 6th month of prenatal life, with centres for the second and third appearing by the 7th or 8th month and that for the fourth sternebra may not appear until the first year *post partum*, although it can be present at birth (Fig. 7.5). Odita *et al.* (1985) summarized that any fetus with two ossified sternal segments (including the manubrium) is at least 30 weeks of age. The presence of three segments indicates an age of around 34 weeks and four segments an age of around 37 weeks.

Therefore, at birth, the sternum may be represented by four or possibly five centres of ossification, as the xiphoid will not commence ossification until between the third and sixth year (Fig. 7.4a). However, the sternebrae will not become recognizable in isolation until after 6 months *post partum*, when they start to take on their characteristic flattened appearance in the antero-posterior plane and are roughly oval or rectangular in outline (Fig. 7.4b).

Fusion

The fusion of the primary ossification centres occurs in a well-documented caudocranial direction (Fig 7.5). The line of fusion of adjacent sternebrae is found at the level of the chondrosternal junction. In fact, the superior half of each costal notch is formed from the sternebra above, while the inferior half is formed from the sternebra below. As a rule, sternebrae three and four are the first to fuse, although there is some confusion in the literature concerning when this actually happens with ages ranging from as young as 4 years to as old as 15 years of age. There is clearly considerable variation in the timing of this event and we have found fusion in a male child as young as 3 years and 4 months (Fig. 7.4b). This unit comprising the fused third and fourth sternebrae will then fuse to the second sternebra around the time of puberty (11–16 years) and this in turn, will finally fuse to the first sternebra towards the end of puberty (15–20 years). It is not uncommon for the manubrium and first sternebra to fuse so that the manubriosternal joint is caudally displaced to occur effectively at the junction between the first and second sternebra at the level of the third costal cartilage.

Pattern of fusion

We have found that when two adjacent sternebrae fuse, the posterior surface fuses first, followed by the anterior surface and the lateral surface, bearing the costal notches, is the last to attain adult form. McKern and Stewart (1957) noted that in the sterna of males between the ages of 17 and 18 years, the delimitation of the individual sternebrae was clear and that only the lower two-thirds were fused. Complete fusion of the mesosternum does not arise until later in adulthood, often approaching 30 years, where remnants of fusion can still be found in the middle of the costal notches. The remains of the site of sternebral fusion may persist as transverse lines seen on the anterior surface of the adult bone. Because of the considerable variation in both the time of appearance of the centres and their subsequent pattern of fusion, the sternum is probably of limited value in the accurate determination of age at death in the juvenile.

Secondary centres

In addition to these primary centres of ossification, a variable number of small secondary centres may occur. These are small, flake-like epiphyses that may not exist as separate entities, but rather fuse to the primary centres as they develop. The appearance and subsequent fusion of these centres are very variable and probably of limited value in age determination. They occur at sites of articulation, namely the sternoclavicular joints and the chondrosternal joints. These epiphyses are not well documented and in fact only Stewart (1954) and McKern and Stewart (1957) seem to have paid them much attention. This is unfortunate as their sample did not contain individuals younger than 17 years of age and so little is documented concerning the earlier development of these centres.

Manubrium

Stewart (1954) and McKern and Stewart (1957) noted that a small, flake-like epiphysis was present on the clavicular surface of the manubrium. We have found that it is not uncommon for more than one epiphyseal flake to form and these fuse as patches in various areas of the articular surface (Fig 7.6). Two epiphyses consistently appear, however, at the anterior and superior margins of the manubrium (suprasternal flakes). It is likely that these are phylogenetic remnants of the epiphyses associated with the embryological presternal and suprasternal masses. McKern and Stewart (1957) noted that these epiphyses fused around 19 years of age, but we have found evidence of epiphyseal fusion in individuals as young as 12 years of age.

Epiphyseal activity was also recorded by McKern and Stewart (1957) in the region of the first costal articulation. They noted that in the immature bone there is a clear interarticular groove separating the articular surfaces of the clavicle above from the first costal cartilage below. With age, this groove gradually obliterates, or indeed a separate ossific nodule may appear, so that by the age of 22–23 years the groove disappears. While this is happening, a thin plaque of bone may be found in the pit of the first costal notch on the manubrium, and McKern and Stewart found this in individuals between the ages of 18 and 24 years.

Mesosternum

Plaques of bone also appear in the remainder of the costal notches of the sternal body. The plaque forms in the pit of the notch, smoothing over the gap between the superior half of the notch formed from the sternebra above

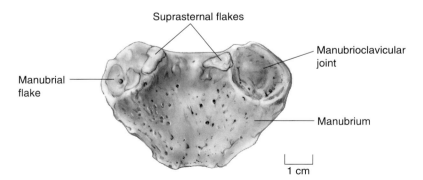

Figure 7.6 The manubrial secondary centres of ossification (approximately 12–14 years).

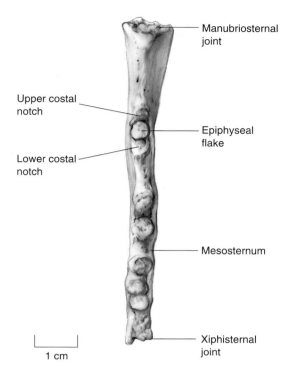

Figure 7.7 The epiphyseal flake of the mesosternal costal notch – male (approximately 17 years).

and the lower half of the notch being formed from the sternebra below (Fig 7.7). These plaques fuse with the body of the sternum in a craniocaudal direction. They form around the time of puberty but remain patent for some not inconsiderable time and certainly into the third decade. The plaques in the upper costal notches close before those in the lower notches and the presence of these plaques will indicate an age that is likely to be younger than 25 years.

The manubriosternal joint

The manubriosternal joint is generally described as either a primary or, more commonly, a secondary cartilaginous joint. The difference between these two classifications is the presence or absence of a fibrocartilaginous disc between two plates of hyaline cartilage. Unlike hyaline cartilage, fibrocartilage does not ossify and so secondary cartilaginous joints tend to remain patent even into late adult life. If the fibrocartilaginous disc is to develop, then a fibrous lamina will appear early in fetal life and the joint will progress to become secondary cartilaginous in form (Fig 7.8). However, if the lamina fails to develop, then a primary cartilaginous joint ensues. In the absence of the fibrocartilaginous barrier, the ossification centres for the manubrium and first sternebra may become juxtaposed and union of the centres will occur (Fig 7.9). This leads to matrical synostosis of the manubriosternal joint, where there is no obvious demarcation between the manubrium and mesosternum either externally or internally, as can be witnessed on X-rays (Fig 7.10). As the potential for this type of fusion arises in the fetus through non-development of a fibrous lamina, its presence should not be considered pathological in nature. It has been shown

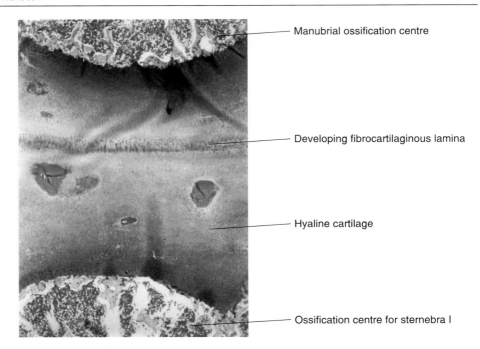

Manubrial ossification centre

Developing fibrocartilaginous lamina

Hyaline cartilage

Ossification centre for sternebra I

Figure 7.8 Histological (H&E) appearance of the manubriosternal joint – male aged 9 months (*post partum*). This shows normal development and a secondary cartilaginous joint will be present in the adult. This is the same specimen as is shown in the radiograph in Fig. 7.3.

that the junction between the manubrium and sternum can slip to the level of the third costal cartilage. This arises when a fibrous lamina develops in this displaced location and not at the level of the second costal cartilage, which represents the normal pattern (Paterson, 1900).

Practical notes

Orientation of the sternum

Reliable orientation of the manubrium can only occur after approximately 6 months *post partum* as before this time it is represented by little more than bony nodules. The bone is flattened in an anteroposterior direction and the posterior surface will be smoother (Fig. 7.4b). Paired, vertical lateral articular facets for the first costal cartilage can be clearly identified as extending for almost half the length of the bone and tend to be located more towards the superior pole. The upper aspect of the manubrium is always broader and more robust than the lower regions. The superior border is rounded and smooth and may show the concavity of the jugular notch, while the inferior extremity is rougher in appearance and tends to be more clearly defined as an oval articular joint surface.

Reliable orientation of the sternebrae is difficult below 2–3 years and the positive identification of a particular segment is extremely difficult unless all the sternebrae are represented and then the attribution will be based on size, with the first tending to be the largest and the fourth the smallest. Each sternebra is flattened in the anteroposterior direction and takes on a roughly rectangular shape when unpaired, but becomes somewhat square in outline when fused with a centre from the opposite side (Fig. 7.4c). The posterior

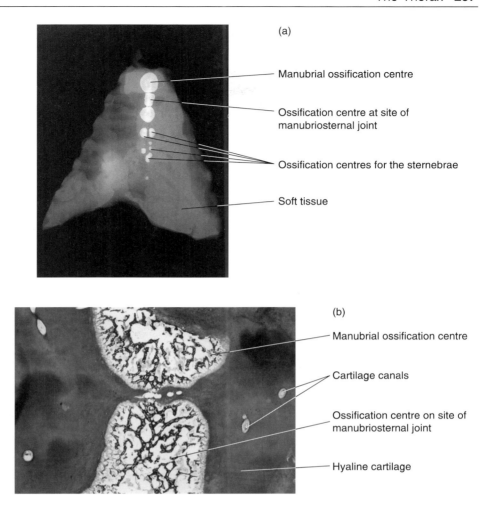

(a)

— Manubrial ossification centre

— Ossification centre at site of manubriosternal joint

— Ossification centres for the sternebrae

— Soft tissue

(b)

— Manubrial ossification centre

— Cartilage canals

— Ossification centre on site of manubriosternal joint

— Hyaline cartilage

Figure 7.9 Matrical manubriosternal synostosis in a 40 week fetus (male). (a) PA radiograph; (b) histological section, Masson's stain × 1 obj. Note that an ossification centre is present at the normal site of the manubriosternal joint, and in the histology there is no fibrous lamina present.

surface is generally flatter than the anterior aspect and the height of the bone is generally in excess of its width.

Bones of a similar morphology

A neonatal basi-occiput may be confused with a more mature manubrium. However, the former possesses a deep concavity for the anterior boundary of the foramen magnum, a mediolateral concavity of the intracranial surface, evidence of part of the occipital condyle and a thickened, D-shaped anterior extremity at the spheno-occipital synchondrosis (see Chapter 4). A basi-occiput and a manubrium from the same individual could never be confused, as the latter will always be smaller and thinner.

The early sternebrae are similar in their morphology to the vertebral centra, but close examination will show that the sternal structures are flatter, more irregular in shape and do not possess the well-developed vascular foramina and radiating grooves seen in the centra (see Chapter 6).

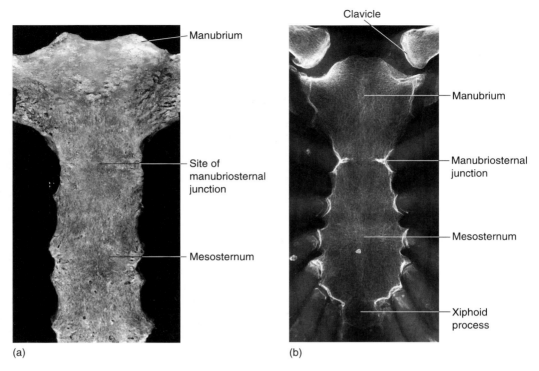

(a)　　　　　　　　　　　(b)

Figure 7.10 Matrical manubriosternal synostosis – female aged 57 years. (a) External appearance of the bone; (b) PA radiograph. Note the continuity of internal architecture between the manubrium and the mesosternum on the radiograph.

Morphological summary (Fig. 7.5)

Prenatal	
Mth 5	Primary centre develops for the manubrium
Mths 5–6	Primary centre develops for first sternebra
Mth 7–8	Primary centres develop for sternebrae 2 and 3
Birth	The sternum is represented by at least four centres of ossification
Yr 1	Primary centre develops for sternebra 4. The manubrium can be identified in isolation
Yrs 3–6	Ossification can commence in the xiphoid. All sternebrae can probably be identified in isolation
Yrs 4–10	Sternebrae 3 and 4 fuse
Yrs 11–16	Sternebra 2 fuses to 3 and 4. Epiphyses appear and commence fusion
Yrs 15–20	Sternebra 1 fuses to rest of mesosternum. Epiphyses continue to fuse
21+ yrs	Sternum essentially complete, although lines of fusion between sternebrae may persist until 25 years or older
25+ yrs	All epiphyseal plaques in costal notches have fused
40+ yrs	Xiphoid process commences fusion to mesosternum

II. THE RIBS AND COSTAL CARTILAGES

Ossification

Primary centres
Primary centres of ossification first appear in ribs 5–7 in the region of the posterior angle between the 8th and 9th weeks of prenatal life (Geddes, 1912; Fazekas and Kósa, 1978; Ogden, 1979). Ossification centres then appear in a bidirectional manner, with the primary centre for the first rib appearing before that of the twelfth. By the 11th and 12th weeks of intra-uterine life, each rib (often with the exception of the twelfth) possesses a single primary centre of ossification. The rib therefore commences ossification in advance of its corresponding vertebra, indicating that in terms of development it is divorced and independent from the primitive mesenchymal vertebra, at a very early fetal age (Fazekas and Kósa, 1978; Ogden, 1979).

Ossification of the cartilage model then ensues, with more rapid development occurring in a ventral, rather than a dorsal, direction. The ventral progression of ossification slows down in the 4th prenatal month, when the proportion of bone to costal cartilage seems to reach equilibrium, reflecting that of the future adult situation (Fazekas and Kósa, 1978).

Between this stage in the ossification process and the presence of secondary centres of ossification at puberty, the only obvious development in the ribs is a change in shape and size. This reflects the gradual development of the juvenile thorax as it comes to adopt a more active role in the mechanism of respiration with the ventral aspect of the rib descending in position whilst the posterior attachment to the vertebral column remains relatively constant. It has long been recognized that the ribs of the neonate are more horizontal in position than those of the adult (Fig 7.11). Breathing is essentially a diaphragmatic and anterior abdominal wall process in the newborn, with the thorax *per se* offering

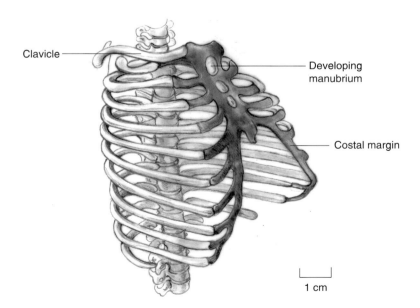

Figure 7.11 The articulated perinatal thoracic skeleton. Note the virtually horizontal ribs and therefore the relatively high position of the thorax.

little more than a relatively fixed container in which the diaphragm's descent induces the movement of air in and out of the respiratory organs. An increase in the obliquity of the rib shaft, and thus a general descent of the thorax, results in a decrease in dependency on diaphragmatic breathing with an increasing ability to incorporate direct thoracic involvement. In the neonate, the transverse diameter of the thorax is relatively smaller than in the adult, but this situation changes at approximately the time when the child begins to walk. The effect of these mechanical factors can in fact be detected in the juvenile rib series, and may act as useful corroborative evidence in the determination of age at death (see below).

Secondary centres

There is very little detailed information concerning the secondary centres of ossification, either in their time of appearance or their time and order of fusion. Stevenson (1924) went so far as to say that the ribs were of little value in age determination. Presumably this was because of the variability in timings and in the fact that these epiphyses are probably the smallest and least readily identifiable in the human body. It is also often very difficult to interpret their status of union, as the appearance of many of the surfaces is much the same both before and after union. It is often only when the epiphysis is actually in the process of fusing that it is readily identifiable and it should be appreciated that this is a very small window of opportunity.

Secondary centres of ossification occur at the sites of articulation. In addition, a centre may be present for the non-articulating area of the tubercle and in fact, these are generally the first to appear at the early stages of puberty (12–14 years). It is unlikely that these epiphyses exist as separate structures, but rather that they fuse with the non-articulating area of the tubercle as they are being formed. Therefore, fusion will also occur at an early age. Ribs that do not possess a tubercle, as they do not articulate with a transverse process (ribs 11, 12 and often 10) will naturally not show epiphyses in this area. The non-articular epiphysis for rib 1 is slightly different in that once it has commenced fusion it extends posteriorly and expands to also become the epiphysis for the articulating region of the tubercle (Fig 7.12a). This arises because of the close proximity of the two surfaces in this rib. In ribs where the two areas are further apart, then two separate centres of ossification will arise and fuse independently.

The epiphysis for the articulating region of the tubercle is next to develop, and in the same way it appears to fuse to the surface while it is actually forming, so it probably never achieves a separate existence (Fig. 7.12b). The appearance and fusion of these epiphyses appears to follow no specific pattern in terms of the sequence of ribs. It is said that they appear and unite in the eighteenth year (Stevenson, 1924), but more detailed information is not available.

The epiphyses for the heads of the ribs are the last to form, with the first of these showing complete fusion around 17 years of age (McKern and Stewart, 1957). The epiphysis appears as a nodule of bone in the superior articular facet and then gradually spreads outwards into the crest and downwards into the inferior facet (Fig. 7.12d). Epiphyses for the heads of the ribs initially appear in the upper and lower members of the series so that the upper and lower ribs are generally more advanced in terms of maturity than the middle ribs. It is generally recognized that complete fusion of the epiphyses of the heads of the ribs is completed by years 22–25 (Stevenson, 1924; McKern and Stewart, 1957).

A summary of the times of appearance and fusion of ossification centers can be seen in Fig. 7.13.

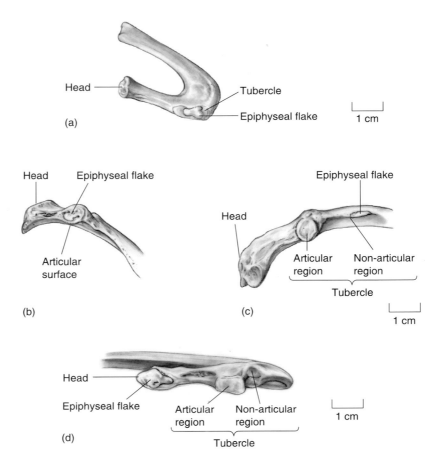

Head

Tubercle

Epiphyseal flake

1 cm

(a)

Head   Epiphyseal flake

Articular
surface

(b)

Epiphyseal flake

Head

Articular   Non-articular
region   region

Tubercle

1 cm

(c)

Head

Epiphyseal flake   Articular   Non-articular
                   region   region

1 cm

(d)   Tubercle

Figure 7.12 Epiphyseal fusion in the ribs: (a) fusion of the epiphysis of rib 1 – male (approximately 17 years); (b) fusion of the articular part of the tubercle (approximately 19 years); (c) fusion of the non-articular part of the tubercle (approximately 21 years); (d) fusion of the head (approximately 22 years).

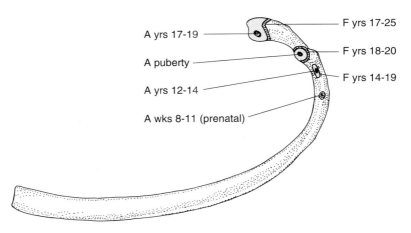

A yrs 17-19   F yrs 17-25

A puberty   F yrs 18-20

A yrs 12-14   F yrs 14-19

A wks 8-11 (prenatal)

Figure 7.13 Appearance (A) and fusion (F) times of the costal ossification centres.

Age changes in rib ends and costal cartilages

The costochondral junction is the region where the bone of the rib merges into the hyaline cartilage of the costal cartilages. This junction represents a developmental anomaly in that the progressive juvenile ossification process falls short of its cartilaginous anlage. Therefore, with increasing age it is perhaps not surprising that continued ossification may proceed in a ventral direction. This process occurs in two ways – morphological alteration of the ventral rib end, and direct ossification of the costal cartilages.

Işcan *et al.*, (1984, 1985) developed a component phase analysis system (rather like that developed for the pubic symphysis) to determine age and establish sex differences in the metamorphosis of the ventral extremity of the fourth right rib. For a full description of this technique, it is advised that the original papers be consulted.

Hyaline cartilage has the ability to mineralize and retains this property even into advancing age. The value of costal cartilage calcification in the prediction of age at death and sex determination has been extensively examined and again it is advised that the original texts are consulted (McCormick, 1980, 1983; McCormick *et al.*, 1985). Patterns of calcification differ between the sexes (Powell and MacLaughlin, 1992) and it is believed that this highly specific sexual dimorphism occurs as a result of both hormonal influences and chemotactic factors, which influence subsequent vascular invasion (Peace, 1992). Deposits of calcium within the costal cartilages can be detected on a radiograph of the chest plate in individuals as young as 18 years of age but obviously the incidence and density of deposition increases dramatically with advancing age (note the similarities to ossification within the laryngeal cartilages – Chapter 4).

Practical notes

Identification of individual juvenile ribs

To understand the functional basis for the identification and orientation of individual juvenile ribs, it is advised that the section on the identification of individual adult ribs is consulted in Scheuer and Black (2000). From the late fetal age, all ribs are readily identifiable, as they have already achieved close to the basic adult morphology. As a result, the identification of a rib is not at issue, only the identification of the position of the specific bone within its series. It should, however, be borne in mind that the cortical shell of juvenile ribs is extremely thin and that both pre- and post-mortem deformation can be major contributory factors in the misidentification of single bones.

Fetal and perinatal – In the fetal and perinatal skeleton, rib 1 is readily identifiable, as it bears the characteristic shape that it will maintain through to adult life. Ribs 2–6 can be identified as their heads generally lie in contact with the horizontal plane when they are placed, inferior border downwards, on a flat surface. Ribs 2 and 3 are somewhat hook-shaped, although this is not as pronounced as in rib 1. The hook shape starts to straighten out in rib 4, as the shaft takes on a gentler curve. In this way, ribs 2 and 3 can be separated from ribs 4–6. Ribs 7–9 are characterized by the fact that their heads have risen above the horizontal plane and so when the rib is placed on a flat surface, the head is elevated. Either rib 7 or 8 will attain the greatest elevation and this is again a phenomenon that is maintained through to adult life.

Ribs 10–12 in the fetal and perinatal skeleton are identifiable first by their smaller size and secondly by the general lack of definition in the region of the head. The head of rib 10 is in the horizontal plane and so lies in direct contact with a flat surface. This also occurs in ribs 11 and 12, but the latter two are markedly more rudimentary in terms of their development.

The fact that so many of the heads of fetal and perinatal ribs will lie in direct contact with a flat surface is readily explained by the common observation that fetal or neonatal ribs lie more horizontally, rather than obliquely in the thorax (Fig. 7.11). It is for this reason that the neonate depends almost entirely on its diaphragm for respiration, as thoracic involvement cannot occur until the ribs adopt a more oblique angle and the thorax descends.

Young child – In the young child, up until approximately 2–3 years of age, the major change that occurs is a descent of the ventral aspect of the thorax by an increasing obliquity of the ribs. This becomes apparent in the morphology of the infant ribs by an increase in the torsion of the shaft and therefore an inclination of the heads to rise above the horizontal plane when the rib is placed, inferior border downwards, onto a flat surface. Within the first year, the heads of ribs 5 and 6 will start to rise, so that by the end of the second or third year of life, all ribs except 1, 2 and 10–12 will show significant shaft torsion that results in an inclination of the heads above the horizontal plane and this persists into the adult situation.

Sideing of juvenile ribs
Typical ribs – As with adult remains, fetal and juvenile ribs are most readily sided by identification of the basic rib morphology. The head of the rib will be posterior and the slightly concave, cup-shaped surface for the costochondral junction will be anterior. The inner surface is concave, the outer surface is convex and the inferior border carries the subcostal groove.

In the absence of the extremities of the rib and given only the shaft, then sideing becomes more difficult. Ribs 2–6 show a twist or torsion at the ventral extremity, so that the outer surface faces more obliquely upwards. This is presumably due to the fact that these ribs articulate directly with the sternum (vertebrosternal). In the lower ribs, the region of the subcostal groove may be of value in identifying the anterior from the posterior extremities when only the shaft is present. Ventral to the region of the posterior angle, the subcostal groove is deeper posteriorly and becomes shallower anteriorly. Those ribs that lack a subcostal groove (ribs 1, 11 and 12) are naturally more difficult to side when fragmentary.

Atypical ribs – In the event of being unable to identify the characteristic morphology of the superior surface of the first rib, when the rib is placed on a horizontal surface, the tip of the head should be in contact with that surface. In this situation, the rib is in its correct position, in that the inferior surface faces downwards and the superior surface faces upwards. If the first rib is placed on a flat surface with the inferior surface facing upwards, then the head of the rib and the outer border will be elevated from the horizontal surface. This general rule holds true from the earliest prenatal stage to the adult situation.

Although the eleventh rib does not posses a readily identifiable subcostal groove, if the inner surface of the rib is examined, a change in shape may be identified, which may aid in side identification. It will be seen that passing from the tubercle in a ventral direction, the shaft increases in height in the region just beyond the posterior angle by an addition of a ledge of bone on the inferior margin for muscle attachment. Again, this morphology holds true from the earliest prenatal material to the adult situation.

The twelfth rib is probably the most difficult to side, but it is possible if the rib is intact. If placed on a horizontal surface, the superior border faces more outwards, while the inferior border faces more inwards. In this way, when looking at the outer surface of the rib, the superior border will overhang the inferior border.

Bones of a similar morphology

Although it is unlikely that the ribs will be confused with any other bone in the body, even when fragmented, some confusion may occur with a fibular shaft fragment, which can be mistaken for the neck region of a rib. Similarly, it is possible for an isolated region of the neck of the acromion of the scapula to be mistaken as a first rib. However, the real difficulty lies in establishing the individual identity of the bone.

Morphological summary (Fig. 7.13)

Prenatal
Wks 8–9	Ossification centres appear for ribs 5–7
Wks 11–12	Ossification centres present in all ribs

Birth	All primary ossification centres present
Yrs 12–14	Epiphyses appear in non-articular region of the tubercle
Yr 18	Epiphyses appear for articular region of the tubercle
Yrs 17–25	Epiphyses appear and fuse for head region
21+ yrs	Ossification may be present in the costal cartilages
25+ yrs	Ribs are fully adult

CHAPTER EIGHT

The Pectoral Girdle

The human pectoral (upper limb) girdle comprises a ventral **clavicle** and a dorsal **scapula** that articulate at the acromioclavicular joint. The clavicle also articulates with the manubrium medially and the scapula articulates with the head of the humerus laterally (Fig. 8.1). Therefore, the only joint between the girdle and the axial skeleton occurs anteriorly with the manubrium and under normal conditions there is no posterior bony connection to the vertebral column. The function of the clavicle is to serve as a strut to steady and brace the upper limb to the thorax, while the scapula achieves maximum mobility by being held in position by muscles and ligaments only. Therefore, the prime function of the pectoral girdle is to increase upper limb mobility through the reduction of articular constraints and so release it for prehensile and manipulative activities.

Early development of the pectoral girdle

The girdle bones are almost entirely derived from the lateral plate mesoderm of the trilaminar embryonic disc (see Chapter 3). Consistent with the fact that the embryo develops in a cephalocaudal direction, the pectoral girdle develops in advance of the pelvic girdle and larger elements tend to chondrify before their smaller counterparts. Mesenchymal cells migrate to the site where the future

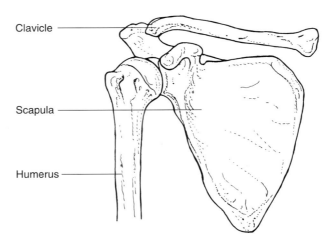

Clavicle

Scapula

Humerus

Figure 8.1 The articulations of the pectoral girdle.

clavicle will develop and maintain a lateral continuity with the mesenchymal condensation that will form the scapula (Hamilton and Mossman, 1972). The scapula develops at the mid-cervical level and neither the embryological nor the fetal clavicle will reach a horizontal position until the shoulders have fully descended (Corrigan, 1960a). Migration of the shoulder commences in the first year and continues until approximately 4 years of age but until full descent is achieved, the clavicle remains elevated at its lateral extremity.

The blastemal stage of clavicular development arises in prenatal week 5, with a fibrocellular proliferation that commences laterally and spreads medially (Gardner, 1968). These cells further condense into a mesenchymal rod that is certainly recognizable by the end of the 5th prenatal week (Gardner and Gray, 1953; Andersen, 1963; O'Rahilly and Gardner, 1975). By around 10 prenatal weeks, cavitation of the acromioclavicular joint is complete (Uhthoff, 1990c). During this early embryonic development of the bone, the supraclavicular nerves can become entrapped in the mesenchymal template (Turner, 1874) and foramina (canaliculi claviculare) will persist in the shaft of the adult clavicle forming tunnels for the passage of the nerves that supply the pectoralis major muscle.

There is a paucity of detailed information concerning the embryological development of the scapula. The upper limb bud arises as a localized differentiation of the lateral plate mesoderm opposite somites 8–10, which corresponds with future cervical vertebrae 5–7 (Streeter, 1942; O'Rahilly et al., 1956; O'Rahilly and Gardner, 1975; Ogden, 1979). The mesenchymal forerunner of the scapula begins to condense around day 33 and is clearly recognizable by day 37 (Lewis, 1901). The scapular anlage (attached to the clavicle via a blastemal connection) then migrates caudally so that by day 44 it lies opposite the first rib, by day 48 it has reached the fifth rib and by day 52 the lower angle has reached the fifth intercostal space (Lewis, 1901; O'Rahilly and Gardner, 1972; Gardner, 1973).

Failure of normal scapular descent results in a congenital elevation of the scapula known as 'Sprengel's deformity'. The aetiology of this maldescent is uncertain, although there may be some predisposing genetic factor. It has even been described as an atavistic representation of a normal condition that was present in man's simian ancestors but this would necessitate it being a bilateral phenomenon and it is usually unilateral. The author who originally described the clinical manifestations of the condition (Sprengel, 1891) suggested that it arose following malpositioning of the fetus *in utero*.

Sprengel's deformity is usually diagnosed in early childhood when the patient presents with an asymmetry at the base of the neck and elevation of the affected shoulder. It is likely that a radiological investigation will reveal that the scapula is not only elevated but also hypoplastic, retaining its fetal form (Livingstone, 1937; Chung and Nissenbaum, 1975; Ogden et al., 1979c). The affected scapula is elevated, reduced in length, occupies a position that is closer to the midline than in the normal situation and the inferior angle is somewhat tilted posteriorly and medially so that the glenoid cavity faces inferiorly. In this position, the mobility of the shoulder joint is affected and the clavicle may not develop its normal characteristic 'S' shape as it is elevated laterally and not in its normal position, which necessitates morphological compensation for the proximity of the neurovascular structures of the upper limb (Chung and Nissenbaum, 1975).

The deformity can be either uni- or bilateral but the incidence tends to be greater on the left. Although some authors state that there is no sex-specific predilection, Ozonoff (1979) considered it to be three times more common in the female. Sprengel's deformity is rare, although it is the most common of all congenital malformations in the shoulder region. In approximately 25% of cases, there is a physical connection between the medial border of the scapula and the cervical part of the vertebral column. This may occur by either a fibrous band or a cartilaginous strip, which may ossify in time to form an 'omovertebral' bone (Smith, 1941; Jeannopoulos, 1952). Some authors consider this bone to be homologous with the suprascapular bone of lower vertebrates and therefore essentially epiphyseal in nature. The omovertebral connection is generally wedge-shaped, being broader medially and attaches to either the spinous processes, transverse processes or laminae of cervical vertebrae 4–7. The omovertebral bone may fuse with the vertebral column or it may form a diarthrodial joint. Corrective surgery is possible, but a significant complication is the subsequent traction that is placed on the brachial plexus by a 'guillotine-like' action of the straightened clavicle. Maldescent of the juvenile scapula can also arise as a deformity following obstetrical brachial plexus paralysis (Pollock and Reed, 1989).

While this condition is normally attributed to failure of descent of the scapula from the neck to the thorax, other authors have attributed it to direct maldevelopment of the vertebrae. For example, Fairbank (1914) remarked that 'the only explanation which seems to account for the deformity is ... faulty segmentation of the mesoblast'. Von Bazan (1979), on the other hand, recognized that this was a relatively common embryological maldevelopment and suggested that it arose from a disturbance of the development of the notochord with abnormal inductive influence on the formation of the upper limb buds. The justification for these propositions is that Sprengel's deformity is normally associated with some form of vertebral maldevelopment (Müller and O'Rahilly, 1986).

The evidence for the cervical origin of the scapula has recently been confirmed through genetic research in mice (Aubin et al., 1998). The authors showed that if the *Hoxa* 5 gene is incorrectly expressed, abnormal development of the vertebral column in the region of C3–T2 occurs concomitant with an abnormal development of the acromion process of the scapula.

The early embryological scapula is somewhat convex on its ventral surface due to the virtual absence of a supraspinous fossa. In the early stages, the supraspinatus muscle is rudimentary and only attaches along the upper limits of the base of the spinous process. However, as the muscle mass increases, so the supraspinous fossa develops in response to the muscle activity. As a result, the two developing plates (supra- and infraspinous) meet at an angle, resulting in an apparent subscapular concavity.

Chondrification of the mesenchymal scapular plate commences in week 6 and ossification may begin around day 57 in the 8th week (Andersen, 1963; O'Rahilly and Gardner, 1972). Cavitation of the glenohumeral joint commences in the 7th prenatal week and is generally completed by the 10th week (Uhthoff, 1990c).

I. THE CLAVICLE

Ossification

Primary centre(s)

There is much controversy over the mode of development of the clavicle during the 6th and 7th prenatal weeks. The most widely accepted view is that ossification commences directly within the membranous structure of the blastemal stage, or at least in a matrix that some authors describe as 'precartilaginous' (Fawcett, 1913; Hanson, 1920; Gardner, 1968; Ogden *et al.*, 1979b; Ogata and Uhthoff, 1990). This membranous origin for the clavicle was previously taken as firm evidence that the clinical condition of craniocleidodysostosis (see later) arose from an early defect in bones formed via intramembranous ossification. This is now considered to be too simplistic a viewpoint, as the condition is more likely to be inherited as an autosomal dominant with a high degree of penetrance.

It has been widely accepted that the lateral aspect of the clavicle may develop from a membranous tissue (as evidenced by its more flattened appearance), while the more medial aspect develops via true endochondral ossification (given its tubular appearance, the presence of an articular disc and a medial epiphysis). This dual origin has also been used to explain the presence of paired centres of ossification.

At around day 39, in the 6th week of intra-uterine life, ossification commences in the precartilage anlage. Although some authors consider there to be only a single primary ossification centre, most agree that there are probably two primary centres (Fig. 8.2), one medial and one lateral. Congenital absence of the lateral half of the clavicle seems to lend some support to a double origin of ossification, as does duplication of the lateral half. Some authors consider the lateral centre to be the larger whilst others state that the medial centre is the larger. Regardless of this debate it is clear that a bony bridge forms shortly after ossification commences and the two centres have generally united by the 7th prenatal week, when vascular invasion of the ossified matrix commences (Fawcett, 1913; Andersen, 1963).

Congenital absence of the clavicle is rare and tends to show a familial tendency, probably arising through failure of the ossification centres to develop. The patient suffers from no power loss in the upper limb and no restriction in movement. In fact, bilateral absence of the clavicles results in hypermobility in this region so that the shoulders can be approximated in the midline when the arms are brought forward and the scapular borders can be made to overlap when the arms are brought behind. In these circumstances, the muscles that would normally attach to the bony clavicle instead find anchorage to an oblique fibrous band.

An inferior displacement of one of the primary centres of ossification can lead to the development of an accessory clavicle (os subclaviculare), which is generally an asymptomatic rudimentary structure. Qureshi and Kuo (1999) suggested that the duplication of the lateral half might be indicative of a previous fracture or injury to the bone. They reported that following lateral physeal separation, full reconstitution of the lateral part could occur.

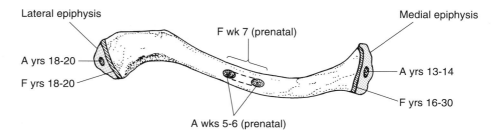

Figure 8.2 Appearance (A) and fusion (F) times of the clavicular ossification centres.

Once the osteoid matrix has been laid down in the precartilage model, then the medial and lateral extremities develop chondrogenous zones of hyaline cartilage so that bone length increases by true endochondral ossification via growth plates (Gardner, 1968). The sternal end grows more rapidly than the acromial end, so that some 80% of the total bone length is derived from growth at the medial end (Ogden *et al.*, 1979b). This explains the disproportionate morphology of the bone in terms of the proportions of the double curvatures and the lateral position of the nutrient artery, which is directed away from the growing end (Ogden *et al.*, 1979b).

The shaft of the clavicle adopts a distinctive 'S' shape by about 8–9 prenatal weeks (Andersen, 1963) and achieves virtual adult morphology by 11 prenatal weeks (Fig. 8.3) (Ogata and Uhthoff, 1990). Increases in bone width then continue by subperiosteal apposition in the shaft and true endochondral ossification at the medial and lateral extremities gives rise to an increase in bone length. This unusually early attainment of adult morphology indicates that the clavicle is not greatly influenced by postnatal mechanical stresses and forces. It is therefore a bone of both considerable phylogenetic and ontogenetic morphological stability (Corrigan, 1960a).

Studies on the fetal growth of the clavicle both by direct examination of the bone (Fazekas and Kósa, 1978) and by ultrasound (Yarkoni *et al.*, 1985) have shown that the clavicle grows at a surprisingly linear rate of approximately 1 mm per week. By term, the clavicle measures some 40–41 mm and then growth appears to slow down, although later growth spurts can be identified between 5–7 years of age and again at puberty (Black and Scheuer, 1996b).

There are two further congenital conditions that affect the clavicle and require additional consideration. The patient with craniocleido (cleidocranial) dysostosis presents with an exaggerated development of the transverse diameter of the cranium concomitant with a retarded ossification of the fontanelles. In addition, the clavicles are either hypoplastic, or indeed absent, leading to marked hypermobility of the shoulder joints (Fitzwilliams, 1910; Heindon, 1951; Tachdjian, 1972). In some instances, only medial and lateral clavicular stumps may develop for the appropriate muscular attachments with an absence of the central section. This can lead to abnormal pressure on the brachial plexus and subclavian arteries, leading to neurological and vascular disturbances. This condition tends to have an autosomal dominant inheritance, although there are some rare cases where it appears to be recessive (Dore *et al.*, 1987).

Fairbank (1949) found that the most common alteration to the clavicle was the absence of the lateral end, whilst Forland (1962) reported that most commonly the central segment would be absent but that medial and lateral stumps would prevail. This latter proposition would corroborate the fact that cranio-

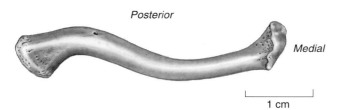

Posterior

Medial

1 cm

Figure 8.3 The right perinatal clavicle. Note the remarkable morphological similarity to the adult form at this very early stage.

cleidodysostosis generally affects those bones that form early in fetal life and, as the medial and lateral extremities of the clavicle develop later, then perhaps they are less affected. Alternatively, it may simply be an indication that the only true functional requirement of the clavicle is to provide a site for muscle attachment.

Congenital pseudo-arthrosis of the clavicle is rare and is generally detected shortly after birth and usually always by 6 years of age, presenting as a painless lump over the clavicle. It does not represent a birth injury, as there is no reactive bone at the site and no callus formation and some authors have taken its presence as being representative of non-union between the two primary centres of ossification. There is no evidence of a genetic link, it is not sex-specific and predominantly affects the right-hand side. In fact, Behringer and Wilson (1972) found that 94% of all cases occurred unilaterally on the right. This pseudo-arthrosis usually occurs just lateral to the midline of the bone, so that the sternal fragment is generally larger. The ends of the bone may be covered by cartilage and may even possess a synovial lining. The aetiology of this condition is unknown, although Lloyd-Roberts et al. (1975) suggested that it might be concerned with the relatively higher position of the fetal right subclavian artery. This would result in the right clavicle being subjected to exaggerated arterial pulsation in the region of the midshaft and this may affect the development of a bony bridge between the primary ossification centres and so alter the normal ossification process. Although painless, except in advancing age, when the condition may cause some aching, surgery is often recommended solely on the grounds of aesthetics.

Secondary centres

Following the pattern displayed by all other major long bones of the limbs, the adult clavicle is derived from a shaft (primary centre(s) of ossification) and medial (sternal) and lateral articular extremities that develop from secondary ossification centres (Todd and D' Errico, 1928). The medial epiphysis is flake-like in appearance and fairly rudimentary in nature, while the lateral epiphysis rarely exists as a separate structure, if indeed it is ever really present.

The **medial** metaphyseal surface of the developing shaft of the clavicle bears the characteristic ridge-and-furrow appearance indicative of vascular activity at a growth plate. Arteries gain access to this region from the periosteal vascular network and penetrate into the zone of hyaline cartilage at the articular extremity. Ossification commences in the epiphyseal cartilage mass around puberty (13–14 years) and has been reported as early as 11 years in females and 12 years in males.

Despite formation at an age that is in accordance with the appearance of other secondary centres in the skeleton, the medial end of the clavicle is, for some unknown reason, a slow-maturing epiphysis and fusion to the diaphysis will not occur until at least 10 years after its initial formation. In fact, it usually caries the accolade of being the final epiphysis to fuse.

The medial epiphysis generally appears as a small nodule in the centre of the sternal cartilage mass of the clavicle (Fig. 8.4). The nodule then begins to flatten out and spread over the articular face, first in a posterior and superior direction. At this stage, the epiphysis may be a separate structure or it may have commenced fusion in the centre of the flake with the metaphyseal surface. The epiphysis rarely covers the entire articular surface and often falls short of the anterior diaphyseal rim (Black and Scheuer, 1996b). Fusion between the diaphysis and the epiphysis begins around 16–21 years (although it has been

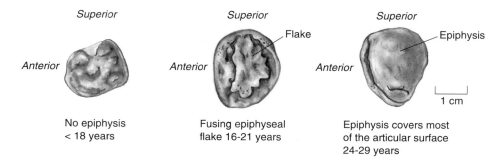

Superior

Anterior

No epiphysis
< 18 years

Superior

Flake

Anterior

Fusing epiphyseal
flake 16-21 years

Superior

Epiphysis

Anterior

1 cm

Epiphysis covers most
of the articular surface
24-29 years

Figure 8.4 Epiphyseal union at the medial end of the right clavicle.

reported as early as 11 years) and completion may not take place until close to 30 years of age (Stevenson, 1924; McKern and Stewart, 1957; Jit and Kulkarni, 1976; Szilvassy, 1980; Webb and Suchey, 1985; MacLaughlin, 1990; Black and Scheuer, 1996b). In summary, a medial end of a clavicle with no evidence of a fused/fusing epiphysis is likely to have come from an individual younger than 18 years of age. The presence of a well-defined fusing flake will occur in individuals between the ages of 16 and 21 years and an epiphysis that covers most of the articular surface will probably occur in an individual between 24 and 29 years. Complete epiphyseal fusion is unlikely to be seen before 22 years and is always complete by 30 years.

Trauma at the medial end of the juvenile clavicle, e.g. dislocation, can result in a separation of the medial epiphysis so that it forms as a separate bone (Denham and Dingley, 1967). Alternatively, the medial end may be resorbed and in this situation the sternal end of the diaphysis will glaze over so that a smooth articular surface is still formed. It is not uncommon to find adult medial clavicular surfaces that show a deep pit at the articular surface. In this situation it is clear that the medial epiphysis has either failed to form or has perhaps been resorbed. This can be quite a common occurrence in some populations (e.g. Kosovar Albanians), suggesting that there may be some genetic influence. It is critical therefore that the observer must first establish whether the metaphyseal surface is active before forming an opinion on the state of development of an epiphysis.

Although there are a number of texts that state that no epiphysis forms at the **lateral** (acromial) end of the clavicle, there are a sufficient number of reports that claim the opposite to be true. When, and if, a lateral epiphysis develops, it tends to be a transitory structure forming at around 19 or 20 years of age and fusing within months of its formation (McKern and Stewart, 1957; Gardner, 1968). Alternatively, the vascular ridge-and-furrow articular surface of the juvenile diaphysis (Fig. 8.5) may simply glaze over as bone is laid down to smooth the articular surface and so a separate entity may never exist (Todd and D'Errico, 1928).

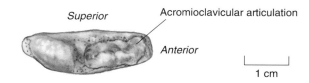

Superior

Acromioclavicular articulation

Anterior

1 cm

Figure 8.5 The lateral epiphyseal surface of the right clavicle.

Practical notes

Sideing of the juvenile clavicle (Fig. 8.3)

The early attainment of the adult-like form ensures that it is relatively easy not only to identify a juvenile clavicle, but also to be sure of its side. Correct orientation relies on being able to identify the superior and inferior surfaces, the anterior and posterior borders and the medial and lateral extremities in exactly the same fashion as one would with an adult bone. It is unlikely that a medial epiphysis could be identified in isolation and so sideing of such a structure is not an issue. Similarly the lateral epiphysis will not be identifiable in isolation, as it probably does not actually attain such a developmental status.

Bones of a similar morphology

A small cross-sectional fragment of a clavicle may be confused with a shaft of one of the long bones in the early stages of development, but the configuration of the medullary cavity should prevent misidentification. Fragments of the lateral end of the clavicle can also be confused with rib fragments.

Morphological summary (Fig. 8.2)

Prenatal

Wks 5—6	Primary ossification centres appear
Wk 7	Two centres fuse to form a single mass
Wks 8—9	Clavicle becomes 'S' shaped
Wk 11	Clavicle adopts adult morphology
Birth	Clavicle is represented by shaft only and is essentially adult in its morphology
Yrs 12—14	Medial epiphyseal flake forms
Yrs 16—21	Fusion of flake commences at medial extremity
Yrs 19—20	Lateral epiphysis may form and fuse
29+ yrs	Fusion of medial epiphysis will be complete in all individuals

II. THE SCAPULA

Ossification

Primary centres

The principal primary centre of ossification for the scapula probably arises in the vicinity of the surgical neck towards the end of the 2nd prenatal month, around 7–8 weeks (Mall, 1906; Noback, 1944; Andersen, 1963; Birkner, 1978). Only Fazekas and Kósa (1978) seem to be in any disagreement with this, stating that ossification commences somewhat later, around the 12th week.

A large nutrient foramen can usually be found in the supraspinous fossa at the thickest part of the lateral boundary of the spinous process. It is for the passage of a branch of the suprascapular artery that pierces the base of the spine at its medial third before dividing into medial and lateral vascular cones, which supply the spinous process. The foramen is usually non-directional and is considered to be the site of the initial nucleus of ossification. However, the primary ossification centre arises in the perichondrium on the ventral aspect of the scapula despite perichondral ossification normally being initiated via muscle-related activity. Laurenson (1964a) has reported that perichondral ossification can commence in advance of normal endochondral ossification when acting in a protective capacity, to prevent damage to well-established nerve pathways. In the fetal scapula, the supraspinous fossa is not well developed and the centre of ossification would correspond closely to the site of the suprascapular nerve as it passes over the superior border. We have consistently found that the largest nutrient foramen is situated in the lateral aspect of the supraspinous fossa at the junction with the spinous process and corresponds closely with the proposed site for the appearance of the primary nucleus of ossification. It is therefore possible that ossification in the scapula is initially perichondral before becoming truly endochondral in nature.

The suprascapular artery is the principal arterial source for the entire scapular region and the aforementioned foramen lies directly in its path, where it passes inferiorly towards the spinoglenoid notch. Therefore, it is likely that a branch directly from the suprascapular artery in the supraspinous fossa is the principal nutrient artery that initiates ossification. Although other nutrient foramina are present in the lateral aspect of both the infraspinous and subscapular fossae, they tend to be both smaller and more variable in position and so are unlikely to be the source of primary ossification.

Ossification expands bidirectionally and reaches the level of the base of the spine by week 9 and the glenoid mass by week 12 (Corrigan, 1960b; Andersen, 1963; Ogden and Phillips, 1983). This pattern of ossification leads to proximal (vertebral) and distal (glenoidal) epiphyseal formation at the end of radiating cones of endochondral ossification (Fig. 8.6). Growth rates are accelerated in the vertebral cone, which results in a greater expansion of the medial border compared to that for the lateral mass (Noback, 1944; Ogden and Phillips, 1983). The spaces between the two endochondral cones are then in-filled by membranous ossification so that much of the 'blade' of the scapula probably does form via intramembranous perichondral ossification, thereby explaining its relatively flat morphology and absence of cancellous bone. The scapula achieves close to adult morphology by 12–14 prenatal weeks and alters little until birth (Corrigan, 1960b; Fazekas and Kósa, 1978; Ogden and Phillips, 1983).

Corrigan (1960b) reported that the concept of 'parturitional proportions' should be considered in relation to growth of the scapula and clavicle, as

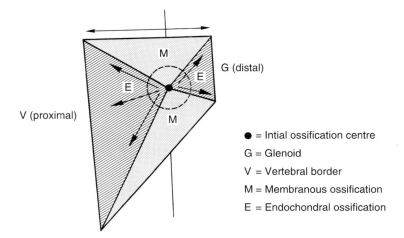

Figure 8.6 Pattern of ossification in the early scapula (redrawn after Ogden and Phillips, 1983).

these dimensions are important in the safe passage of the shoulder region at birth. He found these dimensions to be among the least variable of all measurements of the neonatal clavicle and scapula. Obstetric shoulder arises following trauma to the shoulder region as the fetus passes through the pelvic cavity and this can lead to fractures (most commonly of the clavicle), displacement of the glenohumeral joint or paralysis of upper limb muscles following damage to the brachial plexus. If the trauma passes undetected, then the deformity will persist throughout life and often leads to altered growth at the proximal end of the humerus and to abnormal development of the glenoid cavity.

At birth, the acromion process, coracoid process, medial border, inferior angle and glenoid articular surface are still cartilaginous (Fig. 8.7). The superior margin is often scalloped, the medial margin is convex and the lateral margin is concave. The subscapular fossa is gently concave and the supra- and infraspinous fossae are relatively flat. The infraspinous surface of the spinous process is sharply inclined, while the supraspinous surface is more horizontal. The spinous process ends in a bulbous lateral extension, which bears an epiphyseal surface on its more dorsal aspect. The glenoidal surface is almost oval in shape and slightly convex, with the articular surface extending

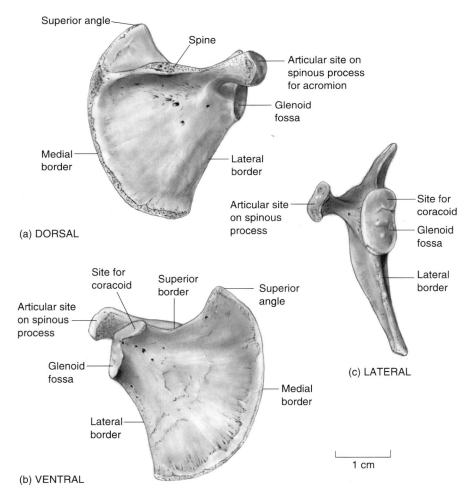

Figure 8.7 The right perinatal scapula.

onto the superior and ventral aspects for articulation with the coracoid process. A notch on the ventral surface clearly demarcates the coracoid from the true scapular regions of the glenoid surface. The glenoidal notch probably arises due to the pressure of the tendon of subscapularis as it passes in front of the joint on its way to attachment at the lesser tubercle of the humerus. The vascular foramina are prominent and the principal foramen is located in the supraspinous fossa at the junction with the spinous process laterally. There is a discernible thickening of the lateral border extending from the glenoid surface above to the inferior angle below.

The primary centre for the coracoid usually appears in the centre of the process within the first year of life (Cohn, 1921a; Smith, 1925; Andersen, 1963; Birkner, 1978; Ogden and Phillips, 1983), although it can be present before birth (Menees and Holly, 1932). The centre is always present by the second year and is certainly recognizable by the third year (Cohn, 1921a) if not before. Depending upon its time of ossification, the coracoid process can usually be identified as a separate structure within the first year, but becomes easier to recognize as it increases in size and the growing surfaces approach the main body of the scapula. The coracoid is hook-shaped, with a broad base and a pointed apex (Fig. 8.8). The base has a large billowed surface for articulation with the body of the scapula and a smaller articular surface on the posterolateral aspect for the subcoracoid centre. The infero-anterior surface is concave and smooth due to the passage of the supraspinatus tendon and the position of the subcoracoid bursa, while the superior surface is ridged for muscular and ligamentous attachments. The posterior surface bears the trapezoid ridge for the attachment of the trapezoid element of the coracoclavicular ligament.

The coracoid centre enlarges progressively and as it nears the scapula (generally in the second year) it develops a bipolar physis (growth plate) permitting growth at both the scapular and coracoid surfaces. Ogden and Phillips (1983) considered this to be a reflection of 'the independence of scapula and coracoid, from an evolutionary standpoint, in most vertebrates'.

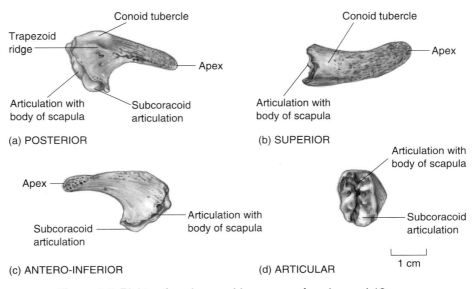

Figure 8.8 Right unfused coracoid process – female aged 12 years.

Fusion of the coracoid to the scapula generally occurs at around 14–15 years (Andersen, 1963) and commences in the region of the coracoid angle (Fig. 8.9). It is completed along the dorsal border in advance of the ventral border and the final area of the coracoid to show union is on the ventral surface of the scapula adjacent to the glenoid mass. This area finally fuses following invasion by a tongue of bone from the subcoracoid centre (Fig. 8.9c). Fusion with the sub- or infracoracoid process requires further consideration (see below). An extremely rare instance of non-fusion of the coracoid has been reported by Gunsel (1951).

Secondary centres

The scapula has at least seven secondary centres of ossification – three associated with the coracoid process, one for the inferior aspect of the glenoid, one at the inferior angle, one (or, more realistically, several small islands) associated with the vertebral border and at least one for the acromion process.

The **subcoracoid** (infracoracoid) centre appears between 8 and 10 years of age and is the first of the scapular secondary centres to commence ossification (Fig. 8.9). It is located in the superior third of the glenoid surface and is dorsal to the base of the coracoid process. It has a double epiphyseal surface for

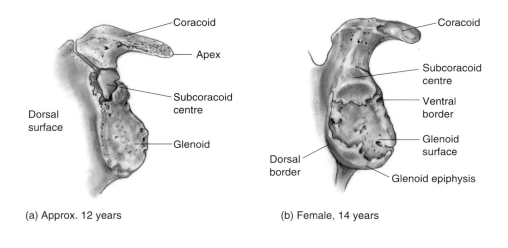

(a) Approx. 12 years

(b) Female, 14 years

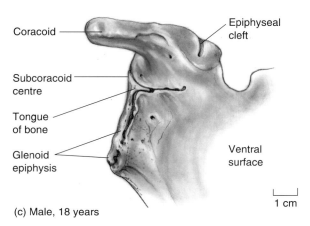

(c) Male, 18 years

Figure 8.9 The development of the right subcoracoid centre.

articulation with both the coracoid process anterosuperiorly and the remainder of the scapula inferiorly. Both of these epiphyseal surfaces commence fusion simultaneously around 14–15 years. Complete fusion between the coracoid and the subcoracoid occurs before complete fusion of the subcoracoid to the remainder of the scapula, as the inferior part of the epiphysis gradually spreads downwards across the upper region of the glenoidal face. The subcoracoid centre is responsible for the formation of the upper third of the glenoidal articular surface. Complete fusion is generally achieved by 16–17 years in both sexes and an indentation remains in the ventral rim of the adult glenoid, which represents the junction between the subcoracoid, coracoid and scapular ossification centres. It is likely that the early commencement of ossification in the subcoracoid centre occurs as a result of the action of the long head of the biceps brachii muscle, which partly attaches to the supraglenoid tubercle on the subcoracoid mass. It is unlikely that this centre is ever recognizable as a separate centre of ossification.

The secondary centre for the remainder of the **glenoid** surface appears around 14–15 years of age, as small islands of ossification around the periphery of the lower aspect of the glenoid rim. These islands eventually coalesce to form a horseshoe-shaped epiphysis, which attaches around the rim of the lower two-thirds of the glenoidal surface and ultimately fuses with the down growths from the subcoracoid centre and with the glenoidal surface of the primary centre (Fig. 8.10). The epiphysis then spreads from the periphery towards the centre of the glenoidal articular surface and complete fusion probably occurs between 17 and 18 years of age. The absence or maldevelopment of this centre gives rise to glenoid dysplasia and an increased incidence of congenital posterior dislocation of the shoulder joint. This hypoplasia or aplasia of the articular surface generally presents as a dentate-shaped glenoidal rim (Sutro, 1967; Chung and Nissenbaum, 1975). Given the size and fragile nature of this secondary epiphysis, it is again unlikely to exist as a recognizable structure in isolation from the glenoid mass.

The epiphysis for the **angle of the coracoid process** appears around 14–15 years of age and fuse by about 20 years. However, it is again unlikely that this epiphysis is ever a separate structure, as it appears to form as an outgrowth from the medial part of the coracoid process, which is in fact 'scapular' in origin (Fig. 8.11). Following fusion of the coracoid process to the sca-

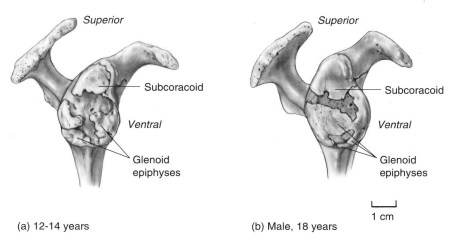

(a) 12-14 years   (b) Male, 18 years

Figure 8.10 Right glenoid epiphyses.

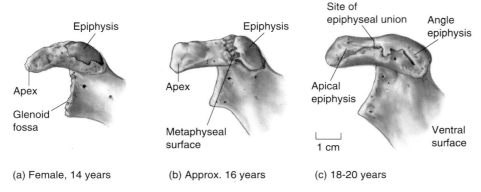

Figure 8.11 The epiphyses of the apex and angle of the right coracoid process.

pula, the thin, scale-like epiphysis passes forwards and laterally across the angle and superior surface of the coracoid process, where it eventually meets and fuses with the **epiphysis of the apex** (Fig. 8.11). This latter epiphysis is also flake-like in appearance and appears between 13 and 16 years and fuses by 20 years of age. Frazer (1948) reported accessory epiphyseal islands associated with the trapezoid ridge on the superior surface of the coracoid, but did not give any ages for either their appearance or fusion.

There is a considerable amount of variation, not only in the times of appearance and fusion of the **acromial epiphyses**, but also in their number and pattern of coalescence (Figs 8.12 and 8.13). Some authors state that there are two secondary centres of ossification, some say four and some say that it is a

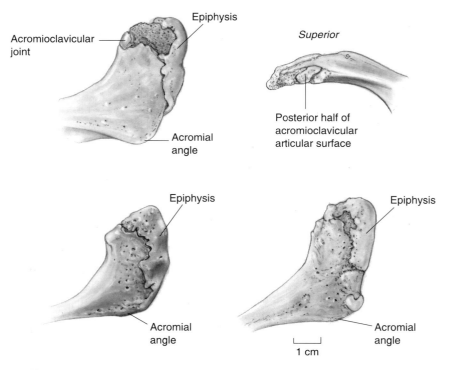

Figure 8.12 Variations in the appearance of the right acromial epiphyses.

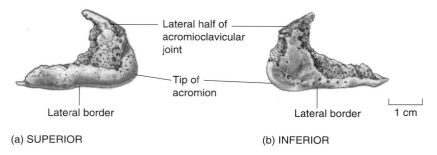

Lateral half of acromioclavicular joint

Tip of acromion

Lateral border

Lateral border

1 cm

(a) SUPERIOR

(b) INFERIOR

Figure 8.13 The right unfused acromial epiphysis.

site of multifocal ossification, but all agree that they appear between 14 and 16 years of age. What is clear is that there is a polarization in the literature depending upon whether the topic under discussion is the normal development of the acromion process or the aetiology of a bipartite acromion process (os acromiale). Papers and texts that deal with the latter state that there are usually four centres, while those of the former state that there are either two or three secondary centres and this corresponds with the situation that we have encountered in our investigation of juvenile remains (Fig. 8.12). The base of the acromion process develops from the lateral extension of the spinous process and generally extends from just medial to the acromial angle across to incorporate the most dorsal third of the acromioclavicular articular facet. An epiphysis (or, more likely, several foci of secondary ossification) develops along the lateral border of the acromion forming a cap that usually extends as far as the apex of the acromion. A second centre forms to fill the gap along the remainder of the anterior and medial borders and indeed a separate centre may form for the acromioclavicular facet. Although this basic pattern was present in all the scapulae we have examined, there is still a considerable amount of variation (Fig. 8.12). **Fusion** of the epiphysis will generally occur by 18–20 years of age.

The acromial epiphysis is distinct in appearance and can probably be identified as a separate structure by around mid- to late puberty (Fig. 8.13). It generally presents as a comma-shaped cap of bone with a rounded and thicker lateral border that forms a prominence at its lateral extremity (tip of the acromion). The anterior border bears the lateral half of the articular surface for the acromioclavicular joint. The lateral border has a shell of compact bone and this extends for a short distance onto the superior surface and for a greater distance onto the inferior surface, thereby forming a distinct plateau.

A bipartite acromion results from a mal-union of the epiphyseal centres to the basal part of the acromion that developed from the spinous process. The condition is often bilateral and results in a usually quadrangular separate piece of bone that articulates with the acromial base. The junction between the two pieces generally arises close to the acromial angle and passes across the middle of the process, often bisecting the acromioclavicular joint. This condition is normally asymptomatic (Chung and Nissenbaum, 1975), although it has been associated with an elevated incidence of rotator cuff injury (Mudge *et al.*, 1984). Some authors have stated that rather than being a developmental defect or in fact the result of traumatic injury, a bipartite acromion can result from repeated occupation-related trauma, which prevents bony union. Many of the original texts on the bipartite acromion state that the acromion arises from four distinct regions – a pre-acromion, meso-acromion, meta-acromion and a basi-acromion (Liberson, 1937) or some similar combination. It is generally held that when non-union arises, it is usually between the meso- and meta-acromial portions (Liberson, 1937). What is in general agreement is that the secondary centres for the acromion arise between 14 and 16 years of age and complete fusion does not tend to occur before 20 years of age, with the most concentrated period of activity being between 18 and 20 years (Ogden and Phillips, 1983). The last site of fusion is to be found on the inferior surface of the acromion, close to the lateral border.

The last scapular epiphyses to commence union are those associated with both the medial border and the inferior angle. Rather than a single centre, it is more likely that the **medial border epiphysis** arises from several small islands, which eventually coalesce to form a fragile narrow strip that commences union in the region of the inferior tip. The islands appear around 15–17 years of age and fusion is generally completed by 23 years of age (Stevenson, 1924; McKern and Stewart, 1957; Birkner, 1978). Fissures can often be found along the medial border in the adult bone and these may represent the sites of incomplete fusion of the epiphyses. It is unlikely that a separate epiphyseal strip can be recovered, as it probably fuses to the medial border as it is forming.

The **inferior angle** of the scapula develops from a secondary centre of ossification, which also appears around 15–17 years of age and generally fuses by 23 years (Stevenson, 1924; McKern and Stewart, 1957; Birkner, 1978). It is a small, crescentic epiphysis that fuses directly at the angle of the scapula and then sends a small tongue for a variable distance along the medial border (Fig. 8.14). A separate infrascapular bone has been reported (McClure and Raney, 1975), where non-union of the epiphysis has occurred. Further, the inferior angle of the scapula may completely fail to develop and this will result in a notched and somewhat foreshortened inferior extremity (Khoo and Kuo, 1948).

While there is much variation in the time of onset, the duration and the final time of closure of the epiphyses of the scapula, there does appear to be a fairly regular order within the individual (Fig. 8.15). At the same time as the coracoid commences fusion with the scapula, the subcoracoid also begins to fuse with

Figure 8.14 Epiphysis at the inferior angle of the left scapula – male aged 17–19 years.

(a)

A yr 1 A yrs 8-10

F approx yr 20

A approx yr 14

F yrs 16-17

F yrs 19-23

F approx yr 20

F yrs 16-17

A yrs 13-16

A yrs 14-16

F yrs 18-20

A yrs 14-15

F yrs 17-18

A yrs 15-17

A wks 7-8 (prenatal)

F yrs 19-23

A yrs 15-17

(b)

F approx yr 20

A yr 1

A yrs 13-16

A yrs 8-10

F yrs 17-18

A yrs 14-15

F yrs 15-20

A wks 7-8 (prenatal)

F yrs 19-23

A yrs 15-17

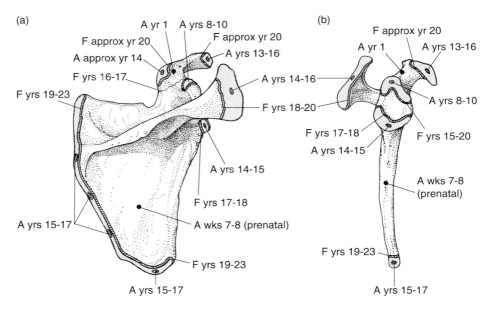

Figure 8.15 The principal primary centre of ossification of the scapula appears during weeks 7–8 of prenatal life and that for the coracoid process during the first year of life. Appearance (A) and fusion (F) of secondary centres – (a) dorsal; (b) lateral.

both the coracoid and the primary centre simultaneously. Before the subcoracoid centre has completed fusion, the ossification centre for the lower two-thirds of the glenoid will commence fusion. Upon completion of the entire glenoid surface, a flake will appear at both the angle and the tip of the coracoid process. Whilst the flake at the coracoid angle is in the process of fusing, the acromion process will commence fusion with the lateral aspect of the spinous process. The epiphyses for the inferior angle and the vertebral border lag behind and do not commence fusion until all other scapular epiphyses have ceased fusion.

Practical notes

Sideing of the juvenile scapula

The main body of the juvenile scapula achieves close to adult morphology by 12–14 weeks of intra-uterine life (Fazekas and Kósa, 1978; Ogden and Phillips, 1983) and so is readily identifiable by birth. Therefore, the same criteria are used to identify side in both juvenile and adult scapulae (Fig. 8.7).

The sideing of juvenile coracoids is not easy and primarily relies on being able to identify the articular surface for the subcoracoid and separate the superior from the inferior surfaces with the former being roughened for muscle attachment and the latter smooth for the passage of the supraspinatus tendon. With the roughened superior surface facing the observer and the conoid tubercle closest, the ventral border (furthest away) is slightly concave whilst the dorsal border (closest) is slightly convex. The apex of the coracoid will then be pointing to the side from which the bone originates (Fig. 8.8).

Sideing of the acromial epiphysis relies on the recognition of the differences between the superior and inferior surfaces, identification of the tip at the junction between the lateral and anterior borders and the position of the acromioclavicular facet. The superior surface is roughened for attachment of the deltoid muscle whilst the inferior surface is smooth due to the presence of the subacromial bursa. The lateral border is generally longer than the anterior border, which will carry one half of the articular surface for the acromioclavicular joint. So that with the superior surface uppermost and the longest border closest, then the comma shape of the epiphysis will point to side from which the bone originates (Figs 8.12, 8.13).

Sideing of the inferior angle epiphysis relies on being able to distinguish between the costal and dorsal surfaces, which is extremely difficult and so if this epiphysis was examined in isolation it is unlikely that a correct sideing could be achieved. The medial aspect of the epiphysis is characterized by a tongue of variable length that courses along the medial border but if unable to separate the dorsal and costal aspects then this will prove of little value (Fig. 8.14).

It is unlikely that any of the other scapular epiphyses can be identified in isolation, either because of their flake-like appearance or because they fuse shortly after formation or indeed actually during formation.

Bones of a similar morphology

Fragmented areas of a juvenile scapula may be confused with various bones of the skull or pelvis due to their flat morphology. The orientation of the bone formation along the extended medial cone should prevent misidentification and, owing to the nature of the spine, this tends to persist to some degree even in badly fragmented remains. If an area of spine is present, then the bone cannot be confused with any other in the skeleton. However, the similarity of the perinatal scapula to the isolated lateral occipital is quite remarkable, although on close examination the differences probably outweigh the similarities (see Chapter 4).

Morphological summary (Fig. 8.15)

Prenatal	
Wks 7–8	Primary ossification centre appears
Wks 12–14	Main body of the scapula has adopted close to adult morphology
Birth	Majority of main body of scapula ossified but acromion, coracoid, medial border, inferior angle and glenoidal mass are still cartilaginous
Yr 1	Coracoid commences ossification
Yr 3	The coracoid is recognizable as a separate ossification centre
Yrs 8–10	Subcoracoid centre appears
Yrs 13–16	Coracoid and subcoracoid commence fusion to body of the scapula
	Epiphyses appear for glenoid rim
	Epiphyses for angle and apex of coracoid appear
	Acromial epiphysis appears
Yrs 15–17	Fusion complete between coracoid, subcoracoid and body of scapula
	Epiphyseal islands appear along medial border
	Epiphysis for inferior angle appears
Yrs 17–18	Fusion of glenoid epiphyses virtually complete
By 20 yrs	Fusion of acromial and all coracoid epiphyses complete
By 23 yrs	Fusion complete at both inferior angle and along medial border; therefore, all scapular epiphyses fused and full adult form achieved

CHAPTER NINE

The Upper Limb

The human upper limb comprises the arm, forearm and hand (Fig. 9.1) and is connected to the axial skeleton by the two elements of the pectoral girdle (Fig. 8.1). The humerus forms the skeleton of the arm. Proximally, it articulates directly with the scapula at the shoulder joint and is indirectly joined to the thorax by scapular muscles and the clavicle. It articulates distally at the elbow joint with the radius and ulna.

The radius forms the skeleton of the lateral part of the forearm. It articulates proximally with the humerus at the elbow joint, distally with the carpus at the wrist joint and medially with the ulna at the proximal and distal radio-ulnar joints.

The ulna forms the skeleton of the medial part of the forearm. It articulates with the humerus at the elbow joint and laterally with the radius at the proximal and distal radio-ulnar joints.

The skeleton of the hand articulates with the forearm at the wrist (radio-carpal) joint with the radius. It comprises at least 27 bones – eight carpals, five metacarpals and 14 phalanges plus a variable number of sesamoids.

Early development of the limbs

There are many structural similarities between the upper and lower limbs. Each limb consists of a proximal segment containing a single bone, a middle segment with two bones and this is joined to a distal segment of five digits by a series of small bones. Although the detailed morphology of the carpus and tarsus can no longer be modelled on the old idea of a basic pentadactyl plan, there are common principles and mechanisms that apply to both limbs. Therefore, the initiation and early development of the limb buds are considered here but the descriptions of the later stages are described with each appropriate bone.

Much of the present knowledge regarding the mechanism of early limb development comes from experimental work on amphibian, reptilian and avian models (Amprino, 1984). More recent work has been undertaken on mammalian models including rodents and it can only be assumed at this time that similar mechanisms occur in the human embryo (Lane and Tickle, 2003). Studies of overlapping *Homeobox* gene domains are gradually providing explanations of the mechanism of control of limb development (Gumpel-Pinot, 1984; Dollé *et al.*, 1989; Izpisua-Belmonte *et al.*, 1991; Tabin, 1992; Lane and Tickle, 2003).

Early accounts of the histogenesis of human embryonic and early fetal limb development can be found in Bardeen and Lewis (1901) and Streeter (1942,

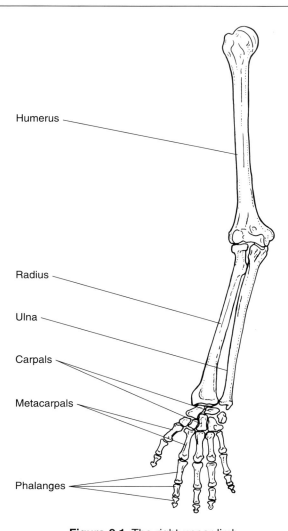

Humerus

Radius

Ulna

Carpals

Metacarpals

Phalanges

Figure 9.1 The right upper limb.

1949). Limb development using terminology of Carnegie stages was first described by O'Rahilly *et al.* (1956, 1957) and O'Rahilly and Gardner (1975).

The upper limb buds are first recognizable at stage 12 (about 30 days of prenatal life) as slight elevations and then as definite ridges opposite the seventh to twelfth somites in the region of the caudal cervical segments C3/4–T1. The lower limb buds are recognizable at stage 13 (about 32 days) opposite somites 25–29 at the L4-S2 level (O'Rahilly and Gardner, 1975; Müller and O'Rahilly, 1986; Fig. 9.2). During the embryonic period, the upper limb is about two days in advance of the lower limb. The constituent parts of both limbs develop sequentially in a proximodistal direction, both in their first appearance and later during chondrification and ossification.

Up to stage 19 (about 7 weeks), the longitudinal axes of the limbs are parallel, with the pre-axial borders facing cranially and the postaxial borders facing caudally (Fig. 9.3). There are several discrepancies in the accounts of embryonic limb rotation, but most describe the upper and lower limbs rotating in opposite directions. However, O'Rahilly and Gardner (1975) stated that the changes in position are complex and ill-understood and involve growth changes

dent formation of the lesser tubercle. The separate centres coalesce early in childhood to form a compound epiphysis, which fuses with the shaft at cessation of growth in length. The growth plate is characteristically cone-shaped, the medial part being intra-articular and lying within the capsule of the shoulder joint. Most of the information concerning times of appearance comes from radiological studies (Flecker, 1932, 1942; Elgenmark, 1946; Christie, 1949; Hansman, 1962; Garn *et al.*, 1967). However, Gray and Gardner (1969) demonstrated histologically that epiphyseal vascularization is present in the fetal period long before the onset of ossification. Early studies showed that the ossification centre for the **head** may be present at birth but usually appears by 6 months *post partum* (Menees and Holly, 1932). Christie (1949) found that the early appearance of the head was positively correlated with weight at birth, and was present more commonly in black females. Lemperg and Liliequist (1972) reported that in Swedish children the humeral head was ossified in over 50% of newborns and a definite correlation existed between time of appearance and weight at birth. Kuhns *et al.* (1973) and Kuhns and Finnstrom (1976) related the appearance of the humeral head to maternal history, birth weight and size as detailed by head circumference and body length, as well as maturity judged by neurological examination. The earliest sign of ossification was at 36 weeks *in utero* but there was wide variability in the onset of ossification and this was only slightly affected by the sex of the neonate. The centre for the humeral head therefore remains unossified in a significant percentage of infants at term and is too variable a feature to be used as a reliable indicator of maturity at birth. From about the end of the first year, the epiphysis for the head is an almost spherical nodule with a smoothly curving, pitted articular surface. It may have the beginning of a bridge of bone to the greater tubercle, which appears as a small downward-pointing beak, or it may remain unjoined to the tubercle for the first few years (Fig. 9.6a).

Reported appearance times for the centre for the **greater tubercle** are very variable and range from 3 months *post partum* to 3 years. Most accounts agree that it is present earlier in girls than in boys (Elgenmark, 1946; Hansman, 1962; Garn *et al.*, 1967). The centre appears laterally and at an angle to that of the head, so that the characteristically conical shape of the proximal epiphysis is present from an early stage. A separate centre for the **lesser tubercle** is described in most anatomy texts but the original source for this information is not well documented. Most radiological accounts (Ogden *et al.*, 1978; Caffey, 1993) only illustrate two centres for the proximal end. Cohn (1924) and Paterson (1929) doubted its separate existence, assuming it to be a downgrowth from the epiphysis for the head. However, Cocchi (1950) described a distinct third centre appearing between the ages of 4 and 5 years. This was not visible radiographically on a normal AP view, as its demonstration required a special axillary projection with the upper limb outwardly rotated. If indeed this third centre has a separate existence in all individuals, it is probably of fairly short duration.

The coalescence of the secondary centres to form a single **compound proximal epiphysis** is described in numerous radiological accounts as occurring between 5 and 7 years and this is the age reported in most anatomy texts. However, Ogden *et al.* (1978) stress that 'studies of postnatal development are virtually non existent' and that the 'appearance of ossification centres in the proximal humerus is not settled'. In their histological study, they describe bone bridging as early as 2 years, long before it can be demonstrated radiologically, which could account for the wide range of reported times of appearance in the literature. We have several compound proximal humeral epiphyses of docu-

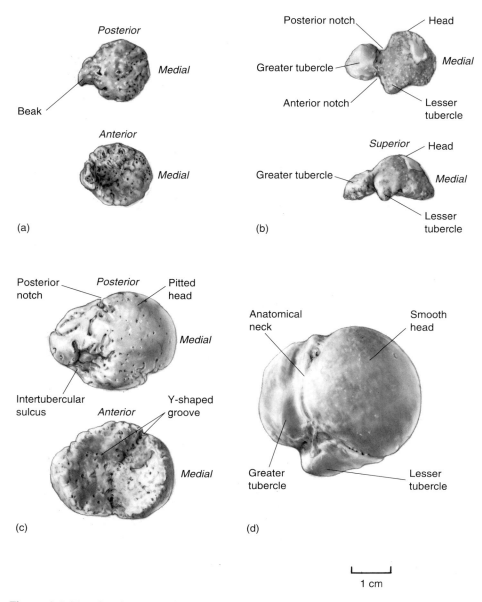

Figure 9.6 The development of the right proximal humeral epiphysis. (a) Head only ossified – 3 years; (b) early compound epiphysis – also 3 years; (c) later compound epiphysis – 8 years; (d) mature epiphysis – adolescent.

mented ages younger than 3 years. The morphology of the recently formed compound epiphysis is consistent with either the lesser tubercle appearing as a separate centre, or as a downgrowth from the capital epiphysis. It is an irregularly shaped bone, with the head joined to the greater tubercle at a constricted waist leaving definite anterior and posterior notches (Fig. 9.6b). The lesser tubercle is attached to the anterior border of the head. At about 7–8 years, the three parts of the epiphysis become more completely fused together and form an irregularly shaped cap (Fig. 9.6c). Anteriorly, the cleft between the greater and lesser tubercles consolidates to form the floor of the intertubercular sulcus, although posteriorly, the junction between the head and greater tubercle persists as an obvious notch. The whole articular surface is formed from porous-looking bone and the metaphyseal surface is deeply divided by a Y-shaped groove into its three constituent parts. By puberty, the three parts consolidate further. The surface of the head is smooth and delimited from the tubercles by an obvious anatomical neck, but there is still a pronounced posterior notch (Fig. 9.6d). From this stage until fusion, the epiphysis takes on the appearance of the adult bone.

Incidence of damage to the proximal humerus is uncommon in children compared to that seen in adults, and subluxation of the glenohumeral joint is rare. Displacement of the entire epiphysis may occur during delivery (Broker and Burbach, 1990) but this injury is not often seen after the age of 5 years. After this age, fractures may include a posteromedial fragment of the metaphysis (Dameron and Rockwood, 1984) or rarely, avulsion of the lesser tuberosity in adolescents (Paschal *et al.*, 1995). Hook-like projections called epiphyseal spurs are sometimes seen at the lateral edge of the epiphysis during childhood and adolescence. They can be mistaken for avulsion fractures but are normal transient phenomena that disappear during late puberty (Keats and Harrison, 1980).

Fusion of the proximal epiphysis coincides with cessation of growth in length, as this is the growing end of the bone. It is responsible for about 80% of growth in length of the shaft (Ozonoff, 1979; Pritchett, 1991). Information on ages of closure from radiographic data are given by Paterson (1929), Flecker, (1932, 1942) and Hansman (1962). These range from 12 to 19 years in females and 15.75 to 20 years in males. The only figures available from observations on skeletal material are those of Stevenson (1924), who does not distinguish between the sexes, and McKern and Stewart's (1957) report on the Korean War dead, which considers only the upper end of the range for males, from 17 to 24 years. They give 24 years for complete union and it thus appears that, from this incomplete set of data, there is a discrepancy (for males, at least) between the appearance of fusion radiographically and those observations made directly on bone, which give an age of about 2 years later.

The stages of closure first described by Stevenson have been used by many authors but the only information on the pattern of closure is from McKern and Stewart (1957), who state that, 'the last site of union for the proximal end appears as a slight groove, posterolaterally'. Ogden *et al.* (1978) suggest that the pattern of closure is variable and may begin in the central region of the epiphysis. In a series of juvenile skeletons we have found a regular pattern of fusion around the periphery. It usually commences in the region of the posterior notch between the head and the greater tubercle by small bridges of bone that eventually coalesce and this was also reported in a specimen by Haines *et al.* (1967). The next area to fuse is anteriorly at the junction of the anatomical and surgical necks. Fusion then progresses medially, thus attaching the head to the shaft, leaving the area under both tubercles open. Bridges of bone at the lateral lip of the sulcus consolidate and fusion spreads to the floor of the sulcus. The last areas remaining open are laterally and posteriorly around the greater tubercle. It thus appears that the pattern of fusion reflects the separate existence of the different parts of the proximal epiphysis.

The **distal epiphysis** of the humerus develops from four separate ossification centres, which appear in the following order: capitulum, medial epicondyle, trochlea and lateral epicondyle. Ranges for the appearance of these centres can be found in Flecker (1932, 1942), Francis *et al.* (1939), Francis, (1940), Elgenmark (1946), Haraldsson (1959) and Hansman (1962). The most useful developmental account is a radiological atlas of the paediatric elbow

(Brodeur *et al.*, 1981), which illustrates stages of maturation at 6-monthly intervals, distinguishing between early and late developers. There is also a radiological and histological study by McCarthy and Ogden (1982a).

The capitulum may appear as early as 6 months *post partum* and is nearly always present by 2 years. It begins as a spherical nodule of bone and by about 3 years its radiological appearance is hemispherical, with a straight superior margin. It appears to be tilted downwards anterior to the lower end of the diaphysis, as the growth plate is always wider posteriorly (Silberstein *et al.*, 1979). A recovered capitular fragment is a substantial wedge-shaped nodule of bone, which is thickest at its lateral base and thinner towards the medial apex. The articular surface is convex anteroposteriorly and the metaphyseal surface is flat. The anterior border is straight and the posterior border is pitted and pointed (Fig. 9.7a).

The medial epicondylar epiphysis can normally be seen on a radiograph by 4 years of age, but is slow to develop. Silberstein *et al.* (1981a) described its appearance as spherical, ovoid, or occasionally multicentric, so it would be difficult to recognize as an isolated epiphysis. The trochlear epiphysis develops initially as multiple foci in the eighth year and soon becomes joined at its lateral edge to the capitulum, from which it is separated by a groove (Fig. 9.7b). The lateral epicondyle is visible on a radiograph at the level of the capitular ossification at the outermost edge of the cartilaginous epiphysis at about 10 years of age (Silberstein *et al.*, 1982). It is occasionally double, but more normally appears as a semilunar sliver, which matures fairly rapidly into a triangular shape with the apex directed medially. The distal part fuses to the lateral edge of the capitulum and often has a nodular articular surface (Fig. 9.7c).

There is a complex pattern of **fusion** but, unlike the proximal end, once the separate centres coalesce, the composite epiphysis does not remain separate from the shaft for very long. The combined capitulum, trochlea and lateral epicondyle are usually united by 10 years in girls and 12 years in boys (Haraldsson, 1959). Brodeur *et al.* (1981) illustrate this fusion as beginning at about 11.5 years in girls and about a year later in boys. Fusion with the shaft begins posteriorly, leaving a line open above the capitulum, lateral trochlea and proximal lateral epicondyle and is usually complete by about 15 years. The centre for the medial epicondyle remains separate from the rest of the compound epiphysis, being isolated from it by a non-articular part of the shaft (Fig. 9.7d). The medial epicondyle is the last of the elbow epiphyses to unite with the shaft, but reported ages of fusion cover a wide time range (Flecker, 1932, 1942; Hansman, 1962) so that it is not a useful indicator of age. Hansman gives a range of 11–16 years in females and 14–19 years for males, but the Brodeur *et al.* (1981) atlas shows that fusion usually occurs by about 15 years of age. It fuses from below upwards, the superior and anterior surfaces being the last to unite, leaving a temporary notch anterosuperiorly (Fig. 9.7e).

After supracondylar fracture, avulsion of the lateral epicondyle is the most common injury at the distal end of the humerus in children (Rutherford, 1985; Nicholson and Driscoll, 1993). If fracture separation of the whole distal epiphysis including the medial epicondyle occurs, it is usually in the young child, when the epiphysis is composed predominantly of cartilage. In the older child the medial epicondyle often remains with the shaft (Wilkins, 1984). The late and separate fusion of the medial epicondyle, with its characteristic notch, can lead to a mistaken diagnosis of fracture in adolescence, but avulsion by muscular action is possible.

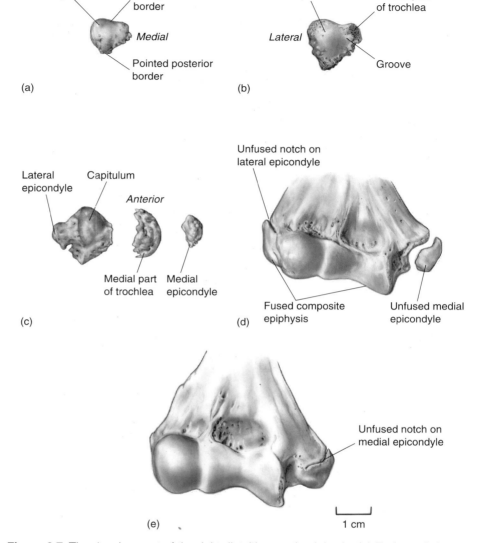

Figure 9.7 The development of the right distal humeral epiphysis. (a) Early capitulum – 7 years; (b) later capitulum – 8 years; (c) three separate parts of epiphysis – late childhood; (d) main part of compound epiphysis fused – adolescent; (e) almost mature distal end – late adolescent.

The appearance and fusion times of the humeral ossification centres are summarized in Fig. 9.8.

Practical notes

Sideing of the juvenile humerus

Diaphysis – the neonatal or infant humerus can be sided using the following features. Proximally, the anterior ridge in the middle of the shaft leads up to the lateral lip of the intertubercular sulcus. The medial border slopes slightly towards the head, whereas the lateral border is straighter. The nutrient fora-

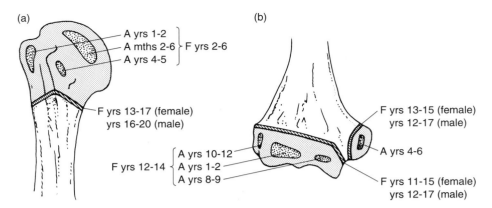

Figure 9.8 The primary ossification centre of the humerus appears during week 7 of prenatal life. Appearance (A) and fusion (F) of secondary centres: (a) proximal end; (b) distal end.

men is usually on the anteromedial side, with its entrance directed distally (Fig. 9.5a,b). Posterodistally, the lateral border of the olecranon fossa is wider than the medial side (Fig. 9.5b).

Proximal epiphysis – the lesser tubercle extends from the head anteriorly and the greater tubercle is lateral, separated by anterior and posterior notches (Fig. 9.6b).

Distal epiphysis – in a young skeleton, the capitulum is usually the only recognizable separate part of the distal epiphysis that is recovered. It is a wedge-shaped nodule of bone, wider at the lateral end. The anterior border is straight and the posterior border is pointed and pitted with nutrient foramina (Fig. 9.7a,b). Once the other parts of the epiphysis have fused to the capitulum, it can be sided in the same manner as the distal end of the adult bone.

Bones of a similar morphology

Perinatal diaphyses – the six major long bones of the limbs can be divided into two groups: the femur, humerus and tibia are larger and look more robust than the radius, ulna and fibula. Taking the bones of a single individual, in the first group, the femur is considerably longer than the humerus and tibia, which are about equal in length (Table 9.1). The humerus can be distinguished from the tibia as it is flattened distally and bears the obvious olecranon fossa posteriorly whereas the tibial shaft is triangular and has flared proximal and distal ends (Figs 9.5 and 11.11). From birth onwards, the growth rate in the lower limb is faster than that of the upper limb and the tibia increases in length faster than the humerus.

Proximal humeral fragment – this may be confused with a proximal femoral fragment or a proximal or distal tibial fragment (Fig. 9.9). The metaphyseal surface of the humerus is roughly circular, with the notch of the intertubercular sulcus visible anteriorly, whereas the metaphyseal surface of the proximal femur is larger and continuous posteriorly onto the lesser trochanteric surface of the shaft. After the neonatal period, the humerus assumes its characteristic peaked proximal end and in the femur the neck begins to develop. The proximal tibia is distinguished from the proximal humerus by its more oval metaphyseal surface, the presence of the tuberosity and, if

Table 9.1 Means and ranges for maximum lengths of diaphyses of major long bones at 10 lunar months

	Mean (mm)	Range (mm)
Humerus	64.9	61.6–70.0
Radius	51.8	47.5–58.0
Ulna	59.3	55.0–65.5
Femur	74.3	69.0–78.7
Tibia	65.1	60.0–71.5
Fibula	62.3	58.0–68.5

Adapted from Fazekas and Kósa (1978)

enough of the shaft is present, the very large nutrient foramen posteriorly. The distal tibial metaphyseal surface is similar in size to that of the humerus but is flatter and has a 'D'-shaped outline with a straight lateral border. The metaphyseal surface of the humerus is raised medially towards the head.

Distal humeral fragment – this can be recognized by the characteristic olecranon fossa posteriorly (Fig. 9.5b,d).

Proximal humeral and femoral head epiphyses – superficially these may look similar but, for a single individual at an early stage, the capital femoral epiphysis is about 1.5 times larger than that of the humerus (Fig. 9.10a,b) and the latter often has either a small laterally pointed beak, which is the beginning of the bridge to the greater tubercle, or has already assumed its tripartite appearance (Figs 9.6c, 9.10e). Later, the composite epiphysis and the femoral head are of similar size, but the humeral epiphysis has assumed its characteristic cap shape with a tripartite groove on its metaphyseal surface

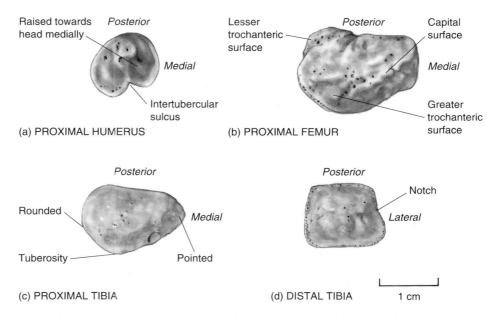

(a) PROXIMAL HUMERUS

(b) PROXIMAL FEMUR

(c) PROXIMAL TIBIA

(d) DISTAL TIBIA   1 cm

Figure 9.9 The metaphyseal surfaces of the right perinatal humeral, femoral and tibial diaphyses.

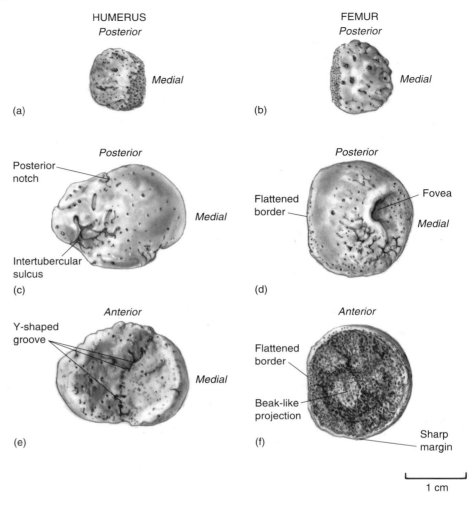

HUMERUS

FEMUR

Figure 9.10 The right humeral and femoral proximal epiphyses. Articular surfaces of (a) humeral head epiphysis and (b) femoral head epiphysis – male aged 3 years. Articular surfaces of (c) humeral proximal epiphysis and (d) femoral head epiphysis – female aged 8 years; (e) and (f) metaphyseal surfaces of (c) and (d), respectively.

(Fig. 9.10e). The femoral head epiphysis is more circular, with a flattened lateral border. The fovea is visible on the articular surface and the beak-shaped projection can be seen on the relatively flat metaphyseal surface (Fig. 9.10d,f).

Morphological summary (Fig. 9.8)	
Prenatal	
Wk 7	Primary ossification centre appears
Wks 36–40	Secondary ossification centre for the head may be visible
Birth	Usually represented by shaft only
2–6 mths	Secondary centre for head appears
1–2 yrs	Secondary centre for greater tubercle appears; secondary centre for capitulum appears
4+ yrs	Secondary centre for medial epicondyle appears and possibly that for lesser tubercle

2–6 yrs	Centres for head, greater and lesser tubercles fuse to form composite epiphysis
By yr 8	Secondary centre for trochlea appears
Yr 10	Secondary centre for lateral epicondyle appears
11–15 yrs	Distal composite epiphysis joins shaft in females
12–17 yrs	Distal composite epiphysis joins shaft in males
13–15 yrs	Medial epicondyle fuses to shaft in females
14–16 yrs	Medial epicondyle fuses to shaft in males
13–17 yrs	Proximal epiphysis fuses in females
16–20 yrs	Proximal epiphysis fuses in males

II. THE RADIUS

The radius forms the skeleton of the lateral part of the forearm and is a long bone consisting of a proximal head, a shaft and an expanded distal end. It articulates proximally with the capitulum of the humerus at the elbow joint, distally with the scaphoid and lunate bones of the carpus at the wrist joint and medially, both proximally and distally, with the ulna, at the superior and inferior radio-ulnar joints.

Early development of the radius

The mesenchymal radius is identifiable at stage 16 (about 8–11 mm/38 days of prenatal life (O'Rahilly et al., 1957). The cartilage anlage starts to form by stage 17 (about 41 days) and by the end of the embryonic period the head, neck and styloid process are all clearly defined (O'Rahilly et al., 1957; O'Rahilly and Gardner, 1975). By stage 21 (about 51 days) there is evidence of early bone collar formation and enlargement of cartilage cells in the centre of the shaft.

Congenital or complete absence of the radius can occur and is usually associated with abnormalities of the hand (Wakeley, 1931; Evans et al., 1950). A radio-ulnar synostosis may also occur and can present with either the proximal radius assimilated with the ulna leaving no recognizable radial head or with the two bones connected by a bony bar, proximal to which a rudimentary radial head may be seen (Hughes and Sweetnam, 1980). This anomaly severely restricts the functional range of the limb as it prevents pronation and supination. Both the absence of a part, or whole, radius and a synostosis probably occurs at the embryological 5–6 week stage which is the normal time for the anlagen of the two bones to separate during the development of the superior radio-ulnar joint.

Ossification

Primary centre

Ossification in the diaphysis is evident during week 8 when a bony collar appears in the midshaft (O'Rahilly and Gardner, 1972). By about 12 weeks of prenatal life, ossification has reached as far as the radial tuberosity, and between 18 and 28 weeks it has extended into the neck proximal to the tuberosity. At term, ossification reaches well into the neck but the tuberosity is still only partially ossified and consists largely of cartilage (Gray and Gardner, 1951). There is a single nutrient foramen in 95% of cases, which is normally situated in the middle of the proximal half of the shaft (Skawina and

Wyczólkowski, 1987). From about the 6th prenatal month, the morphology of the radial diaphysis is sufficiently distinct to permit identification.

The perinatal radius (Fig. 9.11) is rounded in its proximal half and triangular in the distal half and has a very slight lateral curvature. At the proximal end, the neck is directed laterally and the metaphyseal surface is circular and almost flat. Posteriorly, the oblique line is usually visible as a rounded ridge in the middle two quarters and the interosseous border forms a sharp edge. The roughened tuberosity is obvious on the medial side. The shaft flares towards the distal end and its anterior surface is flattened, smooth and slightly concave. The nutrient foramen usually occurs just above the centre of the anterior surface, towards the medial side, and the entrance slopes proximally. The distal metaphyseal surface is oval or triangular with pointed lateral and rounded medial ends. The anterior border is smooth and the posterior border is angled (Fig. 9.11d).

During the first year, a more pronounced lateral curvature develops. The distal metaphyseal surface becomes more angulated posteriorly and flattened medially at the base of the triangle for the ulnar notch. By about 4 years, the

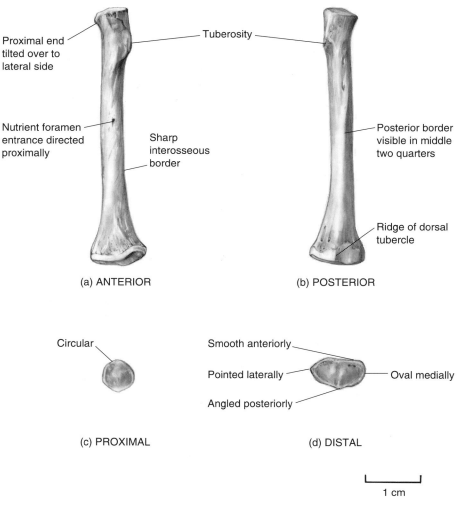

Proximal end tilted over to lateral side

Tuberosity

Nutrient foramen entrance directed proximally

Sharp interosseous border

Posterior border visible in middle two quarters

Ridge of dorsal tubercle

(a) ANTERIOR

(b) POSTERIOR

Circular

Smooth anteriorly

Pointed laterally

Angled posteriorly

Oval medially

(c) PROXIMAL

(d) DISTAL

1 cm

Figure 9.11 The right perinatal radius.

anterior oblique line (the attachment for pronator teres) can be identified. The dorsal tubercle and the groove for the tendon of extensor pollicis longus become apparent with the development of the distal epiphysis and both features extend onto the shaft at about the time of puberty.

The radius is the most commonly fractured bone in children and accounts for almost half of all fractures. The injury usually follows a fall on the outstretched hand, which results in most of the fractures occurring in the distal third (O'Brien, 1984; Thornton and Gyll, 1999).

Secondary centres

The **distal epiphysis** of the radius normally develops from a single centre, which usually appears during the first year and is always present by the middle of the third year. Age ranges for appearance are given by Flecker (1942), Elgenmark (1946), Hansman (1962) and Garn et al. (1967). Detailed radiological standards for girls and boys can be found in the Greulich and Pyle (1959) atlas and a radiological developmental study, including injury patterns, has been described by Ogden et al. (1981). Epiphyseal displacements of the distal radius and ulna are amongst the most common injuries of the growth mechanism in childhood.

The distal ossification centre appears first as a rounded bony nodule, which only gradually takes on the recognizable shape of the distal epiphysis. It begins to flatten out towards the ulnar side during the second year and soon the lateral part becomes thicker so that the epiphysis assumes a triangulated wedge-shaped appearance (Fig. 9.12a). By about 7–8 years the anterior border is straight and the posterior border is angulated in the region of the dorsal tubercle. The medial border is flattened and the thick lateral end is beginning to ossify into the styloid process (Fig. 9.12b). The latter may develop from a separate centre and even remain unfused throughout life (Keats, 1992). By puberty, the ossified area occupies most of the epiphysis and the metaphyseal surface begins to 'cap' the end of the shaft. The dorsal tubercle becomes obvious and bears a groove on its medial side and the medial border forms a definite ulnar notch (Fig. 9.12c). From this stage until fusion, the epiphysis takes on the appearance of the end of the adult bone. Small hook-like projections called epiphyseal spurs, which may simulate avulsion fractures, sometimes develop at the lateral edge of the epiphysis. They are normal variants, probably caused by isolated islands of ossification and disappear by the time of fusion (Harrison and Keats, 1980).

The distal radius is the growing end of the bone and is responsible for 75–80% of the growth in length of the shaft (Ozonoff, 1979; Pritchett, 1991) and the epiphysis is one of the last of the major long bones to fuse. Figures for ages of **fusion** from radiographic observations are given by Flecker (1942) and Hansman (1962). The Greulich and Pyle (1959) radiological wrist atlas gives a series of maturity indicators for the distal end of the radius. They show that fusion begins in the middle of the epiphysis and is usually complete by 15–16 years in females and 17–18 years in males. However, McKern and Stewart (1957) report that 100% fusion was not found in males until the age of 23 years so that, as with the humerus, there is a discrepancy between radiographic and osteological observations.

Fracture separation of the distal epiphysis is the commonest epiphyseal injury (juvenile Colles'). It is not seen much before 6 years of age (Thornton and Gyll, 1999).

The **proximal epiphysis** of the radius normally appears at 5 years of age. It is one of the few epiphyses that are not spherical on first appearance and forms

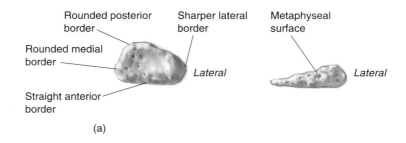

Rounded posterior border
Sharper lateral border
Metaphyseal surface
Rounded medial border
Lateral
Lateral
Straight anterior border

(a)

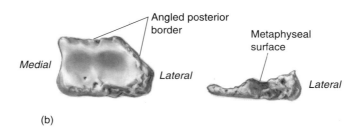

Angled posterior border
Metaphyseal surface
Medial
Lateral
Lateral

(b)

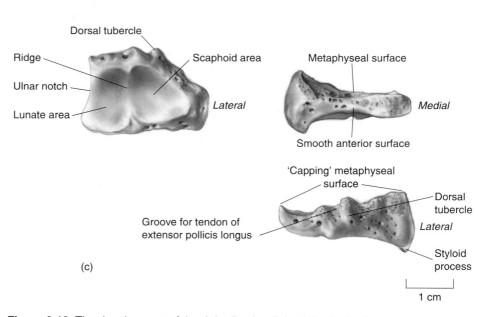

Dorsal tubercle
Ridge
Scaphoid area
Metaphyseal surface
Ulnar notch
Lunate area
Lateral
Medial
Smooth anterior surface

'Capping' metaphyseal surface
Dorsal tubercle
Groove for tendon of extensor pollicis longus
Lateral
Styloid process

(c)

1 cm

Figure 9.12 The development of the right distal radial epiphysis. (a) Early stage – 7 years; (b) later stage – 10 years; (c) mature epiphysis – adolescent. Left row articular surface. Right row (a) and (b) posterior surfaces; (c) anterior and posterior surfaces.

as a flat disc, although it may occasionally develop from two centres lying side by side (Brodeur *et al.*, 1981). Francis *et al.* (1939), Elgenmark (1946), Hansman (1962) and Garn *et al.* (1967) all give separate figures for males and females, which demonstrate that appearance is usually earlier in females and the paediatric elbow atlas (Brodeur *et al.*, 1981) has separate staged radiographs for boys and girls. A detailed radiological account of early development correlated with possible injury patterns can be found in McCarthy and Ogden (1982b). The epiphysis of the radial head (Fig. 9.13a) first appears as a flat sclerotic nucleus slightly posteriorly placed and elliptical in shape when first formed, being wider laterally than in the anteroposterior plane. It has a smooth articular surface and a roughened metaphyseal surface. Ossification gradually expands, first in an elliptical fashion, towards the edge of the epiphysis until its margins and those of the shaft attain the same width, although the joint space is wedge-shaped, being wider on the lateral side. This is related to the fact that, prior to ossification, the metaphyseal surface is not parallel to the articular surface of the capitulum and therefore a line drawn through the long axis of the radial neck projects lateral to the capitulum (Brodeur *et al.*, 1981). The indentation of the fovea is not usually obvious until 10–11 years of age (McCarthy and Ogden, 1982b) and this deepens as the epiphysis matures towards fusion at adolescence (Figs 9.13b,c).

The so-called 'pulled elbow' occurs when the radial head is subluxated out of the annular ligament. It usually occurs in early childhood (15 months to 3 years) when a child is suddenly swung by the arm or steps down from a curb while being held by the hand (Thornton and Gyll, 1999).

Ages for **fusion** of the proximal epiphysis are variable, especially in females, as this is affected by menarche, but all accounts agree that fusion occurs earlier in girls than in boys. Brodeur *et al.* (1981) show a range from radiographs of 11.5–14 years in females and from 13.5–16 years in males. Direct observations on dry bone are incomplete as McKern and Stewart (1957) were able to report ages of fusion during the last part of the range for males only. Even though the proximal radius falls into their Group I of early union, they only found 100% fusion at 19 years. A photograph shows an almost fused epiphysis, with the epiphyseal line still open medially over the tuberosity, and in a series of juvenile skeletons, we have confirmed that this is usually the last part of the head to fuse.

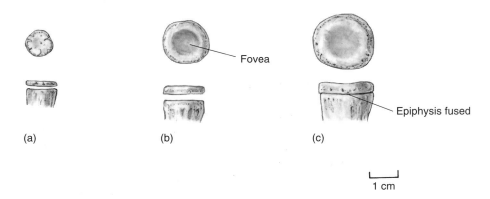

(a) (b) (c)

1 cm

Figure 9.13 The development of the right proximal radial epiphysis. (a) Early stage – 7 years; (b) later stage – 10 years; (c) fused epiphysis – late adolescent. Top row – proximal surface. Bottom row – anterior surface.

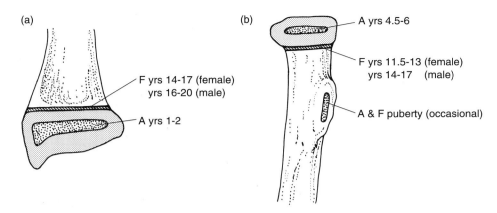

(a)

F yrs 14-17 (female)
yrs 16-20 (male)

A yrs 1-2

(b)

A yrs 4.5-6

F yrs 11.5-13 (female)
yrs 14-17   (male)

A & F puberty (occasional)

Figure 9.14 The primary ossification centre of the radius appears during week 7 of pre-natal life. Appearance (A) and fusion (F) of secondary centres – (a) distal end; (b) proximal end.

The tuberosity of the radius often has the appearance of new bone formation but evidence for a separate epiphysis at this site is conflicting. It is possible that there is a flake epiphysis similar to those for the tubercles of the ribs whose epiphyses look very similar before and after union (see Chapter 7). Flake epi-physes have a short independent life, fusing soon after their formation and are therefore only identifiable during the process of fusion. The appearance and fusion times of the radial ossification centres are summarized in Fig. 9.14.

Practical notes

Sideing of the juvenile radius
Diaphysis – the perinatal or infant radius (Fig. 9.11) can be sided using the following features. Proximally, the bone tilts laterally and the radial tuberosity is on the medial side. In the shaft, the sharp interosseous border is on the medial side. At the distal end, the anterior surface is smooth and slightly concave, whereas the posterior surface is angulated at the dorsal tubercle. The nutrient foramen is usually on the anterior surface of the proximal half of the bone with its entrance directed proximally.

Distal epiphysis – (Fig. 9.12) is wedge-shaped with the thicker end lateral, the anterior border straight and the posterior border rounded or angled. At a later stage, the styloid process can be seen laterally and the dorsal tubercle and groove are on the posterior surface.

Proximal epiphysis – we have not been able to distinguish a right from a left proximal radial epiphysis prior to fusion with the shaft.

Bones of a similar morphology
Perinatal diaphyses – of the diaphyses of the six major long bones, the radius, ulna and fibula are smaller and look less robust than the femur, humerus and tibia (Table 9.1). The radius always remains the shortest of all the long bones. Its tuberosity and flared distal end are characteristic.

Proximal radial fragment – this is distinctive (Fig. 9.11), with the con-stricted neck and circular metaphyseal surface tilted to the lateral side. The tuberosity is obvious just below this. The distal ulna and both ends of the fibula have surfaces of much the same size, but they are at right angles to the shaft.

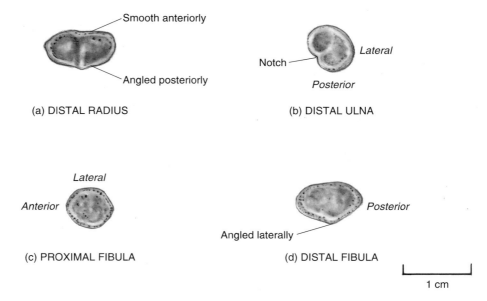

Figure 9.15 The metaphyseal surfaces of right perinatal radial, ulnar and fibular diaphyses.

Distal radial fragment – this is similar to the distal ulnar, proximal fibular or distal fibular fragments. The radial metaphyseal surface is bigger than either the ulna or fibula and has an oval outline, which is usually angled posteriorly. The shaft is flared and has a curved anterior surface (Fig. 9.15).

Morphological summary (Fig. 9.14)

Prenatal
Wk 7	Primary ossification centre appears in shaft

Birth
	Represented by shaft only
1–2 yrs	Secondary centre for distal epiphysis appears
Yr 5	Secondary centre for head appears
By yr 8	Styloid process forms on distal epiphysis
10–11 yrs	Proximal epiphysis shows foveal indentation
11.5–13 yrs	Proximal epiphysis fuses in females
14–17 yrs	Proximal epiphysis fuses in males
Puberty	Flake for tuberosity may form as separate centre
14–17 yrs	Distal epiphysis fuses in females
16–20 yrs	Distal epiphysis fuses in males

III. THE ULNA

The ulna forms the skeleton of the medial part of the forearm and is a long bone consisting of an expanded proximal end, a shaft and a head at the distal end. It articulates proximally with the trochlea of the humerus at the elbow joint and laterally, both proximally and distally, with the radius at the superior and inferior radio-ulnar joints.

Early development of the ulna

The mesenchymal ulna is identifiable at stage 16 (about 38 days of prenatal life) and the cartilage anlage starts to form at stages 17–18 (between 41 and 44 days; O'Rahilly and Gardner, 1975). Chondrification in the olecranon is usually obvious at 46 days and in the styloid process by 49 days. By stage 21 (about 51 days) there is evidence of early bone collar formation in the shaft (O'Rahilly and Gardner, 1975).

As with the radius, the ulna may be congenitally absent (Mann *et al.*, 1998) and this probably occurs at the 5–6 week developmental stage (see Radius – early development).

Ossification

Primary centre

Ossification is first seen at stages 22–23 (during week 8) when a bony collar is seen in the midshaft (O'Rahilly and Gardner, 1975). By 12 weeks of prenatal life, ossification has reached to the same level as the radial tuberosity proximally and between 18 and 28 weeks it has extended almost to the coronoid process and radial notch. There is a single nutrient foramen that is located on the proximal half of the shaft in over 90% of fetuses (Skawina and Wyczólkowski, 1987). The morphology of the ulna is sufficiently distinct to permit identification from about the 6th prenatal month. At term, ossification extends over half the distance between the coronoid and superior limit of the olecranon process (Gray and Gardner, 1951).

The perinatal ulna (Fig. 9.16) looks relatively more robust, although of course smaller, than in childhood or the adult. The shallow trochlear notch with a truncated olecranon is recognizable at the bulky proximal end and the radial notch is obvious on the lateral side. The shaft is flattened mediolaterally in its proximal half and becomes more triangular distally. In the middle two-quarters of the bone, the posterior border is prominent and the interosseous border forms a sharp edge, but the anterior border is not very obvious. The nutrient foramen, whose entrance slopes proximally, is usually on the anterior surface at the junction of the proximal and middle thirds of the bone. At the distal end, the shaft flares slightly towards the oval metaphyseal surface. A faint notch on its posteromedial surface marks the position where the tendon of extensor carpi ulnaris runs towards the styloid process. The supinator crest may be visible on the perinatal bone or become obvious during the first year of life.

In the isolated diaphysis, the trochlear notch appears very wide until about 8 or 9 years of age, as its upper margin is formed from an epiphysis, which does not fuse until adolescence. Superiorly, it appears truncated over the olecranon and inferiorly the coronoid process is not very prominent. The tuberosity is represented by a ridge and hollow and, as a result, the characteristics of the tuberosity in young children are less clearly defined than in the adult (Evans, 1951).

During early childhood, the shaft of the ulna takes on a more elongated sigmoid curvature and becomes more gracile with increasing age. The distal end, together with the radius, is the most common fracture site in children (Thornton and Gyll, 1999). Also the slenderness of the lower half of the shaft makes the ulna one of the least likely long bones to survive inhumation without damage.

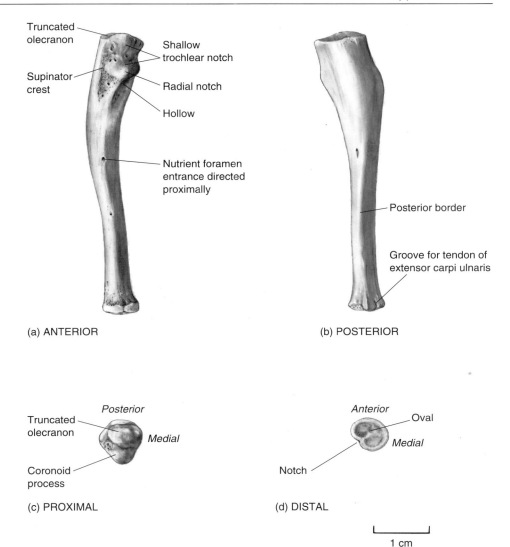

Figure **9.16** The right perinatal ulna.

Secondary centres

The distal epiphysis of the ulna appears between 5 and 7 years, which is considerably later than that of the distal radius (1–2 years). Age ranges for appearance are given by Flecker (1942), Elgenmark (1946), Hansman (1962) and Garn *et al.* (1967). Detailed radiographic standards for girls and boys can be found in the Greulich and Pyle (1959) atlas and a more recent radiological developmental study has been described by Ogden *et al.* (1981). Appearance is normally 1 year to 18 months earlier in girls than in boys.

The ossification centre appears radiologically as an oval bony nodule with smooth margins. The metaphyseal surface soon begins to accommodate itself to the shaft of the bone and becomes flattened and circular in outline with the medial side being thicker than the lateral side (Fig. 9.17a). About 3 years after its first appearance (8–10 years), ossification spreads into the styloid process

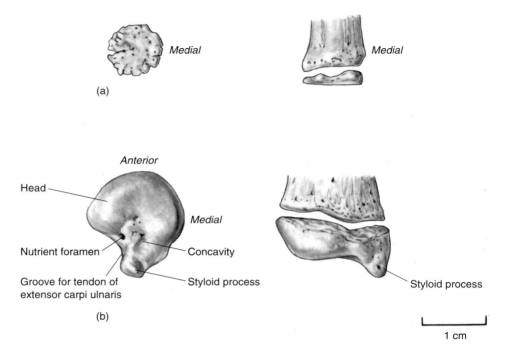

Figure 9.17 The development of the right distal ulnar epiphysis. (a) Early stage – 7 years; (b) later stage – adolescent.

and the metaphyseal surfaces of the diaphysis and epiphysis show reciprocal undulations as the growth plate narrows. Occasionally, there is a separate centre for the styloid process, which may remain separate throughout life (Keats, 1992). Defects, known as epiphyseal clefts, have been reported in the distal ulna and are seen just before fusion when they disappear. They are viewed as normal variants (Harrison and Keats, 1980). By puberty, the epiphysis takes on the appearance of the adult bone (Fig. 9.17b). The articular head is well formed and separated from the styloid process by a shallow concavity pitted with nutrient foramina. The posterolateral end of the concavity bears a groove for the tendon of extensor carpi ulnaris and often has a large nutrient foramen. The articular edge of the epiphysis is now deeper on the anterolateral side.

Fusion of the distal ulnar epiphysis precedes that of the distal radius, beginning in the centre of the epiphyseal plate at 14–15 years in females and 17–20 years in males. This is the growing end of the bone, responsible for 75–85% of growth in length of the shaft (Ozonoff, 1979; Pritchett, 1991). Ranges of fusion times are given by Flecker (1942) and Hansman (1962). The Greulich and Pyle (1959) radiographic standards show complete fusion, with epiphyseal line obliteration soon afterwards, at 16–17 years in females and 17–18 years in males. Thus, the distal ulnar epiphysis has a shorter independent life than its fellow radial epiphysis, appearing about 4 years later and fusing a year earlier. As with the distal radial epiphysis, McKern and Stewart's (1957) observations on male skeletal material show complete union to be later than that described in radiological accounts. They give 23 years for 100% fusion of their specimens, the last traces of peripheral fusion being proximal to the styloid process.

The **proximal epiphysis** of the ulna also appears several years after that for the proximal radius and is usually present by 8 years in females and 10 years in males. The coronoid process and most of the olecranon are formed by extension of ossification from the primary centre in the diaphysis. The olecranon epiphysis forms the superior lip of the articular surface of the trochlear notch and most of the area of bone to which the triceps muscle is attached. Ranges for ages of appearance can be found in Flecker (1942), Hansman (1962) and Garn *et al.* (1967). A detailed radiological description can be found in Cohn (1921b) and Brodeur *et al.* (1981). The account by McCarthy and Ogden (1982b) is based on specialized radiographic techniques and includes possible injury patterns.

The early epiphysis is often composed of a complex collection of ossific nodules and early accounts usually recognize at least two (Fawcett, 1904; Davies and Parsons, 1927; Paterson, 1929). Fawcett described an anterior, or 'beak' centre, which formed part of the articular surface of the trochlear notch, and a second centre which formed the apex of the olecranon process. This description equates with the 'articular' and 'traction' epiphyses of Porteous' (1960) account. Birkner (1978) illustrated the various forms that the olecranon may take in 8–10-year-old children and Brodeur *et al.* (1981) note that the epiphysis is often composed of two, three or more centres, with the upper nucleus, adjacent to the tip, being smaller than the lower. They state that the olecranon has the most predictable age of appearance and final fusion of all the elbow epiphyses and its development is therefore a relatively reliable indicator of age.

However, the pattern of **fusion** at the proximal extremity is variable. Small bony foci may join together before fusing with the shaft, or the smaller proximal articular epiphysis may fuse first, leaving the larger traction part to fuse later. A whole epiphysis (Fig. 9.18a) is a rough, flattened oval piece of bone with a beak pointing to the lateral side. Most of the underside is formed by the irregular metaphyseal surface, but has adjoining it a smooth semilunar part that is the superior rim of the articular surface of the trochlear notch. The upper surface has a rounded, 'bun-like' appearance posteriorly, marking the site of attachment of the tendon of triceps brachii. Fusion starts first on the articular surface at the lateral side and then proceeds posteriorly and medially. The postero-inferior surface is always the last part to remain open (Fig. 9.18b). Silberstein *et al.* (1981b) called the line of fusion the 'wandering physeal line of the olecranon', from its appearance on a lateral radiograph. The epiphyseal plate is first seen proximal to the elbow joint and as the epiphysis increases in size, so the line migrates distally, frequently ending up at the level of the middle of the joint, leaving a wedge-shaped line open inferiorly. Their elbow atlas shows the epiphyseal plate to be half closed by 13 years in females and 14 years in males. It can be complete by 12–14 years in females and 13–16 years in males. Again, McKern and Stewart (1957) find that 100% fusion is later in their skeletal material than is stated in the radiological accounts. Their observations show that the olecranon epiphysis fuses at 19 years in males and is the latest in the range of their Group I early union.

There are reports in the literature of persistent, unfused olecranon epiphyses in the adult (O'Donoghue and Sell, 1942; Skak, 1993). They are usually asymptomatic unless injured after trauma to the elbow, when they can be diagnosed from a lateral radiograph. Kohler *et al.* (1968) distinguish this appearance from so-called 'patella cubiti' which they regard as sesamoid bones in the tendon of the triceps brachii muscle to distinguish them from persistent, unfused epiphyses.

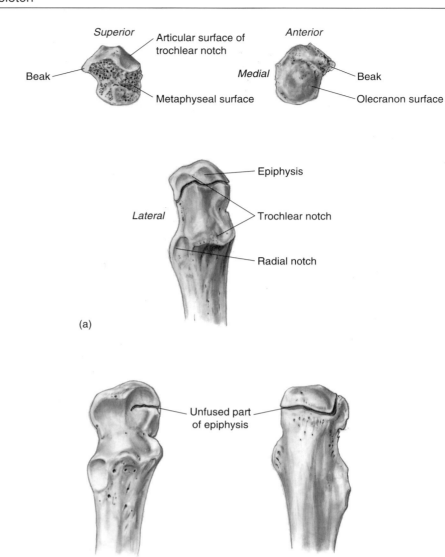

Figure 9.18 The development of the right proximal ulnar epiphysis. (a) Early adolescent; (b) late adolescent.

The appearance and fusion times of the ulnar ossification centres are summarized in Fig. 9.19.

Practical notes

Sideing of the juvenile ulna

Diaphysis – the perinatal or infant ulna can be sided using the following features. Proximally, the trochlear notch bears the articulation for the radius on its lateral side. In the shaft, the sharp interosseous border is lateral and the nutrient foramen is usually in the centre of the anterior upper half with its entrance directed proximally. Distally, the medial surface is slightly concave

(a)

(b)

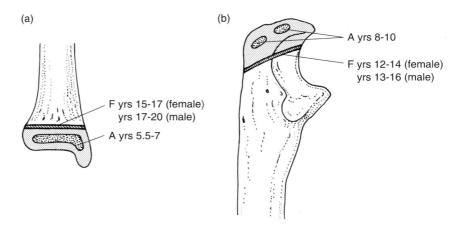

A yrs 8-10

F yrs 12-14 (female)
yrs 13-16 (male)

F yrs 15-17 (female)
yrs 17-20 (male)

A yrs 5.5-7

Figure 9.19 The primary ossification centre of the ulna appears during week 7 of prenatal life. Appearance (A) and fusion (F) of secondary centres – (a) distal end; (b) proximal end.

and the distal metaphyseal surface is oval with a notch on the lateral side for the tendon of extensor carpi ulnaris (Fig. 9.16).

Distal epiphysis – it is difficult to side a distal epiphysis until the styloid process has developed. Looking at the articular surface, the right epiphysis is comma-shaped, with the rounded head towards the top and the groove for the tendon on the left (Fig. 9.17b).

Proximal epiphysis – looking at the metaphyseal proximal epiphysis with the trochlear articular surface superiorly, the beak points to the opposite side from which the bone comes (Fig. 9.18a).

Bones of a similar morphology

Perinatal diaphyses – of the diaphyses of the six major long bones, the radius, ulna and fibula are smaller and look less robust than the femur, humerus and tibia. Up to the age of about 2 months the ulna and fibula are of similar length but the radius is considerably shorter (see Table 9.1). The ulna is distinguishable from the fibula as it is more robust and has the characteristic trochlear notch at the proximal end, whereas the fibula is a slim bone of even width throughout its length (Figs 9.16 and 11.16). After the neonatal period, the fibula is considerably longer than the ulna, as the lower limb increases in length more rapidly than the upper limb.

Proximal fragment – this is distinctive as it bears both trochlear and radial notches (Fig. 9.16a).

Distal fragment – is similar to a proximal fibula, distal fibula or possibly a distal radius. The proximal fibula has a slight neck and the metaphyseal surface is circular, whereas the distal ulna is more oval and may show a notch posteromedially. The distal fibula is flattened mediolaterally and is considerably more gracile than the ulna. The shaft of the radius flares and curves anteriorly towards its end and the metaphyseal surface is angled and larger than that of the ulna (Fig. 9.15).

> ### Morphological summary (Fig. 9.19)
>
> *Prenatal*
> Wk 8   Primary ossification centre appears
>
> *Birth*   Represented by shaft only
> 5–7 yrs   Secondary centre for distal end appears
> About
> 8–10 yrs   Styloid process forms on distal epiphysis
>   Secondary centre(s) for olecranon appear(s)
> 12–14 yrs   Proximal epiphysis fuses in females
> 13–16 yrs   Proximal epiphysis fuses in males
> 17 yrs   Distal epiphysis fuses in females
> 17–20 yrs   Distal epiphysis fuses in males

IV. THE HAND

The hand articulates at the wrist (radiocarpal) joint with the radius and comprises at least 27 bones – eight carpals, five metacarpals and 14 phalanges.

Early development of the hand

Around day 33 of intra-uterine life, the hand plate becomes recognizable as a flattened area of mesenchyme that lies parallel to the median plane (O'Rahilly and Gardner, 1975). By day 37, it clearly shows areas of mesenchymal condensations that will form the region of the carpus, which is surrounded by a crescentic flange that will go on to form the digital plate (Streeter, 1948). By day 38, the digital rays are visible as thickenings in the digital plate and the tips of the future fingers project beyond the crescentic flange, giving it a somewhat crenulated appearance (Fig. 9.20). By day 41, the finger rays are well established and the radial, median and ulnar nerves have penetrated into the hand plate (Blechschmidt, 1969; Uhthoff, 1990b). Between days 38 and 44 the interdigital notches have formed as a result of specific pre-programmed location cell necrosis (apoptosis) as the apical ectodermal ridge thins in this region (Kelley, 1970, 1973). It has been shown that if Janus green is injected at this critical time, then necrosis is inhibited resulting in soft tissue syndactyly (Christ *et al.*, 1986). It has also been shown in mice that following amniotic sac puncture, a transient period of bradycardia is induced, which may produce temporary hypoxia in the distal extremities. When this was performed at a critical gestational age that corresponded with the normal time for chorionic villus sampling in the human, mitotic activity and not apoptosis was observed in the interdigital spaces. It has been postulated that this might explain the phenomenon of syndactyly, which can occur following amniotic sac puncture (Chang *et al.*, 1998).

By day 47 the hand has become tilted so that the pre-axial border is more medial than the post-axial border, i.e. the palm faces caudally and medially and the limb has undergone horizontal flexion so that it lies in a parasagittal, rather than a coronal plane (O'Rahilly and Gardner, 1975).

Chondrification progresses in a well-defined proximodistal direction so that the carpals are formed first and followed in succession by the metacarpals, proximal phalanges, middle and finally distal phalanges (Senior, 1929; O'Rahilly *et al.*, 1957). Of the carpal bones, the capitate and hamate are the first to commence chondrification around day 41, while the lunate at day 47

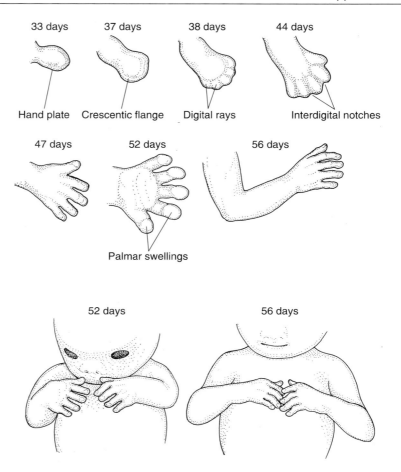

Figure 9.20 The development of the upper limb between 5 and 8 prenatal weeks (redrawn after Larsen, 1993).

and the pisiform at day 50 are the last to commence cartilage anlagen formation (O'Rahilly *et al.*, 1959). By day 52 the digits develop palmar swellings (tactile pads) and the embryological hands now meet in the midline anterior to the cardiac eminence.

From around 48–56 days, interzones appear between the chondrifying bone primordia (Fig. 9.21). This presumptive joint area then develops a distinct three-layered appearance, with future articular cartilage at both ends and a central zone that will differentiate into synovial tissues. Cavitation of this central zone into a true joint space occurs between weeks 9 and 11 (Whillis, 1940; O'Rahilly, 1949; Gray *et al.*, 1957; O'Rahilly *et al.*, 1957; O'Rahilly and Gardner, 1975). It is at this stage that not only are all of the joints in the hand formed, but also the fate of the future carpal pattern is set. So-called 'carpal fusions' are not uncommon but in reality they are really a non-separation of chondrifying zones so that no intercarpal joint space is formed. McCredie (1975) described congenital carpal fusion as arising from 'a disorder of organization of mesenchyme in week 5' and proposed that the structure responsible for organizing the fate of the mesenchyme was the penetrating nerve.

It is generally accepted that in isolated developmental situations, carpal coalitions occur within the same carpal row, whereas if the condition is syn-

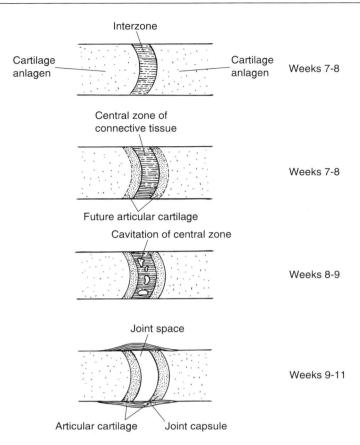

Figure 9.21 Diagrammatic representation of the embryonic development of a synovial joint (redrawn after Larsen, 1993).

drome-related, then the coalitions may cross between the proximal and distal rows (Oner and de Vries, 1994). The coalition of carpal bones and the presence of supernumerary elements that most likely develop from aberrant ossification of small cartilage tags, have been the subject of much debate. Some authors have attempted to explain their presence in terms of phylogenetic evolution, reflecting a primitive atavistic phenomenon, whereas they are in reality more likely to be ontogenetic variants, although there is some evidence for a racial and therefore a genetic predisposition. The nomenclature for these coalitions and supernumerary elements is confusing. O'Rahilly, (1953) describes 28, while Kohler *et al.* (1968) describe 27 separate accessory ossicles and to prevent confusion they are probably best described in terms of their anatomical location, e.g. the os lunatotriquetrum, which is by far the most common carpal coalition with a reported incidence of 2–6% in Negroes and 0.1–0.5% in Caucasians, and although generally asymptomatic, it can permit more extensive ulnar and radial deviation. The lack of a joint space may result in a loss of plasticity of the region and so the bone may be more susceptible to fracture. Cavitation of the joint space between the lunate and triquetral bones occurs around 46–48 days and so from around the 6th week of prenatal life the template has been set for the possibility of lunatotriquetral fusion (Gray *et al.*, 1957).

At approximately day 47, an independent area of chondrification appears at the distal end of the scaphoideum (forerunner of the scaphoid) between the trapezium, trapezoid and capitate. This is known as the 'centrale' and is visible in all embryos up to day 56. Around day 50, an interzone appears between the scaphoideum and the centrale, which eventually narrows until no visible dividing line can be detected around 3–4 prenatal months (Fazekas and Kósa, 1978). If, however, the interzone persists and a joint space does form, then the result will be a separate os centrale (O'Rahilly, 1954). Some authors have considered this to be the phylogenetic remnant of a primitive central carpal row (Poznanski and Holt, 1971) and it is often associated with developmental abnormalities such as Holt Oram syndrome and hand–foot–uterus syndrome. However, in the majority of circumstances the cartilaginous centrale fuses with the scaphoideum and forms the part of the future scaphoid that articulates with the trapezium and the trapezoid. It habitually fuses on its palmar surface first and the dorsal surface eventually fuses some time later (Gray et al., 1957). A tripartite scaphoid can develop when the scaphoideum arises in two parts (naviculare radiale and naviculare ulnare) and remains separate from the centrale (Pfitzner, 1900).

By day 56, the sesamoids of both the first metacarpophalangeal joint and the interphalangeal joints of the thumb are present either as blastemal condensations or may in fact have commenced chondrification (Gray et al., 1957). Even at this early stage of development, the adult shape of the MCP sesamoids is established, with the lateral being more ovoid in shape and the medial more spherical (Gray et al., 1957).

Interzones are generally present in all joints by around day 56 (Gray et al., 1957). Failure of joint formation in the digits results in the congenital interphalangeal fusion, i.e. symphalangism. This is an autosomal dominant condition, which manifests most frequently in the proximal interphalangeal region and in particular that of the fifth digit. It is not surprising that the incidence of this condition is strongly linked to congenital carpal fusions and in particular to both triquetrohamate and capitohamate fusion (Ozonoff, 1979). The absence of the joint space does not result in digital fusion in the fetus, but is delayed until around 6–7 years of age, when epiphyseal activity would be accelerated, resulting in premature and abnormal fusion.

It is interesting to note that up until the time of ossification it is reported that the male hand is in advance of the female hand in terms of maturation and development (Garn et al., 1974). However, it is clear that once ossification commences, the female hand is in advance of the male hand by a matter of weeks initially, but by the end of adolescence this margin has increased to at least 2 years. Garn (1962) and Garn et al. (1969) suggested that this sex-related delay in development could be explained by partial X-chromosome involvement, although Tanner et al (1959) cited the repressive influence of the Y-chromosome as being responsible for the differences.

Ossification

We have been unable to discover a single text that describes in any detail the morphology of the individual developing hand bones. The majority of descriptions refer to the radiological appearance of the bones and this often has little or no bearing on the actual appearance of the dry bone. For this reason, our descriptions of the developing bones have regrettably had to rely on a relatively small sample size of juvenile hands of documented age at death, while the remainder is based on radiographic appearances.

There are at least 48 separate centres of ossification in the hand (Fig. 9.22). Of these, 27 (29 if the sesamoids of the thumb are included) are primary centres and 19 are secondary. However, the pattern of ossification is quite unlike any other region of the skeleton (except the foot of course), as some primary centres arise in the early fetal period and the remainder do not develop until after birth, while the appearance of the secondary centres of ossification are interspersed between the sequential appearance of the primary centres. Therefore, for the sake of both clarity and conformity with the other chapters, the centres will still be considered under the headings of 'primary' and 'secondary', but the reader should be aware that there is no progressive time continuity between these two sections. It should also be appreciated that there has been a considerable amount of research dedicated to the radiographic

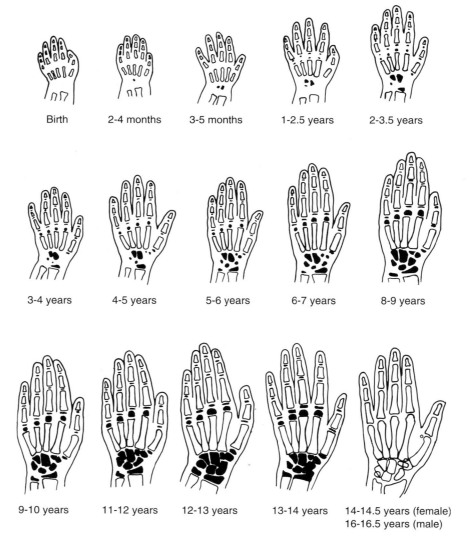

Figure 9.22 Various stages of osseous development in the hand from birth to the end of adolescence (redrawn after Birkner, 1978).

identification of appearance and fusion times in the hand and this has resulted in many slightly conflicting reports of the time of a specific event (see Chapters 1 and 2). It is certain that much of this interest has resulted not only from the ready availability of the hand for radiography but also the large number of centres of ossification provides a considerable amount of information regarding growth and maturity over an extended period of time. There is certainly considerable individual variability in the timing of events in the hand and when this is coupled with racial variation and environmental factors, it is clear that it is impossible to arrive at a universal date for the appearance of a specific centre or its ultimate fusion. Therefore, we have attempted to summarize much of the information available so that a relatively broad time spectrum of events is presented (Fig. 9.22). These timings should not, of course, be considered definitive.

Primary centres
Long bones
Ossification first appears in the distal phalanges, followed closely by the metacarpals, proximal phalanges and finally the middle phalanges (Noback and Robertson, 1951). There is reported to be a tendency for the central digits to ossify in advance of the more marginal fingers (Gray *et al.*, 1957).

It is somewhat surprising that the first centres of ossification to appear in the hand occur in the **distal phalanges** as early as prenatal weeks 7–9. The ossification of a distal phalanx starts at the tip and progresses proximally. A shell of intramembranous perichondral bone is deposited rather like a thimble over the cartilaginous phalanx, commencing in the region of the ungual tuberosity and presumably in response to the attachments of the flexor digitorum profundus tendons (Dixey, 1881; Gray *et al.*, 1957).

Ossification in the **metacarpals** occurs shortly after that of the terminal phalanges, between prenatal weeks 8 and 10 (Gray *et al.*, 1957; O'Rahilly *et al.*, 1959; O'Rahilly and Gardner, 1975) and commences in metacarpals 2 and 3 first, followed by 4 and 5 and finally by the first metacarpal. In all aspects of ossification and fusion the first metacarpal behaves more like a proximal phalanx than a metacarpal. Ossification commences via intramembranous perichondral deposition forming a midshaft collar, which precedes endochondral ossification in the tubular bone.

The primary centres of ossification for the **proximal phalanges** appear very shortly after that for the first metacarpal, in prenatal weeks 9–11 (Brailsford, 1943; Gray *et al.*, 1957; O'Rahilly *et al.*, 1959). The proximal phalanges of digits 2, 3 and 4 are the first to appear, followed by that for the thumb and finally that for digit 5 (Jit, 1957; Kjar, 1974; MacLaughlin-Black and Gunstone, 1995).

The **middle phalanges** are the last of the long bones of the hand to commence ossification. The phalanx for digits 2–4 appears in prenatal weeks 10–12, while that for the fifth digit may not appear until close to term (Gray *et al.*, 1957). This relatively late appearance for this primary centre, in conjunction with premature epiphyseal fusion, may partly explain its susceptibility to growth disorders and its unique involvement in conditions such as brachymesophalangia. In this possibly autosomal recessive inherited disorder it is typically the middle phalanx of digit 5 that is affected and it appears both wider and shorter than in the normal situation (Garn *et al.*, 1976). Not only has a higher incidence of brachymesophalangia-5 has been reported in Asiatic groups (Hertzog, 1967), but it also tends to be prevalent in disorders such as Down's syndrome (Roche, 1961; Greulich, 1973).

In summary, the primary centres of ossification for the metacarpals and phalanges are all present (with the possible exception of the middle phalanx of digit 5) by the beginning of the 4th prenatal month and they are individually recognizable, certainly in a radiograph, by the 5th month. From this stage until birth the only other bones that may start to show ossification are the capitate and hamate although they generally develop within the first 3 or 4 months *post partum*.

From the earliest prenatal age, the first metacarpal is stunted in length compared to the other metacarpals, and it is much more robust (Fig. 9.23). It is certainly identifiable from an early prenatal age as it bears a somewhat rounded distal end with a flattened proximal end that is almost circular in outline and clearly metaphyseal. The remainder of the developing metacarpals are true to the standard morphology of a long bone, bearing diaphyses that are virtually cylindrical in outline, slightly waisted in the middle but expanded at both ends. Unlike other long bones, however, they only bear a metaphyseal surface at their distal extremity, thus in the early stages of development the distal extremities are flat and the proximal are rounded until they develop their characteristic basal articular form.

From early prenatal life, the second metacarpal is usually the longest of the five and it can be readily identified at birth, as its distal end is displaced somewhat laterally, while its proximal end shows a medial displacement, thereby giving the bone a slightly sinuous outline (Fig. 9.23). The bone retains this morphology until approximately 3.5–4.5 years of age when the lateral aspect of the base begins to develop and expand proximally. The second metacarpal adopts its characteristic condylar-shaped proximal extremity around 4–5

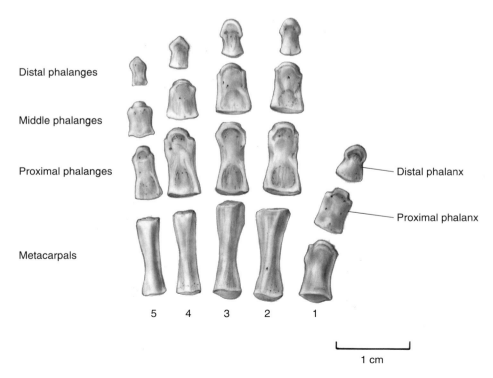

Distal phalanges

Middle phalanges

Proximal phalanges

Metacarpals

Distal phalanx

Proximal phalanx

5   4   3   2   1

1 cm

Figure 9.23 The right perinatal hand.

years of age, concomitant with the appearance of the ossification centre for the trapezoid.

At birth, the third metacarpal is slightly shorter than the second, with a flat distal extremity that is somewhat rectangular in outline with a gently rounded distal extremity (Fig. 9.23). There is no sinuous shape to the diaphysis. Due to its lack of any specific morphology, this metacarpal is not easily distinguished until the intermetacarpal articular sites start to develop. From approximately 5–6 years of age, the proximal surface adopts a roughly triangular outline, although the reciprocal concave lateral border for the second metacarpal may be present slightly earlier at 4 years of age. The styloid process is the most characteristic trait of this metacarpal but it does not develop until around 11–12 years of age and then appears as a slowly developing proximal elongation of the dorsolateral surface (Fig. 9.24). The embryological origin of the styloid process is said to be homologous with a group of cells that fuse with the capitate in Old-World monkeys, but instead fuses with the third metacarpal in man. It is said to stabilize the hand against forces directed towards the palmar aspect of the metacarpal head and so prevent hyperextension of the bone and palmar subluxation of its base (Marzke and Marzke, 1987). A relatively common supernumerary carpal bone, sometimes referred to as the ninth carpal bone, the styloid bone or the hunchback carpal bone, is found in the angle between the base of the third metacarpal, the capitate and the trapezoid bones (Bassoe and Bassoe, 1955). The origin of this bony mass is uncertain but it may well be related to the development of the styloid process of the third metacarpal, although some authors believe it to be acquired rather than congenital. When present it can cause limitations in digit extension, caused by slipping of the extensor tendons over the prominence. Symptoms also include an occasional ache and easy fatigue in the muscles at the wrist, although it is generally asymptomatic.

The fourth metacarpal is considerably shorter than either the second or third and only marginally longer than the fifth (Fig. 9.23). The morphology of the fourth metacarpal is not distinct until the intermetacarpal articulations develop around 4–5 years of age. The fifth metacarpal can be identified at an early age by a number of factors – it is the shortest (true from early prenatal

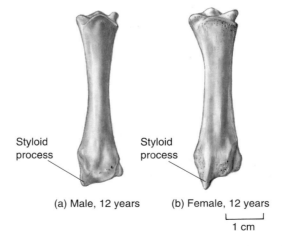

Styloid process   Styloid process

(a) Male, 12 years   (b) Female, 12 years

1 cm

Figure 9.24 The development of the styloid process of the right third metacarpal.

life); the proximal end is slightly bulbous and deviates laterally (true from approximately the first year); there is no articular region on the medial side (identifiable around 4–5 years). These intermetacarpal articulations probably develop at different ages for different joints, but they are certainly apparent in some specimens by 4 years of age.

At birth, the proximal phalanges look too robust and too wide to be associated with the heads of the appropriate metacarpals (Fig. 9.23). The first proximal phalanx is shorter than the others and has three virtually straight sides with a curved distal surface. The remainder of the proximal phalanges are somewhat dumb-bell-shaped with expanded proximal and distal extremities and a constriction in the midshaft. The distal surface is rounded and notched, while the proximal surface is flat with a transversely oval outline that shows a slight concavity on the palmar surface.

The middle phalanges are smaller than their proximal counterparts and they lack the distinctive constriction in the midshaft region (Fig. 9.23). This makes them somewhat dome-shaped, with a rounded but notched distal extremity and medial and lateral borders that flare proximally to terminate at the transversely oval proximal surface, which does not display the concavity seen in the proximal phalanges.

From even the fetal stage of development, the distal phalanges are harpoon-shaped with rounded or pointed distal margins that are flattened on the volar (palmar) surface and display the characteristic barb-like structures that abut onto the shaft (Fig. 9.23). The first distal phalanx is more robust than the others and although it is not necessarily longer, it is obviously wider.

Carpals

The second group of primary centres of ossification in the hand form the carpal bones and these are almost exclusively postnatal in terms of their time of appearance, although Menees and Holly (1932) have reported that the capitate was present at birth in approximately 4% of their male sample and 8% of their female sample, while the hamate was also present in almost identical percentages. The order of appearance of ossification in the carpal region is well documented, although disharmonic patterns do arise in situations of congenital malformations or environmental adversities (Dreizen *et al.*, 1958; Poznanski *et al.*, 1971). Maturation in the hand, and particularly in the carpal region, has assumed considerable clinical significance as a reflection of the stage of skeletal maturation in the rest of the body. For this reason, several atlases of skeletal development in the hand have been developed (e.g. Greulich and Pyle, 1959; Tanner and Whitehouse, 1959; Meschan, 1975; Himes, 1984).

The normal sequence of appearance for the carpal bones is that the capitate appears first, followed closely by the hamate and later by the triquetral and then the lunate. The trapezium, trapezoid and scaphoid all appear at approximately the same time and so their order can be interchangeable, dependent upon the sample under investigation. It is interesting to note that the pattern of appearance of the carpal centres follows an almost circular route. It starts with ossification in the capitate, moves laterally into the hamate and triquetral, before moving proximally into the lunate and finally completing the circuit with the virtually simultaneous appearance of the scaphoid, trapezium and trapezoid. It is not known whether any functional significance can be attributed to this pattern. Last (1973) reported that the carpals ossify in order according to their ultimate adult size, with the largest usually forming first and the smallest last, but this is not strictly true, given that both the lunate and the triquetral are smaller than the scaphoid but they ossify in advance of it by almost 2 years. The sesamoids of the thumb and the pisiform bone are the last primary centres to appear (Beresowski and Lundie, 1952).

When disarticulated and removed from positional identification, the carpal bones are really only identifiable once they take on their adult form. While it is possible to positively identify each bone from radiographs because of its anatomical position, this information is clearly lost when the specimen is only represented by dry bone (Fig. 9.22). Until adult morphology is achieved, carpal bones are represented by small, undifferentiated nodules of bone as they form by endochondral ossification and only adopt their recognisable future shape once the ossification reaches the perichondrium.

The **capitate** is the first carpal to undergo ossification and although a bony centre can be present at birth it most frequently appears between 2 and 3 postnatal months in girls and 3 and 4 postnatal months in boys. It commences as a small, rounded nodule of bone that soon develops a vertically aligned long axis with that of the third metacarpal. Its articular surface with the hamate starts to flatten around 10 months in girls and 12 months in boys and by the first year in girls and 1.5 years in boys it is said to resemble a reversed 'D'. By 1.5 years in girls and 2 years in boys, the articular surface with the hamate begins to show a distinct concavity, but in real terms the bone is fairly indistinct before 2 years of age. At around 2.5 years in girls and 3 years in boys the lateral surface of the capitate shows a distinct indent, which marks the site of attachment of the large interosseous ligament between the trapezoid and scaphoid articular surfaces. The capitate can usually be identified in isolation by 3–4 years of age. At 3 years in girls and 4 years in boys the facet for the second metacarpal has formed an obtuse angle with the articular facet for the trapezoid. The articular surface for the second metacarpal has flattened by 4 years in girls and 5 years in boys and the bone continues to expand, particularly in a vertical direction. At approximately 8.5 years in girls and 9.5 years in boys, there is a sharp angle of demarcation between the articular facets for the second and third metacarpals. The bone has virtually reached its full adult proportions by 11.5 years in girls and 14 years in boys and is essentially adult by 13 years in girls and 15 years in boys.

The ossification centre for the **hamate** appears very shortly after that for the capitate at around 3–4 months in girls and 4–5 months in boys. It appears as a small, roughened nodule, slightly distal to the capitate and aligned with the space between the fourth and fifth metacarpal bones. Some authors have suggested that it can develop from two separate foci of ossification, which reflects its functional position of supporting two metacarpal bases. This somewhat rounded ossific nodule develops a long oblique axis by 6 postnatal months in females and 7 months in males. The capitate surface becomes somewhat flattened around 7 months in girls and 9 months in boys, while flattening of the triquetral surface begins around 10 months and 12 months respectively. The developing hamate assumes the shape of an inverted triangle with a convex capitate margin at approximately 1 year in girls and 1.5 years in boys, but the bone is essentially featureless, like the capitate, until around 2 years of age. The articular surface adjacent to the metacarpals flattens around 3 years in girls and 4 years in boys and the triquetral facet becomes well defined by 4 years and 5 years respectively. It is at this stage that the hamate can be identified in isolation. By 6 years in females and 7 years in males, the triquetral surface shows an indentation and the metacarpal sites are flat. It is not until

7 years in females and 8 years in males that the bone is clearly wedge-shaped with a squared corner at the capitate–metacarpal junction. By 9 years in girls and 11 years in boys the saddle shape of the articular surface for the fifth metacarpal is well defined. The concavity of the triquetral surface is clear by 10 years in girls and 12 years in boys and the saddle-shaped surface for metacarpal 4 is clearly defined. At this stage, the hamulus is visible radiographically but it is not distinct until 11 years and 14 years, respectively. The hamate reaches adult morphology and proportions by 12 years in girls and 15 years in boys.

There is a gap of at least a year until the third carpal centre appears. This is for the **triquetral** and is said to form in the first year by some authors, in the second year by others and even in the third year by others. Not surprisingly, Johnston *et al.* (1968) reported that the variability of time of onset of ossification of the triquetral rendered it of little value in estimating the skeletal age of an individual. It is probably as a result of the considerable degree of variation in timings of events in the hand that many authors have abandoned estimating skeletal age on the basis of appearance and relied more heavily on the number of centres present at any one time. Greulich and Pyle (1959) found that the triquetral became recognizably triangular by around 3.5 years in girls and 4.5 years in boys and by 6 months later the hamate and lunate surfaces had begun to flatten, while the non-articular margin remained convex. A distinct corner was present at the hamate-lunate junction by 6 years in girls and 7 years in boys, and by a year later the bone was distinctly wedge-shaped. The concavity of the hamate surface was visible by 8.5 years in girls and 10 years in boys and it is at this stage that the triquetral can be identified in isolation. They reported that there was little change in either the size or shape of the bone after 12 years in girls and 15 years in boys.

The **lunate** is the fourth carpal to commence ossification and it does so around 3 years in girls and 4 years in boys and often from more than one focus of ossification. The lunate develops a long transverse axis with a bevelled lateral border, a pointed scaphoid region and a rounded triquetral half by 4 years in girls and 5 years in boys. The lunate can be identified in isolation at around 9–10 years of age. Little change in size and shape occurs after 12.5 years in girls and 15 years in boys.

The centres of ossification for the trapezium and trapezoid appear at approximately the same time and there is some conflict in the literature as to which appears first, although the majority seems to agree that it is the **trapezium**. This is said to appear around 4 years in girls and 5 years in boys and it soon develops a long axis, which is directed towards the second metacarpal joint. The margin adjacent to the first metacarpal flattens within the next year and by 6 years in girls and 7 years in boys the bone has developed a squared outline. The concavity of the saddle joint is visible radiologically by 9 years in girls and 10 years in boys and, at this stage, the bone can be positively identified in isolation. The projection of the distal surface between the two metacarpals is well defined by 11.5 years in girls and 14 years in boys. The bone reaches its full adult shape and size by 12.5 years in girls and 15 years in boys.

The **trapezoid** commences ossification at approximately the same age as the trapezium and its angular outline is well defined radiologically by 5 years in girls and 6 years in boys. The convexity of the second metacarpal surface is visible by 7 years in girls and 8 years in boys and the proximal margin is concave by 8.5 and 10 years, respectively. It is at this stage of development that the dry bone can be positively identified in isolation. The bone reaches adult proportions by 12.5 and 15 years, respectively.

The **scaphoid** commences ossification around 5 years in girls and 6 years in boys and a long axis is visible very shortly afterwards. By approximately a year later, the area next to the radial styloid process has flattened and the long axis is clearly aligned with the centre of the radiocarpal joint. Within the next year (7 for girls and 8 for boys) the scaphoid becomes distinctly 'tear-drop'-shaped, with the pointed end lying nearest to the styloid process of the radius and the distal surface has become rounded. The capitate surface is concave and the trapezium and trapezoid surfaces are flattened, with a distinct demarcation angle between them by 8.5 years in girls and 10 years in boys. An indent is clearly visible between the radial and trapezial surfaces by 9.5 years in girls and 11 years in boys and it is at this stage that the dry bone can be identified in isolation. The scaphoid tubercle does not become radiologically distinct until 11 years in girls and 14 years in boys. The bone reaches its adult shape and size by approximately 12.5 years in girls and 15 years in boys.

A non-traumatic divided scaphoid (os scaphoideum bipartitum) is well documented and probably arises from dual centres of ossification, which fail to unite. The division between the two centres occurs across the waist of the bone and it has often been associated with a free os centrale (O'Rahilly, 1953).

The **sesamoids** are the last bones in the hand to commence ossification. The **pisiform** appears radiologically by 8 years in females and by 10 years in males. The bone enlarges to adult size by 12.5 years in females and 15 years in males. The sesamoids associated with both the thumb and the fifth digit appear between 11 and 15 years of age in girls and 13 and 18 years in boys.

Secondary centres
Appearance

There are four morphologically distinct groups of epiphyses in the long bones of the hand – the heads of the metacarpals and the bases of the proximal, middle and distal phalanges. Unlike the situation found in the other long bones of the skeleton, where epiphyses arise at both the proximal and distal poles, in the hand, they are restricted to one end of the bone, although in rare circumstances true supernumerary epiphyses have been documented. Carter and Beaupré (2001) proposed a unique theory that the appearance, of lack of appearance, of a secondary centre associated with a long bone is related to both 'the local intensity of the octahedral shear stress history in the chondroepiphysis and the speed of the approaching primary growth front'. They suggested that the octahedral shear stress in the metacarpals is considerably reduced, through a physical lateral constraint on the developing end, which prevents the 'bulging' of the proximal bone end. As the mechanical stimulus is therefore reduced, the primary growth front simply proceeds unhindered to the end of the bone. They explain the single epiphysis phenomenon found in the phalanges through the fact that they are 'smaller' than the metacarpals and so the growth front can proceed rapidly to the bone end.

It is a general rule that with the exception of the first metacarpal, the heads of all other metacarpals ossify from a separate endochondral secondary centre of ossification. The first metacarpal behaves like a proximal phalanx, as all phalanges ossify from a single centre that forms the shaft and the distal articular surface, while the base of the bone at its proximal extremity forms from a separate secondary centre of ossification.

There are several reports in the literature that state the **order of appearance** of the secondary centres and, of course, few of these actually agree. Therefore, we have summarized the views of many papers and presented the most frequently reported pattern for secondary centre ossification. The general rule is that the secondary centres in the bases of the proximal phalanges are the first to appear, followed closely by those for the metacarpal heads, then the middle phalangeal bases and finally by the distal phalangeal bases (Fig. 9.25). There is, however, a considerable degree of individual and population-related variation within this general pattern.

After birth, it is clear that the capitate and hamate centres of the wrist are the first to show ossification but the base of the third proximal phalanx follows them very shortly at around 10 months in girls and 14 months in boys. The ossification for the base of the second proximal phalanx appears at approximately 14 months in girls and 19 months in boys, while that for the fourth proximal phalanx appears at approximately the same time but marginally

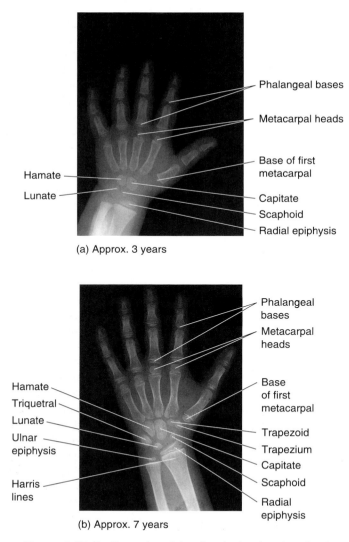

(a) Approx. 3 years

Phalangeal bases
Metacarpal heads
Base of first metacarpal
Hamate
Lunate
Capitate
Scaphoid
Radial epiphysis

(b) Approx. 7 years

Phalangeal bases
Metacarpal heads
Base of first metacarpal
Hamate
Triquetral
Lunate
Ulnar epiphysis
Harris lines
Trapezoid
Trapezium
Capitate
Scaphoid
Radial epiphysis

Figure 9.25 Radiographs of the developing hand and wrist.

later. The head of the second metacarpal appears around 16 months in girls and 22 months in boys, followed by that for the base of the distal phalanx of the first digit at approximately 17 months in girls and 22 months in boys. The head of the third metacarpal appears around 17 months in girls and 24 months in boys, while the fifth proximal phalangeal base appears shortly afterwards at 17 months in girls and 2 years 1 month in boys. The head for the fourth metacarpal appears around 18 months in girls and 2 years 1 month in boys, while that for the base of the middle phalanx of the third digit appears around 19 months and 2 years 4 months, respectively. Ossification of the base of the fourth middle phalanx, the head of the fifth metacarpal and the base of the second middle phalanx all appear around the same time of 19 months in girls and 2 years 5 months in boys. Although the appearance of the triquetral is somewhat variable, it is approximately at this stage of development when the capitate, hamate, heads of metacarpals 2–5, bases of proximal phalanges 2–5, bases of middle phalanges 2–4 and the base of the first distal phalanx have been formed (i.e. 2 years in girls and 2.5 years in boys). The bases of the distal phalanges of the third and fourth digits appear next at approximately 2 years in girls and 2 years 8 months in boys, and the centres for the base of the first metacarpal and the base of the first proximal phalanx coincide at approximately 2 years 1 month in girls and 3 years 2 months in boys. It has been reported that it is not uncommon for the epiphysis at the base of the first proximal phalanx to be formed from more than one focus of ossification (Roche and Sunderland, 1959). It is around this time that the ossification centre appears for the distal end of the radius. The distal phalanx of digit 2 appears around 2 years 4 months in girls and 3 years 7 months in boys, while the centres for the bases of the distal and middle phalanges of digit 5 are the last to appear, at approximately 2 years 5 months in girls and 3 years 7 months in boys. Therefore, by 2.5 years in girls and approximately 3.5 years in boys the secondary ossification centres for the long bones of the hand are all present and it is only the centres for the lunate, trapezium, trapezoid, scaphoid and pisiform bones that are still not present.

The **metacarpal heads** appear as small, undifferentiated endochondral nodules of bone until approximately 5 or 6 years of age. After this time, they become recognizable as metacarpal heads with rounded articular distal surfaces, flattened proximal metaphyseal surfaces and roughly square-shaped outlines. From this age onwards, they continue to approach the adult morphology. Identification of individual metacarpal heads is difficult and confidence will be greatest when only one individual is present (Fig. 9.26). Due to their larger size, the second and third heads can be readily separated from those of the fourth and fifth metacarpals. When the distal articular surfaces are viewed from above, the head of the second metacarpal is almost stellate in appearance, displaying prolongations from each corner. The ventrolateral corner is well developed because of the presence of a sesamoid bone and although the dorsomedial aspect also looks well developed it is mainly due to the fact that its contemporary dorsolateral prolongation is foreshortened, due to the intrusion of the large second metacarpophalangeal ligament that attaches to this surface. The head of the third metacarpal appears squarer in outline, principally due to the lesser development of the ventrolateral corner. However, the dorsomedial prolongation is still well developed, again due to the foreshortening of the dorsolateral corner by the attachment of the relatively strong third metacarpophalangeal ligament. The heads of the third and fourth metacarpals are more difficult to identify, although they are noticeably smaller than those of the more lateral metacarpals. They are both almost square in outline but that

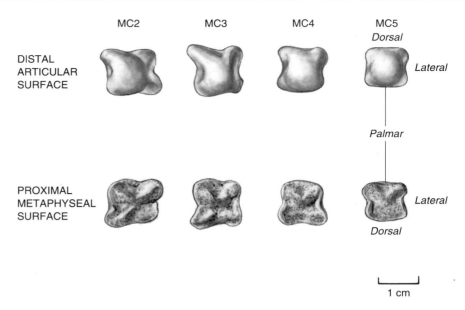

Figure 9.26 The distal and proximal surfaces of right metacarpal heads 2–5.

of the fifth metacarpal displays a slight paring away of the dorsomedial angle of the synovial articular surface. The ventromedial corner can show evidence of prolongation due to the presence of the sesamoid in the abductor tendon. Despite this, the only way to ensure correct identification of a metacarpal head is to be able to fit it securely to a specific metacarpal shaft and this can be achieved only from approximately 9–10 years of age.

The proximal metaphyseal surfaces of the metacarpal heads are quite distinctive (Fig. 9.26). Those of the second and third metacarpals are petaloid with rounded corners and distinct waistings and as a result, four deep crevasses are clearly defined on this surface. The proximal surfaces of metacarpals four and five are flatter and although they do still display the characteristic roundings and constrictions, they are less well developed.

Brailsford (1953) described the epiphyses of the **proximal phalanges** as 'flattened discs having a slightly convex distal surface and a slightly concave proximal surface'. This is certainly true, but there are several details that have not been included and it is somewhat ironic that it is easier to side juvenile proximal phalangeal epiphyses than the equivalent fused adult bone. The epiphysis of the first proximal phalanx is noticeably wider in its transverse than in its ventrodorsal plane (Fig. 9.27). It is almost oval in outline, although the palmar surface is gently concave and the dorsal border is clearly convex. When viewed from the front, this epiphysis displays a slightly sinuous outline with a distally orientated prolongation laterally that will fuse with the shaft and a proximally oriented prolongation medially. As for all these epiphyses, and in agreement with Brailsford (1953), the proximal surface is markedly concave, while the distal metaphyseal surface is very gently convex.

Despite a concavity along the ventral border, the epiphysis of the second proximal phalanx is virtually square in outline (Fig. 9.27). When viewed from the front, it is clearly wedge-shaped, being thicker on its lateral than its medial aspect. The base of the third proximal phalanx also displays this wedge shape and the concavity along the ventral border, but it is clearly wider

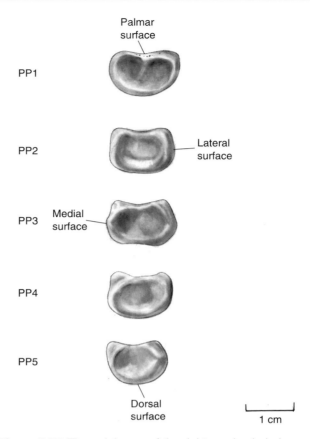

PP1

PP2

PP3

PP4

PP5

Palmar
surface

Lateral
surface

Medial
surface

Dorsal
surface

1 cm

Figure 9.27 The epiphyses of the right proximal phalanges.

in its transverse than in its ventrodorsal plane. In addition, the lateral border is more blunt and the medial border tends to end anteriorly in a sharper projection. The epiphysis of the fourth proximal phalanx displays a semicircular outline with a concave ventral border, which has a more prominent projection on the medial aspect. The epiphysis of the fifth proximal phalanx is the smallest and adopts a more oval outline, with only a gentle hint of a concave ventral border. The lateral aspect of this border is more blunt, while the medial aspect is more pointed.

Brailsford (1953) described the epiphyses of the **middle phalanges** as 'plano-convex shaped discs – the convex surface being opposed to the slightly concave distal extremity of the proximal phalanx'. This description is not quite true, as the discs are essentially biconvex proximally, with a separating ridge that runs from a promontory on the ventral to a similar promontory on the dorsal border (Fig. 9.28). The epiphysis is essentially oval in outline, being longer in the transverse plane, although the ventral border is more gently convex, while the dorsal border is more obviously rounded. The distal metaphyseal surface is convex from ventral to dorsal, with the latter showing a steeper slope down to the dorsal border. From medial to lateral, the distal surface shows a roughly central hollow (corresponding to the ridge on the proximal surface), flanked by a medial and a lateral elevation that correspond with the concavities of the proximal surface. We have found that attempting to side these epiphyses, or indeed assign them to a specific ray, is extremely difficult and in our opinion it cannot be done with any degree of confidence.

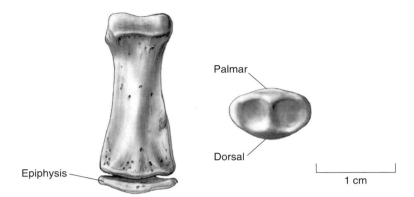

Figure 9.28 The right middle phalangeal epiphysis.

Brailsford (1953) described the epiphyses of the **distal phalanges** simply as 'biconcave discs about the same width as the base of the diaphyses of the terminal phalanges'. This description is somewhat misleading, as the epiphyses of the middle phalanges are more obviously biconcave and, further, the epiphyses tend to be wider than diaphyses (Fig. 9.29). The proximal articular surfaces of the epiphyses of the distal phalanges are concave from ventral to dorsal and slightly convex from medial to lateral.

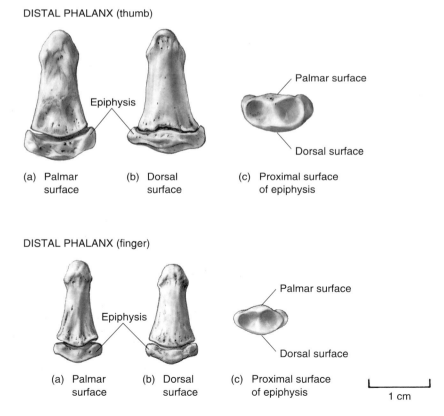

Figure 9.29 The right distal phalangeal epiphyses.

Although essentially biconcave, a delimiting ridge is not so clearly defined as seen in the articular surface of the middle phalanges. At around 10–11 years of age, the ventral border develops a medial and a lateral tongue of bone that pass upwards towards the diaphysis of the phalanx and so form a stable cup-shape in which the diaphysis sits. These tongues presumably form in response to the attachments of the profundus flexor tendon. The dorsal surface does not respond in a similar manner and in fact it dips somewhat proximally, thereby forming a sloping distal metaphyseal surface, which is clearly convex from ventral to dorsal and concave from medial to lateral. We have been unable to correctly assign epiphyses to specific distal phalanges with any degree of reliability, with the exception, of course, of that for the thumb (Fig. 9.29). This is a much larger epiphysis than for any of the other terminal phalanges, is distinctly oval in outline and clearly biconcave. Yet, in all other ways it is identical to the other epiphyses for terminal phalanges.

The epiphysis for the **base of the first metacarpal** is sufficiently different from all the other hand epiphyses to merit a separate description (Fig. 9.30). It is well developed by 7–8 years of age, but can probably not be accurately identified until around 9–10 years. The distal metaphyseal surface is virtually circular in outline and almost planar, although there is a slight slope down towards the dorsal border. The lateral border of the epiphysis develops an upward-projecting tongue of bone that fits into a corresponding recess on the lateral aspect of the diaphysis. The proximal aspect of the ventral border ends in the well-developed styloid process, which is connected to a corresponding process on the dorsal surface and thereby demarcates the bicondylar articular surface.

Fusion

Not surprisingly, the order of **fusion** of the secondary to the primary centres does not mirror their order of appearance and there is much disagreement in

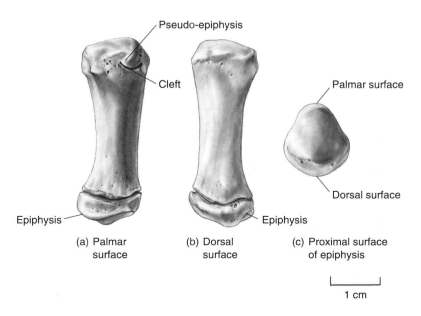

Figure 9.30 The right first metacarpal epiphysis.

the literature. Moss and Noback (1958) state that fusion first occurs in the distal phalanges, with no clear preference for a specific digit or phalanx. Garn *et al.* (1961) and Hansman (1962) both state that the distal epiphyses commence fusion first, followed by the proximal phalanges and the base of the first metacarpal, followed then by the middle phalanges and finally by the remainder of the metacarpals. It should of course be realized that there are no secondary centres associated with the carpal bones.

Joseph (1951) reported that the first digit commenced fusion in advance of all others and the subsequent pattern was for the distal phalanx to fuse first, followed by the metacarpal base and finally by the proximal phalangeal base, while in all the other digits the pattern was for the distal phalanx to fuse first, followed by the middle phalanges, then the proximal phalanges and finally by the remaining metacarpals.

In many ways, it is a purely academic concern as to which epiphysis fuses first as it takes only a matter of 2–4 months for an epiphysis to complete the process of fusion and therefore many studies may well have missed this critically small window of time. Further, it takes only some 13 months for the entire hand to complete epiphyseal fusion from start to finish.

To summarize digital fusion, it can be stated that the distal phalanges are probably the first to commence union at approximately 13.5 years in girls and 16 years in boys and that the first digit seems to fuse about a month in advance of the other distal phalangeal bases. The base of the first metacarpal behaves like the bases of the proximal phalanges in many ways and so it is perhaps not surprising that they tend to commence fusion around the same time. The base of the first metacarpal completes fusion with the diaphysis by approximately 14 years in girls and 16.5 years in boys, while fusion at the bases of the proximal phalanges occurs between 14 and 14.5 years in girls and between 16 and 16.5 years in boys. Fusion of the bases of the middle phalanges ranges from 14 to 14.5 in girls and occurs around 16.5 years in boys. The heads of metacarpals 2–5 are reported to fuse between 14.5 and 15 years in girls and around 16.5 years in boys, with a tendency for metacarpal 5 to be the last bone in the hand to complete epiphyseal fusion.

The epiphyses of the hand have been a contentious issue for hundreds of years, particularly in relation to the so-called 'pseudo-epiphyses' which tend to present as notches or clefts at the non-epiphyseal end of a hand (or foot) long bone and in the position that corresponds with the position of an epiphyseal plate were it to be present (Fig. 9.31). The head of the first metacarpal, the lateral aspect of the base of the second metacarpal and the medial aspect of the base of the fifth metacarpal are reported to be the most common sites for this phenomenon.

Pseudo-epiphyses were first described in the mid-1700s and many papers, particularly radiological, have been concerned with their relevance to specific clinical conditions such as Down's syndrome, hypothyroidism and achondroplasia. Clinicians are also interested in identifying these anatomical variants as they can mimic pathological conditions. However, some anatomists and anthropologists became almost obsessed with the importance of these pseudo-epiphyses in relation to phylogenetic development, seeing the retention of bipolar epiphyses as atavistic evidence for man's evolution from lower life forms.

It is, however, clear that these structures represent normal stages in the physeal invasion of the primary centre into the head of the metacarpal and depending upon their stage of development at a specific time they will appear in a number of guises. In fact, this phenomenon is actually present in most sam-

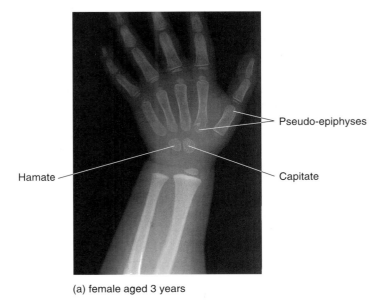

(a) female aged 3 years

Pseudo-epiphysis at distal
extremity of MC1

Cleft

Cleft

Pseudo-epiphysis at proximal
extremity of MC2

1 cm

(b) female aged 8 years 7 months

Figure 9.31 Pseudoepiphyses of the first and second metacarpals.

ples within a particular age range and can actually lend some weight to the observation that it is a normal stage in the development of the bone. For example, ossification into the head of the first metacarpal commences in advance of the appearance of the secondary centre at the proximal pole and its ossification progresses at a much faster rate, indicating that it is different from secondary ossification processes (Ogden *et al.*, 1994). If there is a central invasion into the distal cartilaginous pole, then a mushroom-shaped advancing column of bone can be seen, which is connected by a stalk to the principal ossification centre (Ogden *et al.*, 1994). Proximal to this mushroomed head is a circular notch, which is the constriction where it joins to the shaft and this gives the structure the appearance of an epiphysis. However, the ossification front may be displaced to one side (usually medial), which results in a notch on the lateral side of the bone and as this develops it leaves a deep crescentic cleft on the lateral side, which is referred to as the epiphyseal notch or cleft. These notches can be identified in the first year but do not become well defined until years 2–3 and so they can remain potentially identifiable until the completion of fusion (Fig. 9.31). Complete fusion occurs with the remainder of the structures of the hand at approximately 12 years in females and 14 years in males. These pseudo-epiphyses are therefore transient structures that ultimately align with the remainder of the bone and form a completely normal adult morphology so that retrospective confirmation of their presence is not possible. It is clear from the histological investigations of Haines (1974) and Ogden *et al.* (1994) that the region of the pseudo-epiphysis is associated with an area of cartilage that displays discontinuity of cell columns and so the normal linear progression of ossification is impeded in this region, resulting in so-called 'tide lines', which temporarily halt ossification.

These pseudo-epiphyses are therefore not truly epiphyses at all but normal progressions of the ossification process. However, true supernumerary epiphyses do exist, although they are rare, but they do present in the normal form of an epiphysis as an entirely separate node of ossification in an island of hyaline cartilage.

There are a number of anomalies that appear in the skeletal development of the hand, which relate in particular to the development of the epiphyses. For example, cone-shaped epiphyses have been well documented in the clinical literature and although their aetiology is unknown, it has been linked to conditions such as brachymesophalangia. The epiphysis is best described as possessing a conical projection of the distal border so that it points towards the proximal border of the diaphysis and it has been somewhat artistically likened to 'the indentation in the bottom of a wine bottle'. Interestingly, it shows an incidence that is four times greater in the female than in the male.

Ivory or sclerotic epiphyses are described as epiphyses that appear dense on radiography, making the internal architecture difficult to discern. It is a transitory phase as the epiphysis generally continues to grow and fuse as a normal adult bone. It is thought that the growing epiphyses are particularly sensitive to metabolic alterations and this condition may be radiographic evidence of growth disturbances.

Abnormalities of epiphyseal growth and/or fusion can result in a number of clinical conditions that seem to affect the fifth digit in particular. Brachymesophalangia has been discussed earlier, but conditions such as clinodactyly, where the fifth finger is tilted or crooked, occurs as a growth deformity at the level of the distal interphalangeal joint. Angular deformities can also arise as a result of a condition known as delta phalanx, which is a manifestation of polydactylism. In this condition, a tubular bone of the extremity with a proximal epiphysis becomes the site of origin of an extra skeletal ray. The tethering of the proximal epiphysis by the supernumerary ray creates a peculiar D-shaped phalanx.

The appearance and fusion times of the ossification centres of the hand are summarized in Figure 9.32.

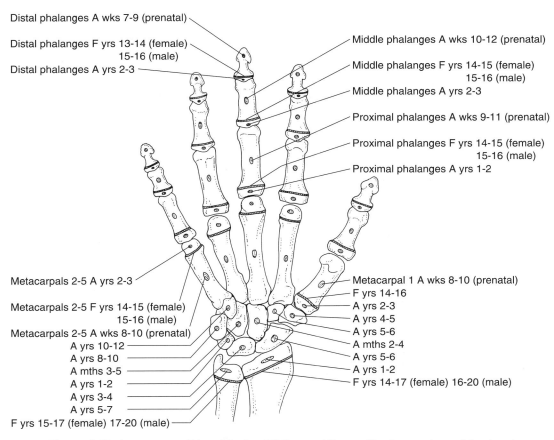

Distal phalanges A wks 7-9 (prenatal)
Distal phalanges F yrs 13-14 (female)
15-16 (male)
Distal phalanges A yrs 2-3

Middle phalanges A wks 10-12 (prenatal)
Middle phalanges F yrs 14-15 (female)
15-16 (male)
Middle phalanges A yrs 2-3
Proximal phalanges A wks 9-11 (prenatal)
Proximal phalanges F yrs 14-15 (female)
15-16 (male)
Proximal phalanges A yrs 1-2

Metacarpals 2-5 A yrs 2-3
Metacarpals 2-5 F yrs 14-15 (female)
15-16 (male)
Metacarpals 2-5 A wks 8-10 (prenatal)
A yrs 10-12
A yrs 8-10
A mths 3-5
A yrs 1-2
A yrs 3-4
A yrs 5-7
F yrs 15-17 (female) 17-20 (male)

Metacarpal 1 A wks 8-10 (prenatal)
F yrs 14-16
A yrs 2-3
A yrs 4-5
A yrs 5-6
A mths 2-4
A yrs 5-6
A yrs 1-2
F yrs 14-17 (female) 16-20 (male)

Figure 9.32 Appearance (A) and fusion (F) times of the ossification centres of the hand.

Practical notes

Sideing

It is a general rule that sideing of the bones of the hand can only be achieved with any degree of confidence as the bone approaches adult morphology around the time of puberty. Before this period, the bones are sufficiently lacking in strong identifiable features making sideing extremely difficult, if not impossible. Certainly, we have found it very difficult to side adult phalanges, so the prospect of correctly assigning side to the bones of the juvenile hand seems tantamount to the search for the Holy Grail! Metacarpals and carpals become more recognizable as puberty approaches and so it is possible, in some cases, that the recognition of developing features that would permit identification of side in the adult might be observed in the juvenile.

Sideing the juvenile first metacarpal relies on being able to identify:

- the nutrient foramen, which is generally located on the distal aspect of the anteromedial surface of the shaft and is directed distally
- demarcation of the volar surface into a larger lateral and a smaller medial area

- identification of the tubercle on the lateral aspect of the proximal extremity for the attachment of the abductor pollicis longus muscle. Once the basal epiphysis is present, then side is easy to establish, as it follows the adult morphology.

Correct identification of side for the second metacarpal relies almost entirely on the development of the base of the bone. However, the head does show marked asymmetry in relation to the attachments of the second metacarpophalangeal ligament, which tends to pare away the dorsolateral aspect. The nutrient foramen is of no value in side identification as it is found with approximately equal frequency on both the anteromedial and anterolateral surfaces.

Identification of side for the third metacarpal is heavily dependent upon identification of the styloid process on the dorsolateral aspect. The nutrient foramen is usually found on the lateral aspect, although variation in its position does not make it a very reliable indicator.

The fourth metacarpal is probably the most difficult to side in the juvenile as correct assignation depends on the morphology of the base. Some additional information may be gleaned from the nutrient foramen, which is generally located on the lateral aspect.

Sideing of the fifth metacarpal also relies heavily on the identification of the non-articular medial surface of the base. The head of the metacarpal tends to be asymmetrical on the palmar aspect, due to the presence of a sesamoid bone on the medial articular surface, which therefore tends to be larger than that of the lateral aspect. The nutrient foramen is generally located on the lateral aspect.

The capitate cannot be identified with any degree of certainty until approximately 3–4 years of age and it is probably not until around 12 years that side can be attributed with any degree of reliability. By an early stage, the bone adopts the shape of a reversed 'D', with a flattened medial surface for articulation with the hamate and a slightly wider distal transverse diameter.

The hamate can probably be identified in isolation from approximately 4–5 years of age, but side cannot be established with confidence until after 9 years of age, when the bone has adopted its characteristic wedge-shaped appearance. In the early years of puberty the hamulus begins to develop and this is located on the palmar surface in a somewhat mediodistal location.

It is unlikely that any of the remainder of the carpals can be attributed correctly to a side until puberty has commenced and the adult morphology is well established (around 12 years in girls and 14–15 years in boys).

Bones of a similar morphology

It is obvious that the appearance of the bones of the hand and the foot are morphologically close and therefore most likely to cause some confusion. It is highly unlikely that any carpal could ever be confused with a tarsal bone, as the latter are considerably larger and much more robust at every age. The metatarsals are generally longer than the metacarpals and the shafts and heads are more slender and slightly compressed in the mediolateral plane. With the exception of the phalanges of the big toe (which are actually larger than those of the thumb), the remaining pedal phalanges are considerably shorter, less well defined and more irregular than their manual counterparts. The pedal phalanges tend to be more rounded in cross-section of the shaft, while the phalanges of the hand show a roughly semicircular outline, due to the volar flattening caused by the close proximity of the long flexor tendons.

Morphological summary (Fig. 9.32)

Prenatal

Wks 7–9	Primary ossification centres appear for distal phalanges
Wks 8–10	Primary ossification centres appear for metacarpals
Wks 9–11	Primary ossification centres appear for proximal phalanges
Wks 10–12	Primary ossification centres appear for middle phalanges

Birth	*All 19 primary centres for the long bones of the hand are present*
	Ossification centres for capitate and hamate may be present
2–3 mths (♀) 3–4 mths (♂)	Ossification centre appears for capitate
3–4 mths (♀) 4–5 mths (♂)	Ossification centre appears for hamate
1–2 yrs	Ossification centre appears for triquetral
10–17 mths (♀) 14–24mths (♂)	Epiphyses for bases of proximal phalanges 2–5 appear
17 mths (♀) 22 mths (♂)	Epiphysis for base of distal phalanx 1 appears
16–19 mths (♀) 22–29 mths (♂)	Epiphyses for heads of metacarpals 2–5 appear
19 mths (♀) 2.5 yrs (♂)	Epiphyses for bases of middle phalanges 2–4 appear
2 yrs (♀) 2–3 yrs (♂)	Epiphyses for bases of distal phalanges 3–4 appear. Epiphyses for base of metacarpal 1 and proximal phalanx 1 appear
2.5 yrs (♀) 3.5 yrs (♂)	Epiphyses for bases of distal and middle phalanges of 5 appear
3 yrs (♀) 4 yrs (♂)	Ossification centre appears for lunate; capitate can be identified
4 yrs (♀) 5 yrs (♂)	Ossification centre appears for trapezium; hamate can be identified
5 years (♀) 6 years (♂)	Ossification centres appear for trapezoid and scaphoid
8 ys (♀) 10 yrs (♂)	Ossification centre appears for pisiform; triquetral can be identified
9–10 yrs	Trapezium, trapezoid and lunate can be identified
9.5–11 yrs	Scaphoid can be identified
10–12 yrs	Hook of hamate appears and fuses to body. Styloid process of metacarpal 3 develops
12 yrs	Pisiform can be identified
11–15 yrs (♀) 13–18 yrs (♂)	Sesamoid bones commence ossification
13.5 yrs (♀) 16 yrs (♂)	Distal phalangeal epiphyses fuse
14–14.5 yrs (♀) 16.5 yrs (♂)	Base of metacarpal 1 fuses; proximal and middle phalangeal epiphyses fuse
14.5–15 yrs (♀) 16.5 yrs (♂)	Heads of metacarpals 2–5 fuse

CHAPTER TEN

The Pelvic Girdle

The pelvic girdle is formed by the articulation of the two innominate bones with the midline sacrum and coccyx, thereby forming the junction between the trunk and the lower limbs (Fig. 10.1).

Early development of the innominate

The lower limb buds appear around day 28 in the region of the lumbar and upper sacral cord segments (Bardeen and Lewis, 1901; O'Rahilly and Gardner, 1975) in response to inductive signals from adjacent somites 24–29. At this stage, the limb bud is comprised of a small proliferating mass of mesenchymal cells lying within a border of ectoderm (O'Rahilly *et al.*, 1956; Laurenson, 1964b; Yasuda, 1973).

Around days 34–36, a core of mesoblast cells starts to condense within an area that is defined by the positions of the obturator, femoral and sciatic nerves, which have already extended deep into the developing limb bud (Laurenson, 1963). It is interesting to note that the position of these major

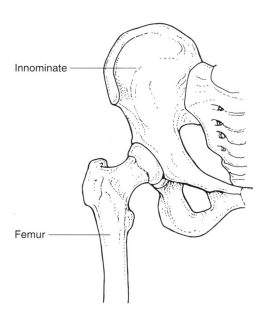

Innominate

Femur

Figure 10.1 The articulations of the pelvic girdle.

nerves is well established *before* the condensation of the pelvic mesenchyme commences, so that the future cartilaginous anlage is forced to form 'around' the already well-established nerve pathways. In situations where a cartilaginous model precedes nervous invasion, then it is the nerve that is forced to adopt a more circuitous route to reach its target. This somewhat precocious development of the three principal nerves of the lower limb may well explain their strikingly linear course in the adult from their origin to their peripheral target site (Laurenson, 1963).

The mesenchymal primordium extends in the form of three processes– an upper iliac, a lower posterior ischial (sciatic) and a lower anterior pubic (Fazekas and Kósa, 1978). The ischial and pubic mesenchymal masses meet and fuse inferiorly around the position of the obturator nerve, thereby forming the obturator foramen. Around days 36–38, the iliac process extends towards the vertebral mesenchymal primordium and fuses with the costal processes of the upper sacral vertebrae (Bardeen, 1905; Fazekas and Kósa, 1978). Eventually, the pubic primordia meet in the midline anteriorly and fuse at the site of the future pubic symphysis.

Chondrification commences in this blastemal structure around weeks 6–7 of intra-uterine development (Bardeen, 1905; O'Rahilly and Gardner, 1975) and appears first in the iliac mass in the region of the acetabulum, cephalad to the greater sciatic notch (Fig. 10.2) (Laurenson, 1964b). Chondrification centres for the pubis and the ischium are well developed by 7–8 weeks and are separated by the course of the obturator nerve (Gardner and O'Rahilly, 1972). Towards the end of the 2nd month, the three chondrification centres meet and fuse to form a shallow acetabulum, with the ischium and ilium fusing in advance of a union with the pubic mass (Adair, 1918). By the end of the 2nd month, the two cartilaginous pubic masses meet and fuse in the midline in the region of the future symphysis (Adair, 1918). In the 8th week, the anterior superior iliac spine, the ischial spine and the ischial tuberosity are well defined (Bardeen, 1905; Andersen, 1962). Therefore, the cartilaginous pelvis is approaching completion by the beginning of the 3rd intra-uterine month (Adair, 1918).

The embryological development and subsequent growth of the acetabulum has been of considerable interest, particularly in relation to congenital dislocation of the hip (Mezaros and Kery, 1980; Gepstein *et al.*, 1984; Portinaro *et al.*, 1994). This condition manifests as a deformity of the acetabulum and dislocation of the hip joint caused mainly by inversion of the fibrocartilaginous labrum and capsular contraction. Ponseti (1978a) noted that following unilateral congenital hip dysplasia, a cartilaginous ridge could be identified within the acetabulum (neolimbus of Ortolani). This was formed by a bulge of the acetabular cartilage that separated the cavity into two sections, with the more lateral of these forming the abnormal shallow site of articulation for the femoral head (Ortolani, 1948). The acetabulum may become shallow or even triangular in shape, with its base directed towards the obturator foramen and its apex looking up and back. Both Harrison (1957) and Ponseti (1978b) have shown that the development of a cup-shaped acetabulum is directly influenced by the presence of the femoral head. If the head is displaced, then an abnormal shape of acetabulum will ensue. Chronic slippage of the femoral head can lead to a permanent dislocation and the development of a rudimentary secondary articulation site, usually located superior to the primary joint site on the dorsal surface of the wing of the ilium. This condition is rare in fetuses younger than 20 weeks and has not been conclusively confirmed prior to the third trimester (Walker, 1983; Lee *et al.*, 1992). It has been suggested that complications at an early embryological stage, perhaps even at the time of limb rotation (6–8 weeks), may interfere with the ordered sequence of development and thereby initiate a train of events that ultimately manifest in an abnormal acetabular design (Gardner and Gray, 1950; Ráliš and McKibbin, 1973). In theory, the fetal hip can dislocate as early as 11 weeks (Watanabe, 1974), as the joint cavity has formed and the hip flexors are active. It is at this time, however, that the acetabulum is at its deepest relative to the femoral head, so this is probably the most stable period in acetabular development (Ippolito *et al.*, 1984). Subsequent normal growth of the acetabulum relies heavily on growth at the triradiate cartilage and so any abnormality in this location will severely affect the appearance and function of the joint (Plaster *et al.*, 1991). Relative to the shape of the femoral head, the acetabulum is at its most shallow around the time of birth and so perhaps it is not surprising that the traumas associated with birth can easily give rise to congenital hip dislocation. After birth, the trend is reversed and the acetabulum deepens and adapts to the more globular femoral head so that the joint becomes more stable.

Frazer (1948) gives an account of an interesting feature of development of the acetabulum that does not appear to have been confirmed by any other text that we can find. He reports that in the embryo, only the ischium and ilium are involved in the articulation with the head of the femur and that the capsule is attached around their ventral margin, while the pubic cartilage remains extra-capsular. Later, the pubis is reported to 'break through' the capsule and so becomes intracapsular, with the synovial cavity extending over it from the ilium. In this way, the original attachment of the capsule is only left on the ischium and this then forms the fibrous basis for the ligament of the head of the femur.

The embryological development of the sacro-iliac joint is particularly interesting. Cavitation of the joint begins in week 6 of intra-uterine life but from the 7th week it develops in a different way from other joints. There is a simultaneous presence of a synovial joint at the caudal part and a synarthrosis at the middle and cranial parts. A clear developmental difference is obvious between the caudal, cranial and middle segments at 14 prenatal weeks. Cavitation at the caudal extremity leads to the formation of a joint space, whereas in the cranial region there is a rich vascular invasion of the tissues separating the sacral and iliac anlagen. In addition, it is interesting to note that at all times during embryological development, the iliac side of the joint is in advance of the sacral side. Further, it is clear that the iliac surface of the joint is covered by fibrocartilage, whereas the sacral side is covered by hyaline cartilage.

The hip joint commences cavitation in week 7, this is complete by week 8 and the entire joint is fully formed by 18 weeks of intra-uterine life (Uhthoff, 1990b).

Ossification

Primary centres

Ossification centres virtually coincide in position with the earlier sites of chondrification and appear in the same order (Fig. 10.2) (Laurenson, 1964a). The centre for the **ilium** is the first to appear around the end of the 2nd and the beginning of the 3rd intra-uterine month. The centre of ossification appears in the perichondrium of the roof of the acetabulum in the vicinity of the future greater sciatic notch (Laurenson, 1964a). By around 9 weeks, the ossification has spread in a cranial direction, covering the internal and external surfaces of

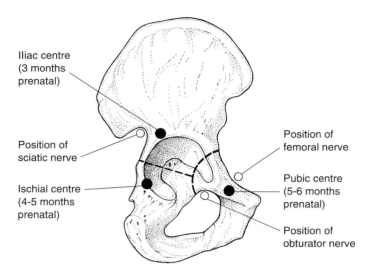

Iliac centre
(3 months
prenatal)

Position of
sciatic nerve

Ischial centre
(4-5 months
prenatal)

Position of
femoral nerve

Pubic centre
(5-6 months
prenatal)

Position of
obturator nerve

Figure 10.2 The position of the primary centres of ossification (and indeed chondrification) and the principal nerves of the lower limb in relation to the right innominate.

the iliac wing without invading the underlying cartilage. Ossification progresses in a radiating fan-like manner laying down bone on both an internal and an external shell (Laurenson, 1965; Birkner, 1978; Delaere *et al.*, 1992). There is evidence to suggest that, while the internal shell develops in advance of the external shell, the external shell tends to be thicker, probably by virtue of the action of the gluteal muscles. By 10–11 weeks, pores develop in the ossified shell and so invading osteoblasts and vascular elements gain access to the internal disintegrating cartilage and so form a primary marrow cavity. Laurenson (1964a) suggested that this unusual form of initial perichondral ossification, followed later by normal endochondral ossification, is indicative of a protective reaction as it tends to occur in regions of the skeleton where the newly developed bone comes into direct contact with a well-established nerve trunk, e.g. the clavicle and ribs. In the ilium, the site of the initial ossification centre coincides with the location of the sciatic nerve. It is possible that the ilium may be recognizable by 4–5 prenatal months through the presence of the upper border of the greater sciatic notch and the characteristic radiating appearance of the iliac shells (Fig. 10.3).

Ossification of the **ischium** is initiated by perichondral ossification that precedes endochondral expansion (Laurenson, 1963) with the initial site appearing in the body of the bone below and behind the position of the acetabulum around 4–5 intra-uterine months. The ischium is certainly identifiable in the third trimester of pregnancy when it appears as a comma- or apple seed-shaped structure, which is broader superiorly and tapers inferiorly to the ramal surface, which points anteriorly. The superior, posterior and inferior borders are convex, while the anterior border is concave. The inner pelvic surface is smooth, while the outer surface bears a depression superiorly for the acetabular surface (Fig. 10.4).

The **pubic** centre is the last to appear between 5 and 6 intra-uterine months and it commences in the region of the superior pubic ramus, anterior to the acetabulum and in close proximity to the passage of both the femoral and obturator nerves. Although in the majority of cases the pubis develops from a single centre of ossification, there are some reports that state that it can

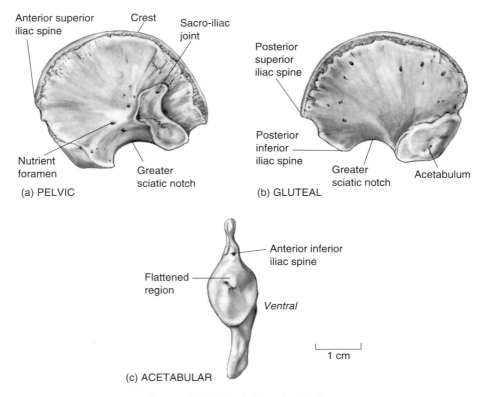

Figure 10.3 The right perinatal ilium.

develop from two or more centres. Even if multiple centres do develop, they are still restricted to the superior ramal region of the pelvis and they unite within the first few months of birth. However, during the process of fusion, they may adopt a sclerotic appearance on radiographs and so be incorrectly diagnosed as fracture sites.

The pubis is rarely recovered from prenatal remains, as it is the last to commence ossification and so is both the smallest and most delicate of the pelvic elements at this stage. In the early stages, it is reported to be dumb-bell-shaped and has even been likened to a Turkish slipper (Fazekas and Kósa, 1978). The lateral (iliac) extremity is more rounded and club-like in appearance and is directed in an infero-oblique direction, while the medial (symphyseal) end is flatter and projects vertically downwards, forming the body of the pubis.

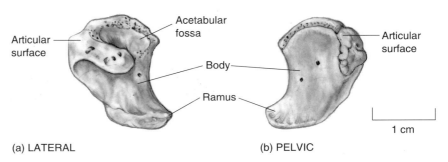

Figure 10.4 The right perinatal ischium.

The inner (pelvic) aspect is relatively featureless, while the outer region clearly shows the line of the pecten pubis passing superomedially across the upper region of the surface and the inferomedially orientated ventral arc of demarcation between the symphyseal surface medially and the lateral surface of the pubic body (Fig. 10.5).

At birth, all three primary centres of ossification are well developed and readily identifiable and each has extended to such a point that it already forms part of the bony acetabular wall (Figs 10.3–10.5). Although the morphology of the primary elements change little within the first few years after birth, each is reported to exhibit rapid growth in the first 3 months, which slows somewhat until 2–3 years of age and then slows even further until the time of puberty, when the secondary sexually related growth changes occur concomitant with the normal adolescent growth spurt. It is said that the pelvic organs descend fully into the pelvic cavity by 6 years of age and presumably this reflects the time at which the complex has grown sufficiently in all diameters to allow complete descent. This descent is readily identified in the living child when their body shape alters from the abdominal distention of the toddler to the slimmer profile of the young child.

Certainly by birth, the ilium has adopted most of the characteristic features of the adult bone (Fig. 10.3). Both the anterior and posterior superior iliac spines are well developed at this stage, although the region of the anterior inferior iliac spine is more poorly defined. Contrary to Wakeley (1929), we have found that both the acetabulocristal buttress and the thickened bar of bone that passes from the auricular surface to the acetabulum are present at birth. Although the crest is distinctly S-shaped, the characteristic concavities and convexities of the iliac and gluteal surfaces do not fully develop until the anterior border bends forward around 2 years of age. This alteration in blade morphology probably results from remodelling associated with body weight transfer in relation to upright posture and locomotion. This is also the time at which England (1990) reports that the sacrum descends between the ilia.

After birth, the appearance of the three centres alters very little, but recognizable changes do occur at the acetabular surface. At birth, the acetabular surface of the ilium is represented by a slight depression in the centre of the somewhat bulbous inferior extremity. By 6 months *post partum*, the iliopectineal line can be distinguished as a distinct promontory on its ventral rim (Fig. 10.6) and by 4–5 years of age a well-defined plaque of bone is present on the ventral aspect of the depression, which represents the future non-articular region of the iliac acetabular fossa. Certainly by 6 years of age, although it can be earlier if ischiopubic fusion is imminent, there is a well-defined line of demarcation between the articulation sites for the pubis and the ischium. Thus, the immature iliac acetabular extremity is basically triangular in

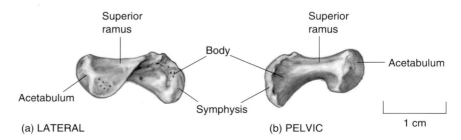

Figure 10.5 The right perinatal pubis.

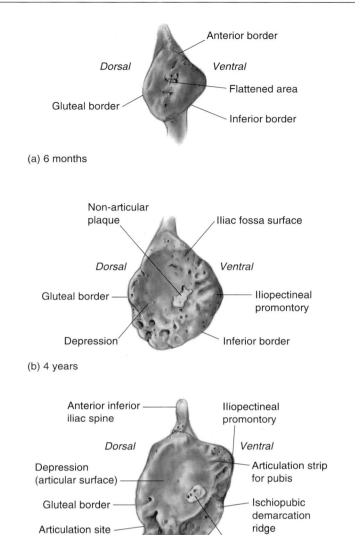

(a) 6 months

(b) 4 years

(c) 6 years

Figure 10.6 The development of the right iliac acetabular surface.

shape, bearing a somewhat dorsally located depression for the articular surface, which is bounded anteriorly and inferiorly by thick strips of metaphyseal bone for articulation with the pubis and ischium respectively (Fig. 10.6). The promontory for the iliopectineal line lies on the anterior border, superior to the line of demarcation between the pubic and ischial articulation sites. The plaque of non-articular bone lies on the anterior aspect of the acetabular depression, lateral to the ischiopubic demarcation line and inferior to the iliopectineal promontory. A highly convoluted area of bone is present at the inferodorsal margin at the point of contact with the descending margin of the greater sciatic notch, and this will be the future site of articulation for the posterior acetabular epiphysis. The gluteal margin of the acetabular extremity is scalloped in appearance and often becomes continuous superiorly with the anterior border of the ilium passing up towards the anterior inferior iliac spine.

In the ischium at birth (Fig. 10.4), the superior pole of the outer lateral surface bears the articular acetabular region, which is restricted to the posterior aspect as a strip of non-articular bone (acetabular fossa) occupies the anterior area. By around 6 months of age, the superior convex border of the ischium develops an angulation so that the site of articulation for the pubis lies anteriorly and that for the ilium lies superiorly (Fig. 10.7). By 1 year of age, the superior border is no longer convex but is straight, so that the articulation site for the ilium lies superiorly and almost horizontally and the site for the pubis lies anteriorly and almost vertically. The most posterior projection of the superior border is thickened and almost triangular in shape and this is the site of articulation for the future posterior acetabular epiphysis (Fig. 10.7). The ischial spine is also well developed by 1 year of age and initially presents as a rounded projection on the posterior margin.

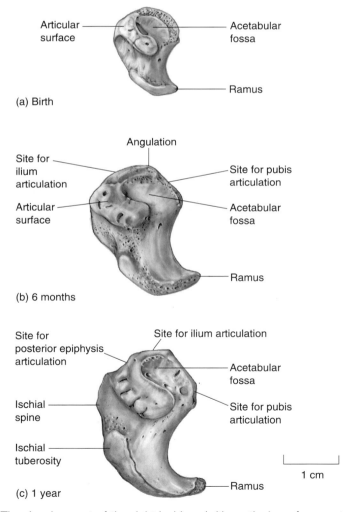

Figure 10.7 The development of the right ischium (with particular reference to the acetabular surface).

The acetabular surface of the immature pubis is roughly oval in outline lying in a somewhat oblique plane. At 6 months of age it is somewhat raised from the remainder of the surface and occupies an anterior location (Fig. 10.8). This elevation is bordered on two sides by metaphyseal surfaces, with the superomedial aspect representing the site for articulation with the ilium and the inferomedial region being the site of articulation with the ischium. The demarcation between these two sites of articulation becomes detectable by around 3–4 years of age and becomes more clearly defined as the time for ischiopubic fusion approaches. By this age, the acetabular region is no longer elevated, but presents as a relatively flat surface that may even be concave in appearance. By 5–6 years of age, a non-articular plaque of bone becomes evident in the acetabular depression on the posterior margin adjacent to the region of articulation with the ischium (Fig. 10.8).

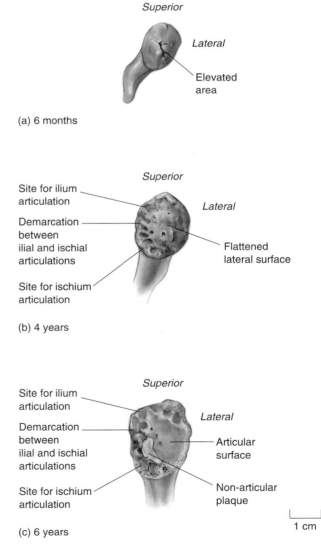

Figure 10.8 The development of the right pubic acetabular surface.

The primary centres of the ischium and the pubis are first to fuse in the region of the rami (Fig. 10.9), and although the timing is extremely variable, as it can arise as early as 3 years of age, it generally occurs between 5 and 8 years. As the time for fusion approaches, the ends of the synchondrosis become enlarged but this 'heaped' appearance has normally diminished by 10 years of age. Although of unknown function and aetiology, an accessory ossicle has been reported in the hyaline cartilage of the joint (Caffey, 1993). It is not clear which surface of the synostosis fuses first as we have found cases where the inner surface is fused but the outer is still open, and indeed cases where the opposite is true. At this early stage, fusion between the ischium and the pubis is restricted to the ramal region, as the vertical flange of the triradiate cartilage is still present between the two bones in the acetabular region and fusion here will not occur until puberty (see below).

Secondary centres

To understand the complex nature of secondary ossification centres in the pelvis, it is useful to consider each of the three constituent parts in terms of normal long bone development where proximal and distal epiphyses develop and fuse to a diaphysis. The secondary centres for the ilium appear at the crest (proximal) and the acetabulum (distal), the pubic secondary centres appear at the acetabulum (proximal) and at the body, crest and ramus (distal) and the ischial epiphyses occur at the acetabulum (proximal) and the ramus and tuberosity (distal). Accessory centres are also reported but they tend to be more variable, e.g. ischial spine and anterior inferior iliac spine.

Clearly, a factor common to all three pelvic elements will be the ossification of the secondary centres in the region of the acetabulum. Acetabular maturation is complex and this has been further complicated by misunderstandings and inconsistent use of nomenclature. An appreciation of the basic histological composition of the developing joint is essential before the pattern of ossification can be fully understood. As with the end of any developing typical long bone, three types of cartilage are represented in the maturing acetabulum: growth, epiphyseal and articular.

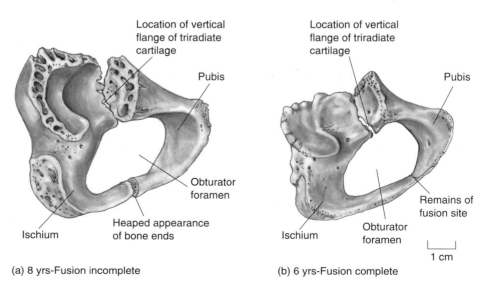

(a) 8 yrs-Fusion incomplete   (b) 6 yrs-Fusion complete

Figure 10.9 Right ischiopubic fusion.

The cartilaginous acetabular anlage is composed of a cup-shaped articular area laterally (deficient inferiorly), which is connected to a medial triradiate unit that is interposed between the ilium, ischium and pubis (Harrison, 1957; Ponseti, 1978b). The articular cartilage lines the inner surface of the cup-shaped region of the anlage and will of course form the site of articulation for the head of the femur at the hip joint. The triradiate unit displays areas of growth cartilage adjacent to the surfaces of the three bony elements and each is separated from its counterpart on the opposite side by a strip of epiphyseal cartilage (Fig. 10.10). In this way, interstitial growth within the triradiate zone causes the acetabulum to expand during childhood and so accommodate the enlarging femoral head (Harrison, 1961).

The triradiate cartilage is comprised of three flanges (Fig. 10.11):

- the anterior flange is located between the ilium and pubis and is slanted superiorly
- the posterior flange is positioned between the ilium and the ischium and is more horizontally placed
- the vertical flange is located between the ischium and the pubis (Ponseti, 1978b).

To understand secondary ossification in the acetabulum it is important to visualize the spatial three-dimensional relationship between the laterally placed cup-shaped acetabular cartilage and the more medially located triradiate complex. Harrison (1957) emphasized the importance of establishing that the cup-shaped acetabular cartilage is not ossified by direct extensions from the triradiate unit but by separate ossicles that form within the cartilaginous zone around the acetabular rim. While Harrison's research was based on the development of the rat pelvis, there is a considerable amount of comparative research that shows a similar pattern throughout most mammals.

There are generally three main epiphyses that form within the cup-shaped cartilage of the acetabulum and these will eventually expand to form both the outer rim of the acetabulum and much of the articular surface, in much the same manner as is seen in the glenoid fossa of the scapula. As these centres enlarge they will ultimately meet with the ossifying triradiate epiphyses and fusion will occur.

The first of the acetabular epiphyses to ossify is the **os acetabuli** (anterior acetabular epiphysis), which appears around 9–10 years of age as a triangular-shaped bone on the ventral acetabular rim, wedged between the pubis and the ilium (Zander, 1943; Ponseti, 1978b). It appears in the thick cartilage of the acetabulum adjacent to the pubis and as it matures it extends into the anterior flange of the triradiate zone between the pubis and the ilium (Fig. 10.12). This

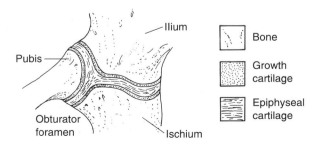

Figure 10.10 A diagrammatic representation of a sagittal section through the immature triradiate zone to show the arrangement of cartilage types.

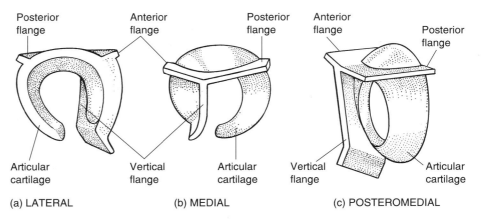

Posterior flange / Anterior flange / Posterior flange / Anterior flange / Posterior flange

Articular cartilage / Vertical flange / Articular cartilage / Vertical flange / Articular cartilage

(a) LATERAL   (b) MEDIAL   (c) POSTEROMEDIAL

Figure 10.11 The right acetabular cartilaginous anlage (redrawn after Harrison, 1958).

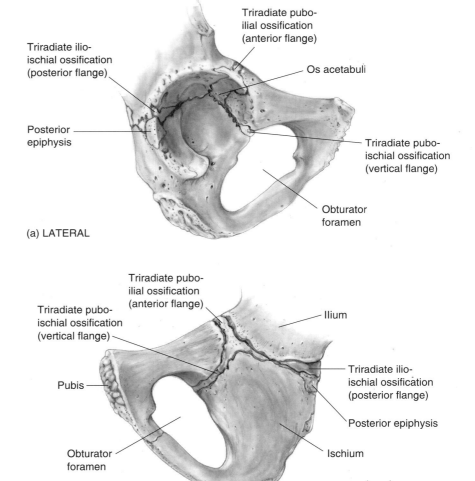

Figure 10.12 Ossification of the right triradiate and acetabular epiphyses (approximately 15 years).

epiphysis forms the anterior aspect of the acetabular rim and extends downward to form both the acetabular articular surface of the pubic element and the upper anterior aspect of the ilium. In time, it will eventually expand upward to fuse with the superior epiphysis of the acetabulum and also with the anterior flange of the triradiate bone (Fig. 10.13).

When well developed and therefore close to the time of union, it is possible that the anterior epiphysis (os acetabuli) of the acetabulum may be identified in isolation (Fig. 10.12). It presents a flattened superior surface for articulation with the ilium, an inferior concave surface for articulation with the pubis, an expanding lateral surface that forms the articular acetabular surface and a triangular-shaped surface that forms at the iliopubic eminence.

A second acetabular epiphysis arises in the posterior acetabular rim at the junction between the ilium and the ischium. Although many radiological texts have also referred to this as the os acetabuli, it is clearly a different structure (Freedman, 1934). Some texts therefore suggest the use of the terms 'anatomical os acetabuli' for the anterior ossific nucleus and 'radiological os acetabuli,' for that on the posterior acetabular rim (Zander, 1943). This is clearly not an ideal situation and so the term 'os acetabuli' tends now to be restricted to the anterior nodule, while the posterior structure has been referred to as the 'os marginalis superior acetabuli,' or indeed the 'nucleus osseous superior marginalis acetabuli' (Zander, 1943). We have named it the **posterior epiphysis** and it tends to be larger than its anterior counterpart and frequently forms from the fusion of several smaller ossicles (Fig. 10.12). It appears around the age of 10–11 years in the posterior aspect of the acetabular cartilage and

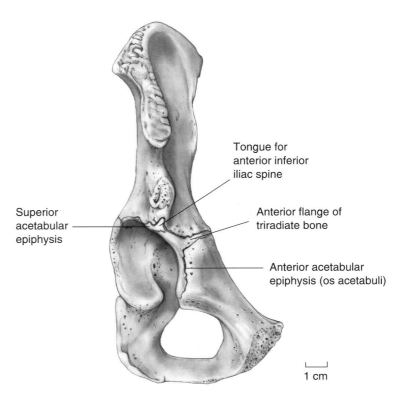

Superior acetabular epiphysis

Tongue for anterior inferior iliac spine

Anterior flange of triradiate bone

Anterior acetabular epiphysis (os acetabuli)

1 cm

Figure 10.13 The development of the right anterior acetabular epiphysis (approximately 15 years).

spreads superiorly and inferiorly to form not only the posterior rim of the acetabulum but also much of the acetabular articular surface of the ischium and a small part of the articular surface of the ilium, as well as fusing with the ossicles in the posterior limb of the triradiate cartilage.

A third, **superior epiphysis** appears in the upper rim of the acetabulum and this has been confusingly referred to as the 'acetabular epiphysis' (Figs 10.13–15). This forms the upper rim of the acetabulum and much of the roof of the acetabular articular surface. This epiphysis does not extend into the triradiate zone but it does frequently pass upward as a tongue of bone to form the lower region of the anterior inferior iliac spine (Fig. 10.14). The epiphysis appears around 12–14 years of age but complete fusion involving the anterior inferior iliac spine may not, in our experience, be completed until 16 or 17 years of age.

From around 9 years of age, a variable number of small ossific islands appear within the true triradiate cartilage and it is likely that these represent the true central epiphyses of the ilium, ischium and pubis (Fig. 10.12). As these centres enlarge, they meet both the expanding acetabular epiphyses and the advancing borders of the three bones of the pelvis and ultimately fuse. There is a tendency for the pelvic aspect of the triradiate zone to fuse in advance of its acetabular aspect, although consolidation is generally complete by mid-puberty. It is reported that acetabular fusion commences around 11 years in females and 14 years in males and is completed by 15 years in females and 17 years in males. In extremely rare circumstances, the epiphyses that form the rim of the acetabulum may persist as isolated nodules of bone (Zander, 1943). Other accessory shell-like ossicles may also develop in the cartilaginous walls of the acetabulum and in rare circumstances they too can persist as permanent separate structures.

The formation of a strong supporting structure for the head of the femur is unquestionably of vital importance for the structural integrity of the hip joint in terms of efficient weight transfer and normal locomotion. It is thought that

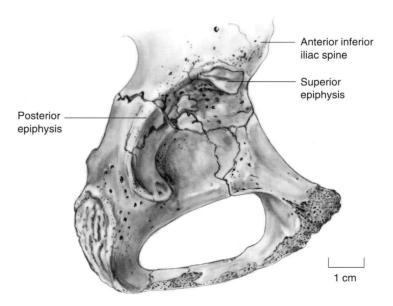

Figure 10.14 The right posterior and superior acetabular epiphyses – female aged 12 years.

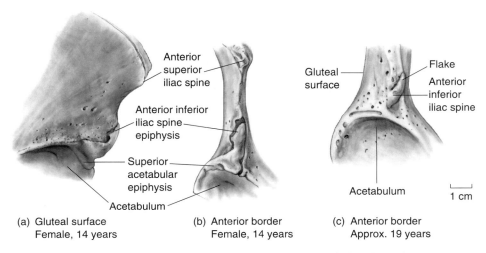

Figure 10.15 The epiphysis of the right anterior inferior iliac spine.

early maturation of the acetabulum may be desirable to enable the joint to withstand the considerable forces that pass through it as body mass and weight increase during puberty. Indeed, Greulich and Thoms (1944) reported that the radiographic appearance of prepubertal pelves was characterized by an 'acetabular constriction' caused by an inward projection of the pelvic wall in the region of the acetabuli. They suggested that this was a manifestation of the medially directed pressure transmitting through the femoral heads to a yielding cartilaginous junction. This radiographic appearance is known as 'juvenile beaking' and is a non-pathological condition resulting from plastic deformity of the triradiate region in relation to normal shear and rotational stress. However, if there is an abnormal progression of triradiate development the clinical condition of 'primary protrusio acetabuli' will arise and this can have many serious implications, not least being obstruction in the midpelvis which can lead to cephalopelvic disproportion during parturition (Alexander, 1965; Gusis *et al.*, 1990).

Trauma to the triradiate cartilage is relatively un-common and is often difficult to diagnose immediately. It generally arises following either a blow to the pubis or ischial ramus resulting in a sheering injury or by crushing/ fracture or impaction-related trauma. The younger the patient is at the time of injury (particularly under 10 years of age), the more likely it is that disruption or arrest of normal growth will occur. Trauma to the cartilage initiates a bridge or graft across the physis, which can result in premature fusion leading to a shallow acetabulum and subluxation of the hip (Hallel and Salvati, 1977). It is only if this graft is broken or resorbed that normal growth can continue. It has also been shown in piglets that if the triradiate cartilage is crossed by an osteotome, for example during Pemberton osteotomy, this will also give rise to a bony bar that traverses the site of injury (Leet *et al.*, 1999). The triradiate cartilage can also be affected by conditions such as suppurative arthritis or even osteochondromas, which will also affect the normal growth of the cartilage.

The comparatively early union of the acetabulum restricts continued growth in the pelvis so that the majority of later pubertal alterations in pelvic shape and size tend to be restricted to the other epiphyseal sites away from the acetabulum. Although much of the initial research on pelvic growth was carried out on the rat pelvis, it is generally recognized that growth at the caudal end of the ischium and at the pubic symphysis is four times faster than the rate of growth exhibited at the acetabulum. Perhaps it is not surprising then, that the joints in these locations continue to show a more prolonged period of growth-related activity and so have become useful as indicators of age at death. This may also go some way towards explaining why the majority of the sexually dimorphic traits in the pelvis are restricted either to the posterior element, e.g. greater sciatic notch, or indeed to the anterior portion, e.g. pubis shape. Increased growth in these two regions in particular may well place undue strain on the ligaments that hold these joints in position and may therefore explain the frequency of pitting and grooving found in these regions in the female in particular, where secondary sexual growth alterations are most prevalent.

Following fusion of the acetabular centres, the order of appearance of the other secondary epiphyses of the pelvis is somewhat variable, but it is generally reported to be – from first to last – anterior inferior iliac spine, iliac crest, ischial tuberosity and pubic symphysis. The order of completion of fusion also tends to follow this pattern.

The epiphysis for the **anterior inferior iliac spine** (AIIS) is reported to commence ossification around 10–13 years of age and fuse by around 20 years. However, there seems to be little information on the variation that can arise in the origin of this epiphysis, its pattern of fusion and its clinical relevance. Major anatomy texts only comment that 'The anterior inferior iliac spine may be ossified as an extension from this centre (os acetabuli) or from a separate centre.' We have found that in the majority of cases the inferior aspect of the anterior inferior iliac spine and the lower aspect of the anterior border of the ilium directly below it, form from an extension of the superior acetabular epiphysis (Fig. 10.15). The position of this epiphysis closely matches the site of attachment of the upper band of the iliofemoral ligament and, as this too passes up towards the AIIS, then perhaps it is not surprising that the lower aspect of the anterior border of the ilium forms in this way. The tongue-like expansion can be found in individuals from around 12 years of age, but it will have fused by around 16–18 years and in all cases by 20 years. The upper aspect of the AIIS can develop as a separate flake-like epiphysis that corresponds with the site of attachment for the straight head of the rectus femoris muscle and is therefore a true traction epiphysis (Fig. 10.15) and a common site of avulsion fracture following violent muscular contraction in athletes.

Despite Francis' (1940) report that the **iliac crest epiphysis** begins to ossify in the middle of the crest and extends outwards in each direction, it is generally recognized that it does indeed form from two separate ossification centres. The anterior epiphysis forms the anterior superior iliac spine and the anterior half of the crest of the ilium, while the posterior epiphysis forms the posterior superior iliac spine and the posterior half of the iliac crest (Stevenson, 1924). The two epiphyses meet in the middle of the crest just posterior to the highest point (Fig. 10.16). The epiphysis obviously assumes the shape of the crest and so adopts a somewhat spiral growth pattern (Birkner, 1978). Unlike the other epiphyses of the innominate, that for the iliac crest is well formed before it commences fusion and so it tends to be somewhat delayed in terms of its maturation.

The iliac crest epiphyses are thin, flat, long, vaguely spiral and, in the early stages, somewhat honeycombed in appearance (Fig. 10.17a,b).The anterior epiphysis is roughly 'S', shaped being concave medially at its ventral extent

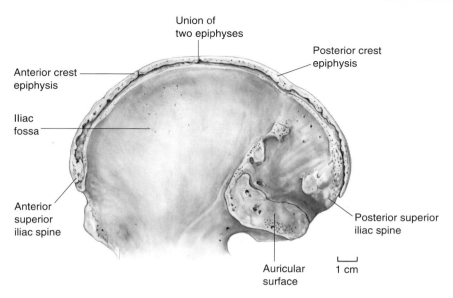

Figure 10.16 The right iliac crest epiphyses (approximately 16 years).

and concave laterally in its dorsal part. The anterior extremity is somewhat expanded and ends in a cap which passes inferiorly to cover the anterior superior iliac spine (Fig. 10.17a). The posterior epiphysis is also somewhat S-shaped, being concave laterally in its anterior part and concave medially in its posterior region. It is broader in its posterior aspect, where it expands to cover the thickened area of bone over the non-articular region of the sacro-iliac articulation (Fig. 10.17b).

Ossification in the crest is said to commence around 12–13 years of age in girls and 14–15 years in boys, with the anterior epiphysis generally forming in advance of the posterior epiphysis. Interestingly, Buehl and Pyle (1942) found that the onset of ossification in the crest consistently occurred within 6 months of the menarcheal date (on average 12.5–13 years), whereas Scoles *et al*. (1988) found that it occurred within 8 months of the onset of menses. The timing of epiphyseal fusion is extremely variable for the crest and this is perhaps not surprising as the epiphysis is almost completely formed before union commences. The anterior and posterior epiphyses fuse to form a single cap for the crest, which tends to commence union initially on the pelvic aspect of the anterior superior iliac spine around 17–20 years of age in males and around 2 years earlier in females (McKern and Stewart, 1957). The pelvic aspect of the anterior epiphysis fuses progressively from anterior to posterior until it reaches the junction with the posterior epiphysis (Fig. 10.18). However, the gluteal aspect of the anterior epiphysis is slower to close as it has a greater surface area to cover as it spreads over the thicker region of the iliac tubercle. The posterior epiphysis seems to commence union in the region of the posterior superior iliac spine and it is the gluteal aspect that fuses in advance of the pelvic aspect. The area of the crest directly adjacent to the region of the sacro-iliac joint is often the last region to fuse as, again, it has to spread over a wider surface area to cover the thickened bar of the crest in this region that marks the attachment of the erector spinae muscle. Partial fusion of the iliac crest is said to range from 15 to 22 years, with complete fusion occurring in 100% of individuals by 23 years of age.

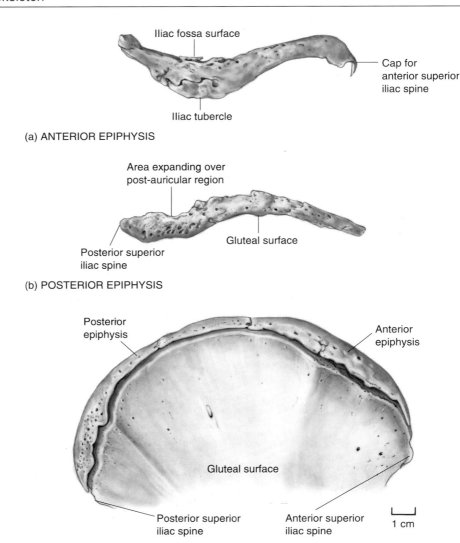

Iliac fossa surface

Cap for
anterior superior
iliac spine

Iliac tubercle

(a) ANTERIOR EPIPHYSIS

Area expanding over
post-auricular region

Gluteal surface

Posterior superior
iliac spine

(b) POSTERIOR EPIPHYSIS

Posterior
epiphysis

Anterior
epiphysis

Gluteal surface

Posterior superior
iliac spine

Anterior superior
iliac spine

1 cm

(c) ANTERIOR AND POSTERIOR CREST EPIPHYSES

Figure 10.17 Isolated right iliac crest epiphyses and their position on the iliac crest (approximately 17 years).

The maturation of the iliac crest epiphysis has proved to be of considerable clinical value in assessing an individual's remaining growth potential (Wagner *et al.*, 1995). This is particularly important when evaluating the necessity for, or indeed against, operative intervention in the management of conditions such as adolescent idiopathic scoliosis. Risser (1958) has shown that the completion of fusion of the iliac crest epiphysis occurs simultaneously with the completion of vertebral growth, which is then concomitant with a static vertebral curvature.

Avulsion of the iliac crest epiphysis has been reported in athletes who undertake sudden contraction of the abdominal muscles.

The **ischial epiphysis** appears as a small flake on the superior aspect of the ischial tuberosity between 13 and 16 years of age and commences union (early in the development of the epiphysis) at the superior rim of the epiphyseal

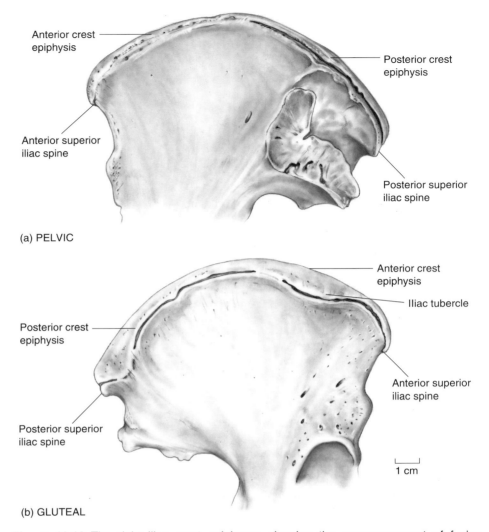

Anterior crest
epiphysis

Posterior crest
epiphysis

Anterior superior
iliac spine

Posterior superior
iliac spine

(a) PELVIC

Anterior crest
epiphysis

Iliac tubercle

Posterior crest
epiphysis

Anterior superior
iliac spine

Posterior superior
iliac spine

1 cm

(b) GLUTEAL

Figure 10.18 The right iliac crest epiphyses showing the commencement of fusion (approximately 19 years).

surface and often slightly directed towards the pelvic border that carries the ischial spine (Fig. 10.19). It is unlikely that this epiphysis is ever separate from the primary ischial centre apart from in its very earliest stages of development.

We have noted that in a small number of individuals there is a distinct bony gutter of communication (Fig. 10.19b) between the upper medial border of the ischial tuberosity and the ischial spine and it is in these individuals that a billowed surface is seen on the lower aspect of the ischial spine. The presence of an epiphysis for the ischial spine has been reported as being somewhat variable (Frazer, 1948) and it is possible that an epiphysis may form only if a line of communication is retained between it and the ischial tuberosity (Fig. 10.19). As the superior border of the ischial tuberosity is the initial site of fusion for the flake-like epiphysis, it can be assumed that if an ischial spine epiphysis is to form, then it will occur in conjunction with that for the tuberosity.

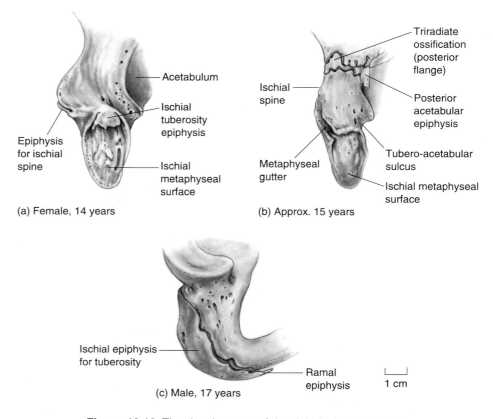

(a) Female, 14 years

Acetabulum

Ischial tuberosity epiphysis

Epiphysis for ischial spine

Ischial metaphyseal surface

(b) Approx. 15 years

Triradiate ossification (posterior flange)

Ischial spine

Posterior acetabular epiphysis

Metaphyseal gutter

Tubero-acetabular sulcus

Ischial metaphyseal surface

(c) Male, 17 years

Ischial epiphysis for tuberosity

Ramal epiphysis

1 cm

Figure 10.19 The development of the right ischial epiphysis.

The ischial epiphysis then spreads across the face of the tuberosity and extends down to its inferior pole, where it continues along the ischial ramus as the thin, tongue-like **ramal epiphysis**. The pelvic surface of the tuberal epiphysis commences union in advance of the lateral aspect so that generally by the time the ramal epiphysis has commenced development (Fig. 10.19c) the pelvic border of the ischial tuberosity is well advanced in terms of fusion and this is said to occur between 16 and 18 years of age. The ramal epiphysis continues forwards along the lower border of the ischial ramus and has generally reached half way along by around 19–20 years of age (Fig. 10.20). By this stage, the epiphysis for the ischial tuberosity has generally completed fusion on all borders and so is fully adult in appearance. The ramal epiphysis will continue edging slowly forwards, ossifying in the cartilage of the margin of the ischiopubic ramus until it approaches the lower lateral aspect of the pubic body. The epiphyseal lines may remain visible for a number of years after fusion is completed, which generally occurs by 20–21 years of age, although fusion in 100% of individuals may not occur until 21–23 years.

Avulsion of the ischial epiphysis is well documented as an athletic injury. It most commonly occurs in track athletes between the ages of puberty and 25 years of age and generally occurs as a result of uncoordinated extension at the hip joint, which puts excessive strain on the hamstring muscles.

Morphological changes at the **pubic symphyseal face** have been the subject of considerable attention in both anthropological and forensic literature.

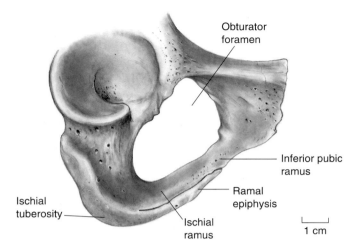

Figure 10.20 The right ischial ramal epiphysis – female aged 19 years.

This is mainly as a result of the prolonged period of age-related change displayed in this region, thereby making it a useful site for the determination of age at death from skeletal remains.

It is reported that the epiphyseal structures associated with the human pubic bone represent remnants of the epipubis and hypo-ischium that occur in many animal groups (Todd, 1921). In fact, all mammalian pubic symphyses, with the exception of man and certain of the higher primates, fuse in the midline via a median bar of bone, which in most cases becomes continuous with the ischial epiphysis (Todd, 1921). In the light of comparative evidence, Todd (1920) proposed that the human symphysis pubis is retrogressive in nature, as the epiphyseal structures involved in the metamorphosis of the joint face, represent bilateral vestiges of this median bar. Many authors have explained this strangely retrogressive phenomenon in terms of a functional requirement to resist fusion and maintain elasticity in this region for the purposes of expansion at parturition. This therefore suggests that the joint is a potential site of weakness in the biomechanics of the bony pelvic ring and so its structure probably reflects a compromise between the rigidity that is essential to maintain normal weight-related stress in conjunction with a certain degree of elasticity, which is essential for the safe passage of a relatively large fetal head.

In the juvenile, there is reported to be a continuous ischiopubic cap of cartilage that begins over the region of the pubic tubercle, lines the crest and ventral aspect of the face of the symphysis and then passes along the conjoint rami to the ischial tuberosity. Ossification then commences in both ends of the cartilaginous strip with that of the ischium arising in advance of that at the pubic end.

McKern and Stewart (1957) noticed that the symphyseal face behaves as two distinct areas and named them the ventral and dorsal demifaces, which may be delimited by a longitudinal groove or ridge. They proposed that only the ventral aspects of the symphysis showed epiphyseal progression, whereas the dorsal aspect only reflects changes in the diaphyseal structure. This morphological delimitation is based on an anatomical premise, where only the ventral aspect of the joint is separated by the interpubic disc of fibrocartilage as it is deficient over the posterior surface of the pubic face. Therefore it is not surprising that the majority of the methods that have employed symphyseal metamorphosis for the evaluation of age at death have relied strongly on the ventral structures of the joint, which Todd considered to be the vestiges of the phylogenetically older median bar.

What is termed the pre-epiphyseal stage by Meindl *et al.* (1985) is characterized by a well-marked ridge-and-furrow appearance of the joint surface (Fig. 10.21a). There is no build-up of bone along the ventral margin and the upper and lower limits of the joint surface are poorly defined. There is generally no epiphysis present for the pubic tubercle, which displays a classic juvenile appearance. This morphological appearance is generally found in individuals up to approximately 20 years of age, but this will of course vary, depending upon the sex and genetic pool from which the individual originated. The first change to occur to this pre-epiphyseal joint is that by a process of gradual accretion, bone is laid directly onto the dorsal face initially, resulting in a smoothing over of the ridge-and-furrow appearance (Fig. 10.21b), and this tends to occur between 15 and 23 years of age. The delimitation of the lower extremity of the joint tends to occur first (around 25 years of age) and this generally arises by the simple accretion of bone in that region. The upper extremity of the face commences delimitation around 23–27 years of age and can arise either by the fusion of a distinct superior ossific nodule in this region (Fig. 10.21c) or by gradual bone accretion. Todd (1921) considered this superior ossific nodule to be homologous with the epipubis of other mammals. Not only does this nodule form the upper limit of the joint surface, but it also extends inferiorly to form the upper aspect of the ventral rampart, a bevelled area of built-up bone that develops along the ventral aspect of the joint separating the articular face medially from the outer surface of the pubic body laterally. The remainder of the rampart is formed either from an upgrowth from an inferior ossific nodule or by simple accretion of bone (Fig. 10.21d). Todd (1921) considered the ventral rampart formation to be homologous with changes that occur in the median bar of other Eutherian mammals and the inferior ossific nodule to be homologous with the hypo-ischium. The variable occurrence of an inferior ossific nodule was taken to be evidence of the removal of the ischium from the anterior midline articulation, which is typical for man and the higher primates.

Frequently, the upper and lower progressions of the rampart fail to meet and so leave a hiatus in the upper ventral rim (Fig. 10.21d,e). Active rampart formation generally occurs between 24 and 30 years of age, although it is often not completed until 35 years of age. The epiphysis for the pubic tubercle can appear as a separate flake between 23 and 25 years of age or indeed it may form from a backward prolongation of the superior ossific nodule.

With increasing age, the dorsal plateau tends to show less dramatic maturation. A slight dorsal margin is said to develop in the middle of the border around 18 years of age and will continue to expand superiorly and inferiorly until the entire border is defined by a rim. This will tend to have occurred by 19–20 years of age. The grooves and ridges of the dorsal face then start to fill in to form the characteristic plateau and vestiges of the billowed surface may remain evident until at least 22–25 years. By around 30 years of age, the dorsal plateau becomes flattened and slightly granular in appearance.

Thus, changes at the symphyseal face show a prolonged period of developmental activity and may not reach a fully matured appearance until 35–40 years of age (Fig. 10.21f). Beyond this age, the changes tend to be degenerative in nature, with breakdown of the symphyseal outline and general degeneration of the texture of the face.

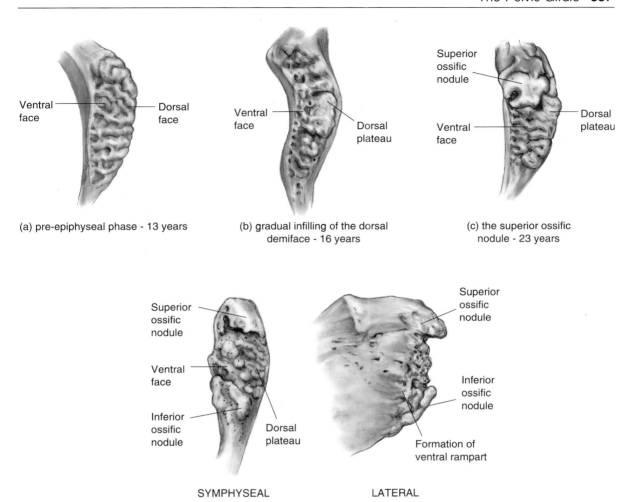

(a) pre-epiphyseal phase - 13 years

(b) gradual infilling of the dorsal demiface - 16 years

(c) the superior ossific nodule - 23 years

SYMPHYSEAL   LATERAL

(d) development of the ventral rampart - 26 years

(e) hiatus in the ventral rampart - 25 years

(f) the mature symphyseal face - 34 years

Figure 10.21 The development of the right pubic symphyseal face.

Sex differences

No discussion of the immature pelvis would be complete without a brief look at sex determination in the juvenile (see also Chapter 1). The pelvis is the area of the human skeleton said to display the greatest levels of sexual dimorphism and, in fact, the innominate is to be preferred over any other single bone for the accurate prediction of sex in the adult. Despite a wealth of literature concerning sex differences in the fetal and juvenile pelvis, it is still generally held that while dimorphism may exist from an early age, it does not reach a sufficiently high level to permit reliable discrimination of sex until after the extensive skeletal modifications of puberty have arisen (Thomson, 1899; Yamamura, 1939; Morton and Hayden, 1941; Morton, 1942; Reynolds, 1945, 1947; Boucher, 1955, 1957; Souri, 1959; Coleman, 1969; Crelin, 1973; Sundick, 1977; Weaver, 1980; Hunt, 1990; Mittler and Sheridan, 1992; Schutkowski, 1993; Holcomb and Konigsberg, 1995).

Interestingly, it has been shown that even in fetal innominates, the sex differences that do arise, tend to parallel those found in the adult, namely sciatic notch proportions, iliac proportions and pelvic inlet and outlet dimensions. Hromada (1939) identified two growth phases in the fetal pelvis where, between the 2nd and the 7th fetal months, there were virtually no discernible sex differences in fetal pelvic dimensions, whereas the dimorphism became increasingly more apparent between 7 months and birth.

The appearance and fusion times of the pelvic ossification centres are summarized in Fig. 10.22.

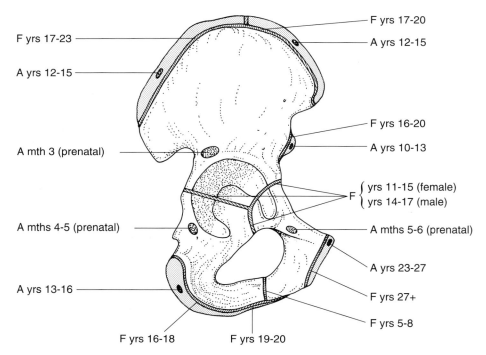

Figure 10.22 Appearance (A) and fusion (F) times of the innominate ossification centres.

Practical notes

Sideing

As the three primary centres adopt close to adult morphology early in fetal development, it is not difficult to identify and side each of the elements. Sideing of the ilium (Fig. 10.3) relies on being able to identify the crest (superiorly), the acetabulum and greater sciatic notch (inferiorly) and the auricular regions (posteriorly) on the inner pelvic surface. If the ilium is held with the iliac fossa facing and the greater sciatic notch inferiorly then the auricular surface will be on the side from which the bone originates, i.e. from the right side if the auricular surface is on the right of the specimen.

Sideing of the ischium (Fig. 10.4) relies on being able to identify the smooth pelvic surface (internally), the acetabular surface on the lateral surface (superiorly and posteriorly), the non-articular region (superiorly and anteriorly) and the thin arm of the ischial ramus inferiorly, which points anteriorly. If the specimen is held with the outer (acetabular) surface facing and with the ramal surface inferiorly, then the ramus will point to the side from which the specimen belongs.

Sideing of the pubis (Fig 10.5) is probably the most difficult and relies on being able to identify the pelvic from the lateral surfaces and the acetabular from the symphyseal surface. The symphyseal surface is longer and thinner than the acetabular extremity, which tends to be thicker and more club-shaped. The pelvic surface is relatively featureless, whereas the lateral surface shows a clear demarcation between the body ventrally and the superior ramus posteriorly. The upper border tends to be more linear than the inferior border, which is has a spiral caused by the passage of the obturator nerve and vessels. Therefore, if the specimen is examined with the lateral surface facing and the and the linear border uppermost, then the symphyseal face will point to the side from which the specimen originates.

Bones of a similar morphology

The immature ilium may be confused with any of the other flat bones of the skeleton if it is in a particularly fragmented state. However, the presence of two distinct compact shells surrounding coarse trabeculae should be sufficiently indicative of ilial origin. It is unlikely that either the ischium or the pubis would be confused with another bone, even from a very early stage.

Morphological summary (Fig. 10.22)

Prenatal

Mths 2–3	Ilium commences ossification
Mths 4–5	Ischium commences ossification and ilium is recognizable
Mths 5–6	Pubis commences ossification
Mths 6–8	Ischium is recognizable in isolation
Birth	All three primary bony components are represented
By 6 mths	The ilium shows a prominence on its acetabular extremity formed by the development of the iliopectineal line and the angulation of the superior border of the ischium has occurred
By yr 1	The superior border of the ischium is square and the ischial spine, pubic tubercle and crest have developed
By yr 2	The anterior border of the ilium has bent forwards in the vertical plane
By yr 3–4	The demarcation of the iliac and ischial articulation sites are clearly defined on the pubis

By yrs 4–5	The non-articular acetabular area is well defined on the ilium
By yrs 5–6	The non-articular acetabular area is well defined on the pubis
5–8 yrs	Fusion of the ischiopubic rami occurs
9–10 yrs	The anterior acetabular epiphysis or 'os acetabuli' appears and ossific islands appear in triradiate cartilage
10–11 yrs	The posterior acetabular epiphysis commences ossification
10–13 yrs	Centre appears for the anterior inferior iliac spine
11–15 yrs	The acetabulum commences and completes fusion in females
12–14 yrs	The superior acetabular epiphysis appears and the iliac crest commences ossification in the female
13–16 yrs	The ischial epiphysis commences ossification
14–17 yrs	The acetabulum commences and completes fusion in males and the iliac crest commences ossification in the male
15–23 yrs	The dorsal plateau of the pubic symphysis may show gradual obliteration of the ridge-and-furrow appearance
16–18 yrs	The ischial tuberosity is complete
17–20 yrs	The iliac crest epiphyses commence fusion
19–20 yrs	The ischial epiphysis extends half way along the ramus
By 20 yrs	The anterior inferior iliac spine has fused
20–23 yrs	Both the ischial epiphysis and the iliac crest complete union. The dorsal margin forms along the dorsal border of the pubic symphyseal surface
23–27 yrs	The epiphysis appears for the pubic tubercle and delimitation of the upper and lower borders of the symphyseal face commence. Epiphysis for pubic tubercle may develop
24–30 yrs	Active ventral rampart formation and obliteration of the ridge-and-furrow appearance of the ventral and dorsal aspects of the pubic symphyseal face
By 35 yrs	Ventral rampart is complete and the symphyseal rim is mature

CHAPTER ELEVEN

The Lower Limb

The lower limbs support the weight of the entire upper body and are the principal organs of locomotion. To fulfil both of these functions satisfactorily, the morphology of the lower limb has been restrained by the necessity of maintaining strength and stability. As a result, the bones of the lower limb tend to be more robust than their upper limb counterparts and the corresponding joints are stronger and more stable. In contrast, the upper limb has effectively relinquished these restrictions to free the limb and thereby maximize its mobility and prehensile capabilities.

The human lower limb comprises the thigh, leg and foot (Fig. 11.1) and is connected to the axial skeleton via the pelvic girdle (Fig. 10.1). The femur forms the skeleton of the thigh. Proximally, it articulates with the innominate at the hip joint and distally, with the tibia and patella at the knee joint.

The tibia forms the skeleton of the medial part of the leg. It articulates proximally with the femur at the knee joint and with the fibula at the superior tibiofibular joint. Distally, it articulates with the foot at the ankle joint and with the fibula at the inferior tibiofibular joint.

The fibula forms the skeleton of the lateral part of the leg. It articulates with the tibia, proximally and distally at the superior and inferior tibiofibular joints and distally, with the foot at the ankle joint.

The skeleton of the foot articulates with the leg at the ankle joint. It consists of 28 constant bones – seven tarsals, five metatarsals, 14 phalanges and two sesamoids.

The **early development** of the lower limb buds closely follows the basic pattern as seen in the upper limb buds. Therefore, the very early development of both limbs has been considered together in the introduction to the upper limb (Chapter 9).

I. THE FEMUR

The femur forms the skeleton of the thigh and is a long bone consisting of proximally, a head, neck and trochanters, and distally, medial and lateral condyles. Proximally, the head articulates with the acetabulum of the innominate at the hip joint (Chapter 10). Distally, the femoral condyles articulate with the tibial plateau and with the patella at the knee joint.

Early development of the femur

The early development of the femur has been much studied and details may be found in Gardner and O'Rahilly (1968) and O'Rahilly and Gardner (1975). The

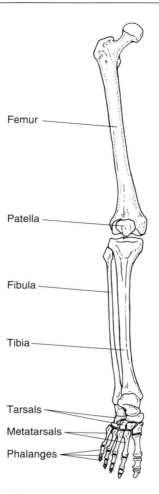

Femur

Patella

Fibula

Tibia

Tarsals

Metatarsals

Phalanges

Figure 11.1 The right lower limb.

mesenchymal femur is visible at stage 17 (about 41 days). Chondrification begins during stages 17 and 18 (about 41–44 days) and is complete by the end of the embryonic period. At 48 days, the head begins to chondrify and by 52 days the neck, both trochanters and the condyles are visible (Gardner and O'Rahilly, 1968; O'Rahilly and Gardner, 1975). At the 8th week of prenatal life the total length of the femur is about 3.5 mm in length (Felts, 1954).

Ossification

Primary centre

Two detailed studies of the later development of the femur, during the fetal period, are by Felts (1954) and Gardner and Gray (1970). A bony collar appears in the midshaft at stages 22 and 23 (weeks 7–8 – Gardner and Gray, 1970; O'Rahilly and Gardner, 1975), and about a week later, endochondral ossification can be identified histologically in the centre of the shaft, although it is not apparent radiologically until about 2 weeks later. At first, periosteal bone occupies more of the length of the diaphysis, but after about 32 weeks, periosteal and endochondral bone formation are co-extensive. Burkus and Ogden

(1984) made a detailed histological study of growth in the distal femur from 9 prenatal weeks to 16 postnatal years. A nutrient canal is first seen at about week 11 but does not necessarily coincide with the definitive later canal(s). In fetuses between the ages of 13 and 28 weeks, over half had two nutrient foramina in the region of the linea aspera (Skawina and Miaskiewicz, 1982).

By about 12–13 weeks, ossification in the shaft has reached almost to the neck region proximally and to the lower epiphysis distally. The fovea in the head becomes obvious at about this time and the linea aspera and the gluteal tuberosity, which are not preformed in cartilage, develop by an increase in thickness of the periosteal bone. The growth zone at the greater trochanter is co-extensive with that in the neck, while that for the lesser trochanter is at right angles to the shaft (Felts, 1954; Gardner and Gray, 1970). From the beginning of the second trimester, the presence of osteoclasts external to the compacta signifies remodelling, which begins proximally, at the level of the lesser trochanter, and distally, around the medial supracondylar line. Resorption and apposition then lead to enlargement in length and width but subsequent growth proceeds rather more slowly. At about this time, the morphology of the femoral diaphysis is sufficiently distinct to permit identification.

During the second part of the prenatal period, there is an increase in robusticity and an alteration in the morphology of the extremities of the ossified part of the shaft. By the 7th prenatal month, the proximal end changes from a convex dome shape to become angulated into two planes which lie under the cartilaginous head and greater trochanter. In the last prenatal month, to coincide with the appearance of the secondary centre (see below), the distal end of the ossified shaft usually develops a central depression (Felts, 1954). Torsion appears to occur throughout the length of the shaft, unlike the humerus, where it is thought to be restricted to the junction of the shaft and proximal epiphysis. It is initially negative but increases markedly to reach a circumnatal value of 30–40° (Elftman, 1945). Both inclination (neck-shaft angle) and obliquity are difficult to determine as they are affected by torsion, but apparent inclination increases slightly throughout the prenatal period and obliquity decreases, so that by term, it is less than in the adult (Felts, 1954). At term, 75–80% of the overall length of the bone is occupied by ossified shaft (Felts, 1954; Gardner and Gray, 1970).

When the perinatal bone (Fig. 11.2) is placed horizontally, resting on the lower metaphysis and epiphyseal surface of the lesser trochanter, the anterior surface is flat and the posterior surface is curved concavely upwards along the long axis of the bone. The shaft is rounded in the upper two-thirds and flattened anteroposteriorly in the lower third. It widens towards the proximal end, curving medially towards the head, which inclines anteriorly. Posteriorly, the linea aspera is usually visible, with a prominent lateral lip that either fades out centrally, or is continued into the lateral supracondylar line. By contrast, on the medial side the lip is smooth and the supracondylar line is rounded. There are usually two nutrient foramina in the upper and middle thirds of the linea aspera whose entrances slope distally. The proximal metaphyseal surface (Fig. 11.2c) is roughly oval in circumference and raised centrally, sloping away on either side to the surfaces for the head and greater trochanter. The surface is continuous at right angles with the metaphyseal surface for the lesser trochanter, which lies laterally on the posterior surface. There is often a large nutrient foramen anteriorly at the proximal end of the shaft beneath the articular surface. The distal metaphyseal surface (Fig. 11. 2d) is oval in circumference, with a flat posterior border and a slightly hollowed anterior border. Most bones have

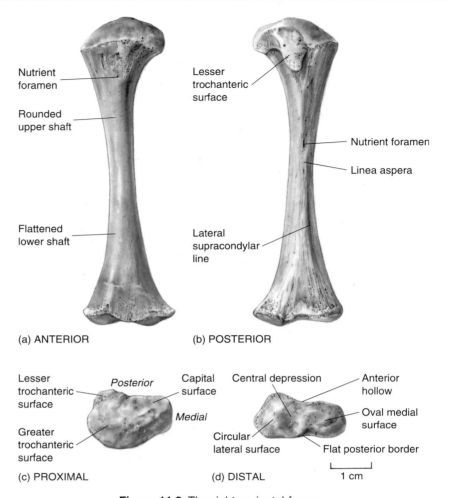

Figure 11.2 The right perinatal femur.

a central depression (see above) dividing the surface into a circular lateral, and an oval medial portion.

The morphology and angulation of the femoral shaft alters considerably during infancy, childhood and adolescence. Initially the neck is more vertical and is formed by early growth of the medial part of the proximal growth plate, but as the hip abductors develop in response to walking, there is a marked lessening of the angle (Humphry, 1889; Morgan and Somerville, 1960). By the age of about 2 years, the neck divides the original single growth plate into two separate metaphyseal growth surfaces for the head and greater trochanter (Fig. 11.3 and 11.4). The neck/shaft angle can be as high as 141° during pre-natal life but declines up to term and continues to do so during childhood to an average of about 127° From birth until about the age of 3 years, the load axis (a perpendicular line from the centre of the femoral head at right angles to the bicondylar plane) passes medial to the axis of the shaft of the bone. After this time, the change in the angle of the neck causes the load axis to intersect the axis of the femoral shaft and brings the knee closer to the midline relative to the hip (Walmsley, 1933). This is usually quantified as an increase in the bicondylar angle and coincides with the adoption of efficient walking at the beginning of childhood (Aiello and Dean, 1990). Tardieu and Trinkaus (1994)

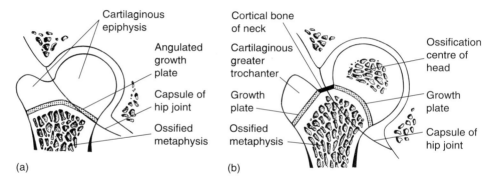

Figure 11.3 The development of the proximal end of the femur. (a) At birth; (b) 3–4 years.

have charted the ontogeny of the bicondylar angle from birth to adolescence in both living humans and skeletal samples. Tardieu (1998) charted the change in angle of obliquity of the shaft and attributed angular remodelling to increased apposition on the medial surface of the distal end of the metaphysis. While this undoubtedly contributes to angulation of the shaft, the change in the morphology and angulation of the femoral neck in infancy is also an important factor.

The trabecular architecture of the neck and shaft also changes during the early years, as remodelling occurs in response to weight bearing as the child begins to stand and then to walk. Osborne *et al.* (1980) and Osborne and Effmann (1981) evaluated the radiological changes from birth to adolescence. During the first year, trabeculae are orientated along the long axis of the shaft but during the second year, as the neck starts to form, principal medial and lateral groups become visible, and by 5 years, secondary trabeculae become obvious. Tobin (1955) showed slab cuts of the proximal femur at this age in which there was no clear-cut triangular area of weak trabeculation, as is apparent in the adult. There is no calcar femorale in the child. This is a spur of bone present in the adult, which projects from the medial cortex into the central

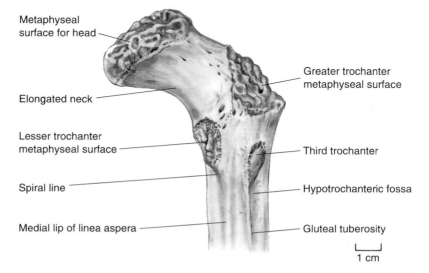

Figure 11.4 Posterior view of the proximal end of a right femur. This is a damaged archaeological fragment of about 11–12 years skeletal age. It has a third trochanter and a hypotrochanteric fossa.

cancellous tissue in the adult thereby strengthening the region. Harty (1957) and Garden (1961) described the details of its development.

The time of appearance of the linea aspera is very variable as it may form a simple ridge in mid-uterine life, but its development is often delayed until after birth, and its distinctive form is sometimes not attained until adolescence. The pilaster is rarely seen as early as late childhood but develops after puberty and is maximal by middle age. A strong linea and pilastry appear to be unrelated (Hrdlička, 1934). On AP radiographs of the adolescent femur, the linea aspera–a–pilaster complex may sometimes appear as the so-called 'track sign'. This shows up as two parallel lines enclosing an area of increased radiodensity in the middle of the shaft (Pitt, 1982).

Anterior curvature also shows a progressive increase with age. Walensky (1965) reported that between 3 and 6 years the femur was relatively straight and a significant curvature developed between 7 and 13 years. In our series of juvenile femora, there appeared to be a visible anterior curvature at about 18 months, which would coincide with weight bearing and walking. By about 7–8 years, the lateral lip of the linea aspera, the spiral line and the gluteal tuberosity become evident.

Normal shaft torsion decreases throughout postnatal life from its circumnatal value of about 35° to about 15° at adolescence. Fabry et al. (1973) noted that there is an accelerated decrease between 1 and 2 years, and another between 14 and 16 years, which correlates with initial walking and then possible modification of walking style caused by adolescent changes in pelvic proportions. Increases beyond the normal range of anteversion are a significant factor in intoeing gait and in many pathological hip conditions of childhood (Engel and Staheli, 1974; Staheli, 1977). A decrease in torsion from 40° at birth to about 12° in adult life has been reported. Although there appeared to be no sexual dimorphism, there was a significant correlation between siblings, which suggested a genetic explanation. Children with a value of more than two standard deviations from the mean showed orthopaedic symptoms and signs (Upadhyay et al., 1990).

The metaphyseal surface of the lower end of the shaft develops changes to mirror the shape of the developing epiphysis. By about 6 months of age, the anterior border develops a hollow, which is co-extensive with the trochlear surface of the epiphysis, and the posterior border becomes notched as the intercondylar fossa ossifies. By 3 years, the lateral surface projects more anteriorly than the medial surface, as the asymmetry of the trochlea develops. By about 4–5 years, condylar and trochlear areas can be distinguished on the metaphyseal surface (Fig. 11.5).

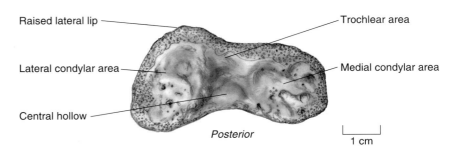

Figure 11.5 The right distal femoral metaphyseal surface – female aged 4 years.

Seventy per cent of fractures are in the midshaft region and are transverse, oblique or spiral, but rarely comminuted. Child abuse is the most common cause in the first 2 years of life (Staheli, 1984).

Secondary centres

The distal end of the femur has the largest and fastest growing epiphysis in the body. It normally develops from a single ossific nucleus, which is the first of the long bone epiphyses to appear and one of the last to fuse. Its ossification is an important marker, both of fetal maturity, and for forensic identification of legal term status (Knight, 1996). The centre normally appears in the last prenatal month, is present in 98% of cases at birth and is therefore sometimes absent in premature infants. It is always obvious by 3 *post partum* months (Francis *et al.*, 1939; Elgenmark, 1946; Kelly and Reynolds, 1947; Christie, 1949; Hansman, 1962). Ossification starts in the proximal half of the cartilaginous epiphysis (Crock, 1967; Gardner and Gray, 1970).

The detailed radiological appearance of the distal femoral epiphysis is shown by Pyle and Hoerr (1955) and Scheller (1960). At birth, the standard for girls is about 2 weeks in advance of that for boys and the discrepancy in developmental timing increases with age so that by puberty, girls are some 2 years in advance of boys. The neonatal epiphysis is an oval nodule of bone lying inferior to the depression in the metaphysis (see above) with its long axis at right angles to the long axis of the bone. For the first 2 weeks, the femoral epiphysis has a larger vertical and horizontal diameter than the tibial epiphysis. In the second half of the first year, the epiphyseal plate begins to develop and the epiphysis becomes ovoid, the lateral side being larger than the medial side. Between 1 and 3 years, the epiphysis grows rapidly in width as ossification spreads into the condylar areas of the cartilage. It takes on a 'wooden shoe' (sabot) appearance radiologically, because of the greater vertical diameter of the lateral condyle. The bony epiphysis becomes recognizable during the second year. It is roughly kidney-shaped with a flat anterior border and an indented posterior border forming the shallow intercondylar fossa. The articular surface is gently rounded and pitted with nutrient foramina, which are numerous within the fossa. On the metaphyseal side, the anterior trochlear third is separated by a faint transverse ridge from the posterior condylar two-thirds, which is itself divided by a central rounded elevation into circular lateral and oval medial areas (Fig. 11.6a).

By the age of 7 years in girls and 9 years in boys, the epiphysis is as wide as the metaphysis (Pyle and Hoerr, 1955). The condyles and intercondylar fossa have now assumed their distinctive shape and the latter is the main site for nutrient foramina. The anterior (trochlear) border has an asymmetrical, sinuous curve, with the lateral lip projecting anteriorly. The trochlear area occupies rather more of the metaphyseal surface than before and this mirrors the distal end of the diaphysis (Fig. 11.6b). Smith (1962a) viewed the transverse ridge separating the two areas of the epiphysis as reflecting the division between weight-bearing compressive forces acting on the condyles and tensile forces pulling downwards on the cruciate ligaments. The adductor tubercle is visible on radiographs at about 8 years in girls and 11 years in boys (Pyle and Hoerr, 1955), by which time it is sometimes also identifiable on the bony epiphysis. Between 8 and 12 years, the epiphysis starts to cap the end of the shaft. The condyles are covered with smooth, cortical bone and the lateral lip of the intercondylar groove projects anterosuperiorly. They are themselves divided into condylar and trochlear areas. The metaphyseal surface is deeply hollowed and grooved and the adductor tubercle is prominent on the poster-

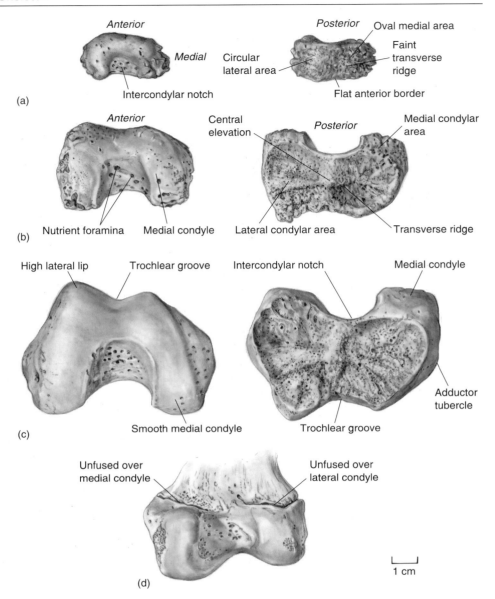

Figure 11.6 Development of the distal right femoral epiphysis. (a) Female aged 2 years; (b) male aged 8 years; (c) male aged 12 years. Left row – articular surfaces. Right row – metaphyseal surfaces; (d) posterior surface of distal right femur from an undocumented adolescent.

omedial border (Fig. 11.6c). From this time until fusion, the distal epiphysis resembles the adult bone.

Fracture separation of the lower femoral epiphysis is relatively uncommon. Infantile separation is associated with breech birth or child abuse, whereas that occurring later is usually related to hyperextension force caused by road traffic accidents or sports injuries (Thornton and Gyll, (1999). Because of the proximity of the large vessels and nerves in the popliteal fossa, there may be acute vascular or neural compromise.

Fusion of the lower end of the femur coincides with cessation of growth in height, as the epiphyses around the knee are the growing ends of the lower limb bones. The distal epiphysis is responsible for about 70% of growth in length of the bone (Digby, 1915; Anderson *et al.*, 1963). Most radiographic observations state that this occurs between the ages of 14 and 18 years in females and 16 and 19 years in males (Flecker, 1932; Hansman, 1962). On the Pyle and Hoerr (1955) radiographic standards, there is definite fusion in the centre of the epiphyseal plate at 14.5 years in females and 17 years in males and the growth plates are replaced by lines of fusion by 15.5 years in females and 18 years in males. However, McKern and Stewart (1957), from observations on dry bone, place the lower end of the femur in their Group II of delayed union and stated that the early stage of union in males can be as late as 20 years and that fusion was not 100% complete in their specimens until 22 years. They describe the last sites for fusion on the posteromedial side of the epiphysis above the medial condyle. In our series of juvenile skeletons, fusion at the periphery always occurred first over the medial and lateral aspects of the epiphysis. It then proceeded across the anterior border and the intercondylar fossa part of the posterior border, leaving the last sites posteriorly over the condyles (Fig. 11.6d).

The **proximal end of the femur** has three, and sometimes four separate secondary centres of ossification but, in contrast to those of the humerus, they do not form a compound epiphysis but develop and fuse independently with the neck or shaft of the bone. At birth, although the whole of the proximal end of the bone is composed of cartilage, the head and both trochanters are well defined. At this stage, the single growth plate can be divided into a medial and a lateral part for the head and greater trochanter. Only a small area of the medial edge of the growth plate is intra-articular, but gradually the neck begins to form by medial extension of the osseous shaft and so more of the growth plate becomes intracapsular. By the age of about 2 years, the growth of the neck has divided the original combined metaphyseal surface into separate areas for the head and greater trochanter (Fig. 11.3). A similar process also separates the metaphyseal surface for the lesser trochanter so that it comes to lie below and medial to the combined metaphyseal surface. Each secondary ossification centre then develops in its own separate cartilaginous territory.

The **centre for the head** is very rarely seen at birth but is present in 60–90% of infants at 6 months and is nearly always visible by the age of 1 year (Walmsley, 1915; Flecker, 1932; Francis *et al.*, 1939; Elgenmark, 1946; Ryder and Mellin, 1966). Hansman (1962) reported the median for girls as 5 months (range – birth to 1 year) and that for boys as 6 months (range – 2 months to 1 year) and Garn *et al.* (1967) gave the 50th percentile as a little earlier than this. Ossification begins above and medial to the centre point of the whole head and, at first, may sometimes be composed of a number of osseous granules (Walmsley, 1915; Trueta, 1957) or a double centre (Keats, 1992).

The ossified part of the epiphysis is spherical for about the first year-and-a-half and then becomes flattened inferiorly as it accommodates itself to the medial section of the proximal end of the shaft and the growth plate is established. At about 3 years of age, it is almost hemispherical in shape, with the lateral side slightly flattened (Fig. 11.7a). The articular surface is rounded and pitted with numerous vascular foramina. The metaphyseal surface is almost flat except for a blunt, beak-like projection that is in line with the posterior surface of the neck. By 6–8 years (Fig. 11.7b), the fovea can be distinguished on the inferomedial side of the articular surface. The almost circular circumfer-

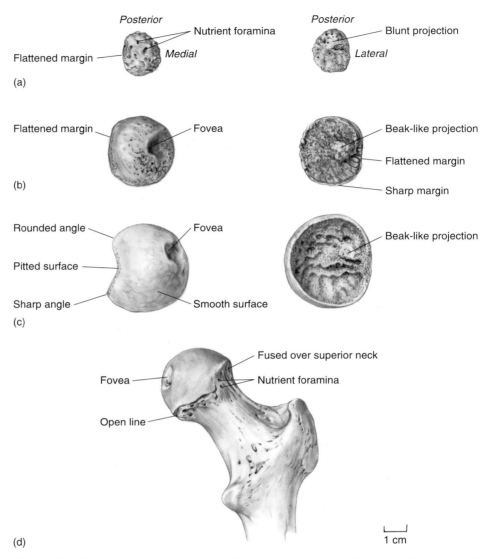

Figure 11.7 The development of the right capital femoral epiphysis. (a) Male aged 3 years; (b) male aged 8 years; (c) undocumented early adolescent. Left row – articular surfaces. Right row – metaphyseal surfaces; (d) posterior surface of right proximal femur from an undocumented late adolescent.

ence has a sharp edge, which extends down over the neck, except for a small, flattened section on the lateral side contiguous with the superior surface of the neck. Smith (1962a) emphasized that the major part of the circumference conforms to the articular margin, while this superior flattened section has large foramina through which the main blood vessels enter the head. The metaphyseal surface is roughened and the beak-like projection is now more obvious at the posterior end of the flattened border. It fits into a reciprocal hollow in the metaphyseal surface of the capital area of the shaft and could possibly act as a locking mechanism to counteract slipping of the epiphysis. By puberty, the articular surface is smooth except for the fovea and consists of about two-thirds of a sphere (Fig. 11.7c). The metaphyseal surface is a shallow cup-shape with sharp edges, as ossification has spread down round the circumference except at the juxtacervical surface. This has an anterior angle, which juts laterally over the anterosuperior margin of the neck, and a more rounded posterior angle, which is in line with the posterosuperior margin. The flat lateral margin is still pitted with nutrient foramina. Ozonoff and Ziter (1985, 1987) described notch-like defects in the femoral head and on the medial side of the neck, which are asymptomatic and occur as normal variants.

The major part of the arterial supply to the epiphysis of the head comes from epiphyseal branches of ascending cervical branches, which in turn arise from the arterial ring of the neck (Crock, 1965, 1967, 1996). There is also a vital supply to a limited area around the fovea, via vessels accompanying the ligament of the head from branches of the obturator or medial circumflex femoral artery (Tucker, 1949). Ogden (1974a) found that at birth, the anterior and posterior halves of the growth plate were supplied equally by the lateral and medial circumflex arteries, respectively. Subsequent vascular changes caused regression of the supply from the lateral artery so that during the transition phase, the capital epiphysis is susceptible to ischaemic necrosis in the event of injury.

Fracture sites at the proximal end of the femur are comparatively rare in children compared to adults and account for fewer than 1% of all paediatric fractures (Hughes and Beaty, 1994). However, epiphysiolysis (slipped epiphysis) and Perthes' disease (Legg–Calvé–Perthes disease/coxa plana) are conditions that result from the particular morphological development of the proximal femur and its vulnerable blood supply. Slipped epiphysis is rarely seen in young children under the age of 3 years, except as a birth injury (Michail *et al.*, 1958; Lindseth and Rosene, 1971), in battered child syndrome or other forms of severe trauma (Ratliff, 1968; Milgram and Lyne, 1975). Early diagnosis and treatment is essential to prevent serious deformity (Ankarath *et al.*, 2002). As the neck/shaft angle alters throughout childhood (see above), it is accompanied by a change in direction of the plane of the epiphyseal growth plate to a more varus and posterior direction. This reaches its maximum between the ages of 10 years and puberty when there is the greatest risk of slipped epiphysis. The previously perpendicular force on the growth plate is altered and it is temporarily placed in a position more susceptible to shear stress as increasing body weight is transmitted down the femur (Ogden, Gossling *et al.*, 1975). Interestingly, this coincides with the appearance of 'juvenile beaking' in the triradiate region of the acetabulum (see Chapter 10). The vulnerability of the blood supply may lead to non-union, varus deformity or premature closure of the growth plate. The highest risk is of avascular necrosis, which is directly related to the amount of displacement. Perthes' disease is also an avascular necrosis of the femoral head of unknown origin. It usually causes flattening of the head, sometimes fragmentation of the epiphysis and thickening of the neck. It occurs uni- or bilaterally, at a peak age of 4 years and more often in boys than girls, in a ratio of about 4:1. Again, it can lead to premature closure of the growth plate and subsequent delay in skeletal development.

Ages for **fusion of the femoral head** as observed on radiographs are given by Flecker (1932) and Hansman (1962). The latter reported the mean for girls as 14 years and 2 months (range 11–16 years) and for boys as 16 years and 3 months (range 14–19 years). Stevenson (1924) and McKern and Stewart (1957) reported observations on dry bone. Stevenson does not distinguish between the sexes and his 'beginning' to 'complete' stages extend from 17 to 18.5 years. McKern and Stewart, reporting on the Korean War dead, are only able to give figures for the latter part of the range in males, as the proximal femoral epiphyses form part of their Group I, early union. They found 88% fused at 17–18 years and 100% fusion by 20 years and note that fusion begins anterolaterally and proceeds to the posteromedial part of the head. Haines *et al.* (1967) and Dvonch and Bunch (1983) described initiation of fusion in the superior aspect of the head, which proceeded inferiorly. This was confirmed in our series of adolescent skeletons, where the head was undergoing union. The flattened section of the epiphyseal edge across the superior surface of the neck always fused first, with the inferomedial aspect being the last part to remain open (Fig. 11.7d).

The centre of ossification appears in the cartilaginous mass of the **greater trochanter** between 2 and 5 years of age, with girls being several months in advance of boys (Paterson, 1929; Flecker, 1932; Francis *et al.*, 1939; Elgenmark, 1946; Garn *et al.*, 1967). Hansman (1962) reported the median for girls as 2 years 10 months (range 18 months to 4 years) and for boys as 4 years (range 2–6 years). By the time that the centre for the trochanter begins to ossify, the growth of the femoral neck has removed it from the vicinity of the head and the two centres subsequently maintain separate development. Ossification begins in the base of the epiphysis next to the growth plate and by about the age of 5–6 years it is a boomerang-shaped ossicle with the anterior limb slightly larger than the posterior limb. It is finely pitted on both surfaces (Fig. 11.8a). By 8–9 years, ossification spreads upwards from the base, it assumes a semilunar shape and the trochanteric fossa is usually obvious (Fig. 11.8b). By puberty, the trochanter has reached its adult morphology (Fig. 11.8c). It is a large, pyramidal-shaped knob of bone with a base and three unequal sides. The original smaller posterior section is now much larger than the anterior part and is attached obliquely at the junction of the neck and shaft. The flat anterior surface is small and reaches further medially onto the neck than the curved posterolateral surface, which is larger. This projects superiorly to form the apex of the trochanter, which overhangs the medial surface where the well-formed trochanteric fossa lies posteriorly. The surface is covered with smooth cortical bone but is still pitted with numerous nutrient foramina, some of them large. The roughened metaphyseal surface is triangular with a long anterior border, a shorter posterolateral border and a curved medial border.

Age ranges for **fusion** of the greater trochanter are wide, but with girls again being in advance of boys. It occurs at about 14–16 years in females and 16–18 years in males. Haines *et al.* (1967) found that the first site of union was in the region of the trochanteric fossa and McKern and Stewart (1957) illustrated the last area of fusion posteromedially. In our series of juvenile skeletons, the greater trochanter always fused around the superior, posterior and anterior borders first with the inferior border being the last to complete union (Fig. 11.8d). In any one individual, its maturity was always slightly in advance of the epiphysis for the head.

Descriptions of the ossification centre of the **lesser trochanter** are extremely variable, times of appearance ranging from 7 to 11 years and of fusion from 16 to 17 years. Some anatomical accounts even throw doubt on its existence as a separate centre and both Paterson (1929) and Flecker (1932, 1936) state that it is not always present, the latter suggesting that it might be more common in males than in females. Puyhaubert (1913) and Paterson (1929) describe it as small and flake-like, which is similar to the epiphysis of the anterior inferior iliac spine (Chapter 10) or the radial tuberosity (Chapter 9), which seems to be in contradiction to its bulky appearance. Haines *et al.* (1967) illustrated a substantial epiphysis fusing at its upper and lower borders, dis-

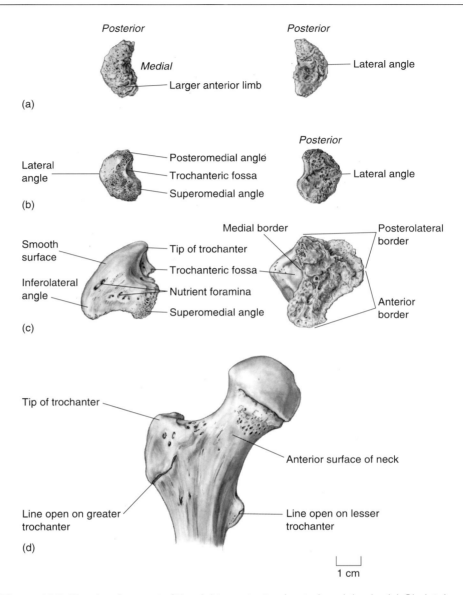

Figure 11.8 The development of the right greater trochanteric epiphysis. (a) Skeletal age 7–8 years; (b) female aged 6 years; (c) undocumented early adolescent. Left row – superior surfaces. Right row – metaphyseal surfaces. Note that the documented 6-year-old trochanter is more mature than that of the 7–8-year-old; (d) anterior surface of right proximal femur from an undocumented late adolescent.

playing an open line in the centre. In our series of juvenile skeletons, the younger specimens usually had an obvious billowed surface at the site of the lesser trochanter on the posterior part of the shaft and the older specimens showed a partially fused epiphysis. Union always began on the lateral border and remained open longer medially (Fig. 11.8d). The only completely separate epiphysis observed was 2 cm long and 1.2 cm in breadth and depth. The fact that an individual epiphysis is rarely seen probably reflects its short existence as a separate entity. McKern and Stewart (1957) reported that 100% fusion did not take place until the age of 20 years. They illustrated a lesser trochanteric

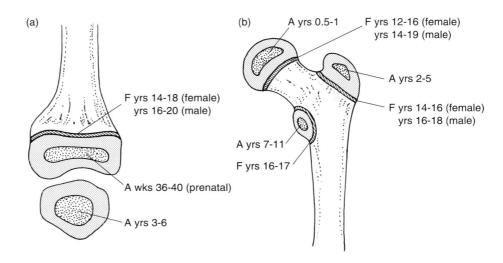

Figure 11.9 The primary ossification centre of the femur appears during weeks 7–8 of prenatal life and the centre for the patella in years 3–6 of postnatal life. Appearance (A) and fusion (F) times of the secondary centres of the femur – (a) proximal end; (b) distal end.

epiphysis partially fused with an open line inferiorly. Avulsion of both the greater and the lesser trochanteric epiphyses are referred to in the clinical literature, usually in connection with sporting injuries in adolescence (Dimon, 1972; Fernbach and Wilkinson, 1981).

Formicola *et al.* (1990) described a very rare skeleton from the Palaeolithic of Italy. Sagitally orientated ridges blending superiorly with the intertrochanteric crest replaced a bilateral absence of the lesser trochanter.

From accounts in the literature it appears that the upper end of the gluteal ridge may ossify separately as a flake at the same time as the lesser trochanter. If this does occur, it could be viewed as the **epiphysis of the third trochanter**. Dixon (1896) described such an epiphysis as a flat, narrow scale of bone, in line with the long axis of the shaft, at the same level as the lowest part of the lesser trochanter. There appears to be no account of its time of fusion.

The appearance and fusion times of the femoral centres of ossification are summarized in Fig. 11.9.

Practical notes

Sideing of the juvenile femur
Diaphysis – sideing the perinatal or early infant femoral diaphysis relies on identifying the medial curve of the shaft towards the head and the surface for the lesser trochanter on the posterior surface (Fig. 11.2). Once the neck of the femur has started to develop at about 2 years of age, the sideing of the diaphysis becomes obvious (Fig. 11.4).

Distal epiphysis – sideing of the epiphysis is possible from about 2 years of age. It depends on identifying the intercondylar fossa posteriorly and the lateral circular and medial oval areas on the metaphyseal surface (Fig. 11.6). After this time, the distal epiphysis rapidly assumes its adult morphology.

Capital epiphysis – from about the age of 3–4 years it is possible to side the epiphysis for the head by recognizing the flattened lateral margin of the circumference and the blunt raised projection at its posterior edge on the metaphyseal surface (Fig. 11.7).

Greater trochanteric epiphysis – sideing of this bony epiphysis at the 'boomerang' stage of development relies on identifying the lateral angle and larger anterior segment. After this time, the superior part of the epiphysis develops and the trochanteric fossa can be seen at the posterior end of the medial surface (Fig. 11.8).

Bones of a similar morphology

Perinatal diaphyses – the six major long bones of the limbs can be divided into two groups: the femur, humerus and tibia are larger and more robust than the radius, ulna and fibula. In the first group, the femur is always bigger than the humerus and tibia, which are almost equal in length (Table 11.1). From birth onwards the femur increases in size rapidly and always remains the longest and largest of the long bones.

Proximal femoral fragment – this may be confused with a proximal humeral fragment (see Humerus – Practical notes, Fig. 9.9).

Distal femoral fragment – this is flattened like a distal humerus but can be distinguished from it by the presence of the olecranon fossa in the humerus (Figs 9.5b,d and 11.2b,d). It is oval like the proximal tibia, but the latter is distinguished by the tuberosity anteriorly (Fig. 11.11a,c).

Proximal femoral and humeral epiphyses – see Humerus – Practical notes, Fig. 9.10.

Table 11.1 Means and ranges for maximum lengths of diaphyses of major long bones at 10 lunar months

	Mean (mm)	Range (mm)
Humerus	64.9	61.6–70.0
Radius	51.8	47.5–58.0
Ulna	59.3	55.0–65.5
Femur	74.3	69.0–78.7
Tibia	65.1	60.0–71.5
Fibula	62.3	58.0–68.5

Adapted from Fazekas and Kósa (1978)

Morphological summary (Fig. 11.9)

Prenatal
Wk 7–8   Primary ossification centre appears in shaft
Wks 36–40   Secondary centre for distal epiphysis appears

Birth   *Represented by shaft and distal epiphysis*
By yr 1   Secondary centre for head appears
2–5 yrs   Secondary centre for greater trochanter appears

By yrs 3—4	Epiphysis of head hemispherical and recognizable
By yrs 3—5	Distal epiphysis recognizable by characteristic shape
6—8 yrs	Greater trochanter becomes recognizable
7—12 yrs	Secondary centre for lesser trochanter appears
12—16 yrs	Head fuses in females
14—19 yrs	Head fuses in males
14—16 yrs	Greater trochanter fuses in females
16—18 yrs	Greater trochanter fuses in males
16—17 yrs	Lesser trochanter fuses
14—18 yrs	Distal epiphysis fuses in females
16—20 yrs	Distal epiphysis fuses in males

II. THE PATELLA

The patella is the largest sesamoid bone in the body. It is contained within the tendon of the quadriceps femoris muscle at the front of the knee and is separated from the skin by the pre-patellar bursa. It articulates with the lower end of the femur at the patellofemoral joint, which is generally considered to be part of the knee joint.

Early development of the patella

Early accounts of the histological development of the patella and knee joint are given by Walmsley (1940) and McDermott (1943) and details of appearance times of the mesenchymal and cartilaginous patella can be found in O'Rahilly et al. (1957), Gardner and O'Rahilly (1968) and O'Rahilly and Gardner (1975). The mesenchymal patella and the patellar retinacula are recognizable on the anterior aspect of the developing knee joint at stages 19 and 20 (week 7). Precartilaginous changes can be seen a week later. Chondrification takes place at stages 21 and 22 (7—8 weeks) (O'Rahilly et al., 1957). At about 11—12 weeks, the perichondrium on the anterior surface is fused to that of the femur. Cavitation of the joint occurs at the end of the embryonic period and soon after this, the knee joint resembles the adult in form and arrangement (Walmsley, 1940).

By 12—13 weeks, a definite suprapatellar pouch is formed. At this stage, the patella is relatively small compared with the distal surface of the femur but growth is then rapid until about 6 months. From this time until birth, it grows at the same rate as the other bones of the lower limb. At about 7 months, the articular surface becomes divided by a vertical ridge into larger lateral and smaller medial areas. It does not acquire the transverse ridges until after birth, when the limb is in use and full extension of the knee joint becomes possible (Walmsley, 1940). Congenital lateral dislocation of the patella before, or soon after, birth is a rare but serious condition. It prevents full active extension of the knee joint and so may cause fixed contractures (Green and Waugh, 1968). At birth, and for the first few years of life, the patella is entirely cartilaginous. It resembles an unossified epiphysis and is surrounded by perichondrium and penetrated by an extensive cartilage canal vascular network (Haines, 1937; Ogden, 1984d).

Ossification

Time of ossification is very variable and can begin as early as 18 months but may not be present until 4 or 5 years. Ranges are 1.5–4 years in girls and 2.5–6 years in boys (Flecker, 1932; Francis *et al.*, 1939; Elgenmark, 1946; Garn *et al.*, 1967; Prakash *et al.*, 1979). Ossification is typically multifocal, but coalescence of separate centres soon takes place. The Pyle and Hoerr (1955) atlas of the knee describes and illustrates the centre at 2 years 8 months in girls and 3 years 6 months in boys. It appears as a vertically elongated nodule in the centre of the knee joint. It rapidly enlarges and the margins may have a granular or irregular radiographic appearance but by about 4 years in girls and 5 years in boys, it is a biconvex disc. By about the age of 9–10 years, the chondro-osseous margins form a defined subchondral plate, indicating a reduction in rate of growth. On section, about one-third of the diameter is seen to be still unossified (Ogden, 1984d). The vertical part of the posterior surface is slightly concave, the postero-inferior surface is flat and the superolateral margin is usually irregular (Pyle and Hoerr, 1955). Over the next 2 years, there is a slow expansion into the rest of the cartilage and trabecular orientation becomes well defined longitudinally in the anterior third. By early adolescence, it is a slim version of the adult bone. The last part to ossify is the superior part of the lateral border, which often remains flat (Fig. 11.10). The patella assumes essentially adult contours by 14 years in females and 16 years in males (Pyle and Hoerr, 1955).

Additional ossification centres may become apparent in the adolescent period, by far the most common being one at the superolateral border, where the margin remains irregular (Wright, 1903; Todd and McCally, 1921). Fusion may occur, with the main centre or ossicle(s) remaining separate to form a bipartite or multipartite patella, with the parts being joined by fibrocartilaginous tissue. The condition may only become obvious if there is disruption caused by minor injury leading to the painful bipartite or multipartite patella in which excision of the fragment(s) may be the preferred option (Devas, 1960; Green, 1975). Multipartite patellae are much less common than the bipartite variety (Wright, 1903; Holland, 1921; Goergen *et al.*, 1979; Johnson and Brogdon, 1982; Ogden *et al.*, 1982; Holsbeeck *et al.*, 1987). Some clinicians believe that the dorsal defect of the patella (DDP) and a bipartite or multipartite patella are stress-induced anomalies of ossification. They both occur in the same characteristic location at the superolateral border, typically in sporting adolescent patients. Abnormal muscular traction by the vastus lateralis, associated with possible vascular insufficiency, was thought to play a part in the condition.

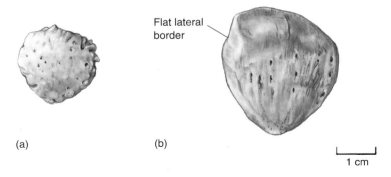

Flat lateral border

(a) (b) 1 cm

Figure 11.10 Juvenile patellae. (a) Skeletal age 7–8 years; (b) 12 years, female.

Sinding–Larson–Johanson syndrome is a traction epiphysitis of the lower pole of the patella, which can occur in vigorous adolescent athletes (Medlar and Lyne, 1978). This proximal attachment of the patellar ligament is subject to similar strains as the tibial tuberosity and irregular calcification or separate ossicles at the inferior pole are not uncommon (Ogden, 1984d). The condition could be viewed as the patellar equivalent of Osgood–Schlatter's disease (see Tibia).

Recurrent lateral dislocation (subluxation) of the patella is a fairly common phenomenon, said to be especially prevalent in adolescent females. However, Hughston (1968) believed it to be an often unrecognized condition in adolescent and young adult athletes of both sexes. It is thought to be exacerbated by a congenital anomalous condition, where there is a failure of full development of the lateral condyle of the femur (Green and Waugh, 1968; Turner and Smillie, 1981).

Rare anomalies of the patella may include complete absence (Kutz, 1949; Bernhang and Levine, 1973). Also uncommon is hypoplasia, as seen in 'small patella syndrome' (Scott and Taor, 1979) or as part of nail-patella syndrome (hereditary onycho-osteodysplasia), which is associated with irregular ossification at the elbow and iliac crest.

Practical notes

Sideing of the juvenile patella

It is difficult to side a juvenile patella until ossification has spread well into the articular surface, which is not until late childhood. Before that time it is a biconvex disc with a slightly pointed apex. Both surfaces are composed of porous bone. In early adolescence the superior part of the lateral border is often flat (Fig. 11.10b).

Morphological summary

Birth	Represented by cartilaginous patella
1.5–3.5 yrs	Multifocal ossification centres appear
4–5 yrs	Becomes biconvex in shape
Puberty	Assumes essentially adult contours
See also Femur (Fig. 11.9).	

III. THE TIBIA

The tibia forms the skeleton of the medial part of the leg and is a long bone consisting of an expanded superior, condylar surface, a shaft and a distal end that extends to form the medial malleolus of the ankle. It articulates proximally with the femoral condyles at the knee joint, distally with the body of the talus at the ankle joint and laterally, both proximally and distally with the fibula at the superior and inferior tibiofibular joints.

Early development of the tibia

Details of the early development of the tibia may be found in Haines (1953), Gardner and O'Rahilly (1968) and O'Rahilly and Gardner (1975). The mesenchymal tibia is visible at stage 17 (about 41 days). Chondrification begins at stage 18 and between stages 19 and 21 the condyles are clearly visible, although the lower end may still be at the blastemal stage (O'Rahilly *et al.*, 1957). By stage 23 (about 56 days) both menisci, collateral ligaments, cruciate ligaments, the ligamentum patellae and the tendon of popliteus are evident.

Ossification

Primary centre

Ossification of the tibia begins at stages 22–23 (week 8), when a bony collar can be seen, and about a week later, endochondral ossification commences in the centre of the shaft and spreads quickly both proximally and distally (O'Rahilly *et al.*, 1957). Vascular canals start to invade at about week 12 and by week 14 the growth plates become established. By week 20, all morphological structures around the knee and ankle are easily recognizable. At birth, 80% of the overall length of the bone is occupied by ossified shaft (Puyhaubert, 1913).

The shaft of the perinatal tibia (Fig. 11.11) is arched somewhat posteriorly in the proximal third and straight in the distal two-thirds. It is widely flared at its proximal end, especially on the medial side. The proximal metaphyseal surface is smoothly convex and roughly oval in outline, with rounded lateral and more pointed medial ends. The outline is straight posteriorly and slopes down anteriorly towards the tuberosity. The anterior border is a sharp ridge turning medially at its distal end. The interosseous and medial borders are rounded in their proximal thirds but become more defined in their distal two-thirds. At the proximal end of the medial surface the area of the tibial tuberosity forms an area of porous bone. Posteriorly, the triangular surface covered by the popliteus muscle is also composed of porous-looking bone. The inferolateral border of the triangle is formed by the soleal line, which is flat at this stage and rarely obvious as a raised ridge before the age of 6–8 years. In over 90% of fetuses there is normally an extremely large, single nutrient foramen below and usually lateral to the popliteal area, whose entrance slopes distally (Skawina and Miaskiewicz, 1982). It is by far the largest vascular foramen found in any of the juvenile long bones and appears out of proportion to the size of the bone. The distal metaphyseal surface is flat. Its outline is either quadrangular with rounded corners or oval. The lateral border is flatter than the other three sides and a faint notch can sometimes be seen in its centre.

By the age of about 6 months, the proximal metaphyseal surface has flattened and by the end of the first year, a depressed area on the anterior surface of the metaphysis can be seen on lateral radiographs. This is deep to the tongue of the epiphysis that will be involved with the formation of the tuberosity (see below). The anterior border of the distal end soon becomes scalloped in the centre. By 4–5 years, both the proximal and distal metaphyseal surfaces are ridged and billowed and reflect the markings of their respective epiphyses (Fig. 11.12). The proximal surface has a groove formed by the posterior cruciate attachment, which runs from the centre to the posterior border and partly divides the surface into a larger, flatter medial and smaller, more sloping lateral section. The anterior intercondylar area slopes forwards on its lateral side to become continuous with the growth area of the tuberosity. The distal surface has a definite D-shaped outline and the medial half of the surface is hollowed out.

The angle that the tibial plateau makes with the shaft varies at different ages. It is known as the angle of retroversion between the plateau and the long

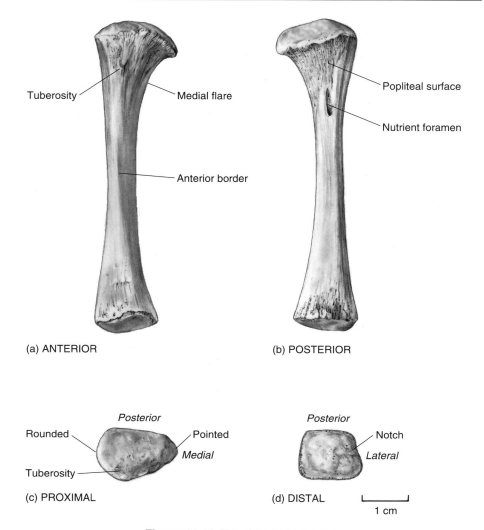

Figure 11.11 The right perinatal tibia.

axis of the shaft, or the angle of inclination between the plateau and the mechanical axis of the shaft. A high angle is seen in fetuses, and at birth can be as high as 27° but normally declines rapidly up to the age of 2 years (Kate and Robert, 1965). High angles in adults have also been observed in populations that spend a large proportion of time in a squatting posture (Charles, 1893; Aitken, 1905; Kate and Robert, 1965) but other mechanical explanations have been suggested for this association (Trinkaus, 1975).

Torsion in the tibial shaft is in a medial direction prenatally, and at birth it may still be medial (internal) or neutral but this changes rapidly in the first year of life, even before attempts at walking are made (Elftman, 1945). Ritter *et al.* (1976) measured an average of 5° internal rotation at birth, which altered to 25° lateral (external) rotation by 2 years. There appeared to be no correlation with sex, race or age of independent walking. Staheli and Engel (1972) reported that there was an external rotation of 5° during the first year, another 10° by mid-childhood and in older children and adults torsion reached 14°. Turner and Smillie (1981) reported that adult torsion is usually reached by the age of 5 years but a significant proportion of individuals do not undergo the full range

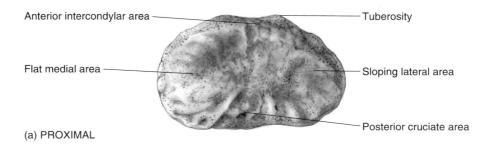

(a) PROXIMAL

Anterior intercondylar area — Tuberosity

Flat medial area — Sloping lateral area

— Posterior cruciate area

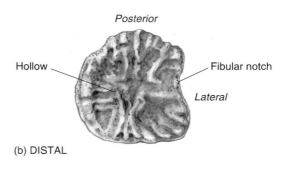

Posterior

Hollow — Fibular notch

Lateral

(b) DISTAL

1 cm

Figure 11.12 The proximal and distal metaphyseal surfaces of a right juvenile tibia – male aged 8 years.

of postnatal lateral torsion and then walk in a 'twine-toed' manner. Hutter and Scott (1949) found that in 50 normal 2-year-olds, 30% had not developed any external rotation and walked with toes turned in. Between the ages of 5 and 7 years, 8–10% of children still had an intoeing walk, with 5% having quite severe deformity. There appeared to be little correction of an internally rotated tibia after the age of 7 years. In a survey of 800 adults, 8% of males and 9% of females showed internal tibial torsion.

Interpretation of these results can be contradictory as the apparent difference in some of these the figures could be due to the differences in terminology or method of measurement. Rosen and Sandick (1955) pointed out that the axial relationship between the foot and thigh, which is the usual measurement made in the living, can be due to either tibiofibular rotation or to a combination of rotation and torsion. Rotation is the turning of one unit upon another at a joint, whereas torsion is measured on dry bone and is the twisting in the axis of a single unit. In addition, some of the measurements in the living were taken with the knee flexed at 90°, thus already involving some medial rotation.

The tibia grows at a fairly uniform rate throughout childhood, in contrast to the femur, which grows more slowly up to puberty and then increases rapidly with the pubertal growth spurt. This means that the crural index (total tibial length × 100/total femoral length) increases from about 6 years to puberty and then decreases after that time (Davenport, 1933). By puberty, the borders and surfaces of the tibial shaft are more clearly defined. The lower end of the metaphysis is distinctly quadrangular, with the lateral border showing the concavity of the fibular notch.

The distal end of the tibial shaft is one of the likeliest places to find Harris lines. These are laid down in infancy and childhood and may persist into adult life (Garn and Schwager, 1967) and so make it possible to calculate their age of formation (Maat, 1984). The hypothesis that lines of increased density are growth arrest lines that cause ultimate retardation in growth was discounted by Gindhart (1969) as no difference in finally attained adult stature was found between heavily and lightly lined individuals.

Fractures of the midshaft or distal third of the tibia are amongst the most common injuries to the lower limb in children of all ages (Thornton and Gyll, 1999). They are usually caused by a rotational force produced whilst the foot is stationary, or by direct violence, such as falls or road traffic accidents. They normally heal readily and delayed union or non-union hardly ever occurs.

Secondary centres

The ossification of the **proximal epiphysis** of the tibia, like that of the distal femur, is an important marker for the estimation of fetal maturity in forensic cases, as it is present in about 80% of full-term infants (Knight, 1996). The centre appears in the majority of fetuses just before birth and is therefore sometimes absent in premature infants. Kuhns and Finnstrom (1976) reported that in North American and Swedish populations the epiphysis was radiographically visible in prenatal week 35 for the 5th percentile and between 2 and 5 postnatal weeks for the 95th percentile. It is always present by 3 months *post partum* (Paterson, 1929; Francis *et al.*, 1939; Pyle and Hoerr, 1955; Hansman, 1962).

Girls are in advance of boys during the whole of postnatal development of the proximal epiphysis and this difference increases from a few weeks at birth to 2–3 years at adolescence. At birth, the tibial ossification centre is an oval nodule aligned vertically below that of the distal femoral epiphysis. Its transverse diameter is less than that of the femoral centre but within 2 weeks the two bony nodules are equal in size (Pyle and Hoerr, 1955). The basic morphology of the whole epiphysis reflects that of the mature shape, but there is a 10–15° posterior tilt of the articular surface (Ogden, 1984e). During the second year, the osseous expansion causes inferior flattening and the growth plate becomes established, while superiorly there is an extension towards the tibial spines.

By 3–4 years of age, the proximal epiphysis is an elongated nodule of bone with a rounded, pitted superior surface, a flattened metaphyseal surface, a scalloped posterior margin and a roughly oval outline (Fig. 11.13a). Growth is rapid and there may be disseminated calcification round the edges of the epiphysis and accessory ossification centres are sometimes seen around the medial and lateral condyles (Scheller, 1960). By 6–7 years, the growth of the centre has stabilized to within 1–3 mm of the periphery of the cartilaginous edge and the margins are smooth (Ogden, 1984e). Ossification has extended into the intercondylar region and the tubercles. The articular surface is smooth and the condyles have reached their characteristic adult shape, the lateral being circular and the medial elongated anteroposteriorly. The triangular anterior intercondylar area and the groove for the posterior cruciate ligament are obvious (Fig. 11.13b). By 7 years in girls and 9 years in boys, the epiphyseal and metaphyseal diameters are equal in width (Pyle and Hoerr, 1955). By 11–13 years, the epiphysis is very substantial (Fig. 11.13c). Both the medial and lateral sides of the epiphysis cap the metaphysis. The medial margin is grooved and pitted with nutrient foramina. The lateral margin has a smooth facet for the attachment of the iliotibial tract at its anterior end and the articular facet

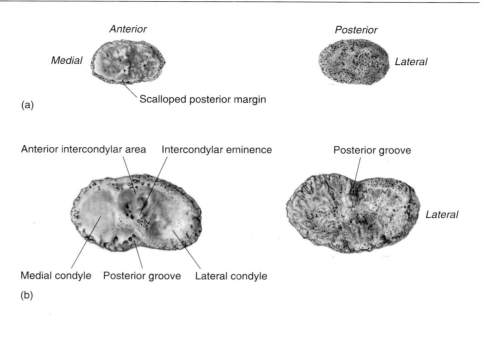

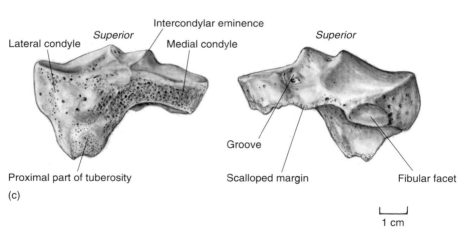

Figure 11.13 The development of the right proximal tibial epiphysis. (a) Male aged 3 years 4 months; (b) male aged 8 years. Left row – articular surfaces. Right row – metaphyseal surfaces; (c) female aged 14 years. Left – anterior; right – posterior of right epiphysis.

for the fibula at its posterior end. The facet is variable in orientation and Ogden (1984e) distinguished two types of joints, each of which had associated clinical sequelae (Ogden, 1974b,c). The posterior margin has a characteristically scalloped appearance in the centre at the attachment of the posterior cruciate ligament. The proximal ossified part of the tibial tuberosity protrudes inferolaterally from the centre of the anterior margin and its length depends on whether fusion has taken place with the distal centre (see below). Prior to fusion or in a damaged specimen, the distal section of the tuberosity is sometimes found as a separate ossicle and can be recognized as an almond-shaped, smooth nodule attached to pitted, porous bone on its superolateral aspect (Fig. 11.13d).

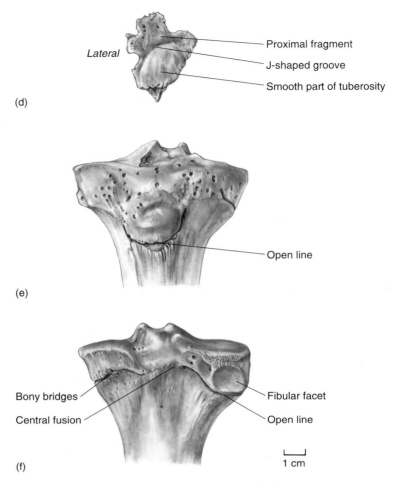

Figure 11.13 (Continued) (d) fragment of tibial tuberosity from an archaeological specimen; (e) anterior surface and (f) posterior surface – male aged 17 years.

Fracture of the proximal tibial epiphysis accounts for only about 3% of physeal injuries as it is well protected by muscles and ligaments. As with injuries to the distal femoral epiphysis, the proximity of the popliteal artery and sciatic and common peroneal nerves carries a potential risk of serious neurovascular complications (Beaty and Kumar, 1994).

Fusion coincides with cessation of growth in height, as the epiphyses around the knee are the growing end of the lower limb bones. The proximal epiphysis is responsible for about 57% of growth in length of the bone (Digby, 1915; Gill and Abbott, 1942; Anderson *et al.*, 1963). In the radiographic knee atlas, the standard for commencement of fusion is 13 years in females and 15.5 years in males, with completion about 1.5 years later (Pyle and Hoerr, 1955). Other observations have rather later times for complete fusion extending to 17 years in females and 19.5 years in males.

McKern and Stewart (1957), reporting on dry bone, found that, in males, there were still 10% and 2% of epiphyses at early stages of union at 17 and 19 years, respectively and that 100% complete fusion did not occur until 23 years. The last site of union was on the posteromedial side of the epiphysis, where there could still be a persistent groove at 24 years. In our series of juvenile skeletons, fusion started on the medial and lateral sides of the condyles and the last open lines were posterior, especially under the fibular facet (Fig. 11.13e).

The **tibial tuberosity** has a unique development as part of, yet distinct from, the main part of the proximal epiphysis (Hughes and Sunderland, 1946; Lewis, 1958; Ehrenborg and Engfeldt, 1961a; Smith, 1962a, Ogden, Hempton *et al.*, 1975; Ogden 1984d). During the 4th month of fetal life, there is an outgrowth of the proximal epiphysis on the anterior part of the shaft of the bone at the level of the proximal growth plate. This forerunner of the tuberosity gradually becomes partially separated from the main shaft by an area of fibrovascular tissue that grows into it from the zone of Ranvier. During the first few months after birth, the tuberosity is slightly distal to the main proximal tibial growth plate, which has bent anterodistally onto the front of the metaphysis. In this area, the proximal part of the growth plate has the typical structure of an endochondral ossification process, except that the cartilage cell columns are shorter than normal. Distal to this is a fibrocartilaginous zone where bone forms directly in the fibrocartilage by intramembranous ossification and yet further distally there is transition from hyaline cartilage to fibrous tissue and subsequent formation of bone. The fibrovascular region contributes to the intramembranous remodelling of the anterior metaphysis (Lewis, 1958; Ogden, Hempton *et al.*, 1975). It is postulated that this specialized cellular arrangement is a response to the very strong tensile stresses imposed on the tissues by the pull of the patellar tendon (Lewis, 1958; Smith, 1962a, 1962b; Ogden, Hempton *et al.*, 1975; Ogden, 1984d). Radiographically, the proximal part of the tuberosity can be seen as a separate tongue, which projects over the anterior surface of the metaphysis as early as 4.5 years in girls and 6 years in boys (Pyle and Hoerr, 1955). In archaeological specimens, however, the central anterior part of the main epiphysis to which the tongue is attached nearly always appears eroded and the tongue is not seen on dry bone until it has reached a more substantial size. Between 8 and 12 years in girls and 9 and 14 years in boys, one or more additional centres for the tuberosity appear in the tip of the cartilaginous tongue and ossification gradually spreads proximally. At adolescence, the proximal tongue is still separated from the distal centre by a cartilaginous bridge, but by the time the separate centres eventually coalesce, the fibrous zone occupies only the most distal part of the growth plate. The line of separation of this combined epiphysis with the diaphysis is gradually obliterated as the oblique and vertical parts of the tuberosity unite with the diaphyseal ledge.

The pattern of **fusion** is variable. Hughes (1948) states that the tip of the beak remains unfused and the Pyle and Hoerr (1955) atlas shows the fusion of the tuberosity occurring a little later than the main part of the proximal epiphysis at 14 years in females and 16.5 years in males. Haines *et al.* (1967) show the tip of the tuberosity fusing first and in our series of juvenile skeletons the sides of the tuberosity were more advanced in fusion than the principal proximal epiphysis, but there was often an open line at the inferior tip (Fig. 11.13e).

This specialized structure and late development of the tuberosity is thought to be a predisposing factor in the aetiology of Osgood–Schlatter's disease. Onset of the condition is seen typically after minor trauma in late childhood or adolescence, when there is maximum activity in the growth plate of the tuberosity (Uhry, 1944; Hughes, 1948; Ogden and Southwick, 1976; Ogden *et al.*, 1980). In spite of the addition of fibrous tissue, there appears to be an inability in some individuals to withstand the large tensile forces that develop in the tendon of the quadriceps muscle and this results in avulsion of segments of the growth plate. It usually occurs when most of the ligamentum patellae is inserted into cartilage, which has a relatively low tensile strength and lacks pain receptors, so that the injury is at first silent (Ehrenborg and Engfeldt, 1961a). Extra bones are sometimes formed in the intervening fibrous tissue and there is often marked nodular irregularity of the tibial tuberosity. Detailed radiological and histological descriptions of the progression of the lesion can be found in Ehrenborg and Lagergren (1961) and Ehrenborg and Engfeldt (1961b).

Reactive bony spurs in the region of the tuberosity have been diagnosed as Osgood–Schlatter's disease in archaeological material (Wells, 1968; Ortner and Putschar, 1985; Stirland, 1991). A related but separate clinical entity, Sinding–Larson–Johansson syndrome, is described under the section on the patella.

The **distal epiphysis** of the tibia starts to ossify during the first year of life. The centre may be seen at 3–4 months of age but often is not obvious until 7–8 months (Francis *et al.*, 1939; Elgenmark, 1946; Hansman, 1962). At first, it is a rounded nodule related to the anterior part of the metaphysis and lying directly above the trochlea of the talus (Hoerr *et al.*, 1962). It rapidly becomes oval in shape, with its long axis lying mediolaterally. By 14 months in girls and 18 months in boys, the centre accommodates itself to the metaphysis and the growth plate becomes established.

The epiphysis first becomes recognizable between 3 and 4 years of age. It is a flattish, oval disc, thicker on the medial side with a projecting beak on the anteromedial aspect of the metaphyseal surface. About a year later, the epiphysis becomes rectangular and the thicker, medial border develops an inferior flange as ossification begins to spread into the base of the medial malleolus. The articular surface is smooth and slightly concave on the medial side. The billowed metaphyseal surface has a raised ridge running anteroposteriorly across the medial side (Fig. 11.14a). Growth is rapid, in keeping with that of the foot, and by 5 years in girls and 6.5 years in boys the epiphyseal and metaphyseal widths are equal. By about 6 years, ossification around the medial side may become irregular as it spreads into the cartilaginous medial malleolus (Ogden and McCarthy, 1983).

Between 8 and 10 years, the epiphysis starts to cap the shaft and the medial malleolar ossification can be seen below the joint surface on radiographs (Hoerr *et al.*, 1962). At this stage, the epiphysis is rhomboidal in outline and the malleolus is obvious on the rounded medial side. The posterior border is flat and joined to the lateral border at a rounded right angle. The anterior border is longer than the posterior border as it slopes medially back to the malleolus, which now extends inferomedially beyond the width of the metaphysis. The metaphyseal surface has a thick, protruding ridge, more obvious anteriorly, under the base of the medial malleolus (Fig. 11.14b).

By puberty, the anterior border is grooved and pitted with numerous nutrient foramina and the lateral border bears the concavity for the fibular notch. The groove for the tendon of tibialis posterior is obvious at the medial end of the posterior surface. The medial malleolus has anterior and posterior colliculi, separated by a notch. The articular surface has assumed its adult sellar shape, being concave sagittally and convex mediolaterally. The metaphyseal surface has furrows radiating from the centre (Fig. 11.14c). Epiphyseal clefts, which normally close spontaneously, have been reported as normal variants in the medial margin of the epiphysis (Harrison and Keats, 1980). Fractures of the distal tibial epiphysis are not common but can lead to asymmetrical growth, shortening of the limb or angular deformity.

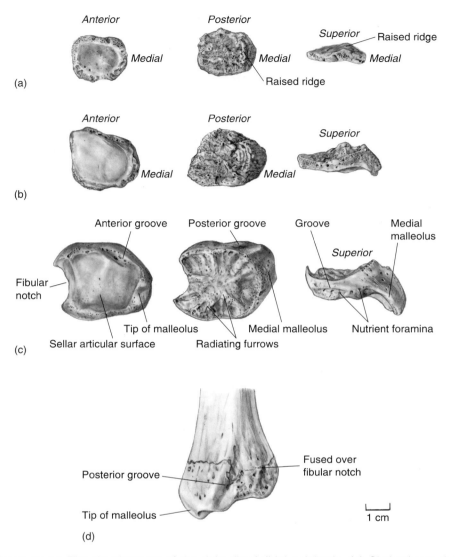

Figure 11.14 The development of the right distal tibial epiphysis. (a) Skeletal age 4–5 years; (b) male aged 8 years; (c) female aged 14 years. Left row – articular surfaces. Middle row – metaphyseal surfaces. Right row – anterior surfaces; (d) posterior surface undocumented adolescent.

It is not unusual for the tip of the medial malleolus to develop from a separate centre of ossification (Den Hoed, 1925; Powell, 1961; Selby, 1961; Coral, 1987; Ogden and Lee, 1990). This seems to be more common in girls, and centres appear between the ages of 7 and 8 years in girls and 9 and 10 years in boys. They usually fuse with the main part of the epiphysis within 2 years. They may be avulsed and cause acute or chronic symptoms which, if not treated, can lead to a fibrous union or pseudoarthrosis (Ogden and Lee, 1990; Ishii *et al.*, 1994). Nomenclature in the literature is confusing as many authors call the extra centre an os subtibiale, but Coral (1987) maintained that this term should be confined to the rare occurrence of a separate bone beneath the medial malleolus persisting after the normal age of fusion. He also stated

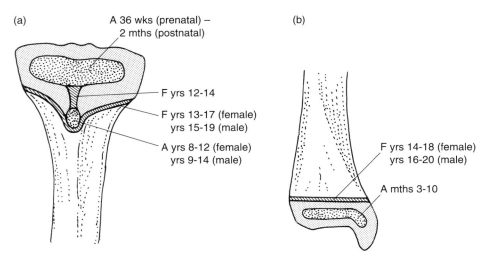

Figure 11.15 The primary ossification centre of the tibia appears during week 7 of prenatal life. Appearance (A) and fusion (F) of the secondary centres – (a) proximal end; (b) distal end.

that the true os subtibiale is related to the posterior colliculus, while an accessory ossification centre occurs distal to the anterior colliculus.

Ages for the initiation of **fusion** of the distal epiphysis are 12–13 years in females and 14–15 years in males and the mean age for completion is 14.5 and 16.5 years, respectively (Hansman, 1962; Hoerr *et al.*, 1962). McKern and Stewart's (1957) observations on dry bone state that there was not 100% union in young males until 20 years of age and this agrees with Hansman's range of 14–20 years in males. Ogden and McCarthy (1983) state that fusion always occurs from medial to lateral and McKern and Stewart (1957) agree with this as the last evidence of fusion is at the anterolateral side of the epiphysis. In our series of juvenile skeletons this was not always so, as there was often a conspicuous line open over the medial malleolus when the rest of the epiphysis had fused (Fig. 11.14d). Epiphyseal separation injuries are relatively common and occur mainly in the 9–14 years range (Thornton and Gyll, 1999).

The appearance and fusion times of the tibial centres of ossification are summarized in Fig. 11.15.

Practical notes

Diaphysis – sideing the perinatal diaphysis relies on identifying the rounded and more flared proximal end and the flatter, less flared distal end. The anterior surface is marked by the sharp border that curves medially at its distal end. The posterior surface has a very large nutrient foramen. At the proximal end the medial border is more concave, and at the distal metaphyseal surface the lateral side is flat and often marked by a small notch (Figs 11.11, 11.12). After the perinatal period, the shaft of the tibia rapidly assumes adult morphology.

Proximal epiphysis – the epiphysis is probably identifiable during the second year as an elongated ossicle, rounded on one side and flat on the other. However, sideing relies on identifying the posterior cruciate groove and lateral and medial condylar areas on the metaphyseal surface, which do not become clear until about 3–4 years of age (Fig. 11.13). An isolated tibial tuberosity, sometimes recovered from an adolescent skeleton, extends infero-laterally from an inverted, 'J'-shaped line (Fig. 11.13d).

Distal epiphysis – this is distinctive from about 3–4 years of age. The medial (malleolar) side of the epiphysis is thicker than the lateral side and has a distinct projection anteriorly on the metaphyseal surface (Fig. 11.14a). From about the age of 6 years the medial malleolus becomes obvious (Fig. 11.14b). The anterior surface has a horizontal groove and from about 11–12 years the oblique groove for the tibialis posterior tendon can be identified on the posterior surface (Fig. 11.14c).

Bones of a similar morphology

Perinatal diaphyses – the six major long bones of the limbs can be divided into two groups: the femur, tibia and humerus are larger and look more robust than the radius, ulna and fibula. The femur is the largest and longest bone in the first group, while the tibia and humerus are very similar in length (see Table 11.1). The distal humerus is flattened and has the obvious olecranon fossa posteriorly, whereas the tibial shaft is triangular and flares out both proximally and distally (Figs 9.5b,d and 11.11). From birth onwards, the tibia increases in length faster than the humerus.

Proximal tibial fragment – is oval like the distal femur but is smaller and distinguished by the presence of the tuberosity anteriorly (Figs 11.11c and 11.2c).

Distal tibial fragment – the metaphyseal surface is about the same size as the proximal humerus but it is flat, with a D-shaped outline and a straight lateral border (Fig. 11.11d). The humerus has a rounded surface with the intertubercular sulcus visible anteriorly (Fig. 9.9).

Morphological summary (Fig. 11.15)

Prenatal

Wks 7–8	Primary ossification centre appears in the shaft
Wks 36–40	Secondary centre for proximal epiphysis appears

Birth

	Represented by shaft and usually proximal epiphysis
By 6 wks	Proximal secondary centre present
3–10 mths	Distal secondary centre appears
3–5 yrs	Medial malleolus starts to ossify
8–13 yrs	Distal part of tuberosity starts to ossify from one or more centres
12–14 yrs	Proximal and distal parts of tuberosity unite
14–16 yrs	Distal epiphysis fuses in females
15–18 yrs	Distal epiphysis fuses in males
13–17 yrs	Proximal epiphysis fuses in females
15–19 yrs	Proximal epiphysis fuses in males

IV. THE FIBULA

The fibula forms the skeleton of the lateral part of the leg and is a slender long bone with an expanded proximal head and a distal end, which extends infer-iorly to form the lateral malleolus of the ankle. It articulates medially, both proximally and distally with the tibia at the superior and inferior tibiofibular joints and also distally with the body of the talus at the ankle joint.

Early development of the fibula

Details of the early development of the fibula may be found in Haines (1953), Gardner and O'Rahilly (1968) and O'Rahilly and Gardner (1975). The mesenchymal fibula is visible by stage 17 (about 41 days) but chondrification lags slightly behind that of the tibia and at stages 18 and 19 has a short chondrified part with both ends still being blastemal. At stage 20 (about 7–8 weeks), a large part of the distal end is still blastemal and is separated from the calcaneus by a dense cellular zone. By stage 23 (about 8 weeks), it is separated from the calcaneus by a small part of the talus. The lateral malleolus extends below that of the medial malleolus by the 5th prenatal month and this increases as development proceeds (Wilgress, 1900).

Of all the long bones, the fibula is the most commonly congenitally absent (Coventry and Johnson, 1952). When this happens, it is usually also associated with serious anomalies in the femur, tibia and foot (Farmer and Laurin, 1960).

Ossification

Primary centre

Ossification of the fibula may begin at stage 23 (week 8), but usually a bone collar does not develop until the beginning of the 3rd prenatal month (O'Rahilly et al., 1957; O'Rahilly and Gardner, 1975). It thus starts to ossify later than all the other major long bones of the limbs.

The perinatal fibula (Fig. 11.16) is a slender, straight bone that is rounded or angled in the proximal half and flattened mediolaterally in the distal half. The anterior and posterior borders are sharp, especially in the distal part, and the interosseous border is usually discernible in the middle third. The anterior border divides distally to enclose the subcutaneous area, which is often covered with porous-looking bone. The shaft flares slightly towards the proximal metaphyseal surface, which is flat and circular. The medial surface at the distal end usually has a roughened triangle for the inferior transverse part of the posterior tibiofibular ligament. The distal metaphyseal surface slopes slightly downwards posteriorly and has a flattened medial border and a rounded or angled lateral border. There are usually one, or sometimes two, nutrient foramina on the medial side in the region of the interosseous border, whose entrances slope distally.

By 2 years of age, the proximal end of the shaft is more flared and consequently the neck also becomes more obvious. The subcutaneous triangle is also more marked and the distal metaphyseal surface is flat. By 6 years, the shaft of the fibula has achieved close to adult morphology and the main borders and surfaces can usually be identified. The distal metaphyseal surface is triangular in outline and the proximal surface is either circular or has a flattened border, which may be dependent on the configuration of the superior tibiofibular joint (Fig. 11.17).

Secondary centres

The order in which the secondary centres of the fibular epiphyses ossify is different from that of other long bones. It is normal for ossification to begin first in those epiphyses at the growing ends of long bones. In the lower limb

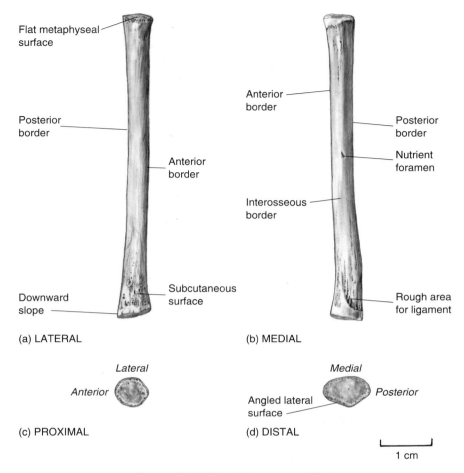

Figure 11.16 The right perinatal fibula.

this takes place around the knee and the distal femur and proximal tibia follow the usual pattern and begin to ossify during the perinatal period. In the fibula, however, the proximal epiphysis does not start to ossify until about 2 years after its distal end, although its union with the diaphysis is in accordance with that of the other knee centres and is considerably later than that of the distal end. Le Gros Clark (1958) suggested that the precocious appearance and fusion

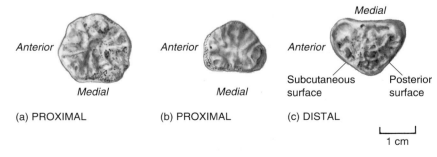

Figure 11.17 Right juvenile fibulae. (a) Proximal metaphyseal surface – female aged 14 years; (b) proximal metaphyseal surface – female aged 12 years; (c) distal metaphyseal surface – female aged 14 years.

of the lower end might be related to infant walking. However, a comparative study in different mammals revealed that the pattern peculiar to the fibula is a widespread mammalian feature and is therefore probably not related to any special feature of the human skeleton (Ellis and Joseph, 1954).

The ossification centre of the **distal epiphysis** appears at the end of the first year or beginning of the second year of life at the time when the infant does indeed start to walk (Paterson, 1929; Flecker, 1932; Francis *et al.*, 1939; Elgenmark, 1946; Hansman, 1962; Hoerr *et al.*, 1962). Even at this early stage, girls are in advance of boys in their development by about 2 months (Hoerr *et al.*, 1962) and this difference increases throughout development, so that by adolescence there is a 3-year difference. In the perinatal period, the epiphyseal/metaphyseal line is at the same level as the epiphysis of the tibia but as development proceeds, there appears to be a distal migration so that by 3 years of age, the growth plate of the fibular epiphysis is level with the tibiotalar articular surface. This relative change in the level of the growth plate coincides with establishment of walking and failure to do this, as for instance in cerebral palsy, may contribute to the valgus deformity characteristic of the condition (Ogden and McCarthy, 1983; Love *et al.*, 1990). At first, the long axis of the epiphysis is transverse and by 18 months in girls and 2 years in boys, the growth plate is established. At 3–4 years, ossification spreads into the region of the malleolar fossa and the epiphyseal cartilage starts to cap the metaphysis.

The bony epiphysis is usually recognizable by this time and is an irregular nodule of bone with a flat metaphyseal surface. The lateral surface is almost flat and has a straight posterior border and a sloping anterior border. The medial surface is angled but has not yet developed an articular facet (Fig. 11.18a). There is often irregular ossification around the margins and also accessory centres may develop but they soon fuse with the main part of the epiphysis (Ogden and McCarthy, 1983). By about 6 years, bone occupies most of the epiphysis. The malleolar fossa is well formed and contains many large and small nutrient foramina (Fig. 11.18b). By adolescence, the tip of the malleolus extends distal to the fossa, the groove for the peroneal tendons can usually be seen and the metaphyseal surface is billowed and has an undulated margin (Fig. 11.18c). Accessory centres are rarer than at the medial malleolus, especially those that fail to fuse, so forming a true os subfibulare (Powell, 1961; Ogden and Lee, 1990).

The distal fibular growth plate contributes a greater percentage of distal leg growth than that of the tibia (Beals and Skyhar, 1984). Bridges of bone start to appear at about 12 years in females and 15 years in males and **fusion** is normally complete by 14 years in females and 16.5 years in males (Paterson, 1929; Hansman, 1962; Hoerr *et al.*, 1962). As with other limb bones, fusion, as judged by inspection of dry bone, is reported at a later age than that seen in radiographs. McKern and Stewart (1957) described 90% and 100% fusion at 17 and 20 years, respectively, in males, with the last fusion medially over the talar articulation. This was confirmed in our series of juvenile skeletons, where the lateral surface of the malleolus was always the first to fuse, leaving an open line over the medial side (Fig. 11.18d).

Ossification in the **proximal epiphysis** of the fibula commences during the fourth year in girls and the fifth year in boys, but timing is more variable than at the distal end (Paterson, 1929; Flecker, 1932; Francis *et al.*, 1939; Elgenmark, 1946; Hansman, 1962; Pyle and Hoerr, 1955). The centre, which may be multinodular, is located distal to that of the tibia. It develops at the same time as ossification is spreading into the intercondylar region of the proximal tibial epiphysis. Ossification spreads slowly, and about 2 years later

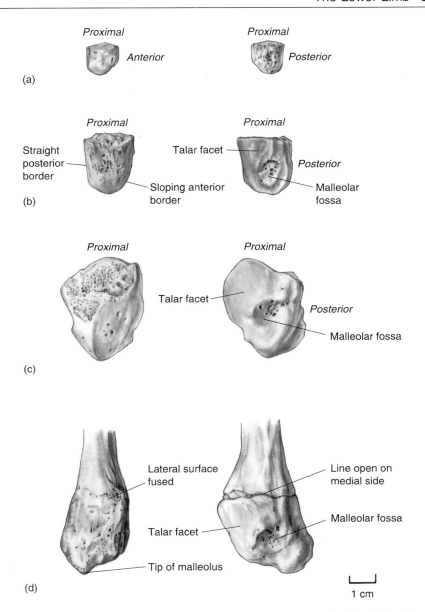

(a)

Proximal

Anterior

Proximal

Posterior

(b)

Proximal

Straight posterior border

Sloping anterior border

Proximal

Talar facet

Posterior

Malleolar fossa

(c)

Proximal

Talar facet

Proximal

Posterior

Malleolar fossa

(d)

Lateral surface fused

Talar facet

Tip of malleolus

Line open on medial side

Malleolar fossa

1 cm

Figure 11.18 The development of the right distal fibular epiphysis. (a) Skeletal age 3 years; (b) female aged 6 years; (c) early adolescent; (d) late adolescent. Left row – lateral surfaces. Right row – medial surfaces.

the ossified epiphysis has a rounded superior border, which is level with the tibial growth plate. The styloid process does not become ossified until about 8 years in girls and 10.5 years in boys (Pyle and Hoerr, 1955). The more common type of circular joint surface lies under and posterior to the tibial condyle. This position provides stability and prevents forward displacement of the fibula, thus making the proximal tibiofibular joint amongst the rarest of epiphyseal childhood injuries. The less common arrangement is for the surfaces to be variable in area and configuration and sometimes a more oblique inclination is associated with subluxation or dislocation (Ogden, 1984e).

The proximal epiphysis is an irregular piece of bone with a rounded superior surface, most of which is occupied by the semilunar tibial facet, which is set at an angle facing anteromedially towards a straight border. The surface slopes away on the other sides. The metaphyseal surface is flat and D-shaped (Fig. 11.19a). Because ossification spreads slowly, it is not until late childhood that the epiphysis shows its distinctive features and even then it can be very variable, having a triangular or rhomboidal shape. The articular facet can be triangular, oval or comma-shaped. The styloid process projects from the posterolateral corner (Fig. 11.19b).

Ages reported for **fusion** of the proximal epiphysis are variable and have a wide range. Flecker (1932) gave 17 years for females and 19 years for males and the equivalent ranges given by Hansman (1962) are 12–17 years for females and 15–20 years for males. McKern and Stewart (1957) recorded 96% fusion by 19 years and 100% by 22 years in males, the last site of fusion being anterolateral. There did not appear to be a constant pattern of fusion in our series of juvenile skeletons.

The appearance and fusion times of the fibular centres of ossification are summarized in Fig. 11.20.

Practical notes

Orientation and sideing of the juvenile fibula
Diaphysis – owing to its fragility, the fibula is the least likely long bone to survive inhumation intact. Even if complete, it is the most difficult of the perinatal long bones to side as it is relatively featureless and may be poorly marked. Proximodistal orientation depends on recognizing the slightly flared and comparatively rounded proximal shaft with a circular metaphyseal surface. The distal half of the shaft is flattened, ending in a more oval or triangular

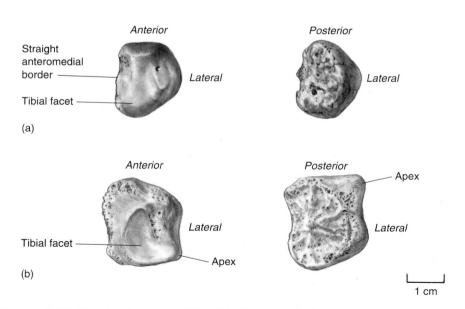

Figure 11.19 The development of the right proximal fibular epiphysis: (a) Male aged 12 years; (b) late adolescent. Left row – articular surfaces. Right row – metaphyseal surfaces.

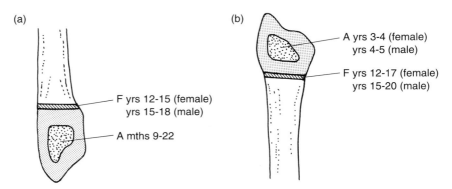

Figure 11.20 The primary ossification centre of the fibula appears during week 8 of pre-natal life. Appearance (A) and fusion (F) of the secondary centres – (a) distal end; (b) proximal end.

metaphyseal surface. Several features may help to distinguish the medial and lateral sides of the bone. Nutrient foramina are nearly always found on the medial side, which may also show an interosseous border in the middle third. The roughened triangle for the inferior part of the posterior tibiofibular ligament runs distally from anterior to posterior on the medial side. The division of the sharp anterior border at the distal end to form the subcutaneous triangle may be seen on the lateral side. The distal metaphyseal surface slopes down posteriorly (Fig. 11.16).

Distal epiphysis – with the metaphyseal surface facing superiorly, the flat surface is medial and the malleolar fossa is posterior (Fig. 11.18b,c).

Proximal epiphysis – this is probably not recognizable until mid-childhood when its distinctive features have developed. The tibial facet and the straight border face anteromedially and the apex projects posterolaterally (Fig. 11.19).

Bones of a similar morphology

Perinatal diaphyses –of the diaphyses of the six major long bones from any one individual, the radius, ulna and fibula are shorter and look less robust than the femur, humerus and tibia (see Table 11.1). The fibula and ulna are of similar length but the ulna, although shorter, is more bulky with its characteristic proximal end. The fibula is straight, narrow and relatively featureless.

Proximal and distal fibular fragments – both these can be difficult to distinguish from each other, a distal ulna or possibly a distal radius. The fibular proximal shaft is rounded and the metaphyseal surface is circular. The distal fibular shaft is flattened mediolaterally and triangles can usually be discerned on the medial and lateral surfaces (see above). Both the upper limb bones are more robust than the fibula. The distal ulna is slightly curved anteriorly and has a notch posteriorly. The distal radius is flared, curved anteriorly and has a larger metaphyseal surface than either the fibula or ulna (Figs 9.11 and 9.15).

Morphological summary (Fig. 11.20)	
Prenatal	
Wk 8	Primary ossification centre appears in the shaft
Birth	Represented by shaft only
9–22 mths	Distal secondary centre appears
During 4th yr	Proximal centre appears in girls
During 5th yr	Proximal centre appears in boys
During 8th yr	Styloid process ossifies in girls
During 11th yr	Styloid process ossifies in boys
12–15 yrs	Distal epiphysis fuses in females
15–18 yrs	Distal epiphysis fuses in males
12–17 yrs	Proximal epiphysis fuses in females
15–20 yrs	Proximal epiphysis fuses in males

V. THE FOOT

The foot articulates with the leg at the ankle (talocrural) joint and is formed from 28 constant bones – seven tarsals, five metatarsals, 14 phalanges and two sesamoids.

Early development of the foot

Given the nature of the pentadactyl limb, it is not surprising that much of the early development of the foot follows the pattern that has already been described in the section on the early development of the hand (Chapter 9). Therefore, it is advised that that section be read in advance, to prevent unnecessary repetition. However, it should be remembered that as a direct result of the proximodistal temporal organization of the human embryo, the development of the foot lags behind that of the hand by approximately 5–6 days from the very earliest embryonic stages (O'Rahilly *et al.*, 1957).

Around day 37 of intra-uterine life, the footplate becomes visible on the caudal end of the lower limb bud (Fig. 11.21). It is slightly tilted so that the pre-axial border is more laterally situated than the postaxial border, i.e. the sole faces cranially and medially (O'Rahilly and Gardner, 1975). Even at this very early stage in the development of the foot, the tibial nerve has penetrated into the region of the footplate.

By day 41, the tarsal region can be recognized as mesenchymal condensations with three or four digital prolongations (digital plate) extending distally from the caudal extremity of the footplate (Gardner *et al.*, 1959; O'Rahilly and Gardner, 1975). The margin of this digital plate is rounded and set off at a slight angle from the crurotarsal region. A slight ventral prominence in the margin indicates the position of the developing first pedal ray (O'Rahilly, 1973). By this stage, the tibial nerve has reached the plantar surface of the developing foot. By day 44, there is a common cellular condensation for the developing tarsal region with distinct digital rays, although the rim of the digital plate may not yet be crenulated (Streeter, 1948; O'Rahilly *et al.*, 1957; Gardner *et al.*, 1959).

Week 7 (days 43–49) is the time of active chondrification of the proximal mesenchymal pedal template. Chondrification generally commences in the cen-

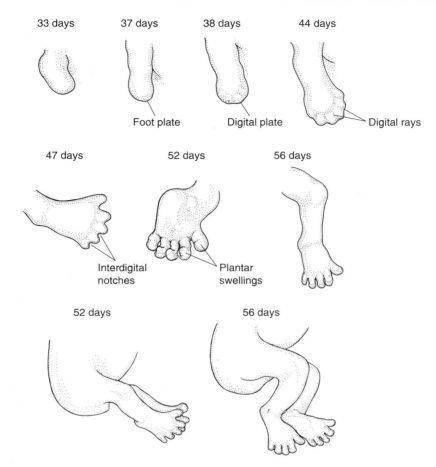

Figure 11.21 The development of the lower limb between 5 and 8 prenatal weeks (redrawn after Larsen, 1993).

tre of a blastemal mass and will continue to develop throughout the embryonic period proper (Gardner *et al.*, 1959; O'Rahilly *et al.*, 1960). There is essentially a proximodistal sequence of chondrification within the digits of the foot, although the pattern in the more proximal segments is a little more irregular. Chondrification is first evident in the region of metatarsals 2–4 followed in order by the cuboid, metatarsal 5, calcaneus, talus, medial cuneiform, intermediate cuneiform, lateral cuneiform, metatarsal 1, navicular, proximal phalanges, middle phalanges and finally by the distal phalanges (Senior, 1929; O'Rahilly *et al.*, 1957; O'Rahilly, 1973). By the end of week 7, each tarsal and metatarsal will have commenced chondrification. The process is simplest in the cuboid and the lateral two cuneiforms as each develops from only a single central nucleus of chondrification. The calcaneus is said to chondrify from two separate centres, with the distal nucleus appearing before the more proximal one. These will ultimately fuse into a single cartilaginous mass by day 48. The talus reportedly chondrifies from three separate regions, with the largest being the first to appear, while the two later centres are considerably smaller. The first centre forms the head and the body of the talus while the second is said to form the lateral process and the third forms the posterior process (Cihák, 1972). The developing medial cuneiform is separated into plantar and dorsal regions by a horizontal strip of non-cartilaginous tissue. This is a constant embryological condition and may explain the divided facets that are sometimes seen on the adult bone and the incidence of bipartite medial cuneiforms (see below). The navicular is the last of the tarsal bones to commence chondrification and it may not in fact begin until well into week 8. It forms from two distinct nuclei, with the most distal and medial forming in advance of that which is more proximal and lateral. Chondrification develops separately in the navicular tuberosity but does eventually fuse with the principal mass. By the end of the 7th week, the lower limb begins to flex towards a parasagittal plane so that the pre-axial (tibial) border is rostral in position and the postaxial (fibular) border is caudal (O'Rahilly et al., 1957).

Week 8 (days 50–56) is the time of active chondrification in the more distal mesenchymal pedal template. Around day 51, the proximal phalanges commence chondrification and interzones (see Chapter 9) are visible in the metatarsophalangeal joints (Gardner et al., 1959; O'Rahilly and Gardner, 1975). The digital plate becomes crenulated and a fan-like arrangement of the toes is evident. When five radiating mesodermal columns have been formed, selective cell necrosis (apoptosis) will occur in the interdigital zones of ectoderm and underlying mesoderm to form the separate toes (Kelley, 1970, 1973; O'Rahilly, 1973). As with the fingers, if a teratogenic agent is introduced at this time or there is some other upset in the normal process of development, then syndactyly of the digits may ensue (Christ et al., 1986). At this time, the tuberosity of the calcaneus is represented by only a mesenchymal condensation and chondrification has not yet commenced in this region (O'Rahilly and Gardner, 1975).

By day 52, chondrification is now evident in the middle phalanges and in the region of the tuberosity of the calcaneus (O'Rahilly et al., 1957; Gardner et al., 1959). Cellular condensations can be seen in the region between the talus and calcaneus at the site of the future sustentaculum tali and also in the tuberosity of the fifth metatarsal (O'Rahilly et al., 1957; Kawashima and Uhthoff, 1990). Homogenous inter-zones are present in the ankle and most of the intertarsal joints (Gardner et al., 1959; O'Rahilly and Gardner, 1975).

By day 54, chondrification has commenced in the sustentaculum tali and this separate centre soon joins with the main mass of the calcaneus (Kawashima and Uhthoff, 1990). The sustentaculum tali is the last of the tarsal elements to commence chondrification but maturation is rapid and development has generally caught up with the main body of the calcaneus by the 9th week. Concurrent with chondrification of the sustentaculum tali, the blastemal tissue at the posterior portion of the future joint between the talus and calcaneus develops into an undifferentiated mesenchymal mass, which by the end of week 8 forms a homogenous cellular interzone (Kawashima and Uhthoff, 1990). In some cases, however, the mesenchymal mass may differentiate into a fibrous structure at the site of the future joint capsule, forming a talocalcaneal bridge (Harris, 1955; Kawashima and Uhthoff, 1990). In the early fetal period the incidence of talocalcaneal bridging is high, but talocalcaneal fusion in the adult is low and it has been suggested that the breakdown of the bridge arises due to the drastic changes that occur in the biomechanical environment after birth and especially following standing and walking (Gardner et al., 1959). Talocalcaneal bridging is a common anomaly associated with peroneal spastic flat foot and although total fusion of the two bones is rare, it has been reported in the literature (Hirschtick, 1951).

As in the carpal region, the pathomechanism of tarsal coalition has been attributed either to a failure of joint formation, or fusion of an accessory ossicle to contiguous tarsal bones. It is within week 8 that cavitation of most of the intertarsal joints will commence and so it is at this stage that future congenital tarsal coalitions may form. Coalitions can theoretically occur between any two contiguous tarsal bones, but it is more common in some than in others. For example, calcaneonavicular synostosis is not uncommon and generally results in a painful spasmodic foot, which can be treated by arthrodesis. It is thought to arise via a specific gene mutation as an autosomal dominant with reduced penetration (Wray and Herndon, 1963). Talocalcaneal and calcaneonavicular coalitions are probably the most common, but fusions do occur, albeit less frequently, in the other tarsals, e.g. talonavicular coalition, naviculocuneiform coalition and cubonavicular coalition.

In addition to the tarsal coalitions, the presence of accessoria adds considerably to the variation that is encountered in the pedal skeleton (O'Rahilly *et al.*, 1960). There are over 50 reported accessoria or supernumerary bones that have been identified in the foot (O'Rahilly, 1953). They are reported to be more common in the fetus than in the adult and it is likely that during development they either disappear or alternatively fuse with other centres to form the tubercles or prominences of the constant tarsal bones. They are also reported to have a relatively high incidence in males between 10 and 15 years and in females between 8 and 12 years, suggesting again a transient nature (Hoerr *et al.*, 1962). They have the potential to persist into adulthood as small supernumerary bones and in many cases there are no clinical symptoms to forewarn their presence but, if necessary, most can be excised with relative ease. In many instances, it is difficult to make a satisfactory distinction between what is truly a supernumerary bone or an inconstant sesamoid and as a result, the naming of these structures is often inaccurate and confusing. As with the carpal bones, it is best to use terms that describe the position of the structure and where possible avoid eponyms such as 'os Vesalii'.

The first and arguably the most common supernumerary element develops around day 54, when an accessory anlage can be identified at the tarsometatarsal border between the primordia of the first and second metatarsals. This dense region of mesenchyme assumes characteristics of a prochondral primordium and may start to commence chondrification but will rapidly de-differentiate and disappear after day 57. It is said that if this structure persists and subsequently ossifies, then it will form an os intermetatarseum, which generally persists as a free ossicle but can fuse to either the medial cuneiform or to either of the adjacent metatarsal bases (Delano, 1941; Cihák, 1972; O'Rahilly, 1973).

By day 57 of intra-uterine life, the foot has reached the end of its embryonic development and all elements have commenced chondrification, including the distal phalanges, the sustentaculum tali and the tuberosity of the fifth metatarsal (O'Rahilly *et al.*, 1957). All inter-zones are present by this stage and cavitation has commenced in the ankle and metatarsophalangeal joints. Therefore, by the end of the embryonic period proper, tarsal coalitions and symphalangism can often be predicted (Gardner *et al.*, 1959). At this time, the soles of the feet face medially and dorsally and the toes of one side are generally in contact with those on the other side (praying feet). The foot is in line with the leg and angulation of the ankle has not really begun, so the foot is in an equinus position. The development of the individual arches of the foot can be detected by the end of the embryonic period (O'Rahilly, 1973).

Talipes equinovarus (clubfoot) is probably one of the most studied congenital abnormalities of the foot and certainly the literature devoted to this condition is voluminous. It is said to occur in one in every 1000 live Caucasian births, to be more frequent in twins and to have a male to female ratio of 2:1. However, its true aetiology is still unknown, although there are several theories as to how this condition arises. Ruano-Gil (1988) reported that in the embryo, the talus and calcaneus sit next to each other in a forced equinus position and that this classical embryological alignment is achieved through the influence of growth at the distal end of the fibula. However, in week 9 the position of the talus relative to the calcaneus alters through the influence of growth at the distal end of the tibia. The talus is said to gradually shift until it finally adopts the characteristic position on top of the calcaneus (Victoria-Diaz, 1979). If this latter phase of growth is halted, then the foot remains in the embryological position, thereby producing talipes equinovarus (clubfoot) where the patient walks on the outer aspect of the talus. Although attractive, arguments against this theory are numerous and it is more likely that 'clubfoot' is really 'a collection of various pathological entities of different aetiology that manifest in a commonly identifiable foot deformity' (Bates and Chung, 1988).

Next to clubfoot, polydactyly is probably the most frequently reported congenital abnormality of the foot, with a frequency of approximately one in every 2000 births (Harrower, 1925). It is frequently the fifth toe that is affected and often there is no bony component, with the additional appendage being composed of only soft tissue (Smith and Boulgakoff, 1923). Oligodactyly (absence of a normal digit) is less common than polydactyly, with a reported incidence of approximately one in every 3000 births (Viladot, 1988).

Ossification

If one ignores the accessoria and the sesamoids, there are potentially 46 separate centres of ossification in the foot. Of these, 26 are primary and 20 (but often less) are secondary. Unlike many other areas of the body (except the hand of course) many of the primary centres arise in the early fetal period and the remainder do not develop until after birth, while the appearance of the secondary centres are interspersed between the sequential appearance of the primary centres. Therefore, for the sake of both clarity and conformity with the other chapters, we will still examine these centres under the headings of primary and secondary, but the reader should be aware that there is no linear temporal continuity between these two sections. It should also be appreciated that there has been a considerable amount of research dedicated to the radiographic identification of appearance and fusion times in the foot and this has resulted in many slightly conflicting reports of the time of a specific event. It is certain that much of this interest has resulted not only from the ready availability of the foot for radiography, but also the large number of centres of ossification provides a substantial volume of information regarding growth and maturity over an extended period of time. There is certainly a considerable degree of individual variability in the timing of events in the foot and when this is coupled with racial variation and environmental factors, it is clear that it is impossible to arrive at a universal time for either the appearance of a specific centre or its subsequent fusion. Therefore, we have attempted to summarize much of the information that is available, so that a relatively broad time spectrum of events is presented. These timings should not, of course, be considered definitive, as variations will inevitably occur.

Primary centres

Within the fetal period, ossification commences first in the metatarsals, followed closely by the distal phalanges, proximal and finally the middle phalanges. It should be noted that this is a different order from that found in the hand, where the distal phalanges are the first to commence ossification (see Chapter 9).

The primary centres for the shafts of the **metatarsals** appear between 8–10 prenatal weeks, which is at a similar time to that for the metacarpals. Metatarsals 2–4 tend to appear before metatarsal 5, while the first metatarsal may not appear until 12 prenatal weeks. This order of appearance is fundamentally in agreement with the pattern of metacarpal appearance found in the hand. As with the first metacarpal, in all aspects of ossification and fusion, the first metatarsal behaves more like a proximal phalanx than a true metatarsal.

The **distal phalanges** appear around the end of the 2nd and throughout the 3rd month of intra-uterine life and so may appear before the shaft of the first metatarsal. The distal phalanx of the first toe appears in advance of the others around 7 weeks according to O'Rahilly *et al.* (1960) or week 9 according to Birkner (1978). Ossification of the distal phalanges of the more lateral toes occurs between 11 and 12 prenatal weeks, while that of the fifth toe may not occur until the 5th or 6th prenatal month. As with the distal phalanges of the hand, ossification commences at the tip and not in the centre, as is found with all other primary centres of long bones. Therefore, ossification can only progress in a proximal direction. A shell of subperiosteal bone is deposited rather like a thimble over the cartilaginous phalanx, while the ungual tuberosity forms by intramembranous ossification on the exterior of the subperiosteal cap. In general, ossification of the distal phalanges of the foot lags behind those of the hand by approximately 3–5 weeks.

The primary centres of ossification for the **proximal phalanges** appear in the 4th prenatal month, around 14–16 prenatal weeks. The centres for the first to the third toes tend to appear in advance of those for the fourth and fifth toe (MacLaughlin-Black and Gunstone, 1995).

As with the hand, the **middle phalanges** of the foot are the last of the long bones to commence ossification. It is well documented that their appearance is somewhat erratic and in the cases of the fourth and fifth toes in particular, ossification may not be detected until after birth. The middle phalanx of the second toe may appear in the 4th prenatal month and that of the third in the 5th prenatal month, but in truth, the time of appearance cannot be stated with any degree of certainty. It is thought that this somewhat unpredictable behaviour of the middle phalanges of the most lateral toes may go some way towards explaining the reduction in the number of phalanges (biphalangism) that can be seen in these toes in particular.

In summary, therefore, the primary centres of ossification for the metatarsals and phalanges are all present (with the probable exception of the middle phalanges of the lateral toes) by the end of the 5th prenatal month (Fig. 11.22).

The second group of primary centres of ossification in the foot give rise to the tarsal bones, and while most develop in the postnatal years, certainly two and often three appear before birth (Figs 11.22 and 11.23). The normal sequence of appearance for the tarsal bones is relatively constant and well documented. The calcaneus appears first, followed closely by the talus and then the cuboid. The remainder of the tarsal bones always appear after birth and the sequence begins with the lateral cuneiform and is followed by the medial and then the intermediate cuneiform, with the navicular being the last to commence ossification.

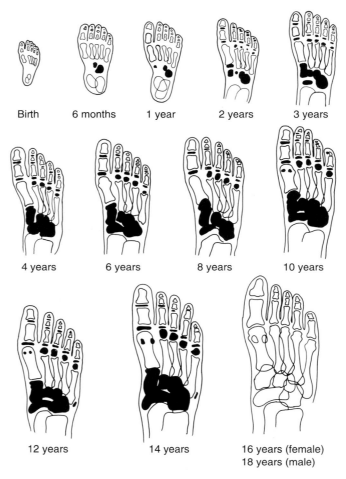

Figure 11.22 Various stages of osseous development in the foot from birth to adolescence (redrawn after Birkner, 1978).

The **calcaneus** is the first of the tarsal bones to commence ossification and frequently does so from two separate centres. The lateral centre is not constant but, when present, it always precedes the formation of the constant medial centre. The former has been described as an osseous shell that develops on the fibular side of the bone and is perichondral in origin. It is located posterior to the site of the future peroneal trochlea and between the lateral process and the retrotrochlear eminence (Meyer and O'Rahilly, 1976). Texts vary on the time of appearance of this centre but it seems to occur around the 4th and 5th prenatal months. The second centre appears somewhat later, around 5–6 prenatal months and is said to be endochondral in nature, as it appears in the centre of the anterior third of the cartilaginous mass of the calcaneus (Meyer and O'Rahilly, 1976). It is clear that the ossification of the calcaneus is a precise sequence of perichondral and endochondral ossification (Fritsch and Eggers, 1999). These authors have found that the ossification grooves of Ranvier differentiate at the margins of the perichondral bone and are accompanied by large cartilage canals that invade the calcaneal anlagen.

A bifid os calcis may arise when the two centres fail to fuse and this is characterized by a deep cleft that separates the anterior third of the bone

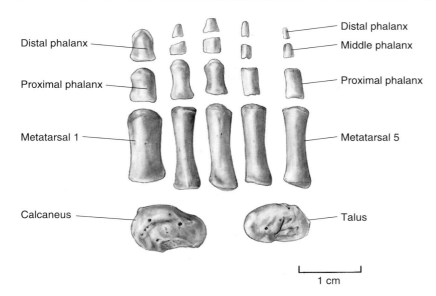

Figure 11.23 The right perinatal foot.

from the posterior two-thirds (Szaboky *et al.*, 1970). This condition is asymptomatic and so does not tend to require any surgical intervention.

As with the bones of the hand, most of the descriptions of changes in the shape of the tarsals have been derived from radiographic texts and not from actual bone specimens. Unlike the carpals, however, we have found that the tarsals adopt a more recognizable form at a younger age and so many can be positively identified at a relatively earlier stage of development.

By around birth, or certainly within the first month *post partum*, the calcaneus can be identified as a piriform-shaped nodule with a shallow indentation on a flattened area, just distal to the centre of the dorsal surface (Fig. 11.24). This is the forerunner of the calcaneal groove that forms the floor of the sinus tarsi and at this early stage of development it displays a large nutrient foramen. The proximal end of the bony nodule is broader than the distal end and is drawn downwards so that the greatest vertical dimension is in the proximal segment of the bone.

The surface of the perinatal calcaneal nodule displays not only flattened regions that do not appear to bear any relevance to future anatomical structures but also various pits, foramina and spiky projections. We have studied this stage extensively and offer the following as a possible explanation for the morphology of the perinatal calcaneus. The uneven surface of the developing nodule is consistent with endochondral bone formation that is occurring in a centrifugal fashion within a cartilaginous precursor. The flattened regions are consistent with perichondral ossification (discussion in Chapter 2). Two constant flat areas are present on every perinatal calcaneus we have examined – one on the medial surface of the bone and one on the lateral aspect of the plantar surface. These coincide with the description of periosteal collars identified from histological sections by Fritsch *et al.* (2001). These plaques are not circumferential as would be found in the shafts of long bones and are surrounded by perichondral ossification grooves which are composed of three distinct layers – an inner osteoprogenitor layer, a middle undifferentiated mesenchymal layer and an outer periosteal layer.

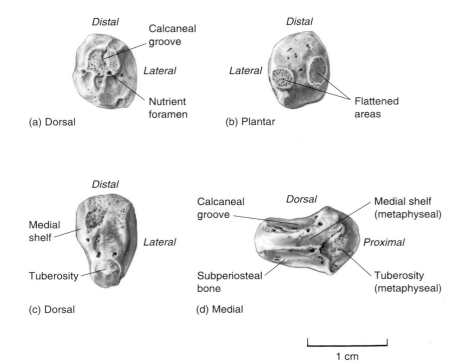

Figure 11.24 The development of the right calcaneus: (a) dorsal surface of perinatal calcaneus; (b) plantar surface of perinatal calcaneus; (c) dorsal surface of calcaneus – child of approximately 3 months *post partum*; (d) medial surface of calcaneus – child of approximately 3 months *post partum*.

This classical perinatal appearance disappears within the first few months of birth as the bone starts to elongate and develop its characteristic morphology (Fig. 11.24c). The distal segment becomes wider, producing a medial shelf that will go on to form the sustentaculum tali. The area of subperiosteal bone below this is fully formed at this stage and corresponds in position with the flattened region seen on the perinatal bone. The lateral surface of the calcaneus is relatively featureless in the first few months and the presence of fully formed subperiosteal bone coincides with the location of the lateral flattening seen in the perinatal bone. Only the proximal posterior segment (tuberosity) of the bone and the region around the developing sustentaculum tali are clearly metaphyseal in nature, displaying characteristic ridges and furrows.

At around 2.5–3 months, the anterior surface of the calcaneus begins to flatten as it assumes a reciprocal shape to the cuboid. By 4–6 months, the plantar tubercles are quite distinct and by 6–7 months the bone has increased considerably in length. Flattening of the talar facets and recognizable development of the sustentaculum tali begins around the end of the first year, which coincides with the onset of unassisted walking. By 3–4 years, the proximal segment displays the characteristic ridge-and-furrow system of an active metaphysis (Fig. 11.25a). By 5–6 years of age the delimitation around the articular facets is clearly defined and the bone is close to its final form (Fig. 11.25b).

The calcaneus can be readily identified at birth but its characteristic morphology is not readily perceived until at least the end of the first year, when it is modified by the influences of locomotion. The bone alters considerably both in shape and size within the first 2 years, but from then until puberty the changes

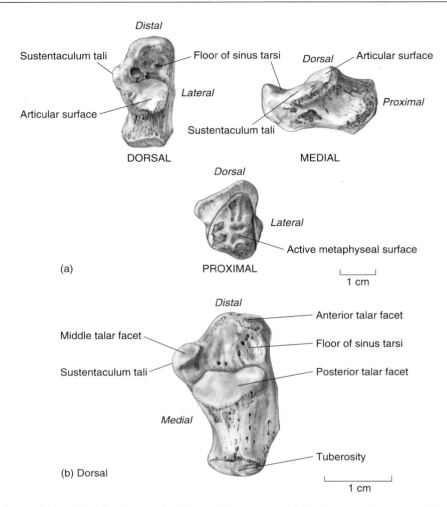

Figure 11.25 The development of the right calcaneus: (a) calcaneus (approximately 3–4 years of age); (b) calcaneus – female aged 6 years.

are gradual and small. Further development of the calcaneus is discussed below in the section on secondary centres.

While the calcaneus may be the first tarsal bone to show ossification, the **talus** is reported to be the first to show evidence of vascular invasion (Gardner *et al.*, 1959). Interestingly, Waisbrod (1973) found that in fetuses with clubfoot, the vascular channels within the talus were less well organized and fewer in number and the ossification centre tended to be smaller. Therefore, he suggested that the aetiology of clubfoot might be blastemal in origin. Ossification of the talus commences in the 6th prenatal month in females and the 7th in males. Goldstein *et al.* (1988) found that the centre was present in 16% of fetuses at 16 weeks and in all fetuses by 23 weeks. However, cases have been reported of the talar centre being absent at birth but appearing shortly afterwards. Ossification may arise from more than one nucleus, but they will rapidly coalesce to form a single centre (Gardner *et al.*, 1959).

The perinatal talus is oval in shape and its radiographic image is said to resemble a 'stubby peanut', with its long axis lying horizontally along the proximodistal plane. Just distal to the centre of the dorsal surface there is a small indentation, which is angled in a distomedial direction. The indentation on the dorsal surface coincides in position with a similar depression on the plantar surface. These two mark the position of the future talar neck and are separated on the lateral surface by a thin dividing bony strip (Fig. 11.26a). The indentation on the dorsal surface separates the future articular portion proximally from the head distally, while the indentation on the plantar surface separates the future anterior and posterior talocalcaneal facets and coincides with the position of the groove for the roof of the sinus tarsi. In the neonate, the angle formed between the neck and head of the talus inclines distally and medially and is reported to be 130–140°. By adulthood this angle will increase to approximately 150°. This reduced angle is thought to account in part for the inverted appearance of the neonatal foot. An increase in the neck angle then becomes associated with the change in the shape of the foot as it comes into

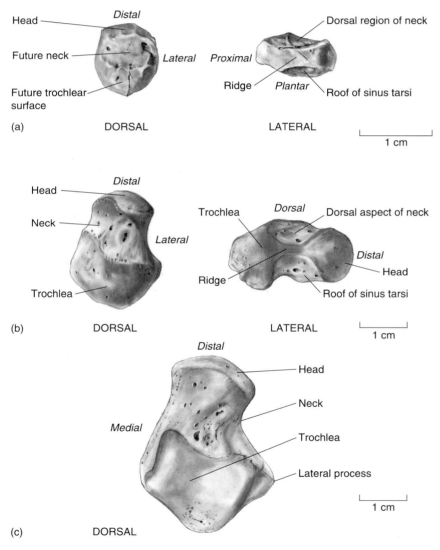

Figure 11.26 The development of the right talus: (a) the perinatal talus; (b) female aged 2 years; (c) female aged 6 years.

contact with the ground in preparation for walking at about 10–12 months. By 2.5–3 months *post partum*, the neck of the talus is well defined.

Ossification of the lateral process of the talus begins around 5 months, as does the development of the sinus tarsi, and by 7 months the neck region is clearly defined and covered by a smooth layer of subperiosteal bone. Around 2 years of age, the posterolateral wall of the sinus tarsi starts to develop as a downward-projecting triangular process. The roundness of the trochlear surface also begins to develop at this age and the bone adopts an identifiable adult morphology (Fig. 11.26b). By around 6 years of age, the articular facets are clearly delimited and only the area around the posterior tubercle shows evidence of continued metaphyseal activity (Fig. 11.26c). The posterior tubercle begins to develop by 7–8 years in girls and 9–10 years in boys, but this will be discussed below in the section on secondary centres.

One of the most frequently discussed congenital conditions of the foot involves the talus and is extremely rare. This is the condition of congenital vertical talus (congenital convex pes valgus or rocker-bottom foot) and its aetiology is unknown, although some authors consider it to be caused by a delay in development early in the first trimester of pregnancy. One of the characteristic features of this condition is a hypoplastic sustentaculum tali on the calcaneus, so there is no support for the head of the talus, which subsequently becomes displaced. Diagnosis can be made at birth by the rocker-bottom appearance of the foot, which is caused by the head of the vertical talus being palpable in the sole. The condition presents with a valgus deviation of the heel, a talar displacement down, forward and medially (hence the 'vertical' talus) and a subsequent dorsal dislocation of the navicular onto the neck of the talus. The abnormal position of the navicular may not be appreciated radiologically until the child is in excess of 3 years of age, as the navicular does not ossify until this time. Congenital vertical talus is idiopathic, but it does show a higher incidence in patients suffering from other conditions, such as cerebral palsy, spina bifida and Down's syndrome. In this clinical condition, the talus is longer than usual, possesses a shorter neck and has a rounded or pointed head. It also displays uncharacteristic articulation facets with both the calcaneus and the navicular. An extremely rare condition of congenital vertical talus in association with talocalcaneal coalition has been reported.

It is well documented in the literature that the neck of the talus changes in direction with the growth of the foot (Goldie, 1988). Gardner (1956) reported that the neck of the talus points towards the medial side of the foot in the young fetus and that the angle between the head and the body increases throughout the fetal period from 16 weeks onwards. Paturet (1951) called this the 'declination angle' and reported it to be between 150 and 160° in the adult. Waisbrod (1973), however, disagreed with this, as he found the angle to be around 150° even in the fetus. He did, however, find that fetuses with clubfoot displayed markedly reduced angles of declination of between 124 and 154°.

The **cuboid** often commences ossification prior to birth but it is not uncommon for it to occur as late as 3 months *post partum* in females and 6 months in males. Menees and Holly (1932) found the cuboid to be present at birth in 35% of males and 56.5% of females. Christie *et al.* (1941) found that is was more commonly present at birth in Negro babies, girls, neonates of a greater maturity and in the offspring of mothers with no recorded pregnancy complications. In addition, they found that the centre was further advanced in the offspring of older (20+ years) and multiparous mothers. For example, the centre was present in 80% of Negro baby girls of high birth weight and only 16% of Negro baby boys of low birth weight.

What is clear is that the presence or absence of the cuboid centre of ossification is not a reliable indicator of a full term fetus. In fact, the cuboid may originate from a cluster of ossific nodules (aligned with the long axis of the calcaneus), which will fuse within the first few months after birth to form a single round homogenous nodule. Between 6 months *post partum* and 1 year, the medial surface that will articulate with the lateral cuneiform begins to flatten. By the end of the second year, the posterior surface that articulates with the calcaneus begins to flatten. Between 3 and 4 years, blunt-angled corners develop so that the characteristic triangular appearance of the bone is achieved (Fig. 11.27a). The distal surface is flat and slopes laterally, the medial surface is virtually straight, the proximal surface is rounded and the lateral surface is clearly non-articular. Also at this stage, the groove for the peroneus longus tendon is evident on the plantar surface. By the end of the fourth year the definition between the articular and non-articular areas of the medial surface are clearly defined and by 8 years of age the bone appears as a miniature of its adult form (Fig. 11.27b). Therefore, the cuboid can be identified in isolation from approximately 3–4 years and develops only in terms of size and definition with advancing age.

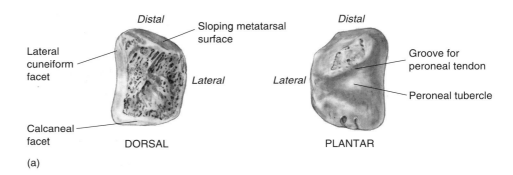

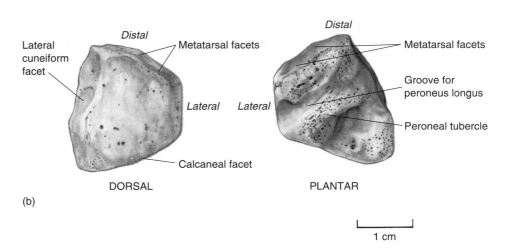

Figure 11.27 The development of the right cuboid: (a) child of approximately 3–4 years; (b) male aged 8 years.

The **lateral cuneiform** generally ossifies within the first year, but in the male it can apparently be delayed until as late as the third year. During the fourth year, a second and even a third nucleus has been reported, lying above and distal to the primary ossific nucleus – this, however, does not seem to be confirmed in any literature other than Stripp and Reynolds (1988). Menees and Holly (1932) found that the centre was present at birth in 3.8% of females and 0.3% of males and this was fundamentally confirmed by Hill (1939). Francis *et al.* (1939) found that, in females, the centre was present in 60% of cases by 3 months, 85% by 6 months and 100% by 24 months. They found that in males, the centre was present in 50% of cases by 3 months *post partum*, 75% by 6 months, 90% by 12 months and 100% by 18 months. Elgenmark (1946) concluded that the centre was always present by 9 months *post partum* in females and 20 months in males. In summary, the appearance of the ossification centre for the lateral cuneiform is variable but it is likely that it will be present in many females by 3–4 months and many males by 5–6 months. Until the end of the first year, when the margins of the bone begin to flatten, the lateral cuneiform appears as either a rounded or oval nodule. It becomes recognizable in isolation around the fourth year, when the individual surfaces can be identified (Fig. 11.28a). The dorsal surface is non-articular, broad and slightly convex from side to side and from proximal to distal. The proximal and distal articular surfaces are convex and not clearly defined. The lateral surface bears a well-defined articular facet proximally and a non-articular region distally. The medial surface shows a well-defined central area of flat subperiosteal bone with numerous nutrient foramina. Between 4 and 6 years of age, the bone gradually adopts its basic adult form.

The **medial cuneiform** commences ossification within the second year in females and often into the third year in males. Elgenmark (1946) reported that the centre was always present in girls by 2 years 11 months and in boys by 4 years 3 months. Francis *et al.* (1939) found that the centre was present in 1% of girls by 6 months *post partum*, 69% by 18 months and 100% by 2 years 6 months. They found that the centre was present in 2% of boys by 6 months *post partum*, 38% by 18 months and 100% by 3 years. Ossification may commence as a single nodule, but it is more likely to arise from a compound centre that may be double or multiple in origin. It is common for the bone to arise from double centres of ossification, one dorsal and one plantar, so that in the absence of synostosis, bipartition (os cuneiforme 1 bipartitum) may occur. It has been reported that the bipartite medial cuneiform is generally larger than its non-bipartite counterpart. The division between the two elements may not be strictly horizontal, but more obliquely placed so that the two bone parts are more correctly labelled as dorsolateral and plantomedial.

Despite its relatively late time of formation, the bone is still identifiable in isolation by between 3 and 4 years of age, when it appears as a roughly piriform-shaped bone with a pointed dorsolateral aspect and a more rounded and thicker plantomedial area (Fig. 11.28b). By approximately 5 years of age, the bone still shows a clearly pointed dorsolateral region and a small patch of smooth subperiosteal bone can be identified on the lateral aspect, indicating the site of the future interosseous ligament connecting to the intermediate cuneiform. By around 6 years of age, this bone has also reached close to its adult morphology.

The **intermediate cuneiform** commences ossification around 2.5 years in females and 3.5 years in males, although it may be delayed in the male until the fourth or even the fifth year. Elgenmark (1946) reported that the centre was always present in girls by 2 years 8 months and in boys by 4 years 3 months.

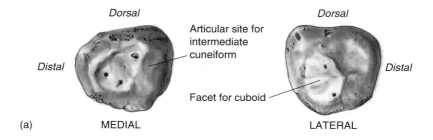

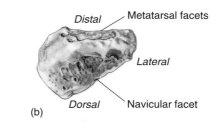

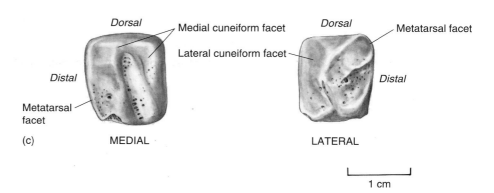

Figure 11.28 The development of the right cuneiforms: (a) lateral cuneiform – female aged 4 years; (b) medial cuneiform – child of approximately 3–4 years; (c) intermediate cuneiform – female aged 6 years.

Francis *et al.* (1939) reported that the centre was present in 2% of girls by 9 months *post partum*, 72% by 2 years and 100% by 3 years of age. They found the centre to be present in 1% of boys by 6 months *post partum*, 59% by 2 years and 100% by 4 years 6 months. The intermediate cuneiform normally arises as a single centre of ossification, although multiple centres have been reported. The intermediate cuneiform cannot be reliably identified in isolation until it has assumed close to adult morphology by around 6 years of age (Fig. 11.28c).

The **navicular** is the last of the tarsal bones to commence ossification and does not tend to do so until the end of the second year in girls and the beginning of the fourth year in boys. There is, however, considerable variation in the reported times of appearance and they range between 2 and 6 years. Elgenmark (1946) reported that the centre was always present in both girls and boys by 4 years 3 months. Ossification may commence from a single nucleus, two nuclei or multiple foci. By around 5 years of age, the bone has a domed distal surface and a flat proximal articular region (Fig. 11.29a) but by 7–8 years the curved arc of the talar surface is well defined and the bone can be readily identified in isolation (Fig. 11.29b). The tuberosity of the navicular does not develop until later and will be described under the section on secondary centres.

Avascular necrosis of the navicular (Köhler's disease) is thought to arise from a combination of mechanical and vascular vulnerability and has a male to female ratio of 6:1 respectively. It has been suggested that because the navicular is the last to commence ossification, it might be more susceptible to the arch compression forces of weight bearing and this, coupled with an inherent vascular insufficiency, may give rise to stress fractures, which leads to subsequent necrosis. This osteochondrosis of the navicular is normally detectable between 4 and 8 years.

The time of ossification of the **sesamoids** associated with the great toe is well documented. It is generally recognized that the lateral (fibular) sesamoid appears before the medial (tibial) sesamoid (by about 2 months) and that they ossify in girls before boys. The sesamoids commence ossification around 9 years in girls and 11–12 years in boys, although they can appear as early as 8 years or as late as 15 years. Ossification occurs most commonly from a single focus, but it is not unusual for it to arise from double or multiple centres. Non-union of multiple centres can lead to partite sesamoids, which surprisingly do not necessarily predispose towards pain but are commonly misidentified as fractures. Partition is more common in the medial sesamoid and more likely to affect females.

Congenital absence (aplasia) of the sesamoids of the great toe is rare, but when it does occur it is more commonly the medial that is affected. While

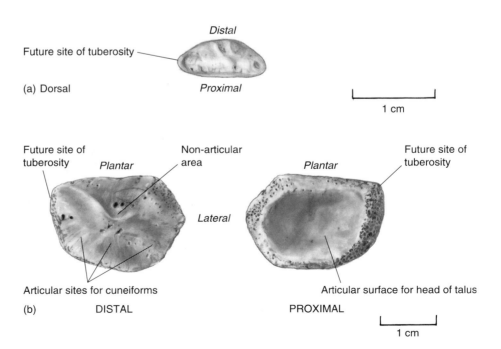

Figure 11.29 Development of the right navicular: (a) child of approximately 5 years; (b) male aged 8 years.

aplasia of the lateral sesamoid is considered to be exceedingly rare, bilateral absence is even less common. Congenital absence of the hallucial sesamoids must be distinguished from resorption following disease. It is interesting that both unilateral and bilateral absence is normally encountered by accident as they rarely display clinical symptoms. Le Minor (1988) reported that bilateral hallucial sesamoids are the norm in most mammalian orders and relatively constant in most of the primate groups. However, they were found to be inconstant in both gorillas and orang-utans and it was suggested that aplasia in the human might be related to a general decline in sesamoids within hominoid primates.

Ossification of the remaining sesamoids in the foot (see above) tends to occur around or after 15 years of age.

Secondary centres

Appearance

The secondary centres of ossification in the foot appear, with at least one and possibly as many as four exceptions, in the cartilaginous extremities of the long bones. There are six morphologically distinct groups of epiphyses in the foot – the heads of the lateral four metatarsals, the base of the first metatarsal, proximal, middle and distal phalanges and the cap-like epiphysis of the calcaneus. Inconstant and perhaps somewhat questionable epiphyses are associated with the talus, navicular and fifth metatarsal (see below). Unlike the situation found in other long bones, where epiphyses arise in both the proximal and distal poles, in the foot, as in the hand, they tend to be restricted to one end of the bone, although in rare circumstances, supernumerary epiphyses have been documented. It is a general rule that, with the exception of the first metatarsal, the heads of all other metatarsals ossify from a separate secondary centre of ossification. The first metatarsal behaves more like a proximal phalanx, as all phalanges ossify from a single centre, which forms the shaft and the distal articular surface, while the base of the bone, at its proximal extremity, develops from a separate secondary centre of ossification.

It is well recognized that many of the epiphyses of the long bones of the foot may commence ossification from more than one locus. Roche and Sunderland (1959) showed that multiple foci (up to eight in some circumstances) are the norm for the development of the epiphyses of the first metatarsal and first proximal phalanx. As a general rule, all metatarsal epiphyses may develop from more than one centre, as indeed may all the epiphyses of the proximal phalanges, although in the female it may be restricted to only the first and fifth proximal phalanges. Multiple foci are not common in either the middle or distal phalanges, although they have been recorded in the second middle phalanx and the first distal phalanx in males only (Roche and Sunderland, 1959). However, by about 4 years of age, the multiple centres will start to consolidate rather like a string of pearls, so that after this date, only a single secondary centre can be detected in these locations.

There are several reports in the literature that state the **order of appearance** of the secondary centres and, of course, few of these agree. Therefore, we have summarized the views of many papers and present the most frequently reported pattern for secondary centre ossification. As a general rule, the secondary centre for the first distal phalanx is usually the first to form, followed loosely in order by the secondary centres for middle phalanges 2–4, all proximal phalanges and the base of the first metatarsal. The appearance of the secondary centres for the metatarsals and distal phalanges of digits 2–4 then follow. The secondary centres for the bases of both the middle and distal phalanges of the fifth digit are very variable with regards to their time of appearance, if in fact they will form at all.

The secondary centre for the base of the first distal phalanx appears at approximately 9 months *post partum* in females and 14 months in males. At this stage, the foot is already represented by the shafts of all the long bones, the calcaneus, talus, cuboid and lateral cuneiform. Few authors have published detailed information on the appearance of the secondary centres for the middle phalanges and this may simply be explained by the fact that they can be masked in many radiographic views of the foot due to the curled nature of the toes and so are difficult to identify with any degree of certainty. The epiphyses of the middle phalanges of digits 2–4 are said to appear between 11 and 14 months in females and 14 and 24 months in boys. There does not appear to be any specific order with relation to the epiphysis of a specific digit appearing first. Some authors state that the epiphyses for the proximal phalanges develop in advance of those for the middle phalanges, while others state the opposite. The epiphyses for the proximal phalanges appear between 11 and 20 months in females and 18 months to 2 years 4 months in males, by which stage the medial cuneiform has commenced ossification. There does seem to be some evidence to suggest that ossification is first detected in the third proximal phalanx, followed in sequence by the fourth, second, first and finally by the fifth. There is some discrepancy in the literature concerning the time of ossification in the epiphysis of the base of the first metatarsal. Francis *et al.* (1939) report it to be 14 months in females and 22 months in males, whereas most other reports place the time at somewhat later between 18 and 20 months in females and 26 and 31 months in males. It is at this stage that the intermediate cuneiform commences ossification. The epiphysis for the head of the second metatarsal commences ossification between 19 months and 2 years in females and between 2 years 3 months and 2 years 10 months in males. The epiphysis for the head of the third metatarsal commences ossification somewhat later at approximately 2 years 5 months in females and 3 years 5 months in males. The epiphysis for the head of the fourth metatarsal commences ossification a little later at 2 years 8 months in females and 4 years in males. By the stage at which all epiphyses of the medial four metatarsals are represented, the navicular has commenced formation.

The epiphyseal centres for the distal phalanges of digits 2–4 appear in the female between 2 years 6 months and 3 years and in males between 4 years and 4 years 7 months. There is some evidence to suggest that if the epiphysis for the distal phalanx of the fifth digit is to develop, then it does so in advance of the other distal phalangeal epiphyses. The epiphysis of the distal phalanx of digit 5 appears at approximately 2 years 3 months in girls and 3 years 11 months in boys. For the remainder of these epiphyses, there is a clear pattern that the fourth digit appears before that of the third, with that for the second being the last to form. The epiphysis for the head of the fifth metatarsal is the last of the constant epiphyses to form and does so almost concomitant with the distal phalangeal epiphyses between 2 years 11 months and 3 years 2 months in females and between 4 years and 4 years 5 months in males.

The epiphysis for the middle phalanx of digit 5 behaves in a similar fashion to the epiphysis for the distal phalanx of the same digit. It may not develop at all, but if it does, then it can appear around 2 years in females and 2 years 11 months in males. However, it has also been reported to appear as late as 5 years of age in both sexes.

The **metatarsal heads** appear as small, undifferentiated nodules of bone until approximately 4–5 years of age. From this time, they become recognizable, with rounded convex articular distal surfaces, flattened proximal meta-physeal surfaces and elongated oval outlines. After this, they continue to approach the adult morphology. It is interesting to note that according to Roche (1964, 1965) between 20 and 30% of shaft growth in the metatarsals occurs at the non-epiphyseal ends. Identification of individual metatarsal heads is difficult and confidence will be greatest when only one individual is present and the individual is close to puberty so that an appropriate head can be fitted to a shaft. The head of the second metatarsal can be readily separated from the others, due to its larger size, while the fifth is the most distinctive due to the difference in angulation. When the articular surfaces are viewed from above, the head of the second metatarsal is somewhat stellate in appearance, display-ing prolongations from each corner, with the plantolateral corner being parti-cularly well developed (Fig. 11.30). The plantar border shows a particularly well-developed notch for the passage of the long flexor tendon. The heads of metatarsals 3 and 4 are very similar in morphology and probably require the presence of a shaft to permit identification via best-fit procedures. When the distal articular surface of the fifth metatarsal head is viewed from above, it is obvious that the entire surface is skewed towards the medial aspect. The med-ial surface of the head is almost vertical, while the lateral surface has a distinct shallow slope. The anterior border displays the characteristic notch for the passage of the long flexor tendon and the medial tubercle is considerably smaller than the lateral.

The proximal metaphyseal surfaces are quite distinctive in appearance and can be readily differentiated from the corresponding metacarpal heads (see

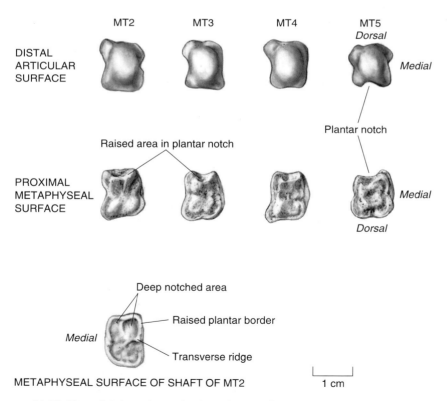

Figure 11.30 The distal and proximal surfaces of the right metatarsal (2–5) head epiphyses (approximately 12 years).

Chapter 9). This surface bears a centrally located raised region that is generally concave, more obviously raised at the plantar border and traversed from medial to lateral by a depression, which corresponds with a ridge on the metaphyseal surface of the metatarsal shaft (Fig. 11.30). This ridge-and-groove mechanism, together with the raised plantar border that locks into a depression on the metatarsal shaft, probably acts as a stop, to prevent both plantar and medial dislocation of the surfaces during locomotion.

Freiberg's infraction is characterized by an osteochondrosis of the second metatarsal head and tends to arise between 10 and 18 years of age. Females are three times more likely to be affected than males and the cause may be attributed to trauma, arterial insufficiency, developmental anomalies, or perhaps a combination of these, although the theory of avascular necrosis tends to be favoured in the clinical literature. In general, the metatarsal is shorter than normal and the head has collapsed (hence infraction) and in severe cases it may even be separate from the shaft.

The epiphyses of the **proximal phalanges** can generally be described as flattened discs that are convex and uneven on their distal surface and smooth and concave on their proximal surface. The hallucial epiphysis is obviously larger and more robust than any of its more lateral counterparts. The articular surface is deeply concave and wider in the transverse than in the dorsoplantar plane. The dorsal, medial and lateral border form an almost uniform disc, while the plantar border is raised into medial and lateral tubercles, with an intervening notch for the passage of the flexor hallucis longus tendon. Until approximately 6–8 years of age, the epiphysis of the proximal hallucial phalanx is disc-shaped and not readily recognizable. But as the epiphysis begins to conform to the shape of the diaphysis by about 7–10 years, its contours become more characteristic (Fig. 11.31a). Epiphyseal clefts or fragmentation are most commonly observed in the basal epiphysis of the proximal phalanx of the great toe. Although their aetiology is unknown, it is thought that they may only appear around the time of puberty and may not be related to multiple foci of ossification, as was originally considered. On a radiographic image, this epiphysis tends to be sclerotic in appearance, which is similar to that seen in the calcaneal epiphysis (see below) and considered to be a normal reaction to the stresses imposed on these structures. It is interesting to note that a sclerotic appearance does not occur in children who never walk.

The remainder of the proximal phalangeal epiphyses are fairly constant in appearance and tend to vary only in size. Assigning a particular epiphysis to a specific proximal phalanx can only be achieved with any degree of accuracy when only one individual is represented and the epiphyses have formed a true cap over the diaphysis to allow a best-fit scenario to be adopted. The proximal articular surface is smooth and concave and slightly wider in the transverse than in the dorsoplantar direction. The plantar margin is straight or slightly concave, while the dorsal margin is gently rounded. The distal (metaphyseal) surface is roughened with a central elevated region that displays at least one, and often two, tooth-like structures close to the region of the plantar notch. These distally directed prolongations probably act as a type of locking mechanism to increase the stability of the joint and so prevent dislocation during locomotion (Fig. 11.32). As with the shafts of the metatarsals, so the shafts of the proximal phalanges also display a deep recess on the plantar border to accommodate the projections from the epiphysis. This phenomenon probably equates with the radiological condition of 'cone-shaped epiphyses'. While this morphology may be more obvious in certain clinical conditions, the frequency of occurrence in normal developing feet, renders them more likely to have a

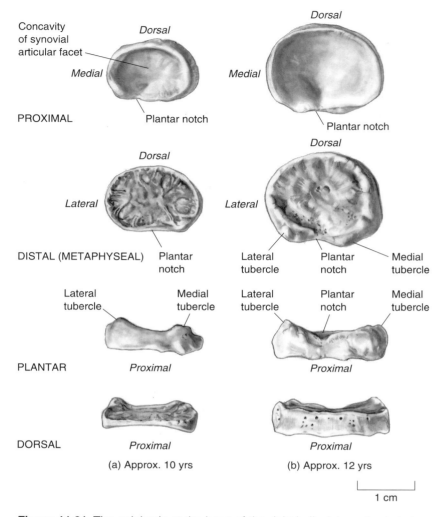

Concavity of synovial articular facet

Dorsal

Medial

PROXIMAL

Plantar notch

Dorsal

Medial

Plantar notch

Dorsal

Lateral

DISTAL (METAPHYSEAL)

Plantar notch

Dorsal

Lateral

Lateral tubercle

Plantar notch

Medial tubercle

Lateral tubercle

Medial tubercle

PLANTAR

Proximal

Lateral tubercle

Plantar notch

Medial tubercle

Proximal

DORSAL

Proximal

Proximal

(a) Approx. 10 yrs

(b) Approx. 12 yrs

1 cm

Figure 11.31 The epiphysis at the base of the right hallucial proximal phalanx.

functional, rather than a pathological, aetiology. So-called conic epiphyses have also been likened in appearance to the indentation on the base of a wine bottle and are reported to be more common in females and fuse at an earlier age than non-conic epiphyses. Interestingly, a similar formation has been described in both the reptilian and avian literature where a long cone or peg of cartilage is described that projects from the epiphysis into the diaphysis. While de Iturriza and Tanner (1969) admit that the aetiology of cone epiphyses is unknown, they do suggest that it may be related to circulation during fetal life. If not circulatory, then they also suggest that it may be related to some tissue metabolic gradient resulting in a difference in cell proliferation and maturation between central and peripheral parts of the epiphysis.

The epiphyses of the **middle phalanges** are often very difficult to identify and assign to a specific digit. These are disc-like structures with a biconcave facet located proximally for articulation with the head of the proximal phalanx (Fig. 11.33a). The two facets are separated by a weak ridge that runs from the plantar to the dorsal rim of the surface. The plantar border is indented to accommodate the passage of the long flexor tendon and the dorsal border is

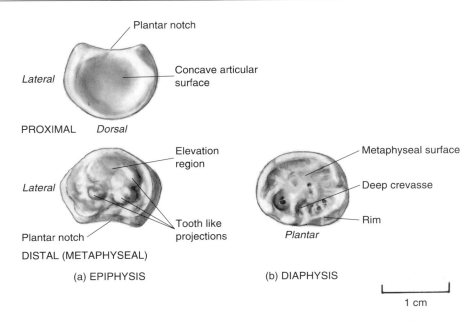

Figure 11.32 The right proximal phalangeal epiphysis (approximately 7 years).

gently rounded. The epiphysis is essentially oval in outline, being longer in its transverse than in its dorsoplantar plane.

The epiphyses of the **distal phalanges** are equally difficult to identify and assign to a specific digit, with the obvious exception of the first digit. The epiphysis of the hallucial distal phalanx is larger and more robust than any of its more lateral counterparts. The concave proximal synovial surface is considerably wider in its transverse than in its dorsoplantar plane, with a wide plantar notch and a gently rounded dorsal border (Fig. 11.34). The medial aspect of the epiphysis is considerably larger than the lateral aspect, presumably due to the influence of the attachment of the flexor hallucis longus tendon. The remainder of the distal phalangeal epiphyses can best be described as small, oval discs (Fig. 11.33b). The proximal synovial articular surfaces are concave, both from plantar to dorsal and medial to lateral. Given the size and unpredictability of these epiphyses, we have not been able to assign an epiphysis to a specific distal phalangeal diaphysis with any degree of reliability.

The epiphysis for the **base of the first metatarsal** is sufficiently different from all the other pedal epiphyses to merit a separate description (Fig. 11.35).

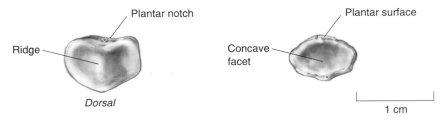

Figure 11.33 The right middle and distal phalangeal epiphyses.

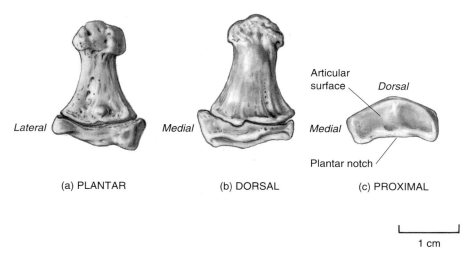

Lateral *Medial* Articular surface *Dorsal* *Medial* Plantar notch

(a) PLANTAR   (b) DORSAL   (c) PROXIMAL

1 cm

Figure 11.34 The right distal hallucial phalanx (approximately 10 years).

It is well developed and recognizable by 6–7 years of age. At this age the proximal articular surface is oval in shape and slightly thicker at the plantar margin. The lateral border is straighter than the more rounded medial border and there is a suggestion of a constriction separating the plantar from the dorsal articular area. By 8 years of age, the readily recognizable form of the epiphysis has developed with its characteristic reniform shape. By approximately 10 years of age, the articular margins of the epiphysis have become clearly defined and the site of attachment of the peroneus longus muscle is identifiable. By approximately 12 years of age, the epiphysis has adopted close to adult morphology and it is interesting to note that a deep crater can be detected in the central region of the distal metaphyseal surface of the epiphysis. This corresponds in position with a centrally located raised mound on the

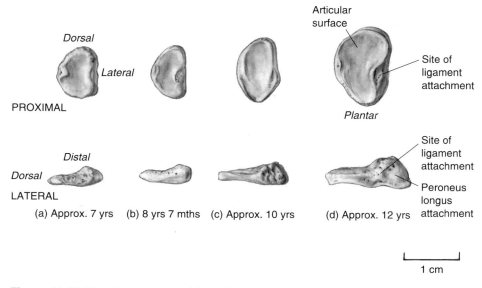

Dorsal *Lateral* PROXIMAL

Articular surface

Site of ligament attachment

Plantar

Dorsal *Distal* LATERAL

Site of ligament attachment

Peroneus longus attachment

(a) Approx. 7 yrs   (b) 8 yrs 7 mths   (c) Approx. 10 yrs   (d) Approx. 12 yrs

1 cm

Figure 11.35 The development of the epiphysis of the base of the right first metatarsal.

metaphyseal surface of the diaphysis and it is likely that they act as a mortice to lock the two developing centres together and prevent movement under the immense forces imposed by locomotion (Fig. 11.36).

So called **'pseudo-epiphyses'** (Fig. 11.37) are commonly reported at the distal end of the first metatarsal. As with those seen in the metacarpals, they tend to appear as notches or clefts in the normally non-epiphyseal end of the bone. While true epiphyses have been reported in this location (Posener *et al.*, 1939), these phenomena generally represent a normal stage in the physeal invasion of the primary centre into the region of the head of the metatarsal and normally appear between the ages of 4 and 5 years (Ogden *et al.*, 1994). For a discussion on pseudoepiphyses see the relevant section in Chapter 9.

While there is no controversy over the fact that the calcaneus is associated with a true secondary centre of ossification, most anatomical texts state that it is the exception within the tarsal bones. However, there is a considerable volume of evidence that shows that epiphyses may also be associated with the talus, navicular and the fifth metatarsal.

The epiphysis of the **calcaneus** is considered to be a traction epiphysis associated with the attachment of the tendo calcaneus and has, confusingly, been likened to the pisiform of the hand. Ossification commences in this epiphysis via multiple centres, which appear between 5 and 6 years in girls and 7 and 8 years in boys, although it has been reported as early as 4 years in girls and as late as 10 years in boys. The centres usually appear below the middle of the posterior border of the calcaneus and spread both proximally and distally until they finally unite to form a cap-like covering around 8 years in girls and 10 years in boys. This cap initially covers the lower two-thirds of the posterior aspect of the calcaneus, while the upper third will form either from a plate-like projection of this epiphysis or from a separate centre. This accessory epiphysis may commence ossification between 10 and 12 years in girls and 11 and 14

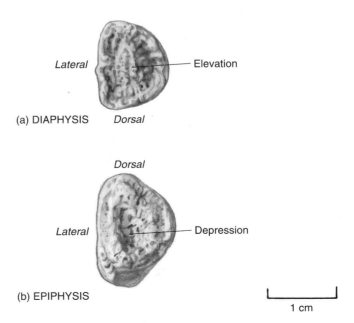

Lateral — Elevation

(a) DIAPHYSIS   Dorsal

Dorsal

Lateral — Depression

(b) EPIPHYSIS

1 cm

Figure 11.36 The metaphyseal surfaces of the diaphysis and epiphysis of the right first metatarsal (approximately 12 years).

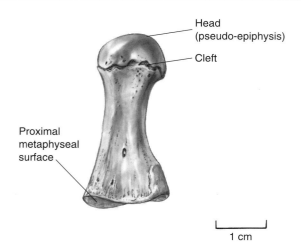

Head
(pseudo-epiphysis)

Cleft

Proximal
metaphyseal
surface

1 cm

Figure 11.37 Pseudo-epiphysis at the distal end of the right first metatarsal – female aged 8 years 7 months.

years in boys. Fusion may occur directly with the body of the calcaneus or inferiorly with the superior border of the principal calcaneal epiphysis.

Painful heels are a relatively common complaint in children between the ages of 9 and 12, especially if they are involved in athletic pursuits. This condition was previously misinterpreted as avascular necrosis of the calcaneal epiphysis or so-called 'Sever's disease' (comparable to Osgood–Schlatter's disease), but is now recognized as stress fractures in the epiphysis following repeated pounding activities. When viewed on a radiograph, the calcaneal epiphysis normally appears denser than the body of the calcaneus and this is recognized as normal and is not attributed to any pathological condition.

It is unlikely that the calcaneal epiphyses could be identified in isolation prior to 8 years in girls and 10 years in boys. Certainly by 10 years of age, the epiphysis has formed a well-defined cap that sits over the lower two-thirds of the posterior surface of the calcaneal metaphysis and may extend down into the region of the lateral tubercle (Fig. 11.38). The epiphysis is convex on its posterior aspect, concave on its metaphyseal surface, thicker in the lower plantar region and more scale-like in its upper extension.

The epiphysis of the **talus** is unlikely to be identified successfully as a separate structure owing to its small size, and indeed it may not always be present. The fact that this structure does exist is borne out by two facts. First, an active metaphyseal surface can be identified on many specimens (Fig. 11.39a) and second, if the structure persists then it becomes known as the os trigonum, which is a well-recognized accessory bone with an incidence of approximately 5% in the general population. When present, this epiphysis is located on the posterior aspect of the talus, in the region of the lateral tubercle. Ossification commences around 8 years in girls and 11 years in boys and fuses within a year or so of appearance. Persistence of the os trigonum can give rise to pain during activities that involve forced plantar flexion (ballet dancers, javelin throwers, footballers, etc.). This os trigonum syndrome or posterior triangle pain can often only be alleviated by removal of the offending ossicle.

The presence of an epiphysis in the **navicular** is more contentious. The region of the tuberosity of the navicular may show evidence of metaphyseal activity (Fig. 11.39b). This is the site of attachment of the tibialis posterior

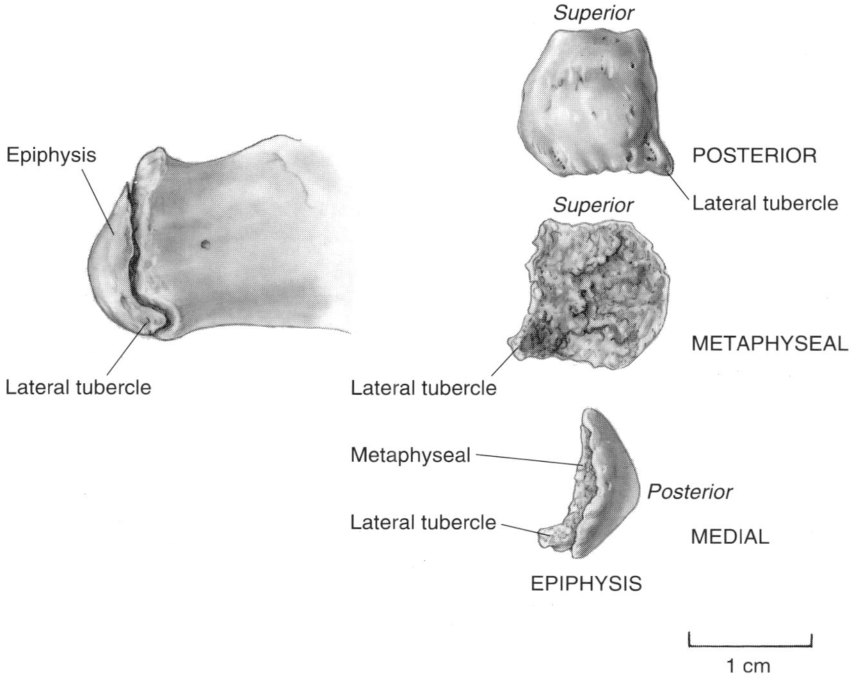

Figure 11.38 The right calcaneal epiphysis (approximately 10 years).

tendon and in approximately 5–10% of the general population it may remain as a separate accessory ossicle (os tibiale externum or prehallux). Persistence of a separate bone usually leads to inflammation of the overlying skin due to shoe pressure and excision is the normal course of action, although care must be taken not to damage the tibialis posterior tendon. The epiphysis is said to commence ossification around 9–10 years in girls and 12–13 years in boys, with fusion occurring shortly thereafter.

The presence of an epiphysis for the tubercle at the base of the **fifth metatarsal** is even more contentious than that for the navicular and is not synonymous with either the os peroneum (a sesamoid in the tendon of peroneus longus) or the os Vesalii. The epiphysis is said to commence ossification around 9–10 years in girls and 12 years in boys and fuses within the next 24 months. It is unlikely that the epiphysis could ever be identified in isolation (Fig. 11.39c).

Fusion

It is not surprising that the order of appearance of the secondary centres of ossification does not mirror their order of fusion to the primary centre. While Birkner (1978) claimed that fusion occurs in a distoproximal sequence, commencing with the fusion of the epiphyses of the distal phalanges and ending with the closure of the metatarsal heads, this is perhaps too simplistic. It is probably true that fusion first commences in the distal phalanges, followed very closely by the middle phalanges, and this occurs between 11 and 12 years of age in females and between 14 and 15 years in males. The heads of metatarsals 2–5 fuse to the diaphyses between 11 and 13 years in females and 14 and 16 years in males, while the proximal phalanges and the base of the first metatarsal are a little later at 13–15 years in females and 16–18 years in males. With the exception of the calcaneal epiphysis, it has been reported that 75% of all females will

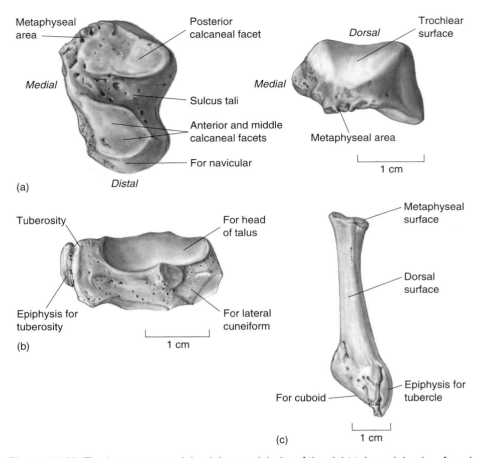

Figure 11.39 The inconstant pedal epiphyses: (a) site of the right talar epiphysis – female aged 8 years 7 months; (b) right navicular epiphysis – female aged 12 years; (c) right fifth metatarsal epiphysis – approximately 10 years.

have completed epiphyseal fusion by 15 years of age and 75% of all males by 17 years of age. It is probably safe to say that epiphyseal fusion is usually always completed by 16 years in females and 18 years in males.

Fusion of the calcaneal epiphysis occurs between 12 and 15 years, but obliteration of the diaphyseo-epiphyseal junction will not be completed until 15–16 years in females and 18–20 years in males. Fusion generally commences in the region of the lateral tubercle, while the final area to close is usually across the margin of the upper border (Fig. 11.40).

The appearance and fusion times of the centres of ossification for the foot are summarized in Figure 11.41.

Growth of the foot

A sound understanding of growth of the foot as a whole is of considerable clinical importance. The length of the fetal foot has been used to predict gestational age and has also been of some value in neonatal anthropology in the study of congenital abnormalities and even to monitor neonates at risk. It is

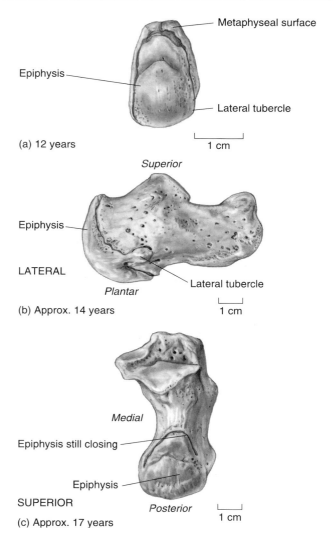

(a) 12 years

(b) Approx. 14 years

(c) Approx. 17 years

Figure 11.40 Fusion of the right calcaneal epiphysis: (a) dorsal surface – female aged 12 years; (b) lateral surface (approximately 14 years); (c) superior surface – adolescent (approximately 17 years).

vital that due consideration be given to the longitudinal growth of the foot prior to pediatric pedal surgery. In fact, the relative growth of different parts of the foot has also been interpreted in terms of its evolutionary significance.

The developing foot is strongly inverted by 2 prenatal months and gradual eversion will occur over the next 7 months, although the foot will remain in an inverted talipes varus position at birth. The neonate has a considerable degree of dorsiflexion at the ankle joint but plantar flexion is limited due to the shortness of the extensor muscles (Crelin, 1973). The foot of the newborn is long and thin in appearance, with no external evidence of longitudinal arches. The average length of the neonatal foot is approximately 8 cm, which is in fact longer than the average length of either the femur or the tibia at this stage. At birth, the foot is approximately 34% of its final adult size. By approximately 1 year of age in females and 1.5 years in males the foot has reached half of its

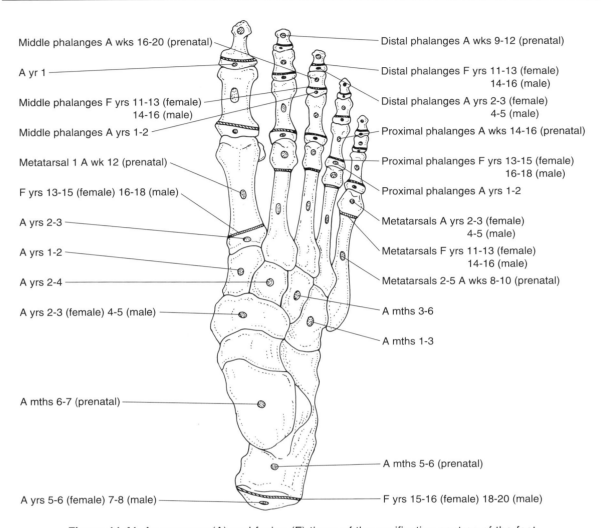

Middle phalanges A wks 16-20 (prenatal)

A yr 1

Middle phalanges F yrs 11-13 (female)
14-16 (male)

Middle phalanges A yrs 1-2

Metatarsal 1 A wk 12 (prenatal)

F yrs 13-15 (female) 16-18 (male)

A yrs 2-3

A yrs 1-2

A yrs 2-4

A yrs 2-3 (female) 4-5 (male)

A mths 6-7 (prenatal)

A yrs 5-6 (female) 7-8 (male)

Distal phalanges A wks 9-12 (prenatal)

Distal phalanges F yrs 11-13 (female)
14-16 (male)

Distal phalanges A yrs 2-3 (female)
4-5 (male)

Proximal phalanges A wks 14-16 (prenatal)

Proximal phalanges F yrs 13-15 (female)
16-18 (male)

Proximal phalanges A yrs 1-2

Metatarsals A yrs 2-3 (female)
4-5 (male)

Metatarsals F yrs 11-13 (female)
14-16 (male)

Metatarsals 2-5 A wks 8-10 (prenatal)

A mths 3-6

A mths 1-3

A mths 5-6 (prenatal)

F yrs 15-16 (female) 18-20 (male)

Figure 11.41 Appearance (A) and fusion (F) times of the ossification centres of the foot.

mature length and by 2 years of age the longitudinal arches have descended to reach the adult form. This precocious development of the foot tends to protect it from future insults (whether they be nutritional, mechanical, metabolic, etc.), so that even if growth in stature is interrupted, there is little effect on foot size. There is a sharp decrease in the rate of growth of the foot from infancy to 5 years of age and from 5–12 years in females and 5–14 years in males there is an increase of only 0.9 cm per year in foot length. The rate of growth decreases rapidly after 12 years in females and 14 years in males, so that 95% of mature length is achieved by 12–13 years in females and 15 years in males. Mature length is generally achieved by 14 years in females and 16 years in males, which naturally coincides with the cessation of epiphyseal growth. There is a small adolescent growth spurt in foot length, which tends to start and finish earlier than that seen either in stature or overall length of the lower limb and precedes normal peak growth spurt by approximately 6–18 months.

Practical notes

Sideing of juvenile foot bones

The bones of the foot tend to mature at an earlier age than their counterparts in the hand and so positive identification can occur at an earlier age (certainly by 6 years).

Tarsals

It is possible to correctly side the neonatal **calcaneus**, although it is much easier to do so by the end of the first year. At birth, the indentation that will form the calcaneal groove is located on the distal aspect of the superior surface and the larger of the two flattened regions is located on the medial aspect of the plantar surface. Within the first few months after birth, the medial projection of the sustentaculum tali begins to form and so the identification of side is apparent.

The **talus** can also be identified and assigned to the correct side of the body by full term, if not slightly before. The position of the talar neck is established early in fetal development and can be seen as depressions on both the dorsal and plantar surfaces that are situated closer to the distal extremity. These two indentations are separated on the lateral aspect by a clearly defined ridge of bone, while on the medial aspect they are separated by a considerable expanse of bone with no distinguishing characteristics.

Although the **navicular** can probably be recognized at around 5 years of age, assigning the specimen to the correct side of the body probably cannot be achieved until closer to 7 or 8 years of age, when the site of the tuberosity can be established. The concavity of the proximal talar surface and the convexity of the distal cuneiform surface are established at an early age, but until the tuberosity develops on the plantomedial aspect of the bone, orientation is extremely difficult.

The **medial cuneiform** is recognizable at 3–4 years of age and can also be assigned to the correct side at this age. It is represented by a thick, rounded plantomedial area and a thin, pointed dorsolateral projection with a relatively flat dorsal surface and a slightly concave plantar surface. The articular region is larger on the distal surface than that on the proximal for articulation with the navicular.

The **intermediate cuneiform** can be readily identified in isolation by around 6 years of age, when it can also be correctly attributed to a specific side of the body. The dorsal surface is flat, the plantar surface is represented by a blunt ridge and the distal surface is generally longer than the proximal. The lateral aspect bears an articulation for the lateral cuneiform along the distal and proximal margins, while the medial aspect bears an articulation for the medial cuneiform that runs almost the entire length of both the dorsal and proximal margins.

The **lateral cuneiform** is recognizable in isolation by around 4 years and at this stage it can successfully be attributed to the correct side of the body. The dorsal surface is flat and the plantar surface ends in a blunt ridge. The medial surface displays a flattened area of subperiosteal bone, with an articulation for the intermediate cuneiform lying proximal to it. The lateral surface bears a rounded articular facet for the cuboid, which is located on the proximal margin of this surface closer to the dorsal surface. This is important to identify, as often it is very difficult to differentiate between the distal articular surface for the third metatarsal and the proximal articulation with the navicular.

The **cuboid** can be identified in isolation and assigned to the correct side by approximately 3–4 years of age, when the nodule starts to develop some of the mature characteristics of the bone. The groove caused by the tendon of peroneus longus can be recognized on the plantar surface, while the dorsal aspect is flattened and clearly non-articular. The distal surface is flat and relatively short compared to the longer and more concave proximal aspect. The lateral border is short with no distinguishing characteristics, while the medial border is longer and bears a well-defined articular facet for the lateral cuneiform.

Metatarsals

Until the metatarsals begin to adopt the adult form of articulations at their bases, it is very difficult to correctly identify both side and specific digit to all except the first. Even at the neonatal stage, the first metatarsal can be separated from all others due to its size and robusticity. The dorsal surface of the shaft is relatively flat, while the plantar surface displays a gentle concavity along its length. The base of the shaft is convex along its medial border and concave along its lateral border. The medial aspect of the head is generally larger than the lateral. The heads of the metatarsals are very difficult to assign to the correct side of the body and can probably only be achieved with any degree of reliability in the second and fifth bones at around 4–5 years of age. The second metatarsal head displays a prominent tubercle at the junction of the plantar and lateral surfaces, while that of the fifth is distinctly skewed towards the medial surface. The epiphysis at the base of the first metatarsal is well developed by 6 years of age and can be readily assigned to a specific side of the body. The medial border tends to be straighter than the lateral border, which displays a slight constriction around the middle of its length. Due to the site of attachment of the peroneus longus tendon on the plantar aspect of the base, this region of the epiphysis tends to be thicker than the dorsal aspect.

Phalanges

Other than the components of the first digit, we have been unable to assign a phalanx to a specific digital ray (let alone side of the body) in the adult, and so it seems a vain hope to attempt to do so in the juvenile. The proximal phalanx of the big toe can be easily attributed to the correct side, as the medial border is always longer than the lateral border. The same is true for the terminal phalanx of this digit and reflects the normal hallux deviation that is present from an early age (Griffiths, 1902).

The only other epiphysis that can be attributed to the correct side of the body is that for the distal hallucial phalanx. Correct sideing relies on being able to identify a relatively larger tubercle on the medial aspect of the epiphysis than occurs on the lateral aspect.

Bones of a similar morphology

Whilst it is true that before 3–4 years of age several tarsals could be mistaken for many developing bones as they appear as relatively undifferentiated nodules, beyond this age, each develops its own characteristic morphology so that close attention to detail should prevent misidentification.

The similarities between the metatarsals and the metacarpals and the manual and pedal phalanges ensure that they are the bones that are most likely to be incorrectly identified. Metatarsals are usually longer than metacarpals, with straighter shafts that are compressed in the mediolateral direction. In addition, the heads of the metatarsals are also compressed in the mediolateral plane. Further, the heads of the metatarsals are relatively smaller compared to their bases than is found in the metacarpals and obviously the arrangement of articular facets on the base will differ from those found in the hand bones. The pedal phalanges are consistently shorter and more slender than those found in the hand and their morphology can be quite irregular. The proximal pedal phalanges have relatively large bases and heads but slender, mediolaterally compressed shafts, whereas those of the hand tend to be longer and more robust. The middle and distal pedal phalanges are very short and have shafts that are concave on both the dorsal and the plantar surfaces, whereas those of the hand are longer and convex on the posterior surface. The distal pedal phalanges tend to have more pronounced ungual tuberosities than the manual distal phalanges, to support the end of the digit.

Morphological summary (Fig. 11.41)

Prenatal

8–10 wks	Primary ossification centres appear for metatarsals 2–5
9–12 wks	Primary ossification centres appear for distal phalanges
12 wks	Primary ossification centre appears for metatarsal 1
14–16 wks	Primary ossification centres appear for proximal phalanges
16–20 wks	Primary ossification centres appear for middle phalanges
5–6 mths	Ossification centre appears for calcaneus
6–7 mths	Ossification centre appears for talus

Birth	At least 16 of the primary centres of ossification for the long bones of the foot are present (middle phalanges of the lateral toes may appear after birth). In addition, both the calcaneus and talus are present and can be identified in isolation (cuboid centre of ossification may be present)
1–3 mths	Ossification centre appears for cuboid
3–6 mths	Ossification centre appears for lateral cuneiform
9 mths (♀) 14 mths (♂)	Epiphysis for base of distal phalanx 1 appears
11–14 mths (♀) 14–24 mths (♂)	Epiphyses for middle phalanges 2–4 appear
11–20 mths (♀) 18–28 mths (♂)	Epiphyses for proximal phalanges appear
12–24 mths (♀) 24–36 mths (♂)	Ossification centre appears for medial cuneiform
18–20 mths (♀) 26–31 mths (♂)	Epiphysis for base of metatarsal 1 appears
19–24 mths (♀) 27–34 mths (♂)	Epiphysis for head of metatarsal 2 appears
24–36 mths (♀) 36–48 mths (♂)	Ossification centre appears for intermediate cuneiform
2 yrs 5mths (♀) 3 yrs 5mths (♂)	Epiphysis for head of metatarsal 3 appears
2 yrs 8 mths (♀) 4 yrs (♂)	Epiphysis for head of metatarsal 4 appears
2–3 yrs (♀) 4–5 yrs (♂)	Ossification centre appears for navicular as do epiphyses for distal phalanges 2–4 and epiphysis for head of metatarsal 5
3–5 yrs (♀) 5–7 yrs (♂)	By this stage, the cuboid, navicular, cuneiforms and metatarsal heads are all identifiable in isolation
5–6 yrs (♀) 7–8 yrs (♂)	Epiphysis for calcaneus appears
8 yrs (♀) 11 yrs (♂)	Epiphysis for talus appears
9 yrs (♀) 12 yrs (♂)	Sesamoids of great toe appear and fusion of talar epiphysis occurs
9–10 yrs (♀) 12–13 yrs (♂)	Epiphysis for navicular may appear (and fuse shortly after)
	Epiphysis at base of metatarsal 5 may appear and will also fuse within the next 24 months
10–12 yrs (♀) 11–14 yrs (♂)	Calcaneal epiphysis commences fusion

11—13 yrs (♀) 14—16 yrs (♂)	Epiphyseal fusion in distal phalanges, middle phalanges and metatarsal heads 2—5
13—15 yrs (♀) 16—18 yrs (♂)	Epiphyseal fusion in proximal phalanges and base of metatarsal 1
15—16 yrs (♀) 18—20 yrs (♂)	Completion of fusion at the calcaneal epiphysis

Bibliography

Acheson, R.M. (1954). A method of assessing skeletal maturity from radiographs: a report from the Oxford Child Health Survey. *Journal of Anatomy* **88**: 498–508.

Acheson, R.M. (1957). The Oxford method of assessing skeletal maturity. *Clinical Orthopaedics and Related Research* **10**: 19–39.

Acheson, R.M. and Archer, M. (1959). Radiological studies of the growth of the pituitary fossa in man. *Journal of Anatomy* **93**: 52–67.

Acheson, R.M. and Hewitt, D. (1954). Oxford Child Health Survey. Stature and skeletal maturation in the pre-school child. *British Journal of Preventive and Social Medicine* **8**: 59–65.

Acsádi G. and Nemeskéri, J. (1970). *History of Human Life Span and Mortality*. Budapest: Akadémiai Kiadó.

Adair, F.L. (1918). The ossification centers of the fetal pelvis. *American Journal of Obstetrics and Diseases of Women and Children* **78**: 175–199.

Adair, F.L. and Scammon, R.E. (1927). Observations on the parietal fontanelle in the newborn and in young infants. *American Journal of Obstetrics and Gynecology* **14**: 149–159.

Adams, J.L. (1934). The supracondyloid variation in the human embryo. *Anatomical Record* **59**: 315–333.

Adams, J.C. and Hamblen, D.L. (1992). *An Outline of Fractures*, 10th edition. Edinburgh: Churchill Livingstone.

Adson, A.W. and Coffey, J.R. (1927). Cervical rib. *Annals of Surgery* **85**: 839–857.

Agarwal, S.K., Malhotra, V.K. and Tewari, S.P. (1979). Incidence of metopic suture in adult Indian crania. *Acta Anatomica* **105**: 469–474.

Ahlqvist, J. and Damsten, O. (1969). A modification of Kerley's method for the microscopic determination of age in human bone. *Journal of Forensic Sciences* **14**: 205–212.

Aiello, L. and Dean, C. (1990). *An Introduction to Human Evolutionary Anatomy*. London: Academic Press.

Aiello, L.C. and Molleson, T. (1993). Are microscopic ageing techniques more accurate that macroscopic ageing techniques? *Journal of Archaeological Science* **20**: 689–704.

Aitken, D.M. (1905). A note on the variations of the tibia and astragalus. *Journal of Anatomy and Physiology* **39**: 489–491.

Ajmani, M.L., Mittal, R.K. and Jain, S.P. (1983). Incidence of metopic suture in adult Nigerian skulls. *Journal of Anatomy* **137**: 177–183.

Akisaka, T., Nakayama, M., Yoshida, H. and Inoue, M. (1998). Ultrastructural modifications of the extracellular matrix upon calcification of growth plate cartilage as revealed by quick-freeze deep etching technique. *Calcified Tissue International* **63**: 47–56.

Albert, A.M. and Maples, W.R. (1995). Stages of epiphyseal union for thoracic and lumbar vertebral centra as a method of age determination for teenage and young adult skeletons. *Journal of Forensic Sciences* **40**: 623–633.

Albinus, B.S. (1737). *Icones ossium foetus humani*. Leidae Batavorum.

Alexander, C. (1965). The aetiology of primary protrusio acetabuli. *British Journal of Radiology* **38**: 567−580.

Ali, S.Y. and Evans, L. (1973). The uptake of [^{45}Ca] calcium ions by matrix vesicles isolated from calcifying cartilage. *Biochemistry Journal* **134**: 647−650.

Alley, R.G. (1936). Enlarged parietal foramina. *Radiology* **27**: 233−235.

Altmann, F. (1955). Congenital atresia of the ear in man and animals. *Annals of Otology, Rhinology and Laryngology* **64**: 824−858.

Alvesalo, L. (1997). Sex chromosomes and human growth. A dental approach. *Human Genetics* **101**: 1−5.

Amprino, R. (1948). A contribution to the functional meaning of the substitution of primary by secondary bone tissue. *Acta Anatomica* **5**: 291−300.

Amprino, R. (1984). The development of the vertebrate limb. *Clinical Orthopaedics and Related Research* **188**: 263−284.

Andersen, H. (1962). Histochemical studies of the development of the human hip joint. *Acta Anatomica* **48**: 258−292.

Andersen, H. (1963). Histochemistry and development of the human shoulder and acromio-clavicular joints with particular reference to the early development of the clavicle. *Acta Anatomica* **55**: 124−165.

Anderson, D.L. and Popovich, F. (1981). Association of relatively delayed emergence of mandibular molars with molar reduction and molar position. *American Journal of Physical Anthropology* **54**: 369−376.

Anderson, D.L., Anderson, G.W. and Popovich, F. (1976). Age of attainment of mineralization stages of the permanent dentition. *Journal of Forensic Sciences* **21**: 191−200.

Anderson, H.C. (1969). Vesicles associated with calcification in the matrix of epiphyseal cartilage. *Journal of Cell Biology* **41**: 59−72.

Anderson, H.C. (1990). The role of cells versus matrix in bone induction. *Connective Tissue Research* **24**: 3−12.

Anderson, H.C. and Morris, D.C. (1993). Mineralization. In: *Physiology and Pharmacology of Bone* (G.R. Mundy and T.J. Martin, Eds), pp. 267−298. Berlin: Springer.

Anderson, J.E. (1960). The development of the tympanic plate. *National Museum of Canada Bulletin* **180**: 143−153.

Anderson, M., Green, W.T. and Messner, M.B. (1963). Growth and the predictions of growth in the lower extremities. *Journal of Bone and Joint Surgery* **45A**: 1−14.

Anderson, M., Messner, M.B. and Green, W.T. (1964). Distribution of lengths of the normal femur and tibia from one to eighteen years of age. *Journal of Bone and Joint Surgery* **46A**: 1197−1202.

Anderson, T. (1988). A medieval hypoplastic dens: a note on its discovery and a review of the previous literature. *Ossa* **13**: 13−37.

Anderson, T. (1995). An anomalous medieval parietal bone. *Journal of Paleopathology* **7**: 223−226.

Anderson, T. (1996). Paracondylar process: manifestation of an occipital vertebra. *International Journal of Osteoarchaeology* **6**: 195−201.

Anderson, T. and Carter, A.R. (1994). Periosteal reaction in a new born child from Sheppey, Kent. *International Journal of Osteoarchaeology* **4**: 47−48.

Ankarath, S., Ng, A.B.Y., Giannoudis, P.V. and Scott, B.W. (2002). Delay in the diagnosis of slipped upper femoral epiphysis. *Journal of the Royal Society of Medicine* **95**: 356−358.

Anson, B.J., Bast, T.H. and Cauldwell, E.W. (1948). The development of the auditory ossicles, the otic capsule and the extracapsular tissues. *Annals of Otology, Rhinology and Laryngology* **57**: 603−632.

Anson, B.J., Bast, T.H. and Richany, S.F. (1955). The fetal and early postnatal development of the tympanic ring and related structures in man. *Annals of Otology, Rhinology and Laryngology* **64**: 802−822.

Anson, B.J., Hanson, J.S. and Richany, S.F. (1960). Early embryology of the auditory ossicles and associated structures in relation to certain anomalies observed clinically. *Annals of Otology, Rhinology and Laryngology* **69**: 427−447.

Anson, B.J., Harper, D.G. and Warpeha, R.L. (1963). Surgical anatomy of the facial canal and facial nerve. *Annals of Otology, Rhinology and Laryngology* **72**: 713−734.

Antonov, A.N. (1947). Children born during the siege of Leningrad in 1942. *Journal of Pediatrics* **30**: 250−259.

Aoki, J., Yamamoto, I., Hino, M., Kitamura, N., Sone, T., Itoh, H. and Torizuka, K. (1987). Reactive endosteal bone formation. *Skeletal Radiology* **16**: 545−551.

Applbaum, Y., Gerard, P. and Bry, K.D. (1983). Elongation of the anterior tubercle of a cervical vertebral transverse process: an unusual variant. *Skeletal Radiology* **10**: 265−267.

Arey, L.B. (1950). The craniopharyngeal canal reviewed and reinterpreted. *Anatomical Record* **106**: 1−16.

Ars, B. (1989). Organogenesis of the middle ear structures. *Journal of Laryngology and Otology* **103**: 16−21.

Arsenault, A.L. (1989). A comparative electron microscopic study of apatite crystals in collagen fibrils of rat bone, dentin and calcified turkey leg tendons. *Bone and Mineral* **6**: 165−177.

Ascenzi, A. and Bonucci, E. (1967). The tensile properties of single osteons. *Anatomical Record* **158**: 375−386.

Ash, M. and Nelson, S.J. (2003). *Wheeler's Dental Anatomy, Physiology and Occlusion*. 8th edition. Philadelphia, PA: W.B. Saunders.

Ashley, G.T. (1956a). The relationship between the pattern of ossification and the definitive shape of the mesosternum in man. *Journal of Anatomy* **90**: 87−105.

Ashley, G.T. (1956b). A comparison of human and anthropoid mesosterna. *American Journal of Physical Anthropology* **14**: 449−462.

Ashley-Montagu, M.F. (1935). The premaxilla in primates. *Quarterly Review of Biology* **10**: 32−59, 181−208.

Ashley-Montagu, M.F. (1937). The medio-frontal suture and the problem of metopism in the primates. *Journal of the Royal Anthropological Institute of Great Britain and Ireland* **67**: 157−201.

Ashley-Montagu, M.F. (1940). Medio-palatine bones. *American Journal of Physical Anthropology* **27**: 139−150.

Atchley, W.R. and Hall, B.K. (1991). A model for development and evolution of complex morphological structures. *Biological Reviews* **66**: 101−157.

Aubin, J.E., Lemieux, M., Tremblay, M., Behringer, R.R. and Jeannotte, L. (1998). Transcriptional interferences at the Hoxa 4/Hoxa 5 locus: importance of correct Hoxa 5 expression for the proper specification of the axial skeleton. *Developmental Dynamics* **212**: 141−156.

Aufderheide, A.C. and Rodriguez-Martin, C. (1998). *The Cambridge Encyclopedia of Human Paleopathology*. Cambridge: Cambridge University Press.

Augier, M. (1931). Squelette céphalique. In: *Traité d'Anatomie Humaine* (P. Poirier and A. Charpy, Eds). Paris: Masson.

Bach-Petersen, S. and Kjær, I. (1993). Ossification of lateral components in the human prenatal cranial base. *Journal of Craniofacial Genetics and Developmental Biology* **13**: 76−82.

Bagnall, K.M., Harris, P.F. and Jones, P.R.M. (1977a). A radiographic study of the human fetal spine. 1. The development of the secondary cervical curvature. *Journal of Anatomy* **123**: 777−782.

Bagnall, K.M., Harris, P.F. and Jones, P.R.M. (1977b). A radiographic study of the human fetal spine. 2. The sequence of development of ossification centres in the vertebral column. *Journal of Anatomy* **124**: 791−802.

Bagnall, K.M., Harris, P.F. and Jones, P.R.M. (1982). Radiographic study of the longitudinal growth of primary ossification centers in limb long bones of the human fetus. *Anatomical Record* **203**: 293−299.

Bagnall, K.M., Higgins, S.J. and Saunders, E.J. (1988). The contribution made by a single somite to the vertebral column; resegmentation using the chick-quail chimera model. *Development* **103**: 69–85.

Balthazard, V. and Dervieux. (1921). Études anthropologiques sur le foetus humain. *Annales de Médicine Legales* **1**: 37–42.

Barclay-Smith, E. (1909). Two cases of Wormian bones in the bregmatic fontanelle. *Journal of Anatomy and Physiology* **44**: 312–314.

Bardeen, C.R. (1905). Studies on the development of the human skeleton. *American Journal of Anatomy* **4**: 265–302.

Bardeen, C.R. and Lewis, W.H. (1901). The development of the limbs, body-wall and back in man. *American Journal of Anatomy* **1**: 1–36.

Bareggi, R., Grill, V., Sandrucci, M.A., Baldini, G., DePol, A., Forabosco, A. and Narducci, P. (1993). Developmental pathways of vertebral centra and neural arches in human embryos and fetuses. *Anatomy and Embryology* **187**: 139–144.

Bareggi, R., Grill, V., Zweyer, M., Sandrucci, M.A., Narducci, P. and Forabosco, A. (1994a). The growth of long bones in human embryological and fetal upper limbs and its relationship to other developmental patterns. *Anatomy and Embryology* **189**: 19–24.

Bareggi, R., Grill, V., Zweyer, M., Narducci, P. and Forabosco, A. (1994b). A quantitative study on the spatial and temporal ossification patterns of vertebral centra and neural arches and their relationship to the fetal age. *Annals of Anatomy* **176**: 311–317.

Bareggi, R., Grill, V., Zweyer, M., Sandrucci, M.A., Martelli, A.M., Narducci, P. and Forabosco, A. (1996). On the assessment of the growth patterns in human fetal limbs: longitudinal measurements and allometric analysis. *Early Human Development* **45**: 11–25.

Barker, D.J.P., Osmond, C., Simmonds, S.J. and Wield, G.A. (1993). The relation of small head circumference and thinness at birth to death from cardiovascular disease in adult life. *British Medical Journal* **306**: 422–426.

Barnes, E. (1994). *Developmental Defects of the Axial Skeleton in Palaeopathology.* Colorado: University Press of Colorado.

Barrett, M.J., Brown, T. and Cellier, K.M. (1964). Tooth eruption sequence in a tribe of central Australian Aborigines. *American Journal of Physical Anthropology* **22**: 79–89.

Barson, A.J. (1970). The vertebral level of termination of the spinal cord during normal and abnormal development. *Journal of Anatomy* **106**: 489–497.

Bassoe, E. and Bassoe, H.H. (1955). The styloid bone and Carpe Bossu disease. *American Journal of Roentgenology* **74**: 886–888.

Bast, T.H. (1930). Ossification of the otic capsule in human fetuses. *Contributions to Embryology* **21**: 53–82.

Bast, T.H. and Forester, H.B. (1939). Origin and distribution of air cells in the temporal bone. *Archives of Otolaryngology* **30**: 183–205.

Bast, T.H., Anson, B.J. and Gardner, W.D. (1947). The developmental course of the human auditory vesicle. *Anatomical Record* **99**: 55–74.

Bates, E.H. and Chung, W.K. (1988). Congenital talipes equinovarus. In: *The Foot* (B. Helal and D. Wilson, Eds), pp. 219–234. Edinburgh: Churchill Livingstone.

Baughan, B. and Demirjian, A. (1978). Sexual dimorphism in the growth of the cranium. *American Journal of Physical Anthropology* **49**: 383–390.

Baur, R. (1969). Zum Problem der Neugliederung der Wirbelsäule. *Acta Anatomica* **72**: 321–356.

Baxter-Jones, A.D.G., Mirwald, R.L., McKay, H.A. and Bailey, D.A. (2003). A longitudinal analysis of sex differences in bone mineral accrual in healthy 8–19-year-old boys and girls. *Annals of Human Biology* **30**: 160–175.

Beals, R.K. and Skyhar, M. (1984). Growth and development of the tibia, fibula and ankle joint. *Clinical Orthopaedics and Related Research* **182**: 289–292.

Beaty, J.H. and Kumar, A. (1994). Fractures about the knee in children. Current concepts review. *Journal of Bone and Joint Surgery* **76A**: 1870–1880.

Beck, F.W. (1963). Paraseptal cartilage in some mammals including man. *Laryngoscope* **73**: 288–305.

Becker, M.J. (1986). Mandibular symphysis (medial suture) closure in modern *Homo sapiens*: preliminary evidence from archaeological populations. *American Journal of Physical Anthropology* **69**: 499–501.

Behrents, R.G. and Harris, E.F. (1991). The premaxillary–maxillary suture and orthodontic mecanotherapy. *American Journal of Orthodontics and Dentofacial Orthopedics* **99**: 1–6.

Behringer, B.R. and Wilson, F.C. (1972). Congenital pseudoarthrosis of the clavicle. *American Journal of Diseases of Children* **123**: 511–517.

Bell, L.S. (1990). Palaeopathology and diagenesis: An SEM evaluation of structural changes using back scattered electron imaging. *Journal of Archaeological Science* **17**: 85–102.

Bell, L.S., Skinner, M.F. and Jones, S.J. (1996). The speed of post mortem change to the human skeleton and its taphonomic significance. *Forensic Science International* **82**: 129–140.

Bellamy, P., Park, W. and Rooney, P.J. (1983). What do we know about the sacro-iliac joint? *Seminars in Arthritis and Rheumatism* **12**: 282–313.

Beltramello, A., Puppini, G., El-Dalati, G., Cerini, R., Sbarbati, A. and Pacini, P. (1998). Fossa navicularis magna. *American Journal of Neuroradiology* **19**: 1796–1798.

Bennett, K.A. (1965). The etiology and genetics of Wormian bones. *American Journal of Physical Anthropology* **23**: 255–260.

Beresowski, A. and Lundie, J.K. (1952). Sequence in the time of ossification of the carpal bones of 705 African children from birth to 6 years of age. *South African Journal of Medical Sciences* **17**: 25–31.

Berkovitz, B.K.B., Holland, G.R. and Moxham, B. J. (2002). *Oral Anatomy, Histology and Embryology*. 3rd edition. Edinburgh: Mosby.

Bernard, G.W. and Pease, D.C. (1969). An electron microscopic study of initial intramembranous osteogenesis. *American Journal of Anatomy* **125**: 271–290.

Bernhang, A.M. and Levine, S.A. (1973). Familial absence of the patella. *Journal of Bone and Joint Surgery* **55A**: 1088–1090.

Berry, A.C. (1975). Factors affecting the incidence of non-metrical skeletal variants. *Journal of Anatomy* **120**: 519–535.

Berry, A.C. and Berry, R.J. (1967). Epigenetic variation in the human cranium. *Journal of Anatomy* **101**: 361–379.

Bertino, E., Di Battista, E., Bossi, A., Pagliano, M., Fabris, C., Aicardi, G. and Milani, S. (1996). Fetal growth velocity: kinetic, clinical and biological aspects. *Archives of Disease in Childhood* **74**: F10-F15.

Bhaskar, S.N. (1953). Growth pattern of the rat mandible from 13 days insemination age to 30 days after birth. *American Journal of Anatomy* **92**: 1–53.

Bhaskar, S.N. (1980). *Orban's Oral Histology and Embryology*. 9th edition. St Louis, MD: Mosby Yearbook.

Bhaskar, S.N., Weinmann, J.P. and Schour, I. (1953). Role of Meckel's cartilage in the development of the rat mandible. *Journal of Dental Research* **32**: 398–410.

Bick, E.M. and Copel, J.W. (1950). Longitudinal growth of the human vertebra: a contribution to human osteogeny. *Journal of Bone and Joint Surgery* **32A**: 803–814.

Bick, E.M. and Copel, J.W. (1951). The ring apophysis of the human vertebra. *Journal of Bone and Joint Surgery* **33A**: 783–787.

Birkbeck, J.A. (1976). Metrical growth and skeletal development of the human fetus. In: *The Biology of Human Fetal Growth* (D.F. Roberts and A.M. Thomson, Eds). pp. 39–68. London: Taylor and Francis.

Birkner, R. (1978). *Normal Radiographic Patterns and Variances of the Human Skeleton – An X-ray Atlas of Adults and Children*. Baltimore (Munich): Urban and Schwarzenberg.

Bisgard, J.D. and Bisgard, M.E. (1935). Longitudinal growth of long bones. *Archives of Surgery* **31**: 568–578.

Björk, A. (1963). Variations in the growth pattern of the human mandible: longitudinal radiographic study by the implant method. *Journal of Dental Research* **42**: 400–411.

Björk, A. and Skieller, V. (1977). Growth of the maxilla in three dimensions as revealed radiographically by the implant method. *British Journal of Orthodontics* **4**: 53–64.

Black, S.M. and Scheuer, J.L. (1996a). A report on occipitalisation of the atlas with reference to its embryological development. *International Journal of Osteoarchaeology* **6**: 189–194.

Black, S.M. and Scheuer, J.L. (1996b). Age changes in the clavicle: from the early neonatal period to skeletal maturity. *International Journal of Osteoarchaeology* **6**: 425–434.

Black, S.M. and Scheuer, J.L. (1997). The ontogenetic development of the cervical rib. *International Journal of Osteoarchaeology* **7**: 2–10.

Blackwood, H.J.J. (1965). The vascularization of the condylar cartilage of the human mandible. *Journal of Anatomy* **99**: 551–563.

Blechschmidt, E. (1969). The early stages of human limb development. In: *Limb Development and Deformity* (C.A. Swinyard, Ed.). Springfield, IL: C.C. Thomas.

Blondiaux, G., Blondiaux, J., Secousse, F., Cotten, A., Danze, P.M. and Ripo, R.M. (1998). Rickets and child abuse: the case of a fourth-century girl from Normandy. *Papers on Paleopathology*, 26–29 August 1998: 4.

Bocquet-Apel, J-P and Masset, C. (1982). Farewell to palaeodemography. *Journal of Human Evolution* **11**: 321–333.

Bocquet-Apel, J-P. and Masset, C. (1985). Matters of moment. *Journal of Human Evolution* **14**: 107–111.

Bocquet-Apel, J-P. and Masset, C. (1996). Paleodemography: expectancy and false hope. *American Journal of Physical Anthropology* **99**: 571–583.

Bogin, B. (1997). Evolutionary hypotheses for human childhood. *Yearbook of Physical Anthropology* **40**: 63–89.

Bolk, L. (1917). On metopism. *American Journal of Anatomy* **22**: 27–47.

Boller, R. (1964). Fetal morphogenesis of the human dentition. *Journal of Dentistry for Children* **31**: 67–97.

Bollobás, E. (1984a). Fissures, canals and syndesmoses in the fetal maxilla. *Acta Morphologica Hungarica* **32**: 231–243.

Bollobás, E. (1984b). The body and processes of the fetal maxilla. *Acta Morphologica Hungarica* **32**: 217–230.

Bonaldi, L.V., De Angelis, M.A. and Smith, R.L. (1997). Developmental study of the round window region. *Acta Anatomica* **159**: 25–29.

Bonneville, J-F., Belloir, A., Mawazini, H., Manzoni, J-M., Runge, M., Monnier, G. and Dietermann, J-L. (1980). Calcified remnants of the notochord in the roof of the nasopharynx. *Radiology* **137**: 373–377.

Bonucci, E. (1967). Fine structure of early cartilage calcification. *Journal of Ultrastructural Research* **20**: 33–50.

Bonucci, E. (1971). The locus of initial calcification in cartilage and bone. *Clinical Orthopaedics and Related Research* **78**: 108–139.

Bonucci, E. (1992). Role of collagen fibrils in calcification. In: *Calcification in Biological Systems* (Bonucci, E. Ed.), pp. 20–39. Boca Raton: CRC Press.

Boreadis, A.G. and Gershon-Cohen, J. (1956). Luschka joints of the cervical spine. *Radiology* **66**: 181–187.

Bossy, J. and Gaillard, L. (1963). Les vestiges ligamentaires du cartilage de Meckel. *Acta Anatomica* **52**: 282–290.

Boucher, B.J. (1955). Sex differences in the foetal sciatic notch. *Journal of Forensic Medicine* **2**: 51–54.

Boucher, B.J. (1957). Sex differences in the foetal pelvis. *American Journal of Physical Anthropology* **15**: 581–600.

Bouvier, M. and Ubelaker, D. (1977). A comparison of two methods for the microscopic determination of age at death. *American Journal of Physical Anthropology* **46**: 391–394.

Bowdler, J.D. (1971). Persistence of the so-called craniopharyngeal canal. *Journal of Anatomy* **110**: 509.

Bowman, J.E., MacLaughlin, S.M. and Scheuer, J.L. (1992). The relationship between biological and chronological age in the juveniles from St Bride's Church, Fleet Street. *Annals of Human Biology* **19**: 216.

Boyan, B.D., Schwartz, Z. and Swain, L.D. (1990). Matrix vesicles as a marker of endochondral ossification. *Connective Tissue Research* **24**: 67–75.

Boyd, G.I. (1930). The emissary foramina of the cranium in man and anthropoids. *Journal of Anatomy* **65**: 108–121.

Boyde, A. (1963). Estimation of age at death of young human skeletal remains from incremental lines in dental enamel. *Third International Meeting in Forensic Immunology, Medicine, Pathology and Toxicology.* London, 16–24 April, 1963. In: *Primate Life History and Evolution* (C. Jean de Rousseau, Ed.). New York: Wiley-Liss.

Brailsford, J.F. (1943). Variations in the ossification of the bones of the hand. *Journal of Anatomy* **77**: 170–175.

Brailsford, J.F. (1953). *The Radiology of Bones and Joints*, 5th edition. Baltimore, MD: Williams and Wilkins.

Bridgeman, G. and Brookes, M. (1996). Blood supply to the human femoral diaphysis in youth and senescence. *Journal of Anatomy* **188**: 611–621.

Brodeur, A.E., Silberstein, M.J. and Graviss, E.R. (1981). *Radiology of the Pediatric Elbow*. Boston, MA: G.K.Hall.

Brodie, A.G. (1941). On the growth pattern of the human head from the third month to the eighth year of life. *American Journal of Anatomy* **68**: 209–262.

Broker, F.H.L. and Burbach, T. (1990). Ultrasonic diagnosis of separation of the proximal humeral epiphysis in the newborn. *Journal of Bone and Joint Surgery* **72A**: 187–191.

Bromage, T.G. and Dean, M.C. (1985). Re-evaluation of the age at death of immature fossil hominids. *Nature* **317**: 525–527.

Brooke, R. (1924). The sacro-iliac joint. *Journal of Anatomy* **59**: 299–305.

Brookes, M. (1957). Femoral growth after occlusion of the principal nutrient canal in day old rabbits. *Journal of Bone and Joint Surgery* **39B**: 563–571.

Brookes, M. (1958). The vascularization of long bones in the human fetus. *Journal of Anatomy* **92**: 261–267.

Brookes, M. (1963). Cortical vascularisation and growth in foetal tubular bones. *Journal of Anatomy* **97**: 597–609.

Brookes, M. (1971). *The Blood Supply of Bone: An Approach to Bone Biology*. London: Butterworth.

Brookes, M. and Harrison, R.G. (1957). The vascularization of the rabbit femur and tibiofibula. *Journal of Anatomy* **91**: 61–72.

Brookes, M. and Revell, W.J. (1998). *Blood Supply of Bone – Scientific Aspects*, 2nd edition. London: Springer.

Brown, T. (1978). Tooth emergence in Australian aboriginals. *Annals of Human Biology* **5**: 41–54.

Brown, W.A.B. (1985). *Identification of Human Teeth*. Bulletin 21/22. London: Institute of Archaeology.

Brown, W.A.B., Molleson, T.I. and Chinn, S. (1984). Enlargement of the frontal sinus. *Annals of Human Biology* **11**: 221–226.

Bruder, S.P. and Caplan, A.I. (1989). Cellular and molecular events during embryonic bone development. *Connective Tissue Research* **20**: 65–71.

Bruyn, G.W. and Bots, G.Th.A.M. (1977). Biparietal osteodystrophy. *Clinical Neurology and Neurosurgery* **80**: 125–148.

Bryce, T.H. and Young, M. (1917). Observations on metopism. *Journal of Anatomy* **51**: 153–166.

Budorick, N.E., Pretorius, D., Grafe, M.R. and Lou, K.V. (1991). Ossification of the fetal spine. *Radiology* **181**: 561–565.

Buehl, C.C. and Pyle, S.I. (1942). The use of age at first appearance of three ossification centres in determining the skeletal status of children. *Journal of Pediatrics* **21**: 335–342.

Buikstra, J.E., Gordon, C.C. and St Hoyme, L. (1984). The case of the severed skull. Individuation in forensic anthropology. In: *Human Identification. Case Studies in Forensic Anthropology* (T.A. Rathbun, and J.E. Buikstra, Eds), pp. 121–135. Springfield, IL: C.C. Thomas.

Burdi, A.R. (1965). Sagittal growth of the nasomaxillary complex during the second trimester of human prenatal development. *Journal of Dental Research* **44**: 112–125.

Burdi, A.R. (1968). Morphogenesis of mandibular arch shape in human embryos. *Journal of Dental Research* **47**: 50–58.

Burdi, A.R. and Silvey, R.G. (1969a). Sexual differences in the closure of the human palatal shelves. *Cleft Palate Journal* **6**: 1–7.

Burdi, A.R. and Silvey, R.G. (1969b). The relation of sex-associated facial profile reversal and stages of human palatal closure. *Teratology* **2**: 297–304.

Burdi, A.R., Garn, S.M. and Miller, R.L. (1970a). Developmental advancement of the male dentition in the first trimester. *Journal of Dental Research* **49**: 889.

Burdi, A.R., Garn, S.M. and Miller, R.L. (1970b). Mesiodistal gradient of mandibular precedence in the developing dentition. *Journal of Dental Research* **49**: 644.

Burdi, A.R., Garn, S.M. and Superstine, J.N. (1975). Mandibular precedence in the prenatal development of four permanent teeth. *American Journal of Physical Anthropology* **43**: 363–366.

Burke, J.T. and Harris, J.H. (1989). Acute injuries of the axis vertebra. *Skeletal Radiology* **18**: 335–346

Burke, A.C., Nelson, C.E., Morgan, A. and Tabin, C. (1995). *Hox* genes and the evolution of vertebrate axial morphology. *Development* **121**: 333–346.

Burkus, J.K. and Ogden, J.A. (1984). Development of the distal femoral epiphysis: a microscopic morphological investigation of the zone of Ranvier. *Journal of Pediatric Orthopedics* **4**: 661–668.

Buschang, P.H., Baume, R.M. and Nass, G.G. (1983). A craniofacial growth maturity gradient for males and females between 4 and 16 years of age. *American Journal of Physical Anthropology* **61**: 373–381.

Buschang, P.H., Tanguay, R., Demirjian, A., La Palme, L. and Goldstein, H. (1986). Sexual dimorphism in mandibular growth of French-Canadian children 6 to 10 years of age. *American Journal of Physical Anthropology* **71**: 33–37.

Butler, P.M. (1967a). Comparison of the development of the second deciduous molar and first permanent molar in man. *Archives of Oral Biology* **12**: 1245–1260.

Butler, P.M. (1967b). Relative growth within the human first upper permanent molar during the prenatal period. *Archives of Oral Biology* **12**: 983–992.

Butler, P.M. (1968). Growth of the human second lower deciduous molar. *Archives of Oral Biology* **13**: 671–682.

Byers, S. (1991). Technical note: calculation of age at formation of radiopaque transverse lines. *American Journal of Physical Anthropology* **85**: 339–343.

Caffey, J. (1953). On the accessory ossicles of the supraoccipital bone. *American Journal of Roentgenology* **70**: 401–412.

Caffey, J. (1993). *Caffey's Pediatric X-ray Diagnosis*, 9th edition (F.N. Silverman and J.P. Kuhns, Eds). St Louis, MO: Mosby Yearbook.

Caffey, J. and Silverman, W.A. (1945). Infantile cortical hyperostoses. Preliminary report on a new syndrome. *American Journal of Roentgenology* **54**: 1–16.

Calonius, P.E.B., Lunin, M. and Stout, F. (1970). Histological criteria for age estimation of the developing human dentition. *Oral Surgery, Oral Medicine and Oral Pathology* **29**: 869–876.

Cameron, N. and Demerath, E.W. (2002). Critical periods in human growth and their relationship to diseases of aging. *Yearbook of Physical Anthropology* **45**: 159–184.

Camp, J.D. and Nash, L.A. (1944). Developmental thinness of parietal bones. *Radiology* **42**: 42–47.

Campbell, L.R., Dayton, D.H. and Sohal, G.S. (1986). Neural tube defects: a review of human and animal studies on the etiology of neural tube defects. *Teratology* **34**: 171–178.

Caplan, A.I., Syftestad, G. and Osdoby, P. (1983). The development of embryonic bone and cartilage in tissue culture. *Clinical Orthopaedics and Related Research* **174**: 243–263.

Carels, C.E.L., Kuipers-Jagtman, A.M., Van der Linden, F.P.G.M. and Van't Hof, M.A. (1991). Age reference charts of tooth formation in Dutch children. *Journal de Biologie Buccale* **19**: 297–303.

Carter, D.R. and Beaupré, G.S. (2001). *Skeletal Form and Function. Mechanobiology of Skeletal Development, Aging and Regeneration.* Cambridge: Cambridge University Press.

Carter, D.R., Mikić, B. and Padiau, K. (1998). Epigenetic mechanical factors in the evolution of long bone epiphyses. *Zoology Journal of the Linnean Society* **123**: 163–178.

Castellana, C. and Kósa, F. (1999). Morphology of the cervical vertebrae in the fetal and neonatal human skeleton. *Journal of Anatomy* **194**: 147–152.

Cave, A.J.E. (1927). Bilateral and unilateral thinning of parietal bone. *Journal of Anatomy* **61**: 486–487.

Cave, A.J.E. (1928). Two cases of congenitally enlarged parietal foramina. *Journal of Anatomy* **63**: 172–174.

Cave, A.J.E. (1930). On fusion of the atlas and axis vertebrae. *Journal of Anatomy* **64**: 337–343.

Cave, A.J.E. (1931). The craniopharyngeal canal in man and anthropoids. *Journal of Anatomy* **65**: 363–367.

Cave, A.J.E. (1934). Cervical intercostal articulations. *Journal of Anatomy* **68**: 521–524.

Cave, A.J.E. (1975). The morphology of the mammalian cervical pleurapophysis. *Journal of Zoology* **177**: 377–393.

Cerný, M. (1983). Our experience with estimation of an individual's age from skeletal remains of the degree of thyroid cartilage ossification. *Acta Universitatis Palackianae Olomucensisi* **3**: 121–144.

Chandraraj, S. and Briggs, C.A. (1991). Multiple growth cartilages in the neural arch. *Anatomical Record* **230**: 114–120.

Chandraraj, S., Briggs, C.A. and Opeskin, K. (1998). Disc herniation in the young and end plate vascularity. *Clinical Anatomy* **11**: 171–176.

Chang, C.H. and Davis, W.C. (1961). Congenital bifid sternum with partial ectopia cordis. *American Journal of Roentgenology* **86**: 513–516.

Chang, H.H., Tse, Y. and Kaufman, M.H. (1998). Analysis of interdigital spaces during mouse limb development at intervals following amniotic sac puncture. *Journal of Anatomy* **192**: 59–72.

Charles, D.K., Condon, K., Cheverud, J.M. and Buikstra, J.E. (1986). Cementum annulation and age determination in Homo sapiens. I. Tooth variability and observer error. *American Journal of Physical Anthropology* **71**: 311–320.

Charles, R.H. (1893). The influence of function as exemplified in the morphology of the lower extremity of the Panjabi. *Journal of Anatomy and Physiology* **28**: 1–18.

Charles, S.W. (1925). The temporo-mandibular joint and its influence on the growth of the mandible. *British Dental Journal* **46**: 845–855.

Chase, S.W. (1942). The early development of the human premaxilla. *Journal of the American Dental Association* **29**: 1991–2001.

Chemke, J. and Robinson, A. (1969). The third fontanelle. *Journal of Pediatrics* **75**: 617–622.

Chen, J.M. (1952). Studies on the morphogenesis of the mouse sternum. II. Experiments on the origin of the sternum and its capacity for self differentiation in vitro. *Journal of Anatomy* **86**: 387–401.

Chilton, L.A., Dorst, J.P. and Garn, S.M. (1983). The volume of the sella turcica in children: new standards. *American Journal of Roentgenology* **140**: 797–801.

Choi, S.C. and Trotter, M. (1970). A statistical study of the multivariate structure and race-sex differences of American White and Negro fetal skeletons. *American Journal of Physical Anthropology* **33**: 307–312.

Chole, R.A. (1993). Differential osteoclast activation in endochondral and intramembranous bone. *Annals of Otology, Rhinology and Laryngology* **102**: 616–619.

Christ, B. and Wilting, J. (1992). From somites to vertebral column. *Annals of Anatomy* **174**: 23–32.

Christ, B., Jacob, H.J. and Brand, B. (1986). Principles of hand ontogenesis in man. *Acta Morphologica Neerlando-Scandinavica* **24**: 249–268.

Christensen, G.J. and Kraus, B.S. (1965). Initial calcification of the human permanent first molar. *Journal of Dental Research* **44**: 1338–1342.

Christie, A. (1949). Prevalence and distribution of ossification centers in the newborn infant. *American Journal of Diseases of Children* **77**: 355–361.

Christie, A.U., Dunham, E.C., Jenss, R.M. and Dippel, A.L. (1941). Development of the center for the cuboid bone in newborn infants: a roentgenographic study. *American Journal of Diseases of Children* **61**: 471–482.

Chung, S.M.K. and Nissenbaum, M.M. (1975). Congenital and developmental defects of the shoulder. *Orthopedic Clinics of North America* **6**: 381–392.

Cihák, R. (1972). *Ontogenesis of the Skeleton and Intrinsic Muscles of the Human Hand and Foot*. New York: Springer.

Clark, G.A., Hall, N.R., Armelagos, G.J., Borkan, G.A., Panjabi, M.M. and Wetzel, F.T. (1986). Poor growth prior to early childhood: decreased health and life-span in the adult. *American Journal of Physical Anthropology* **70**: 145–160.

Cleland, J. (1862). On the relations of the vomer, ethmoid and intermaxillary bones. *Philosophical Transactions of the Royal Society of London* **152**: 289–321.

Cocchi, U. (1950). Zur Frage der Epiphysenossifikation des Humeruskopfes: Das Tuberculum minus. *Radiologica Clinica* **19**: 18–23.

Cockshott, W.P. and Park, W.M. (1983). Observer variation in skeletal radiology. *Skeletal Radiology* **10**: 86–90.

Cohen, J. and Harris, W.H. (1958). The three dimensional anatomy of Haversian systems. *Journal of Bone and Joint Surgery* **40A**: 419–434.

Cohen, J., Currarino, G. and Neuhauser, E.B.D. (1956). A significant variant in the ossification centres of the vertebral bodies. *American Journal of Roentgenology* **76**: 469–475.

Cohn, I. (1921a). Observations on the normally developing shoulder. *American Journal of Roentgenology* **8**: 721–729.

Cohn, I. (1921b). Observations on the normally developing elbow. *Archives of Surgery* **2**: 455–492.

Cohn, I. (1924). Normal bones and joints. *Annals of Roentgenology* **IV**. New York: P.B. Hoeber.

Coleman, W.H. (1969). Sex differences in the growth of the human bony pelvis. *American Journal of Physical Anthropology* **31**: 125–152.

Collins, H.B. (1928). Frequency and distribution of the fossa pharyngea in human crania. *American Journal of Physical Anthropology* **11**: 101–106.

Condon, K., Charles, D.K., Cheverud, J.M. and Buikstra, J.E. (1986). Cementum annulation and age determination in Homo sapiens. II. Estimates and accuracy. *American Journal of Physical Anthropology* **71**: 321–330.

Connor, S.E.J., Chandler, C., Robinson, S. and Jarosz, J.M. (2001). Congenital midline cleft of the posterior arch of the atlas: a rare cause of symptomatic cervical canal stenosis. *European Radiology* **11**: 1766–1769.

Cool, S.M., Hendrikz, J.K. and Wood, W.B. (1995). Microscopic age changes in the human occipital bone. *Journal of Forensic Sciences* **40**: 789–796.

Cooper, P.D., Stewart, J.H. and McCormick, W.F. (1988). Development and morphology of the sternal foramen. *American Journal of Forensic Medicine and Pathology* **9**: 342–347.

Cooper, R.R., Milgram, J.W. and Robinson, R.A. (1966). Morphology of the osteon: An electron microscopic study. *Journal of Bone and Joint Surgery* **48A**: 1239–1271.

Cope, V.Z. (1920). Fusion lines of bones. *Journal of Anatomy* **55**: 36–37.

Coral, A. (1987). The radiology of skeletal elements in the subtibial region: incidence and significance. *Skeletal Radiology* **16**: 298–303.

Corrigan, G.E. (1960a). The neonatal clavicle. *Biologia Neonatorum* **2**: 79–92.

Corrigan, G.E. (1960b). The neonatal scapula. *Biologia Neonatorum* **2**: 159–167.

Covell, W.P. (1927). Growth of the human prenatal hypophysis and the hypophyseal fossa. *American Journal of Anatomy* **38**: 379–422.

Coventry, M.B. and Johnson, E.W. (1952). Congenital absence of the fibula. *Journal of Bone and Joint Surgery* **34A**: 941–955.

Cox, M. (1995). A dangerous assumption: anyone can be a historian! The lessons from Christchurch, Spitalfields. In: *Grave Reflections: Portraying the Past through Cemetery Studies* (S.R. Saunders and A. Herring, Eds), pp.19–29. Toronto: Canadian Scholars' Press.

Cox, M. (2000). Ageing adults from the skeleton. In: *Human Osteology in Archaeological and Forensic Science* (M. Cox and S. Mays, Eds), pp.61–81. London: Greenwich Medical Media.

Crelin, E.S. (1973). *Functional Anatomy of the Newborn*. New Haven, CT: Yale University Press.

Crock, H.V. (1965). A revision of the anatomy of the arteries supplying the upper end of the human femur. *Journal of Anatomy* **99**: 77–88.

Crock, H.V. (1967). *The Blood Supply of the Lower Limbs in Man*. Edinburgh: Churchill Livingstone.

Crock, H.V. (1996). *An Atlas of Vascular Anatomy of the Skeleton and Spinal Cord*. London: Dunitz.

Crock, H.V., Yoshizawa, H. and Kame, S.K. (1973). Observations on the venous drainage of the human vertebral body. *Journal of Bone and Joint Surgery* **55B**: 528–533.

Croft, M.S., Desai, G., Seed, P.T., Pollard, J.I. and Perry, M.E. (1999). Application of obstetric ultrasound to determine the most suitable parameters for the aging of formalin-fixed human fetuses using manual measurements. *Clinical Anatomy* **12**: 84–93.

Crossner, C.G. and Mansfield, L. (1983). Determination of dental age in adopted non-European children. *Swedish Dental Journal* **7**: 1–10.

Cullen, R.L. and Vidić, B. (1972). The dimensions and shape of the human maxillary sinus in the perinatal period. *Acta Anatomica* **83**: 411–415.

Cundy, P., Paterson, D., Morris, L. and Foster, B. (1988). Skeletal age estimation in leg length discrepancy. *Journal of Pediatric Orthopedics* **8**: 513–515.

Cunha, E. (1995). Testing identification records: evidence from the Coimbra identified skeletal collections (nineteenth and twentieth centuries). In: *Grave Reflections: Portraying the Past through Cemetery Studies* (S.R. Saunders and A. Herring, Eds). Toronto: Canadian Scholars' Press.

Curran, B.K. and Weaver, D.S. (1982). The use of the coefficient of agreement and likelihood ratio test to examine the development of the tympanic plate using a known age sample of fetal and infant skeletons. *American Journal of Physical Anthropology* **58**: 343–346.

Currarino, G. (1976). Normal variants and congenital anomalies in the region of the obelion. *American Journal of Roentgenology* **127**: 487–494.

Currarino, G. (1988). Canalis basilaris medianus and related defects of the basiocciput. *American Journal of Neuroradiology* **9**: 208–211.

Currarino, G. and Silverman, F.N. (1958). Premature obliteration of sternal sutures and pigeon-breast deformity. *Radiology* **70**: 532–540.

Currarino, G. and Swanson, G.E. (1964). Developmental variant of ossification of the manubrium sterni in Mongolism. *Radiology* **82**: 916.

Currarino, G., Maravilla, K.R. and Salyer, K.E. (1985). Transsphenoidal canal (large craniopharyngeal canal) and its pathologic implications. *American Journal of Neuroradiology* **6**: 39–43.

Curtis, D.J., Allman, R.M., Brion, J., Holborow, G.S. and Brahman, S.L. (1985). Calcification and ossification in the arytenoid cartilage: incidence and patterns. *Journal of Forensic Sciences* **30**: 1113–1118.

Dahlberg, A.A. and Menegaz-Bock, R.M. (1958). Emergence of the permanent teeth in Pima Indian children. *Journal of Dental Research* **37**: 1123–1140.

Dahm, M.C., Shepherd, R.K. and Clark, G.M. (1993). The postnatal growth of the temporal bone and its implications for cochlear implantation in children. *Acta Oto-Laryngologica (Stockh.)* **505**(Suppl.): 1–27.

Dalgleish, A.E. (1985). A study of the development of thoracic vertebrae in the mouse assisted by autoradiography. *Acta Anatomica* **122**: 91–98.

Dameron, T.B. and Rockwood, C.A. (1984). Fractures and dislocation of the shoulder. In: *Fractures in Children* (C.A. Rockwood, K.E. Wilkins and R.E. King, Eds), pp. 577–682. Philadelphia, PA: Lippincott.

Das, A.C., Saxena, R.C. and Beg, M.A.Q. (1973). Incidence of metopic suture in U.P. subjects. *Journal of the Anatomical Society of India* **22**: 140–143.

Dass, R. and Makhni, S.S. (1966). Ossification of ear ossicles. The stapes. *Archives of Otolaryngology* **84**: 306–312.

Dass, R., Thapar, S.P. and Makhni, S.S. (1969). Foetal stapes. I. General features. *Journal of Laryngology and Otology* **83**: 101–117.

Davenport, C.B. (1933). The crural index. *American Journal of Physical Anthropology* **17**: 333–353.

David, K.M., McLachlan, J.C., Aiton, J.F., Whiten, S.C., Smart, S.D., Thorogood, P.V. and Crockard, H.A. (1998). Cartilaginous development of the human craniovertebral junction as visualised by a new three-dimensional computer reconstruction technique. *Journal of Anatomy* **192**: 269–277.

Davidoff, L.M. (1936). Convolutional digitations seen in roentgenograms of immature human skulls. *Bulletin of the Neurological Institute of New York* **5**: 61–71.

Davies, D.A. and Parsons, F.G. (1927). The age order of the appearance and union of the normal epiphyses as seen by X-rays. *Journal of Anatomy* **62**: 58–71.

Davis, D.B. and King, J.C. (1938). Cervical rib in early life. *American Journal of Diseases of Children* **56**: 744–755.

Dawson, A.B. (1929). A histological study of the persisting cartilaginous plates in retarded or lapsed epiphyseal union in the albino rat. *Anatomical Record* **43**: 109–129.

Dean, M.C. (2000). Progress in understanding hominoid dental development. *Journal of Anatomy* **197**: 77–101.

Dean, M.C. and Beynon, A.D. (1991). Histological reconstruction of crown formation times and initial root formation times in a modern human child. *American Journal of Physical Anthropology* **86**: 215–228.

Dean, M.C., Stringer, C.B. and Bromage, T.G. (1986). Age at death of the Neanderthal child from Devil's Tower, Gibraltar and its implications for studies of general growth and development in Neanderthals. *American Journal of Physical Anthropology* **70**: 301–309.

Dean, M.C., Beynon, A.D., Thackeray, J.F. and Macho, G.A. (1993). Histological reconstruction of dental development and age at death of a juvenile Paranthropus robustus specimen, SK 63, from Swartkrans, South Africa. *American Journal of Physical Anthropology* **91**: 401–419.

de Beer, G.R. (1937). *The Development of the Vertebrate Skull*. Oxford: Clarendon Press.

de Campo, J.F. and Boldt, D.W. (1986). Computed tomography of partial growth plate arrest: initial experience. *Skeletal Radiology* **15**: 526–529.

Dedick, A.P. and Caffey, J. (1953). Roentgen findings in the skull and chest on 1030 newborn infants. *Radiology* **61**: 13–20.

de Iturriza, J.R. and Tanner, J.M. (1969). Cone shaped epiphyses and other minor anomalies in the hands of normal British children. *Journal of Pediatrics* **75**: 265–272.

de La Cruz, A., Linthicum, F.H. and Luxford, W.M. (1985). Congenital atresia of the external auditory canal. *Laryngoscope* **95**: 421–427.

Delaere, O., Kok, V., Nyssen-Behets, C. and Dhem, A. (1992). Ossification of the human fetal ilium. *Acta Anatomica* **143**: 330–334.

Delano, P.J. (1941). Os intermetatarseum: unusual variant. *Radiology* **37**: 102–103.

de Melo e Freitas, M.J. and Salzano, F.M. (1975). Eruption of permanent teeth in Brazilian whites and blacks. *American Journal of Physical Anthropology* **42**: 145–150.

Demirjian, A. (1986). Dentition. In: *Human Growth*, 2nd edition, Vol. 2. Postnatal Growth (F. Falkner and J.M. Tanner, Eds), pp 269–298. New York: Plenum Press.

Demirjian, A. and Goldstein, H. (1976). New systems for dental maturity based on seven and four teeth. *Annals of Human Biology* **3**: 411–421.

Demirjian, A. and Levesque, G.-Y. (1980). Sexual differences in dental development and predictions of emergence. *Journal of Dental Research* **59**: 1110–1122.

Demirjian, A., Goldstein, H. and Tanner, J.M. (1973). A new system of dental age assessment. *Human Biology* **45**: 211–227.

Denham, R.H. and Dingley, A.F. (1967). Epiphyseal separation of the medial end of the clavicle. *Journal of Bone and Joint Surgery* **49A**: 1179–1183.

Den Hoed, D. (1925). Separate centres of ossification of the tip of the internal malleolus. *British Journal of Radiology* **30**: 67–68.

Derry, D.E. (1938). Two skulls with absence of the premaxilla. *Journal of Anatomy* **72**: 295–298.

Deutsch, D., Goultschin, J. and Anteby, S. (1981). Determination of fetal age from the length of femur, mandible and maxillary incisor. *Growth* **45**: 232–238.

Deutsch, D., Pe'er, E. and Gedalia, I. (1984). Changes in size, morphology and weight of human anterior teeth during the fetal period. *Growth* **48**: 74–85.

Deutsch, D., Tam, O. and Stack, M.V. (1985). Postnatal changes in size, morphology and weight of developing postnatal deciduous anterior teeth. *Growth* **49**: 202–217.

Devas, M. (1960). Stress fracture of the patella. *Journal of Bone and Joint Surgery* **42B**: 71–74.

Dietz, F.R. (1989). Effect of denervation on limb growth. *Journal of Orthopedic Research* **7**: 292–303.

Diewert, V.M. (1985). Development of human craniofacial morphology during the embryonic and early fetal periods. *American Journal of Orthodontics* **88**: 64–76.

Digby, K.H. (1915). The measurement of diaphysial growth in proximal and distal directions. *Journal of Anatomy* **50**: 187–188.

Dillaman, R.M. (1984). Movement of ferritin in the 2 day old chick femur. *Anatomical Record* **209**: 445–453.

Dimon, J.H. (1972). Isolated fractures of the lesser trochanter of the femur. *Clinical Orthopaedics and Related Research* **82**: 144–148.

Ditch, L.E. and Rose, J.C. (1972). A multivariate dental sexing technique. *American Journal of Physical Anthropology* **37**: 61–64.

Dixey, F.A. (1881). On the ossification of the terminal phalanges of the digits. *Royal Society of London Proceedings* **31**: 63–71.

Dixon, A.D. (1953). The early development of the maxilla. *Dental Practitioner* **3**: 331–336.

Dixon, A.D. (1958). The development of the jaws. *Dental Practitioner* **9**: 10–18.

Dixon, A.F. (1896). Ossification of the third trochanter in man. *Journal of Anatomy and Physiology* **30**: 502–504.

Dodo, Y. (1980). Appearance of bony bridging of the hypoglossal canal during the fetal period. *Journal of the Anthropological Society of Nippon* **88**: 229–238.

Dodo, Y. (1986). Observations on the bony bridging of the jugular foramen in man. *Journal of Anatomy* **144**: 153–165.

Dollé, P., Izpisua-Belmonte, J.C., Falkenstein, H., Renucci, A. and Duboule, D. (1989). Co ordinate expression of the murine *Hox*-5 complex homeobox-containing genes during limb pattern formation. *Nature* **342**: 767–772.

Doménech-Mateu, J.M. and Sañudo, J.R. (1990). Chondrification of laryngeal cartilages. *Proceedings IVth World Congress of Otorhinolaryngology, Head and Neck Surgery* **2**: 2095–2097.

Donisch, E.W. and Trapp, W. (1971). The cartilage end plates of the human vertebral column (some considerations of postnatal development). *Anatomical Record* **169**: 705–715.

Dore, D.D., MacEwen, G.D. and Boulos, M.I. (1987). Cleidocranial dysostosis and syringomyelia: review of literature and case report. *Clinical Orthopaedics and Related Research* **214**: 229–234.

Doub, H.P. and Danzer, J.T. (1934). Lükenschädel of the newborn. *Radiology* **22**: 532–538.

Dreizen, S., Snodgrasse, R.M., Webb-Peploe, H. and Spies, T.D. (1958). The retarding effect of protracted undernutrition on the appearance of the postnatal ossification centres in the hand and wrist. *Human Biology* **30**: 253–264.

du Boulay, G. (1956). The significance of digital impressions in children's skulls. *Acta Radiologica* **46**: 112–122.

Dubowitz, L.M.S. and Dubowitz, V. (1977). *Gestational Age of the Newborn*. Reading, MA: Addison–Wesley.

Dubowitz, L.M., Dubowitz, V. and Mercuri, E. (1999). *The Neurological Assessment of the Preterm and Full-term Infant*. London: MacKeith Press, distributed by Cambridge University Press.

Duc, G. and Largo, R.H. (1986). Anterior fontanel: size and closure in term and preterm infants. *Pediatrics* **78**: 904–908.

Duckworth, W.L.H. (1902). On an unusual form of nasal bone in a human skull. *Journal of Anatomy and Physiology* **36**: 257–259.

Dvonch, V.M. and Bunch, W.H. (1983). Pattern of closure of the proximal femoral and tibial epiphyses in man. *Journal of Pediatric Orthopedics* **3**: 498–501.

Dyck, P. (1978). Os odontoideum in children: neurological manifestations and surgical management. *Neurosurgery* **8**: 93–99.

Eanes, E. and Hailer, A.W. (1985). Liposome-mediated calcium phosphate formation in metastable solutions. *Calcified Tissue International* **37**: 390–394.

Eby, T.L. and Nadol, J.B. (1986). Postnatal growth of the human temporal bone. Implications for cochlear implants in children. *Annals of Otology, Rhinology and Laryngology* **95**: 356–364.

Ehrenborg, G. and Engfeldt, B. (1961a). The insertion of the ligamentum patellae on the tibial tuberosity. Some views in connection with the Osgood-Schlatter lesion. *Acta Chirurgica Scandinavica* **121**: 491–499.

Ehrenborg, G. and Engfeldt, B. (1961b). Histologic changes in the Osgood–Schlatter lesion. *Acta Chirurgica Scandinavica* **121**: 328–337.

Ehrenborg, G. and Lagergren, C. (1961). Roentgenologic changes in the Osgood–Schlatter lesion. *Acta Chirurgica Scandinavica* **121**: 315–327.

Elftman, H. (1945). Torsion of the lower extremity. *American Journal of Physical Anthropology* **3**: 255–265.

Elgenmark, O. (1946). The normal development of the ossific centres during infancy and childhood. *Acta Paediatrica Scandinavica* **33**(Suppl. **1**).

Eliot, M.M., Souther, S.P. and Park, E.A. (1927). Transverse lines in X-ray plates of the long bones of children. *Bulletin of the Johns Hopkins Hospital* **41**: 364–388.

Ellis, F.G. and Joseph, J. (1954). Time of appearance of the centres of ossification of the fibular epiphyses. *Journal of Anatomy* **88**: 533–536.

El-Najjar, M.Y. and Dawson, G.L. (1977). The effect of artificial cranial deformation on the incidence of Wormian bones in the lambdoidal suture. *American Journal of Physical Anthropology* **46**: 155–160.

Eloff, F.C. (1952). On the relations of the human vomer to the anterior paraseptal cartilages. *Journal of Anatomy* **86**: 16–19.

Engel, G.M. and Staheli, L.T. (1974). The natural history of torsion and other factors influencing gait in childhood. *Clinical Orthopaedics and Related Research* **99**: 12–17.

Engfeldt, B. and Reinholt, F.P. (1992). Structure and calcification of epiphyseal growth cartilage. In: *Calcification in Biological Systems* (Bonucci, E., Ed.), pp. 217–241. Boca Raton, FL: CRC Press.

England, M.A. (1990). *A Colour Atlas of Life Before Birth*. London: Wolfe.

Enlow, D.H. (1963). *Principles of Bone Remodelling*. Springfield, IL: C.C. Thomas.

Enlow, D.H. and Bang, S. (1965). Growth and remodelling of the human maxilla. *American Journal of Orthodontics* **51**: 446–464.

Enlow, D.H. and Hans, M.G. (1996). *Essentials of Facial Growth*. Philadelphia, PA: W.B. Saunders.

Enlow, D.H. and Harris, D.B. (1964). A study of the post-natal growth of the human mandible. *American Journal of Orthodontics* **50**: 25–50.

Epstein, J.A. and Epstein, B.S. (1967). Deformities of the skull surface in infancy and childhood. *Journal of Pediatrics* **70**: 636–647.

Ericksen, M.F. (1991). Histologic estimation of age at death using the anterior cortex of the femur. *American Journal of Physical Anthropology* **84**: 171–179.

Evans, E.M. (1951). Fractures of the radius and ulna. *Journal of Bone and Joint Surgery* **33B**: 548–561.

Evans, F.G., Alfaro, A. and Alfaro, S. (1950). An unusual anomaly of the superior extremities in a Tarascan Indian girl. *Anatomical Record* **106**: 37–48.

Evans, K.T. and Knight, B. (1981). *Forensic Radiology*. Oxford: Blackwells.

Eveleth, P.B. and Tanner, J.M. (1990). *Worldwide Variation in Human Growth*, 2nd edition. Cambridge: Cambridge University Press.

Ewers, S.R. (1968). A study of prenatal growth of the human bony palate from 3 to 9 months. *American Journal of Orthodontics* **54**: 3–28.

Fabry, G., MacEwen, G.D. and Shands, A.R. (1973). Torsion of the femur. *Journal of Bone and Joint Surgery* **55A**: 1726–1738.

Fairbank, H.A.T. (1914). Congenital elevation of the scapula: a series of 18 cases with a detailed description of a dissected specimen. *British Journal of Surgery* **1**: 553–572.

Fairbank, H.A.T. (1949). Cranio-cleido-dysostosis. *Journal of Bone and Joint Surgery* **31B**: 608–617.

Fanning, E.A. (1961). A longitudinal study of tooth formation and root resorption. *New Zealand Dental Journal* **57**: 202–217.

Fanning, E.A. (1962). Effect of extraction of deciduous molars on the formation and eruption of their successors. *Angle Orthodontist* **32**: 44–53.

Farmer, A.W. and Laurin, C.A. (1960). Congenital absence of the fibula. *Journal of Bone and Joint Surgery* **42A**: 1–12.

Fawcett, E. (1904). The presence of two centres of ossification in the olecranon process of the ulna. *Journal of Anatomy and Physiology* **38**: xxvii.

Fawcett, E. (1905a). On the early stages in the ossification of the pterygoid plates of the sphenoid bone in man. *Anatomischer Anzeiger* **26**: 280–286.

Fawcett, E. (1905b). Abstract of paper on the ossification of the lower jaw of man. *Journal of Anatomy and Physiology* **39**: 494–495.

Fawcett, E. (1905c). Ossification of the lower jaw in man. *Journal of the American Medical Association* **45**: 696–705.

Fawcett, E. (1906). On the development, ossification and growth of the palate bone in man. *Journal of Anatomy and Physiology* **40**: 400–406.

Fawcett, E. (1907). On the completion of ossification of the human sacrum. *Anatomischer Anzeiger* **30**: 414–421.

Fawcett, E. (1910a). Description of a reconstruction of the head of a thirty millimetre embryo. *Journal of Anatomy and Physiology* **44**: 303–311.

Fawcett, E. (1910b). Notes on the development of the human sphenoid bone. *Journal of Anatomy and Physiology* **44**: 207–222.

Fawcett, E. (1911). The development of the human maxilla, vomer and paraseptal cartilages. *Journal of Anatomy and Physiology* **45**: 378–405.

Fawcett, E. (1913). The development and ossification of the human clavicle. *Journal of Anatomy and Physiology* **47**: 225–234.

Fawcett, E. (1923). Some observations on the roof of the primordial human cranium. *Journal of Anatomy* **57**: 245–250.

Fawcett, E. (1930). A model of the left half of the human mandible at the 17 mm C.R. stage. *Journal of Anatomy* **64**: 369–370.

Fazekas, I.Gy. and Kósa, F. (1978). *Forensic Fetal Osteology*. Budapest: Akadémiai Kiadó.

Fédération Dentaire International (FDI) (1971). Two-digit system of designating teeth. *International Dental Journal* **21**: 104–106.

Fein, J.M. and Brinker, R.A. (1972). Evolution and significance of giant parietal foramina. *Journal of Neurosurgery* **37**: 487–492.

Felts, W.J.L. (1954). The prenatal development of the human femur. *American Journal of Anatomy* **94**: 1–44.

Ferembach, D., Schwidetsky, I. and Stloukal, M. (1980). Recommendations for age and sex diagnoses of skeletons. Report of the Workshop of European Anthropologists (WEA). *Journal of Human Evolution* **9**: 517–549.

Ferguson, W.R. (1950). Some observations on the circulation in foetal and infant spines. *Journal of Bone and Joint Surgery* **32A**: 640–648.

Fernbach, S.K. and Wilkinson, R.H. (1981). Avulsion injuries of the pelvis and proximal femur. *American Journal of Roentgenology* **137**: 581–584.

Ferrario, V.F., Sforza, C., Guazzi, M. and Serrao, G. (1996). Elliptic Fourier analysis of mandibular shape. *Journal of Craniofacial Genetics and Developmental Biology* **16**: 208–217.

Fielding, J.W. (1965). Disappearance of the central portion of the odontoid process. *Journal of Bone and Joint Surgery* **47A**: 1228–1230.

Fielding, J.W. and Griffin, P.P. (1974). Os odontoideum: an acquired lesion. *Journal of Bone and Joint Surgery* **56A**: 187–190.

Fielding, J.W., Hensinger, R.N. and Hawkins, R.J. (1980). Os odontoideum. *Journal of Bone and Joint Surgery* **62**: 376–383.

Fileti, A. (1927). Embriologia e morfologia del canale ottico. *Annali di Ottalmologia e Clinica Oculistica* **55**: 493–554.

Filipsson, R. (1975). A new method for assessment of dental maturity using the individual curve of number of erupted permanent teeth. *Annals of Human Biology* **2**: 13–24.

Filly, R.A. and Golbus, M.S. (1982). Ultrasonography of the normal and pathologic fetal skeleton. *Radiologic Clinics of North America* **20**: 311–323.

Finnegan, M. (1978). Non-metric variation of the infracranial skeleton. *Journal of Anatomy* **125**: 23–37.

Fischer, K.C., White, R.I., Jordan, C.E., Dorst, J.P. and Neill, C.A. (1973). Sternal abnormalities in patients with congenital heart disease. *American Journal of Roentgenology* **119:** 530–538.

FitzGerald, C.M. (1998). Do dental microstructures have a regular time dependency? Conclusions from the literature and a large-scale survey. *Journal of Human Evolution* **35**: 371–386.

FitzGerald, C., Foley, R.A. and Dean, M.C. (1996). Variation of circaseptan cross striations in the tooth enamel of three modern human populations. *American Journal of Physical Anthropology*, **22**(Suppl.): **104**.

Fitzwilliams, D.C.L. (1910). Hereditary cranio-cleido-dysostosis. *Lancet* **2**: 1466–1475.

Flecker, H. (1932). Roentgenographic observations of the times of appearance of epiphyses and their fusion with the diaphyses. *Journal of Anatomy* **67**: 118–164.

Flecker, H. (1936). Epiphysis for the lesser trochanter. *American Journal of Roentgenology* **35**: 540.

Flecker, H. (1942). Time of appearance and fusion of ossification centres as observed by roentgenographic methods. *American Journal of Roentgenology* **47**: 97–159.

Fleming, A., Keynes, R.A. and Tannahill, D. (2001). The role of the notochord in vertebral column formation. *Journal of Anatomy* **199**: 177–180.

Flickinger, R.A. (1974). Muscle and cartilage differentiation in small and large explants from the chick limb bud. *Developmental Biology* **41**: 202–208.

Ford, E.H.R. (1956). The growth of the foetal skull. *Journal of Anatomy* **90**: 63–72.

Ford, E.H.R. (1958). Growth of the human cranial base. *American Journal of Orthodontics* **44**: 498–506.

Ford, D., McFadden, K.D. and Bagnall, K.M. (1982). Sequence of ossification in human vertebral neural arch. *Anatomical Record* **203**: 175–178.

Forland, M. (1962). Cleidocranial dysostosis. *American Journal of Medicine* **33**: 792–799.

Formicola, V., Frayer, D.W. and Heller, J.A. (1990). Bilateral absence of the lesser trochanter in a late Epigravettian skeleton from Arene Candide (Italy). *American Journal of Physical Anthropology* **83**: 425–437.

Foster, T.D., Grundy, M.C. and Lavelle, C.L.B. (1977). A longitudinal study of dental arch growth. *American Journal of Orthodontics* **72**: 309–314.

Francis, C.C. (1940), The appearance of centres of ossification from 6–15 years. *American Journal of Physical Anthropology* **27**: 127–138.

Francis, C.C., Werle, P.P. and Behm, A. (1939). The appearance of centers of ossification from birth to 5 years. *American Journal of Physical Anthropology* **24**: 273–299.

Frantz, C.H. and O'Rahilly, R. (1961). Congenital limb deficiencies. *Journal of Bone and Joint Surgery* **43A**: 1202–1224.

Frazer, J.E. (1910a). The early development of the Eustachian tube and nasopharynx. *British Medical Journal* **2**: 1148–1150.

Frazer, J.E. (1910b). The development of the larynx. *Journal of Anatomy and Physiology* **44**: 156–191.

Frazer. J.E. (1914). The second visceral arch and groove in the tubo-tympanic region. *Journal of Anatomy and Physiology* **48**: 391–408.

Frazer, J.E. (1922). The early formation of the middle ear and Eustachian tube: a criticism. *Journal of Anatomy* **57**: 18–30.

Frazer, J.E. (1948). *The Anatomy of the Human Skeleton*, 4th edition. London: Churchill.

Freedman, E. (1934). Os acetabuli. *American Journal of Roentgenology* **31**: 492–495.

Freeman, E., Ten Cate, A.R. and Dickinson, J. (1975). Development of a gomphosis by toothgerm implants in the parietal bone of mice. *Archives of Oral Biology* **20**: 139–140.

Freiband, B. (1937). Growth of the palate in the human fetus. *Journal of Dental Research* **16**: 103–122.

Freiberger, R.H., Wilson, P.D. and Nicholas, J.A. (1965). Acquired absence of the odontoid process. *Journal of Bone and Joint Surgery* **47A**: 1231–1236.

Friant, M. (1960). L'evolution du cartilage de Meckel humain, jusqu'a la fin du sixième mois de la vie foetale. *Acta Anatomica* **41**: 228–239.

Frisancho, A.R., Garn, S.M. and Ascoli, W. (1970). Childhood retardation resulting in reduction of adult body size due to lesser adolescent skeletal delay. *American Journal of Physical Anthropology* **33**: 325–336.

Fritsch, H. and Eggers, R. (1999). Ossification of the calcaneus in the normal fetal foot and in club foot. *Journal of Pediatric Orthopedics* **19**: 22–26.

Fritsch, H., Brenner, E. and Debbage, P. (2001). Ossification in the human calaneus: a model for spatial bone development and ossification. *Journal of Anatomy* **199**: 609–616.

Frommer, J. and Margolies, M.R. (1971). Contribution of Meckel's cartilage to the ossification of the mandible in mice. *Journal of Dental Research* **50**: 1260–1267.

Fujioka, M. and Young, L.W. (1978). The sphenoidal sinuses: radiographic patterns of normal development and abnormal findings in infants and children. *Radiology* **129**: 133–136.

Fullenlove, T.M. (1954). Congenital absence of the odontoid process. Report of a case. *Radiology* **63**: 72–73.

Gans, C. and Northcutt, R.G. (1983). Neural crest and the origin of vertebrates: a new head. *Science* **220**: 268–274.

Garden, R.S. (1961). The structure and function of the upper end of the femur. *Journal of Bone and Joint Surgery* **43B**: 576–589.

Gardner, E. (1956). Osteogenesis in the human embryo and foetus. In: *The Biochemistry and Physiology of Bone* (G. Bourne, Ed.), Chapter 13. New York: Academic Press.

Gardner, E. (1963). The development and growth of bone and joints. *Journal of Bone and Joint Surgery* **45A**: 856–862.

Gardner, E. (1968). The embryology of the clavicle. *Clinical Orthopaedics and Related Research* **58**: 9–16.

Gardner, E. (1973). The early development of the shoulder joint in staged human embryos. *Anatomical Record* **175**: 503–519.

Gardner, E. and Gray, D.J. (1950). Prenatal development of the human hip joint. *American Journal of Anatomy* **87**: 163–211.

Gardner, E. and Gray, D.J. (1953). Prenatal development of the human shoulder and acromio-clavicular joints. *American Journal of Anatomy* **92**: 219–276.

Gardner, E. and Gray, D.J. (1970). The prenatal development of the human femur. *American Journal of Anatomy* **129**: 121–140.

Gardner, E. and O'Rahilly, R. (1968). The early development of the knee joint in staged human embryos. *Journal of Anatomy* **102**: 289–299.

Gardner, E. and O'Rahilly, R. (1972). The early development of the hip joint in staged human embryos. *Anatomical Record* **172**: 451–452.

Gardner, E., Gray, D.J. and O'Rahilly, R. (1959). Prenatal development of the skeleton and joints of the human foot. *Journal of Bone and Joint Surgery* **41A**: 847–876.

Garn, S.M. (1962). X-linked inheritance of developmental timing in man. *Nature* **196**: 695–696.

Garn, S.M. (1970). *The Earlier Gain and Later Loss of Cortical Bone in Nutritional Perspective*. Springfield, IL: C.C. Thomas.

Garn, S.M. and Burdi, A.R. (1971). Prenatal ordering and postnatal sequence in dental development. *Journal of Dental Research* **50**: 1407–1414.

Garn, S.M. and Lewis, A.B. (1957). Relationship between the sequence of calcification and the sequence of eruption of the mandibular molar and premolar teeth. *Journal of Dental Research* **36**: 992–995.

Garn, S.M. and Rohmann, C.G. (1963). On the prevalence of skewness in incremental data. *American Journal of Physical Anthropology* **21**: 235–236.

Garn, S.M. and Schwager, P.M. (1967). Age dynamics of persistent transverse lines in the tibia. *American Journal of Physical Anthropology* **27**: 375–378.

Garn, S.M. and Smith, B.H. (1980). Developmental communalities in tooth emergence timing. *Journal of Dental Research* **59**: 1178.

Garn, S.M., Blumenthal, T. and Rohmann, C.G. (1965). On skewness in the ossification centers of the elbow. *American Journal of Physical Anthropology* **23**: 303–304.

Garn, S.M., Lewis, A.B. and Blizzard, R.M. (1965). Endocrine factors in dental development. *Journal of Dental Research* **44**: 243–258.

Garn, S.M., Lewis, A.B. and Bonné, B. (1962). Third molar formation and its developmental course. *Angle Orthodontist* **32**: 270–279.

Garn, S.M., Lewis, A.B. and Kerewsky, R.S. (1965). Genetic, nutritional and maturational correlates of dental development. *Journal of Dental Research* **44**: 228–242.

Garn, S.M., Lewis, A.B. and Polacheck, D.L. (1959). Variability of tooth formation. *Journal of Dental Research* **38**: 135–148.

Garn, S.M., Lewis, A.B. and Shoemaker, D.W. (1956). The sequence of calcification of the mandibular molar and premolar teeth. *Journal of Dental Research* **35**: 555–561.

Garn, S.M., Nagy, J.M., Sandusky, S.T. and Trowbridge, F. (1973). Economic impact on tooth emergence. *American Journal of Physical Anthropology* **39**: 233–238.

Garn, S.M., Rohmann, C.G. and Apfelbaum, B. (1961). Complete epiphyseal fusion of the hand. *American Journal of Physical Anthropology* **19**: 365–371.

Garn, S.M., Rohmann, C.G. and Blumenthal, T. (1966). Ossification sequence polymorphism in skeletal development. *American Journal of Physical Anthropology* **24**: 101–116.

Garn, S.M., Rohmann, C.G. and Hertzog, K.P. (1969). Apparent influence of the x-chromosome on timing of 73 ossification centres. *American Journal of Physical Anthropology* **30**: 123–128.

Garn, S.M., Rohmann, C.G. and Silverman, F.N. (1967). Radiographic standards for postnatal ossification and tooth calcification. *Medical Radiography and Photography* **43**: 45–66.

Garn, S.M., Silverman, F.N., Hertzog, K.P. and Rohmann, C.B. (1968). Lines and bands of increased density. *Medical Radiography and Photography* **44**: 58–89.

Garn, S.M., Sandusky, S.T., Rosen, N.N. and Trowbridge, F. (1973a). Economic impact on postnatal ossification. *American Journal of Physical Anthropology* **38**: 1–3.

Garn, S.M., Sandusky, S.T., Nagy, J.M. and Trowbridge, F. (1973b). Negro-Caucasoid differences in permanent tooth emergence at a constant income level. *Archives of Oral Biology* **18**: 609–615.

Garn, S.M., Babler, W.J. and Burdi, A.R. (1976). Prenatal origins of brachymesophalangia-5. *American Journal of Physical Anthropology* **44**: 413–416.

Garn, S.M., Burdi, A.R. and Babler, W.J. (1974). Male advancement in prenatal hand development. *American Journal of Physical Anthropology* **41**: 353–360.

Geddes, A.C. (1912). The ribs in the second month of development. *Journal of Anatomy and Physiology* **47**: 18–30.

Gepstein, R., Weiss, R.E. and Hallel, T. (1984). Acetabular dysplasia and hip dislocation after selective premature fusion of the triradiate cartilage. *Journal of Bone and Joint Surgery* **64B**: 334–336.

Ghantus, M.K. (1951). Growth of the shaft of the human radius and ulna during the first two years of life. *American Journal of Roentgenology* **65**: 784–786.

Gill, N.W. (1969). Congenital atresia of the ear. *Journal of Laryngology and Otology* **83**: 551–587.

Gill, G.G. and Abbott, L.C. (1942). Practical method of predicting the growth of the femur and tibia in the child. *Archives of Surgery* **45**: 286–315.

Gillett, R.M. (1997). Dental emergence among Zambian school children: an assessment of the accuracy of three methods of assigning ages. *American Journal of Physical Anthropology* **102**: 447–454.

Gindhart, P.S. (1969). The frequency of appearance of transverse lines in the tibia in relation to childhood illness. *American Journal of Physical Anthropology* **31**: 17–22.

Gindhart, P.S. (1973). Growth standards for the tibia and radius in children aged one month through eighteen years. *American Journal of Physical Anthropology* **39**: 41–48.

Giraud-Guille, M.M. (1988). Twisted plywood architecture of collagen fibrils on human compact bone osteons. *Calcified Tissue International* **42**: 167–180.

Girdany, B.R. and Blank, E. (1965). Anterior fontanel bones. *American Journal of Roentgenology* **95**: 148–153.

Gladstone, R.J. and Wakeley, C.P.G. (1932). Cervical ribs and rudimentary first thoracic ribs considered from the clinical and etiological standpoint. *Journal of Anatomy* **66**: 334–370.

Glaser, K.L. (1949). Double contours, cupping and spurring in roentgenograms of long bones in infants. *American Journal of Roentgenology* **61**: 482–492.

Gleiser, I. and Hunt, E.E. (1955). The permanent mandibular first molar: its calcification, eruption and decay. *American Journal of Physical Anthropology* **13**: 253–284.

Glenister, T.W. (1976). An embryological view of cartilage. *Journal of Anatomy* **122**: 323–330.

Goergen, T.G., Resnick, G. and Saltzstein, S.L. (1979). Dorsal defect of the patella: a characteristic radiographic lesion. *Radiology* **130**: 333–336.

Goldbloom, R.B. and Scott Dunbar, J. (1960). Calcification of cartilage in the trachea and larynx in infancy associated with congenital stridor. *Pediatrics* **26**: 669–673.

Goldie, I. (1988). Talar and peritalar injuries. In: *The Foot* (B. Helal, and D. Wilson, Eds), pp. 916–936. Edinburgh: Churchill Livingstone.

Goldstein, H. (1986). Sampling for growth studies. In: *Human Growth, A Comprehensive Treatise*, Vol. 3, 3rd edition (F. Falkner and J.M. Tanner, Eds), pp. 59–78. New York: Plenum Press.

Goldstein, R.S. and Kalcheim, C. (1992). Determination of epithelial half-somites in skeletal morphogenesis. *Development* **116**: 441–445.

Goldstein, I., Reece, E.A. and Hobbins, J.C. (1988). Sonographic appearance of the fetal heel ossification centers and foot length measurements provide independent markers for gestational age estimation. *American Journal of Obstetrics and Gynaecology* **159**: 923–926.

Goode, H., Waldron, T. and Rogers, J. (1993). Bone growth in juveniles: a methodological note. *International Journal of Osteoarchaeology* **3**: 321–323.

Goret-Nicaise, M. and Dhem, A. (1982). Presence of chondroid tissue in the symphyseal region of the growing human mandible. *Acta Anatomica* **113**: 189–195.

Goret-Nicaise, M. and Dhem, A. (1984). The mandibular body of the human fetus. *Anatomy and Embryology* **169**: 231–236.

Gottlieb, K. (1978). Artificial cranial deformation and the increased complexity of the lambdoid suture. *American Journal of Physical Anthropology* **48**: 213–214.

Grant, J.C.B. (1948). *A Method of Anatomy*, 4th edition. London: Ballière, Tindall and Cox.

Gray, D.J. and Gardner, E. (1951). Prenatal development of the human elbow joint. *American Journal of Anatomy* **88**: 429–470.

Gray, D.J. and Gardner, E. (1969). The prenatal development of the human humerus. *American Journal of Anatomy* **124**: 431–445.

Gray, D.J., Gardner, E. and O'Rahilly, R. (1957). The prenatal development of the skeleton and joints of the human hand. *American Journal of Anatomy* **101**: 169–224.

Green, H.L.H.H. (1930). An unusual case of atlanto-occipital fusion. *Journal of Anatomy* **65**: 140–44.

Green, W.T. (1975). Painful bipartite patella. *Clinical Orthopaedics and Related Research* **110**: 197–200.

Green, J.P. and Waugh, W. (1968). Congenital lateral dislocation of the patella. *Journal of Bone and Joint Surgery* **50B**: 285–289.

Greig, D.M. (1892). Congenital and symmetrical perforation of both parietal bones. *Journal of Anatomy and Physiology* **26**: 187–191.

Greig, D.M. (1917). Two cases of congenital symmetrical perforation of the parietal bones. *Edinburgh Medical Journal* **18**: 205–209.

Greig, D.M. (1926). On symmetrical thinness of the parietal bones. *Edinburgh Medical Journal* **33**: 645–671.

Greig, D.M. (1927a). Congenital absence of the tympanic element of both temporal bones. *Journal of Laryngology and Otology* **42**: 309–314.

Greig, D.M. (1927b). Abnormally large parietal foramina. *Edinburgh Medical Journal* **34**: 629–648.

Greulich, W.W. (1973). A comparison of the dysplastic middle phalanx of the fifth finger in mentally normal Caucasians, Mongoloids and Negroes with that of individuals of the same racial groups who have Down's Syndrome. *American Journal of Roentgenology* **118**: 259–281.

Greulich, W.W. and Pyle, S.I. (1959). *Radiographic Atlas of Skeletal Development of the Hand and Wrist*. Stanford, CA: Stanford University Press.

Greulich, W.W. and Thoms, H. (1944). The growth and development of the pelvis of individual girls before, during and after puberty. *Yale Journal of Biology and Medicine* **17**: 91–97.

Griffiths, J. (1902). The normal position of the big toe. *Journal of Anatomy and Physiology* **36**: 344–355.

Grøn, A.-M. (1962). Prediction of tooth emergence. *Journal of Dental Research* **41**: 573–585.

Grube, D. and Reinbach, W. (1976). Das Cranium eines menschlichen Embryo von 80mm Sch.-St.-Länge. *Anatomy and Embryology* **149**: 183–208.

Grüneberg, H. (1963). *The Pathology of Development: A Study of Inherited Skeletal Disorders in Animals*. Oxford: Blackwell Scientific.

Guida, G., Cigala, F. and Riccio, V. (1969). The vascularization of the vertebral body in the human fetus at term. *Clinical Orthopaedics and Related Research* **65**: 229–234.

Gumpel-Pinot, M. (1984). Muscle and skeleton of limbs and body wall. In: *Chimeras in Developmental Biology* (N.A. Le Douarin and A. McLaren, Eds), pp. 281–310. London: Academic Press.

Gunsel, E. (1951). Das os coracoideum. *Fortschritte auf dem Gebiete der Röentgenstrahlen* **74**: 112–115.

Gurdon, J.B., Mohun, T.J., Sharpe, C.R. and Taylor, M.V. (1989). Embryonic induction and muscle gene activation. *Trends in Genetics* **5**: 51–56.

Gusis, S.E., Babini, J.C., Garay, S.M., Garcia Morteo, O. and Maldonado Cocco, J.A. (1990). Evaluation of the measurement methods for protrusio acetabuli in normal children. *Skeletal Radiology* **19**: 279–282.

Gustafson, G. (1950). Age determinations on teeth. *Journal of the American Dental Association* **41**: 45–54.

Gustafson, G. and Koch, G. (1974). Age estimation up to 16 years of age based on dental development. *Odontologisk Revy* **25**: 297–306.

Guy, H., Masset, C. and Baud, C.-A. (1997). Infant taphonomy. *International Journal of Osteoarchaeology* **7**: 221–229.

Gwinn, J.L. and Smith, J.L. (1962). Acquired and congenital absence of the odontoid process. *American Journal of Roentgenology* **88**: 424–431.

Haavikko, K. (1970). The formation and the alveolar and clinical eruption of the permanent teeth. An orthopantographic study. *Proceedings of the Finnish Dental Society* **66**: 101–170.

Haavikko, K. (1973). The physiological resorption of the roots of deciduous teeth in Helsinki children. *Proceedings of the Finnish Dental Society* **69**: 93–98.

Haavikko, K. (1974). Tooth formation age estimated on a few selected teeth: a simple method for clinical use. *Proceedings of the Finnish Dental Society* **70**: 15–19.

Hadley, L.A. (1948). Atlanto-occipital fusion, ossiculum terminale and occipital vertebra as related to basilar impression with neurological symptoms. *American Journal of Roentgenology* **59**: 511–524.

Haeffner, L.S.B., Barbieri, M.A., Rona, R.J., Bettiol, H. and Silva, A.A.M. (2002). The relative strength of weight and length at birth in contrast to social factors as determinants of height at 18 years. *Annals of Human Biology* **29**: 627–640.

Haffajee, M.R. (1997). A contribution by the ascending pharyngeal artery to the arterial supply of the odontoid process of the axis vertebra. *Clinical Anatomy* **10**: 14–18.

Hägg, U. and Matsson, L. (1985). Dental maturity as an indicator of chronological age: the accuracy and precision of three methods. *European Journal of Orthodontics* **7**: 24–34.

Haines, R.W. (1933). Cartilage canals. *Journal of Anatomy* **68**: 45–64.

Haines, R.W. (1937). Growth of cartilage canals in the patella. *Journal of Anatomy* **71**: 471–479.

Haines, R.W. (1953). The early development of the femoro-tibial and tibio-fibular joints. *Journal of Anatomy* **87**: 192–206.

Haines, R.W. (1974). The pseudoepiphysis of the first metacarpal of man. *Journal of Anatomy* **117**: 145–158.

Haines, R.W. (1975). The histology of epiphyseal union in mammals. *Journal of Anatomy* **120**: 1–25.

Haines, R.W. and Mohuiddin, A. (1962). Epiphyseal growth and union in the pigeon. *Journal of the Faculty of Medicine – Baghdad* **4**: 4–21.

Haines, R.W., Mohuiddin, A., Okpa, F.I. and Viega-Pires, J.A. (1967). The sites of early epiphysial union in the limb girdles and major long bones of man. *Journal of Anatomy* **101**: 823–831.

Hale, J.E. and Wuthier, R.E. (1987). The mechanism of matrix vesicle formation: studies on the composition of chondrocyte microvilli and on the effects of microfilament-perturbing agents on cellular vesiculation. *Journal of Biological Chemistry* **262**: 1916–1925.

Hales, S. (1727). *Statical essays. Vol. 1. Vegetable staticks.* London: W. Innys.

Hall, B.K. (1967). The formation of adventitious cartilage by membrane bones under the influence of mechanical stimulation in vitro. *Life Sciences* **6**: 663–667.

Hall, B.K. (1983). *Cartilage Vol. 2. Development, Differentiation and Growth*. New York: Academic Press.

Hall, B.K. (1984). Developmental mechanisms underlying the formation of atavisms. *Biology Reviews* **59**: 89–124.

Hall, B.K. (1988). The embryonic development of bone. *American Science* **76**: 174–181.

Hall, B.K. and Miyake, T. (1992). The membranous skeleton: the role of cell condensations in vertebrate skeletogenesis. *Anatomy and Embryology* **186**: 107–124.

Hallel, T. and Salvati, E.A. (1977). Premature closure of the triradiate cartilage: a case report and animal experiment. *Clinical Orthopaedics and Related Research* **124**: 278–281.

Hamilton, W.J. and Mossman, H.W. (1972). *Hamilton, Boyd and Mossman's Human Embryology – Prenatal Development of Form and Function*. London: Williams and Wilkins.

Hancox, N.M., Hay, J.D., Holden, W.S., Moss, P.D. and Whitehead, A.S. (1951). The radiological 'double contour' effect in the long bones of newly born infants. *Archives of Disease in Childhood* **26**: 534–548.

Hansen, E.S. (1993). Microvascularization, osteogenesis and myelopoiesis in normal and pathological conditions. In: *Bone Circulation and Vascularization in Normal and Pathological Conditions* (A. Shoutens, J.W.M. Gardiniers and S.P.F. Hughes, Eds), pp. 29–41. New York: Plenum Press.

Hansman, C.F. (1962). Appearance and fusion of ossification centres in the human skeleton. *American Journal of Roentgenology* **88**: 476–482.

Hanson, F.B. (1920). The history of the earliest stages in the human clavicle. *Anatomical Record* **19**: 309–325.

Hanson, J.R., Anson, B.J. and Strickland, E.M. (1962). Branchial sources of the auditory ossicles in man – Part II. *Archives of Otolaryngology* **76**: 200–215.

Haraldsson, S. (1959). On osteochondrosis deformans juvenilis capituli humeri including investigation of intra-osseous vasculature in distal humerus. *Acta Orthopaedica Scandinavica* **38**(Suppl.).

Haraldsson, S. (1962). The vascular pattern of a growing and full-grown human epiphysis. *Acta Anatomica* **48**: 156–167.

Harjeet and Jit, I. (1992). Dimensions of the thyroid cartilage in neonates, children and adults in northwest Indian subjects. *Journal of the Anatomical Society of India* **41**: 81–92.

Harris, H.A. (1926). The growth of the long bones in childhood: with special reference to certain bony striations of the metaphysis and to the role of the vitamins. *Archives of International Medicine* **38**: 785–806.

Harris, H.A. (1933). *Bone Growth in Health and Disease*. London: Oxford University Press.

Harris, B.J. (1955). Anomalous structures in the developing human foot. *Anatomical Record* **121**: 399.

Harris, E.F. and Buck, A.L. (2002). Tooth mineralization: a technical note on the Moorrees–Fanning–Hunt standards. *Dental Anthropology* **16**: 15–20.

Harris, R.S. and Jones, D.M. (1956). The arterial supply to the adult cervical vertebral bodies. *Journal of Bone and Joint Surgery* **38B**: 922–927.

Harris, R.I. and MacNab, I. (1954). Structural changes in the lumbar intervertebral discs. Their relationship to low back pain and sciatica. *Journal of Bone and Joint Surgery* **36B**: 304–322.

Harris, A.M.P., Wood, R.E., Nortjé, C.J. and Thomas, C.J. (1987). Gender and ethnic differences of radiographic image of the frontal region. *Journal of Forensic Odonto-Stomatology* **5**: 51–57.

Harrison, T.J. (1957). Pelvic growth. PhD dissertation, University of Belfast.

Harrison, T.J. (1958). The growth of the pelvis in the rat – a mensural and morphological study. *Journal of Anatomy* **92**: 236–260.

Harrison, T.J. (1961). The influence of the femoral head on pelvic growth and acetabular formation in the rat. *Journal of Anatomy* **95**: 12–24.

Harrison, D.F.N. and Denny, S. (1983). Ossification in the primate larynx. *Acta Otolaryngologica* **95**: 440–446.

Harrison, R.B. and Keats, T.E. (1980). Epiphyseal clefts. *Skeletal Radiology* **5**: 23–27.

Harrower, G. (1925). A septdigitate foot in man. *Journal of Anatomy* **60**: 106–109.

Hartley, J.B. and Burnett, C.W.F. (1943a). A study of craniolacunia. *Journal of Obstetrics and Gynaecology of the British Empire* **50**: 1–12.

Hartley, J.B. and Burnett, C.W.F. (1943b). The radiological diagnosis of craniolacunia. *British Journal of Radiology* **16**: 99–108.

Hartley, J.B. and Burnett, C.W.F. (1944). New light on the origin of craniolacunia. *British Journal of Radiology* **17**: 110–114.

Harty, M. (1957). The calcar femorale and the femoral neck. *Journal of Bone and Joint Surgery* **39A**: 625–630.

Hasselwander, A. (1910). Untersuchungen über die Ossifikation des menschlichen Fussskelets. *Zeitschrift für Morphologie und Anthropologie* **12**: 1–140.

Hast, M.H. (1970). The developmental anatomy of the larynx. *Otolaryngologic Clinics of North America* **3**: 413–438.

Hately, W., Evison, G. and Samuel, E. (1965). The pattern of ossification in the laryngeal cartilages: a radiological study. *British Journal of Radiology* **38**: 585–591.

Hattner, R. and Frost, H.M. (1963). Mean skeletal age: its calculation and theoretical effects on skeletal tracer physiology and on the physical characteristics of bone. *Henry Ford Hospital Medical Bulletin* **11**: 201–216.

Havers, C. (1691). *Osteologia Nova*, 2nd edition. London: Smith.

Hawkins, R.J., Fielding, J.W. and Thompson, W.J. (1976). Os odontoideum: congenital or acquired? *Journal of Bone and Joint Surgery* **58A**: 413–414.

Healy, M.J.R. (1986). Statistics of growth standards. In: *Human Growth, A Comprehensive Treatise, Vol. 3*, 2nd edition (F. Falkner and J.M. Tanner, Eds), pp. 47–58. New York: Plenum Press.

Heindon, C.N. (1951). Cleidocranial dysostosis. *American Journal of Human Genetics* **3**: 314–324.

Helm, S. (1969). Secular trends in tooth eruption. A comparative study of Danish school children of 1913 and 1965. *Archives of Oral Biology* **14**: 1177–1191.

Hensinger, R.N. and MacEwan, C. (1975). Congenital anomalies of the spine. In: *The Spine*. Philadelphia, PA: W.B.Saunders.

Hershkovitz, I., Latimer, B., Dutour, O., Jellema, L.M., Wish-Baratz, S., Rothschild, C. and Rothschild, B. (1997). The elusive petroexoccipital articulation. *American Journal of Physical Anthropology* **103**: 365–373.

Hertzog, K.P. (1967). Shortened fifth medial phalanges. *American Journal of Physical Anthropology* **27**: 113–118.

Hesdorffer, M.B. and Scammon, R.E. (1928). Growth of long-bones of human fetus as illustrated by the tibia. *Proceedings of the Society for Experimental Biology and Medicine* **25**: 638–641.

Hess, L. (1945). The metopic suture and the metopic syndrome. *Human Biology* **17**: 107–136.

Hess, A.F., Lewis, J.M. and Roman, B. (1932). A radiographic study of crowns of the teeth from birth to adolescence. *Dental Cosmos* **74**: 1053–1061.

Hewitt, D., Westropp, C.K. and Acheson, R.M. (1955). Oxford Child Health Survey. Effect of childish ailments on skeletal development. *British Journal of Preventive and Social Medicine* **9**: 179–186.

Hill, A.H. (1939). Fetal age assessment by centres of ossification. *American Journal of Physical Anthropology* **24**: 251–272.

Hill, A. (1992). Development of tone and reflexes in the fetus and newborn. In: *Fetal and Neonatal Physiology* (R.A. Polin and W.W. Fox, Eds), pp. 1578–1587. Philadelphia, PA: W.B. Saunders.

Hillson, S. (1996). *Dental Anthropology*. Cambridge: Cambridge University Press.

Himes, J.H. (1984). An early hand–wrist atlas and its implications for secular change. *Annals of Human Biology* **11**: 71–75.

Hindman, B.W. and Poole, C.A. (1970). Early appearance of the secondary vertebral ossification centres. *Radiology* **95**: 359–361.

Hirschtick, A.B. (1951). An anomalous tarsal bone. *Journal of Bone and Joint Surgery* **33A**: 907–910.

Hodges, D.C., Harker, L.A. and Schermer, S.J. (1990). Atresia of the external acoustic meatuses in prehistoric populations. *American Journal of Physical Anthropology* **83**: 77–81.

Hoerr, N.L., Pyle, S.I. and Francis, C.C. (1962). *Radiographic Atlas of Skeletal Development of the Foot and Ankle: A Standard of Reference.* Springfield, IL: C.C. Thomas.

Holcomb, S.M.C. and Konigsberg, L.W. (1995). Statistical study of sexual dimorphism in the human fetal sciatic notch. *American Journal of Physical Anthropology* **97**: 113–125.

Holden, L. (1882). *Human Osteology,* 6th edition. London: Churchill.

Holland, C.T. (1921). On rarer ossifications seen during X-ray examinations. *Journal of Anatomy* **55**: 235–248.

Hollender, L. (1967). Enlarged parietal foramina. *Oral Surgery, Oral Medicine and Oral Pathology* **23**: 447–453.

Hollinshead, W.H. (1965). Anatomy of the spine: points of interest to orthopaedic surgeons. *Journal of Bone and Joint Surgery* **47A**: 209–215.

Holsbeeck, M. van, Vandamme, B., Marchal, G., Martens, M., Victor, J. and Baert, A.L. (1987). Dorsal defect of the patella: concept of its origin and relationship with bipartite and multipartite patella. *Skeletal Radiology* **16**: 304–311.

Hoppa, R.D. (1992). Evaluating human skeletal growth: an Anglo-Saxon example. *International Journal of Osteoarchaeology* **2**: 275–288.

Hoppa, R.D. and Gruspier, K.L. (1996). Estimating diaphyseal length from fragmentary subadult skeletal remains: implications for paleodemographic reconstructions of southern Ontario ossuary. *American Journal of Physical Anthropology* **100**: 341–345.

Horswell, B.B., Holmes, A.D., Barnett, J.S. and Levant, B.A. (1987). Maxillonasal dysplasia (Binder's syndrome): a critical review and case study. *Journal of Oral and Maxillofacial Surgery* **45**: 114–122.

Hrdlička, A. (1934). Contributions to the study of the femur: the crista aspera and the pilaster. *American Journal of Physical Anthropology* **19**: 17–37.

Hromada, J. (1939). Contribution to the study of the growth of the fetal pelvis. *Anthropologie* **18**: 129–170.

Huber, G.C. (1912). On the relation of the chorda dorsalis to the anlage of the pharyngeal bursa or median pharyngeal recess. *Anatomical Record* **6**: 373–404.

Huda, T.F.J. and Bowman, J.E. (1994). Variation in cross-striation number between striae in an archaeological population. *International Journal of Osteoarchaeology* **4**: 49–52.

Huda, T.F.J. and Bowman, J.E. (1995). Age determination from dental microstructure in juveniles. *American Journal of Physical Anthropology* **97**: 135–150.

Hughes, E.S.R. (1948). Osgood–Schlatter's disease. *Surgery, Gynecology and Obstetrics* **86**: 323–328.

Hughes, E.S.R. and Sunderland, S. (1946). The tibial tuberosity and the attachment of the ligamentum patellae. *Anatomical Record* **96**: 439–444.

Hughes, H. (1952). The factors determining the direction of the canal for the nutrient artery in the long bones of mammals and birds. *Acta Anatomica* **15**: 261–280.

Hughes, L.O. and Beaty, J.H. (1994). Fractures of the head and neck of the femur in children. Current concepts review. *Journal of Bone and Joint Surgery* **76A**: 283–292.

Hughes, S. and Sweetnam, R. (1980). *The Basis and Practice of Orthopaedics.* London: Heinemann.

Hughston, J.C. (1968). Subluxation of the patella. *Journal of Bone and Joint Surgery* **50A**: 1003–1026.

Hukuda, S., Ota, H., Okabe, N. and Tazima, K. (1980). Traumatic atlanto-axial dislocation causing os odontoideum in infants. *Spine* **5**: 207–210.

Hummert, J.R and Van Gerven, D.P. (1985). Observation on the formation and persistence of radio-opaque transverse lines. *American Journal of Physical Anthropology* **66**: 297–306.

Humphrey, L.T. (1998). Growth patterns in the modern human skeleton. *American Journal of Physical Anthropology* **105**: 57–72.

Humphry, G.M. (1878). On the growth of the jaws. *Journal of Anatomy and Physiology* **12**: 288–293.

Humphry, G.M. (1889). The angle of the neck with the shaft of the femur at different periods of life and under different circumstances. *Journal of Anatomy and Physiology* **23**: 273–282, 387–389.

Hunt, D.R. (1990). Sex determination in the subadult ilia: an indirect test of Weaver's non-metric sexing method. *Journal of Forensic Sciences* **35**: 881–885.

Hunt, E.E. and Hatch, J.W. (1981). The estimation of age at death and ages of formation of transverse lines from measurements of human long bones. *American Journal of Physical Anthropology* **54**: 461–469.

Hunter, J. (1837). *Collected Works, Vol. 4.* London: Palmer.

Hunter, G.K. (1987). An ion exchange mechanism of cartilage calcification. *Connective Tissue Research* **16**: 111–120.

Hunter, W.S. and Garn, S.M. (1972). Disproportionate sexual dimorphism in the human face. *American Journal of Physical Anthropology* **36**: 133–138.

Hurrell, D.J. (1934). The vascularisation of cartilage. *Journal of Anatomy* **69**: 47–61.

Hutter, C.G. and Scott, W. (1949). Tibial torsion. *Journal of Bone and Joint Surgery* **31A**: 511–518.

Huxley, A.K. and Jimenez, S.B. (1996). Technical note: Error in Olivier and Pineau's regression formulae for calculation of stature and lunar age from radial diaphyseal length in forensic fetal remains. *American Journal of Physical Anthropology* **100**: 435–437.

Hylander, W.L., Picq, P.G. and Johnson, K.R. (1991). Function of the supraorbital region of primates. *Archives of Oral Biology* **36**: 273–281.

Ingervall, B. and Thilander, B. (1972). The human spheno-occipital synchondrosis 1. The time of closure observed macroscopically. *Acta Odontologica Scandinavica* **30**: 349–356.

Inman, V.T. and Saunders, J.B. de C.M. (1937). The ossification of the human frontal bone with special reference to its presumed pre- and post-frontal elements. *Journal of Anatomy* **71**: 383–394.

Ippolito,E., Tovaglia, V. and Caterini, R. (1984). Mechanisms of acetabular growth in the fetus in relation to the pathogenesis and treatment of congenital dislocation of the hip. *Italian Journal of Orthopedics and Traumatology* **10**: 501–510.

Irvine, E.D. and Taylor, F.W. (1936). Hereditary and congenital large parietal foramina. *British Journal of Radiology* **9**: 456–462.

Irwin, G.L. (1960). Roentgen determination of the time of closure of the spheno-occipital synchondrosis. *Radiology* **75**: 450–453.

Işcan, M.Y., Loth, S.R. and Wright, R.K. (1984). Age estimation from the rib by phase analysis: White males. *Journal of the Forensic Science Association* **29**: 1094–1104.

Işcan, M.Y., Loth, S.R. and Wright, R.K. (1985). Age estimation from the rib by phase analysis; White females. *Journal of the Forensic Science Association* **30**: 853–863.

Ishii, T., Miyagawa, S. and Hayashi, K. (1994). Traction apophysitis of the medial malleolus. *Journal of Bone and Joint Surgery* **76B**: 802–806.

Israel, H. and Lewis, A.B. (1971). Radiographically determined linear permanent tooth growth from age 6 years. *Journal of Dental Research* **50**: 334–342.

Izpisua-Belmonte, J.C., Tickle, C., Dollé, P., Wolpert, L. and Duboule, D. (1991). Expression of homeobox *Hox-4* genes and the specification of position in chick wing development. *Nature* **350**: 585–589.

Jacquemin, C., Bosley, T.M., al Saleh, M. and Mullaney, P. (2000). Canalis medularis medianus. *Neuroradiology* **42**: 121–123.

Jacobsen, J., Jørgensen, J.B. and Kjær, I. (1991). Tooth and bone development in a Danish medieval mandible with unilateral absence of the mandibular canal. *American Journal of Physical Anthropology* **85**: 15–23.

Jacobson, A. (1955). Embryological evidence for the non-existence of the premaxilla in man. *Journal of the Dental Association of South Africa* **10**: 189–210.

Jacobson, A.G. and Sater, A. (1988). Features of embryonic induction. *Development* **104**: 341–359.

James, T.M., Presley, R. and Steel, F.L.D. (1980). The foramen ovale and sphenoidal angle in man. *Anatomy and Embryology* **160**: 93–104.

Jarvik, E. (1980). *Basic Structure and Evolution of Vertebrates, Vols 1 and 2*. London: Academic Press.

Jarvis, J.L. and Keats, T.E. (1974). Cleidocranial dysostosis: a review of 40 new cases. *American Journal of Roentgenology* **121**: 5–16.

Jaworski, Z.F.G., Duck, B. and Sekaly, G. (1981). Kinetics of osteoclasts and their nuclei in evolving secondary Haversian systems. *Journal of Anatomy* **133**: 397–405.

Jaworski, Z.F.G., Kimmel, D.B. and Jee, W.S.S. (1983). Cell kinetics underlying skeletal growth and bone tissue turnover. In: *Bone Histomorphometry: Techniques and Interpretation* (R.R. Richer, Ed.), pp. 225–239. Boca Raton, FL: CRC Press.

Jeannopoulos, C.L. (1952). Congenital elevation of the scapula. *Journal of Bone and Joint Surgery* **34A**: 883–892.

Jeanty, P., Dramaix-Wilmet, M., van Kerkem, J., Petroos, P. and Schwers, J. (1982). Ultrasonic evaluation of fetal limb growth. Part II. *Radiology* **143**: 751–754.

Jeanty, P., Kirkpatrick, C., Dramaix-Wilmet, M. and Struyven, J. (1981). Ultrasonic evaluation of fetal limb growth. *Radiology* **140**: 165–168.

Jenkins, F.A. (1969). The evolution and development of the dens of the mammalian axis. *Anatomical Record* **164**: 173–184.

Jensen, E. and Palling, M. (1954). The gonial angle – a survey. *American Journal of Orthodontics* **40**: 120–133.

Jit, I. (1957). Observations on prenatal ossification with special references to the bones of the hand and foot. *Journal of the Anatomical Society of India* **6**: 12–23.

Jit, I. and Kulkarni, M. (1976). Times of appearance and fusion of epiphyses at the medial end of the clavicle. *Indian Journal of Medical Research* **64**: 773–782.

Jit, I. and Shah, M.A. (1948). Incidence of frontal or metopic suture amongst Punjabee adults. *Indian Medical Gazette* **83**: 507–508.

Johanson, G. (1971). Age determination from human teeth. A critical evaluation with special consideration of changes after fourteen years of age. *Odontologisk Revy* **22**(Suppl.): 1–126.

Johnson, J.F. and Brogdon, B.G. (1982). Dorsal defect of the patella. *American Journal of Roentgenology* **139**: 339–340.

Johnson, G.F. and Israel, H. (1979). Basioccipital clefts. *Radiology* **133**: 101–103.

Johnson, D.R. and O'Higgins, P. (1996). Is there a link between changes in the vertebral *Hox* code and the shape of the vertebrae? A quantitative study of shape change in the cervical vertebral column of mice. *Journal of Theoretical Biology* **183**: 89–93.

Johnston, F.E. and Zimmer, L.O. (1989). Assessment of growth and age in the immature skeleton. In: *Reconstruction of Life from the Skeleton* (M.Y. İşcan and K.A.R. Kennedy, Eds), pp. 11–21. New York: Liss.

Johnston, F.E., Whitehouse, R.H. and Hertzog, D.P. (1968). Normal variability in the age and first onset of ossification of the triquetral. *American Journal of Physical Anthropology* **28**: 97–100.

Jones, F.W. (1913). The anatomy of cervical ribs. *Proceedings of the Royal Society of Medicine* **6**: 95–113.

Jones, S.J., Glorieux, F.H., Travers, R. and Boyde, A. (1999). The microscopic structure of bone in normal children and patients with osteogenesis imperfecta: a study using back scattered electron imaging. *Calcified Tissue International* **64**: 8–17.

Joseph, J. (1951). The sesamoid bones of the hand and the time of fusion of the epiphyses of the thumb. *Journal of Anatomy* **85**: 230–241.

Juhl, M.D. and Seerup, K.K. (1983). Os odontoideum. A cause of atlanto-axial instability. *Acta Orthopedica Scandinavica* **54**: 113–118.

Kahane, J.C. (1978). A morphological study of the human prepubertal and pubertal larynx. *American Journal of Anatomy* **151**: 11–20.

Kalla, A.K., Khanna, S., Singh, I.P., Sharma, S., Schnobel, R. and Vogel, F. (1989). A genetic and anthropological study of atlanto-occipital fusion. *Human Genetics* **81**: 105–112.

Kanagasuntheram, R. (1967). A note on the development of the tubotympanic recess of the human embryo. *Journal of Anatomy* **101**: 731–741.

Kapadia, Y.K. (1991). An investigation into Harris lines in the documented juveniles from St Brides. Unpublished BSc dissertation, University of London.

Kapadia, Y.K., Bowman, J.E., MacLaughlin, S.M. and Scheuer, J.L. (1992). A study of Harris lines in the juvenile skeletons from St Bride's. *Annals of Human Biology* **19**: 328–329.

Kate, B.R. and Robert, S.L. (1965). Some observations on the upper end of the tibia in squatters. *Journal of Anatomy* **99**: 137–141.

Kawashima, T. and Uhthoff, H.K. (1990). Prenatal development around the sustentaculum tali and its relation to talocalcaneal coalitions. *Journal of Pediatric Orthopedics* **10**: 238–243.

Keating, D.R. and Amberg, J.R. (1954). A source of potential error in the roentgen diagnosis of cervical ribs. *Radiology* **62**: 688–694.

Keats, T.E. (1992). *Atlas of Normal Roentgen Variants that may Simulate Disease*, 5th edition. St Louis, MO: Mosby Yearbook.

Keats, T.E. and Harrison, R.B. (1980). The epiphyseal spur. *Skeletal Radiology* **5**: 175–177.

Keen, J.A. and Wainwright, J. (1958). Ossification of the thyroid, cricoid and arytenoid cartilages. *South African Journal of Laboratory and Clinical Medicine* **4**: 83–108.

Keleman, E., Jánossa, M., Calvo, W. and Fliedner, T.M. (1984). Developmental age estimated by bone-length measurement in human fetuses. *Anatomical Record* **209**: 547–552.

Kelley, R.O. (1970). An electron microscopic study of mesenchyme during development of interdigital spaces in man. *Anatomical Record* **168**: 43–53.

Kelley, R.O. (1973). Fine structure of the apical rim mesenchyme complex during limb morphogenesis in man. *Journal of Embryology and Experimental Morphology* **29**: 117–131.

Kelly, H.J. and Reynolds, L. (1947). Appearance and growth of ossification centres and increases in the body dimensions of White and Negro infants. *American Journal of Roentgenology* **57**: 479–516.

Kenna, M.A. and Hirose, K. (2003). Embryology and development anatomy of the ear. In: *Pediatric Otolaryngology, Vol. 1*, 4th edition. (C.D. Bluestone, S.E. Stool, C.M. Alper, E.M. Arjmand, H.L. Casselbrant, J.E. Dohar and R.F. Yellon, Eds). pp. 129–145. Philadelphia, PA: Saunders.

Kent, R.L., Reed, R.B. and Moorrees, C.F.A. (1978). Associations in emergence age among permanent teeth. *American Journal of Physical Anthropology* **48**: 131–142.

Kerckring, T. (1717). *Specilegium Anatomicum Osteogeniam Foetuum*. Leiden.

Kerley, E.R. (1965). The microscopic determination of age in human bone. *American Journal of Physical Anthropology* **23**: 149–164.

Kerley, E.R. (1976). Forensic anthropology and crimes involving children. *Journal of Forensic Sciences* **21**: 333–339.

Kerley, E.R. and Ubelaker, D.H. (1978). Revisions in the microscopic method of estimating age at death in human cortical bone. *American Journal of Physical Anthropology* **49**: 545–546.

Kerr, H.D. (1933). Anomalies of the skull in the new-born with special reference to 'relief' or 'lacuna skull' ('Lückenschädel'). *American Journal of Roentgenology* **30**: 458–463.

Kessel, M. and Gruss, P. (1991). Homeotic transformations of murine prevertebrae and concomitant alteration of *Hox* codes induced by retinoic acid. *Cell* **67**: 89–104.

Khoo, F.Y. and Kuo, C.L. (1948). An unusual anomaly of the inferior portion of the scapula. *Journal of Bone and Joint Surgery* **30A**: 1010–1011.

Kieny, M., Mauger, A. and Sengel, P. (1972). Early regionalization of the somitic mesoderm as studied by the development of the axial skeleton of the chick embryo. *Developmental Biology* **28**: 142–161.

Kier, E.L. (1966). Embryology of the normal optic canal and its anomalies. *Investigative Radiology* **1**: 346–362.

Kier, E.L. (1968). The infantile sella turcica. New roentgenological and anatomic concepts based on a developmental study of the sphenoid bone. *American Journal of Roentgenology* **102**: 747–767.

Kier, E.L. and Rothman, L.G. (1976). Radiologically significant anatomic variations of the developing sphenoid in humans. In: *Symposium on the Development of the Basicranium* (J.F. Bosma, Ed.), pp. 107–140. Bethesda, MD: US Department of Health, Education and Welfare.

Kieser, J.A. (1990). *Human Adult Odontometrics*. Cambridge: Cambridge University Press.

King, S.E. and Ulijaszek, S.J. (1999). Invisible insults during growth and development: contemporary theories and past populations. In: *Human Growth in the Past*: *Studies from Bones and Teeth*. (R.D. Hoppa and C.M. FitzGerald. Eds), pp.161–182. Cambridge: Cambridge University Press.

Kirlew, K.A., Hathout, G.M., Reiter, S.D. and Gold, R.H. (1993). Os odontoideum in identical twins: perspectives on aetiology. *Skeletal Radiology* **22**: 525–527.

Kirsch, T and Claassen, H. (2000). Matrix vesicles mediate mineralization of human thyroid cartilage. *Calcified Tissue International* **66**: 292–297.

Kjar, I. (1974). Skeletal maturation of the human fetus assessed radiographically on the basis of ossification sequences in the hand and foot. *American Journal of Physical Anthropology* **40**: 257–276.

Kjær, I. (1975). Histochemical investigations on the symphysis menti in the human fetus related to skeletal maturation in the hand and foot. *Acta Anatomica* **93**: 606–633.

Kjær, I. (1980). Development of deciduous mandibular incisors related to developmental stages in the mandible. *Acta Odontologica Scandinavica* **38**: 257–262.

Kjær, I. (1990a). Ossification of the human fetal basicranium. *Journal of Craniofacial Genetics and Developmental Biology* **10**: 29–38.

Kjær, I. (1990b). Radiographic determination of prenatal basicranial ossification. *Journal of Craniofacial Genetics and Developmental Biology* **10**: 113–123.

Kjær, I. (1990c). Prenatal human cranial development evaluated on coronal plane radiographs. *Journal of Craniofacial Genetics and Developmental Biology* **10**: 339–351.

Kjær, I. (1990d). Correlated appearance of ossification and nerve tissue in human fetal jaws. *Journal of Craniofacial Genetics and Developmental Biology* **10**: 329–336.

Kjær, I. (1997). Mandibular movements during elevation and fusion of the palatal shelves evaluated from the course of Meckel's cartilage. *Journal of Craniofacial Genetics and Developmental Biology* **17**: 80–85.

Kjær, I., Kjær, T.W. and Græm, N. (1993). Ossification sequence of occipital bone and vertebrae in human fetuses. *Journal of Craniofacial Genetics and Developmental Biology* **13**: 83–88.

Klima, M. (1968). Early development of the human sternum and the problem of homologization of the so called suprasternal ossicles. *Acta Anatomica* **69**: 473–484.

Kline, D.G. (1966). Atlanto-axial dislocation simulating a head injury: hypoplasia of the odontoid. Case report. *Journal of Neurosurgery* **24**: 1013–1016.

Knight, B. (1996). *Forensic Pathology*, 2nd edition. London: Arnold.

Knott, V.B. (1974). Birotundal diameter of the human sphenoid bone from age six years to early adulthood. *American Journal of Physical Anthropology* **41**: 279–284.

Knott, V.B. and Johnson, R. (1970). Height and shape of the palate in girls: a longitudinal study. *Archives of Oral Biology* **15**: 849–860.

Knudson, C.B. and Toole, B.P. (1987). Hyaluronate-cell interactions during differentiation of chick embryo limb mesoderm. *Developmental Biology* **124**: 82–90.

Knussmann, R. (1988). *Anthropologie. Handbuch der vergleichenden Biologie des Menschen. Band I*. Stuttgart: Gustav Fisher.

Koch, A.R. (1960). Die Frühentwicklung der Clavicula beim Menschen. *Acta Anatomica* **42**: 177–212.

Kodama, G. (1976a). Developmental studies on the presphenoid of the human sphenoid bone. In: *Symposium on the Development of the Basicranium* (J.F. Bosma, Ed.), pp. 142–154. Bethesda, MD: US Department of Health, Education and Welfare.

Kodama, G. (1976b). Developmental studies on the body of the human sphenoid bone. In: *Symposium on the Development of the Basicranium* (J.F. Bosma, Ed.), pp. 156–165. Bethesda, MD: US Department of Health, Education and Welfare.

Kodama, G. (1976c). Developmental studies on the orbitosphenoid of the human sphenoid bone. In: *Symposium on the Development of the Basicranium* (J.F. Bosma, Ed.), pp. 166–176. Bethesda, MD: US Department of Health, Education and Welfare.

Koebke, J. (1978). Some observations on the development of the human hyoid bone. *Anatomy and Embryology* **153**: 279–286.

Kohler, A., Zimmer, E.F. and Wilk, S.P. (1968). *Borderlands of the Normal and Early Pathologic in Skeletal Radiology*, 3rd edition. New York: Grune and Stratton.

Kolar, J.C. and Salter, E.M. (1997). Preoperative anthropometric dysmorphology in metopic synostosis. *American Journal of Physical Anthropology* **103**: 341–351.

Komlos, J. and Kriwy, P. (2002). Social status and adult heights in the two Germanies. *Annals of Human Biology* **29**: 641–648.

Konie, J.C. (1964). Comparative value of X-rays of the spheno-occipital synchondrosis and of the wrist for skeletal age assessment. *Angle Orthodontist* **34**: 303–313.

Kornberg, M. (1988). MRI diagnosis of traumatic Schmorl's node: a case report. *Spine* **13**: 934–935.

Kósa, F., Antal, A. and Farkas, I. (1990). Electron probe analysis of human teeth for the determination of age. *Medicine, Science and the Law* **30**: 109–114.

Krahl, V.E. (1948). The bicipital groove: a visible record of humeral torsion. *Anatomical Record* **101**: 319–331.

Krahl, V.E. (1976). The phylogeny and ontogeny of humeral torsion. *American Journal of Physical Anthropology* **45**: 595–600.

Krahl, V.E. and Evans, F.G. (1945). Humeral torsion in man. *American Journal of Physical Anthropology* **3**: 229–253.

Kraus, B.S. (1959a). Calcification of the human deciduous teeth. *Journal of the American Dental Association* **59**: 1128–1136.

Kraus, B.S. (1959b). Differential calcification rates in the human primary dentition. *Archives of Oral Biology* **1**: 133–144.

Kraus, B.S. (1960). Prenatal growth and morphology of the human bony palate. *Journal of Dental Research* **39**: 1177–1199.

Kraus, B.S. and Decker, J.D. (1960). The prenatal inter-relationships of the maxilla and premaxilla in the facial development of man. *Acta Anatomica* **40**: 278–294.

Kraus, B.S. and Jordan, R.E. (1965). *The Human Dentition before Birth*. London: Henry Kimpton.

Krogman, W.M. (1951). The problem of 'timing' in facial growth, with special reference to the period of the changing dentition. *American Journal of Orthodontics* **37**: 253–276.

Krogman, W.M. and Işcan, M.Y. (1986). *The Human Skeleton in Forensic Medicine*, 2nd edition. Springfield, IL: C.C. Thomas.

Kronfeld, R. (1935). First permanent molar: its condition at birth and its postnatal development. *Journal of the American Dental Association* **22**: 1131–1155.

Kronfeld, R. and Schour, I. (1939). Neonatal dental hypoplasia. *Journal of the American Dental Association* **26**: 18–32.

Kruyff, E. (1967). Transverse cleft in the basi-occiput. *Acta Radiologica* **6**: 41−48.

Kuettner, K.E. and Pauli, B.U. (1983). Vascularity of cartilage. In: *Cartilage Vol. 1. Structure, Function and Biochemistry* (B.K. Hall, Ed.), pp. 281−312. New York: Academic Press.

Kuhns, L.R. and Finnstrom, O. (1976). New standards of ossification of the newborn. *Radiology* **119**: 655−660.

Kuhns, L.R., Sherman, M.P. and Poznanski, A.K. (1972). Determination of neonatal maturation on the chest radiograph. *Radiology* **102**: 597−603.

Kuhns, L.R., Sherman, M.P., Poznanski, A.K. and Holt, J.F. (1973). Humeral head and coracoid ossification in the newborn. *Radiology* **107**: 145−149.

Kullman, L., Eklund, B. and Grundin, R. (1990). The value of the frontal sinus in identification of unknown persons. *Journal of Forensic Odonto-Stomatology* **8**: 3−10.

Kusiak, J.F., Zins, J.E. and Whitaker, L.A. (1985). The early revascularization of membranous bone. *Plastic and Reconstructive Surgery* **76**: 510−514.

Kutz, E.R. (1949). Congenital absence of the patellae. *Journal of Pediatrics* **34**: 760−762.

Kvinnsland, S. (1969a). Observations on the early ossification of the upper jaw. *Acta Odontologica Scandinavica* **27**: 649−654.

Kvinnsland, S. (1969b). Observations on the early ossification process of the mandible as seen in plastic embedded human embryos. *Acta Odontologica Scandinavica* **27**: 642−648.

Kyrkanides, S., Kjær, I. and Fischer-Hansen, B. (1993). Development of the basilar part of the occipital bone in normal human fetuses. *Journal of Craniofacial Genetics and Developmental Biology* **13**: 184−192.

Lacroix, P. (1951). *The Organization of Bones*. London: Churchill Livingstone.

Landis, W.J. (1995). The strength of a calcified tissue depends in part on the molecular structure and organization of its constituent mineral crystals in their organic matrix. *Bone* **16**: 533−544.

Lane, E.B. and Tickle, C. (2003). Symposium Issue: How to make a hand. *Journal of Anatomy* **202**: 1−174.

Lang, J. (1989). *Clinical Anatomy of the Nose, Nasal Cavity and Paranasal Sinuses* (trans. P.M. Stell). New York: Thieme.

Lang, J. (1995). *Skull Base and Related Structures − Atlas of Clinical Anatomy*. Stuttgart: Schattauer.

Lannigan, F.J., O'Higgins, P., Oxnard, C.E. and McPhie, P. (1995). Age related bone resorption in the normal incus: a case of maladaptive remodelling? *Journal of Anatomy* **186**: 651−655.

Lanz, T. and Wachsmut, W. (1982). *Praktische Anatomie. Zweiter Band, siebter Teil: Rücken*. Berlin: Springer.

Lapayowker, M.S. (1960). An unusual variant of the cervical spine. *American Journal of Roentgenology* **83**: 656−659.

Larsen, W.J. (1993). *Human Embryology*. Edinburgh: Churchill Livingstone.

Last, R.J. (1973). *Anatomy, Regional and Applied*, 5th edition. Edinburgh: Churchill Livingstone.

Latham, R.A. (1966). Observations on the growth of the cranial base in the human skull. *Journal of Anatomy* **100**: 435.

Latham, R.A. (1970). Maxillary development and growth: the septomaxillary ligament. *Journal of Anatomy* **107**: 471−478.

Latham, R.A. (1971). The development, structure and growth pattern of the human mid-palatal suture. *Journal of Anatomy* **108**: 31−41.

Latham, R.A. (1972). The sella point and postnatal growth of the human cranial base. *American Journal of Orthodontics* **61**: 156−162.

Lau, E.C., Mohandas, T.K., Shapiro, L.J., Slavkin, H.C. and Snead, M.L. (1988). Human amelogenin gene loci are on the X and Y chromosomes. *American Journal of Human Genetics* **43**: A149.

Laurenson, R.D. (1963). The chondrification and primary ossification of the human ilium. MD thesis, University of Aberdeen.

Laurenson, R.D. (1964a). The primary ossification of the human ilium. *Anatomical Record* **148**: 209–217.

Laurenson, R.D. (1964b). The chondrification of the human ilium. *Anatomical Record* **148**: 197–202.

Laurenson, R.D. (1965). Development of the acetabular roof in the fetal hip. A histological study. *Journal of Bone and Joint Surgery* **47A**: 975–983.

Lavelle, C.L.B. and Moore, W.J. (1970). Proportionate growth of the human jaws between the fourth and seventh months of intrauterine life. *Archives of Oral Biology* **15**: 453–459.

Lazenby, R.A. (1984). Inherent deficiencies in cortical bone microstructural age estimation techniques. *Ossa* **9**: 95–103.

Lebret, L. (1962). Growth changes in the palate. *Journal of Dental Research* **41**: 1391–1404.

Lechtig, A., Delgado, H., Lasky, R.E., Klein, R.E., Engle, P.L., Yarbrough, C. and Habicht, J.-P. (1975). Maternal nutrition and fetal growth in developing societies. *American Journal of Diseases of Childhood* **129**: 434–437.

Ledley, R.S., Huang, H.K. and Pence, R.G. (1971). Quantitative study of normal growth and eruption of teeth. *Computers in Biology and Medicine* **1**: 231–241.

LeDouble, A.F. (1903). *Traité des Variations des Os du Crâne de l'Homme, Vol. 1*. Paris: Vigot Frères.

Lee, J., Jaruis, J., Uhthoff, H.K. and Avroch, L. (1992). The fetal acetabulum. A histomorphometric study of acetabular anteversion and femoral head coverage. *Clinical Orthopaedics and Related Research* **281**: 48–55.

Lees, S. and Prostak, K. (1988). The locus of mineral crystallites in bone. *Connective Tissue Research* **18**: 41–54.

Leet, A.I., MacKenzie, W.G., Szoke, G. and Harcke, H.T. (1999). Injury to the growth plate after Pemberton osteotomy. *Journal of Bone and Joint Surgery* **81A**: 169–176.

Le Gros Clark, W.E. (1958). *The Tissues of the Body*, 4th edition. Oxford: Clarendon Press.

Le Minor, J.M. (1988). The ventral metacarpo- and metatarsophalangeal sesamoid bones: comparative anatomy and evolutionary aspects. *Morphologisches Jahrbuch* **134**: 693–731.

Lemons, J.A., Kuhns, L.R. and Poznanski, A.K. (1972). Calcification of the fetal teeth as an index of fetal maturation. *American Journal of Obstetrics and Gynecology* **114**: 628–630.

Lemperg, R. and Liliequist, B. (1972). Appearance of the ossification centre in the proximal humeral epiphysis of newborn children. *Acta Radiologica Scandinavica – Diagnosis* **12**: 76–80.

Lengelé, B.G. and Dehm, A.J. (1988). Length of the styloid process of the temporal bone. *Archives of Otolaryngology and Head and Neck Surgery* **114**: 1003–1006.

León, X., Maranillo, E., Mirapeix, R.M., Quer, M. and Sañudo, J.R. (1997). Foramen thyroideum: a comparative study in embryos, fetuses and adults. *Laryngoscope* **107**: 1146–1150.

Letts, M., Smallman, T., Afanasiou, R. and Gouw, G. (1986). Fracture of the pars interarticularis in adolescent athletes: a clinical biometrical analysis. *Journal of Pediatric Orthopedics* **6**: 40–46.

Levesque, G.-Y., Demirjian, A. and Tanguay, R. (1981). Sexual dimorphism in the development, emergence and agenesis of the mandibular third molar. *Journal of Dental Research* **60**: 1735–1741.

Lewin, P. (1917). Congenital absence or defects of bones of the extremities. *American Journal of Roentgenology* **4**: 431–448.

Lewis, W.H. (1901). The development of the arm in man. *American Journal of Anatomy* **1**: 145–183.

Lewis, W.H. (1920). The cartilaginous skull of a human embryo, twenty-one millimeters in length. *Contributions to Embryology* **9**: 301–324.

Lewis, O.J. (1956). The blood supply of developing long bones with special reference to the metaphysis. *Journal of Bone and Joint Surgery* **38B**: 928–933.

Lewis, O.J. (1958). The tubercle of the tibia. *Journal of Anatomy* **92**: 587–592.

Lewis, A.B. and Garn, S.M. (1960). The relationship between tooth formation and other maturational factors. *Angle Orthodontist* **30**: 70–77.

Lewis, M. and Roberts, C.A. (1997). Growing pains: the interpretation of stress indicators. *International Journal of Osteoarchaeology* **7**: 581–586.

Liberson, F. (1937). Os acromiale – a contested anomaly. *Journal of Bone and Joint Surgery* **19**: 683–689.

Limson, M. (1924). Metopism as found in Filipino skulls. *American Journal of Physical Anthropology* **7**: 317–324.

Limson, M. (1932). Observations on the bones of the skull in White and Negro fetuses and infants. *Contributions to Embryology* **23**: 205–222.

Linde, A. (1998). Odontogenesis and Craniofacial Development. *European Journal of Oral Sciences* **106**: Suppl. 1.

Lindseth, R.E. and Rosene, H.A. (1971). Traumatic separation of the upper femoral epiphysis in a newborn infant. *Journal of Bone and Joint Surgery* **53A**: 1641–1644.

Liversidge, H.M. (1994). Accuracy of age estimation from developing teeth of a population of known age (0–5.4 years). *International Journal of Osteoarchaeology* **4**: 37–45.

Liversidge, H.M. (1995). Crown formation times of the permanent dentition and root extension rate in humans. In: *Aspects of Dental Biology: Palaeontology, Anthropology and Evolution* (J.Moggi-Cecchi, Ed.), pp. 267–275. Florence: International Institute for the Study of Man.

Liversidge, H.M. (2003). Variation in modern human dental development. In: *Patterns of Growth and Development in the Genus Homo* (J.L.Thompson, G.E.Krovitz and A.J. Nelson, Eds). Cambridge: Cambridge University Press.

Liversidge, H.M. and Molleson, T.I. (1999). Developing permanent tooth length as an estimate of age. *Journal of Forensic Sciences* **44**: 917–920.

Liversidge, H.M. and Molleson, T.I. (2004). Variation in crown and root formation and eruption of human deciduous teeth. *American Journal of Physical Anthropology* **123**: 172–180.

Liversidge, H.M., Dean, M.C. and Molleson, T.I. (1993). Increasing human tooth length between birth and 5.4 years. *American Journal of Physical Anthropology* **90**: 307–313.

Liversidge, H.M., Herdeg, B. and Rösing, F.W. (1998). Dental age estimation of non-adults. A review of methods and principles. In: *Dental Anthropology, Fundamentals, Limits and Prospects* (K.W. Alt, F.W. Rösing and M. Teschler-Nicola, Eds), pp. 419–442. Vienna: Springer.

Liversidge, H.M., Lyons, F. and Hector, M.P. (2003). The accuracy of three methods of age estimation using radiographic measurement of developing teeth. *Forensic Science International* **131**: 22–29

Livingstone, S.K. (1937). Sprengel's deformity. *Journal of Bone and Joint Surgery* **19**: 539–540.

Lloyd-Roberts, G.C., Apley, A.G. and Owen, R. (1975). Reflections upon the aetiology of congenital pseudoarthrosis of the clavicle. *Journal of Bone and Joint Surgery* **57B**: 24–29.

Logan, W.H.G. and Kronfeld, R. (1933). Development of the human jaws and surrounding structures from birth to the age of fifteen years. *Journal of the American Dental Association* **20**: 379–427.

Lorenzo, R.L., Hungerford, G.D., Blumenthal, B.I., Bradford, B., Sanchez, F. and Haranath, B.S. (1983). Congenital kyphosis and subluxation of the thoraco-lumbar spine due to vertebral aplasia. *Skeletal Radiology* **10**: 255–257.

Loth, S.R. and Henneberg, M. (2001). Sexually dimorphic mandibular morphology in the first few years of life. *American Journal of Physical Anthropology* **115**: 179–186.

Love, S.M., Ganey, T. and Ogden, J.A. (1990). Postnatal epiphyseal development: the distal tibia and fibula. *Journal of Pediatric Orthopedics* **10**: 298–305.

Lovejoy, C.O., Meindl, R.S., Mensforth, R.P. and Barton, T.J. (1985). Multifactorial determination of skeletal age at death: a method and blind tests of its accuracy. *American Journal of Physical Anthropology* **68**: 1–14.

Low, A. (1905). Abstract in Proceedings of the Anatomical Society. *Journal of Anatomy and Physiology* **39**: xxvi-xxix.

Low, A. (1909). Further observations on the ossification of the human lower jaw. *Journal of Anatomy and Physiology* **44**: 83–95.

Lowman, R.M., Robinson, F. and McAllister, W.B. (1966). The craniopharyngeal canal. *Acta Radiologica* **5**: 41–54.

Lucy, D. and Pollard, A.M. (1995). Further comments on the estimation of error associated with the Gustafson dental age estimation method. *Journal of Forensic Sciences* **40**: 222–227.

Lucy, D., Pollard, A.M. and Roberts, C.A. (1994). A comparison of three dental techniques for estimating age at death in humans. *Journal of Archaeological Science* **22**: 151–156.

Lufti, A.M. (1970). Mode of growth, fate and functions of cartilage canals. *Journal of Anatomy* **106**: 135–145.

Luke, D.A., Stack, M.V. and Hey, E.N. (1978). A comparison of morphological and gravimetric methods of estimating human foetal age from the dentition. In: *Development, Function and Evolution of Teeth* (P.M. Butler and K.A. Joysey, Eds), pp. 511–518. London: Academic Press.

Lumsden, A.G.S. (1988). Spatial organization of the epithelium and the role of neural crest cells in the initiation of the mammalian tooth germ. *Development* **103** (Suppl.): 155–169.

Lumsden, A.G.S. and Buchanan, J.A.G. (1986). An experimental study of timing and topography of early tooth development in the mouse embryo with an analysis of the role of innervation. *Archives of Oral Biology* **31**: 301–311.

Lunt, R.C. and Law, D.B. (1974). A review of the chronology of calcification of deciduous teeth. *Journal of the American Dental Association* **89**: 599–606.

Lysell, L., Magnusson, B. and Thilander, B. (1962). Time and order of eruption of the primary teeth: a longitudinal study. *Odontologisk Revy* **13**: 217–234.

Maat, G.J.R. (1984). Dating and rating of Harris lines. *American Journal of Physical Anthropology* **63**: 291–299.

Maat, G.J.R. and Mastwijk, R.W. (1995). Ossification status of the jugular growth plate. An aid for age at death determination. *International Journal of Osteoarchaeology* **5**: 163–168.

Maat, G.J.R., Matricali, B. and Van Meerten, E.L. (1996). Postnatal development and structure of the neurocentral junction. Its relevance for spinal surgery. *Spine* **21**: 661–666.

Macauly, D. (1951). Digital markings in radiographs of the skull in children. *British Journal of Radiology* **24**: 647–652.

Macklin, C.C. (1914). The skull of a human fetus of 40 mm. *American Journal of Anatomy* **16**: 317–385 and 387–426.

Macklin, C.C. (1921). The skull of a human fetus of 43 millimeters greatest length. *Contributions to Embryology* **10**: 57–103.

MacLaughlin, S.M. (1987). An evaluation of current techniques for age and sex determination from adult human skeletal remains. Unpublished PhD dissertation, University of Aberdeen.

MacLaughlin, S.M. (1990). Epiphyseal fusion at the sternal end of the clavicle in a modern Portuguese skeletal sample. *Antropologia Portuguesa* **8**: 59–68.

MacLaughlin, S.M. and Oldale, K.N.M. (1992). Vertebral body diameters and sex prediction. *Annals of Human Biology* **19**: 285–292.

MacLaughlin-Black, S.M. and Gunstone, A. (1995). Early fetal maturity assessed from patterns of ossification in the hand and foot. *International Journal of Osteoarchaeology* **5**: 51–59.

Magriples, U. and Laitman, J.T. (1987). Developmental changes in the position of the fetal human larynx. *American Journal of Physical Anthropology* **72**: 463–472.

Maier, R.J. (1934). Prenatal diagnosis of lacuna skull (Lükenschädel). *Radiology* **23**: 615–619.

Mainland, D. (1953). Evaluation of the skeletal age method of estimating children's development. I. Systematic errors in the assessment of roentgenograms. *Pediatrics* **12**: 114–129.

Mainland, D. (1954). Evaluation of the skeletal age method of estimating children's development. II. Variable errors in the assessment of roentgenograms. *Pediatrics* **13**: 165–173.

Mainland, D. (1957). Evaluation of the skeletal age method of estimating children's development. III. Comparison of methods and inspection in the assessment of roentgenograms. *Pediatrics* **20**: 979–992.

Maj, G., Bassani, S., Menini, G. and Zannini, O. (1964). Studies on the eruption of permanent teeth in children with normal occlusion and malocclusion. *Transactions of the European Orthodontic Society* **40**: 107–130.

Malhotra, V. and Leeds, N.E. (1984). Case report 277. Occipitalization of the atlas with severe cord compression. *Skeletal Radiology* **12**: 55–58.

Mall, F.P. (1906). On ossification centres in human embryos less than one hundred days old. *American Journal of Anatomy* **5**: 433–458.

Malmberg, N. (1944). Occurrence and significance of early periosteal proliferation in the diaphyses of premature infants. *Acta Paediatrica Scandinavica* **32**: 626–633.

Mann, R.W., Symes, S.A. and Bass, W.M. (1987). Maxillary suture obliteration: aging the human skeleton based on intact or fragmentary maxilla. *Journal of Forensic Sciences* **32**: 148–157.

Mann, R.W., Thomas, M.D. and Adams, B.J. (1998). Congenital absence of the ulna with humeroradial synostosis in a prehistoric skeleton from Moundville, Alabama. *International Journal of Osteoarchaeology* **8**: 295–299.

Manzanares, M.C., Goret-Nicaise, M. and Dehm, A. (1988). Metopic sutural closure in the human skull. *Journal of Anatomy* **161**: 203–215.

Maples, W.R. and Rice, P.M. (1979). Some difficulties with the Gustafson dental age estimations. *Journal of Forensic Sciences* **24**: 168–172.

March, H.C. (1944). A vertebral anomaly: Probable persistent neurocentral synchondrosis. *American Journal of Roentgenology* **52**: 408–411.

Maresh, M.M. (1940). Paranasal sinuses from birth to late adolescence. I. Size of the paranasal sinuses as observed in routine postero-anterior roentgenograms. *American Journal of Diseases of Children* **60**: 55–78.

Maresh, M.M. (1943). Growth of major long bones in healthy children. *American Journal of Diseases of Children* **66**: 227–257.

Maresh, M.M. (1955). Linear growth of long bones of extremities from infancy through adolescence. *American Journal of Diseases of Children* **89**: 725–742.

Maresh, M.M. (1970). Measurements from roentgenograms. In: *Human Growth and Development* (R.W. McCammon, Ed.), pp. 157–200. Springfield, IL: C.C. Thomas.

Marins, V.M.R. and Almeida, R.M.V.R. (2002). Undernutrition prevalence and social determinants in children aged 0–59 months, Niterói, Brazil. *Annals of Human Biology* **29**: 609–618.

Martin, R. and Saller, K. (1959). *Lehrbuch der Anthropologie, Vol. 2*, 3rd edition. Stuttgart: Fischer.

Martin, R.B., Burr, D.B. and Sharkey, N.A. (1998). *Skeletal Tissue Mechanics*. New York: Springer.

Marubini, E. and Milani, S. (1986). Approaches to the analysis of longitudinal data. In: *Human Growth, A Comprehensive Treatise, Vol. 3*, 2nd edition (F. Falkner and J.M. Tanner, Eds), pp. 79–94. New York: Plenum Press.

Marvaso, V. and Bernard, G.W. (1977). Initial intramembranous osteogenesis *in vitro*. *American Journal of Anatomy* **149**: 453–468.

Marzke, M.W. and Marzke, R.F. (1987). The third metacarpal styloid process in humans: origin and functions. *American Journal of Physical Anthropology* **73**: 415–431.

Matsumura, G., England, M.A., Uchiumi, T. and Kodama, G. (1994). The fusion of ossification centres in the cartilaginous and membranous parts of the occipital squama in human fetuses. *Journal of Anatomy* **185**: 295–300.

Matsumura, G., Uchiumi, T., Kida, K., Ichikawa, R. and Kodama, G. (1993). Developmental studies on the interparietal part of the human occipital squama. *Journal of Anatomy* **182**: 197–204.

May, D., Jenny, B. and Faundez, A. (2001). Cervical cord compression due to hypoplastic atlas. *Journal of Neurosurgery (Spine 1)* **94**: 133–136.

Mayhall, J.T. (1992). Techniques for the study of dental morphology. In: *Skeletal Biology of Past Peoples: Research Methods* (S.R. Saunders and M.A. Katzenberg, Eds), pp. 59–78. New York: Wiley–Liss.

Mays, S., de la Rua, C. and Molleson, T.I. (1995). Molar crown height as a means of evaluating dental wear scales for estimating age at death in human skeletal remains. *Journal of Archaeological Science* **22**: 659–670.

McCarthy, S.M. and Ogden, J.A. (1982a). Radiology of postnatal skeletal development. V. Distal humerus. *Skeletal Radiology* **7**: 239–249.

McCarthy, S.M. and Ogden, J.A. (1982b). Radiology of postnatal development. Vl. Elbow joint. *Skeletal Radiology* **9**: 17–26.

McClure, J.G. and Raney, R.B. (1975). Anomalies of the scapula. *Clinical Orthopaedics and Related Research* **110**: 22–31.

McCormick, W.F. (1980). Mineralisation of the costal cartilages as an indicator of age: Preliminary observations. *Journal of Forensic Sciences* **25**: 736–741.

McCormick, W.F. (1983). Ossification patterns of costal cartilages as an indicator of sex. *Archives of Pathology and Laboratory Medicine* **107**: 206–210.

McCormick, W.F., Stewart, J.H. and Langford, L.A. (1985). Sex determination from chest plate roentgenograms. *American Journal of Physical Anthropology* **68**: 173–195.

McCredie, J. (1975). Congenital fusion of bones: radiology, embryology and pathogenesis. *Clinical Radiology* **26**: 47–51.

McDermott, L.J. (1943). Development of the human knee joint. *Archives of Surgery* **46**: 705–719.

McGregor, I.A., Thomson, A.M. and Billewicz, W.Z. (1968). The development of primary teeth in children from a group of Gambian villages, and critical examination of its use for estimating age. *British Journal of Nutrition* **22**: 307–314.

McHenry, H. (1968). Transverse lines in long bones of prehistoric Californian Indians. *American Journal of Physical Anthropology* **29**: 1–17.

McIntosh, N. (1998). The newborn. In: *Forfar and Arneil's Textbook of Pediatrics*, 5th edition (A.G.M. Campbell and N. McIntosh, Eds), pp. 93–325. Edinburgh: Churchill Livingstone.

McKern, T.W. and Stewart, T.D. (1957). Skeletal age changes in young American males, analysed from the standpoint of age identification. *Headquarters Quartermaster Research and Development Command, Technical Report* EP-45. Natick, MA.

McRae, D.L. and Barnum, A.S. (1953). Occipitalization of the atlas. *American Journal of Roentgenology* **70**: 23–46.

Medlar, R.C. and Lyne, E.D. (1978). Sinding–Larson–Johansson disease. *Journal of Bone and Joint Surgery* **60A**: 1113–1116.

Meikle, M.C. (2002). *Craniofacial Development, Growth and Evolution*. 2nd edition. Diss, Norfolk: Bateson Publishing.

Meindl, R.S., Lovejoy, C.O., Mensforth, R.P. and Walker, R.A. (1985). A revised method of age determination using the os pubis, with a review and tests of accuracy of other current methods of pubis symphyseal ageing. *American Journal of Physical Anthropology* **68**: 29–45.

Melsen, B. (1969). Time of closure of the spheno-occipital synchondrosis determined on dried skulls. *Acta Odontologica Scandinavica* **27**: 73–90.

Melsen, B. (1972). Time and mode of closure of the spheno-occipital synchondrosis determined on human autopsy material. *Acta Anatomica* **83**: 112–118.

Melsen, B. (1975). Palatal growth studied on human autopsy material. *American Journal of Orthodontics* **68**: 42−54.

Menees, T.O. and Holly, L.E. (1932). The ossification in the extremities of the newborn. *American Journal of Roentgenology* **28**: 389−390.

Merbs, C.F. (1996). Spondylolysis of the sacrum in Alaskan and Canadian Inuit skeletons. *American Journal of Physical Anthropology* **101**: 357−367.

Meredith, H.V. (1957). Change in the profile of the osseous chin during childhood. *American Journal of Physical Anthropology* **15**: 247−252.

Meredith, H.V. (1959). Change in a dimension of the frontal bone during childhood and adolescence. *Anatomical Record* **134**: 769−780.

Meschan, I. (1975). *An Atlas of Anatomy Basic to Radiology*. Philadelphia, PA: W.B. Saunders.

Meyer, D.B. (1978). The appearance of 'cervical ribs' during early fetal development. *Anatomical Record* **190**: 481.

Meyer, D.B. and O'Rahilly, R. (1958). Multiple techniques in the study of the onset of prenatal ossification. *Anatomical Record* **132**: 181−193.

Meyer, D.B. and O'Rahilly, R. (1976). The onset of ossification in the human calcaneus. *Anatomy and Embryology* **150**: 19−33.

Mezaros, T. and Kery, L. (1980). Quantitative analysis of growth of the hip. A radiologic study. *Acta Orthopaedica Scandinavica* **51**: 275−283.

Michaels, L., Prevost, M.J. and Crang, D.F. (1969). Pathological changes in a case of os odontoideum (separate odontoid process). *Journal of Bone and Joint Surgery* **51A**: 965−972.

Michail, J.P., Theodorou, S., Houliaras, K. and Siatis, N. (1958). Two cases of obstetrical separation (epiphysiolysis) of the upper femoral epiphysis. *Journal of Bone and Joint Surgery* **40B**: 477−482.

Milch, R.A., Rall, D.P., Tobie, J.E., Albrecht, J.M. and Trivers, G. (1958). Florescence of tetracycline antibiotics in bone. *Journal of Bone and Joint Surgery* **40A**: 897−910.

Milgram, J.W. and Lyne, E.D. (1975). Epiphysiolysis of the proximal femur in very young children. *Clinical Orthopaedics and Related Research* **110**: 146−153.

Miller, J.Z., Slemenda, C.W., Meany, F.J., Reister, T.K., Hui, S. and Johnston, C.C. (1991). The relationship of bone mineral density and anthropomorphic variables in healthy male and female children. *Bone and Mineral* **14**: 137−152.

Mina, M. and Kollar, E.J. (1987). The induction of odontogenesis in non-dental mesenchyme combined with early murine mandibular arch epithelium. *Archives of Oral Biology* **32**: 123−127.

Mincer, H.H., Harris, E.F. and Berryman, H.E. (1993). The A.B.F.O. study of third molar development and it use as an estimate of chronological age. *Journal of Forensic Sciences* **38**: 379−390.

Mittler, D.M. and Sheridan, S.G. (1992). Sex determination in subadults using auricular surface morphology: A forensic science perspective. *Journal of Forensic Sciences* **37**: 1068−1075.

Molleson, T. and Cox, M. (1993). *The Spitalfields Project. Volume 2 − The Anthropology − The Middling Sort*, Research Report 86. London: Council for BritishArchaeology.

Molleson, T., Cruse, K. and Mays, S. (1998). Some sexually dimorphic features of the human juvenile skull and their value in sex determination in immature juvenile remains. *Journal of Archaeological Science* **25**: 719−728.

Moorrees, C.F.A. and Kent, R.L. (1978). A step function model using tooth counts to assess the developmental timing of the dentition. *Annals of Human Biology* **5**: 55−68.

Moorrees, C.F.A., Fanning, E.A. and Hunt, E.E. (1963a). Formation and resorption of three deciduous teeth in children. *American Journal of Physical Anthropology* **21**; 205−213.

Moorrees, C.F.A., Fanning, E.A. and Hunt, E.E. (1963b). Age variation of formation stages for ten permanent teeth. *Journal of Dental Research* **42**: 1490−1502.

Moradian-Oldak, J., Weiner, S., Addadi, L., Landis, W.J. and Traub, W. (1991). Electron imaging and diffraction study of individual crystals of bone, mineralized tendon and synthetic carbonate apatite. *Connective Tissue Research* **25**: 219−228.

Morgan, J.D. and Somerville, E.W. (1960). Normal and abnormal growth at the upper end of the femur. *Journal of Bone and Joint Surgery* **42B**: 264–272.

Mörnstad, H., Staaf, V. and Welander, U. (1994). Age estimation with the aid of tooth development: a new method based on objective methods. *Scandinavian Journal of Dental Research* **102**: 137–143.

Morreels, C.L., Cherry, J. and Fabrikant, J.I. (1967). Ossified arytenoid cartilage masquerading as a foreign body. *American Journal of Roentgenology* **101**: 837–838.

Morton, D.G. (1942). Observations of the development of pelvic conformation. *American Journal of Obstetrics and Gynaecology* **44**: 799–819.

Morton, D.G. and Hayden, C.T. (1941). A comparative study of male and female pelves in children with a consideration of the etiology of pelvic conformations. *American Journal of Obstetrics and Gynecology* **41**: 485–495.

Moskalewski, S., Oseicka, A. and Maleczyk, J. (1988). Comparison of bone formed intramuscularly after transplantation of scapular and calvarial osteoblasts. *Bone* **9**: 101–106.

Moss, M.L. (1958). The pathogenesis of artificial cranial deformation. *American Journal of Physical Anthropology* **16**: 269–285.

Moss, M.L. and Noback, C.R. (1958). A longitudinal study of digital epiphyseal fusion in adolescence. *Anatomical Record* **131**: 19–32.

Moss, M.L. and Young, R.W. (1960). A functional approach to craniology. *American Journal of Physical Anthropology* **18**: 281–292.

Moss, M.L., Noback, C.R. and Robertson, G.G. (1955). Critical developmental horizons in human fetal long bones. *American Journal of Anatomy* **97**: 155–175.

Moss, M.L., Noback, C.R. and Robertson, G.G. (1956). Growth of certain human fetal cranial bones. *American Journal of Anatomy* **98**: 191–204.

Moss-Salentijn, L. (1975). Cartilage canals in the human spheno-occipital synchondrosis during fetal life. *Acta Anatomica* **92**: 595–606.

Motateanu, M., Gudinchet, F., Sarraj, H. and Schnyder, P. (1991). Case report 665. Congenital absence of posterior arch of atlas. *Skeletal Radiology* **20**: 231–232.

Mudge, M.K., Wood, V.E. and Frykman, G.K. (1984). Rotator cuff tears associated with os acromiale. *Journal of Bone and Joint Surgery* **66A**: 427–429.

Müller, F. and O'Rahilly, R. (1980). The human chondrocranium at the end of the embryonic period, proper, with particular reference to the nervous system. *American Journal of Anatomy* **159**: 33–58.

Müller, F. and O'Rahilly, R. (1986). Somitic-vertebral correlation and vertebral levels in the human embryo. *American Journal of Anatomy* **177**: 3–19.

Müller, F. and O'Rahilly, R. (1994). Occipitocervical segmentation in staged human embryos. *Journal of Anatomy* **185**: 251–258.

Müller, F. and O'Rahilly, R. (1997). The timing and sequence of appearance of neuromeres and their derivatives in staged human embryos. *Acta Anatomica* **158**: 83–99.

Müller, F., O'Rahilly, R. and Tucker, J.A. (1981). The human larynx at the end of the embryonic period proper. 1. The laryngeal and infrahyoid muscles and their innervation. *Acta Otolaryngologica (Stockh.)* **91**: 323–336.

Mundy, G.R. and Martin, T.J. (1993). *Physiology and Pharmacology of Bone. Handbook of Experimental Pharmacology*, Vol. 107. Berlin: Springer.

Muragaki, Y., Mundles, S., Upton, J. and Olsen, B.R. (1996). Altered growth and branching patterns in synpolydactyly caused by mutations in *Hox* 13. *Science* **272**: 548–550.

Murphy, T. (1957). Changes in mandibular form during postnatal growth. *Australian Dental Journal* **2**: 267–276.

Murphy, J. and Gooding, C.A. (1970). Evolution of persistently enlarged parietal foramina. *Radiology* **97**: 391–392.

Mysorekar, V. R. (1967). Diaphyseal nutrient foramina in human long bones. *Journal of Anatomy* **101**: 813–822.

Nabarro, S. (1952). Calcification of the laryngeal and tracheal cartilages associated with congenital stridor in an infant. *Archives of Disease in Childhood* **27**: 185–186.

Nakahara, H., Dennis, J.E., Bruder, S.P., Haynesworth, S.E., Lennon, D.P. and Caplan, A.I. (1991). In vitro differentiation of bone and hypertrophic cartilage from periosteal derived cells. *Experimental Cell Research* **195**: 492–503.

Nayak, U.V. (1931). A case of abnormal atlas and axis vertebra. *Journal of Anatomy* **65**: 399–400.

Nery, E., Kraus, B.S. and Croup, M. (1970). Timing and topography of early human tooth development. *Archives of Oral Biology* **15**: 1315–1326.

Neuman, W.F. and Neuman, M.W. (1953). The nature of the mineral phase of bone. *Chemical Reviews* **53**: 1–45.

Newman, K.J. and Meredith, H.V. (1956). Individual growth in skeletal bigonial diameter during the childhood period from 5 to 11 years of age. *American Journal of Anatomy* **99**: 157–187.

Nicholson, D.A. and Driscoll, P.A. (1993). The elbow. *British Medical Journal* **307**: 1058–1062.

Niida, S., Yamamoto, S. and Kodama, H. (1991). Variation in the running pattern of trabeculae in growing human nasal bones. *Journal of Anatomy* **179**: 39–41.

Niida, S., Yamasaki, K. and Kodama, H. (1992). Interference with interparietal growth in the human skull by the tectum synoticum posterior. *Journal of Anatomy* **180**: 197–200.

Nilsson, A., Isgaard, J. and Lindahl, A. (1987). Effects of unilateral arterial infusion of GH and IGF-1 on tibial longitudinal bone growth in hypophysectionized rats. *Calcified Tissue International* **40**: 91–96.

Njio, B.J. and Kjær, I. (1993). The development and morphology of the incisive fissure and the transverse palatine suture in the human fetal palate. *Journal of Craniofacial Genetics and Developmental Biology* **13**: 24–34.

Noback, G.J. (1922). Simple methods of correlating crown-rump and crown–heel lengths f the human fetus. *Anatomical Record* **23**: 241–244.

Noback, C.R. (1943). Some gross structural and quantitative aspects of the developmental anatomy of the human embryonic, fetal and circumnatal skeleton. *Anatomical Record* **87**: 29–51.

Noback, C.R. (1944). The developmental anatomy of the human osseous skeleton during the embryonic, fetal and circumnatal periods. *Anatomical Record* **88**: 91–125.

Noback, C.R. and Moss, M.L. (1953). The topology of the human premaxillary bone. *American Journal of Physical Anthropology* **11**: 181–187.

Noback, C.R. and Robertson, G.G. (1951). Sequences of appearance of ossification centres in the human skeleton during the first five prenatal months. *American Journal of Anatomy* **89**: 1–28.

Nolla, C.M. (1960). The development of the permanent teeth. *Journal of Dentistry for Children* **27**: 254–266.

Nomata, N. (1964). A chronological study of crown formation of the human deciduous dentition. *Bulletin of the Tokyo Medical and Dental School* **11**: 55–76.

Nonaka, K., Ichiki, A. and Miura, T. (1990). Changes in the eruption order of the first permanent teeth and their relation to the season of birth in Japan. *American Journal of Physical Anthropology* **82**: 191–198.

Norberg, O. (1960). Studies of the human jaws and teeth during the first years of life. II The premaxillary region. *Zeitschrift für Anatomie und Entwicklungsgeschichte* **122**: 1–21.

Northcutt, R.G. and Gans, C. (1983). The genesis of neural crest and epidermal placodes: a reinterpretation of vertebrate origins. *Quarterly Review of Biology* **38**: 1–28.

Nyström, M. and Ranta, H. (2003). Tooth formation and the mandibular symphysis during the first five postnatal months. *Journal of Forensic Sciences* **48**: 373–378.

Nyström, M., Evälahti, M. and Laine, P.O. (1986). Times of natural exfoliation of primary teeth in a group of Finnish children. *Journal of Paediatric Dentistry* **2**: 73–77.

O'Bannon, R.P. and Grunow, O.H. (1954). The larynx and pharynx radiologically considered. *Southern Medical Journal* **4**: 310–317.

O'Brien, T.O. (1984). Fractures of the hand and wrist region. In: *Fractures in Children* (C.A. Rockwood, K.E. Wilkins and R.E. King, Eds), pp. 229–299. Philadelphia, PA: Lippincott.

O'Brien, G.D., Queenan, J.T. and Campbell, S. (1981). Assessment of gestational age in the second trimester by real-time ultrasound measurement of the femur length. *American Journal of Obstetrics and Gynecology* **139**: 540–545.

Odita, J.C., Okolo, A.A. and Omene, J.A. (1985). Sternal ossification in normal human newborn infants. *Pediatric Radiology* **15**: 165–167.

O'Donoghue, D.H. and Sell, L.S. (1943). Congenital talonavicular synostosis. *Journal of Bone and Joint Surgery* **25**: 925–927.

Ogata, S. and Uhthoff, H.K. (1990). The early development and ossification of the human clavicle – an embryological study. *Acta Orthopedica Scandinavica* **61**: 330–334.

Ogden, J.A. (1974a). Changing patterns of proximal femoral vascularity. *Journal of Bone and Joint Surgery* **56A**: 941–950.

Ogden, J.A. (1974b). The anatomy and function of the proximal tibiofibular joint. *Clinical Orthopaedics and Related Research* **101**: 186–191.

Ogden, J.A. (1974c). Dislocation of the proximal tibiofibular joint. *Journal of Bone and Joint Surgery* **56A**: 145–154.

Ogden, J.A. (1979). The development and growth of the musculo-skeletal system. In: *Scientific Basis of Orthopaedics* (J.A. Albright and R. Brands, Eds), New York: Appleton–Century–Crofts, pp. 41–103.

Ogden, J.A. (1981). Injury to the growth mechanisms of the immature skeleton. *Skeletal Radiology* **6**: 237–253.

Ogden, J.A. (1984a). Growth slowdown and arrest lines. *Journal of Pediatric Orthopedics* **4**: 409–415.

Ogden, J.A. (1984b). Radiology of postnatal development. Xl. The first cervical vertebra. *Skeletal Radiology* **12**: 12–20.

Ogden, J.A. (1984c). Radiology of postnatal development. Xll. The second cervical vertebra. *Skeletal Radiology* **12**: 169–177.

Ogden, J.A. (1984d). Radiology of postnatal development. X. Patella and tibial tuberosity. *Skeletal Radiology* **11**: 246–257.

Ogden, J.A. (1984e). Radiology of postnatal development. IX. Proximal tibia and fibula. *Skeletal Radiology* **11**: 168–177.

Ogden, J.A. and Lee, J. (1990). Accessory ossification patterns and injuries of the malleoli. *Journal of Pediatric Orthopedics* **10**: 306–316.

Ogden, J.A. and McCarthy, S.M. (1983). Radiology of postnatal development. VIII. Distal tibia and fibula. *Skeletal Radiology* **10**: 209–220.

Ogden, J.A. and Phillips, S.B. (1983). Radiology of postnatal skeletal development. VII. The scapula. *Skeletal Radiology* **9**: 157–169.

Ogden, J.A. and Southwick, W.O. (1976). Osgood–Schlatter's disease and tibial tuberosity development. *Clinical Orthopaedics and Related Research* **116**: 180–189.

Ogden, J.A., Conlogue, G.J. and Jensen, P. (1978). Radiology of postnatal development: The proximal humerus. *Skeletal Radiology* **2**: 153–160.

Ogden, J.A., Beall, J.K., Conlogue, G.J. and Light, T.R. (1981). Radiology of postnatal development. lV. Distal radius and ulna. *Skeletal Radiology* **6**: 255–266.

Ogden, J.A., Conlogue, G.J., Bronson, M.L. and Jensen, P.S. (1979a). Radiology of postnatal skeletal development. II. The manubrium and sternum. *Skeletal Radiology* **4**: 189–195.

Ogden, J.A., Conlogue, G.J. and Bronson, M.L. (1979b). Radiology of postnatal skeletal development. III. The Clavicle. *Skeletal Radiology* **4**: 196–203.

Ogden, J.A., Conlogue, G.J., Phillips, S.B. and Bronson, M.L. (1979c). Sprengel's deformity. Radiology of the pathological deformation. *Skeletal Radiology* **4**: 204–208.

Ogden, J.A., Ganey, T.H., Light, T.R., Belsole, R.J. and Greene, T.L. (1994). Ossification and pseudoepiphyses formation in the 'non-epiphyseal' ends of bones of the hands and feet. *Skeletal Radiology* **23**: 3–13.

Ogden, J.A., Gossling, H.R. and Southwick, W.O. (1975). Slipped capital femoral epiphysis following ipsilateral femoral fracture. *Clinical Orthopaedics and Related Research* **110**: 167–170.

Ogden, J.A., Hempton, R.F. and Southwick, W.O. (1975). Development of the tibial tuberosity. *Anatomical Record* **182**: 431–446.

Ogden, J.A., McCarthy, S.M. and Jokl, P. (1982). The painful bipartite patella. *Journal of Pediatric Orthopedics* **2**: 263–269.

Ogden, J.A., Tross, R.B. and Murphy, M.J. (1980). Fracture of the tibial tuberosity in adolescents. *Journal of Bone and Joint Surgery* **62A**: 205–215.

O'Halloran, R.L. and Lundy, J.K. (1987). Age and ossification of the hyoid bone: forensic implications. *Journal of Forensic Sciences* **32**: 1655–1659.

Ohtsuki, F. (1977). Developmental changes of the cranial bone thickness in the human fetal period. *American Journal of Physical Anthropology* **46**: 141–154.

Ohtsuki, F. (1980). Areal growth in the human fetal parietal bone. *American Journal of Physical Anthropology* **53**: 5–9.

Olbrantz, K. and Bohrer, S.P. (1984). Fusion of the anterior arch of the atlas and the dens. *Skeletal Radiology* **12**: 21–22.

Olivier, G. (1974). Précision sur la détermination de l'âge d'un foetus d'après sa taille ou la longuer de ses diaphyses. *Médicine Légale et Dommage Corporel* **7**: 297–299.

Olivier, G. and Pineau, H. (1960). Nouvelle détermination de la taille foetale d'après les longeurs diaphysaires des os longs. *Annales de Médicine Légale* **40**: 141–144.

Oner, F.C. and de Vries, H.R. (1994). Isolated capitolunate coalition. *Journal of Bone and Joint Surgery* **76B**: 845–846.

O'Rahilly, R. (1949). Stereographic reconstruction of developing carpus. *Anatomical Record* **103**: 187–193.

O'Rahilly, R. (1951). Morphological patterns in limb deficiencies and duplications. American *Journal of Anatomy* **89**: 135–194.

O'Rahilly, R. (1952). Anomalous occipital apertures. *American Medical Association Archives of Pathology* **53**: 509–519.

O'Rahilly, R. (1953). A survey of carpal and tarsal anomalies. *Journal of Bone and Joint Surgery* **35A**: 626–642.

O'Rahilly, R. (1954). The prenatal development of the human centrale. *Anatomical Record* **118**: 334–335.

O'Rahilly, R. (1959). The development and the developmental disturbances of the limbs. *Irish Journal of Medical Sciences* **397**: 30–33.

O'Rahilly, R. (1973). The human foot. Part 1. Prenatal development. In: *Foot Disorders*. Medical and Surgical Management, 2nd edition (N.J. Giannestras, Ed.), pp. 16–23. Philadelphia, PA: Lea and Febiger.

O'Rahilly, R. (1983). The timing and sequence of events in the development of the human eye and ear during the embryonic period proper. *Anatomy and Embryology* **168**: 87–99.

O'Rahilly, R. (1997). 'Gestational Age' – letter to the Editor. *Clinical Anatomy* **10**: 367.

O'Rahilly, R. and Benson, D.R. (1985). The development of the vertebral column. In: *The Pediatric Spine* (D.S. Bradford and R.M. Hensinger, Eds), pp. 3–18. Stuttgart: Thieme.

O'Rahilly, R. and Gardner, E. (1972). The initial appearance of ossification in staged human embryos. *American Journal of Anatomy* **134**: 291–301.

O'Rahilly, R. and Gardner, E. (1975). The timing and sequence of events in the development of the limbs in the human embryo. *Anatomy and Embryology* **148**: 1–23.

O'Rahilly, R. and Meyer, D.B. (1956). Roentgenographic investigation of the human skeleton during early fetal life. *American Journal of Roentgenology* **76**: 455–468.

O'Rahilly, R. and Müller, F. (1984). The early development of the hypoglossal nerve and occipital somites in staged human embryos. *American Journal of Anatomy* **169**: 237–257.

O'Rahilly, R. and Müller, F. (1986). The meninges in human development. *Journal of Neuropathology and Experimental Neurology* **45**: 588–608.

O'Rahilly, R. and Müller, F. (1996). *Human Embryology and Teratology*, 2nd edition. New York: Wiley–Liss.

O'Rahilly, R. and Müller, F. (2000). Prenatal ages and stages: measures and errors. *Teratology* **61**: 382–384.

O'Rahilly, R. and Müller, F. (2001). *Human Embryology and Teratology*. 3rd edition. New York: Wiley–Liss.

O'Rahilly, R. and Twohig, M.J. (1952). Foramina parietalia permagna. *American Journal of Roentgenology* **67**: 551–561.

O'Rahilly, R. and Tucker, J.A. (1973). The early development of the larynx in staged human embryos. Part 1: embryos of the first five weeks (to stage 15). *Annals of Otology, Rhinology and Laryngology* **82** (Suppl. 7): 3–27.

O'Rahilly, R., Gardner, E. and Gray D.J. (1956). The ectodermal thickening and ridge in the limbs of staged human embryos. *Journal of Embryology and Experimental Morphology* **4**: 254–264.

O'Rahilly, R., Gardner, E. and Gray, D.J. (1959). The skeletal development of the hand. *Clinical Orthopaedics and Related Research* **13**: 42–51.

O'Rahilly, R., Gardner, E. and Gray, D.J. (1960). The skeletal development of the foot. *Clinical Orthopaedics and Related Research* **16**: 7–14.

O'Rahilly, R., Gray, D.J. and Gardner, E. (1957). Chondrification in the hands and feet of staged human embryos. *Contributions to Embryology* **36**: 183–192.

O'Rahilly, R., Müller, F. and Meyer, D.B. (1980). The human vertebral column at the end of the embryonic period proper. 1. The column as a whole. *Journal of Anatomy* **131**: 565–575.

O'Rahilly, R., Müller, F. and Meyer, D.B. (1983). The human vertebral column at the end of the embryonic period proper. 2. The occipitocervical region. *Journal of Anatomy* **136**: 181–195.

O'Rahilly, R., Müller, F. and Meyer, D.B. (1990a). The human vertebral column at the end of the embryonic period proper. 4. The sacro-coccygeal region. *Journal of Anatomy* **168**: 95–111.

O'Rahilly, R., Müller, F. and Meyer, D.B. (1990b). The human vertebral column at the end of the embryonic period proper. 3. The thoracicolumbar region. *Journal of Anatomy* **168**: 81–93.

Ortiz, M.H. and Brodie, A.G. (1949). On the growth of the human head from birth to the third month of life. *Anatomical Record* **103**: 311–333.

Ortner, D.J. and Putschar, W.G.J. (1985). *Identification of Pathological Conditions in Human Skeletal Remains*. Washington, DC: Smithsonian Institute Press.

Ortolani, M. (1948). La Lussazione Congenita dell'anca. *Nuovi Criteri Diagnostici Profilattico Correttivi*. Bologna: Capelli.

Osborne, D. and Effmann, E.L. (1981). Disturbances of trabecular architecture in the upper end of the femur in childhood. *Skeletal Radiology* **6**: 165–173.

Osborne, D.R., Effmann, E.L., Broda, K. and Harrelson, J. (1980). Development of the upper end of the femur with special reference to its internal architecture. *Radiology* **137**: 71–76.

Ossenberg, N.S. (1970). The influence of artificial cranial deformation on discontinuous morphological traits. *American Journal of Physical Anthropology* **33**: 357–371.

Ossenberg, N.S. (1976). Within and between race distances in population studies based on discrete traits of the human skull. *American Journal of Physical Anthropology* **45**: 701–716.

Owsley, D.W. and Jantz, R.L. (1983). Formation of the permanent dentition in Arikara Indians: timing differences that affect dental age assessments. *American Journal of Physical Anthropology* **61**: 467–471.

Ozonoff, M.B. (1979). *Pediatric Orthopedic Radiology*. Philadelphia, PA: W.B. Saunders.

Ozonoff, M.B. and Ziter, F.M.H. (1985). The upper femoral notch. *Skeletal Radiology* **14**: 198–199.

Ozonoff, M.B. and Ziter, F.M.H. (1987). The femoral head notch. *Skeletal Radiology* **16**: 19–22.

Panjabi, M.M., Oxland, R.R., Lin, R-M. and McGowen, T.W. (1994). Thoracolumbar burst fracture. A biomechanical investigation of its multidirectional flexibility. *Spine* **19**: 578–585.

Park, E.A. (1964). The imprinting of nutritional disturbances on the growing bone. *Paediatrics* **33**: 815–862.

Park, E.A. and Richter, C.P. (1953). Transverse lines in bone: mechanism of their development. *Bulletin of the Johns Hopkins Hospital* **93**: 234–248.

Parsons, F.G. (1909). The topography and morphology of the human hyoid bone. *Journal of Anatomy and Physiology* **43**: 279–290.

Paschal, S.O., Hutton, K.S. and Weatherall, P.T. (1995). Isolated avulsion fracture of the lesser tuberosity of the humerus in adolescents. *Journal of Bone and Joint Surgery* **77A**: 1427–1430.

Patake, S.M. and Mysorekar, R. (1977). Diaphyseal nutrient foramina in human metacarpals and metatarsals. *Journal of Anatomy* **124**: 299–304.

Pate, J.R. (1936). An unusual occipito-atloid articulation. *Journal of Anatomy* **71**: 128–129.

Paterson, A.M. (1900). The sternum: its early development and ossification in man and mammals. *Journal of Anatomy and Physiology* **35**: 21–32.

Paterson, A.M. (1904). *The Human Sternum*. London: Williams and Norgate.

Paterson, R.S. (1929). A radiological investigation of the epiphyses of the long bones. *Journal of Anatomy* **64**: 28–46.

Paterson, A.M. and Lovegrove, F.T. (1900). Symmetrical perforations of the parietal bone. *Journal of Anatomy and Physiology* **34**: 228–237.

Paturet, G. (1951). *Traité d'Anatomie Humaine. Tome III*. Paris: Masson et Cie.

Peace, K.A.L. (1992). A morphological, radiological and microscopical investigation of costal cartilage calcification in a cadaveric and an archaeological sample. Unpublished BSc dissertation, University of London.

Peacock, A. (1951). Observations on the prenatal development of the intervertebral disc in man. *Journal of Anatomy* **85**: 260–274.

Pedersen, J.F. (1982). Fetal crown-rump length measurement by ultrasound in normal pregnancy. *British Journal of Obstetrics and Gynaecology* **89**: 926–930.

Pendergrass, E.P. and Pepper, O.H.P. (1939). Observations on the process of ossification in the formation of persistent enlarged parietal foramina. *American Journal of Roentgenology* **41**: 343–346.

Penning, L. (1988). Functional significance of the uncovertebral joints. *Annals of the Royal College of Surgeons of England* **70**: 164.

Pepper, O.H.P. and Pendergrass, E.P. (1936). Hereditary occurrence of enlarged parietal foramina (their diagnostic importance). *American Journal of Roentgenology* **35**: 1–8.

Persson, M. and Thilander, B. (1977). Palatal suture closure in man from 15 to 35 years of age. *American Journal of Orthodontics* **72**: 41–52.

Petrtyl, M., Hert, J. and Fiala, P. (1996). Spatial organization in the Haversian bone in man. *Journal of Biomechanics* **29**: 161–170.

Peyton, W.T. and Peterson, H.O. (1942). Congenital deformities in the region of foramen magnum: basilar impression. *Radiology* **38**: 131–144.

Pfitzner, W. (1900). Beiträge zur Kenntniss des menschlichen Extremitätenskelets. VII. Die Morphologischen Elemente des menschlichen Handskelets. *Zeitschrift für Morphologische und Anthropologie* **2**: 77–157, 365–678.

Pitt, M.J. (1982). Radiology of the femoral linea aspera-pilaster complex: the track sign. *Radiology* **142**: 66.

Plaster, R.L., Schoenecker, P.L. and Capelli, A.M. (1991). Premature closure of the triradiate cartilage: a potential complication of pericapsular acetabuloplasty. *Journal of Pediatric Orthopedics* **11**: 676–678.

Polig, E. and Jee, W.S.S. (1990). A model of osteon closure in cortical bone. *Calcified Tissue International* **47**: 261–269.

Pollanen, M.S. and Chiasson, D.A. (1996). Fracture of the hyoid bone in strangulation: comparison of fractured and unfractured hyoids from victims of strangulation. *Journal of Forensic Sciences* **41**: 110–113.

Pollock, A.N. and Reed, M.H. (1989). Shoulder deformities from obstetrical brachial plexus paralysis. *Skeletal Radiology* **18**: 295–297.

Ponseti, I.V. (1978a). Morphology of the acetabulum in congenital dislocation of the hip: Gross, histological and roentgenographic studies. *Journal of Bone and Joint Surgery* **60A**: 586–599.

Ponseti, I.V. (1978b). Growth and development of the acetabulum in the normal child. *Journal of Bone and Joint Surgery* **60A**: 575–585.

Popich, G.A. and Smith, D.W. (1972). Fontanels: range of normal size. *Journal of Pediatrics* **80**: 749–752.

Porteous, C.J. (1960). The olecranon epiphyses. *Journal of Anatomy* **94**: 286.

Portinaro, N.M.A., Matthews, S.J.E. and Benson, M.K.D. (1994). The acetabular notch in hip dysplasia. *Journal of Bone and Joint Surgery* **76B**: 271–273.

Posener, K., Walker, E. and Weddell, G. (1939). Radiographic studies of the metacarpal and metatarsal bones in children. *Journal of Anatomy* **74**: 76–79.

Pourquie, O. (2001). The vertebrate segmentation clock. *Journal of Anatomy* **199**: 169–175.

Powell, H.D.W. (1961). Extra centre of ossification for the medial malleolus in children. Incidence and significance. *Journal of Bone and Joint Surgery* **43B**: 107–113.

Powell, T.V. and Brodie, A.G. (1963). Closure of the spheno-occipital synchondrosis. *Anatomical Record* **147**: 15–23.

Powell, K.A. and MacLaughlin, S.M. (1992). Costal cartilage calcification as an aid to the identification of sex from human skeletal remains. *Journal of Anatomy* **180**: 357.

Pöyry, M., Nyström, M. and Ranta, R. (1986). Comparison of two tooth formation rating methods. *Proceedings of the Finnish Dental Society* **82**: 127–133.

Poznanski, A.K. and Holt, J.F. (1971). The carpals in congenital malformation syndromes. *American Journal of Roentgenology* **112**: 443–459.

Poznanski, A.K., Garn, S.M., Kuhns, L.R. and Sandusky, S.T. (1971). Dysharmonic maturation of the hand in the congenital malformation syndromes. *American Journal of Physical Anthropology* **35**: 417–432.

Prakash, S., Chopra, S.R.K. and Jit, I. (1979). Ossification of the human patella. *Journal of the Anatomical Society of India* **28**: 78–83.

Pritchett, J.W. (1991). Growth plate activity in the upper extremity. *Clinical Orthopaedics and Related Research* **268**: 235–242.

Proctor, B. (1964). The development of the middle ear spaces and their surgical significance. *Journal of Laryngology and Otology* **78**: 631–649.

Purves, R.K. and Wedin, P.H. (1950). Familial incidence of cervical ribs. *Journal of Thoracic Surgery* **19**: 952–956.

Puyhaubert, A. (1913). Recherchés sur l'ossification des os des membres chez l'homme. *Journal de l'Anatomie et de la Physiologie Normales et Pathologiques de l'homme et des Animaux* **49**: 119–154, 224–268.

Pyle, S.I. and Hoerr, N.L. (1955). *Radiographic Atlas of Skeletal Development of the Knee*. Springfield, IL: C.C. Thomas.

Qureshi, A.A. and Kuo, K.N. (1999). Posttraumatic cleidoscapular synostosis following a fracture of the clavicle. *Journal of Bone and Joint Surgery* **81A**: 256–258.

Ráliš, Z.A. and McKibbin, B. (1973). Changes in shape of the human hip joint during its development and their relationship to its stability. *Journal of Bone and Joint Surgery* **55B**: 780–785.

Rambaud, A. and Renault, Ch. (1864). *Origine et Dévelopment des Os*. Paris: Librairie de F. Chamerot.

Rang, M. (1969). *The Growth Plate and its Disorders*. Edinburgh: Churchill Livingstone.

Ratcliffe, J.F. (1981). The arterial anatomy of the developing human vertebral body. A microarteriographic study. *Journal of Anatomy* **133**: 625–638.

Ratcliffe, J.F. (1982). An evaluation of the intra-osseous arterial anastomoses in the human vertebral body at different ages. A microarteriographic study. *Journal of Anatomy* **134**: 373–382.

Ratliff, A.H.C. (1968). Traumatic separation of the upper femoral epiphysis in young children. *Journal of Bone and Joint Surgery* **50B**: 757–770.

Redfield, A. (1970). A new aid to aging immature skeletons: development of the occipital bone. *American Journal of Physical Anthropology* **33**: 207–220.

Reed, M.H. (1993). Ossification of the hyoid bone during childhood. *Canadian Association of Radiologists Journal* **44**: 273–276.

Reid, D.J. and Dean, M. C. (2000). Brief communication: The timing of linear hypoplasias on human anterior teeth. *American Journal of Physical Anthropology* **113**: 135–139.

Reimann, A.F. and Anson, B.J. (1944). Vertebral level of termination of the spinal cord. *Anatomical Record* **88**: 127–138.

Reinhard, R. and Rösing, F.W. (1985). *Ein Literaturüberblick über Definitionen diskreter Merkmale/anatomischer Varianten am Schädel des Menschen.* Ulm: Selbstverlag.

Reynolds, E.L. (1945). The bony pelvic girdle in early infancy. A roentgenometric study. *American Journal of Physical Anthropology* **3**: 321–354.

Reynolds, E.L. (1947). The bony pelvis in pre-pubertal childhood. *American Journal of Physical Anthropology* **5**: 165–200.

Rezaian, S.M. (1974). Congenital absence of the dens of the axis. A case report with tetraplegia. *Paraplegia* **11**: 263–267.

Richany, S.F., Bast, T.H. and Anson, B.J. (1954). The development and adult structure of the malleus, incus and stapes. *Annals of Otology, Rhinology and Laryngology* **63**: 394–434.

Richenbacher, J., Landolt, A.M. and Theiler, K. (1982). *Applied Anatomy of the Back.* Berlin: Springer.

Risser, J.C. (1958). The iliac apophysis: an invaluable sign in the management of scoliosis. *Clinical Orthopaedics and Related Research* **11**: 111–118.

Ritter, M.A., DeRosa, G.P. and Babcock, J.L. (1976). Tibial torsion? *Clinical Orthopaedics and Related Research* **120**: 159–163.

Roberts, D.F. (1976). Environment and the fetus. In: *The Biology of Human Fetal Growth* (D.F. Roberts and A.M. Thomson, Eds), pp. 267–283. London: Taylor and Francis.

Roche, A.F. (1961). Clinodactyly and brachymesophalangia of the fifth finger. *Acta Pediologica* **50**: 387–391.

Roche, A.F. (1964). Epiphyseal ossification and shaft elongation in human metatarsal bones. *Anatomical Record* **149**: 449–452.

Roche, A.F. (1965). The sites of elongation of the human metacarpals and metatarsals. *Acta Anatomica* **61**: 193–202.

Roche, A.F. (1986). Bone growth and maturation. In: *Human Growth, A Comprehensive Treatise, Vol. 2*, 2nd edition (F. Falkner and J.M. Tanner, Eds), pp. 25–60. New York: Plenum Press.

Roche, A.F. and Barkla, D.H. (1965). The level of the larynx during childhood. *Annals of Otology, Rhinology and Laryngology* **74**: 645–654.

Roche, M.B. and Rowe, G.G. (1951). Anomalous centres of ossification for inferior articular processes of the lumbar vertebrae. *Anatomical Record* **109**: 253–259.

Roche, A.F. and Sunderland, S. (1959). Multiple ossification centres in the epiphyses of the long bones of the human hand and foot. *Journal of Bone and Joint Surgery* **41B**: 375–383.

Rodriguez, J.L., Palacios, J., Garcia-Alix, A. Pastor, I. and Paniagua, R. (1988). Effects of immobilization on fetal bone development. A morphometric study in newborns with congenital neuromuscular diseases with intrauterine onset. *Connective Tissue International* **43**: 335–339.

Rodriguez, J.I., Palacios, J. and Rodriguez, S. (1992). Transverse bone growth and cortical bone mass in the human prenatal period. *Biology of the Neonate* **62**: 23–31.

Roncallo, P. (1948). Researches about ossification and conformation of the thyroid cartilage in man. *Acta Otolaryngologica* **36**: 110–134.

Rosen, H. and Sandick, H. (1955). The measurement of tibiofibular torsion. *Journal of Bone and Joint Surgery* **37A**: 847–855.

Rösing, F.W. (1983). Sexing immature skeletons. *Journal of Human Evolution* **12**: 149–155.

Ross, C.F. and Hylander, W.L. (1996). In vivo and in vitro bone strain in the owl monkey circumorbital region and the function of the postorbital septum. *American Journal of Physical Anthropology* **101**: 183–215.

Ross, J.P. (1959). The vascular complications of cervical rib. *Annals of Surgery* **150**: 340–345.

Rothman, R.H. and Simeone, F.A. (1975). *The Spine*, Vol.1. Philadelphia, PA: W.B.Saunders.

Ruano-Gill, D. (1988). Embryology. In: *The Foot* (B. Helal and D. Wilson, Eds), pp. 25–30. Edinburgh: ChurchillLivingstone.

Rushton, M.A. (1933). On the fine contour lines of the enamel of milk teeth. *Dental Record* **53**: 170–171.

Rushton, M.A. (1944). Growth at the mandibular condyle in relation to some deformities. *British Dental Journal* **76**: 57–68.

Russo, P.E. and Coin, C.G. (1958). Calcification of the hyoid, thyroid and tracheal cartilages in infancy. *American Journal of Roentgenology* **80**: 440–442.

Rutherford, A. (1985). Fractures of the lateral humeral condyle in children. *Journal of Bone and Joint Surgery* **67A**: 851–864.

Ryan, M.D. and Taylor, T.K.F. (1984). Odontoid fractures. A rational approach to treatment. *Journal of Bone and Joint Surgery* **64B**: 416–421.

Ryder, C.T. and Mellin, G.W. (1966). A prospective epidemiological study of the clinical and roentgenological characteristics of the hip joint in the first year of life. *Journal of Bone and Joint Surgery* **48A**: 1024.

Sahni, D., Jit, I., Neelam, and Suri, S. (1998). Time of fusion of the basisphenoid with the basilar part of the occipital bone in northwest Indian subjects. *Forensic Science International* **98**: 41–45.

Salter, R.B. and Harris, W.R. (1963). Injuries including the epiphyseal plate. *Journal of Bone and Joint Surgery* **45A**: 587–622.

Saluja, P.G. (1988). The incidence of spina bifida occulta in a historic and a modern London population. *Journal of Anatomy* **158**: 91–95.

Sandikcioglu, M., Mølsted, K. and Kjær, I. (1994). The prenatal development of the human nasal and vomeral bones. *Journal of Craniofacial Genetics and Developmental Biology* **14**: 124–134.

Sasaki, H. and Kodama, G. (1976). Developmental studies on the post sphenoid of the human sphenoid bone. In: *Symposium on the Development of the Basicranium* (J.F. Bosma, Ed.), pp. 177–191. Bethesda, MD: US Department of Health, Education and Welfare.

Sataloff, R.T. (1990). Embryology of the facial nerve and its clinical applications. *Laryngoscope* **100**: 969–984.

Sauer, G.R. and Wuthier, R.E. (1988). Fourier transform infrared characterization of mineral phases formed during induction of mineralization by collagenase-released matrix vesicles in vitro. *Journal of Biological Chemistry* **263**: 13718–13724.

Saunders, S.R. (1989). Nonmetric skeletal variation. In: *Reconstruction of Life from the Skeleton* (M.Y. Işcan and K.A.R. Kennedy, Eds), pp. 95–108. New York: Alan R. Liss.

Saunders, S.R. (1992). Subadult skeletons and growth related studies. In: *Skeletal Biology of Past Peoples*: *Research Methods* (S.R. Saunders and M.A. Katzenberg, Eds), pp. 1–20. New York: Wiley–Liss.

Saunders, S.R. and Barrans, L. (1999). What can be done about the infant category in skeletal samples? In: *Human Growth in the Past*: *Studies from Bones and Teeth* (R.D.Hoppa and C.M.Fitzgerald, Eds), pp.183–209. Cambridge: Cambridge University Press.

Saunders, S.R. and Hoppa, R.D. (1993). Growth deficit in survivors and non-survivors: biological mortality bias in subadult skeletal samples. *Yearbook of Physical Anthropology* **36**: 127–151.

Saunders, S., DeVito, C., Herring, A., Southern, R. and Hoppa, R. (1993b). Accuracy tests of tooth formation age estimations for human skeletal remains. *American Journal of Physical Anthropology* **92**: 173–188.

Saunders, S., Hoppa, R. and Southern, R. (1993a). Diaphyseal growth in a nineteenth-century skeletal sample of subadults from St Thomas' Church, Belleville, Ontario. *International Journal of Osteoarchaeology* **3**: 265–281.

Scammon, R.E. and Calkins, L.A. (1923). Simple empirical formulae for expressing the lineal growth of the human fetus. *Proceedings of the Society for Experimental Biology and Medicine* **20**: 353–356.

Schaeffer, J.P. (1910a). On the genesis of air cells in the conchae nasales. *Anatomical Record* **4**: 167–180.

Schaeffer, J.P. (1910b). The sinus maxillaris and its relations in the embryo, child and adult man. *American Journal of Anatomy* **10**: 313–368.

Schaeffer, J.P. (1916). The genesis, development and adult anatomy of the nasofrontal region in man. *American Journal of Anatomy* **20**: 125–146.

Scheller, S. (1960). Roentgenographic studies on epiphysial growth and ossification in the knee. *Acta Radiologica Scandinavica* **195** (Suppl.).

Scheuer, J.L. (1998). Age at death and cause of death of the people buried in St Bride's Church, Fleet Street, London. In: *Grave Concerns: Death and Burial in England 1700–1850*, Research Report 113. (M. Cox, Ed.), pp. 100–111. York: Council for British Archaeology.

Scheuer, L. (2002). A blind test of mandibular morphology for sexing mandibles in the first few years of life. *American Journal of Physical Anthropology* **119**: 189–191.

Scheuer, J.L. and Black, S.M. (1995). *The St Bride's Documented Skeletal Collection*, Research Report. London: St Bride's Church.

Scheuer, L. and Black, S. (2000). *Developmental Juvenile Osteology*. London: Academic Press.

Scheuer, J.L. and Bowman, J.E. (1995). Correlation of documentary and skeletal evidence in the St Bride's Crypt population. In: *Grave Reflections: Portraying the Past through Cemetery Studies* (S.R. Saunders and A. Herring, Eds), pp. 49–70. Toronto: Canadian Scholars' Press.

Scheuer, J.L. and MacLaughlin-Black, S.M. (1994). Age estimation from the pars basilaris of the fetal and juvenile occipital bone. *International Journal of Osteoarchaeology* **4**: 377–380.

Scheuer, J.L., Musgrave, J.H. and Evans, S.P. (1980). The estimation of late fetal and perinatal age from limb bone length by linear and logarithmic regression. *Annals of Human Biology* **7**: 257–265.

Schiff, D.C.M. and Parke, W.W. (1973). The arterial supply of the odontoid process. *Journal of Bone and Joint Surgery* **55A**: 1450–1456.

Schour, I. (1936). The neonatal line in the enamel and dentin of the human deciduous teeth and first permanent molar. *Journal of the American Dental Association* **23**: 1946–1955.

Schour, I. and Massler, M. (1941). The development of the human dentition. *Journal of the American Dental Association* **28**: 1153–1160.

Schuller, A. (1943). A note on the identification of skulls by X-ray pictures of the frontal sinuses. *The Medical Journal of Australia* **1**: 554–556.

Schuller, T.C., Kurz, L., Thompson, E., Zemenick, G., Hensinger, R.N. and Herkowitz, H.N. (1991). Natural history of os odontoideum. *Journal of Pediatric Orthopedics* **11**: 222–225.

Schultz, A.H. (1917). Ein paariger Knocken am unterrand der Squama Occipitalis. *Anatomical Record* **12**: 357–362.

Schultz, A.H. (1918a). Observations on the canalis basilaris chordae. *Anatomical Record* **15**: 225–229.

Schultz, A.H. (1918b). The fontanella metopica and its remnants in an adult skull. *American Journal of Anatomy* **23**: 259–271.

Schultz, A.H. (1929). The metopic fontanelle, fissure and suture. *American Journal of Anatomy* **44**: 475–499.

Schunke, G.B. (1938). The anatomy and development of the sacro-iliac joint in man. *Anatomical Record* **72**: 313–331.

Schutkowski, H. (1987). Sex determination of fetal and neonatal skeletons by means of discriminant analysis. *International Journal of Anthropology* **2**: 347–352.

Schutkowski, H. (1993). Sex determination of infant and juvenile skeletons: 1. Morphognostic features. *American Journal of Physical Anthropology* **90**: 199–205.

Schwartz, J.H. (1982). Dentofacial growth and development in *Homo sapiens*: evidence from perinatal individuals from Punic Carthage. *Anatomica Anzeiger* **152**: 1–26.

Schwartz, A.M., Wechsler, R.J., Landy, M.D., Wetzner, S.M. and Goldstein, S.A. (1982). Posterior arch defects of the cervical spine. *Skeletal Radiology* **8**: 135–139.

Scoles, P.V., Salvagno, R., Villalba, K. and Riew D. (1988). Relationship of iliac crest maturation to skeletal and chronologic age. *Journal of Pediatric Orthopedics* **8**: 639–644.

Scott, J.H. (1953). The cartilage of the nasal septum. *British Dental Journal* **95**: 37–43.

Scott, J.H. (1954). The growth of the human face. *Proceedings of the Royal Society of Medicine* **47**: 91–100.

Scott, J.H. (1956). Growth at facial sutures. *American Journal of Orthodontics* **42**: 381–387.

Scott, J.H. (1957). The growth in width of the facial skeleton. *American Journal of Orthodontics* **43**: 366–371.

Scott, J.H. (1958). The cranial base. *American Journal of Physical Anthropology* **16**: 319–348.

Scott, J.H. (1959). Further studies on the growth of the human face. *Proceedings of the Royal Society of Medicine* **52**: 263–268.

Scott, J.H. (1967). *Dento-facial Development and Growth*. London: Pergamon Press.

Scott, C.K. and Hightower, J.A. (1991). The matrix of endochondral bone differs from the matrix of intramembranous bone. *Calcified Tissue International* **49**: 349–354.

Scott, J.E. and Taor, W.S. (1979). The 'small patella' syndrome. *Journal of Bone and Joint Surgery* **61B**: 172–175.

Scott, G.R. and Turner, C.G. (2000). *The Anthropology of Modern Human Teeth. Dental Morphology and its Variation in Recent Human Populations*, 2nd edition. Cambridge: Cambridge University Press.

Seeds, J.W. and Cefalo, R.C. (1982). Relationship of fetal limb lengths to both biparietal diameter and gestational age. *Obstetrics and Gynecology* **60**: 680–685.

Sejrsen, B., Kjr, I. and Jakobsen, J. (1993). The human incisal suture and premaxillary area studied on archaeological material. *Acta Odontologica Scandinavica* **51**: 143–151.

Sejrsen, B., Kjær, I. and Jakobsen, J. (1996). Human palatal growth evaluated on medieval crania using nerve canal openings as references. *American Journal of Physical Anthropology* **99**: 603–611.

Sela, J., Schwartz, Z., Swain, L.D. and Boyan, B.D. (1992). The role of matrix vesicles in calcification. In: *Calcification in Biological Systems* (E. Bonucci, Ed.), pp. 73–105. Boca Raton, FL: CRC Press.

Selby, S. (1961). Separate centre of ossification of the tip of the internal malleolus. *American Journal of Roentgenology* **86**: 496–501.

Selleck, M.A.J. and Stern, C.D. (1991). Fate mapping and cell lineage analysis of Hensen's node in the chick embryo. *Development* **112**: 615–626.

Senior, H.D. (1929). The chondrification of the human hand and foot skeleton. *Anatomical Record* **42**: 35.

Seno, T. (1961). The origin and evolution of the sternum. *Anatomischer Anzeiger* **110**: 97–101.

Sensenig, E. (1949). The early development of the human vertebral column. *Contributions to Embryology* **33**: 23–41.

Serafini-Fracassini, A. and Smith, J.W. (1974). *The Structure and Biochemistry of Cartilage*. Edinburgh: Churchill Livingstone.

Shambaugh, G.E. (1967). *Surgery of the Ear*, 2nd edition. Philadelphia, PA: W.B. Saunders.

Shapiro, R. (1972). Anomalous parietal sutures and the bipartite parietal bone. *American Journal of Roentgenology* **115**: 569–577.

Shapiro, R. and Robinson, F. (1976a). Anomalies of the cranio-vertebral border. *American Journal of Roentgenology* **126**: 1063–1068.

Shapiro, R. and Robinson, F. (1976b). Embryogenesis of the human occipital bone. *American Journal of Roentgenology* **127**: 281–287.

Shapiro, R. and Robinson, F. (1980). *The Embryogenesis of the Human Skull.* Cambridge, MA: Harvard University Press.

Shelby, B. (1992). *Health. World Press Review*, Feb. 4.

Shepherd, W.M. and McCarthy, M.D. (1955). Observations on the appearance and ossification of the premaxilla and maxilla in the human embryo. *Anatomical Record* **121**: 13–28.

Sherk, H.H. and Nicholson, J.T. (1969). Rotary atlanto-axial dislocation associated with ossiculum terminale and mongolism. A case report. *Journal of Bone and Joint Surgery* **51A**: 957–964.

Sherwood, R.J., Meindl, R.S., Robinson, H.B. and May, R.L. (2000). Fetal age: methods of estimation and effects of pathology. *American Journal of Physical Anthropology* **113**: 305–315.

Shock, C.C., Noyes, F.R. and Villanueva, A.R. (1972). Measurement of Haversian bone remodelling by means of tetracycline labelling in rib of rhesus monkeys. *Henry Ford Hospital Medical Bulletin* **20**: 131–144.

Shopfner, C.E. (1966). Periosteal bone growth in normal infants. *American Journal of Roentgenology* **97**: 154–163.

Shopfner, C.E., Wolfe, T.W. and O'Kell, R.T. (1968). The intersphenoidal synchondrosis. *American Journal of Roentgenology* **104**: 184–193.

Shore, L.R. (1931). A report on the spinous processes of the cervical vertebrae in the native races of South Africa. *Journal of Anatomy* **65**: 482–505.

Siegling, J.A. (1941). Growth of the epiphyses. *Journal of Bone and Joint Surgery* **23**: 23–36.

Silau, A.M., Fischer-Hansen, B. and Kjær, I. (1995). Normal prenatal development of the human parietal bone and interparietal suture. *Journal of Craniofacial Genetics and Developmental Biology* **15**: 81–86.

Silau, A.M., Njio, B., Solow, B. and Kjær, I. (1994). Prenatal sagittal growth of the osseous components of the human palate. *Journal of Craniofacial Genetics and Developmental Biology* **14**: 252–256.

Silberstein, M.J., Brodeur, A.E. and Graviss, E.R. (1979). Some vagaries of the capitellum. *Journal of Bone and Joint Surgery* **61A**: 244–247.

Silberstein, M.J., Brodeur, A.E., Graviss, E.R. and Luisiri, A. (1981a). Some vagaries of the medial epicondyle. *Journal of Bone and Joint Surgery* **63A**: 524–528.

Silberstein, M.J., Brodeur, A.E., Graviss, E.R. and Luisiri, A. (1981b). Some vagaries of the olecranon. *Journal of Bone and Joint Surgery* **63A**: 722–725.

Silberstein, M.J., Brodeur, A.E. and Graviss, E.R. (1982). Some vagaries of the lateral epicondyle. *Journal of Bone and Joint Surgery* **64A**: 444–448.

Simms, D.L. and Neely, J.G. (1989). Growth of the lateral surface of the temporal bone in children. *Laryngoscope* **99**: 795–799.

Sinclair, D. (1978). *Human Growth after Birth*, 3rd edition. London: Oxford University Press.

Singh, I.J. and Gunberg, D.L. (1970). Estimation of age at death in human males from quantitative histology of bone fragments. *American Journal of Physical Anthropology* **33**: 373–381.

Skak, S.V. (1993). Fracture of the olecranon through a persistent physis in an adult. *Journal of Bone and Joint Surgery* **75A**: 272–275.

Skawina, A. and Gorczyca, W. (1984). The role of nutrient and periosteal blood vessels in the vascularization of the cortex of shafts of the long bones in human fetuses. *Folia Morphologica (Warszawa)* **43**: 159–164.

Skawina, A. and Miaskiewicz, C. (1982). Nutrient foramina in femoral, tibial and fibular bones in human fetuses. *Folia Morphologica (Warszawa)* **41**: 469–481.

Skawina, A. and Wyczółkowski, M. (1987). Nutrient foramina of humerus, radius and ulna in human fetuses. *Folia Morphologica (Warszawa)* **46**: 17–24.

Skawina, A., Litwin, J.A., Gorczyca, J. and Miodonski, A.J. (1994). The vascular system of human fetal long bones: a scanning electron microscope study of corrosion casts. *Journal of Anatomy* **185**: 369–376.

Skawina, A., Litwin, J.A., Gorczyca, J. and Miodonski, A.J. (1997). The architecture of internal blood vessels in human fetal vertebral bodies. *Journal of Anatomy* **191**: 259–267.

Skinner, M. and Dupras, T. (1993). Variation in birth timing and location of the neonatal line in human enamel. *Journal of Forensic Sciences* **38**: 1383–1390.

Slavkin, H.C. (1988). Gene regulation of oral tissues. 1987 Kreshover lecture. *Journal of Dental Research* **67**: 1142–1149.

Slavkin, H.C., Canter, M.R. and Canter, S.R. (1966). An anatomic study of the pterygomaxillary region in the craniums of infants and children. *Oral Surgery, Oral Medicine and Oral Pathology* **21**: 225–235.

Smith, A.D. (1941). Congenital elevation of the scapula. *Archives of Surgery* **42**: 529–536.

Smith, B.H. (1991). Standards of human tooth formation and dental age assessment. In: *Advances in Dental Anthropology* (M.A. Kelley and C.S. Larsen, Eds), pp. 143–168. New York: Wiley–Liss.

Smith, C.A. (1947). Effects of maternal undernutrition upon the newborn infant in Holland (1944–1945). *Journal of Pediatrics* **30**: 229–243.

Smith, H.D. (1912). Observations on the cranial bone in a series of Egyptian skulls, with especial reference to the persistence of the synchondrosis condylo-squamosa. *Biometrika* **8**: 257–261.

Smith, J.W. (1962a). The relationship of epiphysial plates to stress in some bones of the lower limb. *Journal of Anatomy* **96**: 58–78.

Smith, J.W. (1962b). The structure and stress relations of fibrous epiphysial plates. *Journal of Anatomy* **96**: 209–225.

Smith, S. (1925). Notes on the ossification of the scapula. *Journal of Anatomy* **59**: 387.

Smith, B.H. and Garn, S.M. (1987). Polymorphisms in eruption sequence of permanent teeth in American children. *American Journal of Physical Anthropology* **74**: 289–303.

Smith, J.D. and Abramson, M. (1974). Membranous vs endochondral bone autografts. *Archives of Otolaryngology* **99**: 203–205.

Smith, M.M. and Hall, B. K. (1990). Development and evolutionary origins of vertebral and odontogenic tissues. *Biological Review* **65**: 277–373.

Smith, R.N. and Allcock, J. (1960). Epiphyseal union in the greyhound. *Veterinary Record* **72**: 75–79.

Smith, S. and Boulgakoff, B. (1923). A case of polydactylia shewing certain atavistic characters. *Journal of Anatomy* **58**: 359–367.

Solursh, M. (1983). Cell–cell interactions in chondrogenesis. pp 121–141. In: *Cartilage Vol. 2: Development, Differentiation and Growth* (B.K. Hall, Ed.). New York: Academic Press.

Sontag, L.W. (1938). Evidences of disturbed prenatal and neonatal growth in bones of infants aged one month. *American Journal of Diseases of Children* **55**: 1248–1256.

Souri, S.J. (1959). A morphological study of the fetal pelvis. *Journal of the Anatomical Society of India* **8**: 45–55.

Southam, A.H. and Bythell, W.J.S. (1924). Cervical ribs in children. *British Medical Journal* **2**: 844–845.

Specker, B.L., Brazero, L.W., Tsang, R.C., Levin, R., Searcy, J. and Steichen, J. (1987). Bone mineral content in children 1–6 years of age. *American Journal of Diseases of Children* **141**: 343–344.

Spector, G.T. and Ge, X-X. (1981). Development of the hypotympanum in the human fetus and neonate. *Annals of Otology, Rhinology and Laryngology* **90** (Suppl. 88): 1–20.

Speer, D.P. (1982). Collagenous architecture of the growth plate and perichondrial ossification groove. *Journal of Bone and Joint Surgery* **64A**: 399–407.

Sperber, G.H. (1989). *Craniofacial Embryology*, 4th edition, p. 102. London: Wright, Butterworths.

Spierings, E.L.H. and Braakman, R. (1984). The management of os odontoideum. Analysis of 37 cases. *Journal of Bone and Joint Surgery* **64B**: 422–428.

Spoor, C.F. (1993). The human bony labyrinth: a morphometric description. In: The comparative morphology and phylogeny of the human bony labyrinth. Unpublished PhD dissertation, University of Utrecht.

Sprengel, O.G. (1891). Die angeborne Verschiebung des Schulter blattes nach oben. *Archiv für Klinische Chirurgie* **42**: 545–549.

Sprinz, R. and Kaufman, M.H. (1987). The sphenoidal canal. *Journal of Anatomy* **153**: 47–54.

Spyropoulos, M.N. (1977). The morphogenetic relationship of the temporal muscle to the coronoid process in human embryos and fetuses. *American Journal of Anatomy* **150**: 395–410.

Srivastava, H.C. (1992). Ossification of the membranous portion of the squamous part of the occipital bone in man. *Journal of Anatomy* **180**: 219–224.

Stack, M.V. (1964). A gravimetric study of crown growth rate of the human deciduous dentition. *Biologia Neonatorum* **6**: 197–224.

Stack, M.V. (1967). Vertical growth rate of the deciduous teeth. *Journal of Dental Research* **46**: 879–882.

Stack, M.V. (1968). Relative growth of the deciduous second molar and permanent first molar. *Journal of Dental Research* **47**: 1013–1014.

Stack, M.V. (1971). Relative rates of weight gain in human deciduous teeth. In: *Dental Morphology and Evolution* (A.A. Dahlberg, Ed.), pp. 59–62. Chicago: Chicago University Press.

Staheli, L.T. (1977). Torsional deformity. *Pediatric Clinics of North America* **24**: 799–811.

Staheli, L.T. (1984). Fractures of the shaft of the femur. In: *Fractures in Children* (C.A. Rockwood, K.E. Wilkins and R.E. King, Eds), pp. 845–889. Philadelphia, PA: Lippincott.

Staheli, L.T. and Engel, G.M. (1972). Tibial torsion. A method of assessment and a survey of normal children. *Clinical Orthopaedics and Related Research* **86**: 183–186.

Stallworthy, J.A. (1932). A case of enlarged parietal foramina associated with metopism and irregular synostosis of the coronal suture. *Journal of Anatomy* **67**: 168–174.

Stammel, C.A. (1941). Multiple striae parallel to epiphyses and ring shadows around bone growth centres. *American Journal of Roentgenology* **46**: 497–505.

Steinberg, M.S. (1963). Reconstruction of tissues by dissociated cells. *Science* **141**: 401–408.

Steiner, H.A. (1943). Roentgenologic manifestations and clinical symptoms of rib abnormalities. *Radiology* **40**: 175–178.

Stelling, C.B. (1981). Anomalous attachment of the transverse process to the vertebral body: an accessory finding in congenital absence of a lumbar pedicle. *Skeletal Radiology* **6**: 47–50.

Stevenson, P.H. (1924). Age order of epiphyseal union in man. *American Journal of Physical Anthropology* **7**: 53–93.

Stewart, T.D. (1934). Sequence of epiphyseal union, third molar eruption and suture closure in Eskimos and American Indians. *American Journal of Physical Anthropology* **19**: 433–452.

Stewart, T.D. (1954). Metamorphosis of the joints of the sternum in relation to age changes in other bones. *American Journal of Physical Anthropology* **12**: 519–535.

Stibbe, E.P. (1929). Skull showing perforations of parietal bone or enlarged parietal foramina. *Journal of Anatomy* **63**: 277–278.

Stillwell, W.T. and Fielding, J.W. (1978). Acquired os odontoideum. *Clinical Orthopaedics* **135**: 71–73.

Stirland, A. (1991). Diagnosis of occupationally related palaeopathology. Can it be done? In: *Human Palaeopathology: Current Syntheses and Future Opinions* (D.J. Ortner and A.C. Aufderheide, Eds), pp. 40–47. Washington, DC: Smithsonian Institute Press.

Stone, A.C., Milner, G.R., Pääbo, S. and Stoneking, M. (1996). Sex determination of ancient human skeletons using DNA. *American Journal of Physical Anthropology* **99**: 231–238.

Stout, S.D., Dietze, W.H., Işcan, M.Y. and Loth, S.R. (1994). Estimation of age at death using cortical histomorphometry of the sternal end of the fourth rib. *Journal of Forensic Sciences* **39**: 778–784.

Stovin, J.J., Lyon, J.A. and Clemmens, R.L. (1960). Mandibulofacial dysostosis. *American Journal of Radiology* **74**: 225–231.

Stratemeier, P.H. and Jensen, S.R. (1980). Partial regressive occipital vertebra. *Neuroradiology* **19**: 47–49.

Streeter, G.L. (1918). The histogenesis and growth of the otic capsule and its contained periotic tissue-spaces in the human embryo. *Contributions to Embryology* **7**: 5–54.

Streeter, G.L. (1920). Weight, sitting height, head size, foot length and menstrual age of the human embryo. *Contributions to Embryology* **11**: 143–170.

Streeter, G.L. (1942). Developmental horizons in human embryos. Description of age group XI 13 to 20 somites and age group XII 21 to 29 somites. *Contributions to Embryology* **30**: 211–245.

Streeter, G.L. (1945). Developmental horizons in human embryos. Description of age group XIII, embryos about 4 or 5 millimeters long, and age group XIV, period of indentation of the lens vesicle. *Contributions to Embryology* **31**: 27–63.

Streeter, G.L. (1948). Description of age groups XV, XVI, XVII and XVIII being the third issue of a survey of the Carnegie collection. *Contributions to Embryology* **32**: 133–203.

Streeter, G.L. (1949). Developmental horizons in human embryos (fourth issue). A review of the histogenesis of cartilage and bone. *Contributions to Embryology* **33**: 149–167.

Streeter, G.L. (1951). Description of age groups XIX, XX, XXI, XXII and XXIII, being the fifth issue of a survey of the Carnegie collection. *Contributions to Embryology* **34**: 165–196.

Stricker, M., Van der Meulen, J.C., Raphael, B. and Mazzola, R. (Eds) (1990). *Craniofacial Malformations*. Edinburgh: Churchill Livingstone.

Stripp, W. and Reynolds, C.P. (1988). Radiography and radiology. In: *The Foot* (B. Helal, and D. Wilson, Eds), pp. 146–201. Edinburgh: Churchill Livingstone.

Sullivan, P. and Lumsden, A.G.S. (1981). Embryology and Development. In: *A Companion to Dental Studies*, Vol. 1, Book 2. (J.W. Osborn, Ed.), pp. 35–46. Oxford: Blackwells.

Sullivan, W.G. and Szwajkun, P. (1991). Membranous vs endochondral bone. *Plastic and Reconstructive Surgery* **87**: 1145.

Sunderland, E.P., Smith, C.J. and Sunderland, R. (1987). A histological study of the chronology of initial mineralization in the human deciduous dentition. *Archives of Oral Biology* **32**: 167–174.

Sundick, R.I. (1977). Age and sex determination of subadult skeletons. *Journal of Forensic Sciences* **22**: 141–144.

Sundick, R.I. (1978). Human skeletal growth and age determination. *Homo* **29**: 228–249.

Sutro, C.J. (1967). Dentated articular surface of the glenoid – an anomaly. *Bulletin of Hospital Joint Diseases* **28**: 104–115.

Swischuk, L., Hayden, C.K. and Sarwar, M. (1979). The posterior tilted dens. *Pediatric Radiology* **8**: 27–32.

Sycamore, L.K. (1944). Common congenital anomalies of the bony thorax. *American Journal of Roentgenology* **51**: 593–599.

Syftestad, G.T. and Caplan, A.I. (1984). A fraction from extracts of demineralized adult bone stimulates the conversion of mesenchymal cells into chondrocytes. *Developmental Biology* **104**: 348–356.

Symmers, W. St C. (1895). A skull with enormous parietal foramina. *Journal of Anatomy and Physiology* **29**: 329–330.

Symons, N.B.B. (1951). Studies on the growth and form of the mandible. *Dental Record* **71**: 41–53.

Symons, N.B.B. (1952). The development of the human mandibular joint. *Journal of Anatomy* **86**: 326–332.

Szaboky, G.T., Anderson, J.J. and Wiltsie, R.A. (1970). Bifid os calcis an anomalous ossification of the calcaneus. *Clinical Orthopaedics and Related Research* **68**: 136–137.

Szilvassy, J. (1980). Age determination on the sternal articular faces of the clavicula. *Journal of Human Evolution* **9**: 609–610.

Tabin, C.J. (1992). Why we have (only) five fingers per hand: Hox genes and the evolution of paired limbs. *Development* **116**: 289–296.

Tabin, C.J. (1998). A developmental model for thalidomide defects. *Nature* **396**: 322–323.

Tachdjian, M.O. (1972). *Pediatric Orthopedics*. Philadelphia, PA: W.B. Saunders.

Takahashi, R. (1987). The formation of the nasal septum and the etiology of septal deformity. *Acta Oto-Laryngologica* **443**(Suppl.): 1–160.

Tan, K.L. (1971). The third fontanelle. *Acta Pædiatrica Scandinavica* **60**: 329–332.

Tanaka, T. and Uhthoff, H.K. (1981). Significance of resegmentation in the pathogenesis of vertebral body malformation. *Acta Orthopedica Scandinavica* **52**: 331–338.

Tanaka, T. and Uhthoff, H.K. (1983). Coronal cleft of vertebrae, a variant of normal enchondral ossification. *Acta Orthopaedica Scandinavica* **54**: 389–395.

Tanguay, R., Buschang, P.H. and Demirjian, A. (1986). Sexual dimorphism in the emergence of deciduous teeth: its relationship with growth components in height. *American Journal of Physical Anthropology* **69**: 511–515.

Tanner, J.M. (1962). *Growth at Adolescence*, 2nd edition. Oxford: Blackwell Scientific.

Tanner, J.M. (1978). *Foetus into Man – Physical Growth from Conception to Maturity*. London: Open Books.

Tanner, J.M. and Whitehouse, R.H. (1959). *Standards for Skeletal Maturity Based On A Study of 3000 British Children*. London: Institute of Child Health.

Tanner, J.M., Prader, A., Habich, H. and Ferguson-Smith, M.A. (1959). Genes on the Y-chromosome influencing rate of maturation in man: skeletal age studies in children with Klinefelter's (XXY) and Turner's (XO) syndromes. *Lancet* **2**: 141–144.

Tanner, J.M., Whitehouse, R.H., Cameron, N., Marshall, W.A., Healy, M.J.R. and Goldstein, H. (1983). *Assessment of Skeletal Maturity and Prediction of Adult Height (TW2 Method)*, 2nd edition. London: Academic Press.

Tardieu, C. (1998). Short adolescence in early Hominids: infantile and adolescent growth of the human femur. *American Journal of Physical Anthropology* **107**: 163–178.

Tardieu, C. and Trinkaus, E. (1994). Early ontogeny of the human femoral bicondylar angle. *American Journal of Physical Anthropology* **95**: 183–195.

Taylor, J.R. and Twomey, L.T. (1984). Sexual dimorphism in human vertebral body shape. *Journal of Anatomy* **138**: 281–286.

Ten Cate, A.R. (1998). *Oral Histology: Development, Structure and Function*, 5th edition. London: Mosby Yearbook.

Ten Cate, A.R. and Mills, C. (1972). The development of the periodontium: the origin of alveolar bone. *Anatomical Record* **173**: 69–77.

Thompson, D.D. (1979). The core technique in the determination of age at death in skeletons. *Journal of Forensic Sciences* **24**: 902–915.

Thompson, T.J., Owens, P.D.A. and Wilson, D.J. (1989). Intramembranous osteogenesis and angiogenesis in the chick embryo. *Journal of Anatomy* **166**: 55–65.

Thomson, A. (1899). The sexual differences in the foetal pelvis. *Journal of Anatomy and Physiology* **33**: 359–380.

Thornton, A. and Gyll, C. (1999). *Children's Fractures: a Radiological Guide to Safe Practice*. London: W.B. Saunders.

Tickle, C. (1994). On making a skeleton. *Nature* **368**: 587–588.

Tillmann, B. and Lorenz, R. (1978). The stress at the human atlanto-occipital joint. *Anatomy and Embryology* **153**: 269–277.

Tobin, W.J. (1955). The internal architecture of the femur and its clinical significance. *Journal of Bone and Joint Surgery* **37A**: 57–71.

Todd, T.W. (1920). Age changes in the pubic bone. 1. The male white pubis. *American Journal of Physical Anthropology* **3**: 285–334.

Todd, T.W. (1921). Age changes in the pubic bone. 5. Mammalian pubic metamorphosis. *American Journal of Physical Anthropology* **4**: 334–406.

Todd, T.W. (1930). The anatomical features of epiphyseal union. *Child Development* **1**: 186–194.

Todd, T.W. and D'Errico, J. (1926). The odontoid ossicle of the second cervical vertebra. *Annals of Surgery* **83**: 20–31.

Todd, T.W. and D'Errico, J. (1928). The clavicular epiphysis. *American Journal of Anatomy* **41**: 25–50.

Todd, T.W. and McCally, W.C. (1921). Defects of the patellar border. *Annals of Surgery* **74**: 775–782.

Toldt, C. (1919). *An Atlas of Human Anatomy for Students and Physicians*, English edition, Parts I and II. New York: Rebman.

Tompsett, A.C. and Donaldson, S.W. (1951). The anterior tubercle of the first cervical vertebra and the hyoid bone: their occurrence in newborn infants. *American Journal of Roentgenology* **65**: 582–584.

Töndury, G. and Theiler, K. (1990). *Entwickelungsgeschichte und Fehlbildungen der Wirbelsäule*, 2nd edition. Stuttgart: Hippokrates.

Too-Chung, M.A. and Green, J.R. (1974). The rate of growth of the cricoid cartilage. *Journal of Laryngology and Otology* **88**: 65–70.

Toole, B.P. and Trelstad, R.L. (1971). Hyaluronate production and removal during corneal development in the chick. *Developmental Biology* **26**: 28–35.

Torgersen, J. (1950). A roentgenological study of the metopic suture. *Acta Radiologica* **33**: 1–11.

Torgersen, J. (1951). The developmental genetics and evolutionary meaning of the metopic suture. *American Journal of Physical Anthropology* **9**: 193–210.

Townsend, N. and Hammel, E.A. (1990). Age estimation from the number of teeth erupted in young children: an aid to demographic studies. *Demography* **27**: 165–174.

Traub, W., Arad, T. and Weiner, S. (1992). Growth of mineral crystals in turkey tendon collagen fibers. *Connective Tissue Research* **28**: 99–111.

Travers, J.T. and Wormley, L.C. (1938). Enlarged parietal foramina. *American Journal of Roentgenology* **40**: 571–579.

Trinkaus, E. (1975). Squatting among the Neandertals: a problem in the behavioral interpretation of skeletal morphology. *Journal of Archaeological Science* **2**: 327–351.

Trueta, J. (1957). The normal vascular anatomy of the human femoral head during growth. *Journal of Bone and Joint Surgery* **39B**: 358–394.

Trueta, J. and Cavadias, A.X. (1964). A study of the blood supply of the long bones. *Surgery, Gynaecology and Obstetrics* **118**: 485–498.

Trueta, J. and Morgan, J.D. (1960). The vascular contribution to osteogenesis. I. Studies by the injection method. *Journal of Bone and Joint Surgery* **42B**: 97–109.

Tsou, P.M., Yau, A. and Hodgson, A.R. (1980). Embryogenesis and prenatal development of congenital vertebral anomalies and their classification. *Clinical Orthopaedics* **152**: 211–231.

Tucker, F.R. (1949). Arterial supply to the femoral head and its clinical importance. *Journal of Bone and Joint Surgery* **31B**: 82–93.

Tucker, J.A. and O'Rahilly, R. (1972). Observations on the embryology of the human larynx. *Annals of Otology, Rhinology and Laryngology* **81**: 520–523.

Tucker, J.A. and Tucker, G.F. (1975). Some aspects of laryngeal fetal development. *Annals of Otology, Rhinology and Laryngology* **84**: 49–55.

Tucker, G.F., Tucker, J.A. and Vidić, B. (1977). Anatomy and development of the cricoid. Serial-section whole organ study of perinatal larynges. *Annals of Otology, Rhinology and Laryngology* **86**: 1–4.

Tufts, E., Blank, E. and Dickerson, D. (1982). Periosteal thickening as a manifestation of trauma in infancy. *Child Abuse and Neglect* **6**: 359–364.

Tulsi, R.S. (1971). Growth of the human vertebral column. An osteological study. *Acta Anatomica* **79**: 570–580.

Turk, L.M. and Hogg, D.A. (1993). Age changes in the human laryngeal cartilages. *Clinical Anatomy* **6**: 154–162.

Turner, E.P. (1963). Crown development in human deciduous molar teeth. *Archives of Oral Biology* **8**: 523–540.

Turner, W. (1866). On some congenital deformities of the human cranium. *Edinburgh Medical Journal* **11**: 133–141.

Turner, W. (1874). Further examples of variations in the arrangement of the nerves of the human body. *Journal of Anatomy and Physiology* **8**: 297–299.

Turner, W. (1885). The infra-orbital suture. *Journal of Anatomy and Physiology* **19**: 218–220.

Turner, M.S. and Smillie, I.S. (1981). The effect of tibial torsion on the pathology of the knee. *Journal of Bone and Joint Surgery* **63B**: 296–398.

Ubelaker, D.H. (1978). *Human Skeletal Remains*: *Excavation, Analysis and Interpretation*. Washington, DC: Smithsonian Inst. Press.

Ubelaker, D.H. (1984). Possible identification from radiographic comparison of frontal sinus patterns. In: *Human Identification. Case Studies in Forensic Anthropology* (T.A. Rathbun and J.E. Buikstra, Eds), pp. 399–411. Springfield, IL: C.C. Thomas.

Ubelaker, D.H. (1992). Hyoid fracture and strangulation. *Journal of Forensic Sciences* **37**: 1216–1222.

Ubelaker, D.H. and Pap, I. (1998). Skeletal evidence for health and disease in the Iron Age of northeastern Hungary. *International Journal of Osteoarchaeology* **8**: 231–251.

Uhry, E. (1944). Osgood–Schlatter's disease. *Archives of Surgery* **48**: 406–414.

Uhthoff, H.K. (1990a). The early development of the spine. In: *The Embryology of the Human Locomotor System* (H.K. Uhthoff, Ed.), pp. 34–41. Berlin: Springer.

Uhthoff, H.K. (1990b). The development of the limb buds. In: *The Embryology of the Human Locomotor System* (H.K. Uhthoff, Ed.), pp. 7–14. Berlin: Springer.

Uhthoff, H.K. (1990c). The development of the shoulder. In: *The Embryology of the Human Locomotor System* (H.K. Uhthoff, Ed.), pp. 73–81. Berlin: Springer.

Underwood, L.E., Radcliffe, W.B. and Guinto, F.C. (1976). New standards for the assessment of the sella turcica in children. *Radiology* **119**: 651–654.

Upadhyay, S.S., Burwell, R.G., Moulton, A., Small, P.G. and Wallace, W.A. (1990). Femoral anteversion in healthy children. Application of a new method using ultrasound. *Journal of Anatomy* **169**: 49–61.

Urasaki, E., Yasukouchi, H. and Yokota, A. (2001). Atlas hypoplasia manifesting as myelopathy in a child. *Neurologia Medico-Chirugica (Tokyo)* **41**: 160–162.

Van Alyea, O.E. (1936). The ostium maxillare. Anatomic study of its surgical accessibility. *Archives of Otolaryngology* **24**: 553–569.

Van Alyea, O.E. (1941). Sphenoid sinus. Anatomic study with consideration of the clinical significance of the structural characteristics of the sphenoid sinus. *Archives of Otolaryngology* **34**: 225–253.

Van Beek, G. (1983). *Dental Morphology – an Illustrated Guide*, 2nd edition. Bristol: PSG Wright.

Van der Linden, F.P.G.M. and Duterloo, H.S. (1976). *The Development of the Human Dentition – An Atlas*. Hagerstown, MD: Harper and Row.

Van Gilse, P.H.G. (1927). The development of the sphenoidal sinus in man and its homology in mammals. *Journal of Anatomy* **61**: 153–166.

Van Waalwijk, C.V.D. and Boet, J.N. (1949). Lacuna skull and craniofenestria. *American Journal of Diseases of Children* **77**: 315–327.

Vastine, J.H. and Vastine, M.F. (1952). Calcification in the laryngeal cartilages. *Archives of Otolaryngology* **55**: 1–7.

Vasudeva, N. and Kumar, R. (1995). Absence of foramen transversarium in the human atlas vertebra: a case report. *Acta Anatomica* **152**: 230–233.

Verbout, A.J. (1976). A critical review of the 'Neugliederung' concept in relation to the development of the vertebral column. *Acta Biotheorie (Leiden)* **25**: 219–258.

Verbout, A.J. (1985). The development of the vertebral column. *Advances in Anatomy, Embryology and Cell Biology* **90**.

Verwoerd, C.D.A., Van Loosen, J., Schütte, H.E., Verwoerd-Verhoef, H.L. and Van Velzen, D. (1989). Surgical aspects of the anatomy of the vomer in children and adults. *Rhinology* **9**(Suppl.): 87–96.

Victoria-Diaz, A. (1979). Embryological contribution to the aetiopathology of idiopathic club foot. *Journal of Bone and Joint Surgery* **61B**: 127.

Vidić, B. (1968). The postnatal development of the sphenoidal sinus and its spread into the dorsum sellae and posterior clinoid processes. *American Journal of Roentgenology* **104**: 177–183.

Vidić, B. (1971). The morphogenesis of the lateral nasal wall in the early prenatal life of man. *American Journal of Anatomy* **130**: 121–139.

Vignaud-Pasquier, J., Lichtenberg, R., Laval-Jeantet, M., Larroche, J.C. and Bernard, J. (1964). Les impressions digitales de la naissance à neuf ans. *Biologia Neonatorum* **6**: 250–276.

Viladot, A. (1988). Local Congenital Disorders. In: *The Foot* (B. Helal and D. Wilson, Eds), pp. 235–264. Edinburgh: Churchill Livingstone.

Vogt, E.C. and Wyatt, G.M. (1941). Craniolacunia (Lückenschädel). A report of 54 cases. *Radiology* **36**: 147–152.

Von Bazan, U.B. (1979). The association between congenital elevation of the scapula and diastematomyelia. *Journal of Bone and Joint Surgery* **61B**: 59–63.

Wagner, U.A., Diedrich, V. and Schmitt, O. (1995). Determination of skeletal maturity by ultrasound: a preliminary report. *Skeletal Radiology* **24**: 417–420

Wahby, B. (1903). Abnormal nasal bones. *Journal of Anatomy and Physiology* **38**: 49–51.

Waisbrod, H. (1973). Congenital club foot. An anatomical study. *Journal of Bone and Joint Surgery* **55B**: 796–801.

Wakeley, C.P.G. (1929). A note on the architecture of the ilium. *Journal of Anatomy* **64**: 109–110.

Wakeley, C.P.G. (1931). A case of congenital absence of the radius in a woman. *Journal of Anatomy* **65**: 506–508.

Waldron, T. (1994). The nature of the sample. In: *Counting the Dead. The Epidemiology of Skeletal Populations*, pp. 10–27. Chichester: Wiley.

Walensky, N.A. (1965). A study of anterior femoral curvature in man. *Anatomical Record* **151**: 559–570.

Walker, C. (1917). Absence of premaxilla. *Journal of Anatomy* **51**: 392–395.

Walker, J.M. (1983). Comparison of normal and abnormal human fetal hip joints: a quantitative study with significance to congenital hip disease. *Journal of Pediatric Orthopedics* **3**: 173–183.

Walker, G.F. and Kowalski, C.J. (1972). On the growth of the mandible. *American Journal of Physical Anthropology* **36**: 111–118.

Walker, R.A., Lovejoy, C.O. and Meindl, R.S. (1994). Histomorphological and geometric properties of human femoral cortex in individuals over 50: implications for histomorphological determination of age at death. *American Journal of Human Biology* **6**: 659–667.

Walmsley, T. (1915). The epiphysis of the head of the femur. *Journal of Anatomy and Physiology* **49**: 434–440.

Walmsley, T. (1933). The vertical axes of the femur and their relations. A contribution to the study of posture. *Journal of Anatomy* **67**: 284–300.

Walmsley, R. (1940). The development of the patella. *Journal of Anatomy* **74**: 360–368.

Wang, R-G., Kwok, P. and Hawke, M. (1988). The embryonic development of the human paraseptal cartilage. *Journal of Otolaryngology* **17**: 150–154.

Warkany, J. and Weaver, T.S. (1940). Heredofamilial deviations. II Enlarged parietal foramens combined with obesity, hypogenitalism, microphthalmos and mental retardation. *American Journal of Diseases of Children* **60**: 1147–1154.

Warwick, R. (1950). The relation of the direction of the mental foramen to the growth of the human mandible. *Journal of Anatomy* **84**: 116–120.

Wasson, W.W. (1933). Changes in the nasal accessory sinuses after birth. *Archives of Otolaryngology* **17**: 197–209.

Watanabe, R.S. (1974). Embryology of the human hip. *Clinical Orthopaedics and Related Research* **98**: 8–26.

Watanabe, Y., Konishi, M., Shimada, M., Ohara, H. and Iwamoto, S. (1998). Estimation of age from the femur of Japanese cadavers. *Forensic Science International* **98**: 55–65.

WEA (Workshop of European Anthropologists) (1980). Recommendations for age and sex diagnoses of skeletons. *Journal of Human Evolution* **9**: 517–549.

Weaver, D.S. (1979). Application of the likelihood ratio test to age estimation using the infant and child temporal bone. *American Journal of Physical Anthropology* **50**: 263–270.

Weaver, D.S. (1980). Sex differences in the ilia of a known sex and age sample of fetal and infant skeletons. *American Journal of Physical Anthropology* **52**: 191–195.

Webb, P.A.O. and Suchey, J.M. (1985). Epiphyseal union of the anterior iliac crest and medial clavicle in a modern sample of American males and females. *American Journal of Physical Anthropology* **68**: 457–466.

Weiner, S. and Traub, W. (1989). Crystal size and organization in bone. *Connective Tissue Research* **21**: 259–265.

Weinmann, J.P. and Sicher, H. (1947). *Bone and Bones: Fundamentals of Bone Biology*. London: Henry Kimpton.

Weiss, K.M., Stock, D.W. and Zhao, Z. (1998). In: *The Cambridge Encyclopedia of Human Growth and Development* (S.J. Ulijaszek, F.E. Johnston and M.A. Preece, Eds), pp. 137–138. Cambridge: Cambridge University Press.

Wells, C. (1968). Osgood–Schlatter's disease in the ninth century. *British Medical Journal* **2**: 623–624.

Westhorpe, R.N. (1987). The position of the larynx in children and its relationship to the ease of intubation. *Anaesthesia and Intensive Care* **15**: 384–388.

Weston, W.J. (1956). Genetically determined cervical ribs: a family study. *British Journal of Radiology* **29**: 455–456.

Whillis, J. (1940). The development of synovial joints. *Journal of Anatomy* **74**: 277–283.

White, T.D. (1991). *Human Osteology*. London: Academic Press.

Whitehead, R.H. and Waddell, J.A. (1911). The early development of the mammalian sternum. *American Journal of Anatomy* **12**: 89–106.

Whittaker, D.K. (1992). Quantitative studies on age changes in the teeth and surrounding structures in archaeological material: a review. *Journal of the Royal Society of Medicine* **85**: 97–101.

Whittaker, D.K. and MacDonald, D.G. (1989). *A Colour Atlas of Forensic Dentistry*. London: Wolfe.

Whittaker, D.K. and Richards, D. (1978). Scanning electron microscopy of the neonatal line in human enamel. *Archives of Oral Biology* **23**: 45–50.

Wilgress, J.H.F. (1900). A note on the development of the external malleolus. *Journal of Anatomy and Physiology* **34**: xlii–xliv.

Wilkins, K.E. (1984). Fractures and dislocations of the elbow region. In: *Fractures in Children* (C.A. Rockwood, K.E. Wilkins and R.E. King, Eds), pp. 363–575. Philadelphia, PA: Lippincott.

Willems, G., Van Olmen, A., Spiessens, B. and Carels, C. (2001). Dental age estimation in Belgian children: Demirjian's technique revisited. *Journal of Forensic Sciences* **46**: 893–895.

Williams, P.L., Bannister, L.H., Berry, M.M., Collins, P., Dyson, M. Dussek, J.E. and Ferguson, M.W.J. (1995). *Gray's Anatomy*, 38th edition. Edinburgh: Churchill Livingstone.

Willis, T.A. (1949). Nutrient arteries of the vertebral bodies. *Journal of Bone and Joint Surgery* **31A**: 538–540.

Willock, E.F. (1925). An os interfrontale. *Journal of Anatomy* **59**: 439–441.

Wilsman, N.J. and Van Sickle, D.C. (1972). Cartilage canals, their morphology and distribution. *Anatomical Record* **173**: 79–93.

Wolf, G., Anderhuber, W. and Kuhn, F. (1993). Development of the paranasal sinuses in children: implications for paranasal sinus surgery. *Annals of Otology, Rhinology and Laryngology* **102**: 705–711.

Wollin, D.G. (1963). The os odontoideum. *Journal of Bone and Joint Surgery* **45A**: 1459–1471.

Wong, M. and Carter, D.R. (1988). Mechanical stress and morphogenetic endochondral ossification in the sternum. *Journal of Bone and Joint Surgery* **70A**: 992–1000.

Woo, J-K. (1948). 'Anterior' and 'posterior' medio-palatine bones. *American Journal of Physical Anthropology* **6**: 209–223.

Woo, J-K. (1949a). Racial and sexual differences in the frontal curvature and its relation to metopism. *American Journal of Physical Anthropology* **7**: 215–226.

Woo, J-K. (1949b). Ossification and growth of the human maxilla, premaxilla and palate bone. *Anatomical Record* **105**: 737–761.

Wood, N.K., Wragg, L.E. and Stuteville, O.H. (1967). The premaxilla: embryological evidence that it does not exist in man. *Anatomical Record* **158**: 485–490.

Wood, N.K., Wragg, L.E., Stuteville, O.H. and Oglesby, R.J. (1969). Osteogenesis of the human upper jaw: proof of the non-existence of a separate pre-maxillary centre. *Archives of Oral Biology* **14**: 1331–1341.

Wood, N.K., Wragg, L.E., Stuteville, O.H. and Kaminski, E.J. (1970). Prenatal observations on the incisive fissure and the frontal process in man. *Journal of Dental Research* **49**: 1125–1131.

Wood Jones, F. (1947). The premaxilla and the ancestry of man. *Nature* **159**: 439.

Wood Jones, F. (1953). *Buchanan's Manual of Anatomy*, 8th edition. London: Baillière Tindall and Cox.

Wraith, P. (2003). Letter to the editor. *Annals of Human Biology*. **30**: 109–110.

Wray, J.B. and Herndon, C.N. (1963). Hereditary transmission of congenital coalition of the calcaneus to the navicular. *Journal of Bone and Joint Surgery* **45A**: 365–372.

Wright, W. (1903). A case of accessory patellae in the human subject, with remarks on the emargination of the patella. *Journal of Anatomy and Physiology* **38**: 65–67.

Wuthier, R.E. (1989). Mechanism of *de novo* mineral formation by matrix vesicles. *Connective Tissue Research* **22**: 27–33.

Wyburn, G. (1944). Observations on the development of the human vertebral column. *Journal of Anatomy* **78**: 94–102.

Yamamura, H. (1939). On the fetal pelvis. *Japanese Journal of Obstetrics and Gynaecology* **22**: 268–285.

Yarkoni, S., Schmidt, W., Jeanty, P., Reece, E.A. and Hobbins, J.C. (1985). Clavicular measurement: a new biometric parameter for fetal evaluation. *Journal of Ultrasound Medicine* **4**: 467–470.

Yasuda, Y. (1973). Differentiation of human limb buds in vitro. *Anatomical Record* **175**: 561–578.

Yoshikawa, E. (1958). Changes of the laryngeal cartilages during life and application for determination of probable age. *Japanese Journal of Legal Medicine* **12** (Suppl.): 1–40 (Japanese with English summary).

Yoshino, M., Miyasaka, S., Sato, H. and Seta, S. (1987). Classification system of frontal sinus patterns by radiography. Its application to identification of unknown skeletal remains. *Forensic Science International* **34**: 289–299.

Young, J.W., Bright, R.W. and Whitley, N.O. (1986). Computed tomography in the evaluation of partial growth plate arrest. *Skeletal Radiology* **15**: 530–535.

Young, R.W. (1957). Postnatal growth of the frontal and parietal bone in white males. *American Journal of Physical Anthropology* **15**: 367–386.

Youssef, E.H. (1964). The development of the human skull in a 34 mm human embryo. *Acta Anatomica* **57**: 72–90.

Zander, G. (1943). 'Os acetabuli' and other bone nuclei: periarticular calcifications at the hip joint. *Acta Radiologica* **24**: 317–327.

Zawisch, C. (1956). Missverhältniss zwischen den am auf gehellten Ganzembryo und den aus histologisch-embryologischen Schnittserien gewonnenen Ossifikationdaten. *Anatomischer Anzeiger* **102**: 305–316.

Zawisch, C. (1957). Der ossifikationsprozess des Occipitale und die Rolle des tectum posterius beim menschen. *Acta Anatomica* **30**: 988–1007.

Zimmerman, A.W. and Lozzio, C.B. (1989). Intersection between selenium and zinc in the pathogenesis of anencephaly and spina bifida. *Zeitschrift fur Kinderchirurgie* **44**: 48–50.

Zins, J.E. and Whitaker, L.A. (1979). Membranous vs. endochondral bone autografts: implications for craniofacial reconstruction. *Surgical Forum* **30**: 521–523.

Zins, J.E. and Whitaker, L.A. (1983). Membranous vs. endochondral bone: implications for craniofacial reconstruction. *Plastic and Reconstructive Surgery* **72**: 778–784.

Zoller, H. and Bowie, E.R. (1957). Foreign bodies of food passages versus calcifications of laryngeal cartilages. *Archives of Otolaryngology* **65**: 474–478.

Index

References to illustrations are indicated in **bold** figures.
References to tables are indicated in **bold** *italic* figures